POWER

POWER
A CRITICAL READER

edited by
DANIEL EGAN
University of Massachusetts, Lowell
LEVON A. CHORBAJIAN
University of Massachusetts, Lowell

PEARSON
Prentice Hall

Upper Saddle River, NJ 07458

Library of Congress Cataloging-in-Publication Data
Power : a critical reader / edited by Daniel Egan, Levon Chorbajian.
p. cm.
Includes bibliographical references.
ISBN 0-13-183438-X
1. Power (Social sciences) 2. Political sociology. I. Egan, Daniel, (date) II. Chorbajian, Levon.

HN49.P6P68 2005
303.3–dc22

2004053526

Publisher: Nancy E. Roberts
Executive Editor: Christoper DeJohn
Editorial Assistant: Kristin Haegele
Marketing Manager: Marissa Feliberty
Production Liaison: Marianne Peters-Riordan
Assistant Manufacturing Manager: Mary Ann Gloriande
Cover Design: Bruce Kenselaar
Cover Photo: Lynsey Addario/Corbis
Composition/Full-Service Project Management: GGS Book Services, Atlantic Highlands
Printer/Binder: Phoenix Book Tech
Cover Printer: Phoenix Book Tech

Credits and acknowledgments borrowed from other sources and reproduced, with permission, in this textbook appear on pp. 401–402.

Pearson Education LTD.
Pearson Education Singapore, Pte. Ltd
Pearson Education, Canada, Ltd
Pearson Education—Japan
Pearson Education Australia PTY, Limited
Pearson Education North Asia Ltd
Pearson Educación de Mexico, S.A. de C.V.
Pearson Education Malaysia, Pte. Ltd
Pearson Education, Upper Saddle River, New Jersey

PEARSON
Prentice Hall

10 9 8 7 6 5 4 3 2 1

ISBN 0-13-183438-X

CONTENTS

PREFACE

Together we draw on nearly fifty years of experience as teachers, researchers, and writers in editing this book. The topic, political sociology, is a branch of sociology that focuses on power relations in society and its effects on the distribution of scarce resources. These resources include income and wealth, which in turn determine people's access to nourishment, education, housing, health care, employment, transportation, and communication as well as economic security and a more general sense of well-being.

Common sense tells us that there are great inequalities in the distribution of these goods. Collectively, people in the United States, Canada, Western Europe, Japan, Australia, and New Zealand (the advanced industrial nations) have much more than persons in the Third World. At the same time, within any given country, whether rich or poor, there are further great inequalities between haves and have-nots. We need go no further than the world's richest economy, the United States, to note that 15 percent or more of the population lives in poverty. Conversely, we find that some people in even the world's poorest countries have great resources at their command and live exceedingly well, while hundreds of millions of others live near or even below the edge of survival.

It is when we ask why these conditions exist that common sense fails us. Popular, common sense-based explanations include human nature, God's will, fate, claims of overpopulation, and allegations of different levels of intelligence and motivation among groups of people. The problem with these explanations is that they are not based on the application of scientific principles. Some, such as fate, are purely mystical in nature, while others, such as differential intelligence, are wrapped in pseudoscience. Common sense explanations operate as closed systems. In seeking answers to the question "why?" there are important analytical questions that need to be asked, and popular, common sense explanations do not allow us to ask them. These questions include:

- How do government policies lead to higher or lower levels of poverty?
- What is the connection between great individual and family wealth and the exercise of political power?
- What kinds of ideas and information dominate the educational and mass media systems?
- How do class, racial, and gender oppression come about and what role have they played in the political systems of the past five hundred years?
- What kinds of variations are found in the political parties and party platforms of the advanced industrial nations and what impact do these have on the conditions of life for the residents of these nations?
- What effect do large, transnational corporations and international trade associations such as the World Trade Organization (WTO) have on global development and living standards?
- What are the objectives of an interventionist U.S. foreign policy?
- How and under what conditions have people been able to come together to challenge existing political arrangements and what have been the outcomes of such struggles?

The nine sections of this book cover many of the main issues in political sociology, and they shed much light on the questions posed above. At the same time, we are aware that political sociology covers a vast terrain, and we know that no text can cover all the issues that every instructor considers vital. *Power: A Critical Reader* was designed as a versatile text. Instructors who are satisfied with the coverage can use it as a stand-alone text reader. Others may prefer to combine this book with an authored political sociology text or with one or more monographs on topics of particular import to them. We believe that *Power: A Critical Reader* lends itself easily to each of these options.

We would also like to call attention to features of this book which are special, if not necessarily unique. First, a few words about the word *critical* in the title. Critical is not intended to mean negative and should not be understood in that sense. It refers to a broad range of approaches to the study of societies that focus on the historical and structural foundations of power and the social institutions through which power is exercised. For the past 10,000 years, going back to the beginning of civilization, these social arrangements have conveyed privilege to certain social classes, races, genders, and ethnic, linguistic, and racial groups over others. These arrangements, in turn, have been challenged in a wide variety of ways ranging from small-scale resistance in the form of indifferent and careless work to organized rebellion and revolution. Power, in other words, is tension ridden and sometimes fragile. It is never absolute and always subject to challenge. Critical theories, each in their own way, examine and bring out into the open conditions of oppression and exploitation and modes of resistance. The selections in this book do not represent a single critical theory, but a set of theories that represent this larger perspective we are calling critical.

Second, although *Power: A Critical Reader* was not designed as a class, race and gender reader, we do consider class, race, and gender to be major dimensions of exploitation and tension in premodern, modern, and postmodern societies and as wellsprings of resistance and struggle. We have included many articles that incorporate these perspectives in the sections. However, we have chosen not to gather these selections into separate sections on class, race, and gender but to integrate these selections into the broader issue sections of the text. Our reasoning is that the conditions and struggles of these groups are intimately woven into the political and social fabric of the entire society, and we prefer a format that most closely approximates this reality.

Third, we place great emphasis on the international and global nature of power. Since the expansion into and conquest of Third World regions of the world by European nation-states beginning in the sixteenth century, the modern world has been a global one defined by the movement of people, raw materials, products and services, and culture across national boundaries. Through the linkage of distant parts of the world through air travel and telecommunications, new levels of political and economic consolidation and resistance characterize contemporary capitalism. In addition to having a section on the nation-state and the global economy, we also have readings on revolution, war, and genocide, as well as anti-globalization social movements. We believe it is essential to understand the global foundations of power and how they intersect with nationally-based forms of power.

We would also like to call attention to the section on the mass media. Most political sociologists have failed to consider the mainstream mass media as a highly politicized institution, and as a result a political sociology text or reader that contains a media section is unusual. Our reasoning for including such a section is that there are now unprecedented levels of consolidation and control of the media by giant corporations, and less independence and diversity in the media than in the past. The dependence of the vast majority of the U.S. population on this media for domestic and international news has made the media an institution of critical political import. Section V, "Media and Ideology," is in recognition of this reality.

Several people have been very helpful in bringing this project to completion. The reviewers of the original manuscript devoted serious energy to their task and made valuable contributions in making this a much better book. They are Gregory Hooks, Martin Oppenheimer, William Roy, and Alan Spector. We received encouragement from Corey Dolgon, Jerry Lembcke, Steven Rosenthal, and James Russell. As for our editor, Chris De John of Prentice Hall, little more could have been asked of him. He offered his encouragement and support when it mattered most. He and his staff were sterling from start to finish.

Finally, we recognize our family members for their patience and support. To our spouses Susan Gittelman and Beverly Chorbajian and our children Daniel and Noa Gittelman-Egan, and Monty, Ruby, Garo, Seta, and Von Chorbajian, we owe a great debt.

INTRODUCTION

What Is This Book About?

Until the late eighteenth century, citizens of nations were at the mercy of those who ruled them. People's options were limited. They could try to win the favor of their rulers, they could go about their business and try to stay out of trouble, they could organize and participate in rebellions against entrenched power, and they could hide or flee to other lands. What they could not do was have a say in choosing who ruled them. Nor could they claim legally based rights to freedoms of speech, assembly, and religion that are now the cornerstones of political life in advanced industrial nations. And they could not claim economic rights that are still not well established in a country like the United States—the rights to employment, shelter, education, health care, and labor union organization and union protections (Yates 1999).

The American Revolution and the ratification of the Constitution provided important rights for people to choose their leaders. Nevertheless, the majority of people were left out of the new "democracy." There was no democracy for slaves, Native Americans, women, and white men who were not property owners—in other words, a large majority of the people were excluded. This is because democracy and property are always in tension. Those with property—in other words, those with control over the productive resources of society—try to use the wealth that their property conveys to create power for themselves and to use that power to preserve and extend their privileges. This comes at the expense of others who are kept powerless and without a say in how society is run, what its priorities are, and how society's resources are allocated and used.

Howard Zinn's best-selling history of the United States, *A People's History of the United States* (Zinn 2003), is about the many struggles of working people to extend democracy through the destruction of slavery, the extension of voting rights to women, the creation of a better life for European immigrants, the dismantling of legalized segregation and disenfranchisement that were in place as late as the 1960s, the protests to bring the Vietnam War to an end, and many similar struggles in areas of the environment, occupational safety, and workers' rights. In each instance there has been intense opposition from those who benefited from existing arrangements. These were slave owners, the Robber Barons, and the giant corporations that now dominate national and global economic arrangements. This book examines these themes. It is about power and how it is used to frustrate the democratic aspirations of millions and how that power is challenged to create a fairer and just (we would say democratic) society.

Some Background

Despite the value U.S. culture places on democracy, democracy has been perceived as a threat by dominant social forces since the country's earliest years (Zinn 2003; Parenti 2000). For many, if not most, of the delegates at the Constitutional Convention in 1787, the ownership of property was equated with the right and ability to govern. This should not be surprising since, as historian Charles Beard points out, of the 55 delegates to the Convention, 14 were major land speculators, 15 were slave owners, 24 were owners of public securities, and 11 owned manufacturing, shipping, or mercantile interests (Beard 1935: 73–151). John Jay (New York), coauthor of the *Federalist Papers* and the first chief justice of the Supreme Court, declared, "the people who own the country ought to govern it." Elbridge Gerry (Massachusetts) claimed, "the evils of experience flow from the excess of democracy," while John Dickenson (Delaware) spoke of "the dangerous influence of those multitudes without property and without principle." Roger Sherman of Connecticut stated, "the people should have as little to do as may be about the Government." James McHenry (Maryland) saw democracy as "confusion and licentiousness," and Edmund Randolph (Virginia) referred to "the turbulence and follies of democracy." Alexander Hamilton

(New York), like John Jay a coauthor of the *Federalist Papers*, explained that

> All communities divide themselves into the few and the many. The First are rich and well-born, the other the mass of people. . . . The people are turbulent and changing; they seldom judge or determine right. Give therefore to the first class a distinct permanent share of government. (Beard 1935: 189–216)

In this context, the Constitution's separation of powers, its provision for indirect election of senators (by state legislatures) and presidents (by the Electoral College), and other articles reflect not some abstract commitment to limit the potentially tyrannical power of government, but a very special concern that popular participation in politics, which might threaten the interests of "the few," be constrained (Parenti 2000).

The Framers, no doubt influenced by Plato's description of "the people" as a "large and powerful animal" governed by impulse, emotion, and prejudice rather than reason, equated democracy with mob rule. In more contemporary versions of this argument, fear of mob rule is replaced by fear of the "masses." Today, democracy is recognized as a core value in advanced industrial societies, but only by defining democracy so that it no longer carries the participatory (and, to established elites, potentially threatening) implications of "rule by the people"; democracy now refers to the periodic, competitive selection by citizens of political representatives (Held 1987). Still, a concern that "the people" might demand greater involvement in and control over politics has been a staple of contemporary political theory. Joseph Schumpeter, for example, saw any further participation by citizens beyond voting as political back-seat driving: "the typical citizen drops down to a lower level of mental performance as soon as he enters the political field. He argues and analyzes in a way that we would readily recognize as infantile within the sphere of his real interests. He becomes a primitive again" (Schumpeter 1976: 262). Robert Dahl, whose writings on pluralism have had great influence in political science as well as political sociology, saw the people as "restless and immoderate." For Dahl, a "tyranny of the majority" could be avoided by political competition between various group interests (Dahl 1956). Seymour Martin Lipset, with his concept of "working class authoritarianism," argued that the working class was that class most likely to possess antidemocratic, intolerant attitudes and the least likely to possess the civic orientations Lipset deemed necessary for a pluralist system to work (Lipset 1963). This understanding of democracy is perhaps best represented by a 1975 report by the Trilateral Commission (an organization of academics, corporate executives, and state managers from the United States, Western Europe, and Japan) entitled *The Crisis of Democracy* (Crozier, Huntington, and Watanuki 1975). In this report, the political scientist Samuel Huntington argued that the civil rights, women's, antiwar, environmental, and other social movements that emerged during the 1960s threatened "the governability of democracy" by raising excessive demands on the system: "some of the problems of governance in the United States today stem from an excess of democracy. . . . Needed instead is a greater degree of moderation in democracy" (113). In referring to "the democratic distemper," Huntington suggested that "too much" democracy is dysfunctional.

If one accepts as a given the current distribution of resources in society, then it is easy to see democracy as a threat to stability and order. As we have seen, United States history can be understood as a series of attempts by people, who at various times and for various reasons were excluded from or marginalized by the political process, to make real the promise of democracy. Every advance in democracy and equality in history has been the result of conflict, of mobilization by marginalized, oppressed, and exploited social groups that challenged the legitimacy of existing social institutions.

In their most radical form, labor, feminist, antiracist, and other social movements have all rejected the separation of the political from the social that is characteristic of modern society. Citizens are formally equal in the political sphere (each citizen has one vote, and no citizen's vote counts more than another's), but as individuals in civil society, they are characterized by class, racial, gender, and other forms of inequality. This distinction is problematic for two reasons. First, social inequality creates barriers to meaningful political participation by citizens who occupy subordinate social statuses. To the extent that money is an essential resource for electoral campaigns, for example, class inequality provides wealthy individuals and corporations with a means of political participation that is not available to most citizens. Second, political power is a major means of maintaining social inequality. The state not only engages in repression of critical social movements, it helps to construct common sense ways of looking at the world that legitimize inequality. In response, social movements have sought to socialize politics by seeking to create and (re)distribute the social resources necessary for meaningful participation in politics. This perspective recognizes that citizenship (in the sense of being an active, participating member of a polity) is not defined by law, but rather is constructed socially. At the same time, these movements have sought to politicize society by seeking to extend democracy to the economy, education, popular culture, mass media, and other social institutions. From this perspective, politics is not restricted to government or public policy; *all* social activity is necessarily political.

These ideas were articulated by C. Wright Mills in his book *The Sociological Imagination*, where he argued that the purpose of sociology is to help develop "publics" (Mills 1959). By this Mills meant active, engaged citizens who see their personal troubles as public issues, as the product of social institutions in a particular period of history. With this understanding, people are able to see how their lives are shaped by social forces and, just as importantly, how social institutions can be changed and new ones created. We could not agree more with this, and believe that Mills's point is especially relevant for political sociology. Without publics, democracy becomes formalized at best; at worst, democracy becomes hollow and fragile. By examining the structural limits to and opportunities for extending democracy, political sociology provides invaluable tools to help us understand how to create and maintain publics.

What Is Political Sociology and Where Does It Come From?

Political sociology is the branch of sociology that deals most clearly with power in society and its effects on the allocation of major resources. These resources include education, employment, housing, health care, food, and physical and psychological well-being. The breadth of these resources reveals the very broad definition of politics used by political sociologists. Politics is defined here as any activity that concerns the distribution of rights, responsibilities, or resources, and as such, political activity is not restricted to social arenas that are explicitly defined as political (i.e., the state). Rather, political activity is characteristic of all social institutions. At the same time, political activity has been the principal means by which people have responded to social injustices and sought to change or, more fundamentally, transform social institutions. With its focus on power and the possibilities for social change, political sociology is at the very core of the sociological perspective.

Political sociology, as well as much modern intellectual inquiry, grew out of the massive social changes dating back to the sixteenth century, such as the Protestant Reformation, the rise of modern science, and the origins of capitalism. The declining influence of religion caused mystical modes of thought to be slowly superseded by secular ones. The European Enlightenment represented the beginnings of modern Western thought and contributed to the weakening of religious definitions of the social world. The French Revolution swept away both the power of the Catholic Church and altered many social arrangements both in France and throughout Europe, to which the ideas of the revolution spread from 1789 to 1815 (Lefebvre 1947; Mathiez 1929; Thompson 1963). These changes represented the final death blow to European feudalism and the rise of capitalism as a political economic system based on the private ownership of the means of production and profit based on wage labor as well as the secondary processes of industrialization, urbanization, and global expansion into areas now known as the Third World.[1]

Thus, the short answer to this question is that political sociology developed amid and in response to the rise of capitalism as a political-economic system. After centuries of social conflict and change, capitalism took on its broad outlines in the early nineteenth century.

European feudalism was conclusively defeated. Bourgeois elites took control of the political institutions of the emerging and coalescing nation-states of Europe, and the economic exploitation and immiseration of the European working classes and Third World peoples were evolving toward modern wage labor forms.

This was an enormously disruptive process that took place over the course of several centuries. Beginning at the dawn of the sixteenth century, Third World areas were conquered and colonized. Many people were subjected to genocide at the hands of European colonial powers. Millions of others were enslaved—either transported and enslaved elsewhere as in the case of Africans brought to the Western Hemisphere or effectively enslaved on site (Chomsky 1993; Huberman 1936; Rodney 1974). The thirst for profit that could never be quenched required physical labor to exploit resources, and this effort was provided by laborers mining minerals, harvesting timber, planting crops, and constructing the infrastructure necessary to the colonial enterprise (Williams 1966).

Within industrial societies themselves there was a similar process of creating wage laborers out of former rural dwellers who had provided for themselves in subsistence or limited market economies. These people were driven off the land by making it exceedingly difficult to continue to live there. In England, this was done by passing vagrancy laws that made it unlawful not to be employed and Enclosure Acts that closed off lands known as common lands. These were village lands that had been traditionally used by villagers to hunt, fish, gather food, and graze animals. Closing off these lands and imposing draconian punishments such as long prison terms, exile, or even death made life impossible for many people and forced them to pick up and move, which is exactly what these laws intended. In their new locales, these people took up jobs in mines, factories, transportation, and other industries. In other words, former peasants became what Marx and Engels called the proletariat (or wage laborers) of the new industrial capitalist system (Thompson 1963; Huberman 1936).

Both locales of emergent nineteenth century capitalism, the industrial capitalist states and their colonized areas of the Third World, became centers of resistance. England, in the early nineteenth century, was wracked by demonstrations, food riots, industrial sabotage, and struggles for political rights (Thompson 1963). In 1871, protests in France culminated in the Paris Commune, the largest spontaneous urban rebellion in modern Western history. The people took over the city and held it for ten weeks until subdued by government military forces. Indeed, the history of industrial capitalist states, including the United States, is punctuated by class tensions rooted in the exploitation of labor and expressed as worker resistance, and corporate and governmental repression (Zinn 2003). The forms of resistance and repression have varied widely. Individualistic responses have included indifferent work habits, absenteeism, labor turnover, and sabotage of the workplace. On the collective side, workers have engaged in rallies, demonstrations, marches, strikes, and general strikes, and they have formed labor unions, labor, socialist, and communist political parties, and reformist and revolutionary movements.

The reform movements have generally been more successful than the revolutionary ones, but the two have operated in dynamic interaction wherein the more militant and revolutionary movements have created political space in which the more reformist movements have been able to achieve a measure of success. Among these reforms in the advanced industrial capitalist countries have been recognition of the right to unionize and to strike, and winning the right to vote, the eight-hour workday, government-sponsored pension plans, regulation of corporate activities, overtime pay, and the elimination of legalized segregation. The social welfare reforms have been more generous, far-reaching, and beneficial to the working class in Canada and Europe than they have been in the United States, but there has been some success in the United States as well.

The first successful modern anticolonial struggle was the American Revolution fought against British imperialism. It was soon followed by the revolution in Haiti and then by struggles throughout Central and South America. Anticolonial struggles, nationalist and revolutionary, came later to Asia and Africa, in the twentieth century. By that time, the United States had become a world power, the preeminent one after 1945, and had assumed a counterrevolutionary role that it acted out in China, Korea, Chile,

Cuba, Vietnam, Iraq, and many other locales (Parenti 1989; Blum 1985).

Why Is Political Sociology Relevant Today?

Today we find ourselves in another period of transition and turmoil created by new strategies for extracting profit for the large corporations that now dominate the world's economy. Three interrelated processes define this extraction. The target of the first is roughly 80 percent of the U.S. population that has seen its level of income, share of national wealth, educational opportunity, and economic security slowly, but steadily, drop since the early 1970s (Mishel, Bernstein, and Bushey 2003; Keister 2000). The second is that the globalization process accelerates the extraction of profits from the Third World by using those regions not only in the traditional sense of supplying markets, cheap raw materials, and cheap labor for extractive industries and plantation labor, but increasingly for manufacturing and professional service jobs. Initially this export of jobs from advanced industrial nations to the Third World was for low-level and semi-skilled jobs, but it has increasingly included skilled manufacturing and even professional work. The third process has been one of increased militarization and aggressive intervention in the affairs of other nations. This includes wars, police actions, and invasions as well as covert political interventions. The pacification of the world's governments and peoples for corporate profit is the main objective (ideologically couched as "fighting terrorism," "protecting national security," and "humanitarian intervention") of the U.S. military whose total budget is over ten times larger than that of any other nation (Chomsky 1999; Parenti 2002).

The three processes of declining living standards, job export, and international pacification make the current epoch as much a period of crisis as the early and mid-nineteenth century whose own crises spawned political sociology as a discipline. Now, as then, political sociology provides the analytical tools for understanding social processes that might otherwise appear random, chaotic, natural, inevitable, or beneficial, which they are to corporate America. The understanding provided by political sociology is systematic and integrated, and it can serve as the basis for intelligent political participation, including struggle for social change, equal rights, economic justice, and democratization.

If we define politics as the area where scarce resources are distributed to society's members, then it is political sociology that explains the pattern of distribution. Who gets what, when, where, why, and how is a major concern of political sociologists. In order to accomplish these analytical tasks more effectively and accurately, sociologists employ various models. Each of these models is a tool for organizing and explaining social reality. Before we proceed to the readings that make up this book, we need to take a look at the major models employed in political sociology.

Models in Political Sociology

The first model we will consider is the pluralist model (Dahl 1956; Truman 1951). Pluralism is a term used in political science and is closely related to its sociological counterpart, structural functionalism. Pluralists argue that modern industrial societies contain multiple or plural centers of power. Government, in other words, is not seen as dominated by a single social class or interest group. Rather, a variety of groups, sometimes with opposite and conflicting interests, compete in the political arena for position and influence. The state itself is seen as neutral toward these groups and not predisposed or partisan toward any one or a related group of them. Political decision making in this model is an outgrowth of power and compromise between groups since none is strong enough to win its way consistently and none so weak that it is shut out all the time. In this give-and-take model, industrial corporations may win over environmentalists one day and lose another, and the same goes for corporations and labor unions, pharmaceutical companies and AIDS advocacy groups, and so on. The pluralist model was once the most widely used in political sociology, but it has diminished in popularity among political sociologists in recent years.

The second model is associated with elite theory. It provides a powerful critique of the pluralist model, but before considering its details we note that political sociologist Berch Berberoglu has suggested a useful distinction with regard to elite theory. He divides elite theory into two branches he calls classical elite theory and radical elite theory (Berberoglu 2001). This classification allows us to discuss two types of elite theory that share one major characteristic—society is ruled by elites—and at the same time to remain aware of how they differ on several major dimensions.

Classical elite theory was developed in the early twentieth century by a group of writers of whom Vilfredo Pareto (1968), Gaetano Mosca (1939), and Robert Michels (1962) are the most prominent. Although there are differences among the three, they share a reasonably consistent set of ideas that allow them to be classified together in this school of political thought. Pareto and Mosca insisted on the inevitability and desirability of rule by small selected elites. These elites were viewed as the fittest to rule by virtue of their superior intelligence, character, and skill. The people, the large majority of society, were viewed as unfit to rule because of their general inferiority when compared to elites. Michels agreed that rule by a select elite was inevitable but attributed this outcome less to a natural law of social systems than to the workings of political parties and other bureaucracies that lent themselves to control by the few and made that outcome a predictable one. This is a deeply pessimistic school of political thought, thoroughly antidemocratic. It is not surprising, therefore, that these ideas were influential in the formulation of Italian fascism in the 1920s and 30s.

Radical elite theory is a more recent development associated with two books published in the 1950s, C. Wright Mills best-selling study *The Power Elite* (1957) and Floyd Hunter's less well-known but significant *Community Power Structure* (1953). Mills argued that by the 1950s power in the United States had coalesced around three centers—the corporate sector, the federal government, and the military. The top leadership drawn from all three sectors constituted an interlocking national elite. Mills was impressed with the movement of personnel between sectors, for example, the recruitment of corporate executives to serve in presidential cabinets and high ranking military officers moving on to become top-level corporate executives. Whereas Mills's focus was national, Hunter's, with the exception of his later book *Top Leadership, U.S.A.* (1959), was local. In *Community Power Structure,* Hunter examined the structure of governance in the city of Atlanta, Georgia. Hunter developed a methodology he called the reputational method in which he asked prominent members of the Atlanta community to name its most influential citizens. He found that the names of a narrow core of people associated with business interests kept showing up in the responses. From these results he concluded that the city was governed by a business/financial elite with other groups, even if organized, playing secondary roles in municipal governance.

Radical elite theories are distinguished from classical elite theories in several ways. First, they do not posit the existence of elites as an outgrowth of natural law. For Pareto and Mosca, elite rule was the prevailing pattern of rule in all societies in the past, and they saw no alternative in the future. For Mills and Hunter, elite rule is better explained by examining the history and social structure of particular communities and societies. Second, the classical elite theorists looked down on the masses. For them, the majority is a socially inferior species: less intelligent, petty, feuding, incompetent, apathetic, and, therefore, disqualified to rule. For the radical elite theorists, the citizenry are exploited and manipulated, but that is less a natural condition than a socially conditioned one. In this view, the possibilities for more democratic political structures are open and not excluded by definition. Third, again in contrast to Pareto and Mosca, Mills and Hunter do not celebrate elites. For both of them, elite rule constitutes a disturbing and antidemocratic force in American society because it promotes a narrow band of interests at odds with the best interests of the citizens for economic security, quality education, world peace, environmental integrity, equitable taxes, and freedom from class, race, gender, and ethnic oppression.

The last theoretical perspective is Marxism. In Marxist theory, the core fact for the analysis of society is ownership and control of the means of production. Those who own the productive resources of society—mineral and timber resources, agricultural land, factories and industrial machinery, offices and office equipment, transportation systems, information and information technologies, and large incorporated businesses—constitute the upper class. This class, by virtue of its economic resources, gains control of the state and rules in ways that promote its interests, again as in radical elite theory, at the expense of the working class. Marxism is distinct from the other perspectives in that it is not limited to politics as a single sphere of analysis. It is broader in that it presents a theory of society, arguing that human history can be divided into a few basic modes of production that provide the material resources and social relationships that give that type of society its unique structure of social institutions and ways of life. Furthermore, it is in the resolution of class struggles within societies that social change is rooted and that we have the progression through history of one type of society evolving out of earlier forms.

Whereas the pluralist model posits the existence of at least a minimum of shared interests between all members of society, Marxist theory sees the upper and working classes in opposition to one another. The former exploits and lives off of the labor of the latter, and this leads to conflict known as class struggle. This conflict is manifested in ways large and small, ranging from careless work habits to armed revolution. As in classical elite theory, Marxism promotes the existence of laws of society, but instead of elite rule it is class struggle that becomes the engine of social conflict and change. Finally, although Marxist theory bears similarities to radical elite theory, Marxist theory differs in important ways. Instead of stressing rule by an elite, Marxism traces the origins of power to ownership patterns in society and insists that those who actually do rule do not do so as an elite but as representatives of a small class that owns and controls the means of production. Marxism also offers a theory of society and not just a theory of politics. The existence of social classes based on differential ownership of the means of production defines (though not absolutely) the nature of other social institutions such as law, education, work, the media, and the family. These other spheres are granted a degree of autonomy, but the key idea is that economic relationships and not other variables such as values, to name an alternative widely promoted in the United States, have the major causal influence in structuring the nature of social institutions (Barrow 1993; Carnoy 1984).

In his text on sociological theory, Irving Zeitlin recognizes Marx's position as the giant of nineteenth-century critical social theory. It is in this body of work that we find a theory of the development of capitalism, an understanding of the social and political organization of society, and an explanation of social change. Zeitlin argues that because of the preeminence of Marx's work, all subsequent social theory is a dialogue with Marx (Zeitlin 2000). We are sympathetic to this interpretation, which is illustrated by our early selections in Sections I and II of this book. We also draw on other later traditions that have tried to revise Marx's theory to fit the more contemporary developments and nuances of advanced industrial capitalist societies or to address important gaps in that theory. These perspectives include radical elite theory, neo-Marxism, critical theory, feminist theory, critical race theory, and postmodernism.

Vernacular Pluralism

Although the influence of pluralist theory has seriously declined in the last quarter century, pluralism has always extended far beyond the confines of academic journals, libraries, and conferences. Academic pluralism has always been linked to a popular or vernacular pluralism that has not declined at all. It is healthy and robust although as inaccurate as its academic version. Much K–12 and university level teaching about government and social issues is based on the assumptions, explicit or implied, of the pluralist model. These assumptions also serve as the foundation for much editorial writing and political speech making. In all these sectors we find the underlying assumptions of the pluralist model made explicit.

Vernacular pluralism consists of the commonplace, foundational assumptions about the civic life of society. In the United States this means assuming that society is democratic. It means assuming that corporate and political leaders (except for an occasional bad apple) have everyone's best interests at heart. It also means assuming that in its relationships with other nations, the United States promotes freedom and democracy and fights tyranny and oppression. Vernacular pluralism embodies an overriding belief in a shared national interest by all the citizenry and the many groups and organizations in which they participate. This assumed, shared collective interest is frequently expressed through the use of first person plural pronouns by political and corporate leaders, as in "We Americans" or "Our interests in the Middle East."

The fallacy of vernacular pluralism is easily brought out when we examine a specific case history. Early in his first term as president, Bill Clinton tried to create a national health insurance system. The United States is the only advanced industrial country without one, which means that Americans have no legal right to health care. For a time in 1993–94, health care was a public issue regularly reported in the mass media. Most participants claimed that their position offered "the best health care plan for America." The fallacy of this format is exposed when we consider two hypothetical people. The first is a single mother, raising two children, and working as a waitress in a middle-level restaurant. The other is the president of a major insurance company. They are both Americans, but there is no best health-care plan for America that is the best health-care plan for both of them. This is because they belong to different social classes. Vernacular pluralism assumes that we are all in the same boat when we are not.

This becomes clear when we consider the needs of the waitress/mother and the insurance company president. Her need for health insurance is personal, while his is structural. She needs health insurance that she can afford and that provides protection for her and her children. He needs health insurance that is privately sold and administered through his company and companies like it and that generates the highest level of profit. If we look at the four major components of health insurance—cost (how much is it?), coverage (what does it cover and what does it exclude?), deductibles (how much does the person have to pay before the insurance company pays?), and limits (what is the maximum the company will pay for a single illness, hospitalization, etc.?)—we can quickly see that what is best for the waitress/mother is the worst for the insurance company president. The best insurance for her is the insurance that is inexpensive, covers all physical and mental illness, has no deductibles, and no limits on insurance payments. The insurance that is best for him, that allows him to please his board of directors and stockholders and guarantees him his job with generous raises and stock options, is just the opposite. What is true of health insurance is true of every area of policymaking—foreign policy, tax policy, education policy, transportation policy, antitrust policy, pension policy, etc.

As long as there are social classes and other social divisions, there will be different and opposing class interests. Vernacular pluralism conceals this and contributes to making people naïve or apathetic and ultimately easier to manipulate and control. In this sense it is dangerous and holds back rather than promotes the strengthening and extension of democracy.

The Readings

The readings for this book have been selected with this danger in mind. All of the readings are written from a critical perspective, broadly defined. Each sheds light on an important aspect of the political system.

The book itself is divided into nine sections. Sections I and II contain more theoretical selections. Section I addresses the concept of power from several different perspectives, including Marxism and neo-Marxism, critical theory, feminism, critical race theory, and postmodernism. These readings examine the material and cultural foundations of power as well as the ways in which power shapes individual identity. The four readings in Section II examine the state. Each offers a leading perspective on the relationship of the state to the larger society developed by researchers over the past half-century. These selections extend the theories of power to the central political institutions of society.

Over the past two centuries, there have been major political struggles concerning elections, gaining the right to vote for excluded groups and extending the right to vote universally in advanced industrial societies. These struggles and the victories that have resulted have raised their own controversies over the role of campaign contributions, rules about voting, and whether electoral politics is even a viable mechanism for bringing about political and social change. In Section III, four authors examine different aspects of electoral politics and the franchise.

Many political struggles during the twentieth century in industrialized nations have focused on winning and defending entitlement benefits (pensions, health insurance, decent working conditions, educational benefits, etc.) for the working class. Victories in these areas—to a lesser degree in the United States than elsewhere—resulted in the creation of the welfare state. Since the early 1970s, these benefits have come under increasing attack from the right, and have been scaled back, in some cases dramatically, over what they had been. The readings in Section IV focus attention on the rise of the welfare state and the current attacks on it.

By the mid-twentieth century, the mass media, print and electronic, had become people's primary source of news and information, especially national and international, and also of entertainment. Among other things, these media serve as important conduits of political ideas and policies that are designed to simultaneously address social issues and protect upper-class interests. It is clear that the media play an important political role in shaping political opinion and manufacturing consent for elite policies. For this reason, Section V is devoted to the topic of the media and ideology.

Nation-states and the global economy are the subject matter of Section VI. Beginning in the 1990s, globalization became the new buzzword for international relations in the political, economic, and cultural spheres. Establishment writers have defined globalization as desirable and inevitable, the wave of the future, bringing with it the free movement of people (workers), raw materials, and goods and services. Yet despite glowing accounts, the process of globalization has not gone uncontested. There have been demonstrations in advanced industrial countries and rebellions in the Third World, indicating that significant numbers of people are unwilling to accept globalization as the beneficial/benign and inevitable process its promoters allege. Globalization has also raised questions about the role of the nation-state in the global economy. Is it obsolete or much less important than in the past? In Section VI we examine the various dimensions of globalization.

Many of the earlier readings have dealt with the economic and ideological power of the state. Any discussion of the role of the state in organizing and maintaining social inequality would be inadequate without an examination of the state's coercive power. In Section VII we turn our attention to the coercive power of the state with an examination of war as an interstate activity; genocide, which in the last century has targeted peoples within and between states; and repression, which also victimized residents of particular states. These are the most humanly tragic expressions of political power, and we intend for these readings to provide a critical, structural analysis of political violence rather than a simply moralistic one.

In the last two sections we move from the institutional bases of power to the possibilities for social change. Power is always contradictory, with weaknesses that may offer people opportunities to organize resistance. The next two sections address these concerns. In Section VIII, "Revolution," we evaluate the successes and failures of twentieth-century revolutions and their relevance into the twenty-first century. In Section IX, "Social Movements," we look at movements for social change in nonrevolutionary situations and pay attention to the structural forces that produce social movements and the internal dynamics of these movements.

We believe that these topics provide a sound introduction to political sociology with a mix of classic and cutting-edge readings. We do recognize though that there are topics not represented here. We also recognize that while we have tried to represent a range of critical theories, most of the selections are written from a radical elite or Marxist perspective. Furthermore, each perspective actually contains a range of writers and ideas. There is no single Marxist, feminist, or postmodern position on power and its workings. The field of political sociology is simply too broad to cover every issue from every critical perspective. Nevertheless, we do believe that these selections will provide readers with the necessary critical analytical tools to realize Mills's call for a sociology that creates publics and tools they can apply to current and future political issues that affect themselves and millions of others worldwide.

Notes

1. We are using the term "Third World" in preference to newer concepts such as "semi-periphery" and "periphery" and the "global South" because it is better established and known. We do recognize that the group of Third World nations contains far more diversity in levels of industrialization, military capabilities, and standards of living than when the term was coined in the 1950s.

References

Barrow, Clyde W. 1993. *Critical Theories of the State: Marxist, Neo-Marxist, Post-Marxist.* Madison: University of Wisconsin Press.

Beard, Charles. 1935. *An Economic Interpretation of the Constitution of the United States.* New York: Macmillan.

Berberoglu, Berch. 2001. *Political Sociology.* Dix Hills, NY: General Hall.

Blum, William. 1985. *Killing Hope: U.S. Military and CIA Interventions Since World War II.* Monroe, Maine: Common Courage Press.

Carnoy, Martin. 1984. *The State and Political Theory.* Princeton: Princeton University Press.

Chomsky, Noam. 1993. *Year 501.* Boston: South End Press.

———. 1999. *The New Military Humanism.* Monroe, Maine: Common Courage Press.

Crozier, Michael J., Samuel P. Huntington, and Joji Watanuki. 1975. *The Crisis of Democracy.* New York: New York University Press.

Dahl, Robert. 1956. *A Preface to Democratic Theory.* Chicago: University of Chicago Press.

———. 1971. *Polyarchy.* New Haven: Yale University Press.

Held, David. 1987. *Models of Democracy.* Stanford: Stanford University Press.

Huberman, Leo. 1936. *Man's Worldly Goods: The Story of the Wealth of Nations.* New York: Harper & Brothers.

Hunter, Floyd. 1953. *Community Power Structure.* Chapel Hill: University of North Carolina Press.

———. 1959. *Top Leadership, U.S.A.* Chapel Hill: University of North Carolina Press.

Keister, Lisa. 2000. *Wealth in America.* New York: Cambridge University Press.

Lefebvre, Georges. 1947. *The Coming of the French Revolution.* Princeton: Princeton University Press.

Lipset, Seymour Martin. 1963. *Political Man.* New York: Doubleday.

Mathiez, Albert. 1929. *The French Revolution.* New York: Alfred A. Knopf.

Michels, Robert. 1962. *Political Parties.* New York: Free Press.

Mills, C. Wright. 1957. *The Power Elite.* New York: Oxford University Press.

———. 1959. *The Sociological Imagination.* New York: Oxford University Press.

Mishel, Lawrence, Jared Bernstein, and Heather Bushey. 2003. *The State of Working America, 2002–2003.* Ithaca: Cornell University Press.

Mosca, Gaetano. 1939. *The Ruling Class.* New York: McGraw-Hill.

Parenti, Michael. 1989. *The Sword and the Dollar.* New York: St. Martin's Press.

———. 2000. *Democracy for the Few.* New York: St. Martin's Press.

———. 2002. *The Terrorism Trap: September 11 and Beyond.* San Francisco: City Lights Books.

Pareto, Vilfredo. 1968. *The Rise and Fall of the Elites.* Totowa, NJ: Bedminster Press.

Perrucci, Robert, and Earl Wysong. 2003. *The New Class Society.* Lanham, MD: Rowman & Littlefield.

Rodney, Walter. 1974. *How Europe Underdeveloped Africa.* Washington: Howard University Press.

Schumpeter, Joseph. 1976. *Capitalism, Socialism, and Democracy.* London: Allen and Unwin.

Thompson, E. P. 1963. *The Making of the English Working Class.* New York: Random House.

Truman, David. 1951. *The Governmental Process.* New York: Knopf.

Williams, Eric. 1966. *Capitalism and Slavery.* New York: G.P. Putnam's Sons.

Yates, Michael. 1999. *Why Unions Matter.* New York: Monthly Review Press.

Zeitlin, Irving M. 2000. *Ideology and the Development of Social Theory.* Upper Saddle River, NJ: Prentice-Hall.

Zinn, Howard. 2003. *A People's History of the United States, 1492–Present.* New York: Harper-Collins.

POWER

Chapter 1

Important People:

Robert Dahl = power - non-hierarchical/competative distribut

Steven Lukes = 3D limit + prevent discussion/emergence of issues

SECTION I
CRITICAL THEORIES OF POWER

In our introduction we identified power as the central concept in political sociology. Here we develop this concept by offering selections that illustrate the varying interpretations of power held by critical social theorists. Conventional definitions of power refer to the ability of an actor to achieve aims in the face of opposition from others. Robert Dahl (1956), for example, defines power "as A's capacity for acting in such a manner as to control B's responses" (13). Implicit in Dahl's definition is the idea that power is generally dispersed throughout society. An actor's capacity for power will depend on the specific resources they possess and the specific issue being decided, and so "power is non-hierarchically and competitively arranged" (Held 1987:189) with no one actor dominant on all (or most) issues.

Steven Lukes (1974) sees this as a "one-dimensional" view of power because of its focus on observable behavior by actors in the making of decisions on specific issues over which there is some observable conflict of interest. For Lukes, power implies much more than the ability to make decisions. First, it also means the ability to place limits on the kind of issues that can be discussed and decided upon in the first place. What Lukes calls a "two-dimensional" view of power "involves examining both *decision-making* and *nondecision-making*" (18), by which he means the exclusion of issues or interests from political debate. This exclusion can occur through such means as coercion, influence, the acceptance of legitimate authority, force, and manipulation. As we shall see later in the section on electoral politics, voters may exercise decision-making power by selecting one candidate for political office over another, but nondecision-making power lies with those who are able to shape the rules of the electoral process in the first place. To the extent that potential candidates do not run in or candidates drop out of electoral contests because of a lack of money, the options available to voters have already been shaped by other actors. Those actors who can set the agenda for decision making by admitting certain issues and interests and excluding others by granting or withholding the financial contributions necessary to run a political campaign have a degree of power that extends beyond that found in the decision-making process itself.

Second, and more significantly, power also means the ability to prevent the emergence of issues in the first place. Even the two-dimensional view of power is limited, according to Lukes, by its focus on excluding *existing* issues from the decision-making process. But what if people feel no grievances, and are unaware of an issue? As Lukes eloquently states,

> is it not the supreme and most insidious exercise of power to prevent people, to whatever degree, from having grievances by shaping their perceptions, cognitions and preferences in such a way that they accept their role in the existing order of things, either because they can see or imagine no alternative to it, or because they see it as natural and unchangeable, or because they value it as divinely ordained and beneficial? (24)

In this "three-dimensional" view of power, Lukes suggests that actors' location in historically specific social institutions shapes what they see and experience in the world and shapes their understanding of the possibilities for social change. The absence of observable conflict does not necessarily imply a social consensus, but rather a generalized acceptance of a socially constructed "common sense" that reinforces fundamental social relations.

The readings in this section provide important critical statements of this three-dimensional view of power. With the concept of commodity fetishism, Karl Marx explained how people tend to see the products of their labor as having an existence and value independent of their human creation or the way in which they satisfy human needs.

In capitalism, objects are produced and exchanged not to satisfy specific human needs, but as a means to the end of increased capital accumulation. Because workers do not control the process of production or the products they produce, they are likely to experience the product of their labor not as an expression of their individuality or as a contribution to the welfare of others, but as an alien object that oppresses them. Likewise, the social relations through which objects are produced are obscured to the extent that the monetary value of commodities serves as the basis for exchange. Marx argued that commodity fetishism characterized all social relationships in capitalism. Social institutions and relations that are created and reproduced by people come to be experienced as natural, universal, and absolute, beyond the ability of their creators to change them. Thus, although capitalism is a historically specific creation of human actors, it appears to people as an inevitable and unchangeable force.

One of the central questions for the Frankfurt School of critical theorists that emerged prior to the Second World War was to understand why groups that might have an objective interest in transforming society may either be unaware of those interests or not act on them. What Herbert Marcuse called "two-dimensional thought" recognizes contradictions between what is and what could be, but modern capitalist society suppresses the development of two-dimensional thought. Instead, "one-dimensional thought" closes off criticism and an understanding of possible alternatives. We internalize a technological rationality that enslaves us to a life of alienated labor and alienated consumption and that destroys the environment. We are, in a world characterized by one-dimensional thought, unable to see how technology could be used to free people and satisfy human needs. The desire for freedom itself becomes a commodity (think about the number of advertisements that emphasize freedom and individuality), thereby ensuring that it is safely contained and managed on terms favorable to dominant social forces.

Antonio Gramsci, writing from a prison cell in fascist Italy, developed the concept of hegemony to understand how the power of dominant classes is reproduced. Gramsci argued that coercion is an insufficient base for power. Although coercion is an important element of power (as we shall see in the section on war, genocide, and repression), power in modern, advanced capitalist societies is expressed through the construction of hegemony, which refers to the cultural and intellectual dominance of the ruling class through a coherent system of values, beliefs, norms, and symbols that are supportive of the established order. The power of dominant classes requires that their worldview be accepted and internalized by subordinate groups as "common sense," thereby limiting opportunities for subordinate groups to be critical and conceive of social alternatives. Hegemony is not imposed, but rather is a negotiated process in which dominant groups must often grant concessions to subordinate groups in order to ensure the latter's continued consent. Thus, even though the state is a major means by which dominant groups exercise their power, Gramsci directs our attention to the institutions of civil society (such as religion, education, the media, and family) that generate a cultural "common sense."

The selections by George Lipsitz and Anne Phillips examine how power determines the construction of racial and gender identities. Lipsitz's article on race makes clear that it is a system constructed to justify the exploitation of labor through slavery, colonialism, and restrictive immigration policies. Although the specific forms and victims of this exploitation have changed over time, exploitation remains the central feature of race. Race is a particularly modern social phenomenon that appears to us as if it is a fixed, biological fact. Because of this, the racialized nature of social institutions is rarely acknowledged. His focus on whiteness is a call to reveal the taken-for-granted material and cultural benefits that define "white" in opposition to "nonwhite." For her part, Phillips discusses a central theme in feminist theory: how the separation between public and private spheres transforms biological differences between males and females into social, gendered differences between men and women. Gender is a social construction in which men's oppression of women is made to appear natural or inevitable by virtue of a supposed biologically determined division of labor. In both cases, race and gender are seen as systems that are imposed by dominant groups to justify and normalize their oppression of subordinate groups.

Finally, postmodernists like Michel Foucault reject the idea that power has a center. What many people have seen as the failure of revolutionary movements to successfully transform society or, once taking power, their degeneration into bureaucratic and often self-destructive systems is explained, for Foucault, by the fact that such movements are misdirected. Because power is diffuse and fragmented, a network with threads that extend everywhere, there are no commanding heights (such as the state) whose overthrow would mark a new era. Foucault is more interested in how power operates at the local level to construct individuals. His concept of "political anatomy" emphasizes the way in which power is a productive (rather than destructive) force that organizes human bodies, and is associated with the construction of specific knowledges or discourses (such as psychiatry or medicine) through which these bodies are known.

Each of these readings, by examining the unspoken assumptions through which power is organized, conveys a sense of how social institutions organize power in the interests of dominant groups. These readings provide the theoretical foundation with which to understand the more empirical works in the remaining sections of the book.

References

Dahl, Robert. 1956. *A Preface to Democratic Theory.* Chicago: Chicago University Press.

Held, David. 1987. *Models of Democracy.* Stanford: Stanford University Press.

Lukes, Steven. 1974. *Power: A Radical View.* London: Macmillan.

capitalism/commodity fetishism
↳ objects production/exchange does not satisfy human need ⇒ only for making $
• workers feel oppressed/view it as unchangeable

Herbert Marcuse
→ use tech. to satisfy human needs
1-D vs 2D though
↳ enslaves
freedom becomes a commodity

antonio Gramsci
• hegemony (of the ruling class)
• generate cultural "Common Sense" (lower internalizes)
• make sm. concessions ⇒ consent

George Lipsitz - race
Anne Phillips - gender
both used by dominant groups to justify oppression

Michel Foucault - "political anatomy"

THE FETISHISM OF COMMODITIES

KARL MARX

A commodity appears, at first sight, a very trivial thing, and easily understood. Its analysis shows that it is, in reality, a very queer thing, abounding in metaphysical subtleties and theological niceties. So far as it is a value in use, there is nothing mysterious about it, whether we consider it from the point of view that by its properties it is capable of satisfying human wants, or from the point that those properties are the product of human labour. It is as clear as noon-day, that man, by his industry, changes the forms of the materials furnished by Nature, in such a way as to make them useful to him. The form of wood, for instance, is altered, by making a table out of it. Yet, for all that, the table continues to be that common, every-day thing, wood. But, so soon as it steps forth as a commodity, it is changed into something transcendent. It not only stands with its feet on the ground, but, in relation to all other commodities, it stands on its head, and evolves out of its wooden brain grotesque ideas, far more wonderful than "table-turning" ever was.

The mystical character of commodities does not originate, therefore, in their use-value. Just as little does it proceed from the nature of the determining factors of value. For, in the first place, however varied the useful kinds of labour, or productive activities, may be, it is a physiological fact, that they are functions of the human organism, and that each such function, whatever may be its nature or form, is essentially the expenditure of human brain, nerves, muscles, &c. Secondly, with regard to that which forms the ground-work for the quantitative determination of value, namely, the duration of that expenditure, or the quantity of labour, it is quite clear that there is a palpable difference between its quantity and quality. In all states of society, the labour-time that it costs to produce the means of subsistence, must necessarily be an object of interest to mankind, though not of equal interest in different stages of development. And lastly, from the moment that men in any way work for one another, their labour assumes a social form.

Whence, then, arises the enigmatical character of the product of labour, so soon as it assumes the form of commodities? Clearly from this form itself. The equality of all sorts of human labour is expressed objectively by their products all being equally values; the measure of the expenditure of labour-power by the duration of that expenditure, takes the form of the quantity of value of the products of labour; and finally, the mutual relations of the producers, within which the social character of their labour affirms itself, takes the form of a social relation between the products.

A commodity is therefore a mysterious thing, simply because in it the social character of men's labour appears to them as an objective character stamped upon the product of that labour; because the relation of the producers to the sum total of their own labour is presented to them as a social relation, existing not between themselves, but between the products of their labour. This is the reason why the products of labour become commodities, social things whose qualities are at the same time perceptible and imperceptible by the senses. In the same way the light from an object is perceived by us not as the subjective excitation of our optic nerve, but as the objective form of something outside the eye itself. But, in the act of seeing, there is at all events, an actual passage of light from one thing to another, from the external object to the eye. There is a physical relation between physical things. But it is different with commodities. There, the existence of the things *quâ* commodities, and the value-relation between the products of labour which stamps them as commodities, have absolutely no connexion with their physical properties and with the material relations arising therefrom. There it is a definite social relation between men, that assumes, in their eyes, the fantastic form of a relation between things.

{Ask Him}

In order, therefore to find an analogy, we must have recourse to the mist-enveloped regions of the religious world. In that world the productions of the human brain appear as independent beings endowed with life, and entering into relation both with one another and the human race. So it is in the world of commodities with the products of men's hands. This I call the Fetishism which attaches itself to the products of labour, so soon as they are produced as commodities, and which is therefore inseparable from the production of commodities.

This Fetishism of commodities has its origin, as the foregoing analysis has already shown, in the peculiar social character of the labour that produces them.

commodity
- product of human labor & can sat. wants/useful

THE NEW FORMS OF CONTROL

HERBERT MARCUSE

A comfortable, smooth, reasonable, democratic unfreedom prevails in advanced industrial civilization, a token of technical progress. Indeed, what could be more rational than the suppression of individuality in the mechanization of socially necessary but painful performances; the concentration of individual enterprises in more effective, more productive corporations; the regulation of free competition among unequally equipped economic subjects; the curtailment of prerogatives and national sovereignties which impede the international organization of resources. That this technological order also involves a political and intellectual coordination may be a regrettable and yet promising development.

The rights and liberties which were such vital factors in the origins and earlier stages of industrial society yield to a higher stage of this society: they are losing their traditional rationale and content. Freedom of thought, speech, and conscience were—just as free enterprise, which they served to promote and protect—essentially *critical* ideas, designed to replace an obsolescent material and intellectual culture by a more productive and rational one. Once institutionalized, these rights and liberties shared the fate of the society of which they had become an integral part. The achievement cancels the premises.

To the degree to which freedom from want, the concrete substance of all freedom, is becoming a real possibility, the liberties which pertain to a state of lower productivity are losing their former content. Independence of thought, autonomy, and the right to political opposition are being deprived of their basic critical function in a society which seems increasingly capable of satisfying the needs of the individuals through the way in which it is organized. Such a society may justly demand acceptance of its principles and institutions, and reduce the opposition to the discussion and promotion of alternative policies *within* the status quo. In this respect, it seems to make little difference whether the increasing satisfaction of needs is accomplished by an authoritarian or a non-authoritarian system. Under the conditions of a rising standard of living, non-conformity with the system itself appears to be socially useless, and the more so when it entails tangible economic and political disadvantages and threatens the smooth operation of the whole. Indeed, at least in so far as the necessities of life are involved, there seems to be no reason why the production and distribution of goods and services should proceed through the competitive concurrence of individual liberties.

Freedom of enterprise was from the beginning not altogether a blessing. As the liberty to work or to starve, it spelled toil, insecurity, and fear for the vast majority of the population. If the individual were no longer compelled to prove himself on the market, as a free economic subject, the disappearance of this kind of freedom would be one of the greatest achievements of civilization. The technological processes of mechanization and standardization might release individual energy into a yet uncharted realm of freedom beyond necessity. The very structure of human existence would be altered; the individual would be liberated from the work world's imposing upon him alien needs and alien possibilities. The individual would be free to exert autonomy over a life that would be his own. If the productive apparatus could be organized and directed toward the satisfaction of the vital needs, its control might well be centralized; such control would not prevent individual autonomy, but render it possible.

This is a goal within the capabilities of advanced industrial civilization, the "end" of technological rationality. In actual fact, however, the contrary trend operates: the apparatus imposes its economic and political requirements for defense and expansion on labor time and free time, on the material and intellectual culture. By virtue of the way it has organized its technological base, contemporary industrial society tends to be totalitarian. For "totalitarian" is not only a terroristic political coordination of society, but also a nonterroristic economic-technical coordination which operates through the manipulation of needs by vested interests. It thus precludes the emergence of an effective opposition against the whole. Not only a specific form of government or party rule makes for totalitarianism, but also a specific system of production and distribution which may well be compatible with a "pluralism" of parties, newspapers, "countervailing powers," etc.

Today political power asserts itself through its power over the machine process and over the technical organization of the apparatus. The government of advanced and advancing industrial societies can maintain and secure itself only when it succeeds in mobilizing, organizing, and exploiting the technical, scientific, and mechanical productivity available to industrial civilization. And this productivity mobilizes society as a whole, above and beyond any particular individual or group interests. The brute fact that the machine's physical (only physical?) power surpasses that of the individual, and of any particular group of individuals, makes the machine the most effective political instrument in any society whose basic organization is that of the machine process. But the political trend may be reversed; essentially the power of the machine is only the stored-up and projected power of man. To the extent to which the work world is conceived of as a machine and mechanized accordingly, it becomes the *potential* basis of a new freedom for man.

Contemporary industrial civilization demonstrates that it has reached the stage at which "the free society" can no longer be adequately defined in the traditional terms of economic, political, and intellectual liberties, not because these liberties have become insignificant, but because they are too significant to be confined within the traditional forms. New modes of realization are needed, corresponding to the new capabilities of society.

Such new modes can be indicated only in negative terms because they would amount to the negation of the prevailing modes. Thus economic freedom would mean freedom *from* the economy—from being controlled by economic forces and relationships; freedom from the daily struggle for existence, from earning a living. Political freedom would mean liberation of the individuals *from* politics over which they have no effective control. Similarly, intellectual freedom would mean the restoration of individual thought now absorbed by mass communication and indoctrination, abolition of "public opinion" together with its makers. The unrealistic sound of these propositions is indicative, not of their utopian character, but of the strength of the forces which prevent their realization. The most effective and enduring form of warfare against liberation is the implanting of material and intellectual needs that perpetuate obsolete forms of the struggle for existence.

The intensity, the satisfaction and even the character of human needs, beyond the biological level, have always been preconditioned. Whether or not the possibility of doing or leaving, enjoying or destroying, possessing or rejecting something is seized as a *need* depends on whether or not it can be seen as desirable and necessary for the prevailing societal institutions and interests. In this sense, human needs are historical needs and, to the extent to which the society demands the repressive development of the individual, his needs themselves and their claim for satisfaction are subject to overriding critical standards.

We may distinguish both true and false needs. "False" are those which are superimposed upon the individual by particular social interests in his repression: the needs which perpetuate toil, aggressiveness, misery, and injustice. Their satisfaction might be most gratifying to the individual, but this happiness is not a condition which has to be maintained and protected if it serves to arrest the development of the ability (his own and others) to recognize the disease of the whole and grasp the chances of curing the disease. The result then is euphoria in unhappiness. Most of the prevailing needs to relax, to have fun, to behave and consume in accordance with the advertisements, to love and hate what others love and hate, belong to this category of false needs.

Such needs have a societal content and function which are determined by external powers over which the individual has no control; the development and satisfaction of these needs is heteronomous. No matter how much such needs may have become the individual's own, reproduced and fortified by the conditions of his existence; no matter how much he identifies himself with them and finds himself in their satisfaction, they continue to be what they were from the beginning—products of a society whose dominant interest demands repression.

■ ■ ■ ■

In the last analysis, the question of what are true and false needs must be answered by the individuals themselves, but only in the last analysis; that is, if and when they are free to give their own answer. As long as they are kept incapable of being autonomous, as long as they are indoctrinated and manipulated (down to their very instincts), their answer to this question cannot be taken as their own. By the same token, however, no tribunal can justly arrogate to itself the right to decide which needs should be developed and satisfied. Any such tribunal is reprehensible, although our revulsion does not do away with the question: how can the people who have been the object of effective and productive domination by themselves create the conditions of freedom?

The more rational, productive, technical, and total the repressive administration of society becomes, the more unimaginable the means and ways by which the administered individuals might break their servitude and seize their own liberation. To be sure, to impose Reason upon an entire society is a paradoxical and scandalous idea—although one might dispute the righteousness of a society which ridicules this idea while making its own population into objects of total administration. All liberation depends on the consciousness of servitude, and the emergence of this consciousness is always hampered by the predominance of needs and satisfactions which, to a great extent, have become the individual's own. The process always replaces one system of preconditioning by another; the optimal goal is the replacement of false needs by true ones, the abandonment of repressive satisfaction.

The distinguishing feature of advanced industrial society is its effective suffocation of those needs which demand liberation—liberation also from that which is tolerable and rewarding and comfortable—while it sustains and absolves the destructive power and repressive function of the affluent society. Here, the social controls exact the overwhelming need for the production and consumption of waste; the need for stupefying work where it is no longer a real necessity; the need for modes of relaxation which soothe and prolong this stupefication; the need for maintaining such deceptive liberties as free competition at administered prices, a free press which censors itself, free choice between brands and gadgets.

Under the rule of a repressive whole, liberty can be made into a powerful instrument of domination. The range of choice open to the individual is not the decisive factor in determining the degree of human freedom, but *what* can be chosen and what *is* chosen by the individual. The criterion for free choice can never be an absolute one, but neither is it entirely relative. Free election of masters does not abolish the masters or the slaves. Free choice among a wide variety of goods and services does not signify freedom if these goods and services sustain social controls over a life of toil and fear—that is, if they sustain alienation. And the spontaneous reproduction of superimposed needs by the individual does not establish autonomy; it only testifies to the efficacy of the controls.

■ ■ ■ ■

We are again confronted with one of the most vexing aspects of advanced industrial civilization: the rational character of its irrationality. Its productivity and efficiency, its capacity to increase and spread comforts, to turn waste into need, and destruction into construction, the extent to which this civilization transforms the object world into an extension of man's mind and body makes the very notion of alienation questionable. The people recognize themselves in their commodities; they find their soul in their automobile, hi-fi set, split-level home, kitchen equipment. The very mechanism which ties the individual to his society has changed, and social control is anchored in the new needs which it has produced.

The prevailing forms of social control are technological in a new sense. To be sure, the technical structure and efficacy of the productive and destructive apparatus has been a major instrumentality for subjecting the population to the established social division of labor throughout the modern period. Moreover, such integration has always been accompanied by more obvious forms of compulsion: loss of livelihood, the administration of justice, the police, the armed forces. It still is. But in the contemporary period, the technological controls appear to be the very embodiment of Reason for the benefit of all social groups and interests—to such an extent that all contradiction seems irrational and all counteraction impossible.

■ ■ ■ ■

In this process, the "inner" dimension of the mind in which opposition to the status quo can take root is whittled down. The loss of this dimension, in which the power of negative thinking—the critical power of Reason—is at home, is the ideological counterpart to the very material process in which advanced industrial society silences and reconciles the opposition. The impact of progress turns Reason into submission to the facts of life, and to the dynamic capability of producing more and bigger facts of the same sort of life. The efficiency of the system blunts the individuals' recognition that it contains no facts which do not communicate the repressive power of the whole. If the individuals find themselves in the things which shape their life, they do so, not by giving, but by accepting the law of things—not the law of physics but the law of their society.

I have just suggested that the concept of alienation seems to become questionable when the individuals identify themselves with the existence which is imposed upon them and have in it their own development and satisfaction. This identification is not illusion but reality. However, the reality constitutes a more progressive stage of alienation. The latter has become entirely objective; the subject which is alienated is swallowed up by its alienated existence. There is only one dimension, and it is everywhere and in all forms. The achievements of progress defy ideological indictment as well as justification; before their tribunal, the "false consciousness" of their rationality becomes the true consciousness.

This absorption of ideology into reality does not, however, signify the "end of ideology." On the contrary, in a specific sense advanced industrial culture is *more* ideological than its predecessor, inasmuch as today the ideology is in the process of production itself. In a provocative form, this proposition reveals the political aspects of the prevailing technological rationality. The productive apparatus and the goods and services which it produces "sell" or impose the social system as a whole. The means of mass transportation and communication, the commodities of lodging, food, and clothing, the irresistible output of the entertainment and information industry carry with them prescribed attitudes and habits, certain intellectual and emotional reactions which bind the consumers more or less pleasantly to the producers and, through the latter, to the whole. The products indoctrinate and manipulate; they promote a false consciousness which is immune against its falsehood. And as these beneficial products become available to more individuals in more social classes, the indoctrination they carry ceases to be publicity; it becomes a way of life. It is a good way of life—much better than before—and as a good way of life, it militates against qualitative change. Thus emerges a pattern of *one-dimensional thought and behavior* in which ideas, aspirations, and objectives that, by their content, transcend the established universe of discourse and action are either repelled or reduced to terms of this universe. They are redefined by the rationality of the given system and of its quantitative extension.

HEGEMONY

ANTONIO GRAMSCI

What we can do, for the moment, is to fix two major superstructural "levels": the one that can be called "civil society," that is the ensemble of organisms commonly called "private," and that of "political society" or "the State." These two levels correspond on the one hand to the function of "hegemony" which the dominant group exercises throughout society and on the other hand to that of "direct domination" or command exercised through the State and "juridical" government. The functions in question are precisely organisational and connective. The intellectuals are the dominant group's "deputies" exercising the subaltern functions of social hegemony and political government. These comprise:

1. The "spontaneous" consent given by the great masses of the population to the general direction imposed on social life by the dominant fundamental group; this consent is "historically" caused by the prestige (and consequent confidence) which the dominant group enjoys because of its position and function in the world of production.
2. The apparatus of state coercive power which "legally" enforces discipline on those groups who do not "consent" either actively or passively. This apparatus is, however, constituted for the whole of society in anticipation of moments of crisis of command and direction when spontaneous consent has failed.

■ ■ ■ ■

In my opinion, the most reasonable and concrete thing that can be said about the ethical State, the cultural State, is this: every State is ethical in as much as one of its most important functions is to raise the great mass of the population to a particular culture and moral level, a level (or type) which corresponds to the needs of the productive forces for development, and hence to the interests of the ruling classes. The school as a positive educative function, and the courts as a repressive and negative educative function, are the most important State activities in this sense: but in reality, a multitude of other so-called private initiatives and activities tend to the same end—initiatives and activities which form the apparatus of the political and cultural hegemony of the ruling classes.

Government with the consent of the governed—but with this consent organised, and not generic and vague as it is expressed in the instant of elections. The State does have and request consent, but it also "educates" this consent, by means of the political and syndical associations; these, however, are private organisms, left to the private initiative of the ruling class.

■ ■ ■ ■

The revolution which the bourgeois class has brought into the conception of law, and hence into the function of the State, consists especially in the will to conform (hence ethicity of the law and of the State). The previous ruling classes were essentially conservative in the sense that they did not tend to construct an organic passage from the other classes into their own, i.e. to enlarge their class sphere "technically" and ideologically: their conception was that of a closed caste. The bourgeois class poses itself as an organism in continuous movement, capable of absorbing the entire society, assimilating it to its own cultural and economic level. The entire function of the State has been transformed; the State has become an "educator," etc.

THE POSSESSIVE INVESTMENT IN WHITENESS

GEORGE LIPSITZ

Blacks are often confronted, in American life, with such devastating examples of the white descent from dignity; devastating not only because of the enormity of white pretensions, but because this swift and graceless descent would seem to indicate that white people have no principles whatever.

—JAMES BALDWIN

Shortly after World War II, a French reporter asked expatriate Richard Wright for his views about the "Negro problem" in America. The author replied, "There isn't any Negro problem; there is only a white problem."[1] By inverting the reporter's question, Wright called attention to its hidden assumptions—that racial polarization comes from the existence of blacks rather than from the behavior of whites, that black people are a "problem" for whites rather than fellow citizens entitled to justice, and that, unless otherwise specified, "Americans" means "whites."[2] But Wright's formulation also placed political mobilization by African Americans during the civil rights era in context, connecting black disadvantages to white advantages and finding the roots of black consciousness in the systemic practices of aversion, exploitation, denigration, and discrimination practiced by people who think of themselves as "white."

Whiteness is everywhere in U.S. culture, but it is very hard to see. As Richard Dyer suggests, "[W]hite power secures its dominance by seeming not to be anything in particular."[3] As the unmarked category against which difference is constructed, whiteness never has to speak its name, never has to acknowledge its role as an organizing principle in social and cultural relations.[4] To identify, analyze, and oppose the destructive consequences of whiteness, we need what Walter Benjamin called "presence of mind." Benjamin wrote that people visit fortune-tellers less out of a desire to know the future than out of a fear of not noticing some important aspect of the present. "Presence of mind," he suggested, "is an abstract of the future, and precise awareness of the present moment more decisive than foreknowledge of the most distant events."[5] In U.S. society at this time, precise awareness of the present moment requires an understanding of the existence and the destructive consequences of the possessive investment in whiteness that surreptitiously shapes so much of our public and private lives.

Race is a cultural construct, but one with sinister structural causes and consequences. Conscious and deliberate actions have institutionalized group identity in the Untied States, not just through the dissemination of cultural stories, but also through systematic efforts from colonial times to the present to create economic advantages through a possessive investment in whiteness for European Americans. Studies of culture too far removed from studies of social structure leave us with inadequate explanations for understanding racism and inadequate remedies for combating it.

Desire for slave labor encouraged European settlers in North America to view, first, Native Americans and, later, African Americans as racially inferior people suited "by nature" for the humiliating subordination of involuntary servitude. The long history of the possessive investment in whiteness stems in no small measure from the fact that all subsequent immigrants to North America have come to an already racialized society. From the start, European settlers in North America established structures encouraging a possessive investment in whiteness. The colonial and early national legal systems authorized attacks on Native Americans and encouraged the appropriation of their lands. They legitimated racialized chattel slavery, limited naturalized citizenship to "white" immigrants, identified Asian immigrants as expressly unwelcome (through legislation aimed at immigrants from China in 1882, from India in 1917, from Japan in 1924, and from the Philippines in 1934), and provided pretexts for restricting the voting, exploiting the labor, and seizing the property of Asian Americans, Mexican Americans, Native Americans, and African Americans.[6]

The possessive investment in whiteness is not a simple matter of black and white; all racialized minority groups have suffered from it, albeit to different degrees and in different ways. The African slave trade began in earnest only after large-scale Native American slavery proved impractical in North America. The abolition of slavery led to the importation of low-wage labor from Asia. Legislation banning immigration from Asia set the stage for the recruitment of low-wage labor from Mexico. The new racial categories that emerged in each of these eras all revolved around applying racial labels to "nonwhite" groups in order to stigmatize and exploit them while at the same time preserving the value of whiteness.

Although reproduced in new form in every era, the possessive investment in whiteness has always been influenced by its origins in the racialized history of the United States—by its legacy of slavery and segregation, of "Indian" extermination and immigrant restriction, of conquest and colonialism. Although slavery has existed in many countries without any particular racial dimensions to it, the slave system that emerged in North America soon took on distinctly racial forms. Africans enslaved in North America faced a racialized system of power that reserved permanent, hereditary, chattel slavery for black people. White settlers institutionalized a possessive investment in whiteness by making blackness synonymous with slavery and whiteness synonymous with freedom, but also by pitting people of color against one another. Fearful of alliances between Native Americans and African Americans that might challenge the prerogatives of whiteness, white settlers prohibited slaves and free blacks from traveling in "Indian country." European Americans used diplomacy and force to compel Native Americans to return runaway slaves to their white masters. During the Stono Rebellion of 1739, colonial authorities offered Native Americans a bounty for every rebellious slave they captured or killed. At the same time, British settlers recruited black slaves to fight against Native Americans within colonial militias.[7] The power of whiteness depended not only on white hegemony over separate racialized groups, but also on manipulating racial outsiders to fight against one another, to compete with each other for white approval, and to seek the rewards and privileges of whiteness for themselves at the expense of other racialized populations.

Aggrieved communities of color have often curried favor with whites in order to make gains at each other's expense. For example, in the nineteenth century some Native Americans held black slaves (in part to prove to whites that they could adopt "civilized" European American ways), and some of the first chartered African American units in the U.S. army went to war against Comanches in Texas or served as security forces for wagon trains of white settlers on the trails to California. The defeat of the Comanches in the 1870s sparked a mass migration by Spanish-speaking residents of New Mexico into the areas of West Texas formerly occupied by the vanquished Native Americans.[8] Immigrants from Asia sought the rewards of whiteness for themselves by asking the courts to recognize them as "white" and therefore eligible for naturalized citizenship according to the Immigration and Naturalization Act of 1790; Mexican Americans also insisted on being classified as white. In the early twentieth century, black soldiers accustomed to fighting Native Americans in the Southwest participated in the U.S. occupation of the Philippines and the punitive expedition against Pancho Villa in Mexico.[9] Asian American managers cracked down on efforts by Mexican American farm workers to unionize, while the Pullman Company tried to break the African American Brotherhood of Sleeping Car Porters by importing Filipinos to work as porters. Mexican Americans and blacks took possession of some of the property confiscated from Japanese Americans during the internment of the 1940s, and Asian Americans, blacks, and Mexican Americans all secured advantages for themselves by cooperating with the exploitation of Native Americans.

Yet while all racialized minority groups have sometimes sought the rewards of whiteness, they have also been able to come together in interethnic antiracist alliances. Native American tribes often harbored runaway slaves and drew upon their expertise in combat against whites, as in 1711 when an African named Harry helped lead the Tuscaroras against the British.[10] Native

Americans secured the cooperation of black slaves in their attacks on the French settlement near Natchez in colonial Louisiana in 1729, and black Seminoles in Florida routinely recruited slaves from Georgia plantations to their side in battles against European Americans.[11] African Americans resisting slavery and white supremacy in the United States during the nineteenth century sometimes looked to Mexico as a refuge (especially after that nation abolished slavery), and in the twentieth century the rise of Japan as a successful non-white world power often served as a source of inspiration and emulation among African American nationalists. Mexican American and Japanese American farm workers joined forces in Oxnard, California, in 1903 to wage a successful strike in the beet fields, and subsequently members of the two groups organized an interracial union, the Japanese Mexican Labor Association.[12] Yet whether characterized by conflict or cooperation, all relations among aggrieved racialized minorities stemmed from recognition of the rewards of whiteness and the concomitant penalties imposed upon "nonwhite" populations.

Yet today the possessive investment is not simply the residue of conquest and colonialism, of slavery and segregation, of immigrant exclusion and "Indian" extermination. Contemporary whiteness and its rewards have been created and recreated by policies adopted long after the emancipation of slaves in the 1860s and even after the outlawing of *de jure* segregation in the 1960s. There has always been racism in the United States, but it has not always been the same racism. Political and cultural struggles over power have shaped the contours and dimensions of racism differently in different eras. Antiracist mobilizations during the Civil War and civil rights eras meaningfully curtailed the reach and scope of white supremacy, but in each case reactionary forces engineered a renewal of racism, albeit in new forms, during succeeding decades. Racism has changed over time, taking on different forms and serving different social purposes in each time period.

The present political culture in this country gives broad sanction for viewing white supremacy and antiblack racism as forces from the past, as demons finally put to rest by the passage of the 1964 Civil Rights Act and the 1965 Voting Rights Act.[13] Jurists, journalists, and politicians have generally been more vocal in opposing what they call "quotas" and "reverse discrimination"—by which they usually mean race-specific measures, designed to remedy existing racial discrimination, that inconvenience or offend whites—than in challenging the thousands of well-documented cases every year of routine, systematic, and unyielding discrimination against minorities. It is my contention that the stark contrast between nonwhite experiences and white opinions during the past two decades cannot be attributed solely to individual ignorance or intolerance, but stems instead from liberal individualism's inability to describe adequately the collective dimensions of our experience.[14] As long as we define social life as the sum total of conscious and deliberative individual activities, we will be able to discern as racist only *individual* manifestations of personal prejudice and hostility. Systemic, collective, and coordinated group behavior consequently drops out of sight. Collective exercises of power that relentlessly channel rewards, resources, and opportunities from one group to another will not appear "racist" from this perspective, because they rarely announce their intention to discriminate against individuals. Yet they nonetheless give racial identities their sinister social meaning by giving people from different races vastly different life chances.

The gap between white perception and minority experience can have explosive consequences. Little more than a year after the 1992 Los Angeles rebellion, a sixteen-year-old high school junior shared her opinions with a reporter from the *Los Angeles Times*. "I don't think white people owe anything to black people," she explained. "We didn't sell them into slavery, it was our ancestors. What they did was wrong, but we've done our best to make up for it." A seventeen-year-old senior echoed those comments, telling the reporter, "I feel we spend more time in my history class talking about what whites owe blacks than just about anything else when the issue of slavery comes up. I often received dirty looks. This seems strange given that I wasn't even alive then. And the few members of my family from that time didn't have the luxury of owning much, let alone slaves. So why, I ask you, am I constantly made to feel guilty?"[15]

More ominously, after pleading guilty to bombing two homes and one car, vandalizing a synagogue, and attempting to start a race war by planning the murder of Rodney King and the bombing of Los Angeles's First African Methodist Episcopal Church, twenty-year-old Christopher David Fisher explained that "sometimes whites were picked on because of the color of their skin. . . . Maybe we're blamed for slavery."[16] Fisher's actions were certainly extreme, but his justification of them drew knowingly and precisely on a broadly shared narrative about the victimization of "innocent" whites by irrational and ungrateful minorities.

The comments and questions raised about the legacy of slavery by these young whites illuminate broader currents in our culture, with enormous implications for understanding the enduring significance of race in our country. These young people associate black grievances solely with slavery, and they express irritation at what they perceive as efforts to make them feel guilty or unduly privileged because of things that happened in the distant past. The claim that one's own family did not own any slaves is frequently voiced in our culture. It is almost never followed with a statement to the effect that of course some people's families did own slaves and we will not rest until we track them down and make them pay reparations. This view never acknowledges how the existence of slavery and the exploitation of black labor after emancipation created opportunities from which immigrants and others benefited, even if they did not personally own slaves. Rather, it seems to hold that, because not all white people owned slaves, no white people can be held accountable or inconvenienced by the legacy of slavery. More important, having dispensed with slavery, they feel no need to address the histories of Jim Crow segregation, racialized social policies, urban renewal, or the revived racism of contemporary neoconservatism. On the contrary, Fisher felt that his discomfort with being "picked on" and "blamed" for slavery gave him good reason to bomb homes, deface synagogues, and plot to kill black people.

Unfortunately for our society, these young whites accurately reflect the logic of the language of liberal individualism and its ideological predispositions in discussions of race. In their apparent ignorance of the disciplined, systemic, and collective *group* activity that has structured white identities in U.S. history, they are in good company. In a 1979 law journal article, future Supreme Court justice Antonin Scalia argued that affirmative action "is based upon concepts of racial indebtedness and racial entitlement rather than individual worth and individual need." and is thus "racist."[17] Yet liberal individualism is not completely color-blind on this issue. As Cheryl I. Harris demonstrates, the legacy of liberal individualism has not prevented the Supreme Court from recognizing and protecting the group interests of *whites* in the Bakke, Croson, and Wygant cases.[18] In each case, the Court nullified affirmative action programs because they judged efforts to help blacks as harmful to whites: to white expectations of entitlement, expectations based on the possessive investment in whiteness they held as members of a group. In the Bakke case, for instance, where the plaintiff argued that medical school affirmative action programs disadvantaged white applicants like himself, neither Bakke nor the Court contested the legitimacy of medical school admissions standards that reserved five seats in each class for children of wealthy donors to the university or that penalized Bakke for being older than most of the other applicants. The group rights of not-wealthy people or of people older than their classmates did not compel the Court or Bakke to make any claim of harm. But they did challenge and reject a policy designed to offset the effects of past and present discrimination when they could construe the medical school admission policies as detrimental to the interests of whites as a group—and as a consequence they applied the "strict scrutiny" standard to protect whites while denying that protection to people of color. In this case, as in so many others, the language of liberal individualism serves as a cover for coordinated collective group interests.

Group interests are not monolithic, and aggregate figures can obscure serious differences within racial groups. All whites do not benefit from the possessive investment in whiteness in precisely the same ways; the experiences of members of minority groups are not interchangeable. But the possessive investment in whiteness always affects individual and group life chances and opportunities. Even in cases where minority groups secure political and economic power through collective mobilization, the terms and conditions of their collectivity and the logic of group solidarity are always influenced and intensified by the absolute value of whiteness in U.S. politics, economics, and culture.[19]

In the 1960s, members of the Black Panther Party used to say that "if you're not part of the solution, you're part of the problem." But those of us who are "white" can only become part of the solution if we recognize the degree to which we are already part of the problem—not because of our race, but because of our possessive investment in it. Neither conservative "free market" policies nor liberal social welfare policies can solve the "white problem" in the United States, because both reinforce the possessive investment in whiteness. But an explicitly antiracist interethnic movement that acknowledges the existence and power of whiteness might make some important changes. Antiracist coalitions also have a long history in the United States—in the political activism of John Brown, Sojourner Truth, and the Magon brothers among others, but also in our rich cultural tradition of interethnic antiracism connected to civil rights activism of the kind detailed so brilliantly in rhythm and blues musician Johnny Otis's book, *Upside Your Head! Rhythm and Blues on Central Avenue.* These all too infrequent but nonetheless important efforts by whites to fight racism, not out of sympathy for someone else but out of a sense of self-respect and simple justice, have never completely disappeared; they remain available as models for the present.[20]

Walter Benjamin's praise for "presence of mind" came from his understanding of how difficult it may be to see the present. But more important, he called for presence of mind as the means for implementing what he names "the only true telepathic miracle"—turning the forbidding future into the fulfilled present.[21] Failure to acknowledge our society's possessive investment in whiteness prevents us from facing the present openly and honestly. It hides from us the devastating costs of disinvestment in America's infrastructure over the past two decades and keeps us from facing our responsibility to reinvest in human resources by channeling resources toward education, health, and housing—and away from subsidies for speculation and luxury. After two decades of disinvestment, the only further disinvestment we need is from the ruinous pathology of whiteness, which has always undermined our own best instincts and interests. In a society suffering so badly from an absence of mutuality, an absence of responsibility and an absence of justice, presence of mind might be just what we need.

Notes

The epigraph is from James Baldwin, *The Devil Finds Work* (New York: Dell, 1976), 1.

1. Raphael Tardon, "Richard Wright Tells Us: The White Problem in the United States," *Action*, October 24, 1946. Reprinted in Kenneth Kinnamon and Michel Fabre, *Conversations with Richard Wright* (Jackson: University Press of Mississippi, 1993), 99. Malcolm X and others used this same formulation in the 1960s, but I believe that it originated with Wright, or at least that is the earliest citation I have found.

2. Toni Morrison points out the ways in which African Americans play an essential role in the white imagination, how their representations both hide and reveal the terms of white supremacy upon which the nation was founded and has been sustained ever since. See *Playing in the Dark: Whiteness in the Literary Imagination* (Cambridge: Harvard University Press, 1992).

3. Richard Dyer, "White," *Screen* 29, 4 (fall 1998): 44.

4. I thank Michael Schudson for pointing out to me that since the passage of civil rights legislation in the 1960s whiteness dares not speak its name, cannot speak in its own behalf, but rather advances through a color-blind language radically at odds with the distinctly racialized distribution of resources and life chances in U.S. society.

5. Walter Benjamin, "Madame Ariane: Second Courtyard on the Left," in *One-Way Street* (London: New Left Books, 1969), 98–99.

6. See Lisa Lowe, *Immigrant Acts: On Asian American Cultural Politics* (Durham, N.C.: Duke University Press, 1996), 11–16; Gary B. Nash, *Red, White, and Black: The Peoples of Early America* (Englewood Cliffs, N.J.: Prentice-Hall, 1974); Ronald Takaki, *A Different Mirror: A History of Multicultural America* (Boston: Little, Brown, 1993), 177–83.

7. Nash, *Red, White, and Black*, 292–93.

8. Howard R. Lamar, *Texas Crossings: The Lone Star State and the American Far West, 1836–1986* (Austin: University of Texas Press, 1991), xiii.

9. Cedric J. Robinson, *Black Movements in America* (New York and London: Routledge, 1997), 44.

10. Nash, *Red, White, and Black*, 294.

11. Robinson, *Black Movements in America*, 43–44.

12. Takaki, *A Different Mirror*, 187–88; Peter Narvaez, "The Influences of Hispanic Music Cultures on Afro-American Blues Music," *Black Music Research Journal* 14, 2 (fall 1994): 206; Ernest V. Allen, " 'When Japan Was Champion of the Darker Races': Satokata Takahishi and the Flowering of Black Messianic Nationalism," *Black Scholar* 24, 1: 27–31.

13. Nathan Glazer makes this argument in *Affirmative Discrimination* (New York: Basic Books, 1975).
14. I borrow the term "overdetermination" from Louis Althusser, who uses it to show how dominant ideologies become credible to people in part because various institutions and agencies independently replicate them and reinforce their social power.
15. Rogena Schuyler, "Youth: We Didn't Sell Them into Slavery," *Los Angeles Times,* June 21, 1993, sec. B.
16. Jim Newton, "Skinhead Leader Pleads Guilty to Violence, Plot," *Los Angeles Times,* October 20, 1993, sec. A.
17. Antonin Scalia, "The Disease as Cure," *Washington University Law Quarterly,* no. 147 (1979): 153–54, quoted in Cheryl I. Harris, "Whiteness as Property," *Harvard Law Review* 106, 8 (June 1993): 1767.
18. Harris, ibid., 1993.
19. The rise of a black middle class and the setbacks suffered by white workers during deindustrialization may seem to subvert the analysis presented here. Yet the black middle class remains fragile, far less able than other middle-class groups to translate advances in income into advances in wealth and power. Similarly, the success of neoconservatism since the 1970s has rested on securing support from white workers for economic policies that do them objective harm by mobilizing countersubversive electoral coalitions against busing and affirmative action, while carrying out attacks on public institutions and resources by representing "public" space as black space. See Melvin Oliver and Tom Shapiro, "Wealth of a Nation: A Reassessment of Asset Inequality in America Shows At Least One-Third of Households Are Asset Poor," *Journal of Economics and Sociology* 49, 2 (April 1990). See also John R. Logan and Harvey Molotch, *Urban Fortunes: The Political Economy of Place* (Berkeley: University of California Press, 1994).
20. Johnny Otis, *Upside Your Head! Rhythm and Blues on Central Avenue* (Hanover, N.H.: Wesleyan/University Press of New England, 1993). Mobilizations against plant shutdowns, for environmental protection, against cutbacks in education spending, and for reproductive rights all contain the potential for panethnic antiracist organizing, but too often neglect of race as a central modality for how issues of employment, pollution, education, or reproductive rights are experienced isolates these social movements from their broadest possible base.
21. Benjamin, "Madame Ariane," 98, 99.

PUBLIC SPACES, PRIVATE LIVES

ANNE PHILLIPS

The representation of women is about who gets elected, and even in the most optimistic scenarios it still deals with a political elite. This does not stop it mattering, but for the majority of feminists the questions of democracy have been wider in scope, revolving around prior issues of what "politics" and "political" should mean. The significance feminism attaches to the distinctions between public and private should by now be clear, for the boundary (if any) is continually contested, and most have argued that the relationship must be redefined. To put it with rather more dramatic panache, the women's movement has claimed that "the personal is political." As Iris Young notes, the women's movement "has made public issues out of many practices claimed too trivial or private for public discussion: the meaning of pronouns, domestic violence against women, the practice of men's opening doors for women, the sexual assault on women and children, the sexual division of housework and so on" (1987:74). Things that used to be dismissed as trivial can no longer be viewed as the haphazard consequence of individual choice, for they are structured by relations of power. Things once shrouded in the secrecies of private existence are and should be of public concern. The sexual division of labour and the sexual distribution of power are as much part of politics as relations between classes or negotiations between nations, and what goes on in the kitchen and bedroom cries out for political change.

The conventional distinction between public and private conjures up an image of the public as occupying a specific place: the grandiose chambers of the national assembly; the scaled-down versions of the local town hall. And while political scientists have occasionally played with the idea that politics exists wherever there is conflict—a more expansive notion that could accommodate some women's movement concerns—most fall back into circularity. Politics is about public decisions, and it occurs in a public space. It refers to ministers and cabinets, parliaments and councils; it means parties and pressure groups, civil service and courts. Under the rubric of public opinion, the concept can stretch itself to take on the media, political culture, the schools. But politics is not a question of who looks after the children and who goes out to work, or of who addresses the meeting and who makes the tea. These are private affairs.

It is a measure of the changes that feminism has helped bring about that my contrast already sounds forced, and if I am re-erecting some ancient monument just in order to tear it down. The competing notion that everything is political also has wide currency today (perhaps the noun still attaches itself to definite places, while the adjective will go any old where?). Though the women's movement has no copyright on this, it can certainly claim some credit for spreading the idea around. This is the more extraordinary when we consider the context out of which "the personal is political" came.

It was initially a riposte to male politicos in the civil rights and socialist/radical movements: activists whose conception of politics was far too grand to admit the pertinence of merely sexual concerns. From the middle of the 1960s, women in a number of advanced capitalist countries (though most markedly in the USA) were beginning to question their treatment in Left organizations. The men made the decisions while the women typed the leaflets, and despite the supposed joint commitment to liberating the world, the women were still regarded as just a good time in bed. As David Bouchier has noted, the phrase "women's liberation" was first adopted (round about 1964) with mildly satirical intent (1983:52). Liberation was the word of the moment, and in applying to themselves a term usually reserved for heroic peoples struggling against imperialist aggression, women hoped to establish parallels that no good militant could deny.

Deny it they did, amid gales of laughter and patronizing sneers, and it was against this background that women so much needed to claim their concerns as "political." (The context is revealing, for who else except dedicated radicals would have thought political the thing to be?) A lengthier version of the slogan dating from a 1967 women's newsletter helps fill in the details. After a major conference on the so-called New Politics which had brought together various Left groups but denied any platform to women, Chicago feminists launched the *Voice of the Women's Liberation Movement.* Attacking the blinkered horizons of their erstwhile comrades, they announced that "the liberation of women from their oppression is a problem as worthy of political struggle as any other that the New Politicians were considering" (cited in Bouchier 1983:53). Women's problems are political, too.

The "political" to which these women were laying claim was not the world of elections or governments or theories of the state. Politics worked as shorthand for all those structures (in the language of the time, this would be institutions), of exploitation and oppression against which struggle must be waged. In describing the personal as political, women were contesting those activists who had sneered at their "trivial" concerns. It *did* matter that women were treated as sexual objects to be consumed by the more powerful men. It *did* matter that wives had to pander to their husbands because they could not earn enough to live on their own. It *did* matter that organizations whose rhetoric leapt from one grand proclamation of freedom to another still refused to consider the inequalities of women. Men had power over women, and where there was oppression, there politics came in.

Beyond its early history in 1960s radicalism, the personal is political came to assume a whole complex of meanings. In its most combative forms it dissolved all distinction between public and private, personal and political, and came to regard all aspects of social existence as if they were an undifferentiated expression of male power. This was the version most associated with radical feminism, where patriarchal power came to be viewed as the primary form of oppression (either *the* primary or at least of equal status with class), and the hitherto private sphere of reproduction was identified as the site of this power. Politics and power then came to mean almost the same thing. In *Sexual Politics* (1970), for example, Kate Millett defined power as the essence of politics and patriarchal government as "the institution whereby that half of the populace which is female is controlled by the half which is male" (p. 25). Though she refers to an institution, it is not one located in a particular place—we are a long way here from any conventional institutions of power.

For other feminists, this was a fearful collapse of public and private. Deploying "the personal is political" to more sober effect, they used it to claim not identity but rather a relationship between two spheres. The key point here was that public and private cannot be dealt with as separate worlds, as if the one exists in a rhythm independent from the other. Thus relations inside family and household are knocked into the appropriate shape by a battery of public policies (on housing, for example, social security, education); conversely, relations at the workplace and in politics are moulded by the inequalities of sexual power. From this perspective, it is a nonsense to think of the "personal" as something outside of politics, or to conceive of politics as immune to sexuality and "private" concerns. And when the distinction is employed to deny social responsibility for what goes on behind so-called private doors, it is not only nonsense but directly oppressive.

Various inflections can be put on "the personal is political," and each has implications for the way democracy is conceived. At its minimum, new topics are being placed on the political agenda, and in many cases this redefinition of what counts as public concerns has transformed the opportunities for women to become politically active. The politics that once seemed defined by alien abstractions has been reshaped to include the texture of daily life, offering what was to many a first opening into "political" debate. When feminism turned its spotlight on family and household, it queried the places within which politics occurs, extending the demand for democracy to cover many more arenas. As Sheila Rowbotham has noted, feminism shifts attention towards the sphere of everyday life and widens the meaning of democracy "to include domestic inequality, identity, control over sexuality, challenge to cultural representation, community control over state welfare and more equal access to public resources" (1986:85–6). When politics is redefined, so too is democracy.

But to say that feminism questions, transforms and in some instances dissolves the relationship between public and private is to beg rather a lot of questions. In assessing the implications for the theory and practice of democracy we need to consider which variant is involved.

■ ■ ■ ■

Refashioning this relationship is so much at the heart of feminist politics that you could almost define the tradition in these terms. But so far I have used the phrase somewhat loosely, and mostly in discussing other traditions. I want now to examine the variety of ways in which feminists have queried the division into public and private spheres—and what I shall take to cover similar ground, the different meanings they have attached to the slogan that "the personal is political." I have separated out those aspects that have particular bearing on the problems of democracy, different inflections that may not have equal weight in feminist theory or practice but are the most pertinent in this context. To those who have lived through the last two decades of the women's movement, my emphasis may seem eccentric, or even to miss the point, for while some of what I say will be instantly recognizable as part of the politics of the last twenty years, the rest is phrased in terms that derive from other traditions. The relevance will nonetheless emerge.

Private Constraints on Public Involvement

The first aspect is the one that will come easiest to those versed in mainstream democratic debate. It links the feminist imperative on the relationship between public and private to existing arguments about the degrees of control people exert through their working lives. In this version, "the personal is political" draws attention to the dependence of one sphere on the other, noting that democracy in the home is a precondition for democracy abroad. Supporters of participatory democracy have told us that the experience of hierarchy and subordination at work undercuts our equal development as citizens. If this is so, how much more so does the experience of subordination and submission at home?

Feminists have explored two aspects here, one of them brutally practical and the other to do with our identity and sense of our selves. In the first place women are prevented from participating in public life because of the way their private lives are run. The division of labour between women and men constitutes for most women a double burden of work.

■ ■ ■ ■

The mere pressures of time will keep most women out of any of the processes of decision-making on offer. The active citizenry of the ancient world was freed for participation in public affairs by a vast army of women and slaves who performed the necessary household labour. Today, the most foolhardy of democrats would not risk resurrecting that ideal, for given the contemporary equation of democracy with equality, we must all be more modest in our ideas of what active citizenship entails. But the way our private lives are organized promotes male involvement and reduces female participation. Who collects the children and who makes the tea is a vital political concern.

Often more numbing than the sheer accumulation of practical obstacles is the different experience men and women have of power. Women have only to walk down the street to be reminded of their physical vulnerability and lack of social power, and the night-time scurry from one lighted area to another does not enhance one's feelings of confidence or control. Inside each household there may be too much variation by class, region, race or religion to hazard a generalization over who takes the major family decisions—but the men earn more money and all too often they abuse their greater physical power. Most women's experience at work certainly fits the routinized pattern that has been identified by advocates of workplace democracy as destroying any sense of efficacy or control, while the dominance of nature in women's home lives (by which I mean both the grander experiences of pregnancy and childbirth and the more mundane level of feeding and washing and changing the nappies) does not encourage women to believe they can reshape their world.

■ ■ ■ ■

This is part then of what feminism has to contribute to the debates on democracy: the importance of transforming the familial, domestic, "private" sphere; of laying the groundwork for a democratic society by democratizing sexual relations in the home. But the arguments so far follow a well-worn track, extending established connections between social and political life. Equality in the household is being presented as a means to an end, as a necessary condition for what we really want, which is democracy in the wider sphere. To this extent, the argument does not capture the full flavour of "the personal is political." Taking an analogy from more general debates between socialists and feminists, it is as if the equality of the sexes is being promoted because it has been discovered that it contributes to the development of socialism, but is not valued as an end in itself. Yet the personal is political has usually meant more than that the personal *affects* the political; even in its most sober guises, it is saying that the personal is political too. The second meaning attached to the slogan is thus one that stresses the ubiquity of power. Never mind the learning process, never mind the equalization of time, never mind the cumulative effects of household equality on political participation outside. Democracy is *as* important in the household as anywhere else, for in the household there is unequal power.

Power as All-Pervasive

When the women's movement re-emerged in the late 1960s, it was particularly insistent on women's unhappiness in the family—through boredom, lack of control and because of violence. While the external world of jobs and pay and media and politics figured significantly in campaigns and on the agenda of demands, the more burning preoccupations were often closer to home. In the consciousness-raising groups that were so vital in this period, women began to grapple with their sense of identity and frustration, and, as Sheila Rowbotham describes in her account of the British movement, moved from a puzzled indictment of men's emotional incapacity and women's emotional dependence to a starker sense of coercion and control (1989:6–10). Men and women were supposed to be related through love, but sexuality seemed to be distorting our relations with those who were not our lovers and bringing vulnerability and pain with those who were. Heterosexual love began to look like a trap. Stripped of its romantic gloss, the family began to emerge as a site of male power, a power that in its more benign aspects got women working excessively long hours for minimal reward, and in its worst could expose them to physical and sexual abuse. The family was no haven in a heartless world, the lover no guarantee of harmony or bliss.

This harsher view of family and sexual relations carried with it a more pervasive definition of power. Many had thought of problems they had with husbands or lovers in terms of individual psychology—maybe we're not compatible? maybe I want what's impossible? maybe he just doesn't care?—but in the process of exploring individual experiences, they came to identify general patterns of power. Feminists then disagreed profoundly over who was responsible (was it men or capitalism or structures or roles?) but were reasonably united in stressing the subordination of women in the home. In relation to democracy, this implied a good deal more than the idea that equality in the household is a condition for democracy in the state. It was not just that women were prevented from participating in external activities by the pressures and constraints of the home; women's impotence and subordination, their submission and dependence, crucially mattered in themselves. The personal was *as* political as anything else, and as devastatingly destructive of our human development as anything that governments could do.

■ ■ ■ ■

All this makes it sound a good deal simpler than it is and leaves us with some uneasy questions about the differences between democratizing the family, household or community, democratizing the workplace, and democratizing the state. The democratization of the workplace, for example, can occur through state intervention, through legislation that requires firms to set up decision-making structures that will involve employees or their representatives, that dictates the nature and range of decisions that must be put to the employees, or, more ambitiously, that enforces a transfer of ownership to the workers. The "democratization of everyday life" is not open to the same kind of process. We can perhaps imagine the kind of decision-making structures that would equalize power within the household, but would we welcome the household inspectorate whose job it might be to enforce them? In the first case, we can regulate for democracy. In the second, we are calling on participants to take democracy into their own hands. It is one thing to say that both spheres are characterized by democratically unaccountable power, but once we turn to what might be the democratic solutions, there are important distinctions of kind.

■■■■

A Woman's Right to Choose

The contemporary women's movement has tended to see a woman's right to abortion—her right to decide for herself whether or not to continue with a pregnancy—as the quintessentially feminist demand. A woman who cannot choose what is done with her body is no better than a slave; how could anyone else claim to make this decision? Yet almost as soon as it was articulated, "a woman's right to choose" became a source of anxiety. It was such a defiant assertion of individual rights, such a refusal of social intervention. In most of the issues that have provoked feminist campaigns, the division between public and private was being identified as a crucial element in the subordination of women, something that excused society from its responsibility for caring for the young and old, that confined women to a (lesser) realm they had not chosen to inhabit and, in such phrases as "the Englishman's home is his castle," legitimated domestic violence. Over abortion, feminism seemed to be going the opposite way.

■■■■

Feminists have long been uneasy with the implications. Commenting on the breadth of support for a woman's right to decide for herself whether to have an abortion or not, Susan Himmelweit suggests that "the popularity of the idea of private choice in reproduction is a reflection and acceptance of the existing division," in which having babies is a private, and of course female, concern (1980:67). People respond readily enough because it fits with their existing convictions—and yet these convictions themselves are part of what feminism has attacked. The case for greater social provision for children, for example, has often been argued on the grounds that children are *not* exclusively their mother's concern. With the exception of babies conceived by artificial insemination by donor, each child has both a father and a mother, so why is it only the latter who takes care of the child? Each child will grow up to contribute to the society, so why doesn't society do more to help? The modern counter-argument can all too easily be fuelled by the woman's right to choose whether or not to have babies: "well, you chose to have them, so stop complaining and get on with the job." It is hard (though not impossible) to argue both cases simultaneously, hard to call on fathers and/or society to shoulder more responsibility for those children who are born, and yet in the same breath deny the father or society any voice in making the decision.

■■■■

If abortion is the testing ground for dissolving all differences between public and private, then most feminists fail. When it comes down to it, they do want to retain distinctions between some areas or activities that are open to public decision and others that should remain personal concerns. The argument does not usually depend on how democratically public decisions are made, for women will want to retain control over certain aspects of their lives no matter how impressive the procedures have become. At the same time, however, feminists have wanted to challenge the enforced separation between public and private, and though this may sound too much like having one's cake and eating it, it is not, in fact, inconsistent. As Iris Young has argued (1987), there ought to be certain aspects of our lives from which we are entitled to exclude others, about which we can say they are nobody's affair but our own. (We will argue endlessly about what fits into this category, but that is not to say the category itself is absurd.) Equally important, however, is that there should be no aspect of our lives which we are compelled to keep private. There is no inconsistency, for example, in saying that our sexuality should be our private concern but that homophobia should be on the public agenda. In similar vein, there is no inconsistency in saying that abortion is a decision we must make for ourselves, but that the treatment of children should be a public concern.

Most feminist writing implies a distinction of sorts between public and private. . . . In terms of democracy, this means that the sphere of sexual and family relations cannot be treated in exactly the same way as the sphere of work or the sphere of conventional politics. First, there are some decisions that must be regarded as an individual and not a social affair, and under any conditions that I can envisage, a woman's right to decide for herself whether or not to continue with a pregnancy remains the clearest example of this. When women are denied access to abortion, they are being denied the freedom to make this choice themselves, and are being treated as if their bodies belonged to somebody else. Democracy is not supposed to coexist with slavery, and no society can present itself as fully democratic if it compels women into unwanted pregnancy and childbirth. This seems to be indisputable, but it is worth noting that this version of democracy has a markedly liberal tone.

In the more mundane (if often more pressing) areas of who cleans the house and who cooks the meals, the women's movement has certainly said that democracy should be extended to the private sphere. People rarely make any formal analogy between the equal right to vote in elections and an equal say in household affairs: it is hardly a question of secret ballots on who cleans the bathroom, or formal majorities on what to have for tea. But when women have noted that men presume the authority to take major decisions because they bring in the money on which the household survives, there are strong resonances of what is a classic argument for democracy. Income and wealth should be entirely irrelevant; each individual should have an equal voice. (Women also, of course, argue that incomes should be equalized, and query the complacent formalism of liberal ideas. But the claim on equal standing in household decisions is not made to depend on this.)

■ ■ ■ ■

On abortion, women have demanded the right to take a decision by themselves and not be dictated to by what others say or do. But in other aspects, too, there is a limit to how much we can assimilate private and public spheres. "Household" democracy, in particular, is not really a matter of regulation, imposition, guarantee. There are all kinds of social intervention that can help make relations between the sexes more democratic, and various ways in which public policy or public resources can contribute to a process of change. The provision of refuges and affordable accommodation can give more women a choice about leaving relationships that are beyond redemption; changes in the hours that men and women work can increase the chances for equalizing the distribution of household tasks; changes in the practices of mortgage companies, landlords and insurance offices can give women more of a say. All these can empower women, making it more possible for them to claim their place as equals and encouraging the practices of democracy in the home. None of these, however, can dictate what goes on between lovers or husbands and wives—and with the exception of bodily injury, most people prefer it this way. At the end of the day, what happens will depend on the individuals themselves, on how much they insist on change.

Means and Ends

This is no news to the women's movement, and indeed it is much of what "the personal is political" has meant to feminists over the last twenty years. Part of the slipperiness of the slogan is that it takes us out of our personal preoccupations and experiences, and simultaneously lets us treat these experiences as the political centre of our life. Thus, on the one hand, it has helped women see that what they thought of as peculiar to themselves (personal, unique and perhaps basically their fault) may be part of a general pattern of sexual relations that is then available to political change. On the other hand, it gives women the confidence to claim the kind of changes they can already make (refusing to cook the dinner or type the leaflet, maybe even throwing him out) as politically important. Politics then becomes something other than procedures or rules or programmes for change. It is what we do in our everyday life.

Politics had become associated with alien or grandiose concerns, either because it was thought to happen in particular places (from which women were absent), or because it dealt with matters of earth-shattering importance (on which women could have nothing to say). Contemporary feminism has challenged this, theoretically in terms of the abstract way men have thought about power, and practically in saying politics has no integrity until it is grounded in everyday life. Drawing attention to the detailed texture of our daily lives, "the personal is political" has claimed a continuum between those things that were previously considered the most trivial and minor and those to which the term politics could be confidently attached. But instead of referring to a particular place (the household), this version of "the personal" stresses aspects that will be present in every activity, no matter where or when it takes place. This is perhaps the most characteristic of all the meanings associated with the slogan and the one that will be most familiar to those who have been active in the women's movement over the last decades. What implications does it have for democracy?

When women in the civil rights or socialist movement said the personal was political, part of what they were stressing was the relationship between means and ends. There was something pretty suspect about organizations that could see themselves as dedicated to liberation but treated the women involved as if they had no abilities or minds of their own. The ideals were being subverted by the daily practice, and yet most men seemed to think this a silly complaint. The new women's movement was convinced that it did indeed matter and consistently emphasized the ways women related to one another as a crucial part of what the movement was about. You could not claim to be involved in a politics of liberation if you unthinkingly exploited other people's time and energies and continually put people down. The division of labour mattered, so did inequalities in confidence or capacities, and so did any separation into leaders and led. Feminism meant thinking about all these issues, regarding the way you organized as something that was as important and revealing as your goals.

■ ■ ■ ■

For a variety of reasons, then, I am arguing that we *do* need a distinction between private and public, and that rather than abandoning this distinction, the emphasis should be on uncoupling it from the division between women and men. First, there are some decisions which will remain individual ones, and no matter how thoroughly democratized public debate and decision-making may become, there are matters we will want to reserve to ourselves. The clearest example of this is a woman's decision about continuing or terminating a pregnancy, but a less gender-specific example might be the choices we make about our sexuality. Second, even within the much larger category of decisions where a number of people are involved and each is then entitled to an equal voice, there is a distinction between spheres within which democracy can be imposed and spheres within which it should be enabled. If we take the simplest definition of democracy as saying that everyone should have a vote and nobody more than one, there will be certain areas where this can and should be enforced by law (it should be illegal to vote twice in elections) and others where it would be nonsense to have formal regulation. Feminism has brought the domestic sphere much more clearly into the orbit of democratic debate, but the argument is that women should be empowered so that they can insist on the equality themselves, and in this sense it still retains a distinction.

Finally, the equation of the personal with the political has drawn attention to the details of how people relate and organize and has thus been linked to the democratization of whatever association (including places of work) we find ourselves in. On this point, however, feminists have sometimes acted as if there were an amorphous continuum in which there are no distinctions beyond those of size. Here, too, we need to differentiate. There is a difference between extending control over decisions to everyone involved in a particular venture or place of work, and increasing participation in what has been traditionally defined as politics. The one does not lead inexorably to the other. Feminism rightly queries the exclusive emphasis on "politics" as conventionally defined and has stressed the often more immediate issues of taking control where we work and live. This positive insistence on the democratization of everyday life should not become a substitute for a more lively and vital political life.

References

Bouchier, David 1983: *The Feminist Challenge: The Movement for Women's Liberation in Britain and the United States.* Macmillan.

Himmelweit, Susan 1980: Abortion: individual choice and social control. *Feminist Review*, 5.

Millett, Kate 1970: *Sexual Politics.* Jonathan Cape.

Rowbotham, Sheila 1986: Feminism and democracy. In David Held and Christopher Pollitt (eds.), *New Forms of Democracy*, Open University and Sage.

———1989: *The Past Is Before Us: Feminism in Action Since the 1960s.* Pandora.

Young, Iris Marion 1987: Impartiality and the civic public. In Seyla Benhabib and Drucilla Cornell (eds.), *Feminism as Critique.* Polity.

THE BODY OF THE CONDEMNED

MICHEL FOUCAULT

Historians long ago began to write the history of the body. They have studied the body in the field of historical demography or pathology; they have considered it as the seat of needs and appetites, as the locus of physiological processes, and metabolisms, as a target for the attacks of germs or viruses; they have shown to what extent historical processes were involved in what might seem to be the purely biological base of existence; and what place should be given in the history of society to biological "events" such as the circulation of bacilli, or the extension of the life-span. But the body is also directly involved in a political field; power relations have an immediate hold upon it; they invest it, mark it, train it, torture it, force it to carry out tasks, to perform ceremonies, to emit signs. This political investment of the body is bound up, in accordance with complex reciprocal relations, with its economic use; it is largely as a force of production that the body is invested with relations of power and domination; but, on the other hand, its constitution as labour power is possible only if it is caught up in a system of subjection (in which need is also a political instrument meticulously prepared, calculated and used); the body becomes a useful force only if it is both a productive body and a subjected body. This subjection is not only obtained by the instruments of violence or ideology; it can also be direct, physical, pitting force against force, bearing on material elements, and yet without involving violence; it may be calculated, organized, technically thought out; it may be subtle, make use neither of weapons nor of terror and yet remain of a physical order. That is to say, there may be a "knowledge" of the body that is not exactly the science of its functioning, and a mastery of its forces that is more than the ability to conquer them: this knowledge and this mastery constitute what might be called the political technology of the body. Of course, this technology is diffuse, rarely formulated in continuous, systematic discourse; it is often made up of bits and pieces; it implements a disparate set of tools or methods. In spite of the coherence of its results, it is generally no more than a multiform instrumentation. Moreover, it cannot be localized in a particular type of institution or state apparatus. For they have recourse to it; they use, select or impose certain of its methods. But, in its mechanisms and its effects, it is situated at a quite different level. What the apparatuses and institutions operate is, in a sense, a micro-physics of power, whose field of validity is situated in a sense between these great functionings and the bodies themselves with their materiality and their forces.

Now, the study of this micro-physics presupposes that the power exercised on the body is conceived not as a property, but as a strategy, that its effects of domination are attributed not to "appropriation," but to dispositions, manoeuvres, tactics, techniques, functionings; that one should decipher in it a network of relations; constantly in tension, in activity, rather than a privilege that one might possess; that one should take as its model a perpetual battle rather than a contract regulating a transaction or the conquest of a territory. In short this power is exercised rather than possessed; it is not the "privilege," acquired or preserved, of the dominant class, but the overall effect of its strategic positions—an effect that is manifested and sometimes extended by the position of those who are dominated. Furthermore, this power is not exercised simply as an obligation or a prohibition on those who "do not have it"; it invests them, is transmitted by them and through them; it exerts pressure upon them, just as they themselves, in their struggle against it, resist the grip it has on them. This means that these relations go right down into the depths of society, that they are not localized in the relations between the state and its citizens or on the frontier between classes and that they do not merely reproduce, at the level of individuals, bodies, gestures and behaviour, the general form of the law or government. . . . Lastly, they are not univocal; they define innumerable points of confrontation, focuses of instability, each of which has its own risks of conflict, of struggles, and of an at least temporary inversion of the power relations. The overthrow of these "micro-powers" does not, then, obey the law of all or nothing; it is not acquired once and for all by a new control of the apparatuses nor by a new functioning or a destruction of the institutions; on the other hand, none of its localized episodes may be inscribed in history except by the effects that it induces on the entire network in which it is caught up.

Perhaps, too, we should abandon a whole tradition that allows us to imagine that knowledge can exist only where the power relations are suspended and that knowledge can develop only outside its injunctions, its demands and its interests. Perhaps we should abandon the belief that power makes mad and that, by the same token, the renunciation of power is one of the conditions of knowledge. We should admit rather that power produces knowledge (and not simply by encouraging it because it serves power or by applying it because it is useful); that power and knowledge directly imply one another; that there is no power relation without the correlative constitution of a field of knowledge, nor any knowledge that does not presuppose and constitute at the same time power relations. These "power-knowledge relations" are to be analysed, therefore, not on the basis of a subject of knowledge who is or is not free in relation to the power system, but, on the contrary, the subject who knows, the objects to be known and the modalities of knowledge must be regarded as so many effects of these fundamental implications of power-knowledge and their historical transformations. In short, it is not the activity of the subject of knowledge that produces a corpus of knowledge, useful or resistant to power, but power-knowledge, the processes and struggles that traverse it and of which it is made up, that determines the forms and possible domains of knowledge.

SECTION II
STATE THEORY

In Western political theory, the state is seen as the representative of the common good. The writings of the early social contract theorists, such as Thomas Hobbes and John Locke, present the state as a neutral arbiter of conflicting individual interests, one that is necessary to ensure social peace and order (Carnoy 1984; Held 1987). Contemporary theorists such as Joseph Schumpeter and Robert Dahl make a similar argument. For Schumpeter, citizens (who, you will recall, Schumpeter thought were incapable of direct participation in politics) choose legislators to serve as representatives of the general will (Schumpeter 1976). For Dahl, the diversity of citizen interests, and the assumption that no one interest is consistently dominant, suggests that the state serves to mediate these differences and produce policy outcomes that take these interests into account (Dahl 1956). The writings in this section challenge this assumption, and instead argue that the state represents the interests of dominant groups. In doing so, critical theories of the state can be understood as specific applications of the theories of power discussed in the previous section.

Because "[Karl] Marx did not develop a single, coherent theory of politics and/or the State"(Carnoy 1984:45), there has been considerable debate among critical theorists of the state. Hal Draper provides a concise statement of how Karl Marx and Friedrich Engels conceptualized the state. For Marx and Engels, the state emerges from the relations of production characteristic of a specific society. As such, the state does not represent the common interest, but rather the fundamental interests of the dominant class. The state is a coercive system of specialized institutions that, in class-dominated societies, separates out from the general body of society and protects the property relations that serve as the foundation of the power of the ruling class. The specific mechanisms by which the state acts as an instrument of the dominant class, however, are not clearly specified in their writing. We saw in the last section how, for Gramsci, the state serves as an educator, building consent for its rule among members of subordinate groups by granting concessions (such as the right to unionize, civil rights for African-Americans, etc.) in a strategic manner. We will see later on, in the section on war, genocide, and repression, how the repressive power of the state is used to preserve fundamental social relations.

The selections by G. William Domhoff and Fred Block are representative of two major directions that more contemporary authors have taken in examining the state. Domhoff argues that a power elite, by which he means a leadership group consisting of members of the social upper class, representatives from major corporations and financial institutions, and participants in the policy formation organizations supported by the other two, is itself a governing class. Domhoff's class dominance framework suggests that the state serves capital because its representatives are directly involved in the state. As we will see in the next section (on electoral politics), this involvement takes a number of forms, including serving as appointees to top government positions and participating in the social networks through which corporate-oriented policies are developed.

Block provides an alternative analysis of the state, one that acknowledges the state's role in reproducing capitalism while simultaneously asserting that a considerable degree of autonomy exists in terms of the specific ways in which the state undertakes this role. Block challenges the idea, which he sees as common on both the right and the left, that the economy is autonomous from politics; for the right, such an assumption leads to a desire to minimize state intervention in markets, while for the left it leads to a kind of economic determinism in which politics is derivative of economic forces. Block instead argues that markets are constructed by the state; indeed, the imperatives of a market economy would destroy society if not for the structure imposed by the state. He does not deny that economic forces help to shape state policy. As Block argues elsewhere (Block 1987), state managers, in pursuit of their own interests, have little choice but to pursue policies that privilege the ruling class. In a capitalist economy, state managers are dependent on private capital to generate the tax revenue they need to fund state functions and provide for the employment and economic security of its citizens that give state managers political legitimacy. However, in this article Block argues that the state's central role in constructing the economy means that there is no one general "logic" of capitalism. Instead, differences in the internal balance of political forces and in a state's position in the world capitalist system will lead to differences in the specific institutional forms taken by a capitalist economy.

Mimi Abramovitz also rejects the traditional concept of the state as a neutral representative of the common good, but her critique is based on a socialist feminist rather than a Marxist perspective; indeed, she is critical of Marxism for what she sees as its inadequate analysis of gender. Abramovitz argues that the state is simultaneously capitalist and patriarchal, upholding both class and gender domination and mediating contradictions between the two. As Phillips suggested in the previous section, the state intervenes in the family and gender relations to maintain the family's role as an institution that contributes to the reproduction of capitalism, and state regulation of women's domestic and market labor contributes to the reproduction of a patriarchal gender division of labor. At the same time, however, Abramovitz suggests that the contradictions between these two roles make the state a contested terrain in which subordinate groups can challenge what she calls "patriarchal capitalism."

Although critical debates about the nature of the state peaked during the 1970s and 1980s, they are still quite relevant today (see Aronowitz and Bratsis 2002). Conservatives have for over twenty-five years led an assault against "big government," but in fact the state has in many ways become stronger during this period. It has, as we will see in Section IV on the welfare state, escalated its efforts to stigmatize poor people as lazy welfare cheats, thereby leading to the creation of a more restrictive and punitive set of welfare policies. It has also been more aggressive in efforts to undermine labor unions by refusing to enforce or strengthen existing labor laws, privatizing public services, and imposing cuts in wages and benefits on unionized public employees. Our discussion of war, genocide, and repression later in the book will examine the increasing significance of coercive state power in the context of the "war on terrorism" and the increasingly militarized and repressive criminal justice system. Finally, we will see how, despite the widespread argument that the state is decreasing in importance in the context of the global economy, the major capitalist states are in many ways in the driver's seat of globalization; the United States has long played a leadership role in multilateral institutions such as the World Bank and the International Monetary Fund, and its refusal to accept other institutions such as the International Criminal Court effectively renders them moot. Failure to appreciate the continued significance of the state will be costly, not only in terms of the fullness of our sociological analysis but also in terms of our efforts to expand democracy and social equality.

References

Aronowitz, Stanley, and Peter Bratsis. 2002. *Paradigm Lost: State Theory Reconsidered.* Minneapolis: University of Minnesota Press.

Block, Fred. 1987. "The Ruling Class Does Not Rule: Notes on the Marxist Theory of the State." *Revising State Theory.* Philadelphia: Temple University Press.

Carnoy, Martin. 1984. *The State and Political Theory.* Princeton: Princeton University Press.

Dahl, Robert. 1956. *A Preface to Democratic Theory.* Chicago: University of Chicago Press.

Held, David. 1987. *Models of Democracy.* Stanford: Stanford University Press.

Schumpeter, Joseph. 1976. *Capitalism, Socialism, and Democracy.* London: Allen and Unwin.

THE STATE AS SUPERSTRUCTURE

HAL DRAPER

The state, then, comes into existence insofar as the institutions needed to carry out the common functions of the society require, for their continued maintenance, the separation of the power of forcible coercion from the general body of society.

■ ■ ■ ■

The state is the institution, or complex of institutions, which bases itself on the availability of forcible coercion by special agencies of society in order to maintain the dominance of a ruling class, preserve existing property relations from basic change, and keep all other classes in subjection.

"In subjection" does not mean cowering under a whip—not necessarily and not usually. More generally it means also: in willing compliance, in passive acquiescence, or in ingrained dependence. The ruling class relies in the first place on its economic pressures:

> The possessing classes [wrote Engels] . . . keep the working class in servitude not only by the might of their wealth, by the simple exploitation of labor by capital, but also by the power of the state—by the army, the bureaucracy, the courts.[1]

Direct state measures are, to begin with, an auxiliary method, and in the end an *ultima ratio.*

Here is a summary which continues a passage from Engels cited above:

> The state . . . is a product of society at a certain stage of development; it is the admission that this society has become entangled in an insoluble contradiction with itself, that it is cleft into irreconcilable antagonisms which it is powerless to dispel. But in order that these antagonisms, classes with conflicting economic interests, might not consume themselves and society in sterile struggle, a power seemingly standing above society became necessary for the purpose of moderating the conflict, of keeping it within the bounds of "order"; and this power, arisen out of society, but placing itself above it, and increasingly alienating itself from it, is the state.[2]

In this sense, politics is concentrated economics: "the power of the state," wrote Marx, is "the concentrated and organized force of society"; in this sense the state is "the summing up of bourgeois society."[3] The relations it sums up "are *economic* before everything else."[4] It is "a reflection, in concentrated form, of the economic needs of the class controlling production," wrote Engels.[5] The "concentration" metaphor emphasizes the social essence of state power but, as we shall see, cannot do equal justice to all its aspects. Marx suggested another metaphor: the state is "the political superstructure" which rests on the socioeconomic organization of society; the formalist, eyes bent only on the political forms, refuses to become acquainted with the "economic realities" that underlie those forms; but "All real progress in the writing of modern history has been effected by descending from the political surface into the depths of social life."* In modern history, says Engels, "the state—the political order—is the subordinate, and civil society—the realm of economic relations—the decisive element."[8]

*The quotations here are from an article by Marx in 1858.[6] This base superstructure metaphor, sometimes treated as a late invention by Engels, was first set down in *The German Ideology*: "The social organization, evolving directly out of production and commerce, . . . in all ages forms the basis of the state and of the rest of the ideological superstructure, . . ."[7]

Special Characteristics of the State

The new political institution, the state, differs from the primitive (protopolitical) organizing authorities of tribal communities in a number of important respects.

1. The state is a power over a given *territory* (thereby including the people in the territory), rather than over a kinship group of related people. The equation of a political structure with a given territory or slice of the earth was once an innovation.

The state had to be based on territory because of the rise of private property and the social consequences of this change. Consider the way in which Engels traces this process, in a little detail, in the specific case of Athens.[9] As new economic relations (slavery, exchange of products, money, and so on) disintegrated the old kinship social groups over a period of time, the very members of the kinship groups were scattered over the whole of Attica, instead of concentrating around their communally owned land. In the city of Athens itself, commercial interests mingled them all helter skelter. New occupations divided the population into new types of interest groups which had no relationship to the old kinship structure. The new slave class was outside the old structure altogether, as were also strangers and foreigners who settled in Athens for the new commercial purposes. Thus the old social structure based on kinship was progressively destroyed, and the new institutions developing to organize the new social relations could work only by taking people by where they lived, not by blood relationships.

Marx makes the further point that a state can scarcely arise as long as family units are (say) scattered singly through a forest area as among the old Germanic tribes. A certain amount of *urban* concentration is required to form the unity that corresponds to a state. In the old German case, there may indeed be a community formed by such rurally scattered family units connected by kinship ties; but while this community structure may serve to unify them, it does not turn them into such a unity. In Marx's words:

> The *community* therefore appears as a *unification*, not as a *union*; as a unification in which the owners of land form independent subjects, not as a unity. Hence the community does not exist "in fact" as a *state*, a *state entity*, as in antiquity, because it does not exist as a *town*. In order for the community to come into actual existence, the free landowners must hold an *assembly*, whereas—for example in Rome—it *exists* apart from such assemblies in the very existence of the *town itself* and the officials heading it, etc.[10]

2. The second characteristic we have already stressed: the creation of *specialized* institutions and instruments of coercion divorced from the communal whole.

> The second is the establishment of a *public power* which no longer directly coincides with the population organizing itself as an armed force. This special public power is necessary because a self-acting armed organization of the population has become impossible since the cleavage into classes. The slaves also belonged to the population; the 90,000 citizens of Athens formed only a privileged class as against the 365,000 slaves. The people's army of the Athenian democracy was an aristocratic public power against the slaves, whom it kept in check; however, a gendarmerie also became necessary to keep the citizens in check. . . . This public power exists in every state; it consists not merely of armed men but also of material adjuncts, prisons and institutions of coercion of all kinds, of which gentile [kinship] society knew nothing. It may be very insignificant, almost infinitesimal, in societies where class antagonisms are still undeveloped and in out-of-the-way places as was the case at certain times and in certain regions in the United States of America.* It grows stronger, however, in

*The coming of state power to these regions is a characteristic theme of the Hollywood Western: the man with the badge or the cavalry detachment galloping to the rescue represents state power (the white man's). Part of the Western's fascination for overcivilized people no doubt stems from a primitive situation existing in relatively recent times.

proportion as class antagonisms within the state become acute, and as adjacent states become larger and more populous. We have only to look at our present-day Europe, where class struggle and rivalry in conquest have screwed up the public power to such a pitch that it threatens to devour the whole of society and even the state itself. [11]

Marx, commenting on the fact that the official title of a Hohenzollern ruler is *Kriegsherr*, "Lord of War," says it means

that the true prop of their kingly power must be sought for, not in the people, but in a portion of the people, separated from the mass, opposed to it, distinguished by certain badges, trained to passive obedience, drilled into a mere instrument of the dynasty which owns it as its property and uses it according to its caprice.[12]

3. The new state institution, from the very beginning, is more expensive than the old ways of organizing society. It has to be paid for by special contributions from the citizens: *taxes.*

These were absolutely unknown in gentile society, but we know enough about them today. As civilization advances, these taxes become inadequate; the state makes drafts on the future, contracts loans, *public debts.*[13]

These are all different means by which the state conscripts the citizens' purse to finance itself. It follows that the old saw, "Nothing is certain but death and taxes," is a product of class society, not of human nature.

4. The new and special functions of the state require a new officialdom on an unprecedented scale, which becomes a bureaucracy—a *ruling* officialdom. Now it is true that even in the protopolitical authorities of the tribal communities, the division of labor required that certain individuals become functionaries, devoting most of their time to public functions (religious and tribal chieftains, and so on), but this was often a temporary status, it did not necessarily confer ruling power, and the number involved was small. However, the main difference between such functionaries and the typical state bureaucracy lies in something else. The state makes special efforts to separate its bureaucratic personnel from the population as a whole, to erect a special social wall around them, to elevate them above society, to invest them with an aura of unquestionable privilege.

Having public power and the right to levy taxes, the officials now stand, as organs of society, *above* society. The free, voluntary respect that was accorded to the organs of the gentile constitution does not satisfy them, even if they could gain it; being the vehicles of a power that is becoming alien to society, respect for them must be enforced by means of exceptional laws by virtue of which they enjoy special sanctity and inviolability. The shabbiest police servant in the civilized state has more "authority" than all the organs of gentile [clan] society put together; but the most powerful prince and the greatest statesman, or general, of civilization may well envy the humblest gentile chief for the unstrained and undisputed respect that is paid to him. The one stands in the midst of society, the other is forced to attempt to represent something outside and above it.[14]

While the status of the bureaucracy in society varies considerably according to time and place, it has never been clearer than today that it is this characteristic of officialdom which is increasingly the mark of exploitative societies.

The State as Class Executive

Engels recognized the class role played by the mystique of "the sanctity of the law" very early, before he was much influenced by Marx, that is, in the pages of his *Condition of the Working Class in England*:

Certainly the law is sacred to the bourgeois, for it is of his own making, put through with his approval and for his

> protection and benefit. He knows that even if a particular law may injure him as an individual, still the complex of legislation as a whole protects his interests; and that above all the strongest support of his social position is the sanctity of the law and the inviolability of the order established by the active expression of will by one part of society and passive acceptance by the other. It is because the English bourgeois sees his own image in the law, as he does in his God, that he holds it to be holy and that the policeman's club (which is really his own club) holds a power for him that is wonderfully reassuring. But for the worker it certainly does not. The worker knows only too well and from too long experience that the law is a rod that the bourgeois holds over his head, and he does not bother himself about it unless he has to.[15]

Marx noted the pattern of sanctification in a discussion which applied immediately to the justification of private property in land but would apply equally to all private property:

> . . . they [jurists, philosophers, and political economists] disguise the original fact of conquest under the cloak of "Natural Right." If conquest constituted a natural right on the part of the few, the many have only to gather sufficient strength in order to acquire the natural right of reconquering what has been taken from them. In the progress of history the conquerors attempt to give a sort of social sanction to their original title derived from brute force, through the instrumentality of laws imposed by themselves. At last comes the philosopher who declares those laws to imply the universal consent of society.[16]

Engels sums up the general analysis as follows:

> Because the state arose from the need to hold class antagonisms in check, but because it arose, at the same time, in the midst of the conflict of these classes, it is, as a rule,* the state of the most powerful, economically dominant class, which, through the medium of the state, becomes also the politically dominant class, and thus acquires new means of holding down and exploiting the oppressed class. Thus, the state of antiquity was above all the state of the slave owners for the purpose of holding down the slaves, as the feudal state was the organ of the nobility for holding down the peasant serfs and bondsmen, and the modern representative state is an instrument of exploitation of wage-labor by capital.[18]

The best-known summary statement is in the *Communist Manifesto.* This is not directed generally to the nature of the state, but specifically to the situation where

> . . . the bourgeoisie has at last, since the establishment of Modern Industry and of the world market, conquered for itself, in the modern representative State, exclusive political sway. The executive of the modern State is but a committee for managing the common affairs of the whole bourgeoisie.[19]

And at the end of Part II of the Manifesto: "Political power, properly so called, is [**] the organized power of one class for oppressing another."[21]

There is a common paraphrase of this, sometimes given (mistakenly) as an actual quotation from Marx, namely "The state is the executive committee of the ruling class." Similar summary sentences will be found elsewhere in Marx and Engels.[22]

The most useful short statement of the role of the state is the one suggested by the Manifesto formulation: the state is the institution "for

*Note the qualification "as a rule": immediately following this section as quoted, Engels goes on to discuss exceptions to the rule. A similar qualification occurs in his *Origin of the Family*: "The cohesive force of civilized society is the state, which in all typical periods is exclusively the state of the ruling class. . . ."[17]

**The standard Marx-Engels translation inserts the word *merely* at this point; it is not in the German original. Like the *but* (*nur*) in the preceding citation ("The executive of the modern state is but a committee . . . "),[20] the word is an intensive.

managing the common affairs" of the ruling class. For Marx, there is no doubt that its basic task ("above all," as Engels says) is to "hold down and exploit the oppressed class." But whenever necessary they make clear that this is not its *only* task, not its *only* role, despite the occurrence of emphatic words like *merely*, *nothing but*, and so on in short aphoristic formulations.

Subsidiary Tasks of the State

This state, which manages the common affairs of the ruling class, has other tasks too. Three other tasks, in fact, and it is not necessary to go far to find them. They are analogues of the same three tasks we listed a few pages back as characteristic of *any* organizing authority in a society, even in a stateless community. Translated into state terms, these subsidiary tasks may be described as follows:

1. There are certain functions which any government must perform in order to keep the society going, even if we assume they are of no special advantage to the ruling class. Sanitation departments prevent epidemics; policemen find lost babies; help is given to areas struck by natural disasters like hurricanes or earthquakes. These may take on the appearance of nonclass functions even in a class-bound state.

2. The state developed from the beginning on a national or imperial basis; it exists within territorial boundaries. As a national state, it manages the common affairs of the ruling class of that particular state as against the rival ruling classes of other national states. Entrenched behind national boundaries, the separate states vie for trade, raw materials, investment, commercial advantage, and so on. Behind each boundary, one of the tasks of the state is to safeguard and advance the interests of its own ruling class against all rivals.

3. The ruling class itself is not a monolithic block; it is shot through with criss-crossing interest blocs, as well as ordinary individual competitive antagonisms. Particularly under capitalism—which begins as dog-eat dog competition—one of the tasks of the state is to mediate, reconcile, in some way settle the internecine disputes and conflicts *within* the ruling class. This does not imply that the state institutions act as impartial Solomons even in intracapitalist terms: for there is a hierarchy of economic power as well as political influence. But some kind of settlement of intraclass disputes there must be, in order to avoid tearing the whole social fabric apart in an unregulated melee.

What is the relationship between the basic task of the state ("holding down and exploiting the oppressed class") and the three subsidiary tasks which we have described? There are two differences to be noted.

1. The most obvious difference is that, from Marx's standpoint, the state's task of class domination is not only basic but its specific *reason for existence*. The other three are tasks which the state has taken over from its preceding protopolitical institutions; it is not these tasks which bring the state into existence.

Operationally, this difference has a profound consequence for the historical reactions of the ruling class; for experience shows that in practice the ruling class *does subordinate* the three subsidiary tasks to the first (basic) task, where there is a clash. It will forget internal class differences to make common cause against a threat from below, and it will conspire with the national enemy if its own working class threatens its rear. As Marx noted that the Prussians were aiding the French Versailles government in crushing the Paris Commune, he added:

> It was only the old story. The upper classes always united to keep down the working class. In the eleventh century there was a war between some French knights and Norman knights, and the peasants rose in insurrection; the knights immediately forgot their differences and coalesced to crush the movement of the peasants.[23]

About the same time, he entered in his notebook:

> The *Paris-Journal*, the most ignoble of the Versailles papers, says: "the peace has been signed.—With our enemies? No, with the Prussians. And, however great our hatred may be of those who ruined us [Prussians], we must say that it cannot

> equal the horror with which we are filled by those who dishonor us [Parisians]."[24]

In domestic affairs, wrote Marx, the same bourgeois liberals who condemn government intervention are the first to demand it if the target is the working class:

> These same "gallant" free-traders, renowned for their indefatigability in denouncing government interference, these apostles of the bourgeois doctrine of *laissez-faire,* who profess to leave everything and everybody to the struggles of individual interests are always the first to appeal to the interference of Government as soon as the individual interests of the working-man come into conflict with their own class-interests. In such moments of collision they look with open admiration at the Continental States where despotic governments, though, indeed, not allowing the bourgeoisie to rule, at least prevent the working-men from resisting.[25]

2. The second difference is that the three subsidiary tasks, unlike the basic task, may convey the appearance of being nonclass in character, as if simply actuated by the need of society or nation as a whole rather than by the self-interest of the dominant class. On this ground it has been common to attack the Marxist "exaggeration" which views the state as primarily a class instrument. This is not the place to argue the question, but only to establish what Marx's viewpoint is.

It should be clear from what has already been explained that there is no question about one thing: the state really does have nonclass tasks, and it carries them out. *But it carries them out inevitably in class-distorted ways, for class ends, with class consequences.*

The Class Nature of the State

The position has nothing to do with denying that there are all kinds of nonclass *aspects* to society. What is important is understanding that the class character of a society permeates every aspect of the society, including these.

One illustration: it is certainly in the interest of society as a whole, that epidemics be prevented; hence sanitation can be regarded as a nonclass task of government. But in historical fact the ruling powers embraced city-wide sanitation only when it was impressed on them that plagues originating among the poor also killed the rich. Marx noted in *Capital* that "the mere fear of contagious diseases which do not spare even 'respectability,' brought into existence from 1847 to 1864 no less than ten Acts of Parliament on sanitation," and "the frightened bourgeois" in the big cities took municipal measures.[26] Engels describes what happened as science proved that such ravaging diseases as cholera and smallpox incubated their germs in the pestilential conditions of the poor districts before spreading to the other side of the tracks:

> As soon as this fact had been scientifically established the philanthropic bourgeois became inflamed with a noble spirit of competition in their solicitude for the health of their workers. Societies were founded, books were written, proposals drawn up, laws debated and passed, in order to stop up the sources of the ever-recurring epidemics. The housing conditions of the workers were investigated and attempts made to remedy the most crying evils.

The capitalist state exerts itself to do the workers good, and its professors can now easily prove that the class bias of the state is grossly exaggerated. But to this day the class character of sanitation can be observed with the naked eye by comparing any workers' district with any rich residential district. The dominant economic interests certainly will not allow conditions so bad as to breed plagues:

> Nevertheless, the capitalist order of society reproduces again and again the evils to be remedied, and does so with such inevitable necessity that even in England the remedying of them has hardly advanced a single step.[27]

The next remedial step is "urban renewal" or slum clearance, in the name of such obviously nonclass aspirations as "civic improvement." This pattern was already an old story to Marx, who pointed out in *Capital*:

> "Improvements" of towns, accompanying the increase of wealth, by the demolition of badly built quarters, the erection of palaces for banks, warehouses, &c., the widening of streets for business traffic, for the carriages of luxury [automobile freeways], and for the introduction of tramways, &c. [rapid-transit projects], drive away the poor into even worse and more crowded hiding places.[28]

Engels pointed to the Bonapartist prefect of Paris, Haussmann, as the model for

> the practice, which has now become general, of making breaches in the working-class quarters of our big cities, particularly in those which are centrally situated, irrespective of whether this practice is occasioned by considerations of public health and beautification or by the demand for big centrally located business premises or by traffic requirements, such as the laying down of railways, streets, etc. No matter how different the reasons may be, the result is everywhere the same: the most scandalous alleys and lanes disappear to the accompaniment of lavish self-glorification by the bourgeoisie on account of this tremendous success, but—they appear again at once somewhere else, and often in the immediate neighborhood.[29]

In sum: the class nature of the state is attested not by the fact that every act is necessarily, equally, and exclusively in the direct interest of the ruling class only, but by the fact that all other interests are regularly *subordinated* to the interests of the ruling class, that the acts of the state are decisively shaped by what the ruling class and its representatives conceive its interests to be, and take place only within the framework of those interests. Along these lines Engels makes a comparison:

> As all the driving forces of the actions of any individual person must pass through his brain, and transform themselves into motives of his will in order to set him into action, so also all the needs of civil society—no matter which class happens to be the ruling one—must pass through the will of the state in order to secure general validity in the form of laws. . . . If we inquire into this we discover that in modern history the will of the state is, on the whole, determined by the changing needs of civil society, by the supremacy of this or that class, in the last resort, by the development of the productive forces and relations of exchange.[30]

The needs of society, no matter how class-neutral in origin or intention, cannot be met without passing through the political (and other) institutions set up by a class-conditioned society; and it is in the course of being processed through these channels that they are shaped, sifted, skewed, molded, modeled, and modulated to fit within the framework established by the ruling interests and ideas. This is how the class nature of the state and the society asserts itself, even without malevolent purposes or sinister plots.

Notes

1. Letter, Engels to Spanish Federated Council of the International Working Men's Association, 13 February 1871, in Marx and Engels *Selected Correspondence*, 260.
2. Engels, *The Origin of the Family, Private Property, and the State*, in Marx and Engels *Selected Works* Volume 3, 326–327.
3. Marx, *Capital*, Volume I, 751; Marx, *Grundrisse*, 28–29.
4. Marx, *Notebook on Maine*, 329.
5. Engels, *Ludwig Feuerbach and the End of Classical German Philosophy*, in Marx and Engels *Selected Works* Volume 3, 370.
6. Marx, "Mazzini and Napoleon," in *New York Tribune*, 11 May 1858.
7. Marx and Engels, *The German Ideology*, Marx and Engels *Werke* Volume 3, 36.
8. Engels, *Ludwig Feuerbach and the End of Classical German Philosophy*, in Marx and Engels *Selected Works* Volume 3, 369.
9. Engels, *The Origin of the Family, Private Property, and the State*, in Marx and Engels *Selected Works* Volume 3, 280–283.
10. Marx, *Grundrisse*, 383.
11. Engels, *The Origin of the Family, Private Property, and the State*, in Marx and Engels *Selected Works* Volume 3, 327.
12. Marx, "Preparations for War in Russia," in *New York Tribune*, 8 November 1860.

13. Engels, *The Origin of the Family, Private Property, and the State,* in Marx and Engels *Selected Works* Volume 3, 328.
14. Ibid.
15. Engels, *The Condition of the Working Class in England,* Marx and Engels *Werke* Volume 2, 443–444.
16. Marx, "The Nationalization of the Land," in *Labour Monthly* reprint, 415.
17. Engels, *The Origin of the Family, Private Property, and the State,* in Marx and Engels *Selected Works* Volume 3, 332.
18. Ibid., 328.
19. Marx and Engels, *The Communist Manifesto,* in Marx and Engels *Selected Works,* Volume 1, 110–111.
20. For the German original, see Marx and Engels *Werke,* Volume 4, 464.
21. Marx and Engels, *The Communist Manifesto,* in Marx and Engels *Selected Works,* Volume 1, 127.
22. For example, Engels, *The Housing Question,* in Marx and Engels *Selected Works* Volume 2, 347; Marx, *The Civil War in France,* in Marx and Engels *Selected Works* Volume 2, 218.
23. Marx, "Report at 23 May 1871 session of the General Council of the International Working Men's Association," in *G.C.F.I.* 70–71 [4], 201.
24. Marx, "Notebook on the Paris Commune," April–May 1871, 150.
25. Marx, "English Prosperity-Strikes-The Turkish Question-India," in *New York Tribune,* 1 July 1853.
26. Marx, *Capital* Volume I, 658.
27. Engels, *The Housing Question,* in Marx and Engels *Selected Works* Volume 2, 324.
28. Marx, *Capital* Volume I, 657.
29. Engels, *The Housing Question,* in Marx and Engels *Selected Works* Volume 2, 350.
30. Engels, *Ludwig Feuerbach and the End of Classical German Philosophy,* in Marx and Engels *Selected Works* Volume 3, 369–370.

DEFINING THE CLASS DOMINANCE VIEW

G. William Domhoff

Introduction

My most general assumption is that social power is rooted in organizations. I define organizations simply as sets of rules, roles, and routines developed to accomplish some particular purpose.

Since human beings have a vast array of "purposes," they have formed an appropriately large number of organizations. But only a few of these purposes and organizations weigh heavily in terms of generating social power. According to Mann's analysis, Western civilization and the current power configurations within it are best understood by determining the intertwinings and relative importance at any given time of organizations based in four "overlapping and intersecting sociospatial networks of power" (1986:1). These networks are labeled ideological, economic, military, and political, and placed in that particular order only because it makes for a handy memory device—IEMP. This lack of concern with order of presentation is possible because no one of these organizational networks is more fundamental than the others. Each one presupposes the existence of the others, which vindicates philosopher Bertrand Russell's (1938:10–11) earlier demonstration that power cannot be reduced to one basic form; in that sense, says Russell, power is like the idea of energy in the natural sciences.

This starting point immediately puts Mann at odds with schools of thought operating in terms of the ultimate primacy of historical materialism or the state, but it allows him to have agreements with the Marxists for some eras and the state autonomists for others. Mann's view thus puts an enormous emphasis on history, and hence on empirical studies.

Before I explain each of the four major organizational networks, I want to stress that the theory is not derived from any psychological assumptions about the importance of different human purposes. Instead, the point is strictly sociological: these four networks happen to be the most useful organizational bases for generating social power. In Mann's words, "Their primacy comes not from the strength of human desires for ideological, economic, military, or political satisfaction but from the particular organizational means each possesses to attain human goals, whatever they may be" (1986:2).

In the American vernacular, we can say each organizational network is in the business of selling some service or product needed by many members of a society. The ideology network sells meaning, answers to universal concerns about the origins of humanity, death, the purpose of life, and other existential questions. Churches are the primary salespeople in this area, and some of them have developed into formidable power generators, such as the Catholic church in Europe for many centuries. In the United States, secular organizations like self-help groups and psychotherapy cults have enjoyed some success in marketing meaning to the college-educated middle class, but churches remain the most important organizations in fulfilling this human need for Americans. Protestant churches in particular always have had an enormous role in producing American morality and culture. However, their constant splintering into new denominations, and then further schisms within the denominations, has limited them as a source of social power. The historical role of churches also has been limited through the separation of church and state by the Founding Fathers, reflecting both the weak nature of the church network at the time and the Founders' own secular tendencies. True, the Catholic church was a power base in some urban areas in the late nineteenth and early twentieth centuries through the Democratic party, often making alliances with the political machines, but more recently its power has been limited to realms like abortion and school prayer. Religious values end up for the most part as one of the many hooks used in the symbolic politics played by economic rivals in trying to further their own interests.

The economic network is in the business of selling material goods and personal services. It creates classes defined in terms of their power over the different parts of the economic process from extraction of raw materials to manufacturing to distribution. Since these economic classes are also social relationships between groups of people who often have different interests, the economic network also can generate class conflict, by which I mean disagreements over such matters as ownership, profit margins, wage rates, working conditions, and unionization that manifest themselves in ways that range from workplace protests and strikes to industrywide boycotts and bargaining to nationwide political actions. However, class conflict is not always present because both owners and workers, the most likely rival classes in recent times, have to have the means to organize themselves over an extended area of social space for conflict to occur. For much of Western history, there have been "ruling classes," defined by Mann as any "economic class that has successfully monopolized other power sources to dominate a state-centered society at large" (1986:25). However, because nonowning classes usually find it difficult to organize, class conflict has been important only in certain periods of history, such as ancient Greece, early Rome, and the present capitalist era. In other words, Mann does not see class conflict as the "motor" of history, putting his theory in disagreement with Marxism once again.

In the United States, the economic network leads to the corporations, banks, plantations, agribusinesses, and trade unions of primary concern of this book. The nationwide nature of the transportation and communication systems, and the commonality of language, education, and culture, mean that the bases for class solidarity and class conflict are present in the United States. Moreover, I believe that such class conflict has frequently manifested itself since the late nineteenth century and has been the single most important factor (but not the only factor) driving American politics in the twentieth century. This standpoint may seem to put me at odds with the great majority of social scientists and historians, who see the basic conflict as one between conservatives and liberals, but I will try to show that this conservative/liberal conflict is more fully analyzed as a class conflict. Conservatism is the ideology of the corporate rich and their allies, liberalism the ideology of the working class and its allies. More specifically, I will try to show that a corporate-conservative coalition contends with a liberal-labor coalition for the allegiance of voters from the many occupational, ethnic, and religious groups comprising the American working class. As historians emphasize, the content of conservatism and liberalism does evolve over time: one side is the party of order, the other the party of hope, as the saying goes, but I think the different interests of capitalists and their employees are at the heart of the conflict.

The third network of social power, the military, is in the business of organized violence, sometimes for the benefit of its own members, as in what Mann calls empires of domination, but more often in recent centuries as a service to ideological, economic, or political networks. Organizations of violence are most often attached to a state, but they are sometimes separate from it, which is one reason why the state autonomy theorists' emphasis on the monopolization of legitimate coercion in defining the state is not general enough as a starting point (Skocpol 1993:43). In the United States in the late nineteenth century, for example, corporations often created their own organizations of violence to break strikes or resist unions, or else hired private specialists in such work. The largest of the private armies in that era, the Pinkerton Detective Agency, "had more men than the U.S. Army" (Mann 1993:646). The state did not interfere with organized corporate violence until the 1930s because most of the unionization efforts by workers were defined by judges as violations of property rights and/or the right to freedom of contract; employers thus had a legitimate right to "defend" their property and hire replacement workers and private armies (pp. 645–48).

As for the American government's own army, it had a large role historically in taking territory from Native Americans, Spain, and Mexico, but it was never big enough for long enough until the Second World War to be considered a serious contender for social power. True, several famous generals became presidents starting with George Washington (who was also a large landholder of his day), but there has been no sustained organizational base for turning military power into social power. The generals who became presidents had "name recognition" and prestige as war heroes, but it was not the military who carried them to political victory.

The fourth and final network, the state, which Mann calls the political network, is in the business of selling territorial regulation, which means order, dispute resolution, and regularity within a fixed area of land. This task of regulation within a bounded area most fundamentally defines the state and makes it potentially autonomous. The economic network, and people in general, desperately need this service, but no other network is capable of providing it for sustained periods of time.

The lack of emphasis on coercion and domination in explaining the origins of the state once again places Mann's theory in historical disagreement with Marxism, which sees the origins of the state in class conflict between owners and workers, making it an organization of class domination from the outset. Archaeological and historical evidence does not presently support the Marxist view (e.g., Claessen and Skalnik 1978; Cohen and Service 1978; Mann 1986:49–63, 84–87). Lest I seem to be giving hostages here to state autonomy theorists, let me quickly add that Mann sees the American state of the late nineteenth and early twentieth centuries (which is where his account ends for now) as a capitalist-liberal formation embodying basic capitalist principles, using its courts and armies to crush labor organizing, and responding to political parties wherein capitalists have at the least a large amount of influence (1993:635–59, 705).

Historically, states were not highly important in the Western world in the one thousand years following the fall of the Roman Empire. They gradually grew in power in the fifteenth and sixteenth centuries in the context of the growth of capitalism on the one hand and the development of an arms race on another. A highly competitive system of nation-states arose in Europe in which only the militarily powerful states survived, usually in alliance with economic elites willing to pay for the necessary armies in exchange for protection of property rights and the regulation of markets. Within this context, states usually came to have the monopoly on legitimate violence that state autonomy theorists emphasize (i.e., armies capable of policing the state territory and defending it against outsiders). States also gained dominance over ideology networks: nationalism and idolization of the head of state gradually mingled with Christianity in providing meaning for the lives of ordinary citizens. The question of social power narrowed to the relative power of economic and state elites, which is a good part of the story of Western history in the past few hundred years. Thus, the American case I am focusing on here is but one in a much larger set, and the outcomes vary greatly from country to country (Mann 1993).

In the United States, the political network has been decentralized and fragmented to a degree unique among industrialized societies for a variety of reasons taught in junior high school. It also is highly unusual in the degree to which it is staffed by a certain kind of specialist, the lawyer. Lawyers already were important in colonial America, and thirty-three of the fifty-five delegates to the Constitutional Convention in 1789 were lawyers, although they were well-born property owners as well (Mann 1993:157). They remained equally important ever after as the Constitution and the Supreme Court became central features of the American state, and involvement in a political party became the main avenue to a judicial appointment. Twenty-six of the forty-two American presidents have been lawyers, as have a majority of national-level legislators (Eulau and Sprague 1964).

■ ■ ■ ■

But are these lawyer/politicians acting primarily in terms of the independent interests of the state, as the state autonomy theorists would say, or instead making sure that the needs of the top economic class are being met even while doing the necessary minimum of regulating and adjudicating? Are lawyer/politicians specialists in smoothing over class conflict? With those questions we can take leave of this general discussion of the four networks of social power and turn to the . . . class dominance theory of power in the United States.

■ ■ ■ ■

I want to demonstrate the value of a specific theoretical framework: class dominance.

Specifically I want to show there is (1) a small social upper class (2) rooted in the ownership and control of a corporate community that (3) is integrated with a policy-planning network and (4) has great political power in both political parties and dominates the federal government in Washington. That may appear to be a tall order because terms like "social upper class" and "corporate community" may seem hard to specify, and evidence for "great influence" in political parties and "domination" of the federal government difficult to come by. But it can be done with a fair amount of rigor.

Specifying the Class Dominance Framework

Introduction

In this section I am going to define all the concepts used in my theory, and show how they are studied. I am also going to explain how my theory involves a synthesis of a class theory with what is often thought to be its antithesis in American sociology, an organizational theory, thereby creating what I call a class/organizational synthesis. As I will argue, this synthesis takes place through boards of directors, the legal holders of power in virtually every profit and nonprofit organization in this country.

Social Class/Upper Class

Formally speaking, a social class is a network of interacting and intermarrying families who see each other as equals and accord each other social respect. For my purposes, though, social classes as networks of interacting and intermarrying families are only a starting point. If and when such social classes are found, it is then possible to take the next step and see if they are based in one or more economic classes, and to determine the underlying economic and political relationships between social classes. Within this context it also is possible to talk of segments within the underlying economic classes, meaning groupings within an economic class that have somewhat different interests due to their particular position within the overall social structure. In the case of the ownership class in the United States, these segments have different bases of wealth and partially conflicting interests on some issues while sharing strong common concerns in the face of initiatives by nonowners or agencies within the state.

As far as an upper social class, everyone agrees that one exists in the United States, but they disagree on what, if anything, it has to do with economic classes or power. Is it a mere status group with little or no power, or is it also a capitalist (ownership) class whose members dominate the state, as determined by one or more agreed-upon indicators of power? In order to answer these questions, we first of all need an empirical or operational definition of the upper class, that is, a set of indicators of upper-class standing.

We can talk of the upper class as an institutional network of schools, clubs, and resort areas (Domhoff 1983:17–18). This institutional network has persisted in roughly its present form for a little over one hundred years now, although there have been some additions, subtractions, and alterations. New clubs spring up when the young men do not want to be in the "stuffy" clubs of the older men; a Junior League is developed as women of the upper class gain more independence; a prep school becomes too liberal and loses support; a resort area starts to be frequented by members of the middle class. These are ebbs and flows: the institutional network remains intact.

We know far less about the continuity of the families who create and utilize this institutional network. We found in a sample of 5,900 families in the 1980 *Social Register* that 9 percent listed themselves as members of one of four ancestral societies dating back at least to the American Revolution (Domhoff 1983:22). Baltzell's (1958) work shows continuity back to the seventeenth century in several elite Philadelphia families. Two studies of families in Detroit demonstrated continuity over three generations (Schuby 1975; Davis 1982), as did a study of families involved in the steel industry in the late nineteenth and early twentieth centuries (Ingham 1978:230–31). We know that some members of the upper class marry outside their class, usually someone from the upper-middle class they met at college, but the best general picture for now is a stable family group within the upper class that incorporates new members, including newly wealthy capitalists whatever their social origins (Domhoff 1983:34–36).

The existence of the network of upper class institutions makes it possible to determine if and to what extent members of this class are involved in corporations, political parties, government, and other institutions of the society. Through this tracing outward we can determine overrepresentation and discover other institutional networks. For any systematic research seeking to link social class with the power centers of the society, the upper-class institutions are truly the bedrock starting point.

■ ■ ■ ■

Our many studies of the membership networks generated from the *Social Register*, private club membership lists, and private school alumni lists demonstrate beyond a doubt that the upper-class network is nationwide in its scope and surprisingly dense (Domhoff 1970:chap. 4). So does the outstanding study of women of the upper class by Susan Ostrander (1984). It is likely that most members of the upper class have connections in most major cities through common schooling, clubs, or resorts, and can reach a wide array of people through friends of friends. If we think of meetings at clubs, resorts, and alumni gatherings as a series of constantly changing small groups, then research findings in social psychology on social cohesion in small groups become relevant to issues of power because socially cohesive groups are better able to solve problems than less cohesive groups due to a greater desire to reach common understanding. My inference from this research is that social cohesion facilitates policy cohesion within the upper class (Domhoff 1974: chap. 3).

■ ■ ■ ■

The Power Elite

Members of the upper class, if they rule America, certainly do not do so alone. There are not that many of them to begin with, especially when half of them have been excluded by sexism from pursuing traditional pathways to power. Moreover, many members of the upper class are not interested in ruling. They prefer to live the good life based on their inherited wealth, even leaving the management of their stock portfolios to hired experts. They spend their time breeding dogs or horses, traveling, or mingling with celebrities at glitzy social events. Now, there are fewer such people than meet the eye, but the first issue we face in claiming that the upper class is a ruling—or governing—class is that many of its members do not seem to be involved in ruling.

Moreover, America seems to be an organizational society, not a class one. What is most obvious about it are the large "institutional hierarchies," as Mills (1956) called them, that developed throughout the twentieth century—large corporations, the Pentagon, the executive branch of the federal government, but also large public university systems like the University of California (nine campuses), hospital complexes like the Mayo Clinic, charitable foundations like the Ford Foundation and Rockefeller Foundation, and more. How could members of a small upper class dominate such a vast array of diverse and apparently independent institutions, each with its own history, traditions, purposes, and internal methods of operation?

At this point the boards of directors of these institutions come into the picture as the official repository of final authority in them. I believe the class and organizational dimensions of American society meet on these boards. Board members from the upper class bring a class perspective to the management of the organization, while the managers of the organization who have risen within it to serve on the board of directors bring an organizational perspective. The board is thus one nexus for a synthesis of the class and organizational viewpoints. Its members strive to keep the organization viable in terms of organizational principles while incorporating the class perspectives of the upper-class directors.

This viewpoint provides an empirical starting point for linking studies of class-based social power to organizations: if there is evidence that a board of directors is controlled by members of the upper class, then we can say the institution itself is controlled by members of the upper class. We can determine this control by studying the history of the board, the funding of the organization, or the composition of the board. In practice we usually end up studying the composition of the board when it comes to the large number of corporations. However, more attention has been paid to history and funding with other organizations, partly because there are fewer of them, partly because the relevant information is more accessible.

Generally speaking, board members wield their power through hiring and firing the leadership level of organizations. They pick and choose among the organizational executives striving to reach the top, whom they know from serving on board-based committees with them, or they bring in a new top executive made known to them by their network of upper-class friends serving on other boards of directors. Boards are especially important in times of crisis or potential mergers (e.g., Mace 1971; Bowen 1994). Board committees often do far more than meets the eye (Lorsch and MacIver 1989).

If boards of directors are given their due, then we have one key to the means by which the upper class exerts its influence: a leadership group I call the *power elite*. I define the power elite as active, working members of the upper class and high-level employees in institutions controlled by members of the upper class. High-level employees are defined as those selected or approved directly by the board of directors, which usually means the chairperson and president, along with a few other high-level employees who may be asked to serve on the board. It follows that all those executives serving on a board of directors in an institution controlled by members of the upper class are members of the power elite. A few senior members of long standing may have no present institutional affiliations, but for the most part members of the power elite are directors or high-level employees of one or more organizations in the institutional network.

But what institutions in American society are controlled by members of the upper class according to this definition? Every type of institution from major businesses to private universities to cultural and fine arts organizations to private welfare agencies, which is possible because some people sit on many different boards. For my purposes, though, I want to focus on those organizations I think are most involved in the exercise of power.

The Corporate Community

The corporate community is defined in network terms as all those corporations connected into one network by people who serve on two or more boards of directors. Below this visible level there are also common stock ownership, shared lawyers and investment bankers, and other linkages that help make the idea of a corporate community a sociological reality.

The corporate community can be traced back in American history as far as there are adequate records, to 1816, where David Bunting's (1983) important archival work shows that the ten largest banks and ten largest insurance companies in New York City were completely connected; eighteen directors with three or more positions linked 95 percent of the companies in the sample. There were, of course, other interlocks as well. Bunting's sample of the twenty largest banks, ten largest insurance companies, and ten largest railroads for 1836 generated a corporate community that included 95 percent of the sample firms; this time 30 men held 103 directorships linking 73 percent of the corporations (Bunting 1983:133–38). His samples for later in the century show similar results, which are supplemented by Roy's (1983) detailed study of a sample of firms in eleven industries between 1886 and 1904, showing that the corporate community grew out from a core of railroads, banks, coal, and telegraph companies in 1886 to encompass all the industries in his sample by 1904. Work by Mizruchi (1982, 1983) picks up the story at that point and shows the stability of these findings until 1974. Railroads gradually become more peripheral to the network as the importance of railroads in the American economy declined, and industrial corporations became more central, but throughout the seventy-year period the network remained intact, with banks at the center. The four most central banks in 1974 were also the central banks in the 1904 network, created by either the Morgan financial interests or the Rockefeller family (e.g., Mizruchi 1983:176–77).

According to our indicators of upper-class membership, the upper class was overrepresented by a factor of fifty-three in a sample of the largest corporations in three sectors for 1963; the figure for the top fifteen banks was sixty-two; for the top fifteen insurance companies, forty-four; and for the twenty largest industrials, fifty-four (Domhoff 1967:52–55). Dye (1976:151–52), using a sample of 201 corporations for 1970, estimates that 30 percent of the directors had upper-class origins. The figure is even higher for the inner circle, where two to three times as many directors are members of the upper class in different samples (Soref 1980; Domhoff 1983:71–72).

The findings on the overlap between the upper class and the corporate community reinforce my earlier conclusion based on the great wealth possessed by members of the upper class: this social group is also a capitalist class. This fact makes the conceptual and terminological arguments between Marxists and other social scientists over class vs. status groups into moot ones for at least the top level of American society in the twentieth century because the highest status group is rooted in the ownership and control of large banks and corporations. In the phrase coined by Mills (1956:147), we are dealing with a "corporate rich." This may not seem like news in the 1990s, but from the 1940s through the 1970s the widespread belief in the alleged separation of ownership and control, with managerial specialists from the middle class supposedly controlling the corporations, was one of the main reasons mainstream social scientists rejected the idea of a power elite or ruling class.

In addition to the upper-class overrepresentation on the boards of directors, there are many board members who are not members of the upper class. Most of these other directors are executives who have risen through the corporate ranks, but there also are college presidents, academic experts, former politicians, former military men, celebrities, and in recent years, various kinds of "tokens" [see Domhoff (1967:51–52) and Zweigenhaft and Domhoff (1982:25–46) for discussions of the pathways to board status]. The important point about the upwardly mobile executives is that they are chosen on the basis of their ability to realize goals determined for the corporation by members of the upper class, meaning first and foremost producing a profit, but also corporate expansion and good public relations as well. Through their educations at top business schools, their experience in the corporate world, and their gradual accrual of stock through generous option plans, they are assimilated into the social life and worldview of the corporate rich (Domhoff 1983:73–76).

■ ■ ■ ■

Skocpol and other state autonomists constantly try to narrow the argument to the power of business executives compared to state officials and experts, but my theory is much more general, as the foregoing discussion demonstrates. I am talking about a social upper class and an economic class (i.e., a corporate community in its current form) that are two sides of the same coin, not simply about executives. Further evidence for the greater breadth of my perspective will be presented in the next section on the policy-planning network that is based in the upper class and corporate community. Power in twentieth-century America cannot be discussed in any faintly realistic way without an understanding of the role played by this important network.

The Policy-Planning Network

Tracing out the nonbusiness directorships of wealthy men and corporate directors led me to the discovery of what I came to call the policy-planning network (Domhoff 1967, 1970: chaps. 5 and 6). It consists of (1) foundations, (2) think tanks, (3) specialized research institutes at major universities, and (4) general policy discussion groups, where members of the upper class and corporate community meet with experts from the think tanks and research institutes, journalists, and government officials to discuss policy, ideology, and plans (PIP) concerning the major issues facing the country (Domhoff 1979: chap. 3; Alpert and Markusen 1980; Useem 1984). The general way in which I think people, money, and ideas flow through the network is shown in Figure 1.1.

The organizations in the policy-planning network are nonprofit and tax-free, and are therefore portrayed by their leaders as separate from the corporate community. They are also said to be nonpartisan or bipartisan, above the political fray, not tied to either major party. Contrary to these claims, the policy-planning network is, in fact, the programmatic political party for the upper class and the corporate community, a major element

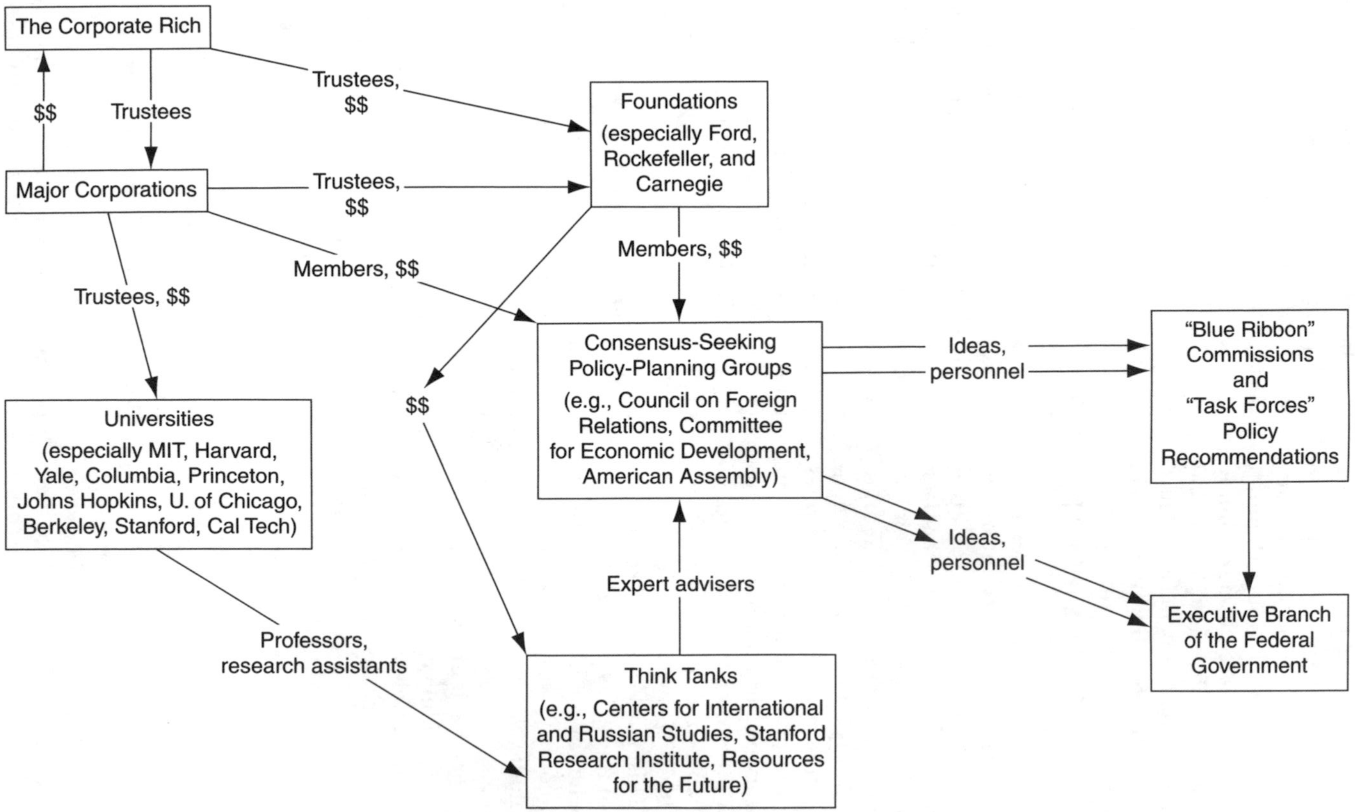

Figure 1.1 The flow of policy from corporations and their owners to government. *(From G. William Domhoff, "How the Power Elite Set National Goals," in Robert Perrucci and Marc Pilisuk [eds.], The Triple Revolution Emerging, Boston, Little, Brown, 1971, p. 213.)*

in the power elite. There are differences of opinion between different parts of the network, for reasons that I have admitted are not well understood (Domhoff 1983:91), and even between individuals in the same organization, but the general stance of the network ranges from moderate conservative to ultra-conservative. The existence of this network leads me to believe the upper class and corporate community are organized above and beyond the interest group level stressed by most theorists. To the degree that case studies on its operation are convincing (e.g., Weinstein 1968; Shoup and Minter 1977; Domhoff 1979: chap. 3; 1990; Peschek 1987), then my view is supported, but more case studies are clearly needed.

The specification of a policy-planning network also provides us with a way to deal with claims by the state autonomy theorists about the importance of independent experts. For them, of course, all experts are independent because they are not capitalists or corporate executives. Thanks to the policy-planning network, we can say a person is a *corporate expert* if he or she is an employee of a foundation, think tank, or discussion group in the network, and even a member of the power elite if on the board of directors of one of these organizations.[1]

The main financial engine for the policy-planning network is a set of charitable foundations that began to appear on the landscape in the early twentieth century. They have been conducting studies, funding think tanks and universities, and providing grants for individual scholars ever since. In the 1950s, when the huge Ford Foundation joined the network, this foundational complex seemed to be complete, but in the 1970s very conservative members of the corporate community created a new set of foundations that fueled the rise of the New Right (Colwell 1980, 1993; Jenkins and Shumate 1985; Allen 1992).

■ ■ ■ ■

The think tanks in the network are highly specialized research groups that produce the PIP that are argued about in the policy discussion groups. They compete with each other for grants from the foundations and government agencies. There is a very limited market for their output—essentially corporations and government. If think tanks are looked at as if they were business firms competing in a market, it can be readily understood why they could not stray very far from the corporate community and the foundations even if they did not have people from the business and foundational networks on their boards of directors [Alpert and Markusen (1980) provide this insight].

■ ■ ■ ■

The policy discussion groups, consisting of several hundred or even a few thousand members, only some of whom are active at any given time, are the integrating centers within the policy-planning network. They are not places of power, nor even of ideas, but meeting grounds for those with power and those with PIP. Although they sponsor speakers, large conferences, and written policy statements, their most important method of operation is through smaller discussion groups that meet on a weekly or monthly basis. I see these organizations as having several major functions not appreciated by either interest group or state autonomy theorists. If rival theorists took these functions more seriously, they would see why businessmen bring a general power elite perspective when they serve in government and why many experts are known personally by members of the upper class and corporate community.

First, the discussion organizations provide an informal training ground for new leadership within the power elite. The various small discussion groups within each of them are in effect seminars for corporate leaders conducted by experts from the think tanks and university research institutes. Second, it is within these organizations that members of the power elite sort out in an informal fashion which of their peers are best suited for government positions. This is valuable information when they are asked by friends who serve as financial angels to politicians to suggest people for government appointments. Third, corporate experts learn the perspectives of business leaders on the issues of the day, which helps in fitting the PIP to corporate needs. Fourth, the upper-class and corporate members of these organizations have the opportunity to become acquainted with the corporate experts, sizing them up for possible service in government. In a little study I did of members of the Council of Economic Advisers, I found that eleven of its first thirteen chairs came from the policy-planning network; six had been advisers for one policy discussion organization alone, the Committee for Economic Development (Domhoff 1987:195–96).

In addition, these organizations have two major functions in relation to the rest of society: First, they legitimate their members as persons capable of government service and selfless pursuit of the national interest. Members are portrayed as giving up their free time for no reimbursement to take part in highly selective organizations that are nonprofit and nonpartisan in nature. Second, through such avenues as books, journals, policy statements, press releases, and speakers, these groups influence the climate of opinion both in Washington and the country at large. That is, they have ideological as well as policy functions.

■■■■

Now that the relationship of the policy-planning network to the upper class and corporate community is clearly established, I want to close this section with a visual representation of how the three networks are interconnected. As Figure 1.2 shows, some people are members of only one of the three, others of two, and a few of all three. Those who are members of all three are certainly at the heart of the power elite, but we also see that people who are neither upper class nor corporate leaders can be members of it by virtue of their high-level positions in the policy-planning network. This diagram reinforces what I explained in my earlier discussion about the relationship of the upper class and the power elite. On the one hand, a person can be a member of the upper class, but not involved in governing. Conversely, a person can be a member of the power elite, but not in the upper class. Thus,

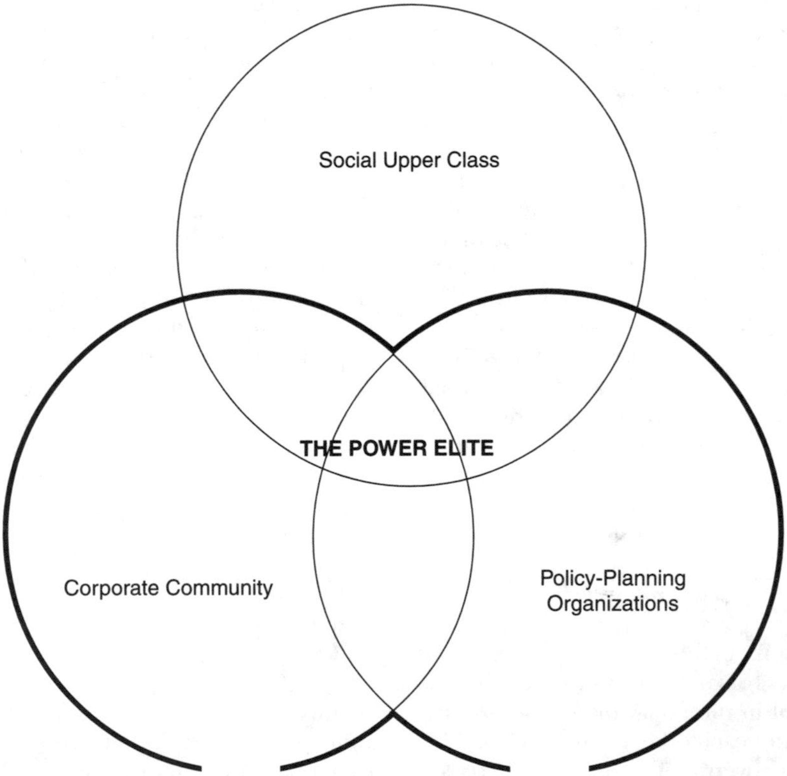

Figure 1.2 A multinetwork view of the relationship between the upper class and the power elite, showing the overlaps of the social upper class, corporate community, and policy-planning network. The power elite is defined by the thick lines.

this diagram provides a detailed view of the networks that make up the power elite, showing the people involved in the class/organizational synthesis. It warns again that to reduce my view to one of dominance by business executives, as the state autonomy theorists do, is inaccurate.

Conservatives, Liberals, and Class Conflict

If we were able to do a membership network analysis that included every person in the United States, we would find very few people in any institutional network. This conclusion follows from studies showing that only one-third participate in any policy-oriented organization even at the local level, and only 10 percent give any money to a political party (e.g., Hamilton 1972:chap. 2; Flacks 1988:chap. 2). However, if we look more narrowly at the networks created by the shared memberships, financing, and policy positions of lobbying and advocacy groups, we find two coalitions competing for the attention, allegiance, and votes of the Great Unorganized (e.g., McCune 1956; Deakin 1966; Ross 1967; Hall 1969; Melone 1977).

The first coalition is based in the upper class and power elite, which reach out to and fund a very large number of conservative groups concerned with tax reduction, patriotism, religion, and morality. It has the support of the real estate and development interest ("growth elites") that dominate local and county governments (Molotch 1976, 1979; Logan and Molotch 1987). I call this the corporate-conservative coalition.

The second of these coalitions is based in liberal organizations and trade unions. This liberal-labor coalition is less well financed and is of more recent vintage, roughly the second term of Roosevelt's presidency. It came into being because of the Great Depression as one part of the larger Roosevelt coalition, which already included southern plantation elites, who were the mortal enemies of the liberal-labor coalition. True, there were liberals (often called reformers) before the New Deal, and they sometimes worked with unions, but many of the reformers were still Progressive Republicans, and the unions did not like social policies that brought the federal government into the picture until well into the depression.

When we compare the corporate-conservative and liberal-labor coalitions, we can safely say the former is more organized than the latter. However, this kind of a claim is still too strong for historians like Gabriel Kolko and his students, who claim business is highly fragmented (e.g., Kolko 1963; Vittoz 1987; Gordon 1994), or for those participants in the power elite who see nothing but chaos and personal rivalry all around them. To accommodate their concerns, we can approach the point about organization in terms of how the world looks from the individual viewpoint: the corporate-conservative coalition is slightly less disorganized, confused, and shortsighted than its opponents. Both sides, that is, are made up of struggling, muddled, egotistical individuals. However, when it comes to the exercise of power, either perspective adds up to the same conclusion. The corporate-conservative coalition generally is more cohesive than the liberal-labor one. From a sociological point of view, the Kolko school of business history and the participant-observers in the power elite are letting the day-to-day noise of rhetoric and personal ambition obscure the stability of the class and institutional structure of American society.

■ ■ ■ ■

When we look at the issues dividing the two coalitions, they add up to what is meant by class conflict, because they involve fundamentally opposed views on how the revenues taken in by corporations, plantations, and other profit-making entities that employ wage labor should be divided up. The liberal-labor coalition wants the corporate rich to pay higher wages to workers and higher taxes to government. The corporate-conservative coalition rejects these two objectives completely, claiming they endanger the freedom of individuals and the workings of the free market. The desire for higher wages and bigger government social programs leads the liberal-labor coalition to take two organizational steps. The first is unionization of the work force, which is opposed vehemently by the corporate-conservative coalition in every way possible. The second is politics, which takes place in the liberal wing of the Democratic party because of the great difficulties in sustaining a third party in a presidential system that also elects legislators from districts (i.e., a series of "winner-take-all" elections makes a vote for a liberal third party a vote for the coalition's least favorite (Republican) choice between the two major parties due to the fact that it is one less vote for the Democratic candidate).

One of the political demands made of the state by the liberal-labor coalition—help in unionizing—is in my view the single most important factor in determining the antigovernment stance of the corporate-conservative coalition. Despite all that the state does for the corporate-conservative coalition in promoting and subsidizing businesses, and in providing protection for private property, it is nonetheless viewed with suspicion and watched with care by the power elite because it is a real threat to corporate control of labor markets, either by employing unemployed workers or supporting unionization.[2] Fear of losing control of labor markets, I believe, is the power issue that links class conflict to the antigovernment orientation of the power elite.

The fundamental differences of opinion on unions and government aid to unionization also allow us to distinguish between corporate experts in the policy-planning network and liberal experts.

Notes

1. I will not count affiliates of university research institutes as corporate experts because they are employees of universities. However to see how the Russian Research Institute at Harvard University was controlled by the Carnegie Corporation on key issues, see O'Connell (1989).

2. Welfare is the conservative solution to unemployment, given begrudgingly only in times of disruption, always accompanied by stigmatization and victim-blaming in order to reinforce work norms (Piven and Cloward 1971). Liberals much preferred government employment to welfare during the New Deal, but lost to conservatives on the issue (Rose 1994:53–56, 77–80).

References

Allen, Michael P. 1992. "Elite Social Movement Organizations and the State: The Rise of the Conservative Policy-Planning Network." *Research in Politics and Society* 4:87–109.

Alpert, Irvine, and Ann Markusen. 1980. "Think Tanks and Capitalist Policy." In *Power Structure Research*, edited by G. William Domhoff. Beverly Hills: Sage.

Baltzell, E. Digby. 1958. *Philadelphia Gentlemen: The Making of a National Upper Class.* New York: Free Press.

Bowen, William. 1994. *Inside the Boardroom.* New York: Wiley.

Bunting, David. 1983. "Origins of the American Corporate Network." *Social Science History* 7:129–42.

Claessen, Henri, and Peter Skalnik, eds. 1978. *The Early State.* The Hague: Mouton.

Cohen, Ronald, and Elman R. Service, eds. 1978. *Origins of the State.* Philadelphia: Institute for the Study of Human Issues.

Colwell, Mary. 1980. "The Foundation Connection: Links among Foundations and Recipient Organizationas." In *Philanthropy and Cultural Imperialism.* Boston: Hall.

Davis, Donald. 1982. "The Price of Conspicuous Production: The Detroit Elite and the Automobile Industry, 1900–1933." *Journal of Social History* 16:21–46.

Deakin, James. 1966. *The Lobbyists.* Washington, DC: Public Affairs Press.

Domhoff, G. William. 1967. *Who Rules America?* Englewood Cliffs, NJ: Prentice-Hall.

Domhoff, G. William. 1970. *The Higher Circles.* New York: Randon House.

Domhoff, G. William. 1974. *The Bohemian Grove and Other Retreats.* New York: Harper & Row.

Domhoff, G. William. 1979. *The Powers That Be.* New York: Random House.

Domhoff, G. William. 1983. *Who Rules America Now?* New York: Simon and Schuster.

Domhoff, G. William. 1987. "Where Do Government Experts Come From?" In *Power Elites and Organizations*, edited by G. William Domhoff and Thomas R. Dye. Beverly Hills: Sage.

Dye, Thomas R. 1976. *Who's Running America?* Englewood Cliffs, NJ: Prentice-Hall.

Eulau, Heinz, and John Sprague. 1964. *Lawyers in Politics.* Indianapolis, IN: Bobbs-Merrill.

Flacks, Richard. 1988. *Making History.* New York: Columbia University Press.

Gordon, Linda. 1994. *Pitied But Not Entitled.* New York: Free Press.

Hall, Donald. 1969. *Cooperative Lobbying.* Tucson: University of Arizona Press.

Hamilton, Richard. 1972. *Class and Politics in the United States.* New York: Wiley.

Heclo, Hugh. 1978. "Issue Networks and the Executive Establishment." In *The New American Political System*, edited by Anthony King. Washington, DC: American Enterprise Institute.

Ingham, John. 1978. *The Iron Barons.* Westport, CT: Greenwood.

Jenkins, J. Craig, and Teri Shumate. 1985. "Cowboy Capitalists and the Rise of the 'New Right': An Analysis of Contributors to Conservative Policy Formation Organizations." *Social Problems* 33:130–45.

Kolko, Gabriel. 1963. *The Triumph of Conservatism.* New York: Free Press.

Laumann, Edward, and David Knoke. 1987. *The Organizational State.* Madison: University of Wisconsin Press.

Logan, John, and Harvey Molotch. 1987. *Urban Fortunes.* Berkeley: University of California Press.

Lorsch, Jay, and Elizabeth MacIver. 1989. *Pawns or Potentates?* Cambridge, MA: Harvard Business School.

Mace, Myles. 1971. *Directors: Myth and Reality.* Cambridge, MA: Harvard University Press.

Mann, Michael. 1986. *The Sources of Social Power.* Vol. 1. New York: Cambridge University Press.

Mann, Michael. 1993. *The Sources of Social Power.* Vol. 2. New York: Cambridge University Press.

McCune, Wesley. 1956. *Who's Behind Our Farm Policy?* New York: Praeger.

McQuaid, Kim. 1982. *Big Business and Presidential Power from FDR to Reagan.* New York: Morrow.

Melone, Albert. 1977. *Lawyers, Public Policy and Interest Group Politics.* Washington, DC: University Press of America.

Mills, C. Wright. 1956. *The Power Elite.* New York: Oxford University Press.

Mizruchi, Mark. 1982. *The Structure of the American Corporate Network, 1904–1974.* Beverly Hills, CA: Sage.

Mizruchi, Mark. 1983. "Relations among Large American Corporations, 1904–1974." *Social Science History* 7:165–82.

Molotch, Harvey. 1976. "The City as a Growth Machine." *American Journal of Sociology* 82:309–30.

O'Connell, Charles. 1989. "Social Structure and Science: Soviet Studies at Harvard." Ph.D. dissertation, University of California, Los Angeles.

Ostrander, Susan. 1984. *Women of the Upper Class.* Philadelphia: Temple University Press.

Peschek, Joseph. 1987. *Policy-Planning Organizations.* Philadelphia: Temple University Press.

Piven, Frances, and Richard Cloward. 1971. *Regulating the Poor.* New York: Pantheon.

Rose, Nancy. 1994. *Put to Work: Relief Programs in the Great Depression.* New York: Monthly Review.

Ross, Robert L. 1967. "Dimensions and Patterns of Relating among Interest Groups at the Congressional Level of Government." Ph.D. dissertation, Michigan State University, East Lansing.

Roy, William. 1983. "Interlocking Directorates and the Corporate Revolution." *Social Science History* 7:143–64.

Russell, Bertrand. 1938. *Power: A New Social Analysis.* London: Allen and Unwin.

Schuby, T. D. 1975. "Class Power, Kinship and Social Cohesion: A Case Study of a Local Elite." *Sociological Focus* 8:243–55.

Shoup, Laurence, and William Minter. 1977. *Imperial Brain Trust.* New York: Monthly Review.

Skocpol, Theda. 1993. "Gendered Identities in Early U.S Social Policy." *Contention* 2:157–82.

Soref, Michael. 1980. "The Finance Capitalists." In Maurice Zeitlin, ed., *Class, Conflict, and the State.* Cambridge: Winthrop.

Sweezy, Paul. 1953. "The American Ruling Class." In Paul Sweezy, ed., *The Present As History.* New York: Monthly Review Press.

Useem, Michael. 1984. *The Inner Circle.* New York: Oxford University Press.

Vittoz, Stanley. 1987. *New Deal Labor Policy and the American Industrial Economy.* Chapel Hill: University of North Carolina Press.

Weinstein, James. 1968. *The Corporate Ideal in the Liberal State.* Boston: Beacon.

Zweigenhaft, Richard, and G. William Domhoff. 1982. *Jews in the Protestant Establishment.* New York: Praeger.

POLITICAL CHOICE AND THE MULTIPLE "LOGICS" OF CAPITAL

FRED BLOCK

With growing intensity during the seventies and eighties, economists and publicists advanced the argument that problems of high inflation and slowing productivity growth were the inevitable consequence of excessive growth of government—too much regulation, tax rates pegged so high as to discourage initiative, and the proliferation of social programs that insulated individuals from the discipline of the labor market. They insisted that deregulation, tax cuts, and the reduction of social spending were necessary to restore the integrity of the free market, so that the conditions for stable economic growth could be restored.[1]

In fact, analysts on the left frequently cited these conservative arguments as evidence for their claim that capitalism and democracy were in conflict.[2] They suggested that if the various forms of state regulation and state social welfare spending that had been won through popular struggles did actually interfere with the "logic of capitalism," then this would constitute proof of the necessity and desirability of a transition to socialism. For adherents of this position, a transition to socialism represented the only way to preserve the gains that had come through democratic struggles within capitalism.

Yet the persuasiveness of both leftist and rightist arguments that posited a conflict between democracy and state action on the one hand and the logic of the economy on the other depended on developments in the world economy. After all, it had been the conventional wisdom for the previous twenty years that the "mixed economy"—a combination of private ownership and state intervention—was the optimal institutional form for achieving economic efficiency and social welfare. It took a series of international economic shocks to undermine this conventional wisdom.

In the seventies with growing international economic competition, the demise of the Bretton Woods international monetary order, and OPEC's oil price rises, American citizens and politicians were suddenly confronted with the reality of international economic interdependence. The scholarly community reflected this shift by rediscovering the constraints placed on national societies by the discipline of the world economy. During the seventies, American academics elaborated both "world system theory" and "international political economy," both of which had at their core the analysis of the pressures placed on national societies by the world economy.

The international economy that American academics rediscovered had changed from the self-regulating gold standard of the nineteenth century, but the international currency markets continued to operate as constraints on national policymakers. If, for example, a particular country were following expansionary policies when those around it were contracting, it would likely face a balance-of-payments crisis and severe downward pressure on its currency. Moreover, citizens in country after country were told during the seventies by politicians and business leaders that they could not afford various types of social-policy measures because of their potential damage to the country's international competitive position in a context of increased conflicts over markets. And in periods of economic contraction, such as 1974–1975 and 1980–1983, existing redistributive policies came under attack on the grounds that they prevented the readjustments that were necessary for improved performance in world markets.[3]

These pressures were highlighted by the efforts of the Mitterrand government in France to go against the tide of the world economy in the early eighties. The French Socialist government pursued redistributive and expansionary policies while the rest of the major economies were still in recession. The results were higher rates of inflation and mounting balance-of-payments difficulties for France. The currency markets forced a series of devaluations of the franc and ultimately the Mitterrand government was forced to reverse many of its policies and pursue a program of austerity.

These experiences provided persuasive support for the idea of a fundamental conflict between government policies designed to increase legitimation and the logic of capitalist accumulation. The evidence appeared overwhelming that in the context of a highly competitive capitalist world economy, there exist strict limits to the types of governmental policies that are possible in any particular country. Moreover, as competition mounts within that world economy, there are powerful pressures to reduce the level of taxes and social welfare in any particular country toward the lowest international common denominator.

To be sure, leftist and free market theorists use different concepts to describe the tension between politics and the logic of the economy. Where one would discuss "the logic of accumulation," the other would refer to "the logic of the market." Yet the difference in language conceals an analytic similarity. The two sets of theorists share two central ideas in common. The first is a rejection of optimistic, Keynesian ideas about the mixed economy in favor of the view that there is no "free lunch"—efforts to improve social welfare through government action interfere with either the logic of the market or the imperatives of accumulation.

The second common idea is that there is such a thing as an economy that is autonomous and that has a single logic. This assumption, which can be called the economistic fallacy, was sharply critiqued in a book published more than forty years ago, *The Great Transformation.*[4] In that book, Karl Polanyi challenged the idea that the economy is autonomous and obeys a single logic. . . .

Polanyi develops his argument about the autonomy of the economy by directly challenging economic liberalism's account of the evolution of capitalism. Adam Smith and others argued that capitalism evolved out of an innate human desire to truck and barter. While archaic social institutions had placed limits on the market, a process began in the late Middle Ages through which the market gained increasing strength and autonomy, until political institutions finally evolved that maximized market freedom. As one would expect, this history rests on the idea of an autonomous economy that needs only to be given its freedom; the process is one of natural evolution from restrictions on the human desire to trade to a society organized around that desire.

In contrast, Polanyi highlights the unnaturalness and discontinuity in the historical changes that gave rise to capitalism. The traditional account asserts that the growth of both local and international trade in the late Middle Ages resulted naturally in the development of integrated national markets. But Polanyi insists that both local and international trade could flourish indefinitely without the creation of integrated national markets. Under mercantilism, local and international markets were subordinate to political control, so there was no natural dynamic leading to integrated markets.

Polanyi emphasizes instead the importance of political intervention for the rise of modern capitalism. The emergence of national markets was not the result of spontaneous evolution but of the deliberate political interventions of the Crown.[5] Later on, the development of a market economy also depended on action by the state. The particular example that he analyzed most extensively was the role of the English Poor Law Reform in creating a modern labor market. He described in detail the consequences of the Speenhamland Act—a system of welfare relief instituted in 1795 by rural squires to maintain order in the countryside. By providing relief in supplement to wages, the act had the effect of lowering wages and productivity in the countryside, while also discouraging migration to the urban areas. Hence, Speenhamland became a significant obstacle to the full development of capitalism. Only the imposition of the Poor Law Reform created the mobile and compelled labor force that allowed industrial capitalism to flourish.[6]

In the analysis of Speenhamland, Polanyi rejects the view that welfare policies are external or supplementary to the economy; rather he sees them as fundamentally constitutive of the market economy. The emphasis on the importance of Crown policies in creating national markets or on the centrality of welfare policies for creating labor markets is aimed at demonstrating that the economy is not an autonomous entity but that it has always been profoundly shaped by state action.

As to the logic of the economy, Polanyi's analysis is more implicit than explicit. Polanyi did insist that the nineteenth-century ideal of a self-regulating market was utopian, in the sense of being unachievable. He argued that if markets were left to themselves, they would quickly destroy human society and the natural environment. In pursuit of short-term gains, entrepreneurs would exploit the labor force so brutally that it would not be able to reproduce itself, they would devastate the environment, and they would destroy the trust necessary for a system of contracts to survive. While longer-term considerations might lead individual capitalists to oppose such actions, the pressures of a competitive market would quickly force even the most enlightened either to engage in such destructive practices or to risk bankruptcy. The only alternative is the imposition of regulations by the state that would place legal limits binding on all entrepreneurs.[7] For Polanyi, the classical example of such regulations were the Factory Acts that were passed very soon after the Poor Law Reform.[8] The Factory Acts were the first step of what Polanyi terms the protective counter-movement—the movement to preserve human society from the devastation caused by the self-regulating market.

The implicit argument is that the behaviors of economic actors do not—by themselves—aggregate into a whole that is either rational or sustainable, and it is, therefore, only state action that assures a reasonable outcome. One might say that the economy has a logic that is shaped by individual pursuit of profits, but it is a semantic error to assume that this logic produces a rational or coherent outcome at the aggregate level. For example, individual employers struggle to expand output while limiting wage increases, but the result is an expansion in output without sufficient demand and the economy slips into severe depression. Only state action can redirect these economic patterns into a coherent whole.

It must be stressed that this type of argument is not the same as classical Marxist formulations. While Marx stresses the irrationality of capitalism and its tendency toward periodic crises, he emphasizes the purifying nature of those crises, reflecting his fundamental respect for the capitalist economy's capacity to regulate itself. Even in the discussion in *Capital*[9] of the importance of the Factory Acts in placing a limit on the working day and forcing employers to shift toward technological innovation, he fails to address this critical state intervention in theoretical terms. In brief, Marx was a product of his time in perceiving economic logic as aggregating into a coherent—albeit irrational—whole without the need for state action.[10]

Recognition that economic logics by themselves do not aggregate into coherent wholes deepens the importance of the insight that the economy is never fully autonomous. It suggests that what we generally call "the economy" is always the product of a combination of state action and the logic of individual or institutional economic actors. It follows, as well, that crises or dysfunctions in "the economy" cannot be traced solely to interference with economic logics, because those economic logics have never—by themselves—produced a coherently functioning whole. Rather, one would expect to find one root of economic crises in the particular fit between economic logics and state action. In brief, instead of assuming, as does the conservative wisdom, that the problem is too much state intervention, this Polanyian view suggests that the issue is the specific structure of state intervention, with the distinct possibility that more intervention might be necessary to overcome crises.

In this view, government policies—including redistributive social policies—are not superstructures built on top of some economic base. Rather, they are constitutive of the capitalist economy—without them, there would be no functioning capitalist society. Hence, it no longer makes sense to speak of a contradiction between government policies and some essential logic of accumulation because the latter is a meaningless abstraction. Some government economic policies are more effective than others, but the explanation for the less effective ones has to be sought at a more concrete level of analysis than interference with the basic logic of the economy.

Analyzing the Diversity of Capitalist Institutional Arrangements

The diversity of the conditions under which capitalism has flourished provides considerable support for this line of argument. If the economy were autonomous and had a single logic, one would expect that there would be a very narrow range of difference in governmental policies and institutional arrangements among capitalist countries. But the reality is that capitalism flourishes in such diverse settings as Sweden and South Korea. The extent of government regulation, the rates of taxation, and the nature of social policies varies across different capitalist countries far more than can be explained by different levels of development or different positions within the world economy.

The explanation for this diversity is not difficult to see. Individual capitalists tend to be opportunistic and pragmatic. While they might have a tendency to prefer the minimal state of laissez-faire ideology, they also tend to adapt to the political realities that they face. If their efforts to shape the political environment to their liking are unsuccessful, they will generally figure out ways to make profits in the new circumstances. It is precisely this adaptability of capital that makes it understandable how capitalism has flourished despite the enormous growth of the state in the twentieth century.

But while private ownership of capital is consistent with a broad range of different governmental policies, any particular set of policies must have some coherence if stable growth is to be achieved. If, for example, policies that encouraged production of consumer goods were combined with policies that restricted the growth of domestic and international markets, then one would anticipate serious problems and little growth. This idea of the need for some coherence in the institutional environment in which capitalists operate is captured in the concept of "social structures of accumulation."[11]

According to Gordon et al., each long period of capitalist expansion involves a particular set of social arrangements to sustain the dynamic of capitalist accumulation. The "social structure of accumulation" comprises particular configurations of urban growth, particular types of financial and governmental mechanisms for structuring demand, and specific ways of organizing the relations between workers and employers. It is the social structures of accumulation that assure that economic logics aggregate into a coherent and sustainable whole. As long as we remember that there is not one unique social structure of accumulation at a given moment, but multiple possibilities, then this conceptualization reinforces the Polanyian idea that one cannot simply separate out economic development from the political-economic context that makes it possible.

If, for example, we consider the experience of the Depression of the thirties in the United States, it becomes clear that a host of government policies laid the basis for a new period of capitalist expansion after World War II. The combination of social insurance programs and the extensive federal role in subsidizing suburbanization played a key role in supporting aggregate demand. Similarly, social insurance provisions and the recognition of industrial unions created the conditions for a relatively successful period of labor management relations in basic industry.

That the specific social structures of accumulation that were put in place in the thirties and forties ultimately came to grief in the sixties and seventies is not evidence that there was too much interference in the free market. Rather, social structures of accumulation are always time-limited in their effectiveness. As with the development of organisms, there is a process of growth and decay shaped by several factors. Particular patterns of social and economic development will face a law of diminishing returns—as, for example, when suburban development becomes increasingly problematic because available empty land is so far from the central city. And over an extended period of time, people will also become dissatisfied with some of the institutional arrangements that are part of particular social structures of accumulation. Industrial employees might grow restive with particular ways of organizing the workplace or a feminist movement might emerge that challenges the established place of women in the society. Finally, some of the positive synergies that occurred during the phase of expansion can turn negative under changing historical circumstances, as when a structure of accumulation that relied heavily on cheap energy faces systematic oil price rises.[12] Through these dynamics, particular social structures of accumulation become dysfunctional—they produce slower growth and more political-economic difficulties. The combination of vested interests and general resistance to change makes it unlikely that decaying social structures of accumulation will be effectively reformed. Usually, dramatic political-economic deterioration is necessary before forces are mobilized to establish new social structures of accumulation.

In short, the political-economic difficulties that both leftists and rightists have identified as a product of the conflict between state intervention and the logic of the economy can better be understood as the result of decaying social structures of accumulation. This latter diagnosis leads to very different prescriptions. Whereas the conventional view sees the necessity of a reduction in the government's role in the economy, and particularly a sharp reduction in its efforts to redistribute income, a focus on decaying social structures of accumulation suggests that an expanded role of the state, and particularly an increased role of the state in redistributing income to the less well-off, could be part of the new social structures of accumulation. Whereas redistributive social policies were central to the last period of expansion because of the tendency of the society's capacity to produce to outstrip market-generated demand, it seems logical to suggest that they could be even more central to new social structures of accumulation in a period when computerization has the potential to expand output far faster than employment.[13]

The International Dimension

However, any argument that stresses the multiplicity of possibilities for organizing particular capitalist societies must deal with the issue of the world economy. As was noted earlier, the rediscovery of the ways in which the international economy constrains national choices played a key role in the revival of the economist fallacy. These constraints have been seen as part of the fundamental economic structure of capitalism; according to this view, they cannot be altered without significant costs in reduced efficiency. I argue to the contrary that these constraints are actually political and ideological; they have little to do with efficiency and they can be altered without significant efficiency costs.

The pressures of the world economy fall into two categories—the impact of competition in international trade and the impact of international capital movements. While there are obvious interactions between these dimensions, they can be discussed separately.

The standard argument that is made about international trade is simply an extension of the argument that wage levels are critical to international competitiveness. It is argued that a country that has more generous social policies will be forced to have higher tax rates to finance these benefits. If these higher taxes fall on firms that produce products that are internationally traded, the firms will be at a competitive disadvantage in relation to firms from countries with lower taxes and less generous social policies.

One problem with this argument, as with many popular economic ideas, is that it traces out only one side of a causal sequence. The positive effects on economic efficiency of social policies are completely neglected, even though it is well known that higher levels of health, education, and general welfare are associated with higher levels of output per employee in manufacturing.[14] Sweden, for example, was able to "afford" more developed social welfare spending through most of the post–World War II period while maintaining a very strong position in international trade. The reason was that Swedish industry was able to use the high-quality "human capital" in the society to produce goods that were internationally competitive by virtue of their technological sophistication and quality.

Furthermore, the experience of the United States in terms of medical care suggests that the failure of the government to take an active role in delivering social services can be even more damaging to international competitiveness. It is well known that health-care costs for employees is one of the largest expense items for American automobile firms.[15] It seems highly likely that had the United States instead created a system of national health insurance, the burden on industries in international competition would be less great than it is now.

The conventional argument also forgets that productivity gains in internationally competitive production are closely linked to overall rates of economic growth.[16] If redistributive social policies contribute to rapid economic growth in a particular country, it is possible that that country's industries will improve their international competitiveness more rapidly than firms in another country that remains bogged down in slow growth.[17]

Above all, this conventional wisdom vastly exaggerates the importance of wage costs—both direct and indirect—in determining international competitiveness.

■ ■ ■ ■

In advanced economies, the international competitiveness of a country's products is influenced by many factors, including a broad range of government policies. And in the face of adversity, there are strategies to pursue for improved trade performance other than reductions in wages, benefits, and government welfare expenditures.

Arguments about capital movements tend to play a more central role in the conventional wisdom because the impact of capital movements can be much more immediate and dramatic than changes in a country's competitiveness in international trade. For example, a country that institutes generous social policies that require higher taxes on business or that imposes stricter regulations on business than its neighbors will likely experience significant capital flight. Not only will international capital be less likely to invest in such a country, but domestic capital is likely to seek safer and more lucrative opportunities abroad. In its mild form, such net capital outflows can lead to a domestic economic slowdown, a negative balance of payments, and a deterioration in the value of the country's currency. This devalued currency, in turn, means a relative reduction in the citizenry's standard of living. When capital outflows accelerate, the result can be even more serious economic turmoil that usually can force either a change of government or a change of governmental policy.

For adherents of the economistic fallacy, these consequences flow directly from the negative efficiency consequences of the original governmental actions. The increase in taxes or the increase in regulations will impose such burdens on firms that they will not be able to achieve adequate profit levels, so that they have no choice but to shift to foreign investments. It is here, also, that the trade arguments are invoked. Because it is assumed that the government moves will assure a deterioration in the international competitiveness of domestic industry, it would make little sense for a shrewd businessperson to invest there rather than abroad.

But with investments, as with trade, the actual effects of any particular set of governmental initiatives are extremely difficult to predict. Again, redistributive policies might strengthen the domestic market and create all kinds of new investment opportunities. Forms of regulation might spawn new industries, as in pollution control, and even contribute to greater consumer and business confidence. One thinks, for example, of the negative investment climate created by proximity to toxic waste dumps.

The classic example of this unpredictability were Roosevelt's New Deal reforms. While the business community was almost unanimous in its condemnation of Roosevelt's initiatives on the grounds that he was destroying the conditions for an efficient capitalist order, the reality was that the reforms created the conditions for the great post–World War II economic expansion. There was, to say the least, a large gap between what was perceived to be efficient in the short term and what was efficient over the long term.

The point, however, is that the actual effects of more generous social policies on the country's international trade and investment position are basically irrelevant. Usually domestic and international business will not wait to see whether the policies strengthen or weaken the balance of payments; they will proceed immediately as though the impact of the policies will be negative. In most circumstances, they are then able to make the prediction into a self-fulfilling prophecy. If producers have predicted that higher taxes will be inflationary, they can then prove the accuracy of this forecast by accelerating the pace of price rises. If they have warned of negative effects on the trade balance, these too can be produced by "leads and lags" in payments that are justified through the imminence of a devaluation. If business has warned of an outflow of capital and a reduction in international investment, these too can be arranged by signaling that the business climate has turned bad under the new government.

The claim, however, is that each of these prophecies is soundly based in an economic theory that emphasizes the international trade and capital constraints on domestic economic actions. The reality is that both the self-fulfilling prophecies and the economic theory must be understood for what they are—stratagems in an ongoing political struggle. The business community tends to oppose redistributive social policies and higher taxes for very simple reasons. Redistributive policies can improve the bargaining power of certain sectors of the labor force with a possible negative effect on profit levels. Similarly, higher taxes appear to threaten profit levels and the income of the wealthy. For any particular firm, the impact on profits is not inevitable—it simply means that greater effort might be necessary to generate the same amount of profit. But an inconvenience for particular capitalists is not the same as impairing the logic of capitalism. The gap between system logic and short-term self-interest emerges when capitalists who are "inconvenienced" by various types of government intervention are forced to be more aggressive and imaginative in finding ways to turn a profit, thus contributing to the efficiency with which the society produces.[18]

But in opposing these types of measures, the business community uses its two complementary weapons—the self-fulfilling prophecy and the claims of economic theory. If business simply warned on the basis of theory that a particular policy would have disastrous consequences without being able to confirm its own predictions, it would not be taken seriously. Alternatively, if the business community fulfilled its own prophecies without the support of a persuasive theory that explained why those outcomes were inevitable, its maneuvers would likely be seen as obvious power plays. And there would be the opportunity to respond to such power plays in the realm of politics. In short, the special potency of economic theory is that it gives business arguments that appear to lie outside of politics and that preclude, in advance, political responses.

To be sure, even if the veil of economic ideology were stripped away, governments would be able to respond effectively to some, but not all, of the self-fulfilling prophecies. If business raises prices to fulfill a prediction of inflation, price controls could be imposed or a tax incentive scheme could be enacted that rewarded those firms that limited their price increases. Through such measures a government could gain time to demonstrate that the actual economic effects of its policies are positive. However, if capital flight and massive disinvestment are predicted, it is difficult—in most cases—for a single government, acting alone, to respond effectively. Even if capital controls are imposed to slow the flight of domestic capital, it is fairly certain that there will be a net and sizable loss of international capital, which can represent a crippling blow to a government's prospects.

However, much depends at this point on which government is involved. If we are discussing the United States government, it is difficult to foresee conditions under which it would be unable to pursue alternative policy directions because of the pressures of flight capital. Even in a period of significant domestic reforms, the United States would still appear a safer haven for international capital than most other places in the world. In addition, the United States has the capacity to mobilize its allies and international institutions such as the IMF to help it resist speculative pressures against the dollar. Moreover, the United States has on earlier occasions successfully controlled the outflow of capital by its own international banks and multinational corporations.[19]

The real problem comes with less powerful countries who find their domestic plans foiled by international capital movements. But it is in these cases that most analysts make the mistake of assuming that the free movement of international capital is a fundamental and necessary part of capitalist world economy. Even without returning to the age of mercantilism, it must be recalled that capitalism flourished at the domestic level through the two World Wars despite substantial controls over international capital movements. Moreover, the early plans of J.M. Keynes and Harry Dexter White for the postwar international monetary order contemplated substantial controls over international capital mobility. White, in particular, feared that the free movement of capital could doom efforts within particular countries to pursue full-employment policies, so he proposed international arrangements through which other countries would agree to repatriate flight capital that left a country in violation of its domestic capital controls.[20] While these plans were not implemented, their demise reflected the political balance of forces at the time—particularly, the power of internationally oriented business in the United States—rather than the fundamental logic of the system. Moreover, despite the triumph of those forces favoring the free movement of capital, it was not until 1958 that most European countries restored the convertibility of their currencies. Hence, much of the postwar recovery of European capitalism occurred under a system of controls over the outflow of capital.

In fact, too much freedom for international capital movements is irrational even on capitalist terms. The huge quantities of "stateless" capital in the Eurodollar market that quickly shift from one currency to another have created turmoil in the currency markets and have repeatedly interfered with the effectiveness of national economic policies. And on numerous occasions, major countries have found it necessary to peg interest rates at excessively high rates—with the resulting slowdown in growth and increases in unemployment—simply because of the pressures of international capital markets. While it was once hoped that the shift in the seventies from fixed exchange rates to flexible rates would make possible international monetary stability even with these massive pools of speculative capital, floating rates have not solved the problem.

Moreover, the free movement of international capital has also created significant problems of instability in international banking. During the seventies, the international banks fell over each other making excessive loans to Third World countries creating the present debt crisis. And there is continuing fear of a spreading international financial crisis resulting from the failure of a subsidiary or offshore bank that is subject to little or no regulation by national banking authorities.

These problems have created strong pressures for increased regulation of international banking and even some establishment figures have made policy proposals designed to discourage speculative capital flows.[21] The point is that the degree to which the international economic order regulates and restricts international capital flows is itself a matter of political choice, and the efficiency arguments for complete freedom of capital movement are deeply flawed.[22] Hence, it is a political possibility that the international monetary order be reformed to limit speculative capital flows or to establish means to offset such flows.[23] Such reforms would result in a reduction in the political leverage that comes from the threat or reality of massive capital flight. Governments would then have expanded possibilities for pursuing alternative domestic policies.

In sum, the international argument has the same flaws as the domestic one—it mistakes the political preferences of an extremely powerful interest group for the fundamental logic of an economic system. In doing so, it simply reinforces the political strength of business by denying the real political choices that are available for organizing the international economic order and national political economies.

Notes

1. See Robert Bacon and Walter Eltis, *Britain's Economic Problems: Too Few Producers* (London: Macmillan, 1978); Organization for Economic Cooperation and Development, *Towards Full Employment and Price Stability* (Paris: OECD, 1977); George Gilder, *Wealth and Poverty* (New York: Basic Books, 1981).
2. See Alan Wolfe, *The Limits of Legitimacy* (New York: Free Press, 1978), chap. 10.
3. For an influential statement of these arguments, see Barry Bluestone and Bennett Harrison, *The Deindustrialization of America* (New York: Basic Books, 1982), especially chap. 6.
4. The original publication was in 1944, but references are to the Beacon Press edition, Boston, 1957. For an extended discussion of Polanyi's thought, see Fred Block and Margaret Somers, "Beyond the Economistic Fallacy: The Holistic Social Science of Karl Polanyi," in *Vision and Method in Historical Sociology*, ed. Theda Skocpol (New York: Cambridge University Press, 1984).
5. Polanyi, *Transformation*, 63–67.
6. Polanyi, *Transformation*, 77–85.
7. Polanyi, *Transformation*, 73.
8. Polanyi, *Transformation*, 165–166.
9. Volume 1, chap. 8, 15.
10. See Adam Przeworski, "The Ethical Materialism of John Roemer," *Politics & Society* 11, 3 (1982): 289–313, for a critique of the Marxist tendency to see the economy as a self-operating automaton.
11. See David Gordon, Richard Edwards, and Michael Reich, *Segmented Work, Divided Workers* (New York: Cambridge University Press, 1982). While I make use of their concept, there is much in their argument with which I disagree.
12. This list of factors is far from complete; it is meant only to be illustrative.
13. The argument is that if computerization reduces the demand for labor while output rises, there could be a significant shortfall in demand. While such an outcome is not inevitable, a weakening of the labor market from technological displacement can reduce employee bargaining power so that wage gains fail to keep pace with the growth of output. On problems of employment generation in advanced capitalism, see Fred Block, "Technological Change and Employment: New Perspectives on an Old Controversy," *Economia & Lavoro* (Aug.–Sept. 1984).
14. See Denison's classic work in growth accounting, Edward F. Denison, *Accounting for United States Economic Growth, 1929–1969* (Washington: Brookings, 1974).

15. In 1984, Chrysler Corporation budgeted $460 million for health-insurance premiums. This amounts to $5,000 per employee or $275 per vehicle. "Chrysler Program Saves Millions in Health Costs," *New York Times* (April 29, 1985).
16. "In general, there is a logical correlation between increases in production and in productivity, with productivity speeding up as production accelerates and slowing down as production is retarded." Harry Magdoff and Paul Sweezy, "Productivity Slowdown: A False Alarm," *Monthly Review* 31, 2 (June 1979): 11.
17. The actual outcome depends, of course, on other variables such as the rate of inflation, exchange rates, and the propensity to import. But my point is that the impact of social policies on international competitiveness is indeterminate and depends on other variables some of which can be effectively manipulated by governments.
18. This now neglected line of argument has a distinguished lineage in the economics literature. For example, in his classic study of manufacturing employment, Fabricant argues that reductions in the length of the working day imposed by government or unions can have the effect of inducing greater entrepreneurial effort by the employer. Solomon Fabricant, *Employment in Manufacturing, 1899–1939* New York: NBER, 1942) 13.
19. The system of capital controls imposed during the Vietnam War is described briefly in Fred Block, *The Origins of International Economic Disorder* (Berkeley: University of California Press, 1977) 182–184.
20. Block, *Origins*, 42–46.
21. While the Reagan administration's obstinate commitment to free markets and deregulation has discouraged initiatives in this direction, steps were being taken in the late seventies toward greater international cooperation to regulate banking. See Hugo Colje, "Bank Supervision on a Consolidated Basis," *The Banker* (June 1980): 29–34. Robert Dunn writes that, "Prohibitions or limitations on capital flows have been widely discussed as a possible route to a less volatile exchange market . . . ," and he reports a proposal by James Tobin to discourage speculative capital flows by taxing exchange market transactions. Robert M. Dunn Jr., *The Many Disappointments of Flexible Exchange Rates*, Princeton Essays in International Finance, no. 154, Dec. 1983, 24–26.
22. The argument that the new technologies of capital transfer make controls impossible is clearly specious. The reality is that such electronic transfers leave more traces than traditional currency transactions.
23. The natural coalition for such reforms would bring together progressive social forces in Western Europe and the United States with Third World nations that are currently suffering from their indebtedness to international banks.

A FEMINIST THEORY OF THE STATE

MIMI ABRAMOVITZ

Building on the Marxist analysis of capitalism and the radical feminist analysis of patriarchy, socialist feminism maintains that the state is neither a neutral mediator of interest group conflict nor simply procapital. Rather, the state protects the interests of both capital and patriarchy by institutionalizing capitalist class and property relations and upholding patriarchal distinctions. According to Zillah Eisenstein,

> The formation of the state institutionalizes patriarchy; it reifies the division between public and private life as one of sexual differences . . . The domain of the state has always signified public life and this is distinguished in part from the private realm by differentiating men from women . . . The state formalizes the rule by men because the division of public and private life is at one and the same time a male-female distinction . . . The state's purpose is to enforce the separation of public and private life and with it the distinctness of male and female existence.[1]

The state protects capitalism and patriarchy by enforcing their respective requirements, but also by mediating any conflicts that arise from the state's simultaneous commitment to both. The state steps in to create order and cohesion especially when the heterogeneous and frequently divided dominant class cannot agree on how best to resolve these tensions.[2]

Including patriarchy complicates the otherwise useful analysis of the origins and development of the welfare state put forward by Gough, Dickinson, O'Connor, and other contemporary Marxists who suggest that the welfare state operates to mediate conflicts between the capitalist requirements of production and reproduction. They see the welfare state as assisting capitalist accumulation and the legitimacy of the prevailing social order by assuring the reproduction of the labor force, the maintenance of society's non-working members, and securing the social peace. If Marxism argues that the welfare state arose to mediate reproductive relations on behalf of the productive needs of capital, socialist feminism holds that the welfare state originated to meet the changing requirements of patriarchy *and* capitalism and to mediate their conflicts. Drawing on various parts of the socialist-feminist discourse, a new but far from singular and still incomplete perspective can be envisioned which suggests that the origins and functions of the welfare state represent not only the need to reproduce and maintain the labor force as observed by the Marxists, but also to uphold patriarchal relations and to regulate the lives of women. From this perspective, the welfare state operates to uphold patriarchy and to enforce female subordination in both the spheres of production and reproduction, to mediate the contradictory demands for women's home and market labor, and to support the nuclear family structure at the expense of all others.

Upholding Patriarchal Control in the Family and the Market

Socialist feminists maintain that state intervention in work and family life reflects the changing requirements of patriarchy as well as those of capitalism and the historical intervention of the state on behalf of "proper" family life. Both Brown and Ursel[3] argue that the advance of capitalism gradually shifted the center of patriarchal control from the private family headed by a man to the state. In pre-industrial society, where the household was both the productive and reproductive unit, patriarchal authority was private or familial, that is, grounded in the gender organization of the family. Public or social patriarchy, rooted in the state, was more facilitative than direct, providing only the structural supports for private patriarchy in the home. By law, custom, and economics, male heads of household controlled the labor of women and other family members as well as their access to most economic resources. Marriage, property, inheritance, and public aid laws were local and operated primarily to enforce such control by the patriarch who, in turn, was obliged to maintain the nuclear family and women's place in the home.

Public or social patriarchy became stronger as the rise of industrial capitalism began to weaken the economic and political underpinnings of male authority. The separation of production and reproduction, the growth of factories, the creation of a wage labor force (which employed women and children as well as men), and the emergence of new ideas about individual freedom, equality, and opportunity shifted the basis of patriarchal authority from the male head of household to the employer and the state. As market relations slowly lessened men's ability to control the labor of family members and increased their wives' and children's access to economic resources, familial patriarchy alone no longer sufficed to maintain male domination and the gender division of labor.

The decline of patriarchal authority modified the state's relationship to private family life. As familial patriarchy gave way to social or public patriarchy, the state assumed regulatory functions previously confined to the family including greater regulation of marriage, inheritance, child custody, and employment.[4] The growth of the social welfare system and its "reform" in the early nineteenth century also marked the shift from familial to social patriarchy, at least for the poor. The transition, signaled by an attack on public aid (outdoor relief) and the rise of institutional care (indoor relief) made public aid very harsh and punitive. The Marxist explanation of these "reforms" suggests that state-regulated deterrence became necessary to discipline the newly industrialized labor force. The feminist analysis adds that the social welfare changes also operated to enforce new ideas about proper family life. Punitive relief programs assured that women chose any quality of family life over public aid. Welfare recipients whose families did not comply with prevailing norms were considered undeserving and treated even more poorly by the system. Given women's responsibility for maintaining the home, poor, immigrant, and female-headed households suspected of being unable to properly socialize their children were frequently defined as unworthy of aid. If an institutional placement resulted, it could tear "undeserving" families apart, often for reasons of poverty alone.

In the early twentieth century, the entry of more women into the labor force challenged patriarchal patterns and was viewed as competitive with men. The new labor and social welfare legislation that emerged enforced the gender division of labor and otherwise re-asserted patriarchal structures in the family and the market. Protective labor laws, Mothers' Pension programs, and other new social legislation excluded women from the labor market and relegated them to the home where they worked to reproduce and maintain the labor force. These and other laws also supported a sex-segregated occupational structure and established male-dominated hierarchies at the workplace (which mirrored and reinforced those already in place in the home).

During the rest of the twentieth century, the expanding welfare state continued to support patriarchal dominance while mediating reproductive relations on behalf of the productive needs of capital. The emergence of the modern welfare state, marked by the enactment of the 1935 Social Security Act, signaled the institutionalization of public or social patriarchy. Instead of simply assuming patriarchal control, the state began to systematically subsidize the familial unit of production through the provision of economic resources to the aged, the unemployed, and children without fathers. The major income maintenance programs of the Social Security Act also incorporated patriarchal family norms. They each presumed and reinforced marriage, the male breadwinner/female homemaker household type and women's economic dependence on men. Mary McIntosh[5] points out that even the special programs for female heads of households indirectly buttressed the ideal family type by substituting the state for the male breadwinner. By helping this "deviant" family approximate the "normal" one, programs for female-headed families "solved" one of patriarchy's major problems, that of the so-called "broken home" or female-headed home. At the same time, the program's low benefits and stigma penalized husbandless women for their departure from prescribed wife and mother roles. This kept unmarried motherhood and the breakup of the two-parent family from appearing too attractive to others. Until very recently, when they began to falter in this regard, the programs of the Social Security Act implicitly supported family structures that conformed to the patriarchal model and penalized those that did not. The historical intervention by the state on behalf of "proper" family life suggests the family's importance to the survival of capitalism and patriarchy. Indeed, families absorb the cost and responsibility for bearing and socializing the next generation, for managing consumption and other household matters, for organizing sexual relations, for providing care to the aged, sick, and young who cannot work, and for producing income to meet all these needs. The attack on the welfare state can be understood partly as an effort to restore the ability of the welfare state to uphold traditional patriarchal arrangements in face of recent threats derived from major changes in both the family system and the political economy.

Regulating the Labor of Women

Socialist feminists agree with contemporary Marxists that the welfare state helps to assure reproduction of the labor force and the maintenance of the non-working members of the population. But they stress that from the start, programs serving women have had a more complicated role. The activities necessary to secure the physical, economic, and social viability of the working class depend heavily on women's unpaid domestic labor as do prevailing patriarchal family patterns. But because this competes with capital's ongoing demand for women's low paid market labor, socialist feminism forces us to see that the welfare state must regulate the lives of women in a unique way.

The demands for women's domestic and market labor have contradicted each other since the separation of household and market production in the early nineteenth century. Women's domestic labor assures capital fit, able, and properly socialized workers on a daily and a generational basis as well as the care of those unable to work. This unpaid domestic labor absorbs the costs that industry or government would otherwise have to pay to reproduce and maintain a productive labor force. Women's domestic labor also reinforces patriarchal arrangements. It relieves individual men of household tasks, services their physical, sexual, and emotional needs, keeps women economically dependent, stops them from competing with men in the job market, and defines women's place in the home. By the end of the colonial period, however capital's need for cheap market labor had combined with the impoverishment of the working class to draw increasingly large numbers of women into the wage labor market. Paradoxically, their entry conflicted with the benefits received by capital from women's unpaid domestic labor. Combined with fewer marriages and more female-headed households, the growing labor force participation of women, which held the possibility of greater economic independence, also contained a challenge to male dominance and patriarchal family patterns.

Socialist feminism argues that, from colonial times to the present, social welfare programs serving women have had to deal with these contradictory pulls. Given the twin benefits of female labor, the welfare state, in most historical periods, has played a central role in mediating the resulting conflict, especially among poor and working-class women. Social welfare policies have always regulated the lives of women, channelling some into the home to devote full time to reproducing and maintaining the labor force and others into the labor market where they also create profits for capital. By distinguishing among women as "deserving" and "undeserving" of aid, the policies also reinforced divisions among women along lines of race, class, and marital status.

Arena of Struggle

Like some Marxists, some socialist feminists conclude that the paradoxes of the welfare state make it a productive arena for feminist as well as class struggle. On the one hand, welfare state policies assist capital and patriarchy by reproducing the labor force, regulating the competing demands for female labor, enforcing female subordination, maintaining women's place in the home, and sustaining the social peace. On the other hand, welfare state benefits threaten patriarchal arrangements. They redistribute needed resources, offer non-working women and single mothers a means of self-support, and provide the material conditions for the pursuit of equal opportunity. Welfare state benefits that help women to survive without male economic support subsidize, if not legitimize, the female-headed household and undermine the exclusivity of the male-breadwinner, female-homemaker family structure. As a social wage, welfare state benefits increase the bargaining power of women relative to men. Eisenstein[6] argues that the very existence of the welfare state, especially its deep involvement in family life, is potentially subversive to capitalism, liberalism, and patriarchy. Whether or not and how the welfare state carries out its abstract tasks or exposes its roots in patriarchal capitalism, however, is not predetermined. Rather it reflects the degree of prevailing struggle over who (capital or labor) "pays" for these benefits and the extent to which the welfare state policies can be made to change rather than reproduce the conditions necessary to perpetuate patriarchal capitalism. In the final analysis, the outcome of the struggle reflects the relative power of the contesting forces at any moment in time.

The Role of Ideology: The Family Ethic and the Regulation of Women

The welfare state functions identified by socialist feminists are carried out, in part, by the codification of the family ethic or the ideology of women's roles in its rules and regulations. Indeed, the family ethic is one way in which the welfare state regulates the lives of women. Ideology, or the relatively coherent system of beliefs and values about human nature and social life generated by a society for itself, is found in the realm of ideas, the actions of individuals, and in the practices of societal institutions, including the welfare state. The power of ideology lies in its ability to influence the thinking and behavior of individuals, the practices of institutions, and the organization of society. In the case of women, the family ethic, articulates expected work and family behavior and defines women's place in the wider social order. Embodied in all societal institutions, this dominant norm is enforced by the laws and activities of the state.

The family ethic derives from patriarchal social thought that sees gender roles as biologically determined rather than socially assigned and from standard legal doctrine that defines women as the property of men. It is grounded in the idea that natural physical differences between the sexes determine their differential capacities. The idea of natural differences between the sexes causes individuals to see their femininity and masculinity solely as part of human nature[7] rather than as the product of socialization. The sense of "naturalness" legitimizes socially constructed gender distinctions and enables individuals to participate, without question, in gender-specific roles. The implication that biology is destiny also obscures the historical impact of differential socialization and unequal opportunities on the choices made by individuals of different sexes, races, and ages. By making these choices seem natural and rational, the family ethic helps to justify discrepancies between societal promises and realities, to rationalize prejudice, discrimination, and inequalities, and to promote the acquiescence of the oppressed in their oppression. Finally, the direct appeal to nature as the source of gender differences minimizes the cultural determination of women's sexuality, the significance of changes in women's position over time, and the importance of women's private domestic labor to both capitalist production and patriarchal arrangements.

Like most ideologies, the ideology of women's roles represents dominant interests and explains reality in ways that create social cohesion and maintain the *status quo.* The family ethic articulates and rationalizes the terms of the gender division of labor. Despite its long history, the lynchpin of the family ethic—the assignment of homemaking and childcare responsibilities to women—has remained reasonably stable.

A family ethic telling women about their proper place existed in colonial America. This pre-industrial code placed women in the home and subordinate to the male head of household. Women were expected to be economically productive, but to limit their productive labor to the physical boundaries of the home. Between 1790 and 1830, changes in the political economy that accompanied the rise of industrial capitalism caused a dramatic shift in women's roles. The emerging market economy removed production from the home and created gender-based separate spheres. As men took their place in the market, the work ethic followed them there; but the new "industrial family ethic" continued to define women's place as in the home.

The industrial family ethic resembled its colonial predecessor in many ways, except that it denied women a recognized productive role. Told not to engage in market labor at all, the family ethic defined women's place as exclusively in the home. Reflecting the needs of the new social order, their domestic work included creating a comfortable retreat for the market-weary breadwinner, socializing children to assume proper adult work and family roles, managing household consumption, offering emotional nurturance to family members, caring for the aged and the sick, taming male sexuality, and providing moral guardianship to the family and the wider community. At the same time, and reflecting patriarchal rules, women were viewed as the "weaker sex" in need of male support and protection. The subordination of women became grounded in their economic dependence on men and in the law. The latter continued to define women as male property and to grant men control of women's labor and access to resources.

The idea of the family ethic draws on what other scholars have labeled the "cult of domesticity" or the "cult of true womanhood."[8] But as developed here, the concept goes beyond earlier descriptions, to examine the codification of the ideology of women's roles in societal institutions and to analyze its regulatory powers. Indeed, the family ethic which "protects" the white middle-class family also operates a mechanism of social regulation and control.

On the individual level, the family ethic keeps women in line. Fulfilling the terms of the family ethic theoretically entitles a woman to the "rights of womanhood" including claims to femininity, protection, economic support, and respectability. Non-compliance brings penalties for being out of role. Encoded in all societal institutions, the family ethic also reflects, enforces, and rationalizes the gender-based division of society into public and private spheres and helps to downgrade women in both. The ideology of women's roles helps to keep women at the bottom of the hierarchies of power in both the public and the private spheres.

Indeed, the idea that women belong at home has historically sanctioned the unequal treatment of women in the market. The resulting economic insecurity has channeled them back into the home. The need for women's domestic labor and the ideological presumption of a private sphere to which women rightfully belong has helped to rationalize their subordination in the public sphere. When industry's need for inexpensive labor drew women out of their "proper place," the idea that they belonged in the home justified channelling them into low-paid, low-status, gender segregated sectors of the economy and into jobs whose functions paralleled those tasks traditionally performed by women at home. Women's inability to earn a livable wage made men, marriage, and family life into a necessary and a more rational source of financial support. Lacking a material basis for independence, a women easily became economically, if not psychologically, dependent on men which, in turn, created the conditions for women's subordinate family role.

In brief, the family ethic, which locked women into a subordinate family role also rationalized women's exploitation on the job. By devaluing women's position in each sphere, the ideology of women's work and family roles satisfied capital's need for a supply of readily available, cheap, female labor. By creating the conditions for continued male control of women at home and on the job, the economic devaluation and marginalization of women also muted the challenge that increased employment by women posed to patriarchal norms.

Targeted to and largely reflecting the experience of white, middle-class women who marry and stay home, the family ethic denied poor and immigrant women and women of color the "rights of womanhood" and the opportunity to embrace the dominant definition of "good wife" and mother because they did not confine their labor to the home.[9] Forced by dire poverty to work for wages outside the home, they also faced severe exploitation on the job, having to accept the lowest wages, longest hours, and most dangerous working conditions. Instead of "protecting" their femininity and their families' social respectability, the notion of separate spheres placed poor and immigrant women and women of color in a double bind at home and reinforced their subordinate status in the market. Separate spheres, which recognized and sustained the household labor that white women performed for their families, offered no such support to non-white women.[10] Both Dill and Glenn point out that society's treatment of women of color clearly indicated that their value as laborers took precedence over their domestic and reproductive roles. On all fronts, the families of poor and immigrant women and women of color experienced a series of assaults not faced by middle-class white women.

Perhaps this is why some of the families of poor, employed, husbandless, immigrant women, and women of color tried so hard to comply with the terms of the family ethic. Indeed, working-class men struggled to keep their wives at home even when this involved major sacrifices in the organization and comfort of their family life. To stay out of the labor force, working-class women typically limited family consumption, sent their children to work, sacrificed the privacy of their homes to take in boarders, increased production of household goods and/or took in paid piece-work which burdened their already long work day.[11]

The ideology of women's roles is deeply encoded in social welfare policy. It is well-known that social welfare laws categorize the poor as deserving and undeserving of aid based on their compliance with the work ethic. But the rules and regulations of social welfare programs also treat women differentially according to their perceived compliance with the family ethic. Indeed, conforming to the ideology of women's roles has been used to distinguish among women as deserving or undeserving of aid since colonial times. Assessing women in terms of the family ethic became one way the welfare state could mediate the conflicting demands for women's unpaid labor in the home and her low paid labor in the market, encourage reproduction by "proper" families, and otherwise meet the needs of patriarchal capitalism. Recognizing the role of the family ethic in social welfare policy permits us to uncover the long untold story of the relationship between women and the welfare state.

Notes

1. Zillah R. Eisenstein, *Feminism and Sexual Equality: Crisis in Liberal America* (New York: Monthly Review Press, 1984), p. 92.
2. *Ibid.*, pp. 89–92.
3. Jane Ursel, "The State and the Maintenance of Patriarchy: A Case Study of Family, Labour and Welfare Legislation in Canada," in James Dickinson and Bob Russell (eds.), *Family, Economy, & State* (New York: St. Martins Press, 1986), pp. 154–155, 157; Carol Brown, "Mothers Fathers and Children: From Private to Public Patriarchy," in Lydia Sargent (ed.), *Women and Revolution: A Discussion of the Unhappy Marriage of Marxism and Feminism* (Boston: South End Press, 1981), pp. 239–267.
4. Ursel, p. 158.
5. Mary McIntosh, "The State and the Oppression of Women," in Annette Kuhn and Ann Marie Wolpe (eds.), *Feminism and Materialism: Women and Modes of Production* (London: Routledge and Kegan Paul, 1978), pp. 254–289.
6. Zillah Eisenstein, *The Radical Future of Liberal Feminism* (New York: Longman, 1981), pp. 104–105.
7. Julie A. Matthaei, *An Economic History of Women in America* (New York, Shocken Books, 1982), pp. 3–7.
8. See for example: Nancy F. Cott, *The Bonds of Womanhood: "Woman's Sphere" in New England, 1780–1835* (New Haven: Yale University Press, 1977); Barbara Welter, "The Cult of True Womanhood: 1820–1860," in Michael Gordon (ed.), *The American Family in Socio-Historical Perspective* (New York: St. Martin's Press, 1978), pp. 313–333; Barbara Epstein, "Industrialization and Femininity: A Case Study of Nineteenth Century New England," in Rachel Kahn-Hut, Arlene Kaplan Daniels, Richard Colvard (eds.), *Women and Work: Problems and Perspectives* (New York: Oxford University Press, 1982), pp. 88–100; Barbara J. Harris, *Beyond Her Sphere: Women and the Professions in American History* (Westport, CT: Greenwood Press, 1983), pp. 32–72; Laurel Thatcher Ulrich, *Good Wives: Image and Reality in the Lives of Women in Northern New England* (New York: Oxford University Press, 1982).
9. Bonnie Thornton Dill, *Our Mothers' Grief: Racial Ethnic Women and the Maintenance of Families*, Research Paper #4, May 1986, Center for Research on Women, Memphis State University, Memphis Tennessee 38152, pp. 48–49.
10. Evelyn Nakano Glenn "Racial Ethnic Women's Labor: The Intersection of Race, Gender and Class Oppression," *Review of Radical Political Economics*, 17 (3) (Fall 1985), pp. 86–104.
11. Dill, p. 15.

SECTION III
ELECTORAL POLITICS

When we talk with our students about politics and voting, we are struck by how few students say they vote in major elections. In this regard, our students are similar to their peers across the country. In the 2000 presidential election, only 28.4 percent of eligible 18- to 20-year-olds reported that they voted, and only 24.2 percent of eligible 21- to 24-year-olds did so. These figures are considerably lower than any other age group; the next lowest reported voter turnout, for 25- to 34-year-olds, was 43.7 percent (U.S. Census 2001: 251). Students also report low levels of participation in other forms of political activity, such as contacting elected representatives about an issue, volunteering in an election campaign, or attending a rally. When we ask students why they choose not to be involved in politics, the major responses are either that they are not interested in politics or they are cynical about politicians and the political system. As sociologists, we reject the idea that the students themselves are to blame for this; this all too frequent conclusion lets political institutions off the hook. Instead, we are interested in the social forces that produce these responses. If students say they are not interested in politics, then why have political institutions not captured their interest in the first place? If students express cynicism about politics, perhaps this is not so much a reflection of their personalities as it is a rational (although unproductive) appraisal of how political institutions actually operate in the United States.

Critical studies of the U.S. electoral system are based on the assumption that the expansion of democratic control over the state and other social institutions (such as the economy) is a desirable goal. From this perspective, the electoral system is characterized by structural inequalities that place limits on the effective political participation of subordinate groups and provide important benefits to dominant groups. By defining the boundaries of political debate, these inequalities reveal the limits of the one-dimensional model of decision-making power discussed in Section I of the book. The readings in this section illustrate how these inequalities operate.

The selection by Frances Fox Piven and Richard A. Cloward addresses a major contradiction in U.S. society: How is it that, in a society that proclaims the value of democracy and sees itself as a democratic model for the rest of the world, citizen participation in electoral politics should be so low? In the 2000 presidential election, voter turnout was 52 percent, and this was an improvement over 1996, when just 49 percent of eligible voters actually voted (U.S. Census Bureau 2001:253). In comparative terms, voter turnout in the United States is the lowest of the major countries (Kloby 2003). Nonvoting tends to be explained in relatively individualistic terms (apathy, laziness) or as an expression of contentment with the status quo. Piven and Cloward reject these explanations, and instead argue that electoral laws, particularly those concerning registration, have resulted in a major demobilization of working class and poor citizens over the past one hundred years. Institutionalized efforts to reduce voter turnout have the consequence of benefiting dominant groups materially by limiting the political participation of those who might have interests in major economic redistribution.

G. William Domhoff's examination of the specific mechanisms with which the power elite secures its interests in public policy also helps us to understand low voter turnout. Although all citizens have one vote, members of the power elite control access to important political resources not available to other citizens. Their direct involvement in government as cabinet officers, for example, ensures that the interests of the power elite are better represented in constructing and implementing policy. Members of the power elite provide information (either directly or through the use of lobbyists) to secure advantages in the writing of specific legislation, and they seek to influence public policy more generally through their involvement in policymaking organizations (such as the Council on Foreign Relations, the Business Roundtable, and the Committee for Economic Development) that generate ideas and programs to address major economic, political, and social issues (see also Perrucci and Wysong 2003). These mechanisms construct the boundaries that average citizens encounter when they participate in politics, allowing some issues to come to the fore and excluding others, and defining the limits of debate on those issues that are defined as meaningful. Low voter turnout can be seen as a rational response to the recognition that voters' decision-making power (the one-dimensional model of power) is constrained by the power elite's monopoly of more fundamental forms of power.

The selection by Dan Clawson, Alan Neustadtl, and Mark Weller examines the role of money in the U.S. electoral system. In the 2000 election, for example, almost $1 billion was spent on all congressional races (U.S Census Bureau 2001:256), and about $500 million in unregulated "soft money" contributions were made to the two major political parties (U.S. Census Bureau 2001:254). Given the strong likelihood that the candidate who raises more money in a race will win, the need for campaign finance gives extraordinary influence to those individuals and organizations that can provide this money. Although citizens are legally equal in that their votes count the same, they are not equal economically, and this class inequality plays a major role in limiting the democratic character of the U.S. electoral system; indeed, the low voter turnout that Piven and Cloward speak of can be seen as a rational response to this. As Clawson, Neustadtl, and Weller point out, less than one-fourth of 1 percent of the population gives contributions of $200 or more to federal candidates, and the great bulk of the money contributed by organizations comes from corporations. Contributors and recipients enter into a social relationship of mutuality and reciprocity in which the perspectives of the former take on the mantle of "common sense," and therefore exercise dominant influence on the development of public policy. The problem of campaign finance, therefore, is less often specific acts of corruption in which money is offered in return for support for specific policies, but rather the less obvious, taken-for-granted access that comes from being part of a social network.

Finally, Lani Guinier points to the way that different electoral systems have different consequences for political participation by and representation for racial minorities in the United States. The existing winner-take-all electoral system, in which those with the majority of votes win all of the representation, is formally race-neutral in that all voters are defined as having an equal vote. However, given voting patterns that tend to reflect group interests, members of racial minorities will consistently be unable to elect representatives that reflect their interests, and so this race-neutral electoral system in fact produces racially discriminatory results. One of the benefits of whiteness, then, is the ability to maximize white political representation, and to have the whiteness of political representation obscured by reference to "majority rule." Alternative electoral systems such as cumulative voting (giving voters multiple votes that can be allocated however they wish) and supermajority voting (requiring more than a majority of votes) are race-neutral ways of making minority votes matter while not violating the fundamental democratic principle of one person–one vote.

There is one more point that is worthy of note here. For many of the authors in this section, their critique of electoral politics is presented in the context of political action. Piven and Cloward, for example, were active in the effort to pass the National Voter Registration Act of 1993 (the "Motor Voter" law) that made it easier for citizens to register to vote, while the book from which Clawson, Neustadtl, and Weller's article is taken was written as part of the movement for campaign finance reform. Domhoff has contributed to debates on the proper role that the Democratic Party should play in progressive political strategy (Domhoff 2003), and Guinier has been active in campaigns for legal and electoral reform. All too often, we find that students recognize the inequalities in the political system but respond with cynicism or withdrawal from politics. The critical perspective offered here avoids this tendency toward political demobilization by integrating a structural and historical analysis of politics with recognition of the possibility and necessity for people to act collectively to change politics.

References

Domhoff, G. William. 2003. *Changing the Powers That Be: How the Left Can Stop Losing and Win.* Lanham, MD: Rowman & Littlefield.

Kloby, Jerry. 2003. *Inequality, Power, and Development.* 2nd ed. Amherst, NY: Humanity Books.

Perrucci, Robert, and Earl Wysong. 2003. *The New Class Society.* Lanham, MD: Rowman & Littlefield Publishers.

U.S. Census Bureau. 2001. *Statistical Abstract of the United States 2001.* Washington, DC: Government Printing Office.

DOES VOTING MATTER?

FRANCES FOX PIVEN AND RICHARD A. CLOWARD

The right to vote is the core symbol of democratic politics. Of course, the vote itself is meaningless unless citizens have other rights, such as the right to speak, write, and assemble; unless opposition parties can compete for power by offering alternative programs, cultural appeals, and leaders; and unless diverse popular groupings can gain some recognition by the parties. And democratic arrangements that guarantee formal equality through the universal franchise are inevitably compromised by sharp social and economic inequalities. Nevertheless, the right to vote is the feature of the democratic polity that makes all other political rights significant. "The electorate occupies, at least in the mystique of [democratic] orders, the position of the principal organ of governance."[1]

Americans generally take for granted that ours is the very model of a democracy. Our leaders regularly proclaim the United States to be the world's leading democracy and assert that other nations should measure their progress by the extent to which they develop electoral arrangements that match our own. At the core of this self-congratulation is the belief that the right to vote is firmly established here. But in fact the United States is the only major democratic nation in which the less-well-off, as well as the young and minorities, are substantially underrepresented in the electorate. Only about half of the eligible population votes in presidential elections, and far fewer vote in off-year elections. As a result, the United States ranks at the bottom in turnout compared with other major democracies. Moreover, those who vote are different in politically important respects from those who do not. Voters are better off and better educated, and nonvoters are poorer and less well educated. Modest shifts from time to time notwithstanding, this has been true for most of the twentieth century and has actually worsened in the last three decades. In sum, the active American electorate overrepresents those who have more and underrepresents those who have less.

Despite the central role that political scientists typically assign to electoral processes in shaping politics, some scholars deny that important political consequences follow from the constriction of the electorate. In one variant of this argument, nonvoting is defined as a kind of voting, a tacit expression of satisfaction with the political status quo. Since many people abstain and are apparently satisfied, the size of the nonvoting population actually demonstrates the strength of the American democracy. Of course, no one has offered an adequate explanation of why this "politics of happiness"[2] is consistently concentrated among the least well-off.

Another variant of the no-problem position asserts that mass abstention contributes to the health of a democratic polity not because it is a mark of satisfaction but because it reduces conflict and provides political leaders with the latitude they require for responsible governance. A functioning democracy, the argument goes, requires a balance between participation and nonparticipation, between involvement and noninvolvement.[3] The "crisis of democracy" theorists of the 1970s, for example, reasoned that an "excess" of participation endangered democratic institutions by "overloading" them with demands, especially economic demands.[4] This rather Olympian view of the democratic "functions" of nonvoting fails, of course, to deal with the decidedly undemocratic consequences of muffling the demands of some groups in the polity and not others.

A bolder but kindred argument fastens on the characteristics of nonvoters—especially their presumed extremism and volatility—to explain why their abstention is healthy for the polity. To cite a classic example, Lipset (1960) points to evidence that nonvoters are more likely to have antidemocratic attitudes.[5] Similarly, George Will, writing "In Defense of Nonvoting," says that "the fundamental human right" is not to the franchise but "to good government"; he points to the high turnouts in the late Weimar Republic as evidence of the dangers of increased voter participation, an example often favored by those who make this argument.[6] Will's point of view is reminiscent of the arguments of nineteenth-century reformers who proposed various methods of *reducing* turnout—by introducing property qualifications on the vote, for example—in order to improve the quality of the electorate. Consider, for example, the *New York Times* in 1878: "It would be a great gain if people could be made to understand distinctly that the right to life, liberty, and the pursuit of happiness involves, to be sure, the right to good government, but not the right to take part, either immediately or indirectly, in the management of the state."[7]

The Contested Vote

American history has been marked by sharp contests over the question of who may vote, the conditions under which they may vote, or just which state offices they may vote for, and how much some votes will weigh in relation to other votes. These questions were hard fought because they were a crucial dimension of struggles for political advantage.

The United States was the first nation in the world in which the franchise began to be widely distributed,[8] a historical achievement that helps to explain the democratic hubris we display to this day. That achievement occurred at a time when the hopes of peasants, artisans, and the urban poor everywhere in the West were fired by the essential democratic idea, the idea that if ordinary people had the right to participate in the selection of state leaders, their grievances would be acted upon.[9] That hope was surely overstated, as were the fears of the propertied classes that the extension of the vote would give the "poor and ignorant majority" the power to "bring about a more equitable distribution of the good things of this world."[10] Nevertheless, the large possibilities associated with democracy help to explain why the right of ordinary people to vote was sharply contested. And if the franchise was ceded earlier in the United States, it was because post-Revolutionary elites had less ability to resist popular demands. The common men who had fought the Revolution were still armed and still insurgent. Moreover, having severed their connection with England, American men of property were unprotected by the majesty and military forces of a traditional state apparatus.

The political institutions that developed in the context of an expanded suffrage did not remedy many popular grievances. Still, a state influenced by political parties and election did not merely replicate traditional patterns of class domination either. It also reflected in some measure the new social compact embodied in the franchise. Contenders for rulership now needed votes, and that fact altered the dynamics of power, modestly most of the time, more sharply some of the time. In the early nineteenth century, the electoral arrangements that forced leaders to bid for popular support led to the gradual elimination of property, religious, and literacy qualifications on the franchise and to the expansion of the number of government posts whose occupants had to stand for election. By the 1830s, virtually all white men could vote. And, for a brief period after the Civil War, black men could as well. As the century wore on and the political parties developed systematic patronage operations to win elections, wide voting rights meant that common people received at least a share of the largesse, distributed in the form of Civil War pensions, friendly interventions with the courts or city agencies, and sometimes county or municipal poor relief—a reflection, if somewhat dim, of the electoral compact.

But at the beginning of the twentieth century, a series of changes in American electoral arrangements—such as the reintroduction of literacy tests and poll taxes, the invention of cumbersome voter registration requirements, and the subsequent withering of party efforts to mobilize those who were confronted by these barriers—sharply reduced voting by the northern immigrant working class and virtually eliminated voting by blacks and poor whites in the South. By World War I, turnout rates had fallen to half the eligible electorate and, despite some rises and dips, they have never recovered.

The purging of lower-strata voters from the electorate occurred at precisely that time in our history when the possibilities of democratic electoral politics had begun to enlarge. Indeed, we think it occurred *because* the possibilities of popular influence were expanding. First, as the economy industrialized and nationalized, government intervened more, so that at least in principle, the vote bore on a wide range of issues that were crucial to economic elites. Of course, government policies had always played a pivotal role in economic development: policies on tariffs and currency, slavery, immigration and welfare, internal improvements, and the subsidization of the railroads had all shaped the course of American development. But as the twentieth century began, the scale and penetration of government activity, especially regulatory activity, grew rapidly. It grew even more rapidly during the Great Depression.

Second, government's expanding role in the economy came to influence popular political ideas, and popular organizational capacities, in ways that suggested a new potential for popular struggle and electoral mobilization. Thus, a more pervasively and transparently interventionist state undermined the old laissez-faire idea that economy and polity necessarily belonged to separate spheres[11] and encouraged the twentieth-century idea that political rights include economic rights, particularly the right to protection by government from the worst instabilities and predations of the market.

Expanded state activities created new solidarities that became the basis for political action, including action in electoral politics. For example, government protection of the right to collective bargaining, ceded in response to mass strikes, reinforced the idea that workers had rights, promoted the unionization of millions of industrial workers, and made possible a large role for unions in electoral politics; Social Security reinforced the idea that government was responsible for economic well-being and promoted the organization of millions of "seniors" and the disabled; increased expenditures on social services nourished the growth of a voluntary sector that contracted to provide these services; and the enormous expansion of public programs gave rise to a vast network of public employee organizations, which were naturally keenly interested in electoral politics and had the organizational capacity to express that interest. In other words, new and expanded state activities gave rise to new political understandings and new political forces, and to the possibility that these new understandings and forces would become an influence in electoral politics.[12]

But while the enlarged role of government and the new popular ideas and solidarities that resulted created the possibility that electoral politics would become a major arena for the expression of working- and lower-class interests, that possibility was only partly realized. One reason was that vast numbers of those who might have been at the vortex of electoral discontents were, for all practical purposes, effectively disenfranchised at the beginning of the twentieth century. In Western Europe, the pattern was virtually reversed. There working-class men were enfranchised at the beginning of the twentieth century, and their enfranchisement led to the emergence of labor or socialist or social democratic parties that articulated working class interests and ultimately exerted considerable influence on the policies and political culture of their nations. In the United States, by contrast, the partial disfranchisement of working people during the same period helps explain why no comparable labor-based political party developed here, and why public policy and political culture remained more narrowly individualistic and property-oriented.[13]

The costs of exclusion were also indirect, for exclusion helped to sustain the distinctive southern system. Southern states had been especially aggressive in promulgating legal and administrative barriers to the vote, arrangements that of course disfranchised blacks, and most poor whites as well, and ensured that the quasi-feudal plantation system and the regular use of terror on which it depended would remain unchallenged within the South. But the consequences went beyond the South to the nation as a whole, Southern representatives always wielded great influence in national politics, largely as a result of the terms of the sectional compromise through which a nation had been formed in 1789. The compromise not only guaranteed the "states' rights" through which the southern section managed their own affairs before the Civil War, and afterward as well. It also laid out the several arrangements that guaranteed the South enduring predominance in national politics, including the three-fifths rule, which weighted slaves, a form of property, in allocating representation in the Congress, and a system of allocating representation to the states in the electoral college and in the Senate without regard to population. After the Civil War, and especially after the election of 1896, party competition disappeared from the South, and the subsequent disfranchisement of blacks and poor whites made its reemergence unlikely, with the consequence that unfailingly reelected southern congressmen gained the seniority that permitted them to dominate congressional committees.

If the peculiar development of the South was made possible by disfranchisement, southern representatives used their large influence in national government to steadfastly resist any federal policies that threatened the southern system. In particular, they vigorously resisted the labor and welfare policies that might have nourished the development of working-class politics during the New Deal and thereafter, as a matter of sectional and class interest and also as a matter of ideology. National welfare and labor policies were weakened as a result, and, even then, southern states were often granted exemption from coverage, with the further consequence that the South with its low wages and draconian labor discipline became—and remains today—a haven for industries eager to escape from the unionized workforces and more liberal state policies in the non-South.[14]

The South also illustrates the important political consequences that followed from the expansion of the franchise. Consider, for example, the impact of the Twenty-fourth Amendment of 1964 and the Voting Rights Act of 1965, which together eliminated poll taxes, literacy tests, and voter-registration obstructions that had kept blacks and many poor whites from the polls. In the aftermath of these reforms, both black and white voter participation rose sharply, and as it did, state and local policies became less discriminatory. More important, once politicians had to face blacks at the polls, the age-old use of violence against blacks, which had been the linchpin of southern apartheid, declined sharply, signaling the inevitable transformation of the southern system.[15]

We do not mean by these comments to overstate the importance of the ballot. Voters have limited ability to affect policy, and that limited influence is tempered by other influences. In the United States, a weak party system penetrated by moneyed interest groups and a strong laissez-faire culture were and are constraints on the political influence of the less-well-off, no matter the shape of the electorate.[16] Nevertheless, a full complement of lower-strata voters would have at least moderated the distinctively harsh features of American capitalist development in the twentieth century. Corporate predations against workers and consumers probably would have been curbed more effectively. Enlarged electoral influence from the bottom might have blocked public policies that weakened unions and inhibited their ability to organize. And an effectively enfranchised working class almost surely would have prodded political leaders to initiate social welfare protections earlier and to provide more comprehensive coverage in a pattern more nearly resembling that of Western Europe. Not least important, the enfranchisement of blacks and poor whites would have prevented the restoration of the caste labor system in the South after Reconstruction and the development of a one-party system whose oligarchical leaders wielded enormous power in national politics for most of the twentieth century. The influence of the South, in turn, effectively countered what influence the working-class electorate in the North, its strength reduced by disfranchisement, was able to exert. And finally, the exclusion from electoral politics of large sectors of the working class, as well as the rural poor of the South, precluded the emergence of a political party that could have stimulated greater class consciousness among American workers and the poor by articulating their interests and cultural orientations.[17] In other words, the distinctive pattern of American political development at least partly stems from the fact that the United States was not a democracy, in the elementary sense of an effective universal suffrage, during the twentieth century.

The politics of the closing decades of the twentieth century also illustrate the pivotal role of a skewed electorate. Numerous commentators have pointed out that beginning in the 1970s and continuing through the 1980s and 1990s, American corporations mobilized for politics with a focus and determination rare in the American experience. True, large corporations had always maintained a political presence to guard their particular firm and sector interests in legislative and bureaucratic spheres. However, the economic instabilities of the 1970s and the sagging and uncertain profits that resulted spurred business leaders to coordinate their efforts and to develop a broad legislative program calling for tax and regulatory rollbacks, cuts in spending on social programs, a tougher stance toward unions, and increases in military spending. The scale of this agenda demanded a new and broad-ranging political mobilization, including the creation of an extensive infrastructure of business associations, policy institutes, and think tanks that functioned as lobbying and public relations organizations.[18]

During the same years that business leaders were organizing to break the constraints of post–World War II public policies, and especially the constraints of the regulatory and social policy expansion of the 1960s, the Christian Right movement was emerging. The movement was also a reaction to the politics of the 1960s, albeit less to the public policies of the decade than to the cultural assaults on traditional sexual and family mores with which the sixties movements were associated. This late-twentieth-century revival movement turned out to be, at least during the 1970s and 1980s, an opportunity for newly politicized corporate leaders. Business organization and money are of course themselves formidable political resources, especially when campaign contributions are coordinated to achieve party influence as they began to be in the 1970s.[19] But elections are ultimately won by voters at the polls, and the Christian Right provided the foot soldiers—the activists and many of the voters—who brought a business-backed Republican party to power.

These several developments came together in the election of 1980. . . . Reagan's victory was made possible by the coordination of business campaign contributions on the one hand, and on the other the voter registration and mobilization efforts of the growing Christian Right with a network of fundamentalist churches at its base. However achieved, the election made it possible for the new Republican-business-fundamentalist alliance to claim that their agenda was in fact demanded by the American people. Among other things, Reagan was said to have tapped deep popular resentments against the public policies that were singled out for attack, as well as vast popular support for tax cuts and a military buildup. In fact, postelection polls showed that Reagan won not because of his campaign broadsides against big government[20] but because of popular discontent with the Carter administration's policies, especially anger over high unemployment.[21] Americans believe that presidents are responsible for the state of the economy, and by that criterion, Carter had failed.[22]

But the truncated electorate may have mattered even more than the formidable corporate campaign mobilization, the surge of activism among Christian fundamentalists, and Carter's failure to manage the "political business" cycle.[23] The underrepresentation of working and poor people, whose living standards were the target of much of the business program, helped to explain the weakness of political opposition to the Reagan administration's agenda during the 1980 campaign and thereafter. Elections were being won in the teeth of public opposition to the programmatic goals of the victors, and one reason was simply that the electorate did not represent the public.[24] The 1980 evidence was clearcut. Polls showed the voters tilted toward Reagan by 52 percent over Carter's 38 percent. But nonvoters, who were nearly as numerous, tilted toward Carter by 51 percent over 37 percent. In a close study of that election, Petrocik concluded that the "margin for Ronald Reagan in 1980 was made possible by a failure of prospective Carter voters to turn out on election day."[25]

To be sure, over the course of the next decade and more, a dominant conservative regime did succeed in promoting a conservative swing in public opinion and in the Democratic party. Nevertheless, fast-forward to 1994, the year of another historic victory, the takeover of the House of Representatives by the same Republican-business-fundamentalist coalition, with the fundamentalists now even more prominent and more assertive. The data repeat the pattern of 1980: while the Democrats won only 47 percent of the actual vote, they scored 58 percent among nonvoters, according to the National Election Studies, a percentage-point spread sufficient to throw the election to them. In a definitive study of that election, Joel Lefkowitz (1999) concludes that "Republicans won, then, not because more potential voters preferred their party, but because more of those who preferred Republicans voted."[26] In sum, nonvoting is important not merely for the intellectual queries it suggests but for its role in patterning American politics.

Movements and Electoral Participation

With their voting numbers depleted and without a labor party, whatever influence poor and working-class people have exerted in American politics has depended mainly on the emergence of mass insurgency. Protest movements dramatized the issues that parties detached from a lower class base could ignore, galvanized broad public attention to those issues, and threatened to cause the dissensus that parties dependent on broad coalitions feared. In *Poor People's Movements* (1977), we argued that it was when political discontent among the lower classes "breaks out of the confines of electoral procedures that the poor may have some influence."[27] Our view, in brief, was that poor and working-class people sometimes exercised power when they mobilized in mass defiance, breaking the rules that governed their participation in the institutions of a densely interdependent society. As evidence for this thesis, we summoned our studies of the role of protest movements of the 1930s and 1960s in winning major reforms. Consistently, the virtual absence of large-scale protest during the 1980s made it possible to initiate domestic policies that dramatically increased the bias of public policy against working-class and lower-class groups.

But the electoral context matters, nevertheless, for it is a crucial influence on the emergence and success of movements in contemporary democracies. This point needs a little explaining, because movements and voting are sometimes treated simply as conflicting and alternative forms of political expression. The bearing of each on the other is, however, multifaceted; some aspects of electoral politics undermine movements, as many observers have emphasized. But other aspects of electoral politics are crucial to the growth and success of movements.

On the one hand, there are features of a vigorous and inclusive electoral politics that tend to suppress collective protest. Electoral arrangements promulgate powerful meanings and rituals which define and limit the appropriate forms of political action. The very availability of the vote and the ritual of the periodic election are like magnets attracting and channeling popular political impulses. Other forms of collective action, and especially defiant collective action, are discredited precisely because voting and electioneering are presumably available as the normative ways to act on political discontent. In addition to constraining the forms of popular political action, the electoral system tends to restrict the goals of popular politics, and even the orientations of popular political culture, to the political alternatives generated by the dominant parties. Further, involvement in electoral politics can weaken the solidarities which undergird political movements, a development which takes its most extreme form under clientelist or machine modes of appealing to voters. And finally, electoral political institutions can seduce people away from any kind of oppositional politics. People are hypnotized by the circuses of election campaigns, while their leaders are enticed by the multiple opportunities to gain positions in the electoral representative system. In short, involvement in electoral politics can channel people from movement politics.

Despite the hyperbole with which this sort of view is sometimes expressed, it is supported by a long and serious intellectual tradition. Reinhard Bendix (1964), for example, argued that the class consciousness of European workers was enhanced precisely because they were barred from electoral participation during most of the nineteenth century; Ted Robert Gurr (1968) and other movement analysts explicitly posited that electoral institutions channel people away from protest; and Murray Edelman (1971) stressed the symbolic manipulation associated with electoral participation. And there is clearly some broad historical fit between the idea that electoral arrangements constrain protest movements and the actual course of movements in American history. For example, as electoral participation expanded in the first third of the nineteenth century, particularly with the emergence of machine-style political organization, early workingmen's insurgencies did in fact tend to become absorbed in regular party politics. At the end of the nineteenth century, the Populist movement was fragmented, diminished, and ultimately destroyed by its venture into national electoral politics. Much of the momentum of the labor movement of the 1930s was lost as it became absorbed in Democratic party politics. Similarly, the black movement dissipated as it turned from protest to politics in the 1970s. And historical trends in European politics also suggest that strong electoral organization tends to supplant mass protest.

However, we think the bearing of electoral politics on movement politics is more complex and multifaceted than these simple oppositions suggest. Electoral politics also constitutes the principal environment of contemporary movements, and aspects of that environment nurture rather than suppress movements. After all, the idea of popular rights associated with democratic electoral arrangements encourages the belief that change is possible, and by the efforts of ordinary people. This is the implication of the very core democratic idea, the idea that ordinary people have the right to participate in governance by choosing their rulers. Furthermore, movements may also gain protection from electoral politics, since the anticipation of adverse voter reactions often restrains state leaders from resorting to repression as a way of dealing with political defiance.

Some electoral conditions are more conducive to movements than others. Movements tend to arise when electoral alignments become unstable, usually as a result of changes in the larger society that generate new discontents or stimulate new aspirations and thus undermine established party allegiances. Electoral volatility is particularly associated with large-scale economic change, especially change that generates widespread hardship. When the allegiance of key voter blocs can no longer be taken for granted, contenders are likely to raise the stakes in electoral contests by employing campaign rhetoric that acknowledges grievances and gives voice to demands as a way to building majorities. In other words, movements are more likely to emerge when a climate of political possibility has been created and communicated through the electoral system.

Movements also win what they win largely as a result of their impact on electoral politics. The issues raised when masses of people become defiant sometimes break the grip of ruling groups on political interpretations so that new definitions of social reality, and new definitions of the possible and just, can be advanced. In turn, these issues and understandings, raised and communicated by masses of defiant people, activate and politicize voters and sometimes attract new voters to the polls who alter electoral calculations. It is in fact mainly by their ability to galvanize and polarize voters, with the result that electoral coalitions fragment or threaten to fragment, that protest movements score gains in electoral-representative systems.[28] When political leaders issue new rhetorical appeals to attract or hold voters or go on to make policy concessions, it is to cope with threats of electoral defection and cleavage or to rebuild coalitions when faced with the threat or reality of electoral defections. In this way, the electoral system not only protects and nourishes movements but also yields them leverage on state leaders. The influence of voters is also enhanced, for movements activate electoral constituencies and make their allegiance conditional on policy responses. In short, the life course of contemporary movements can be understood only in relation to the electoral environment in which they emerge and on which they have an impact.

There is broad historical confirmation for this aspect of the relationship between movements and electoral politics. In the 1930s, striking industrial workers were able to force a wavering New Deal administration to support government protection for collective bargaining. The strike movement had so antagonized business groups as to eliminate any possibility that the New Deal could recover their support, and it also threatened to put at risk the votes of the working class, on which the New Deal depended. Similarly, in the 1950s and 1960s, the southern civil rights movement forced national Democratic leaders to throw their weight behind legislation that would dismantle the southern caste system and strike down the procedures by which blacks and most poor whites had been disfranchised. The reason is that the civil rights movement simultaneously precipitated defections among southern whites to the Republican party and jeopardized the votes of growing numbers of blacks in the cities of the border states and the North.

Thus, while a vigorous electoral politics probably dampens the tendency to protest, electoral politics is nevertheless also critical to movement success. When we wrote *Poor People's Movements* (1977) it was in part to specify some of the ways in which this was so, if only because earlier analyses of protest movements tended to ignore their electoral environment. But there was one major feature of the American electoral system with which we did not deal. We did not call attention to the distinctive pattern of lower-strata exclusion in the United States or explore its implications for the emergence and evolution of protest movements.

How, then, did the twentieth-century history of massive nonvoting by poorer and minority people bear on the fate of movements in American politics? At first glance, one might expect large-scale nonvoting to reduce the effectiveness of the electoral system in absorbing discontent and suppressing movements. However, the methods by which people are made into nonvoters matter. When whole categories of people are denied the vote as a matter of acknowledged state policy—as southern blacks were—their exclusion may well strengthen their collective identity, provoke their indignation, and legitimate defiant forms of political action. But in the United States, the formal right to the franchise has been virtually universal, a condition much celebrated in the political culture. Only those who are aliens, felons, not yet of age, or undomiciled are denied the vote as a matter of acknowledged policy. At the same time, the effectiveness of the franchise for the bottom strata has been reduced by the failure of the parties to make the appeals and deploy the outreach strategies that would mobilize these voters and by residual procedural obstructions embedded in the voting process. This pattern of demobilization and obstruction was selective in that it was more likely to reduce voting by the poor and unlettered than by the better-off and educated. Still, entire categories of the population were not legally denied the franchise, and the administrative methods by which the exercise of the franchise is impeded remained obscure and indeed seemed to be the fault of the nonvoters themselves, of their apathy or poor education. Under these circumstances, the *idea* that voting and elections provided the means for acting on political grievances remained largely intact, even though the means were not in fact available to tens of millions of people. The demobilization of large sectors of the American electorate was thus secured at less cost to the legitimacy of electoral processes as the prescribed avenue for political change than would otherwise have been the case.

At the same time, the constriction of the electorate weakened the complementarities between electoral politics and protest movements. The interactions between movements and the electoral context that encouraged the growth of movements and sometimes led to movement victories depended on the existence of voter constituencies inclined to be responsive to the appeals of protesters. Thus protests from below were more likely to arise in the first place when contenders for office were forced to employ rhetoric that appealed to less-well-off voters and thus gave courage to the potential protesters. Such movements were more likely to grow when they were at least somewhat safe from the threat of state repression because political leaders were constrained by fear of adverse reactions by working-class or lower-class or minority voters. Finally, protesters were more likely to win when the issues they raised stirred support among significant numbers of these voters, threatening to lead to voter defections. The complementary dynamic between movements and electoral politics thus depended both on the composition and orientation of movements and on the composition and orientation of significant blocs in the electorate. In other words, the sharp underrepresentation of poor and minority people in the American electorate created an electoral environment that also weakened their ability to act politically through movements. This is another important way in which massive nonvoting has shaped American politics.

Notes

1. Key (1955:3).
2. This phrase is taken from the title of an article by Eulau (1956). Gary Orren (1987:52, n. 2) quotes a *Boston Globe* columnist writing in the same vein: "Low voter turnout is . . . a symptom of political, economic, and social health. . . . If you'd rather watch "All My Children" or "Family Feud" than nip over to the firehouse to vote, then you can't be feeling terribly hostile toward the system." Will (1983:96) also defines nonvoting as a "form of passive consent." See Jackman's (1987:418) review of this perspective.
3. See, for example, Almond and Verba (1965:343–65, 402–69, 472–505); Eckstein (1966); Dahl (1961); and Huntington (1974).
4. This perspective is set out in Crozier et al. (1975); Huntington (1975); Brittan (1975); and Bell (1978).

5. Lipset (1960). Prothro and Grigg (1960) are also pertinent. But see Rogin (1967) for a rebuttal.
6. Will (1983:96). For another study that draws the lesson of the dangers of high participation from the fall of Weimar, see Brown (1987).
7. Cited in McGerr (1986:47). Petrocik (1987:244) contains a discussion of the literature that claims that new or irregular voters are more volatile.
8. The exception to this assertion is France, where universal manhood suffrage was won during the Revolution, albeit only briefly.
9. The vote was the core demand of the Chartists, for example. Ernest Jones explained at a Chartist Council meeting in January of 1848 that "there are some gentlemen who tell the people that they must grow rich and then they will be free. . . . No, my friends, above all we need the vote. . . . Go in person and knock at the doors of St. Stephen's, knock till your privileged debtors give you back, trembling, what they have owed you for centuries! Go knock, and go on knocking until justice has been done." Quoted in Sheila Rowbotham, "The Tale That Never Ends," *Socialist Register*, 1999.
10. The warning was issued by the historian J. A. Froude in an address to the Liberty and Property Defence League in London in the aftermath of the passage of the Third Reform Bill in England. See Brittan (1975:146).
11. Chapter 3 of *The New Class War* (Piven and Cloward 1985) contains an extended discussion of the distinctive political arrangements—including constitutionalism, a complex but flexible federal system, fragmented and bureaucratized government authorities, and clientelism—that contributed to the vigor of laissez-faire in the nineteenth-century United States, both by obscuring government activities in the interests of business and by creating a realm of government and politics within which politics did indeed seem to be separate from the larger economy.
12. The argument that broad and pervasive government interventions in the twentieth century generated new political forces is developed in *The New Class War* (Piven and Cloward 1985).
13. For recent discussions of the correlation of low levels of electoral turnout and a class bias in party politics and public policy, see Arend Lijphart (1977:1–14); and Rosenstone and Hansen (1993:234–35). For an analysis that goes part of the way toward explaining why attitudinal survey data is not a good measure of the potential impact of higher turnout from the bottom on politics, see Verba et al. (1993:303–18).
14. DuBois (1989:704) makes this point strongly, attributing the weak labor movement in the United States to the intransigence of the South.
15. On the impact of voting on public policy in the South, see Bensel and Sanders (1986:52–70).
16. We discuss these multiple influences as they shaped American welfare state policies in *Regulating the Poor* (1993: chapter 12).
17. On the role of political parties in shaping class consciousness, see Przeworski (1977). We do not do justice here to the diverse arguments in the literature on "American exceptionalism." More recent work fastens on the distinctiveness of American working-class ideology in the antebellum period, and particularly on the vigor of working-class "republicanism." See for example Dawley (1976); Faler (1981); Montgomery (1981); Wilentz (1984); and Steffen (1984).
18. The sources on the business mobilization are numerous. See for example Edsall (1984); Ferguson and Rogers (1986); Vogel (1989); Plotke (1996); Martin (1994); Phillips (1994).
19. On the coordination of business contributions and the increasing scale of those contributions, see Edsall (1984); Vogel (1989); and Clawson et al. (1998).
20. In any case, the meaning of "big government" was unclear. Republican politicians used it as a euphemism for New Deal interventions. But its meaning to survey respondents was ambiguous. See Nie et al. (1976); and Petrocik (1987).
21. Using data from the 1980 National Election Study surveys, Markus (1982) finds no evidence for the contention that the election was a referendum on Reagan's policy positions. The data indicate instead that voters shifted because of dissatisfaction with Carter's economic performance. Burnham's (1981) analysis of exit poll data from the 1980 election concludes that the paramount issue among voters who swung to Reagan was unemployment. See also Miller and Wattenberg (1985).
22. The argument that incumbents are judged by performance was originally put forward by Key (1966), and is authoritatively examined by Fiorina (1981). The significance of the state of the economy in assessing performance and determining the reelection chances of incumbents is stressed by Tufte (1978). The pattern appears to be common to democratic and industrialized nations. See for example Hibbs (1977 and 1982), who showed the critical importance of the economic performance of government in British elections during the same period we are discussing here. The importance of high unemployment levels in recent European elections that displaced conservative governments would seem to confirm this point.
23. Tufte ((1978).
24. In fact, surveys indicated that opposition to the Reagan program intensified as time went on. See for example Lipset (1985 and 1986); Navarro (1985); and Ferguson and Rogers (1986: chapter 1).
25. Petrocik (1987:240–253) maintains that both the 1980 and 1984 elections broke with a pattern in which irregular voters or nonvoters who are "without settled habits and, therefore, sensitive to short-term tides" surge in the

direction of the majority. He goes on to show that while there was a smaller discrepancy between voters and non-voters in 1984, "again nonvoters were less supportive of the winner than voters were."

26. Lefkowitz (1999:42).
27. Piven and Cloward (1979:15).
28. Charles Tilly (1984:310–11).

References

Almond, Gabriel, and Sidney Verba. 1965. *The Civic Culture: Political Attitudes and Democracy in Five Nations.* Boston: Little, Brown.

Bell, Daniel. 1978. *Cultural Contradictions of Capitalism.* New York: Basic Books/Harper Colophon Books.

Bendix, Reinhard. 1964. *Nation Building and Citizenship.* New York: John Wiley.

Bensel, Richard Franklin, and Elizabeth Sanders. 1986. "The Impact of the Voting Rights Act on Southern Welfare Systems." In Benjamin Ginsberg and Allan Stone, eds., *Do Elections Matter?* New York: M. E. Sharpe.

Brittan, Samuel. 1975. "The Economic Contradictions of Democracy." *British Journal of Political Science* 5, 22 (April).

Brown, Courtney. 1987. "Voter Mobilization and Party Competition in a Volatile Electorate." *American Sociological Review* 52, 1 (February).

Burnham, Walter Dean. 1981. "The 1980 Earthquake: Realignment, Reaction, or What?" In Thomas Ferguson and Joel Rogers, eds., *The Hidden Election: Politics and Economics in the 1980 Presidential Campaign.* New York: Pantheon Books.

Clawson, Dan, Alan Neustadl, and Mark Weller. 1998. *Dollars and Votes.* Philadelphia, Pa.: Temple University Press.

Crozier, Michael, Samuel P. Huntington, and Joji Watanuki. 1975. *The Crisis of Democracy: Report on the Ungovernability of Democracies to the Trilateral Commission.* New York: New York University Press.

Dahl, Robert. 1961. *Who Governs?* New Haven, Conn.: Yale University Press.

Dawley, Alan. 1976. *Class and Community: The Industrial Revolution in Lynn.* Cambridge: Harvard University Press.

DuBois, W. E. B. 1989 [1903]. *Souls of Black Folk.* New York: Bantam Books.

Eckstein, Harry. 1966. *Division and Cohesion in Democracy: A Study of Norway.* Princeton, N.J.: Princeton University Press.

Edelman, Murray. 1971. *Politics as Symbolic Action.* New Haven, Conn.: Yale University Press.

Edsall, Thomas B. 1984. *The New Politics of Inequality.* New York: W. W. Norton.

Eulau, Hans. 1956. "The Politics of Happiness." *Antioch Review* 16.

Faler, Paul. 1981. *Mechanics and Manufacturers in the Early Industrial Revolution: Lynn, Massachusetts, 1780–1860.* Albany, N.Y.: State University of New York Press.

Ferguson, Thomas, and Joel Rogers. 1986. *Right Turn.* New York: Hill & Wang.

Fiorina, Morris. 1981. *Retrospective Voting in American Presidential Elections.* New Haven, Conn.: Yale University Press.

Gurr, Ted Robert. 1968. "A Casual Model of Civil Strife: A Comparative Analysis Using New Indices." *American Political Science Review* 62, 4 (December).

Hibbs, Douglas A. 1977. "Political Parties and Macroeconomic Policy." *American Political Science Review* 71, 4 (December).

———. 1982. "Economic Outcomes and Political Support for British Governments Among Occupational Classes: A Dynamic Analysis." *American Political Science Review* 76, 2 (June).

Huntington, Samuel. 1974. "Postindustrial Politics: How Benign Will It Be?" *Comparative Politics* 6, 2 (January).

———. 1975. "Chapter 3—The United States." In Michael Crozier, Samuel P. Huntington, and Joji Watanuki, *The Crisis of Democracy: Report on the Ungovernability of Democracies to the Trilateral Commission.* New York: New York University Press.

Jackman, Robert W. 1987. "Political Institutions and Voter Turnout in the Industrial Democracies." *American Political Science Review* 81, 2 (June).

Key, V. O., Jr. 1955. "A Theory of Critical Elections." *Journal of Politics* 17, 1 (February).

———. 1966. *The Responsible Electorate.* Cambridge: Harvard University Press.

Lefkowitz, Joel. 1999. "Winning the House: Re-election Strategies, Challenger Campaigns, and Mobilization Against Incumbents." Ph.D. diss., Graduate School, City University of New York.

Lijphart, Arend. 1977. "Unequal Participation: Democracy's Unresolved Dilemma," *American Political Science Review* 91, 1 (March).

Lipset, Seymour Martin. 1960. *Political Man: The Social Bases of Politics.* Garden City, N.Y.: Doubleday.

———. 1985. "The Elections, the Economy, and Public Opinion: 1984." *PS: The Journal of the American Political Science Association* 18, 1 (Winter).

———. 1986. "Beyond 1984: The Anomalies of American Politics." *PS: The Journal of the American Political Science Association* 19, 2 (Spring).

Markus, Gregory B. 1982. "Political Attitudes During an Election Year: A Report on the 1980 NES Study." *American Political Science Review* 76, 3 (September).

Martin, Cathie Jo. 1994. "Business and the New Economic Activism: the Growth of Corporate Lobbies in the Sixties." *Polity* 27, 1 (Fall).

McGerr, Michael E. 1986. *The Decline of Popular Politics: The American North, 1865–1928.* New York: Oxford University Press.

Miller, Arthur H., and Martin P. Wattenberg. 1985. "Throwing the Rascals Out and Performance

Evaluations of Presidential Candidates, 1952–1980." *American Political Science Review* 79, 2 (June).

Montgomery, David. 1981. *Beyond Equality: Labor and the Radical Republicans, 1862–1872.* Urbana: University of Illinois Press.

Navarro, Vicente. 1985. "The 1980 and 1984 U.S. Elections and the New Deal: An Alternative Interpretation." *International Journal of Health Services* 15, 3 (Fall).

Nie, Norman H., Sidney Verba, and John H. Petrocik. 1976. *The Changing American Voter.* Cambridge: Harvard University Press.

Orren, Gary R. 1987. "Political Participation and Public Policy: The Case for Institutional Reform." In Alexander Heard and Michael Nelson, eds., *Presidential Selection.* Durham, N.C.: Duke University Press.

Petrocik, John R. 1987. "Voter Turnout and Electoral Preference: The Anomalous Reagan Elections." In Kay Schlozman, ed., *Elections in America.* London: Allen & Unwin.

Phillips, Kevin P. 1994. *Arrogant Capital.* Boston: Little, Brown.

Piven, Frances Fox, and Richard A. Cloward. 1993. *Regulating the Poor.* New York: Vintage Books.

———. 1979. *Poor People's Movements: Why They Succeed, How They Fail.* New York: Vintage Books.

———. 1985. *The New Class War.* Revised and expanded ed. New York: Vintage Books.

Plotke, David. 1996. *Building a Democratic Political Order.* New York: Cambridge University Press.

Prothro, James W., and Charles M. Grigg. 1960. "Fundamental Principles of Democracy: Bases of Agreement and Disagreement." *Journal of Politics* 22, 2 (May).

Przeworski, Adam. 1977. "Proletariat into a Class: The Process of Class Formation from Karl Kautsky's *The Class Struggle* to Recent Controversies." *Politics & Society* 7, 4.

Rogin, Michael Paul. 1967. *Intellectuals and McCarthy: The Radical Specter.* Cambridge: M.I.T. Press.

Rosenstone, Steven J., and John Mark Hansen. 1993. *Mobilization, Participation, and Democracy in America.* New York: Macmillan.

Rowbotham, Sheila. 1999. "The Tale That Never Ends," *Socialist Register.* New York: Monthly Review Press.

Steffen, Charles. 1984. *The Mechanics of Baltimore: Workers and Politics in the Age of Revolution, 1703–1812.* Urbana: University of Illinois Press.

Tilly, Charles. 1984. "Social Movements and National Politics." In Charles Bright and Susan Harding, *Statemaking and Social Movements.* Ann Arbor: University of Michigan Press.

Tufte, Edward R. 1978. *Political Control of the Economy.* Princeton, N.J.: Princeton University Press.

Verba, Sidney, Kay Lehman Schlozman, Henry Brady, and Norman H. Nie. 1993. "Citizen Activity: Who Participates? What Do They Say?" *American Political Science Review,* 87, 2 (June).

Vogel, David. 1989. *Fluctuating Fortunes: The Political Power of Business in America.* New York, Basic Books.

Wilentz, Sean. 1984. *Chants Democratic: New York City and the Rise of the Working Class, 1788–1850.* New York: Oxford University Press.

Will, George F. October 10, 1983. "In Defense of Nonvoting." *Newsweek,* p. 96.

HOW THE POWER ELITE DOMINATE GOVERNMENT

G. WILLIAM DOMHOFF

The power elite build on their structural economic power, their storehouse of policy expertise, and their success in the electoral arena to dominate the federal government on the issues about which they care. Lobbyists from corporations, law firms, and trade associations play a key role in shaping government on narrow issues of concern to specific corporations or business sectors, and the policy-planning network supplies new policy directions on major issues, along with top-level governmental appointees to implement those policies.

However, victories within government are far from automatic. As is the case in the competition for public opinion and electoral success, the power elite face opposition from a minority of elected officials and their supporters in labor unions and liberal advocacy groups. These liberal opponents are sometimes successful in blocking the initiatives of ultraconservatives or the New Christian Right, but the corporate-conservative coalition itself seldom loses when it is united. In fact, most of the victories for the liberal-labor coalition come because of support from moderate conservatives, usually in situations of extreme social disruption, such as economic depressions or wars.

■ ■ ■ ■

The Role of Governments

Governments are potentially autonomous because they have a unique function: territorial regulation. They set up and guard boundaries and then regulate the flow of people, money, and goods in and out of the area for which they have responsibility. They also have regulatory functions within a territory, such as settling disputes through the judicial system and setting the rules that shape the economic marketplace.[1]

Neither business, the military, nor churches are organized in such a way that they could provide these necessary functions. The military sometimes steps in—or forces its way in—when a government is weak or collapsing, but it has a difficult time carrying out routine regulatory functions for very long. Nor can competing businesses regulate themselves. There is always some business that will try to improve its market share or profits by adulterating products, reducing wages, colluding with other companies, or telling half-truths. As most economists and all other social scientists agree, a business system could not survive without some degree of market regulation. Contrary to claims about markets being free, they are historically constructed institutions dependent upon governmentally sanctioned enforcement of property and contract rights.[2]

Sometimes the federal government has to act to protect markets from being completely destroyed by the anticompetitive practices of a company that thereby grows very large. That is what happened in 1911, when the Supreme Court ordered the break-up of the Rockefellers' huge Standard Oil of New Jersey because of the illegal strategies used by John D. Rockefeller, Sr., to destroy rivals. It is also what happened in the case of Microsoft, when Netscape sent the Department of Justice a 222-page paper in 1996, which was later backed up by testimony from representatives of Sun Microsystems, AOL, and others. What seemed at first to be innovation turned out to be manipulation and intimidation in the tradition of Rockefeller, Sr.[3]

Governments are also essential in creating money, setting interest rates, and shaping the credit system. Although the United States tried to function without a central bank for much of the nineteenth century, the problems caused by a privately controlled money system were so great that the most powerful bankers of the day worked together to create the Federal Reserve System in 1912.[4] The system was improved during the 1930s and is now an essential tool of the corporate community in keeping a highly volatile business system from careening off in one direction or another. When the stock market crashed in 1987, for example, the Federal Reserve made sure there would be no repeat of the Great Depression by instructing large New York banks to keep making loans to temporarily insolvent debtors. Similar bailouts were performed in the 1990s for problems in Mexico, Korea, and a Wall Street investment firm, Long Term Capital Management, that could have caused large-scale bankruptcies.[5]

The federal government also is essential in providing subsidy payments to groups in trouble, such as farmers and low-income workers, in ways that bolster the market system and benefit large corporations. Farmers received a record $28 billion in direct payments in 2000, which is half of all farm income. This program allows large corporations to buy commodities at low prices, while at the same time providing purchasing power in rural communities throughout the South, Midwest, and Great Plains.[6] Low-income employees who work full time and have children received $30 billion in 2000 through a program called *Earned Income Tax Credits.* Both corporate leaders and Republicans prefer these year-end government bonus payments to the old system of welfare payments because they increase the labor pool and reinforce the work ethic.[7]

Nor is the state any less important in the context of a globalizing economy. If anything, it is even more important because it has to enforce rules concerning patents, intellectual property, quality of merchandise, and much else in an unregulated international arena. The international economy simply could not function without the agreements on monetary policy and trade that the governments of the United States, Japan, Canada, and Western Europe uphold through the International Monetary Fund, World Trade Organization, and other international agencies. For the American corporate community, domination of the state on economic issues also remains essential because the laws favoring American corporations that move production overseas could be easily changed. Tax breaks to offset taxes paid overseas could be eliminated, for example, or laws could be passed stipulating that goods could not enter the United States from countries that ban unions and use government force to suppress wages.

Appointees to Government

The first way to see how the power elite shapes the federal government is to look at the social and occupational backgrounds of the people who are appointed to manage the major departments of the executive branch, such as state, treasury, defense, and justice. If the power elite is as important as this book claims, they should come disproportionately from the upper class, the corporate community, and the policy-planning network.

There have been numerous studies of major governmental appointees under both Republican and Democratic administrations, usually focusing on the top appointees in the departments that are represented in the president's cabinet. These studies are unanimous in their conclusion that most top appointees in both Republican and Democratic administrations are corporate executives and corporate lawyers, and hence members of the power elite. Moreover, they are often part of the policy-planning network as well, supporting the claim that the network plays a central role in preparing members of the power elite for government service.[8]

Two major historical studies of cabinet appointees provide relevant background information on major government appointees from the founding of the country through the Carter Administration. A comparison of the top appointees in the Clinton and George W. Bush administrations brings the information forward to 2000. The most ambitious of these studies—a three-volume work that covers cabinet officers, diplomats, and Supreme Court justices from 1789 to 1980—defines the economic elite as those who were among the top wealth holders or sat on the boards of the largest companies of their era. It shows that (1) 96 percent of the cabinet and diplomatic appointees from 1789 to 1861 were members of the economic elite, with a predominance of landowners, merchants, and lawyers; (2) from 1862 to 1933, the figure was 84 percent, with an increasing number of financiers and corporate lawyers; and (3) from 1934 to 1980, the overall percentage was 64, but with only 47 percent during the New Deal.[9] The second large-scale study, which focuses on the 205 individuals who served in presidential cabinets between 1897 and 1972, reports that 60 percent were members of the upper class and 78 percent members of the corporate community. There are no differences in the overall percentages for Democrats and Republicans or for the years before and after 1933.[10]

The most systematic study of the factors leading to appointments shows that corporate executives who have two or more outside directorships are four times more likely to serve in a federal government advisory position than executives from smaller companies. In addition, participation of corporate directors in at least one policy group increases their chances of an appointment by a factor of 1.7. An accompanying interview study supported the quantitative findings by showing that chief executive officers often mention participation in a policy group as a qualification for an appointment to government.[11]

Reflecting the different coalitions that make up the two parties, there are some differences between the second-level and third-level appointees in Republican and Democratic administrations. Republicans frequently appoint ultraconservatives to agencies that are thoroughly disliked by the appointee, such as the Environmental Protection Agency, the Occupational Safety and Health Administration, The National Highway Traffic Safety Administration, and the Office of Civil Rights. Democrats, on the other hand, often place liberals in the same agencies, creating a dramatic contrast when a Democratic administration replaces a Republican one. The Clinton Administration's appointments to the Office of the Attorney General, for example, were far more vigorous in using the antitrust laws to challenge monopolistic corporate practices than those of the Reagan and Bush administrations.[12] As an even more dramatic example, the Food and Drug Administration took on the tobacco companies during the Clinton years and won, to the amazement of everyone.[13]

The way in which presidents rely on corporate leaders and experts from the policy groups in making appointments can be seen in both the Clinton and Bush administrations. President Clinton's first secretary of state was a director of Lockheed Martin, Southern California Edison, and First Interstate Bancorp, a trustee of the Carnegie Corporation, a recent vice-chair of the Council on Foreign Relations, and officially a corporate lawyer. The second secretary of state, the daughter of a Czechoslovakian diplomat who immigrated to the United States and became a dean at the University of Denver, married into great wealth, earned a Ph.D. in international relations, raised money for the Democratic Party, and became active in several foreign policy groups. The first secretary of defense, a former professor and longtime member of Congress, came from a business family in Wisconsin. The first secretary of treasury inherited millions from his rancher father and founded his own insurance company in Texas. He was succeeded by a codirector of the Wall Street investment banking firm of Goldman, Sachs who was also a trustee of the Carnegie Corporation and had a net worth between $50 and $100 million in 1992. The first director of the CIA was a corporate lawyer and a director of Martin Marietta, a large defense contractor; the second CIA director, a professor and administrator at MIT, was a director of Citicorp, Perkins-Elmer, and CMS Energy.

The secretary of agriculture was an African-American from the Mississippi Delta whose grandfather and father were major landowners and business owners. The secretary of commerce, also an African-American, came from a family that owned a hotel in Harlem; at the time of his appointment he was a lawyer with one of the leading corporate firms in Washington, which paid him $580,000 in 1992 even though he spent most of his time as chairman of the Democratic Party. The secretary of energy was both African-American and female; she is also the former executive vice president of Northern States Power, a utility company in Minnesota, and the daughter of two physicians. The secretary of housing and urban development, a Mexican-American who had been mayor of San Antonio, was the chair of an investment firm, the head of an air charter company, and a trustee of the Rockefeller Foundation at the time of his appointment. The least-connected major figure who was in the Clinton cabinet, the attorney general, is the daughter of journalists in Florida and was once a state attorney in Miami.

The administration drew many of its key members from a small group of current or recent directors on the board of the Council on Foreign Relations. In addition to the secretary of state, who was a Council director from 1982 to 1991, three other Council directors held top positions in the State Department at one point or another. The secretary of health and human services was a Council director at the time of her appointment, as well as the chancellor of the University of Wisconsin, a trustee of the Committee for Economic Development, and a trustee of the Brookings Institution. Other Council directors who served in the Clinton Administration at the one point or another were the White House special counsel, the director of the Office of Management and Budget, and the head of the Federal Reserve Board.

The top levels of the Bush Administration are as directly connected to the corporate community as any set of high government officials could be, but President Bush's cabinet also contains a significant number of ultraconservatives with strong views on a wide range of social issues. President Bush and his father are both graduates of Andover and Yale, and the younger Bush is also a graduate of Harvard Business School. Both owned oil companies before they went into politics, and the new president is a former owner of the Texas Rangers baseball team as well, thanks to the generosity of some of Bush, Sr.'s, main campaign donors.[14] Vice President Richard Cheney spent the eight years prior to his appointment as president of Halliburton, an oil drilling company, where he made several million dollars a year and exercised over $20 million in stock options when he left. He was also on the board of directors of Electronic Data Systems, Procter & Gamble, and Union Pacific. He served as a director of the Council on Foreign Relations from 1987 to 1989, and was vice-chair of the board of the American Enterprise Institute when he became vice president.

The president's chief of staff, Andrew Card, came to his position after seven years as the chief lobbyist for General Motors, where his title was vice president for governmental affairs. The national security advisor, Condoleezza Rice, an African-American woman from the middle class in Birmingham, with a Ph.D. in international relations from the University of Denver, was the provost of Stanford University and a director of Chevron and Transamerica. The head of the Office of Management and Budget, Mitchell E. Daniels, Jr., was a senior executive at Eli Lilly & Co., the former president of a conservative think tank, and a former aide in the Reagan White House.

The secretary of state, retired army general Colin Powell, the chair of the Joint Chiefs of Staff during the Persian Gulf War, and an African-American, made millions after his retirement as a speaker to corporate employees at $60,000 to $75,000 an appearance. He served as a director of Gulfstream Aerospace until its merger with General Dynamics in 1999, where he earned $1.49 million from stock options in exchange for helping the company sell its corporate jets in Kuwait and Saudi Arabia.[15] He was a director of America Online at the time of his appointment to the state department, walking away with $8.27 million in stock options, and his overall worth since retiring from the army came to over $28 million in 2001. Powell is also a member of the Council on Foreign Relations.

The secretary of defense, Donald Rumsfeld, who held numerous positions in the Nixon and Ford administrations, including secretary of defense for eighteen months between 1975 and 1977, spent eight years as the chief executive officer of G.D. Searle & Co., and three years in the same position for General Instruments. He sat on 4 corporate boards in 1998: Kellogg, Sears Roebuck, The Tribune Publishing Co., and Gulfsteam Aerospace (where, he like his fellow director, General Powell, he made over $1 million from stock options for his help in selling corporate jets). He was a trustee of 2 think tanks, the American Enterprise Institute and the Rand Corporation. In 1998, he headed a bipartisan congressional commission to assess the ballistic missile threat from North Korea and Iran, which concluded that the United States was in great danger.

The secretary of treasury, Paul H. O'Neill, was the recently retired chair of Alcoa and a director of Lucent Technologies. He holds over $50 million in Alcoa stock. He was a member of the Business Council and the Business Roundtable, the chair of the board of trustees at the Rand Corporation, where he rubbed elbows with Rumsfeld, and a trustee of the American Enterprise Institute, where he served with Rumsfeld and Cheney. The secretary of commerce, Donald L. Evans, a long-time friend of President Bush and his chief fundraiser for the 2000 campaign, bringing in

$100 million, is the son of a Shell Oil manager and the chief executive officer of Tom Brown, Inc., a mid-sized oil company in Midland, Texas.

The secretary of transportation, Norman Mineta, an Asian-American and former Democratic congressman, inherited his father's insurance agency in San Jose, where he was elected to the city council and the office of mayor before going to Congress in 1975. He resigned from Congress and then worked as a vice president at Lockheed Martin from 1995 until July 2000, when President Clinton appointed him secretary of commerce. The secretary of labor, Elaine Chao, a Chinese-American, is a daughter of wealthy immigrants from Taiwan. She graduated from Mount Holyoke and the Harvard Business School, worked in management for the Bank of America and Citicorp, and served as deputy secretary of transportation and then head of the Peace Corps in the George H. W. Bush Administration. She has served on the boards of Clorox, Dole Foods, and Northwest Airlines and is affiliated with the Heritage Foundation.

The secretary of agriculture, Ann Veneman, is the daughter of a well-to-do California farmer who worked as the undersecretary of health, education, and welfare in the Nixon Administration. She is a lawyer and served as a deputy to the undersecretary of agriculture in the Reagan Administration. After her service in the Reagan Administration, she joined a corporate law lobbying firm in Washington for two years before going to Sacramento to practice corporate law. The director of the Environmental Protection Agency, Christine Todd Whitman, the governor of New Jersey at the time of her appointment, is from a very wealthy family. She is a member of the Council on Foreign Relations.

The secretary of education, Rod Paige, an African-American born and raised in Mississippi, has a doctorate in physical education from Indiana University, and was the dean of the School of Education at Texas Southern University before becoming the superintendent of schools in Houston, where his firm approach caught the eye of George W. Bush while he was governor of Texas. The secretary of housing and urban development, Melquiades Martinez, was the highest elected official in the Florida county that encompasses the city of Orlando. He is the first Cuban-American to be appointed to the cabinet. He has a net worth of $3 million from his personal-injury law practice.

The secretary of veterans affairs, Anthony J. Principi, a decorated Vietnam War veteran with an undergraduate degree from the U.S. Naval Academy and a law degree from Seton Hall, is a longtime advocate for veterans. He was deputy secretary of veterans affairs from 1989 to 1992 and acting secretary of veterans affairs in 1992 and 1993. After leaving government, he joined a corporate law firm in San Diego for two years, then moved into the corporate world as a vice president at a subsidiary of Lockheed Martin and the head of a telecommunications company. He was president of QTC Medical Services, Inc., in San Diego at the time of his appointment.

The remainder of the Bush cabinet is from the ultraconservative wing of the party. The attorney general, John Ashcroft, the son and grandson of ministers, is a former governor and senator from Missouri, but he did spend 6 years in private law practice before going into politics. He is a strong opponent of abortion, except when a woman's own life is endangered, and is very close to leaders in the New Christian Right. The secretary of health and human services, Tommy G. Thompson, the longtime governor of Wisconsin at the time of his appointment, also is strongly opposed to abortion and has been a leader in cutting back on welfare. He has close ties with tobacco and brewing companies, which made his appointment to the department that looks after health of great concern to liberals.

The secretary of energy, Spencer Abraham, strongly in the ultraconservative camp on all issues, is the grandson of a Christian Lebanese immigrant and the first Arab-American to serve in the cabinet. Ironically, during his term as the Republican senator from Michigan, he advocated the abolishment of the department he now heads. The secretary of the interior, Gale Norton, served as the attorney general of Colorado from 1992 to 1998 when she joined a corporate law firm in Denver and became a registered lobbyist for NL Industries, a major manufacturer of lead-based paint. She spent much of her earlier career fighting court battles against environmental regulations in the West. Her husband is a commercial real estate developer.

As these thumbnail sketches show, the ethnic, racial, and gender diversity of Bush's appointments is at least as wide as Clinton's, but the political orientations are even more corporate and conservative, and dramatically so on social issues. The nature of the Bush Cabinet suggests that the diversity fought for by liberal women, minorities, and gays and lesbians since the 1960s does not necessarily transfer into a liberal social outlook. It may even be that the power elite has been strengthened by calls for diversity that did not include an emphasis on the liberal social philosophy that energized the activists. Leaders in the power elite have been able to defuse criticism based on gender, ethnicity, and race while at the same time appointing people with the class backgrounds and values that are important in reinforcing the structure and distribution of power.[16]

The general picture that emerges from this information on the overrepresentation of members of the corporate community and policy network in appointed governmental positions is that the highest levels of the executive branch, especially in the State, Defense, and Treasury departments, are interlocked constantly with the corporate community through the movement of executives and corporate lawyers in and out of government. Although the same person is not in governmental and corporate positions at the same time, there is enough continuity for the relationship to be described as one of revolving interlocks. Corporate leaders resign from their numerous directorships to serve in government for two or three years, then return to the corporate community.

This practice gives corporate officials temporary independence from the narrow concerns of their own companies and allows them to perform the more general roles they have learned in the policy-discussion groups. However, it does not give them the time or inclination to become fully independent from the corporate community or to develop a perspective that includes the interests of other classes and groups. In terms of the *Who governs?* indicator of power, then, it is clear that the power elite are the predominant voice in top-level appointive positions in the executive branch.

Supreme Court Appointments

The Supreme Court has a special and unique role in the American system of governance. As the final arbiter in major disputes, it has been imbued with a mystique of reverence and respect that makes it the backstop for the American power elite.[17] While its members are to some extent constrained by legal precedent, there is in fact a fair degree of discretion in what they decide, as seen in the numerous great reversals of opinion down through the years.[18] Such reversals have occurred most dramatically on the issue of rights for African-Americans. Then, too, a switch in precedents in 1937 by two members of the court legitimated the crucial legislation having to do with union organizing. . . .[19] Coming closer to home, the independent power of the Supreme Court was on display for all Americans in the 2000 elections: A highly conservative court that preached against judicial activism and emphasized states rights nonetheless overrode the Florida Supreme Court and found a way to put a stop to the counting of uncounted votes that might have tipped the presidential election to the Democrats. As constitutional scholars argued vociferously about the legal reasoning behind the court's majority, the Democratic Party and most ordinary Americans accepted the decision.

As the court's prevention of the Florida recount shows, Supreme Court appointments, and deference to their decisions, do matter, which is yet another reason why the power elite work so hard to win elections. As standard sources conclude from an examination of Supreme Court appointments, virtually all appointees have shared the ideological and political views of the presidents who appointed them.[20] In effect, this means that the Supreme Court reflects the range of acceptable opinion within the corporate-conservative coalition. The appointees are also primarily from the upper and upper-middle classes, and an "inordinate number had served as corporate attorneys before their appointments."[21] However, they also tend to be from elite law schools, to have experience as lower-level judicial appointments or as professors at prestigious law schools, and to have been active in a political party. They are subject to strong scrutiny by leaders of the American Bar Association and confirmation by the Senate.[22]

The current court reflects most of these generalities. Four are graduates of Harvard Law School, including three Reagan-Bush appointments and one Clinton appointment. Two are from Stanford Law School, one from Yale Law

School, and one from Columbia Law School. The justice most clearly from the upper class, a corporate lawyer appointed by President Gerald Ford, received his law degree at Northwestern. Most had corporate law experience, except for the two women justices, who found it difficult to find positions in a law firm despite their high rankings upon graduation from Stanford and Columbia. Six of the nine are millionaires, including the two Clinton appointees. Some inherited their wealth, some married into wealth, and others acquired wealth from their corporate law practices.

Two of the nonmillionaires, Antonin Scalia and Clarence Thomas, are also the most conservative justices. Scalia worked for a corporate law firm for six years after graduation from Harvard, then became a law professor. Thomas's work experience after graduation from Yale included two years as a corporate attorney for Monsanto Chemical Company, followed by two years as a legislative assistant to the millionaire Republican senator from Missouri, John C. Danforth, who later urged his appointment to the Supreme Court as the African-American replacement for the first African-American ever appointed to the Supreme Court, civil rights lawyer Thurgood Marshall. The third nonmillionaire, Anthony M. Kennedy, is the son of a corporate lawyer and a graduate of Harvard, and was a corporate lawyer before he became a judge.

[T]he biggest differences among the justices concern volatile social issues. Women's rights, affirmative action, civil liberties, and the separation between church and state are the main targets of the ultraconservatives on the court. There is much less disagreement on issues of concern to the corporate community. On these issues, court opinions can be seen as the best rationales that can be constructed for the defense of the corporate economic system.

The Special-Interest Process

The special-interest process consists of the many and varied means by which specific corporations and business sectors gain the favors, tax breaks, regulatory rulings, and other governmental assistance they need to realize their narrow and short-run interests. The process is carried out by people with a wide range of experiences: former elected officials, experts who once served on congressional staffs or in regulatory agencies, employees of trade associations, corporate executives whose explicit function is government liaison, and an assortment of lawyers and public-relations specialists. The process is based on a great amount of personal contact, but its most important ingredients are the information and financial support that the lobbyists have to offer. Much of the time this information comes from grassroots pressure generated by the lobbyists to show that voting for a given measure will or will not hurt a particular politician.[23]

The most powerful lobbyists are gathered into a few large firms that are large businesses in themselves. The 10 biggest firms reported fees of $67 million for the first six months of 2000. These firms, in turn, are often owned by the public relations firms that have a major role in the opinion-shaping network. Two former Senate majority leaders, one Democratic and one Republican, are the leading figures in the second-largest lobbying firm, whose many clients include Citigroup, Merrill Lynch, and Brown & Williamson Tobacco. The issues these firms handle are typical of the special-interest process. For example, Pfizer, a pharmaceutical manufacturer, paid one firm $400,000 to try to work against a National Transportation Safety Board proposal to ban the use of antihistamines by truck drivers. The Magazine Publishers of America paid another firm $520,000 to oppose a possible 15 percent increase in magazine postal rates.[24]

Intricate and arcane tax breaks are one of the most important aspects of the special interest process. Thanks to successful efforts in 1993 to relax rules concerning minimum corporate taxes, and changes in 1997 making it possible for corporations to spread tax breaks over several years, 12 of 250 profitable large firms studied for the years 1996 to 1998 paid no federal income taxes. Seventy-one of the 250 paid taxes at less than half the official rate during those three years. General Electric alone saved $6.9 billion.[25] Examples such as this could be multiplied endlessly.

Special interests also work through Congress to try to hamstring regulatory agencies or reverse military purchasing decisions they do not like. When the Federal Communications Commission tried to issue licenses for over 1,000 low-power FM stations for schools and community groups,

Congress blocked the initiative at the behest of big broadcasting companies, setting standards that will restrict new licenses to a small number of stations in the least populated parts of the country. When the Food and Drug Administration tried to regulate tobacco, Congress refused authorization in 2000 in deference to the tobacco industry. In 1989, the Pentagon tried to cancel a new helicopter that was considered too costly and dangerous, but Congress deferred to the defense industry, allocating funds to keep it in production, and there have been three deadly crashes since.[26]

Some special-interest conflicts pit one sector of business against another, such as when broadcasters jockey for advantage against movie or cable companies. Sometimes the arguments are within a specific industry, as occurred when smaller insurance companies moved their headquarters to Bermuda in 1999 and 2000 to take advantage of a tax loophole worth as much as $4 billion annually. Since the bigger insurance companies cannot take advantage of this opportunity, they support bipartisan legislation to end the tax benefits of setting up in Bermuda. They have hired a lobbying firm, several law firms, and a public relations firm to press their cause. The small companies countered by hiring a different set of law firms and public relations companies.[27]

The special-interest process often is used to create loopholes in legislation that is accepted by the corporate community in principle. "I spent the last 7 years fighting the Clean Air Act," said a corporate lobbyist in charge of PAC donations, who then went on to explain why he gave money to elected officials who voted for the strengthening of the Clean Air Act in 1990:

> How a person votes on the final piece of legislation is not representative of what they have done. Somebody will do a lot of things during the process. How many guys voted against the Clean Air Act? But during the process some of them were very sympathetic to some of our concerns.[28]

Translated, this means there are forty pages of exceptions, extensions, and other loopholes in the 1990 version of the act after a thirteen-year standoff between the Business Roundtable's Clean Air Working Group and the liberal-labor coalition's National Clean Air Coalition. For example, the steel industry has thirty years to bring twenty-six large coke ovens into compliance with the new standards. Once the bill passed, lobbyists went to work on the Environmental Protection Agency to win the most lax regulations possible for implementing the legislation. As of 1998, after twenty-eight years of argument and delay, the agency had been able to issue standards for less than ten of the many hazardous chemicals emitted into the air.[29]

Although most studies of the special-interest process recount the success of one or another corporation or trade association in gaining the tax or regulatory breaks it seeks, or discuss battles between rival sectors of the corporate community, there are occasional defeats for corporate interests at the hands of liberals and labor within this process. In 1971, for example, environmentalists convinced Congress to end taxpayer subsidies for construction of a supersonic transport. In 1997, a relatively strong antistrip mine bill was adopted over the objections of the coal industry. Laws that improved auto safety standards were passed over automobile industry objections in the 1970s, as were standards of water cleanliness opposed by the paper and chemical industries.[30]

The liberal-labor coalition also can claim some victories for its own initiatives in Congress. For example, the Family and Medical Leave Act of 1993 allows both male and female employees of companies with fifty or more employees to take up to twelve weeks of unpaid leave a year for child care or family illness. The bill was opposed by corporate groups when it was first introduced in 1986, and vetoed twice by President George H. W. Bush before President Clinton came into office. The act covers 55 percent of American workers if government agencies are included. The fact that the leaves are unpaid limits the number of workers who can take advantage of them, and conservatives were able to exempt small companies and reduce the amount of leave from eighteen weeks to twelve, but health benefits are still in place during the leave. Seventeen percent of the workforce took advantage of this opportunity over an eighteen-month period during 1994 and 1995.[31]

The special-interest process is the most visible and frequently studied aspect of governmental activity in Washington. It also consumes the lion's share of the attention devoted to legislation by elected officials. There is general agreement among a wide range of theorists about the operation of this dimension of American politics. The special-interest process is very important to the corporate community, but it is not the heart of the matter when it comes to a full understanding of corporate power in the United States.

The Policy-Making Process

General policy-making on issues of concern to the corporate community as a whole is the culmination of work done in the policy network. However, the differences between moderate conservatives and ultraconservatives sometimes lead to major conflicts over new policies within the executive branch and the legislative process. This was especially the case before the mid-1970s, although the moderate conservatives stopped ultraconservatives from going too far on some issues during the Reagan Administration. In addition, the power elite have to fend off alternative legislative proposals put forward by the liberal-labor coalition at this point in the policy process.

The recommendations developed in the policy-planning network reach government in a variety of ways. On the most general level, their reports, news releases, and interviews are read by elected officials and their staffs, if not in their original form, then as they are summarized by commentators and columnists in the *Washington Post, New York Times,* and *Wall Street Journal.* Members of the policy organizations also appear before congressional committees and subcommittees that are writing legislation or preparing budget proposals. During one calendar year, for example, 134 of the 206 trustees of the Committee for Economic Development testified at least once before Congress on issues ranging from oil prices to tax reductions to cutting regulatory red tape. Not all of this testimony related directly to CED projects, but all of it related to issues of concern to the corporate community. In several instances, the testimony was written for the trustees by CED staff members; three of these staff members also presented their own testimony on behalf of CED.

Impressive as these numerous appearances before legislative committees are, the most important contacts with government are more direct and formal in nature. First, people from the policy-planning network are often members of the many unpaid committees that advise specific departments of the executive branch on general policies. Second, they are prominent on the presidential and congressional commissions that have been appointed from time to time since World War II to make recommendations on a wide range of issues from highway construction to Social Security to a new missile defense system. Third, corporate leaders have personal contact with both appointed and elected officials as members of the two policy organizations with the most access to government, the Business Council and the Business Roundtable. Fourth, they serve as informal advisers to the President in times of foreign policy crisis. Finally, they are appointed to government positions with a frequency far beyond what would be expected if all groups had an equal chance, putting them in a position to endorse the policy suggestions brought to them by their colleagues and former employees in the policy-planning network.

For the most part, the positions taken by moderate conservatives determine the outcome of policy battles. If they do not wish to see any change, they side with their ultraconservative counterparts in the power elite to defeat any programs suggested by liberals or labor. There were only a few instances in the twentieth century when the conservative voting bloc did not unite to block class-oriented liberal-labor legislation through an outright majority, maneuvering within key congressional committees, or a filibuster in the Senate.*

If the moderate conservatives favor policy changes opposed by the ultraconservatives, they seek the backing of liberal-labor elected officials for a program developed in moderate think tanks or policy-discussion groups, or else they modify a plan advocated by liberals. They are especially likely to take this course in times of extreme social disruption like the late 1960s,

*It was not until 1917 that a filibuster could be ended with a two-thirds vote. Since 1974, it takes three-fifths of the votes to end a filibuster. Because both Republicans and Democrats now resort to filibusters more frequently than they did in the past, in effect it is now necessary to have 60 votes in the Senate to pass highly liberal or highly conservative legislation.

when they were dealing simultaneously with an antiwar movement, major upheaval in inner cities, and an overheated economy. In this context, for example, many corporate leaders welcomed the idea for the first Earth Day in 1970, and openly sponsored it, although many came to regret the "excesses" of the environmental movement just a few years later.[32]

Sometimes general policy battles pit one or two industries against the rest of the corporate community, with the aggrieved industries eventually losing out. This is what happened to a large extent in the 1950s and 1960s when the textile and chemical sectors blocked attempts to reduce tariff barriers and increase world trade. When leaders from the Committee for Economic Development were able to forge a compromise with textile and chemical spokespersons, the opposition in Congress disappeared immediately.[33] The same thing happened in 1987 when the U.S. Chamber of Commerce and the National Federation of Independent Business objected on general principle to a call by the American Electronics Association, the Chemical Manufacturers Association, and organized labor for a federal program to monitor and notify workers exposed to toxic substances in the workplace. The legislation was defeated by a Republican filibuster in the Senate because the corporate community as a whole feared that such a program might provide a thin entering wedge for further demands for regulation.[34]

None of this means that congressional voting coalitions develop any more quickly and easily on large-scale issues than they do on special-interest ones. Instead, each coalition has to be carefully constructed by elected officials, with the help of corporate lobbyists and grassroots publicity. It is here that the political leaders do their most important work. They are specialists in arranging trades with other politicians for votes, and in being sensitive to the electoral risks for each colleague in voting for or against any highly visible piece of legislation. They are also experts at sensing when the moment is right to hold a vote, often keeping the final outcome hanging in the balance for weeks or months at a time. Sometimes they wait until a lame-duck session shortly after elections have been held, or slip controversial legislation into omnibus bills that are hard for voters to fathom. Finally, their constant interaction with constituents and the media gives them the experience and sensitivity to create the rhetoric and symbols needed to make the new legislation palatable to as many people as possible.

■ ■ ■ ■

Why Business Leaders Feel Powerless

Despite the strong *Who governs?* and *Who wins?* evidence that the power elite have great power over the federal government on the issues of concern to them, many corporate leaders feel they are relatively powerless in the face of government. To hear them tell it, the Congress is more responsive to organized labor, environmentalists, and consumers than it is to them. They also claim to be harassed by willful and arrogant bureaucrats who encroach upon the rightful preserves of the private sector, sapping them of their confidence and making them hesitant to invest their capital.

These feelings have been documented by a journalist and political scientist who observed a series of meetings at a policy discussion group in which the social responsibilities of business were being discussed. The men at these meetings were convinced that everybody but them was listened to by government. Government was seen as responsive to the immediate preferences of the majority of citizens. "The have-nots are gaining steadily more political power to distribute the wealth downward," complained one executive. "The masses have turned to a larger government." Some even wondered whether democracy and capitalism are compatible. "Can we still afford one man, one vote? We are tumbling on the brink," said one. "One man, one vote has undermined the power of business in all capitalist countries since World War II," announced another. "The loss of the rural vote weakens conservatives.[35]

The fear business leaders express of the democratic majority leads them to view recessions as a saving grace, because recessions help to keep the expectations of workers in check. Workers who fear for their jobs are less likely to demand higher wages or government social programs. For example, different corporate executives made the following comments:

> This recession will bring about the healthy respect for economic values that the Great Depression did.
>
> People need to recognize that a job is the most important thing they can have. We should use this recession to get the public to better understand how our economic system works. Social goals are OK, provided the public is aware of their costs.
>
> It would be better if the recession were allowed to weaken more than it will, so that we would have a sense of sobriety.[36]

The negative feelings these corporate leaders have toward government are not a new development in the corporate community. A study of business leaders' views in the nineteenth century found that they believed political leaders to be "stupid" and "empty" people who go into politics only to earn a living. As for the ordinary voters, they are "brutal, selfish, and ignorant." A comment written by a businessman in 1886 could have been made at the meetings just discussed: "In this good, democratic country where every man is allowed to vote, the intelligence and the property of the country is at the mercy of the ignorant, idle and vicious."[37] Even in the 1920s, when everyone agrees that business was at the zenith of its powers, corporate leaders sang the same tune.[38] These findings undercut any claim that business hostility toward government stems largely from the growth of government programs during the New Deal.

The emotional expressions of businesspeople about their lack of power cannot be taken seriously as power indicators, although they give pause to thoughts on how corporate leaders might react in the face of a large-scale democratic social and political movement that seriously challenges their prerogatives and privileges. The investigation of power concerns actions and their consequences, which are in the realm of sociology, economics, and politics, not in the realm of subjective feelings. Still, it is worthwhile to try to understand why corporate leaders complain about a government they dominate. There are three intertwined aspects to the answer.

First of all, complaining about government is a useful power strategy, a form of action in itself. It puts government officials on the defensive and forces them to keep proving that they are friendly to business, out of concern that corporate leaders will lose confidence in economic conditions and stop investing. A political scientist makes this point as follows:

> Whether the issue is understood explicitly, intuitively, or not at all, denunciations serve to establish and maintain the subservience of government units to the business constituencies to which they are actually held responsible. Attacks upon government in general place continuing pressure on governmental officers to accommodate their activities to the groups from which support is most reliable.[39]

There also seems to be an ideological level to the corporate stance toward government, which is based in a fear of the populist, democratic ideology that underlies American government. Since power is in theory in the hands of all the people, there is always the possibility that some day the people, in the sense of the majority, will make the government into the pluralist democracy it is supposed to be. In the American historical context, the great power of the dominant class is illegitimate, and the existence of such power is therefore vigorously denied.[40]

The most powerful reason for this fear of popular control is revealed by the corporate community's unending battle with unions. It is an issue-area like no other in evoking angry rhetoric and near-perfect unity among corporate leaders. It also has generated more violence than any other issue except civil rights for African-Americans. The uniqueness of the corporate community's reaction to any government help for unions supports the hypothesis that the corporate community, small businesses, and the growth coalitions are antigovernment because they fear government as the only institution that could challenge corporate control of labor markets, thereby changing the functioning of the system to some extent and reducing the power of employers. The federal government can influence labor markets in five basic ways:

1. The government can hire unemployed workers to do necessary work relating to parks, schools, roadways, and the environment. Such government programs were a great success during the New Deal, when unemployment reached 25 percent and social disruption seemed imminent, but they were quickly shut down at the insistence of business leaders when order was restored and the economy began to improve.[41]

2. It can support the right to organize unions and bargain collectively, as described in the previous section. This kind of government initiative is opposed even more strongly than government jobs for the unemployed because it would give workers a sustained organizational base for moving into the political arena.

3. Although the power elite appreciate the value of old-age, disability, and unemployment insurance, they worry that politicians might allow these programs to become too generous. In fact, these programs expanded in response to the turmoil of the 1960s and 1970s to the point where the Reagan Administration felt it necessary to cut them back in order to reduce inflation and make corporations more profitable.[42]

4. The government can tighten labor markets by limiting immigration. The immigration of low-wage labor has been essential to the corporate community throughout American history. When conservative Republicans began to think about passing anti-immigration legislation in the mid-1990s, as called for in their campaign rhetoric, they were met with a barrage of employer opposition, particularly from leaders in agribusiness, and quickly retreated.

5. Government can reduce unemployment and tighten labor markets by lowering interest rates through the operations of the Federal Reserve System. This fact has been made obvious to a large percentage of the public by the way in which the Federal Reserve increases unemployment by increasing the interest rates whenever the unemployment rate dips too low. Although the issue is cast in terms of inflation, the economics of inflation are often the politics of labor markets.

Given the many ways that the government could tighten labor markets and thereby reduce profits and increase the economic power of American workers, it is understandable that the corporate community would be fearful of the government it dominates.

The Limits of Corporate Domination

Involvement in government is the final and most visible aspect of corporate domination, which has its roots in the class structure, control of the investment function, and the operation of the policy-planning network. If the government officials did not have to wait on corporate leaders to decide where and when they will invest, and if government officials were not further limited by the general public's acceptance of policy recommendations from the policy-planning network, then power elite involvement in elections and government would count for a lot less than it does under present conditions.

Domination by the power elite does not negate the reality of continuing conflict over government policies, but few conflicts involve challenges to the rules that create privileges for the upper class and the corporate community. Most of the numerous battles within the interest-group process, for example, are only over specific spoils and favors; they often involve disagreements between competing business interests.

Similarly, conflicts within the policy-making process sometimes concern differences between the moderate conservatives and ultraconservatives in the power elite. Many issues that at first appear to be legislative defeats for the corporate community turn out to be situations where the moderate conservatives decided for their own reasons to side with the liberal-labor coalition. At other times, the policy disagreements involve issues where the needs of the corporate community as a whole come into conflict with the needs of specific industries, which is what happened in the past on trade policies and also on some environmental legislation.

Notes

1. Michael Mann, "The Autonomous Power of the State: Its Origins, Mechanisms, and Results," *Archives of European Sociology* 25 (1984): 185–213; Michael Mann, *The Sources of Social Power: A History of Power From the Beginning*

to A.D. 1760, vol. 1 (New York: Cambridge University Press, 1986).

2. Roger Friedland and A. F. Robertson, *Beyond the Marketplace: Rethinking Economy and Society* (New York: Aldine de Gruyter, 1990).

3. Steve Lohr, "U.S. Pursuit of Microsoft: Rare Synergy With Company's Rivals," *New York Times*, 12 June 2000, C1.

4. James Livingston, *Origins of the Federal Reserve System: Money, Class, and Corporate Capitalism, 1890–1913* (Ithaca: Cornell University Press, 1986).

5. Bob Woodward, *Maestro: Greenspan's Fed and the American Boom* (New York: Simon & Schuster, 2000).

6. Timothy Egan, "Failing Farmers Learn to Profit From Wealth of U.S. Subsidies," *New York Times*, 25 December 2000, 1.

7. John Myles and Jill Quadagno, "'Envisioning a Third War: The Welfare State in the Twenty-First Century," *Contemporary Sociology* 29 (2000): 156–167.

8. G. William Domhoff, *Who Rules America?*, 1st ed. (Englewood Cliffs, N.J.: Prentice-Hall, 1967); G. William Domhoff, *Who Rules America Now?* (New York: Simon & Schuster, 1983); Harold Salzman and G. William Domhoff, "The Corporate Community and Government: Do They Interlock?," in *Power Structure Research*, ed. G. William Domhoff (Beverly Hills: Sage Publications, 1980), 227–254.

9. Philip H. Burch, *Elites in American History: The New Deal to the Carter Administration*, vol. 3 (New York: Holmes & Meier, 1980); Philip H. Burch, *Elites in American History: The Civil War to the New Deal*, vol. 2 (New York: Holmes & Meier, 1981); Philip H. Burch, *Elites in American History: The Federalist Years to the Civil War*, vol. 1 (New York: Holmes & Meier, 1981).

10. Beth Mintz, "The President's Cabinet, 1897–1972: A Contribution to the Power Structure Debate," *Insurgent Sociologist* 5 (1975): 131–148.

11. Michael Useem, "Which Business Leaders Help Govern?," in *Power Structure Research*, ed. G. William Domhoff (Beverly Hills: Sage Publications, 1980), 199–225; Michael Useem, *The Inner Circle: Large Corporations and the Rise of Business Political Activity in the U.S. and U.K.* (New York: Oxford University Press, 1984).

12. James Grimaldi, "The Antitrust Administration," *Washington Post Weekly*, 10 July 2000, 18.

13. David Kessler, *A Question of Intent: How a Small Government Agency Took on America's Most Powerful and Deadly Industry* (New York: Public Affairs Press, 2000).

14. Joe Conason, "Notes on a Native Son: The George W. Bush Success Story," *Harper's Magazine*, February 2000, 39–53.

15. Thomas Toch, "A Savior for Washington's Has-Beens," *New Republic*, 21 December 1998, 10.

16. Richard L. Zweigenhaft and G. William Domhoff, *Diversity in the Power Elite: Have Women and Minorities Reached the Top?* (New Haven: Yale University Press, 1998).

17. Michael Mann, *The Sources of Social Power: The Rise of Classes and Nation-States, 1760–1914*, vol. 2 (New York: Cambridge University Press, 1993).

18. Morris Leopold Ernst, *The Great Reversals: Tales of the Supreme Court* (New York: Weybright & Talley, 1973).

19. Richard Cortner, *The Wagner Act Cases* (Knoxville: University of Tennessee Press, 1964).

20. Robert Carp and Ronald Stidham, *Judicial Process in America*, 4th ed. (Washington: CQ Press, 1998); Lawrence Baum, *The Supreme Court*, 6th ed. (Washington, D.C.: CQ Press, 1998).

21. Robert Carp and Ronald Stidham, *Judicial Process in America*, 4th ed. (Washington, D.C.: CQ Press, 1998), p. 217.

22. Lawrence Baum, *The Supreme Court*, 6th ed. (Washington, D.C.: CQ Press, 1998).

23. Kenneth M. Goldstein, *Interest Groups, Lobbying, and Participation in America* (Cambridge, England and New York: Cambridge University Press, 1999).

24. Shawn Zeller, "Cassidy Captures the Gold," *National Journal*, 21 October 2000, 3332–3334.

25. David Johnston, "Study Finds That Many Large Corporations Pay No Taxes," *New York Times*, 29 October 2000, C2.

26. James Dao, "After a Crash in North Carolina, Marines Ground Osprey Program," *New York Times*, 13 December 2000, 1; Stephen Labaton, "Congress Severely Curtails Plan for Low-Power FM Stations," *New York Times*, 19 December 2000, 1.

27. Peter Stone, "A Bermuda Brouhaha for Insurers," *National Journal*, 14 October 2000, 3262.

28. Dan Clawson, Alan Neustadtl, and Mark Weller, *Dollars and Votes: How Business Campaign Contributions Subvert Democracy* (Philadelphia: Temple University Press, 1998), p. 6.

29. Dan Clawson, Alan Neustadtl, and Mark Weller, *Dollars and Votes: How Business Campaign Contributions Subvert Democracy* (Philadelphia: Temple University Press, 1998), p. 7.

30. Mark Green, ed., *The Monopoly Makers* (New York: Grossman, 1973); David Vogel, *Fluctuating Fortunes: The Political Power of Business in America* (New York: Basic Books, 1989).

31. Ilana DeBare, "A Time for Caring," *San Francisco Chronicle*, 3 August 1998, B1–B3.

32. David Vogel, *Fluctuating Fortunes: The Political Power of Business in America* (New York: Basic Books, 1989); G. William Domhoff, *The Power Elite and the State: How Policy Is Made in America* (Hawthorne, N.Y.: Aldine de Gruyter, 1990), chapter 10.

33. G. William Domhoff, *The Power Elite and the State: How Policy Is Made in America* (Hawthorne, N.Y.: Aldine de Gruyter, 1990), chapter 8.

34. David C. Jacobs, *Business Lobbies and the Power Structure in America: Evidence and Arguments* (Westport, Conn.: Quorum Books, 1999).

35. Leonard S. Silk and David Vogel, *Ethics and Profits: The Crisis of Confidence in American Business* (New York: Simon & Schuster, 1976), pp. 50, 75.
36. Leonard S. Silk and David Vogel, *Ethics and Profits: The Crisis of Confidence in American Business* (New York: Simon & Schuster, 1976), p. 64
37. Leonard S. Silk and David Vogel, *Ethics and Profits: The Crisis of Confidence in American Business* (New York: Simon & Schuster, 1976), p. 193.
38. James W. Prothro, *The Dollar Decade: Business Ideas in the 1920's* (Baton Rouge: Louisiana State University Press, 1954).
39. Grant McConnell, *Private Power & American Democracy* (New York: Alfred A. Knopf, 1966), p. 294.
40. David Vogel, "Why Businessmen Mistrust Their State: The Political Consciousness of American Corporate Executives," *British Journal of Political Science* 8 (1978): 45–78.
41. Frances Fox Piven and Richard A. Cloward, *Regulating the Poor: The Functions of Public Welfare*, updated ed. (New York: Vintage Books, 1993); Nancy Ellen Rose, *Put to Work: Relief Programs in the Great Depression* (New York: Monthly Review Press, 1994).
42. Frances Fox Piven and Richard A. Cloward, *The New Class War: Reagan's Attack on the Welfare State and Its Consequences* (New York: Pantheon Books, 1982).

FOLLOW THE MONEY

Dan Clawson, Alan Neustadtl, and Mark Weller

The Money Primary

Imagine the November election is just a few weeks away, and your friend Sally Robeson is seriously considering running for Congress two years from now. This year the incumbent in your district, E. Chauncey DeWitt III, will (again!) be reelected by a substantial margin, but you and Sally hate Chauncey's positions on the issues and are convinced that with the right campaign he can be beaten. Sally is capable, articulate, well informed, respected in the community, politically and socially connected, charming, good at talking to many kinds of people, and highly telegenic. She has invited you and several other politically active friends to meet with her immediately after the election to determine what she would need to do to become a viable candidate.

The meeting that takes place covers a host of topics: What are the key issues? On which of these are Sally's stands popular, and on which unpopular? What attacks, and from what quarters, will be launched against her? What individuals or groups can she count on for support? How, why, and where is the incumbent vulnerable? But lurking in the background is the question that cannot be ignored: *Can Sally (with the help of her friends and backers) raise enough money to be a contender?*

This is the *money primary, the first, and, in many instances, the most important round of the contest.* It eliminates more candidates than any other hurdle. Because it eliminates them so early and so quietly, its impact is often unobserved. To make it through, candidates don't have to come in first, but they do need to raise enough money to be credible contenders. Although having the most money is no guarantee of victory, candidates who don't do well in the money primary are no longer serious contenders. Certainly, plenty of well-funded candidates lose—Michael Huffington spent $25 million of his own money in an unsuccessful 1994 race for the Senate. But in order to be viable, a candidate needs to raise a substantial minimum.

How much is needed? If Sally hopes to win, rather than just put up a good fight, she, you, and the rest of her supporters will need to raise staggering amounts. (At least they are staggering from the perspective of most Americans; Ross Perot, Steve Forbes, or Michael Huffington may view the matter differently.) In order to accumulate the *average* amount for major-party congressional candidates in the general election, you will collectively need to raise $4,800 next week. And the week after. And *every* week for the next two years.

But even that is not enough. The average amount includes many candidates who were never "serious"; that is, they didn't raise enough to have a realistic hope of winning. If you and your friends want to raise the average amount spent by a *winning* candidate for the House, you'll have to come up with $6,730 next week and every single week until the election, two years away.

Well, you say, your candidate is hardly average. She is stronger, smarter, more politically appealing, and more viable than the "average" challenger. You think she can win even if she doesn't raise $6,730 a week. Let's use past experience—the results of the 1996 elections—to consider the likelihood of winning for challengers, based on how much money they raised. In 1996 more than 360 House incumbents were running for reelection; only 23 of them were beaten by their challengers. The average successful challenger spent $1,045,361—that is, he or she raised an average of over $10,000 every week for two years. What were the chances of winning without big money? Only one winning challenger spent less than $500,000, 12 spent between a half-a-million and a million dollars, and 10 spent more than a million dollars. Furthermore, 13 of the 23 winning challengers outspent the incumbent. A House challenger who can't raise at least a half-million dollars doesn't have a one percent chance of winning; the key primary is the money primary. The

Boston Globe reported that "House candidates who headed into the final three weeks with the most in combined spending and cash on hand won 93 percent of the time."[1] What about that one low-spending winner? She is Carolyn Cheeks Kilpatrick, who won election by beating an incumbent in the primary and then having a walkover in the general election; the district, in Detroit, is the fourth poorest in the nation and consistently votes more than 80 percent Democratic. Although Kilpatrick spent only 174,457, few other districts make possible a similar election strategy.

In the Senate, even more money is needed. Suppose your candidate were going to run for the Senate, and started fundraising immediately after an election, giving her six years to prepare for the next election. How much money would she need to raise each and every week for those *six* years? The average winning Senate candidate raised approximately $15,000 per week.

For presidential candidates, the stakes are, of course, much higher: "The prevailing view is that for a politician to be considered legitimate, he or she must collect at least $20 million by the first of January 2000."[2] Presumably any candidate who does not do so is "illegitimate" and does not belong in the race.

If you collectively decide that the candidate you plan to back will need to raise $7,000 per week (for the House; $15,000 per week for the Senate), how will you do it? Suppose you hold a $10-per-person fundraiser—a barbecue in the park on Memorial Day or Labor Day. Even if 500 people attend, the affair will gross only $5,000, and net considerably less, no matter how cheap the hot dogs and hamburgers. And that takes no account of the problems of persuading 500 people to attend—just notifying them of the event is a major undertaking—or what it would mean to hold such an event every week, not just on Labor Day. In order to get through the money primary, an alternative strategy is needed, so candidates, especially incumbents, increasingly prefer to raise money at "big ticket" events.[3] Selling 10 tickets for a $1,000-per-person fundraiser brings in more than twice as much as the 500-person barbecue in the park.

Who is likely to cough up a thousand bucks to attend a fundraiser? Although practically anyone *could* come up with a thousand dollars . . . a disproportionate number of such contributors are corporate political action committees (PACs), executives, and lobbyists. One typical version of the $1,000-per-person fundraiser is a breakfast: The candidate and 10 to 30 PAC officers and lobbyists from a particular industry (trucking, banking, oil and gas exploration). Even with a lavish breakfast, the candidate's net take is substantial. If enough lobbyists and corporate executives can be persuaded to come, perhaps the candidate could get by on one fundraiser every couple of weeks.

Coming up with the money is a major hassle; even for incumbents, it requires constant effort. *National Journal*, probably the single most authoritative source on the Washington scene, reports that "there is widespread agreement that the congressional money chase has become an unending marathon, as wearying to participants as it is disturbing to spectators," and quoted an aide to a Democratic senator as observing, "During hearings of Senate committees, you can watch senators go to phone booths in the committee rooms to dial for dollars." Just a few years ago—in 1990, the date of this statement—soliciting funds from federal property, whether Congress or the White House, was routine, openly discussed, and not regarded as problematic. The activity had always been technically illegal, but only in 1997 did it become an issue, with President Clinton and (especially) Vice President Gore singled out as if they were the only offenders.

But long before the 1996 election, politicians felt that they had no choice: The Senate majority leader reported that "public officials are consumed with the unending pursuit of money to run election campaigns."[4] Senators not only leave committee hearings for the more crucial task of calling people to beg for money. They also chase all over the country, because their reelection is more dependent on meeting rich people two thousand miles from home than on meeting their own constituents. Thomas Daschle, the current Democratic leader in the Senate, reports that, in the two years prior to his election to the Senate, he "flew to California more than 20 times to meet with prospective contributors," going there almost as often as he went to the largest city in his home state of South Dakota.[5] This process is sometimes carried to an extreme: Representative John Murtha, Democrat of Pennsylvania, was criticized because at one point he had raised nearly $200,000, of which only $1,000 came from his district. The same processes operate at the presidential level, where donors hold the key to success at the polls. The day after the 1996 Iowa caucuses propelled Lamar Alexander's candidacy into the first tier, he took time off from campaigning in New Hampshire for a phone conference call to tell 250 supporters that he needed each of them to raise $5,000 by the end of the week "to help keep his campaign afloat."[6] The *New York Times* headlined one 1996 story, "In New Jersey, Meeting the Voters Is a Luxury," and declared that "the real campaign" was "raising money for a barrage of television ads," with both major party candidates admitting that they spent "at least half a day, two or three days a week, on the telephone asking for money."[7]

Not only is it necessary to raise lots of money; it is important—for both incumbents and challengers—to raise it early. Senator Rudy Boschwitz, Republican of Minnesota, was clear about this as a strategy. He spent $6 million getting reelected in 1984, and had raised $1.5 million of it by the beginning of the year, effectively discouraging the most promising Democratic challengers. After the election he wrote, and typed up himself, a secret evaluation of his campaign strategy:

> "Nobody in politics (except me!) likes to raise money, so I thought the best way of discouraging the toughest opponents from running was to have a few dollars in the sock. *I believe it worked. . . . From all forms of fundraising I raised $6 million plus and got 3 or 4 (maybe even 5) stories and cartoons* that irked me," he said. "In retrospect, I'm glad I had the money."[8]

Similarly, in March 1996 Bill Paxon, chair of the House Republican campaign committee, said, "We've been pounding on members[9] to raise more money by the filing deadline; if they show a good balance, that could ward off opponents."[10]

The Contributors' Perspective

Candidates need money, lots of it, if they are to have any chance of winning. The obvious next question . . . is who gives, why, and what they expect for it.

Contributions are made for many different reasons. The candidate's family and friends chip in out of loyalty and affection. Others contribute because they are asked to do so by someone who has done favors for them. People give because they agree with the candidate's stand on the issues, either on a broad ideological basis or on a specific issue. Sometimes these donations are portrayed as a form of voting—people show that they care by putting their money where their mouth is, anyone can contribute, and the money raised reflects the wishes of the people. Even for these contributions, however, if voting with dollars replaces voting at the ballot box, then the votes will be very unequally distributed: the top 1 percent of the population by wealth will have more "votes" than the bottom 90 percent of the population. In the 1996 elections, less than one-fourth of one percent of the population gave contributions of $200 or more to a federal candidate.[11] PACs and large contributors provide most of the money, however; small contributors accounted for under one-third of candidate receipts.[12]

It is not just that contributions come from the well-to-do. Most contributors have a direct material interest in what the government does or does not do. Their contributions, most of them made directly or indirectly by business, provide certain people a form of leverage and "access" not available to the rest of us. The chair of the political action committee at one of the twenty-five largest manufacturing companies in the United States explained to us why his corporation has a PAC:

> The PAC gives you access. It makes you a player. These congressmen, in particular, are constantly fundraising. Their elections are very expensive, and getting increasingly expensive each year. So they have an ongoing need for funds.
>
> It profits us in a sense to be able to provide some funds because in the provision of it you get to know people, you help them out. There's no real quid pro quo. There is nobody whose vote you can count on, not with the kind of money we are talking about here. But the PAC gives you access. Puts you in the game.
>
> You know, some congressman has got X number of ergs of energy and here's a

> person or a company who wants to come see him and give him a thousand dollars, and here's another one who wants to just stop by and say hello. And he only has time to see one. Which one? So the PAC's an attention getter.

So-called soft money, where the amount of the contribution is unlimited, might appear to be an exception: Isn't $100,000 enough to buy a guaranteed outcome? We will argue that it is *not*, at least not in any simple and straightforward way. PAC contributions are primarily for members of Congress; they are for comparatively small amounts, but enough to gain access to individual members of Congress. The individual member, however, has limited power. Soft money donations are best thought of as a way of gaining access to the president, top party leaders, and the executive branch. These individuals are more powerful than ordinary members of Congress, so access to them comes at a higher price. That privileged access is invaluable, but, as we will try to show, it does not—and is not expected to—*guarantee* a quid pro quo.

In business–government relations most attention becomes focused on instances of scandal. The real issue, however, is not one or another scandal or conflict of interest, but rather the *system* of business–government relations, and especially of campaign finance, that offers business so many opportunities to craft loopholes, undermine regulations, and subvert enforcement. Still worse, many of these actions take place beyond public scrutiny. . . .

Why Business?

[We focus] on business and the way it uses money and power to subvert the democratic process. This runs counter to the conventional wisdom, which treats all campaign contributions as equally problematic. A "balanced" and "objective" approach would, we are told, condemn both business and labor; each reform that primarily restricts business should be matched by one that restricts labor. We've heard these arguments, thought them over, and rejected them. They assume that what we have now is "balance" and that all changes should reinforce the existing relations of power. We see no reason to accept that as an a priori assumption.

Why are business campaign contributions more of a problem than contributions by labor (or women, or environmentalists)? First, because business contributes far more money. According to a study by the Center for Responsive Politics,[13] in the last election business outspent labor by an 11 to 1 margin. Most reports about campaign finance give the impression that labor contributes roughly as much as business—a distortion of the reality.

Second; . . . beyond the world of campaign finance, business has far more power than labor, women's groups, or environmentalists.

Third, business uses campaign contributions in a way few other groups do, as part of an "access" process that provides corporations a chance to shape the details of legislation, crafting loopholes that undercut the stated purpose of the law. Other groups do this on rare occasions; business does so routinely. Businesses are far more likely than other donors to give to *both* sides in a race; nearly all the soft money donors who gave to both sides were corporations.

Fourth, there is a fundamental difference between corporate and labor PAC contributions. That difference is democracy; unions have it, corporations don't. This overwhelmingly important distinction is concealed by almost all public discussion. No one talks about it, no one seems to take it seriously. There is a virtual embargo on any mention of this fact, but it merits serious consideration.

The original legislation ratifying the creation of PACs, passed in 1971 and amended in 1974 after Watergate, intended that corporations and labor unions be treated in parallel fashion. In each case, the organization was permitted a special relationship to the group that democratically controlled it—stockholders in the case of corporations, members in the case of labor unions. The organization was permitted to communicate with those individuals and their families on any issue (including political issues), to conduct registration and get-out-the-vote campaigns, and to ask those people for voluntary contributions to a political action committee.

In the 1975 SUN–PAC decision, the Federal Election Commission, for almost the only time in its existence, took a bold step. In fact, it essentially threw out a key part of the law and then rewrote it, permitting corporations to solicit PAC contributions not just from their stockholders but also from their managerial employees. This had two consequences. First, corporate PACs—but no others—are able to coerce people to contribute. Second, corporate PACs are not, even in theory, democratically controlled. Each of these consequences needs to be examined.

Neither stockholders nor union members can be coerced to contribute—the organization doesn't have power over them, they have power over the organization. Managers, however, can be coerced. As a result, virtually all corporate PAC money comes from employees rather than stockholders. If your boss comes to you and asks for a contribution, saying he or she hopes that all team players will be generous, it's not easy for you, an ambitious young manager, to say no. Some companies apparently do not pressure employees to contribute, but others do. For example, at one company we studied, the head of government relations told us that each year he and the company's lobbyist go to each work unit and hold an employee meeting: "We talk about the PAC and what it means to the company and what it means to them as individuals, and we solicit their membership; if they are members, we solicit an increase in their gift." Then the employees' boss is asked "to get up and say why they are members and why they think it's important for an employee to be a member." The upper-level manager clearly has no confidentiality, which in itself sends a key message to others. A number of coercive elements converge in this solicitation: The meeting is public, employees are to commit themselves then and there in the public meeting, the boss recommends that subordinates contribute, and an impression is probably conveyed that the boss will be evaluated on the basis of his or her employees' participation rate. The PAC chair insists there is no pressure, but admits employees feel differently:

> And yet regardless of how many times you say that, there's always going to be some employees who feel that you got them into that meeting to put pressure on. But if they feel pressure it's self-imposed from the standpoint of the solicitation. Because there will be several of us, including myself, who will get up and say, we want you to be a member and here's why.

However, even his definition of "no pressure" is cause for concern: "But as far as a manager or anybody getting up and telling you that if you don't participate we're going to fire you, . . . there's no pressure." No one is told they will be fired for failing to contribute, but it seems probable that they will assume their boss will be disappointed and that their contribution or noncontribution will be remembered at promotion time.

The second consequence of the 1975 SUN–PAC decision is even more important. Corporate PACs are *not* democratic. Many corporations have steering committees that vote to decide to whom the PAC will contribute, but the committees are appointed, the corporate hierarchy selects individuals who are expected to take the corporate purpose as their own, and managers know that they will be evaluated on their performance on the committee. As one senior vice president explained: "Policy is made by the top of the company, and it filters down. They tell you what they want, and you do it."

The internal functioning of corporate PACs suggests how they relate to and value democracy. Most aspects of the political system are beyond the *direct* control of corporations, but they *can* determine how their PACs operate and make decisions. As a result, in all but a handful of corporate PACs democratic control is not even a theoretical possibility. The PAC raises its money from employees, but employees do not and cannot vote on the leadership or direction of either the PAC or the corporation. The PAC officer who is responsible for the day-to-day details of running the PAC is appointed. *No* corporation elects its PAC officer—any more than corporate employees elect any other official. While PACs do sometimes change political direction, this happens because the corporation is acquired or because a new CEO takes office, not because contributors are dissatisfied.[14]

Not only the PAC officer is appointed. Virtually all PAC steering committees are appointed, not elected. The chair of one of the handful with elections explained:

> We have a steering committee that's elected by the members. We send out ballots for the steering committee. It's a Russian election[15] admittedly—there is a slate of nominees and there is an opportunity for people to write in but as a practical matter it's almost impossible for a write-in to win.

The only corporation that reported having *some* contested elections agreed that, in general: "It is an elected-appointive; it's kind of a pseudo-election I guess is what it amounts to."

We might expect those ideological corporations that stress general principles of support for democracy and the "free" enterprise system to be exceptions to the undemocratic organization of corporate PACs. Not at all. At one corporation that boasted about its wholehearted support of the "free enterprise system," the chair of the PAC Committee matter-of-factly noted: "If our [company] chairman said we are going to have a certain kind of PAC, then we'd have an option of resigning or doing it the way he wanted." At another ideological corporation, *all* members of the PAC committee are among the top ten corporate officers. In PAC committee deliberations, we were told, "It's never heated because it's not a very democratic system."

The nondemocratic character of corporate PACs is consistent with the principles guiding the corporation as a whole. Corporations are not run on democratic principles; employees don't vote on corporate leadership or policies. Many corporate executives are dubious about democracy in general. Leonard Silk and David Vogel attended a set of meetings organized by the Conference Board for top executives. They concluded:

> While critics of business worry about the atrophy of American democracy, the concern in the nation's boardrooms is precisely the opposite. For an executive, democracy in America is working all too well—*that is the problem.*[16]

Campaign contributions are (part of) the solution to the "problem" of democracy.

■ ■ ■ ■

The Current Law

The most provocative and also probably the most accurate beginning point is that there is, in effect, no law. Or, rather, an untold number of laws and regulations exist, but a determined donor can get around them. The morass of regulations creates enormous hassles for both candidates and donors, makes life more difficult for those attempting to use money to dominate the system, and provides a significant measure of public disclosure. But it does not prevent outrageous abuses, and it sanctions a system whose normal operation involves exchanging money for special influence. In practice, campaign finance is today *less* regulated than it has been at any time since 1907 (when the Tillman Act was passed). That is the starting point for any discussion of the law; the rest should be thought of as a map showing the obstacles placed in the way of smart lawyers, candidates, and donors.

We won't try to cover all the technicalities of the current law; the outlines are confusing enough. *Individuals* may contribute $1,000 per candidate per election. But since most candidates face both a primary and a general election, that limit doubles; the creative use of family members can further expand it. No individual may contribute more than $25,000 in total (to all candidates) per year, though people may also contribute $5,000 per year to a PAC.

Political action committees, or PACs, are entities that collect money from many contributors, pool it, and then make donations to candidates. Corporations, unions, and trade associations may sponsor PACs, paying all of their operating expenses (rent, phone, mailings, the salaries of individuals who work only on the PAC), but they can't put their own money directly into the PAC, because all PAC money must come from voluntary donations. PACs may contribute up to $5,000 per candidate per election (with primaries again doubling the limit), and may give an unlimited total amount.

Candidates must *disclose* all PAC donations (of any size), the names of all individuals who donate $200 or more, and the total amount spent and received (including the amounts received from donations of less than $200). PACs must disclose all donations, and report the names of all individuals who contribute $200 or more.

By far the most important recent change in campaign finance is the explosion of so-called soft money. "Hard money" refers to donations made (more or less) within the framework of the law as it was originally intended; "soft money"—which could equally well be called "loophole money"—is money that escapes the requirements of federal law. Like most such distinctions, it's less clear than it seems—for example, a 1991 federal regulation requires that soft money contributions be reported: That reporting is itself a (minimal) form of regulation.

Soft money differs from hard money in two critical ways. First, there is absolutely no limit on the amount of the contribution. A corporation can give one hundred thousand dollars, a million dollars, or more. Second, corporations, unions, and other organizations can take the money directly from their central treasuries. PACs must get their money from (at least supposedly) voluntary donations by individuals to the PAC. That placed some limit on corporate giving. Stockholders contributed very little, and although corporations could successfully coerce the money out of their managers, doing so became, at least, a problem. Now corporations may take the money directly out of their treasuries—and they have astonishingly deep pockets.

The Federal Election Commission (FEC) is supposed to monitor candidates and contributors and enforce the rules, but it is underfunded and takes—literally—years to reach decisions. In terms of action, the FEC is paralyzed on most important issues, since by law its commissioners are evenly balanced—three Democrats and three Republicans—but it requires a majority vote to act. Typically, the FEC takes (roughly) forever to officially consider a violation. Then it either fails to reach any decision or imposes a minimal fine.*

▪ ▪ ▪ ▪

What Is Power?

Our analysis is based on an understanding of power that differs from that usually articulated by both business and politicians. The corporate PAC directors we interviewed insisted that they have no power.

> If you were to ask me what kind of access and influence do we have, being roughly the 150th largest PAC, I would have to tell you that on the basis of our money we have zero. . . . If you look at the level of our contributions, we know we're not going to buy anybody's vote, we're not going to rent anybody, or whatever the clichés have been over the years. We know that.

The executives who expressed these views clearly meant these words sincerely.[17]. . . Power, in this common conception, is the ability to make someone do something against their will. If that is what power means, then corporations rarely have any in relation to members of Congress, nor does soft money give the donor power over presidents. As one senior vice president said to us: "You certainly aren't going to be able to buy anybody for $500 or $1,000 or $10,000—it's a joke." Soft money donations of a million dollars might seem to change the equation, but we will argue they do not: Just as $10,000 won't buy a member of Congress, $1,000,000 won't buy a president. In this regard we agree with the corporate officials we interviewed: A corporation is not in a position to say to a member of Congress, "Either you vote for this bill or we will defeat your bid for reelection." Rarely do they even say: "You vote for this bill or you won't get any money from us."

▪ ▪ ▪ ▪

Power, we would argue, is not just the ability to force someone to do something against their will; it is most effective (and least recognized) when it shapes the field of action. Moreover, business's vast resources, influence on the economy, and general legitimacy place it on a different footing from other campaign contributors. Every day a member of Congress accepts $1,000 donation from a corporate PAC, goes to a committee hearing, proposes "minor" changes in a bill's wording, and has those changes accepted without discussion or examination. The changes "clarify" the language of the bill, legalizing higher levels of pollution for a specific pollutant, or exempting the company from some tax. The media do not report this change and no one speaks against it. On the other hand, if a PAC were formed by Drug Lords for Cocaine Legalization, no member would take their money. If a member introduced a "minor" wording change to make it easier to sell crack without bothersome police interference, the proposed change would attract massive attention, the campaign contribution would be labeled a scandal,

*See editors' note at end of reading.

the member's political career would be ruined, and the changed wording would not be incorporated into the bill. Drug Lords may make an extreme example, but approximately the same holds true for many groups: At present, equal rights for gays and lesbians could never be a minor and unnoticed addition to a bill with a different purpose.

Even groups with great social legitimacy encounter more opposition and controversy than business faces for proposals that are virtually without public support. One example is the contrast between the largely unopposed commitment of tens or hundreds of billions of dollars for the savings and loan bailout, compared to the sharp debate, close votes, and defeats for the rights of men and women to take *unpaid* parental leaves. The classic term for something noncontroversial that everyone must support is "a motherhood issue," and while it costs little to guarantee every woman the right to an *un*paid parental leave, this measure nonetheless generated intense scrutiny and controversy—going down to defeat under President Bush, passing under President Clinton, and then again becoming a focus of attack after the 1994 Republican takeover of Congress. Few indeed are the people publicly prepared to defend pollution or tax evasion. Nonetheless, business is routinely able to win pollution exemptions and tax loopholes. Although cumulatively some vague awareness of these provisions may trouble people, most are allowed individually to pass without scrutiny. *No* analysis of corporate political activity makes sense unless it begins with a recognition of this absolutely vital point. The PAC is a vital element of corporate power, but it does not operate by itself. The PAC donation is always backed by the wider power and influence of business.

Corporations are unlike other "special interest" groups not only because business has far more resources, but also because of its acceptance and legitimacy. When people feel that "the system" is screwing them, they tend to blame politicians, the government, the media—but rarely business. In terms of campaign finance, while much of the public is outraged at the way money influences elections and public policy, the issue is almost always posed in terms of politicians, what they do or don't do. This is part of a pervasive double standard that largely exempts business from criticism. We, however, believe it is vital to scrutinize business as well.

We did two dozen radio call-in shows after the appearance of our last book, *Money Talks.* On almost every show, at least one call came from someone outraged that members of Congress had recently raised their pay to $125,100. (For 1998, it will be about $137,000.) Not a single person even mentioned corporate executives' pay. *Business Week* calculated that in 1996 corporate CEOs were paid an average of $5.8 million (counting salary, bonuses, and stock option grants), or more than 200 times the average worker's pay, and more than 40 times what members of Congress are paid.[18] More anger is directed at Congress for delaying new environmental laws than at the companies that fight every step of the way to stall and subvert the legislation. When members of Congress do favors for large campaign contributors, anger is directed at the senators who went along, not at the business owner who paid the money (and usually initiated the pressure). The public focuses on the member's receipt of thousands of dollars, not on the business's receipt of millions (or hundreds of millions) in tax breaks or special treatment. It is a widely held belief that "politics is dirty." But little public comment and condemnation is generated when companies get away—quite literally—with murder. This disparity is evidence of business's success in shaping public perceptions. Lee Atwater, George Bush's 1988 campaign manager, saw this as a key to Republican success:

> In the 1980 campaign, we were able to make the establishment, insofar as it is bad, the government. In other words, big government was the enemy, not big business. If the people think the problem is that taxes are too high, and the government interferes too much, then we are doing our job. But, if they get to the point where they say that the real problem is that rich people aren't paying taxes, . . . then the Democrats are going to be in good shape.[19]

We argue that corporations are so different, and so dominant, that they exercise a special kind of power, what Antonio Gramsci called hegemony.[20] Hegemony can be regarded as the ultimate example of a field of power that structures what people and groups do. It is sometimes referred to as a worldview, a way of thinking about the world that influences every action, and makes it difficult to even consider alternatives. But in Gramsci's analysis it is much more than this, it is a culture and set of institutions that structure life patterns and coerce a particular way of life. Susan Harding[21] gives the example of relations between whites and blacks in the South prior to the 1960s. Black inferiority and subservience were not simply ideas articulated by white racists, they were incorporated into a set of social practices: segregated schools, restrooms, swimming pools, restaurants; the black obligation to refer to white men as "Mister"; the prohibition on referring to black men as "Mister"; the use of the term "boy" for black males of any age and social status; the white right to go to the front of any line or to take the seat of any African American, and so on. Most blacks recognized the injustice and absurdity of these rules, but this did not enable them to escape, much less defy, them. White hegemony could not be overthrown simply by recognizing its existence or articulating an ideal of equality; black people had to create a movement that transformed themselves, the South, and the nation as a whole.

Hegemony is most successful, and most powerful, when it is unrecognized. White hegemony in the South was strong, but never unrecognized and rarely uncontested. White southerners would have denied, probably in all sincerity, that they exercised power: "Why our nigras are perfectly happy, that's the way they want to be treated." But many black southerners would have vigorously disputed this while talking to each other.[22] In some sense, gender relations in the 1950s embodied a hegemony even more powerful than that of race relations. Betty Friedan titled the first chapter of *The Feminine Mystique* "The Problem That Has No Name," because women literally did not have a name for, did not recognize the existence of, their oppression.[23] Women as well as men denied the existence of inequality or oppression, denied the systematic exercise of power to maintain unequal relations.

We argue that today business has enormous power and exercises effective hegemony, even though (perhaps because) this is largely undiscussed and unrecognized. *Politically*, business power today is similar to white treatment of blacks in 1959—business may sincerely deny its power, but many of the groups it exercises power over recognize it, feel dominated, resent this, and fight the power as best they can. At least until very recently, *economically*, business power was more like gender relations in 1959: Virtually no one saw this power as problematic. The revived labor movement is beginning to change this, and there are signs that a movement is beginning to contest corporate power. Nonetheless, if the issue is brought to people's attention, many still don't see a problem: "Well, so what? how else could it be? maybe we don't like it, but that's just the way things are." . . .

Hegemony is never absolute. African Americans and women both were (and are) forced to live in disadvantaged conditions, but they simultaneously fought for dignity and respect. Unusual individuals always violated conventions and tested limits. A hegemonic power is usually opposed by a counterhegemony. Thus, while children in our society are taught to compete with each other to earn the praise of authority figures, and while most children engage in this process much of the time, it is also true that the "teacher's pet" is likely to face ostracism. . . .

The Limits to Business Power

We have argued that power is more than winning an open conflict, and that business is different from other groups because its pervasive influence on our society shapes the social space for all other actors. These two arguments, however, are joined with a third: a recognition—in fact an insistence—on the limits to business power. Though we stress the power of business, business does not feel powerful. As one executive said to us:

> I really wish that our PAC in particular, and our lobbyists, had the influence that is generally perceived by the general population. If you see it written in the press, and you talk to people, they tell you about all that influence that you've got, and frankly I think that's far overplayed, as far as the influence goes. Certainly you can get access to a candidate, and certainly you can get your position known; but as far as influencing that decision, the only way you influence it is by the providing of information.

Executives believe that corporations are constantly under attack, primarily because government simply doesn't understand that business is crucial to everything the society does, but can easily be crippled by well-intentioned but unrealistic government policies. A widespread view among the people we interviewed is, "Far and away the vast majority of things that we do are literally to protect ourselves from public policy that is poorly crafted and nonresponsive to the needs and realities and circumstances of our company." These misguided policies, they feel, can come from many sources: labor unions, environmentalists, the pressure of unrealistic public interest groups, the government's constant need for money or the weight of its oppressive bureaucracy. Therefore, simply to stay even requires a pervasive effort. If attention slips for even a minute, an onerous regulation will be imposed or a precious resource taken away. To some extent such a view is an obvious consequence of the position of the people we interviewed: If business could be sure of always winning, the government relations unit (and thus the jobs of its members) would be unnecessary; if it is easy to win, PAC directors deserve little credit for company victories and much blame for defeats. But evidently the corporation agrees with them, since it devotes significant resources to political action of many kinds, including the awareness and involvement of top officials. Chief executive officers and members of the board of directors repeatedly express similar views.

Both the business view of their vulnerability, and our insistence on their power, are correct. . . .

Like the rest of us, they can usually think of other things they'd like to have but know they can't get at this time, or could win but wouldn't consider worth the price that would have to be paid. More important, the odds may be very much in their favor, their opponents may be hobbled with one hand tied behind their backs, but it is still a contest requiring pervasive effort. Once upon a time, perhaps, business could simply make its wishes known and receive what it wanted; today, corporations must form PACs, give soft money, actively lobby, make their case to the public, run advocacy ads, and engage in a whole range of costly and degrading activities that they wish were unnecessary. From the outside, we are impressed with their high success rates over a wide range of issues and with the absence of a credible challenge to the general authority of business. From the inside, corporations are impressed with the serious consequences of their occasional losses and with the unremitting effort needed to maintain their privileged position.

We have stressed that business power does not rest *only* on campaign contributions. But campaign contributions remain crucial to business power. A football analogy may be appropriate: Business's vast resources and its influence on the economy may be thought of as equivalent to a powerful offensive line, able to clear the opposition out of the way and create huge openings. But someone then has to take the ball and run through that opening. The PAC and the government relations operation are, in this analogy, like a football running back. When they carry the ball, they have to move quickly, dodge attempts to tackle them, and, if necessary, fight off an opponent and keep going. The analogy breaks down, however, because it implies a contest between evenly matched opponents. Most of the time the business situation more closely approximates a contest between an NFL team and high school opponents. The opponents just don't have the same muscle. Often they are simply intimidated, or have learned through past experience the best thing to do is get out of the way. Occasionally, however, the outclassed opponents will have so much courage and determination that they will at least score—if not win.

Notes

Editors' note: Since this article was written, there have been some changes in campaign finance law. The Bipartisan Campaign Finance Act of 2002 prohibited national parties from soliciting or spending soft money. The Federal Election Commission has, however, interpreted BCFA as permitting state and local parties to continue raising and spending soft money, and the FEC allowed national parties to set up 'independent' committees which could continue to raise and spend soft money. In return for this loophole-ridden limit on the use of soft money, individual contributions to candidates were increased to $2000 per election, with an upper limit of $37,500 contributed to candidates in an election cycle. As a result, BCFA appears to be, at best, a cosmetic change to the role that money plays in election campaigns.

1. *Boston Globe*, November 8, 1996, p. A26.
2. *New York Times*, September 3, 1997, p. A18.

3. In 1976, 48 percent of House members' campaign receipts came from individual contributions of less than $500; in 1988, only 27 percent did ("Money and Politics: A Special Report," *National Journal*, June 16, 1990). In the 1996 elections, this remained nearly constant at approximately 28 percent (FEC online WWW publication).

4. For quotations in this and the preceding paragraph, see, "Money and Politics," *National Journal*, p. 1448.

5. "Money and Politics," *National Journal*, pp. 1462, 1460.

6. *Boston Globe*, February 14, 1996, p. A11.

7. *New York Times*, November, 1, 1996, p. A1.

8. Boschwitz, quoted in Brooks Jackson, *Honest Graft: Big Money and the American Political Process* (New York: Knopf, 1988), pp. 251–252. Emphasis in book. (Obviously, the secret memo didn't stay secret.) Boschwitz's 1990 strategy backfired. He discouraged the most "promising" Democratic candidates, but Paul Wellstone—a true long shot by all accounts—beat him, despite Boschwitz's 4 to 1 spending advantage. In the 1996 rematch between the two candidates, Wellstone outspent Boschwitz and won handily.

9. "Members" is the term most often used to refer to what once were called "congressmen." The term has the advantage of being gender neutral, and can refer either to senators or to House representatives. It will be our term of choice in this book, though some corporate executives still use the older form, so it will appear in some quotations.

10. Quoted in Elizabeth Drew, *Whatever it Takes: The Real Struggle for Political Power in America* (New York: Viking, 1997), pp. 19–20.

11. David Donnelly, Janice Fine, and Ellen S. Miller, "Going Public," *Boston Review*, April–May 1997. Larry Makinson, "The Big Picture: Money Follows Power Shift on Capitol Hill" (Washington, D.C.: Center for Responsive Politics, 1997, www.crp.org).

12. www.fec.gov.

13. Makinson, "The Big Picture."

14. While most new CEOs do not ask for any changes in PAC behavior, their right to do so is not contested. One PAC official identified himself as a conservative Republican who had attended the 1988 Republican National Convention as a delegate. Until recently the PAC had followed roughly that same orientation, but he told us that the PAC was going to become much more bipartisan due to the accession of a new CEO with strong ties to the Democratic party. As a loyal corporate employee (who wanted to keep his job), he strongly endorsed this shift.

15. His reference is to a bygone era.

16. Leonard Silk and David Vogel, *Ethics and Profits* (New York: Simon & Schuster, 1976), p. 43.

17. Their views on this, as on other issues, are sometimes complicated and contradictory, and at other points in the same interview the respondent might take a different position.

18. In Japan CEOs get an average of $300,000, or 17 times as much as workers. For an analysis of CEO pay, and information on how to get details on the pay for specific CEOs, see *America@Work* (May/June 1997), published by the AFL–CIO.

19. Quoted in Kevin Phillips, *The Politics of Rich and Poor: Wealth and the American Electorate in the Reagan Aftermath* (New York: Random House, 1990), p. 32.

20. Antonio Gramsci, *Selections From The Prison Notebooks of Antonio Gramsci*, ed. and trans. Quintin Hoare and Geoffrey Nowell Smith (New York: International Publishers, 1972).

21. Susan Harding, "Reconstructing Order through Action: Jim Crow and the Southern Civil Rights Movement." In *Statemaking and Social Movements: Essays in History and Theory*, ed. Charles Bright and Susan Harding (Ann Arbor: University of Michigan Press, 1984), pp. 378–402.

22. Or if talking to whites in circumstances where they felt secure in articulating their real feelings.

23. Betty Friedan, *The Feminine Mystique* (New York: Norton, 1963).

THE TYRANNY OF THE MAJORITY

Lani Guinier

I have always wanted to be a civil rights lawyer. This lifelong ambition is based on a deep-seated commitment to democratic fair play—to playing by the rules as long as the rules are fair. When the rules seem unfair, I have worked to change them, not subvert them. When I was eight years old, I was a Brownie. I was especially proud of my uniform, which represented a commitment to good citizenship and good deeds. But one day, when my Brownie group staged a hatmaking contest, I realized that uniforms are only as honorable as the people who wear them. The contest was rigged. The winner was assisted by her milliner mother, who actually made the winning entry in full view of all the participants. At the time, I was too young to be able to change the rules, but I was old enough to resign, which I promptly did.

To me, fair play means that the rules encourage everyone to play. They should reward those who win, but they must be acceptable to those who lose. The central theme of my academic writing is that not all rules lead to elemental fair play. Some even commonplace rules work against it.

The professional milliner competing with amateur Brownies stands as an example of rules that are patently rigged or patently subverted. Yet, sometimes, even when rules are perfectly fair in form, they serve in practice to exclude particular groups from meaningful participation. When they do not encourage everyone to play, or when, over the long haul, they do not make the losers feel as good about the outcomes as the winners, they can seem as unfair as the milliner who makes the winning hat for her daughter.

Sometimes, too, we construct rules that force us to be divided into winners and losers when we might have otherwise joined together. This idea was cogently expressed by my son, Nikolas, when he was four years old, far exceeding the thoughtfulness of his mother when she was an eight-year-old Brownie. While I was writing one of my law journal articles, Nikolas and I had a conversation about voting prompted by a *Sesame Street Magazine* exercise. The magazine pictured six children: four children had raised their hands because they wanted to play tag; two had their hands down because they wanted to play hide-and-seek. The magazine asked its readers to count the number of children whose hands were raised and then decide what game the children would play.

Nikolas quite realistically replied, "They will play both. First they will play tag. Then they will play hide-and-seek." Despite the magazine's "rules," he was right. To children, it is natural to take turns. The winner may get to play first or more often, but even the "loser" gets something. His was a positive-sum solution that many adult rule-makers ignore.

The traditional answer to the magazine's problem would have been zero-sum solution: "The children—all the children—will play tag, and only tag." As a zero-sum solution, everything is seen in terms of "I win; you lose." The conventional answer relies on winner-take-all majority rule, in which the tag players, as the majority, win the right to decide for all the children what game to play. The hide-and-seek preference becomes irrelevant. The numerically more powerful majority choice simply subsumes minority preferences.

In the conventional case, the majority that rules gains all the power and the minority that loses gets none. For example, two years ago Brother Rice High School in Chicago held two senior proms. It was not planned that way. The prom committee at Brother Rice, a boys' Catholic high school, expected just one prom when it hired a disc jockey, picked a rock band, and selected music for the prom by consulting student preferences. Each senior was asked to list his three favorite songs, and the band would play the songs that appeared most frequently on the lists.

Seems attractively democratic. But Brother Rice is predominantly white, and the prom committee was all white. That's how they got two proms. The black seniors at Brother Rice felt so shut out by the "democratic process" that they organized their own prom. As one black student put it: "For every vote we had, there were eight votes for what they wanted. . . . [W]ith us being in the minority we're always outvoted. It's as if we don't count."

Some embittered white seniors saw things differently. They complained that the black students should have gone along with the majority: "The majority makes a decision. That's the way it works."

In a way, both groups were right. From the white students' perspective, this was ordinary decisionmaking. To the black students, majority rule sent the message: "we don't count" is the "way it works" for minorities. In a racially divided society, majority rule may be perceived as majority tyranny.

That is a large claim, and I do not rest my case for it solely on the actions of the prom committee in one Chicago high school. To expand the range of the argument, I first consider the ideal of majority rule itself, particularly as reflected in the writings of James Madison and other founding members of our Republic. These early democrats explored the relationship between majority rule and democracy. James Madison warned, "If a majority be united by a common interest, the rights of the minority will be insecure." The tyranny of the majority, according to Madison, requires safeguards to protect "one part of the society against the injustice of the other part."

For Madison, majority tyranny represented the great danger to our early constitutional democracy. Although the American revolution was fought against the tyranny of the British monarch, it soon became clear that there was another tyranny to be avoided. The accumulations of all powers in the same hands, Madison warned, "whether of one, a few, or many, and whether hereditary, self-appointed, or elective, may justly be pronounced the very definition of tyranny."

■ ■ ■ ■

The debate about majority tyranny reflected Madison's concern that the majority may not represent the whole. In a homogeneous society, the interest of the majority would likely be that of the minority also. But in a heterogeneous community, the majority may not represent all competing interests. The majority is likely to be self-interested and ignorant or indifferent to the concerns of the minority. In such case, Madison observed, the assumption that the majority represents the minority is "altogether fictitious."

Yet even a self-interested majority can govern fairly if it cooperates with the minority. One reason for such cooperation is that the self-interested majority values the principle of reciprocity. The self-interested majority worries that the minority may attract defectors from the majority and become the next governing majority. The Golden Rule principle of reciprocity functions to check the tendency of a self-interested majority to act tyrannically.

So the argument for the majority principle connects it with the value of reciprocity: You cooperate when you lose in part because members of the current majority will cooperate when they lose. The conventional case for the fairness of majority rule is that it is not really the rule of a fixed group—The Majority—on all issues; instead it is the rule of shifting majorities, as the losers at one time or on one issue join with others and become part of the governing coalition at another time or on another issue. The result will be a fair system of mutually beneficial cooperation. I call a majority that rules but does not dominate a Madisonian Majority.

The problem of majority tyranny arises, however, when the self-interested majority does not need to worry about defectors. When the majority is fixed and permanent, there are no checks on its ability to be overbearing. A majority that does not worry about defectors is a majority with total power.

In such a case, Madison's concern about majority tyranny arises. In a heterogeneous community, any faction with total power might subject "the minority to the caprice and arbitrary decisions of the majority, who instead of consulting the interest of the whole community collectively, attend sometimes to partial and local advantages."

"What remedy can be found in a republican Government, where the majority must ultimately decide," argued Madison, but to ensure "that no one common interest or passion will be likely to unite a majority of the whole number in an unjust pursuit." The answer was to disaggregate the majority to ensure checks and balances or fluid, rotating interests. The minority needed protection against an overbearing majority, so that "a common sentiment is less likely to be felt, and the requisite concert less likely to be formed, by a majority of the whole."

Political struggles would not be simply a contest between rulers and people; the political struggles would be among the people themselves. The work of government was not to transcend different interests but to reconcile them. In an ideal democracy, the people would rule, but the minorities would also be protected against the power of majorities. Again, where the rules of decisionmaking protect the minority, the Madisonian Majority rules without dominating.

But if a group is unfairly treated, for example, when it forms a racial minority, *and* if the problems of unfairness are not cured by conventional assumptions about majority rule, then what is to be done? The answer is that we may need an *alternative* to winner-take-all majoritarianism. . . .

In my legal writing, I follow the caveat of James Madison and other early American democrats. I explore decisionmaking rules that might work in a multi-racial society to ensure that majority rule does not become majority tyranny. I pursue voting systems that might disaggregate The Majority so that it does not exercise power unfairly or tyrannically. I aspire to a more cooperative political style of decisionmaking to enable all of the students at Brother Rice to feel comfortable attending the same prom. In looking to create Madisonian Majorities, I pursue a positive-sum, taking-turns solution.

Structuring decisionmaking to allow the minority "a turn" may be necessary to restore the reciprocity ideal when a fixed majority refuses to cooperate with the minority. If the fixed majority loses its incentive to follow the Golden Rule principle of shifting majorities, the minority never gets to take a turn. Giving the minority a turn does not mean the minority gets to rule; what it does mean is that the minority gets to influence decisionmaking and the majority rules more legitimately.

Instead of automatically rewarding the preferences of the monolithic majority, a taking-turns approach anticipates that the majority rules, but is not overbearing. Because those with 51 percent of the votes are not assured 100 percent of the power, the majority cooperates with, or at least does not tyrannize, the minority.

The sports analogy of "I win; you lose" competition within a political hierarchy makes sense when only one team can win; Nikolas's intuition that it is often possible to take turns suggests an alternative approach. Take family decisionmaking, for example. It utilizes a taking-turns approach. When parents sit around the kitchen table deciding on a vacation destination or activities for a rainy day, often they do not simply rely on a show of hands, especially if that means that the older children always prevail or if affinity groups among the children (those who prefer movies to video games, or those who prefer baseball to playing cards) never get to play their activity of choice. Instead of allowing the majority simply to rule, the parents may propose that everyone take turns, going to the movies one night and playing video games the next. Or as Nikolas proposes, they might do both on a given night.

Taking turns attempts to build consensus while recognizing political or social differences, and it encourages everyone to play. The taking-turns approach gives those with the most support more turns, but it also legitimates the outcome from each individual's perspective, including those whose views are shared only by a minority.

In the end, I do not believe that democracy should encourage rule by the powerful—even a powerful majority. Instead, the ideal of democracy promises a fair discussion among self-defined equals about how to achieve our common aspirations. To redeem that promise, we need to put the idea of taking turns and disaggregating the majority at the center of our conception of representation. Particularly as we move into the twenty-first century as a more highly diversified citizenry, it is essential that we consider the ways in which voting and representational systems succeed or fail at encouraging Madisonian Majorities.

To use Nikolas's terminology, "it is no fair" if a fixed, tyrannical majority excludes or alienates the minority. It is no fair if a fixed, tyrannical majority monopolizes all the power all the time. It is no fair if we engage in the periodic ritual of elections, but only the permanent majority gets to choose who is elected. Where we have tyranny by The Majority, we do not have genuine democracy.

My life's work, with the essential assistance of people like Nikolas, has been to try to find the rules that can best bring us together as a democratic society. . . . I have a predisposition, reflected in my son's yearning for a positive-sum solution, to seek an integrated body politic in which all perspectives are represented and in which all people work together to find common ground. I advocate empowering voters and their representatives in ways that give even minority voters a chance to influence legislative outcomes.

But those in the majority do not lose; they simply learn to take turns. This is a positive-sum solution that allows all voters to feel that they participate meaningfully in the decisionmaking process. This is a positive-sum solution that makes legislative outcomes more legitimate.

My work did not arise in a vacuum. . . . There have been three generations of attempts to curb tyrannical majorities. The first generation focused directly on access to the ballot on the assumption that the right to vote by itself is "preservative of all other rights." During the civil rights movement, aggrieved citizens asserted that "tyrannical majorities" in various locales were ganging up to deny black voters access to the voting booth.

The 1965 Voting Rights Act and its amendments forcefully addressed this problem. The act outlawed literacy tests, brought federal registrars to troubled districts to ensure safe access to polls, and targeted for federal administrative review many local registration procedures. Success under the act was immediate and impressive. The number of blacks registered to vote rose dramatically within five years after passage.

The second generation of voting rights litigation and legislation focused on the Southern response to increased black registration. Southern states and local subdivisions responded to blacks in the electorate by switching the way elections were conducted to ensure that newly voting blacks could not wield any influence. By changing, for example, from neighborhood-based districts to jurisdiction-wide at-large representatives, those in power ensured that although blacks could vote, and even run for office, they could not win. At-large elections allowed a unified white bloc to control all the elected positions. As little as 51 percent of the population could decide 100 percent of the elections, and the black minority was permanently excluded from meaningful participation.

In response, the second generation of civil rights activism focused on "qualitative vote dilution." Although everyone had a vote, it was apparent that some people's votes were qualitatively less important than others. The concerns raised by the second generation of civil rights activists led Congress to amend the Voting Rights Act. In 1982, congressional concern openly shifted from simply getting blacks the ability to register and vote to providing blacks a realistic opportunity to elect candidates of their choice. Thus, the new focus was on electing more black officials, primarily through the elimination of at-large districts, and their replacement by majority-black single-member districts. Even if whites continued to refuse to vote for blacks, there would be a few districts in which whites were in the minority and powerless to veto black candidates. The distinctive group interests of the black community, which Congress found had been ignored in the at-large, racially polarized elections, were thus given a voice within decisionmaking councils.

The second generation sought to integrate physically the body politic. It was assumed that disaggregating the winner-take-all at-large majority would create political access for black voters, who would use that access to elect black representatives.

In many places, second-generation fights continue today. A number of redistricting schemes have been challenged in court, and not all courts agree on the outcomes, let alone the enterprise itself. Nevertheless, few disagree that blacks continue to be underrepresented in federal, state, and local government.

Even in governments in which minority legislators have increased, the marginalization of minority group interests has often stubbornly remained. Third-generation cases have now begun to respond. Third-generation cases recognize that it is sometimes not enough simply to ensure that minorities have a fair opportunity to elect someone to a legislative body. Under some unusual circumstances, it may be necessary to police the legislative voting rules whereby a majority consistently rigs the process to exclude a minority.

The Supreme Court's recent decision in *Presley v. Etowah County* heralds the arrival of this concern. Although black representatives for the first time since Reconstruction enjoyed a seat on the local county commission in Etowah and Russell counties in Alabama, they did not enjoy much else. Because of second-generation redistricting, black county commissioners were elected to county governing bodies in the two counties. Immediately upon their election, however, the white incumbents changed the rules for allocating decisionmaking authority. Just like the grandfather clauses, the literacy tests, the white primary, and other ingenious strategies devised to enforce white supremacy in the past, rules were changed to evade the reach of the earlier federal court decree.

In one county the newly integrated commission's duties were shifted to an appointed administrator. In the other county, its duties were shifted from individual commissioners to the entire commission voting by majority rule. Because voting on the commission, like voting in the county electorate followed racial lines, "majority rule" meant that whites controlled the outcome of every legislative decision. The incumbents defended this power grab as simply the decision of a bona-fide majority.

This happened as well in Texas when the first Latina was elected to a local school board. The white majority suddenly decided that two votes were henceforth necessary to get an item on the agenda. In Louisiana, the legislature enacted a districting plan drawn up by a group of whites in a secret meeting in the subbasement of the state capital, a meeting from which all black legislators were excluded.

Through these three generations of problems and remedies, a long trail of activists has preceded me. In 1964, ballot access was defended eloquently by Dr. Martin Luther King, Jr., and Fannie Lou Hamer. In 1982, redistricting was the consensus solution to electoral exclusion championed by the NAACP, the League of Women Voters, the Mexican-American Legal Defense Fund, and many others.

My ideas follow in this tradition. They are not undemocratic or out of the mainstream. Between 1969 and 1993, the Justice Department under both Democratic and Republican presidents disapproved as discriminatory over one hundred sets of voting rules involving changes to majority voting. None of these rules was unfair in the abstract, but all were exclusionary in practice. President Bush's chief civil rights enforcer declared some of them to be "electoral steroids for white candidates" because they manipulated the election system to ensure that only white candidates won.

This history of struggle against tyrannical majorities enlightens us to the dangers of winner-take-all collective decisionmaking. Majority rule, which presents an efficient opportunity for determining the public good, suffers when it is not constrained by the need to bargain with minority interests. When majorities are fixed, the minority lacks any mechanism for holding the majority to account or even to listen. Nor does such majority rule promote deliberation or consensus. The permanent majority simply has its way, without reaching out to or convincing anyone else.

Any form of less-than-unanimous voting introduces the danger that some group will be in the minority and the larger group will exploit the numerically smaller group. This is especially problematic to defeated groups that do not possess a veto over proposals and acts that directly affect them or implicate concerns they value intensely. Thus, the potential for instability exists when any significant group of people ends up as permanent losers.

The fundamentally important question of political stability is how to induce losers to continue to play the game. Political stability depends on the perception that the system is fair to induce losers to continue to work within the system rather than to try to overthrow it. When the minority experiences the alienation of complete and consistent defeat, they lack incentive to respect laws passed by the majority over their opposition.

. . . The problem is that majoritarian systems do not necessarily create winners who share in power. Politics becomes a battle for total victory rather than a method of governing open to all significant groups.

This is what happened in Phillips County, Arkansas, where a majority-vote runoff requirement unfairly rewarded the preferences of a white bloc-voting majority and, for more than half a century, excluded a permanent voting minority. Predominantly rural and poor, Phillips County has a history of extremely polarized voting: Whites vote exclusively for white candidates and blacks vote for black candidates whenever they can. In many elections, no white person ever publicly supports or endorses a black candidate. Although qualified, highly regarded black candidates compete, local election rules and the manipulation of those rules by a white bloc have meant that no black person in over a century had been elected to any countywide office when I brought a lawsuit in 1987. Yet blacks were just less than half of the voting-age population.

Reverend Julious McGruder, a black political candidate and a former school board member, testified on the basis of fifteen years of working in elections that "no white candidate or white person has come out and supported [a] black." Black attorney Sam Whitfield won a primary and requested support in the runoff from Kenneth Stoner, a white candidate he had defeated in the first round. In a private conversation, Stoner told Whitfield that he personally thought Whitfield was the better remaining candidate but that he could not support him. As Whitfield recounted the conversation at trial, Stoner said, "He could not support a black man. He lives in this town. He is a farmer. His wife teaches school here and that there is just no way that he could support a black candidate."

Racially polarized voting is only one of the political disadvantages for blacks in Phillips County. Blacks, whose median income is less than three thousand dollars annually, also suffer disproportionately from poverty, which works to impede their effective participation in the political process. For example, 42 percent of blacks have no car or truck, while only 9 percent of the white population are similarly encumbered; and 30 percent of blacks, compared to 11 percent of whites, have no telephone. Thus isolated by poverty, black voters are less able to maneuver around such obstacles as frequent, last-minute changes in polling places. County officials have moved polling places ten times in as many elections, often without prior notice and sometimes to locations up to twelve to fifteen miles away, over dirt and gravel roads. Moreover, because of the relative scarcity of cars, the lack of public transportation in the county, and the expense of taxis, the election campaigns of black candidates must include a get-out-and-vote kind of funding effort that a poor black community simply cannot afford.

Black candidates who win the first round come up against one particular local election rule—the majority vote runoff law—that doubles the access problem, by requiring people to get to the polls two times within a two-week period. Because this rule combines with local racism, almost half the voters for over a century never enjoyed any opportunity to choose who represents them. As a numerical, stigmatized, and racially isolated minority, blacks regarded the majority vote requirement as simply a tool to "steal the election"—a tool that had the effect of demobilizing black political participation, enhancing polarization rather than fostering debate, and in general excluding black interests from the political process. As Rev. McGruder testified, running twice to win once "*just kill*[*s*] *all the momentum, all of the hope, all of the faith, the belief in the system.*" Many voters "really can't understand the situation where you say 'You know, Brother Whitfield won last night' and then come up to a grandma or my uncle, auntie and say 'Hey, you know, we're going to have to run again in the next 10 days and—because we've got a runoff.'"

In fact, between the first and second elections, turnout drops precipitously, so that the so-called majority winner in the runoff may receive fewer votes than the plurality winner in the first primary. In fact, in all three black-white runoff contests in 1986, the white runoff victor's majority occurred only because the number of people who came out to vote in the second primary went down.

Indeed, the district court that heard the challenge in 1988 to the Arkansas law did not dispute the facts: that no black candidate had ever been elected to countywide or state legislative office from Phillips County and that "race has frequently dominated over qualifications and issues" in elections. The court, nonetheless, preferred to stick with this obviously unfair electoral scheme, reasoning that The Majority should prevail even when The Majority is the product of a completely artificial and racially exclusionary runoff system. It is decisions like this one that continue to inspire me to work for a better way.

The court failed to see that the unfairness wrought by winner-take-all majority rule was inconsistent with democratic fair play in this county. At first blush, the unfairness of 51 percent of the people winning 100 percent of the power may not seem obvious. It certainly seems to be much less than the unfairness of a professional hatmaker's competing against kids. But in some ways it is worse. For example, when voters are drawn into participating by seemingly fair rules, only to discover that the rules systematically work against their interests, they are likely to feel seduced and abandoned. Moreover, those Brownies who made their own hats could at least be assured that others would sympathize with their having been taken advantage of. People who have been systematically victimized by winner-take-all majority rules usually get little sympathy from a society that wrongfully equates majority tyranny with democracy.

As the plaintiffs' evidence demonstrated, this was precisely the situation in Phillips County, where the fairness of the majority requirement was destroyed by extreme racial polarization, the absence of reciprocity, and the artificial majorities created in the runoffs. Judge Richard Arnold put it simply in a related case: Implementation of the majority vote requirement in eastern Arkansas represented a pattern of actions in which "a systematic and deliberate attempt" was made to "close off" avenues of opportunity to blacks in the affected jurisdictions.

In other words, my project has been to return the inquiry to its most authoritative source—the voters themselves. For example, Milagros Robledo, a Latino voter in Philadelphia, is one of many voters who say they are angry, confused and more cynical than ever about the political process. After a recent scandal involving the solicitation of absentee ballots in a hotly contested local election, Mr. Robledo lamented, "After going through this whole thing, I now really know the value of my vote. It means nothing to me, and it means a lot to the politicians." For Mr. Robledo, his community has continuously been shortchanged by elected officials who are more interested in getting elected than in representing the people.

I take my cue from people like Milagros Robledo. I seek to keep their faith that votes should not count more than voters. I struggle to conceptualize the representatives' relationship with voters to make that relationship more dynamic and interactive.

It is in the course of this struggle that I made my much maligned references to "the authenticity assumption." Authenticity is a concept I describe within my general criticism of conventional empowerment strategies. The Voting Rights Act expressly provides that black and Latino voters must be afforded an equal opportunity "to participate in the political process and to elect representatives of their choice." The question is: which candidates are the representatives of choice of black or Latino voters?

Authenticity subsumes two related but competing views to answer that question. The first version of authenticity seeks information from election results to learn how the voters perceive elected officials. In this view, voting behavior is key. Authentic representatives are simply those truly chosen by the people. The second authenticity assumption is that voters trust elected officials who "look like" or act like the voters themselves. In this view, authenticity refers to a candidate who shares common physical or cultural traits with constituents. In this aspect of authenticity, the nominally cultural becomes political.

Despite the importance of voter choice in assessing minority preferred or minority sponsored candidates, those who support the second authenticity assumption substitute the concept of presumptive or descriptive representativeness in which candidates who look like their constituents are on that basis alone presumed to be representative. In the name of authenticity, these observers have argued that the current voting rights litigation model is effective because it provides blacks or Latinos an opportunity to elect physically black or culturally Latino representatives. This is an understandable position, and I present it as such, but it is not *my* position. Indeed, I term it "a limited empowerment concept."

My preference is for the first view of authenticity, the one that focuses on the voter, not the candidate. In *Thornburg v. Gingles*, a 1986 Supreme Court opinion, Justice William Brennan stressed that it is the "status of the candidate as the chosen representative of a particular racial group, not the race of the candidate, that is important."

This leads to two complementary conclusions that are firmly embedded in the caselaw and the literature. First, white candidates can legitimately represent nonwhite voters if those voters elected them. . . . And second, the election of a black or Latino candidate or two will not defeat a voting rights lawsuit, especially if those black or Latino elected officials did not receive electoral support from their community. Just because a candidate is black does not mean that he or she is the candidate of choice of the black community.

Borrowing from the language of the statute, I say voters, not politicians, should count. And voters count most when voters can exercise a real choice based on what the candidates think and do rather than what the candidates look like.

■ ■ ■ ■

. . . I look at the *procedural* rules by which preferences are identified and counted. Procedural rules govern the process by which outcomes are decided. They are the rules by which the game is played.

I have been roundly, and falsely, criticized for focusing on outcomes. Outcomes are indeed relevant, but *not* because I seek to advance particular ends, such as whether the children play tag or hide-and-seek, or whether the band at Brother Rice plays rock music or rap. Rather, I look to outcomes as *evidence* of whether all the children—or all the high school seniors—feel that their choice is represented and considered. The purpose is not to guarantee "equal legislative outcomes"; equal opportunity to *influence* legislative outcomes regardless of race is more like it.

For these reasons, I sometimes explore alternatives to simple, winner-take-all majority rule. I do not advocate any one procedural rule as a universal panacea for unfairness. Nor do I propose these remedies primarily as judicial solutions. They can be adopted only in the context of litigation after the court first finds a legal violation.

Outside of litigation, I propose these approaches as political solutions if, depending on the local context, they better approximate the goals of democratic fair play. One such decision-making alternative is called cumulative voting, which could give all the students at Brother Rice multiple votes and allow them to distribute their votes in any combination of their choice. If each student could vote for ten songs, the students could plump or aggregate their votes to reflect the intensity of their preferences. They could put ten votes on one song; they could put five votes on two songs. If a tenth of the students opted to "cumulate" or plump all their votes for one song, they would be able to select one of every ten or so songs played at the prom. The black seniors could have done this if they chose to, but so could any other cohesive group of sufficient size. In this way, the songs preferred by a majority would be played most often, but the songs the minority enjoyed would also show up on the play list.

Under cumulative voting, voters get the same number of votes as there are seats or options to vote for, and they can then distribute their votes in any combination to reflect their preferences. Like-minded voters can vote as a solid bloc or, instead, form strategic, cross-racial coalitions to gain mutual benefits. This system is emphatically not racially based; it allows voters to organize themselves on whatever basis they wish.

Corporations use this system to ensure representation of minority shareholders on corporate boards of directors. Similarly, some local municipal and county governments have adopted cumulative voting to ensure representation of minority voters. Instead of awarding political power to geographic units called districts, cumulative voting allows voters to cast ballots based on what they think rather than where they live.

Cumulative voting is based on the principle of one person–one vote because each voter gets the same total number of votes. Everyone's preferences are counted equally. It is not a particularly radical idea; thirty states either require or permit corporations to use this election system. Cumulative voting is certainly not antidemocratic because it emphasizes the importance of voter choice in selecting public or social policy. And it is neither liberal nor conservative. Both the Reagan and Bush administrations approved cumulative voting schemes pursuant to the Voting Rights Act to protect the rights of racial- and language-minority voters.

But, as in Chilton County, Alabama, which now uses cumulative voting to elect both the school board and the county commission, any politically cohesive group can vote strategically to win representation. Groups of voters win representation depending on the exclusion threshold, meaning the percentage of votes needed to win one seat or have the band play one song. That threshold can be set case by case, jurisdiction by jurisdiction, based on the size of minority groups that make compelling claims for representation.

Normally the exclusion threshold in a head-to-head contest is 50 percent, which means that only groups that can organize a majority can get elected. But if multiple seats (or multiple songs) are considered simultaneously, the exclusion threshold is considerably reduced. For example, in Chilton County, with seven seats elected simultaneously on each governing body, the threshold of exclusion is now one-eighth. Any group with the solid support of one-eighth the voting population cannot be denied representation. This is because any self-identified minority can plump or cumulate all its votes for one candidate. Again, minorities are not defined solely in racial terms.

As it turned out in Chilton County, both blacks and Republicans benefited from this new system. The school board and commission now each have three white Democrats, three white Republicans, and one black Democrat. Previously, when each seat was decided in a head-to-head contest, the majority not only ruled but monopolized. Only white Democrats were elected at every prior election during this century.

■ ■ ■ ■

As a solution that permits voters to self-select their identities, cumulative voting also encourages cross-racial coalition building. No one is locked into a minority identity. Nor is anyone necessarily isolated by the identity they choose. Voters can strengthen their influence by forming coalitions to elect more than one representative or to select a range of music more compatible with the entire student body's preferences.

Women too can use cumulative voting to gain greater representation. Indeed, in other countries with similar, alternative voting systems, women are more likely to be represented in the national legislature. For example, in some Western European democracies, the national legislatures have as many as 37 percent female members compared to a little more than 5 percent in our Congress.

There is a final benefit from cumulative voting. It eliminates gerrymandering. By denying protected incumbents safe seats in gerrymandered districts, cumulative voting might encourage more voter participation. With greater interest-based electoral competition, cumulative voting could promote the political turnover sought by advocates of term limits. In this way, cumulative voting serves many of the same ends as periodic elections or rotation in office, a solution that Madison and others advocated as a means of protecting against permanent majority factions.

A different remedial voting tool, one that I have explored more cautiously, is supermajority voting. It modifies winner-take-all majority rule to require that something more than a bare majority of voters must approve or concur before action is taken. As a uniform decisional rule, a supermajority empowers any numerically small but cohesive group of voters. Like cumulative voting, it is race-neutral. Depending on the issue, different members of the voting body can "veto" impending action.

Supermajority remedies give bargaining power to all numerically inferior or less powerful groups, be they black, female, or Republican. . . . The same concept of a minority veto yielded the Great Compromise in which small-population states are equally represented in the Senate.

I have never advocated (or imagined) giving an individual member of a legislative body a personal veto. Moreover, I have discussed these kinds of exceptional remedies as the subject of court-imposed solutions only when there has been a violation of the statute and only when they make sense in the context of a particular case. I discuss supermajority rules as a judicial remedy only in cases where the court finds proof of consistent and deeply engrained polarization. It was never my intent that supermajority requirements should be the norm for all legislative bodies, or that simple majority voting would ever in itself constitute a statutory or constitutional violation.

Both the Reagan and Bush administrations took a similar remedial approach to enforcement of the Voting Rights Act. In fact, it was the Reagan administration that *approved* the use of supermajority rules as a remedial measure in places like Mobile, Alabama, where the special five-out-of-seven supermajority threshold is still in place today and is credited with increasing racial harmony in that community.

But—and here I come directly to the claims of my critics—some apparently fear that remedies for extreme voting abuses, remedies like cumulative voting or the Mobile supermajority, constitute "quotas"—racial preferences to ensure minority rule. While cumulative voting, or a supermajority, is quite conventional in many cases and race neutral, to order it as a remedy apparently opens up possibilities of nonmajoritarianism that many seem to find quite threatening.

Indeed, while my nomination was pending, I was called "antidemocratic" for suggesting that majority voting rules may not fairly resolve conflict when the majority and minority are permanently divided.* But alternatives to majority voting rules in a racially polarized environment are too easily dismissed by this label. As Chief Justice Burger wrote for the Supreme Court, "There is nothing in the language of the Constitution, our history, or our cases that requires that a majority always prevail on every issue." In other words, there is *nothing inherent in democracy that requires majority rule.* It is simply a custom that works efficiently when the majority and minority are fluid, are not monolithic, and are not permanent.

Other democracies frequently employ alternatives to winner-take-all majority voting. Indeed, only five Western democracies, including Britain and the United States, still use single-member-district, winner-take-all systems of representation. Germany, Spain, the Netherlands, and Sweden, among other countries, elect their legislatures under some alternative to winner-take-all majority voting. As the *New Yorker*, in a comment on my nomination, observed, President Clinton was right in calling some of my ideas "difficult to defend," but only because "Americans, by and large, are ignorant of the existence, let alone the details, of electoral systems other than their own."

No one who had done their homework seriously questioned the fundamentally democratic nature of my ideas. Indeed, columnists who attacked my ideas during my nomination ordeal have praised ideas, in a different context, that are remarkably similar to my own. Lally Weymouth wrote, "There can't be democracy in South Africa without a measure of formal protection for minorities." George Will has opined, "The Framers also understood that stable, tyrannical majorities can best be prevented by the multiplication of minority interests, so the majority at any moment will be just a transitory coalition of minorities." In my law journal articles, I expressed exactly the same reservations about unfettered majority rule and about the need sometimes to disaggregate the majority to ensure fair and effective representation for all substantial interests.

The difference is that the minority I used to illustrate my academic point was not, as it was for Lally Weymouth, the white minority in South Africa. Nor, did I write, as George Will did, about the minority of well-to-do landlords in New York City. I wrote instead about the political exclusion of the black minority in many local county and municipal governing bodies in America.

Yet these same two journalists and many others condemned me as antidemocratic. Apparently, it is not controversial to provide special protections for affluent landlords or minorities in South Africa but it is "divisive," "radical," and "out of the mainstream" to provide similar remedies to black Americans who, after centuries of racial oppression, are still excluded.

■ ■ ■ ■

. . . My vision of fairness and justice imagines a full and effective voice for all citizens. . . . I have tried to show that democracy in a heterogeneous society is incompatible with rule by a racial monopoly of any color.

■ ■ ■ ■

I hope we rediscover the bold solution to the tyranny of The Majority, which has always been more democracy, not less.

Note

Editors' note: During Bill Clinton's first term, Lani Guinier was nominated to be assistant attorney general for civil rights. In the face of vicious and unfounded criticism of her work by the right, her nomination was withdrawn.

*See editors' note at end of reading.

SECTION IV
THE WELFARE STATE

As we have seen, the state is one of, and perhaps the most, important institutions through which the power of the dominant class is organized. At the same time, however, officials must be sensitive to the need to ensure that citizens see state policies as legitimate; public policy that is too blatantly supportive of the dominant class at the expense of others will likely cause social unrest. Thus, the state is caught in a contradiction: In its support of capitalism it contributes to the expansion of social inequality, while its need for legitimacy requires that its policies (at least marginally) acknowledge and reduce social inequality. The development of the modern welfare state following the Great Depression of the 1930s was an attempt to resolve this contradiction. The mass unemployment and poverty that characterized that period brought with it an explosion of organizing efforts among the poor, the unemployed, small farmers, and industrial workers that threatened the fundamental social relations of capitalism (Zinn 1995). In Gramscian terms, the creation of a welfare state was a concession made by the dominant class to maintain hegemony during a period of crisis for U.S. capitalism.

After a long history in which the necessity for nonmarket forms of social provision was denied by political, economic, and cultural authorities, the creation of the welfare state was a powerful victory. That this victory simultaneously reproduced existing social inequalities is clear from examining its structure. The United States has a two-tiered welfare state consisting of social insurance programs such as Social Security and Medicare, which are financed through payroll taxes and provide benefits to all regardless of income on the basis of citizenship, and public assistance ("welfare") programs such as Temporary Assistance for Needy Families (which replaced Aid to Families with Dependent Children in 1996), Medicaid, and food stamps, which are financed through general revenues and are available only to those who have incomes below a certain level. The recipients of social insurance have historically been seen by major social institutions as "deserving," by which is meant they have paid into the system through their payroll taxes and their need is based on circumstances, such as age or illness, that are beyond their control. In contrast, the recipients of welfare have been defined as "undeserving" in that they are seen as not contributing to society through work (and so working citizens are said to bear the cost of caring for them) and the causes of their poverty are assumed to lie in their own misbehavior (Gans 1995). This distinction between "deserving" and "undeserving" recipients of state assistance is the main organizing principle of a welfare state that is the least comprehensive and least generous, and has the least effect in reducing poverty, of any major capitalist country (Kloby 2003; Marger 2002).

Frances Fox Piven and Richard A. Cloward argue that the history of welfare is one of enforcing low wages and class inequality. They argue that welfare is a form of social control that expands during periods of social conflict (for example, the 1930s and 1960s) and contracts during periods in which business dominance has been restored (for example, the 1980s and 1990s). Welfare is thus seen as a material concession that the ruling class makes to reintegrate subordinate groups and demobilize potentially threatening challenges to its authority. At the same time, however, welfare cannot be so comfortable that it attracts people away from work. As a result, welfare programs tend to be inadequate for long-term provision of human needs, and the intricate and often intimidating procedures for receiving welfare benefits ensure that large proportions of potentially eligible people never apply. Poor people are thus compelled to accept whatever low-wage jobs are available, and the large pool of low-wage labor helps to depress wages throughout the economy.

Linda Gordon argues that the welfare state reproduces the gender division of labor that Phillips discussed earlier, one that privileges men at the expense of women. It devalues work that has historically been performed by women by suggesting that the care poor single mothers provide to their children is not work, and that they are really working only when they work for a wage. Poor women are placed in a no-win situation. If they stay at home to care for their children, they are seen as lazy. If they work in the paid economy at one or more low-wage jobs, they are likely to be criticized for not fulfilling their role as mother (for example, "latchkey children" come home from school to no adult supervision). The welfare state also punishes women for perceived violations of sexual and family norms. "Deserving" women are poor because of the death of a male spouse, who is presumed to be the major source of family income. In contrast, "undeserving" women are poor because they are sexually active and become pregnant outside of marriage. The distinction between social insurance and welfare is thus a gendered one in which women who uphold patriarchal definitions of women's roles and the nature of the family are rewarded, both materially and symbolically, while women who deviate from these definitions are stigmatized.

Kenneth J. Neubeck and Noel A. Cazenave see the welfare state as contributing to the social construction of race. In this context, the association of whiteness with work and productivity and blackness with laziness is one of the privileges of whiteness that Lipsitz spoke of earlier. This reproduction of the "deserving"–"undeserving" dichotomy is perhaps best illustrated by how the New Deal social programs excluded African Americans (for example, Social Security's exclusion of agricultural and domestic workers, the great majority of whom were black) and reinforced existing patterns of racial segregation (for example, the Federal Housing Administration's refusal to insure mortgages in integrated neighborhoods). Neubeck and Cazenave's examination of the Personal Responsibility and Work Opportunity Reconciliation Act of 1996 (more popularly known as "welfare reform") finds that a racialized welfare recipient—the black "welfare queen"—was a central theme of efforts to restructure the welfare state. In the context of this racialized subject, the argument offered by conservatives of both major political parties that welfare had to be made more restrictive because it provided incentives for dependency and "illegitimate" children was in fact an argument for race population control.

Gøsta Esping-Andersen provides an important comparative analysis of welfare states that helps us to understand just how minimal the U.S. welfare state is in addressing poverty. Liberal welfare states such as the United States are contrasted with corporatist welfare states (such as France and Germany) that provide strong social rights to citizens, but in ways that maintain existing class and status differences, and social democratic welfare states (found, for example, in the Scandinavian countries) that exhibit a commitment to broad social equality in the provision of welfare. Despite the differences between corporatist and social democratic welfare states, their understanding of welfare as a social right and their extensive nonmarket provision of welfare explain the dramatically lower rates of poverty and less severe stigma associated with poverty found in these countries relative to the United States. These are countries that, in contrast to the United States, have relatively stronger labor movements as well as labor, social democratic, or communist political parties that organized for more complete forms of social provision. Even as left political parties in Great Britain, France, and Germany have begun to scale back their commitment to social welfare, labor unions have remained strong supporters of these policies and have often successfully challenged efforts to reduce social welfare.

The articles in this section are critical of the welfare state, but in a different way from those whose criticism led to the "welfare reform" of the mid-1990s. For these conservative critics who emphasize the importance of market values, the goal of welfare reform has been a reduction in social provision; as Marger (2002) makes clear, reductions in welfare spending and in the number of people receiving welfare are evidence of success in achieving this goal. The criticisms of welfare presented in this section are based on the failure of welfare state policies in the United States to reduce poverty and inequality. For these critics, Esping-Andersen's typology of welfare states provides some hope that a different balance of political forces can produce a welfare state that more adequately addresses the consequences of poverty and inequality.

References

Gans, Herbert J. 1995. *The War Against the Poor: The Underclass and Antipoverty Policy.* New York: Basic Books.

Kloby, Jerry. 2003. *Inequality, Power, and Development.* 2nd ed. Amherst, NY: Humanity Books.

Marger, Martin. 2002. *Social Inequality: Patterns and Processes.* New York: McGraw-Hill.

Zinn, Howard. 1995. *A People's History of the United States.* 2nd ed. New York: HarperCollins.

RELIEF, LABOR, AND CIVIL DISORDER: AN OVERVIEW

FRANCES FOX PIVEN AND RICHARD A. CLOWARD

Since the early sixteenth century, many Western governments have come to make provision for the care of the destitute, often known as poor relief. (In the United States, such provisions are now called public assistance or public welfare.) . . .

Relief arrangements are ancillary to economic arrangements. Their chief function is to regulate labor, and they do that in two general ways. First, when mass unemployment leads to outbreaks of turmoil, relief programs are ordinarily initiated or expanded to absorb and control enough of the unemployed to restore order; then, as turbulence subsides, the relief system contracts, expelling those who are needed to populate the labor market. Relief also performs a labor-regulating function in this shrunken state, however. Some of the aged, the disabled, the insane, and others who are of no use as workers are left on the relief rolls, and their treatment is so degrading and punitive as to instill in the laboring masses a fear of the fate that awaits them should they relax into beggary and pauperism. To demean and punish those who do not work is to exalt by contrast even the meanest labor at the meanest wages. These regulative functions of relief, and their periodic expansion and contraction, are made necessary by several strains toward instability inherent in capitalist economies.

Problems of Controlling Labor by Market Incentives

All human societies compel most of their members to work, to produce the goods and services that sustain the community. All societies also define the work their members must do and the conditions under which they must do it. Sometimes the authority to compel and define is fixed in tradition, sometimes in the bureaucratic agencies of a central government. Capitalism, however, relies primarily upon the mechanisms of a market—the promise of financial rewards or penalties—to motivate men and women to work and to hold them to their occupational tasks.

Basic to capitalist economic arrangements is change. The economy is kept in constant flux by entrepreneurs searching out new and bigger markets and cheaper methods of production and distribution. These changes in the organization of production and distribution create continuous shifts in manpower needs: workers must acquire new skills; they must move to new locales; a stream of uninitiated people must be made to fill new and different occupations in a changing productive system. Because of this fluidity, work roles under capitalism cannot be assigned by tradition. Nor can responsibility for the allocation of labor conveniently be lodged in the bureaucracies of a central government, for in a market system a great variety of dispersed entrepreneurs control production and define labor requirements. In the place of tradition or governmental authority, capitalist societies control people and work tasks precisely as they control goods and capital—through a market system.

Under capitalism, manpower distribution is mainly the result of monetary incentives or disincentives: profits or wages, or the threat of no profits or no wages. As these incentives ebb and flow in response to economic changes, most people are more or less continuously induced to change and adapt. Continual change in labor requirements also means that, at any given moment, some people are left unemployed. In subsistence economies everyone works; the labor force is virtually synonymous with the population. But capitalism makes labor conditional on market demand, with the result that some amount of unemployment becomes a permanent feature of the economy.[1] In other words, change and fluctuation and unemployment are chronic features of capitalism.

But periodically change takes on catastrophic proportions. Sometimes this is the result of the natural disasters that afflict all societies, such as crop failures or rapid population growth, which disturb the ongoing pattern of work and its rewards. To such travails capitalism adds abrupt, erratic, and extreme fluctuations in production and distribution, leading to massive and precipitous modifications in the requirements for labor. The two main sources of the catastrophic changes that distinguish capitalism are depression and rapid modernization.

During the economic downturns or depressions that have marked the advance of capitalism, the structure of market incentives simply collapses; with no demand for labor, there are no monetary rewards to guide and enforce work. During periods of rapid modernization—whether the replacement of handicraft by machines, the relocation of factories in relation to new sources of power or new outlets for distribution, or the demise of family subsistence farming as large-scale commercial agriculture spreads—portions of the laboring population may be rendered obsolete or at least temporarily maladjusted. Market incentives do not collapse; they are simply not sufficient to compel people to abandon one way of working and living in favor of another.

In principle, of course, these dislocated people become part of a labor supply to be drawn upon by a changing and expanding labor market. As the history of Western market systems shows, however, people do not adapt so readily to drastically altered methods of work and to the new and alien patterns of social life dictated by that work. They may resist leaving their traditional communities and the only life they know. Bred to labor under the discipline of sun and season, however severe that discipline may be, they may resist the discipline of factory and machine, which, though it may be no more severe, may seem so because it is alien. The process of human adjustment to these economic changes has ordinarily entailed generations of mass unemployment, distress, and disorganization.

Now, if human beings were invariably given to enduring these travails with equanimity, there would be no governmental relief systems at all. But often they do not, and for reasons that are not difficult to see. The regulation of civil behavior in all societies is intimately dependent on stable occupational arrangements. So long as people are fixed in their work roles, their activities and outlooks are also fixed; they do what they must and think what they must. Each behavior and attitude is shaped by the reward of a good harvest or the penalty of a bad one, by the factory paycheck or the danger of losing it. But mass unemployment breaks that bond, loosening people from the main institution by which they are regulated and controlled.

Moreover, mass unemployment that persists for any length of time diminishes the capacity of other institutions to bind and constrain people. Occupational behaviors and outlooks underpin a way of life and determine familial, communal, and cultural patterns. When large numbers of people are suddenly barred from their traditional occupations, the entire structure of social control is weakened and may even collapse. There is no harvest or paycheck to enforce work and the sentiments that uphold work; without work, people cannot conform to familial and communal roles; and if the dislocation is widespread, the legitimacy of the social order itself may come to be questioned. The result is usually civil disorder—crime, mass protests, riots—a disorder that may even threaten to overturn existing social and economic arrangements. It is then that relief programs are initiated or expanded.

However, simply providing aid to quiet the unemployed will not stop disorder: it may even permit it to worsen, for although the remedy may prevent workers' starvation, the trigger that sets off disorder is not economic distress itself but the deterioration of social control. To restore order, the society must create the means to reassert its authority. Because the market is unable to control men's behavior, at least for a time, a surrogate system of social control must be evolved, at least for a time. Moreover, if the surrogate system is to be consistent with normally dominant patterns, it must restore people to work roles. Thus, even while obsolete or unneeded laborers are temporarily given relief, they are generally succored only on condition that they labor, whether in public workhouses and labor yards or by being contracted and indentured to private entrepreneurs. To illustrate these views we turn to some examples of the emergence and expansion of relief-giving in early European capitalist societies. . . .

Civil Disorder and the Initiation or Expansion of Relief-Giving

Western relief systems originated in the mass disturbances that erupted during the long transition from feudalism to capitalism beginning in the sixteenth century. As a result of the declining death rates in the previous century, the population of Europe grew rapidly; as the population grew, so did transiency and beggary. To deal with these threats to civil order, many localities legislated severe penalties against vagrancy. Even before the sixteenth century, the magistrates of Basel had defined twenty-five different categories of beggars, together with appropriate punishments for each. But penalties alone did not deter begging, especially when economic distress was severe and the numbers affected were large. Consequently, some localities began to augment punishment with provisions for the relief of the vagrant poor.

As early as 1516, the Scottish theologian John Major, who taught at the University of Paris, declared: "If the Prince or Community should decree that there should be no beggar in the country, and *should provide for the impotent*, the action would be praiseworthy and lawful."[2] In 1520, Martin Luther urged the German nobility not only to abolish beggary but to provide for their own poor. In 1523 Luther published a detailed relief scheme for Leisnig, in Saxony, which prohibited begging and provided for a common chest to aid the old, the weak, and those poor householders who had "honourably labored at their craft or in agriculture" but who could no longer find the means to support themselves. Ordinances modeled on Luther's injunctions were rapidly instituted in the German municipalities[3] and in 1530 the German emperor Charles the Fifth issued an edict outlawing beggary and directing each municipality to maintain its poor.[4]

A French town that initiated such an arrangement early in the sixteenth century was Lyons,[5] which was troubled both by a rapidly growing population and by the economic instability associated with the transition to capitalism. By 1500 Lyons' population had already begun to increase. During the decades that followed, the town became a prosperous commercial and manufacturing center—the home of the European money market and of expanding new trades in textiles, printing, and metalworking. As it thrived it attracted people, not only from the surrounding countryside, but even from Italy, Flanders, and Germany. All told, the population of Lyons probably doubled between 1500 and 1540.

All this was very well as long as the newcomers could be absorbed by industry. But not all were, with the result that the town came to be plagued by beggars and vagrants. Moreover, prosperity was not continuous: some trades were seasonal and others were periodically troubled by foreign competition. With each economic downturn, large numbers of workers were thrown out of work. They—and especially their children, who were preferred as beggars for the sympathy they elicited—recurrently took to the streets to plead for charity, cluttering the very doorsteps of the better-off classes. Lyons was most vulnerable during periods of bad harvest, when famine not only drove up the cost of bread for urban artisans and journeymen but brought hordes of peasants into the city, where they sometimes paraded through the streets in great numbers to exhibit their misfortune.

Thus the economic distress resulting from population changes and agricultural and other natural disasters which had characterized life throughout the Middle Ages was exacerbated by the vagaries of an evolving market economy. Consequently, turbulence among the poor reached a new pitch. In 1529 food riots erupted, with thousands of Lyonnais looting granaries and the homes of the wealthy; in 1530, artisans and journeymen armed themselves and marched through the streets; in 1531, mobs of starving peasants literally overran the town.

Such charity as had previously been given in Lyons was primarily the responsibility of the church or of those of the more prosperous who sought to purchase their salvation through almsgiving. If almsgiving were to serve a religious end for the prosperous, the destitute could hardly be prohibited from begging. But this method of caring for the needy obviously stimulated rather than discouraged begging and created a public nuisance to the better-off citizens (one account of the times describes famished peasants so gorging themselves as to die on the very doorsteps where they were fed). Moreover, to leave charity to church or citizen meant that few got aid, and those not necessarily according to their need. The result was that mass disorders periodically erupted.

The increase in disorder led the rulers of Lyons to conclude that the giving of charity should no longer be governed by private whim. Consequently, in 1534, churchmen, notables, and merchants joined together to establish a centralized administration for disbursing aid. All charitable donations were consolidated under a central body, the "Aumône-Générale," whose responsibility was to "nourish the poor forever." A list of the needy was established by a house-to-house survey, and tickets for relief were issued to those who qualified. Standards were fixed in allotting bread and money, the sick were sent to a hospital for free medical care, and not least, begging was strictly prohibited.

Indeed, most of the features of modern welfare—from criteria to discriminate the worthy poor from the unworthy to strict procedures for surveillance of recipients and measures for their rehabilitation—were present in Lyons' new relief administration. By the 1550's, about 10 per cent of the town's population was receiving relief, while the number of patients in the Lyons hospital for the poor had tripled.[6] The notables and merchants who promoted this scheme did not so much take pride in their charity as in their aspiration to make of Lyons "a vision of peace."

Within two years of the establishment of relief in Lyons, King Francis I ordered each parish in France to register its poor and to provide for the "impotent" out of a fund of contributions. Elsewhere other townships began to devise similar systems to deal with the vagrants and mobs cast up by famine, rapid population growth, and the transition from feudalism to capitalism. . . .

England also felt these disturbances, and just as it pioneered in developing an intensively capitalist economy, so it was at the forefront in developing nation-wide, public relief arrangements to replace purely local and private charity. During the closing years of the fifteenth century, the emergence of the wool industry in England began to transform the economic and social arrangements governing agriculture. As sheep raising became more profitable, much land was converted from tillage to pasturage, and large numbers of peasants were displaced by an emerging entrepreneurial gentry which either bought their land or cheated them out of it. The impact on the dispossessed farmers was one that was to become familiar in successive periods of agricultural modernization. Sir Thomas More described their plight in 1516:

> The husbandmen be thrust out of their own, or else either by covin or fraud, or by violent oppression they be put besides it, or by wrongs and injuries they be so wearied, that they be compelled to sell all: by one means therefore or by other, either by hook or crook they must needs depart away, poor, silly, wretched souls, men, women, husbands, wives, fatherless children, widows, woeful mothers, with their young babes, and their whole household small in substance and much in number, as husbandry requireth many hands. Away they trudge, I say, out of their known and accustomed houses, finding no place to rest in. All their household stuff, which is very little worth, though it might well abide the sale, yet being suddenly thrust out, they be constrained to sell it for a thing of naught. And when they have wandered abroad till that be spent, what can they then else do but steal, and then justly pardy be hanged, or else go about a begging. And yet then also they be cast in prison as vagabonds, because they go about and work not: whom no man will set at work, though they never so willing profer themselves thereto.[7]

A statute of 1488–1489 comments with alarm on the resulting disorders:

> [F]or where in some towns two hundred persons were occupied and lived by their lawful labors, now be there occupied two or three herdsmen, and the residue fall in idleness, the husbandry which is one of the greatest commodities of this realm is greatly decayed, churches destroyed, the service of God withdrawn, the bodies there buried not prayed for, the patron and curates wronged, the defense of this land against our enemies outward feebled

> and impaired; to the great displeasure of God, to the subversion of the policy and good rule of this land, and remedy be not hastily therefore purveyed.[8]

Early in the sixteenth century, the national government moved to try to forestall such disorders. In 1528 the Privy Council, anticipating a fall in foreign sales as a result of the war in Flanders, tried to induce the cloth manufacturers of Suffolk to retain their employees.[9] In 1534, a law passed under Henry VIII attempted to limit the number of sheep in any one holding in order to inhibit the displacement of farmers and agricultural laborers and thus forestall potential disorders. Beginning in the 1550's, the Privy Council attempted to regulate the price of grain in poor harvests. But the entrepreneurs of the new market economy were not so readily curbed, so that during this period another method of dealing with labor disorders, especially vagrancy, was evolved.

Until this time, communities in England, as in other European countries, sanctioned almsgiving as a means of personal salvation, and one third of parish church funds was set aside for this purpose. Early in the sixteenth century, however, the national government moved to replace parish arrangements for charity with a nationwide system of relief. In 1531, an act of Parliament decreed that local officials search out and register those of the destitute deemed to be impotent, and give them a document authorizing begging. Almsgiving to others was outlawed. As for those who sought alms without authorization, the penalty was public whipping till the blood ran.

Thereafter, other arrangements for relief were rapidly instituted. An act passed in 1536, during the reign of Henry VIII, required local parishes to take care of their destitute and to establish a procedure for the collection and administration of donations for that purpose by local officials.[10] (In the same year Henry VIII began to expropriate monasteries, helping to assure secular control of charity.[11]) With these developments, the penalties for beggary were made more severe, including an elaborate schedule of branding, enslavement, and execution for repeated offenders. Even so, by 1572 beggary was said to have reached alarming proportions, and in that year local responsibility for relief was more fully spelled out by the famous Elizabethan Poor Laws, which established a local tax, known as the poor rate, as the means for financing the care of paupers and required that justices of the peace serve as the overseers of the poor.

In the closing years of the sixteenth century, the price of grain rose almost continuously, causing considerable hardship among the laborers. After 1594, bad harvests sharpened their miseries, especially in 1596–1597, when "Unemployment was frequent, poverty was everywhere . . . there was . . . constant danger of revolt."[12] When Parliament convened in October 1597, it acted to clarify and systematize the provisions for relief, especially the system of taxation, and the practice of making relatives responsible for paupers. "The coincidence between the coming of the free wage-labourer and an organised public provision for the destitute cannot, in the nature of things, be exactly proved," write the Webbs[13] but the indications are convincing, and were to become more convincing still as the system of free labor expanded and changed.

After this period of activity, the parish relief machinery lapsed into disuse. But then a depression in cloth manufacture in 1620, followed by bad harvests and high prices in 1621–22, produced new outbreaks of disorder. The Privy Council established a special commission charged with enforcing the Poor Laws,[14] and by the 1630's the relief rolls had expanded enormously.[15] Relief was curtailed again with the onset of the Civil War, when high pay enticed much of the surplus agricultural population into the army. A long period of contraction then ensued, apparently accounted for by rising wages under Cromwell and by the paralysis of the central machinery of government after the war.

Relief arrangements were reactivated and expanded again, however, during the massive agricultural dislocations of the late eighteenth century. Most of the English agricultural population had by then lost its landholdings; in place of the subsistence farming found elsewhere in Europe, a three-tier system of landowners, tenant farmers, and agricultural workers had evolved in England. The vast majority of the people were a landless proletariat, hiring out by the year to tenant farmers. The margin of their subsistence, however, was provided by common and waste lands, on which they gathered kindling, grazed animals, and hunted game to supplement their meager wages. Moreover, the use of the commons was part of the English villager's birthright, his sense of place and pride. It was the disruption of these arrangements and the ensuing disorder that led to the new expansion of relief.

By the middle of the eighteenth century, an increasing population, advancing urbanization, and the growth of manufacturing had greatly expanded markets for agricultural products, mainly for cereals to feed the urban population and for wool to supply the cloth manufacturers. These new markets, together with the introduction of new agricultural methods (such as cross-harrowing), led to large-scale changes in agriculture. To take advantage of rising prices and new techniques, big landowners moved to expand their holdings still further by buying up small farms and, armed with parliamentary "Bills of Enclosure," by usurping the common and waste lands which had enabled many small cottagers to survive.[16] Although this process began much earlier, it accelerated rapidly after 1750; by 1850, well over 6 million acres of common land—or about one quarter of the total arable acreage—had been consolidated into private holdings and turned primarily to grain production.[17] Half of this acreage was enclosed between 1760 and 1800, a period during which the rate of parliamentary acts of enclosure ran ten times higher than in the previous forty years. For great numbers of agricultural workers, enclosure meant no land on which to grow subsistence crops to feed their families, no grazing land to produce wool for home spinning and weaving, no fuel to heat their cottages, and new restrictions against hunting. It meant, in short, deprivation of a major source of subsistence for the poor.

New markets also stimulated a more businesslike approach to farming. Landowners demanded the maximum rent from tenant farmers, and tenant farmers in turn began to deal with their laborers in terms of cash calculations. Specifically, this meant a shift from a master-servant relationship to an employer-employee relationship, but on the harshest terms. Where laborers had previously worked by the year and frequently lived with the farmer, they were now hired for only as long as they were needed and were then left to fend for themselves.[18] Pressures toward short-term hiring also resulted from the large scale cultivation of grain crops for market, which called for a seasonal labor force, as opposed to mixed subsistence farming, which required year-round laborers. The use of cash rather than produce as the medium of payment for work, a rapidly spreading practice, encouraged partly by the long-term inflation of grain prices, added to the laborer's hardships.[19] Finally, the rapid increase in rural population[20] at a time when the growth of woolen manufacturing continued to provide an incentive to convert land from tillage to pasturage produced a larger labor surplus, leaving agricultural laborers with no leverage in bargaining for wages with their tenant-farmer employers.[21] The result was widespread unemployment and terrible hardship among agricultural workers.

None of these changes took place without resistance from small farmers and laborers who, while they had known hardship before, were now being forced out of a way of life and even out of their villages. Some rioted when "Bills of Enclosure" were posted; some petitioned the Parliament for their repeal. During the last decade of the eighteenth century, when hardship was made more acute by a succession of poor harvests, there were widespread food riots. But their protests could not curb the market processes that were at work. As for the distress of the displaced laborers, the laissez-faire commentators of the time pontificated that this was the necessary concomitant of economic productivity and progress.

A solution to disorder was needed, however, and that solution turned out to be relief.[22] During the late eighteenth and early nineteenth centuries, the English countryside was periodically besieged by turbulent masses of the displaced rural poor and the towns were racked by Luddism, radicalism, trade-unionism, and Chartism,[23] even while the ruling classes worried about what the French Revolution might augur for England.

> If compassion was not a strong enough force to make the ruling classes attend to the danger that the poor might starve, fear would certainly have made them think of the danger that the poor might rebel. . . . Thus fear and pity united to sharpen the wits of the rich, and to turn their minds to the distresses of the poor.[24]

It was at this time that the poor relief system—first created in the sixteenth century to control the earlier disturbances caused by population growth and the commercialization of agriculture—became a major institution.[25] Between 1760 and 1784, taxes for relief—the "poor rate"—rose by 60 per cent; they doubled by 1801, and rose by 60 per cent more in the next decade.[26] By 1818, the poor rate was over six times as high as it had been in 1760. Hobsbawm estimates that up to the 1850's, upwards of 10 percent of the English population were paupers.[27] The relief system, in short, was expanded in order to absorb and regulate the masses of discontented people uprooted from agriculture but not yet incorporated into industry.

■ ■ ■ ■

Enforcing Low-Wage Work During Periods of Stability

Even in the absence of cataclysmic change, market incentives may be insufficient to compel all people at all times to do the particular work required of them. Incentives may be too meager and erratic, or people may not be sufficiently socialized to respond to them properly. To be sure, the productivity of a fully developed capitalist economy would allow wages and profits sufficient to entice the population to work; and in a fully developed capitalist society, most people would also be reared to want what the market holds out to them. They would expect, even sanctify, the rewards of the marketplace and acquiesce in its vagaries.

But no fully developed capitalist society actually exists. (Even today, in the United States, the most advanced capitalist country, certain regions and population groups—such as Southern tenant farmers—remain on the periphery of the wage market and are only partially socialized to the ethos of the market.) Capitalism evolved slowly and spread slowly. During most of this evolution, the market provided meager rewards for most workers, and none at all for some. For many, this is still so. And during most of this evolution, large sectors of the laboring classes were not fully socialized to the market ethos. The relief system, we contend, has made an important contribution toward overcoming these persisting weaknesses in the capacity of the market to direct and control men.

Once an economic convulsion subsides and civil order is restored, relief systems are not ordinarily abandoned. The rolls are reduced, to be sure, but the shell of the system usually remains, ostensibly to provide aid to the aged, the insane, the disabled, and such other unfortunates as may be without economic utility. However, the manner in which these "impotents" have always been treated, in the United States and elsewhere, suggests a purpose quite different from remediation of their destitution. For these residual persons have been universally degraded for lacking economic value and ordinarily relegated to the foul quarters of the workhouse, with its strict penal regimen and its starvation diet. Such institutions were repeatedly proclaimed the sole source of aid during times of stability, and for a reason bearing directly on the maintenance of work norms in a market system.

Conditions in the workhouse were intended to ensure that no one with any conceivable alternatives would seek public aid. Nor can there be any doubt of that intent. This statement by the Poor Law Commissioners in 1834, for example, admits of no other interpretation:

> Into such a house none will enter voluntarily; work, confinement, and discipline, will deter the indolent and vicious; and nothing but extreme necessity will induce any to accept the comfort which must be obtained by the surrender of their free agency, and the sacrifice of their accustomed habits and gratifications. *Thus the parish officer, being furnished an unerring test of the necessity of applicants, is relieved from his painful and difficult responsibility; while all have the gratification of knowing that while the necessitous are abundantly relieved, the funds of charity are not wasted by idleness and fraud.*[28]

The method worked. Periods of relief expansion were generally followed by "reform" campaigns to abolish all "outdoor" aid and restrict relief to those who entered the workhouse—as in England in 1722, 1834, and 1871 and in the United States in the 1880's and 1890's—and these campaigns almost invariably resulted in a sharp reduction in the number of applicants seeking aid.

The harsh treatment of those who had no alternatives except to fall back upon the parish and accept "the offer of the House" terrorized the impoverished masses.[29] That, too, was a matter of deliberate intent. The workhouse was designed to spur men to contrive ways of supporting themselves by their own industry, *to offer themselves to any employer on any terms.* It did this by making pariahs of those who could not support themselves; they served as an object lesson, a means of celebrating the virtues of work by the terrible example of their agony.[30] Three years after the Poor Law Commissioners of 1834 decreed the abolition of outdoor relief and the expansion of the system of workhouses, Disraeli accurately said of this reform that "it announces to the world that in England poverty is a crime."

The deterrent doctrine of relief enunciated in 1834 provided a formula for relief-giving in the urban industrial labor market, which is known as the principle of "less eligibility:"

> The first and most essential of all conditions, a principle which we find universally admitted, even by those whose practice is at variance with it, is, that his [the relief recipient's] situation on the whole shall not be made really or apparently so eligible [i.e., desirable] as the situation of the independent laborer of the lowest class.[31]

Deterrent relief practices have their contemporary equivalents. For while the conditions of relief in the United States today are less harsh, the main tendency is still far from progressive liberalization. Rather, the pattern is cyclical: long periods of restrictiveness are interrupted periodically by short periods of liberalization. Thus the relief system created by the Social Security Act of 1935 in the United States was administered for more than two decades to ensure that as few of the poor as possible obtained as little as possible from it. The principle of "less eligibility" was reflected in statute, policy, and day-to-day practice: not only were grants kept at levels "more severe than that of the lowest class of laborers who obtain their livelihood by honest industry," which meant in some states that the recipients received too little to sustain life, but the punishment and degradation that the Poor Law authorities were confident would make relief recipients "less eligible" had their modern parallel in such practices as mass searches and raids of recipients' homes. During the 1960's, however, . . . many of these restrictions collapsed and the rolls rose precipitiously. But even as this occurred, pressures to reorganize the system also mounted.

■■■■

Relief and the Political Process

■■■■

The modernization of any society generally entails expansion of the power and authority of its national government. However, when disruptions in the economy lead to occupational dislocation, causing widespread distress and discontent, it is usually local government that first experiences the tremors and moderates them by extending relief. The necessary incremental adjustments are made by local legislative bodies or by local officials who possess discretion over relief arrangements.

But institutions do not ordinarily adjust easily, not only because of internal bureaucratic rigidities but also because change requires that the fiscal and political supports for the institution must be revised: for example, if local relief rolls rise, the parish poor rate or the state sales tax must be increased, and that may anger local taxpayers. Accordingly, the ability of local government to respond to such crises is inhibited even while the limited expansion of relief that is taking place strains and overloads the fiscal, administrative, and political underpinnings of the relief system. When local relief practices and capacities begin to break down, the national government is likely to intervene.

Correlatively, if expanding local relief begins to intrude on the operations of the labor market, the national government will intervene to force the contraction of relief, especially if disorder is not widespread. The national government of England intervened to assure the provision of local relief in the 1530's and again in the 1630's, but it enforced the contraction of relief in 1722 and 1834; the Federal Government in the

United States intervened to assure a massive expansion of relief during the Great Depression (and again in the 1960's), but moved to contract relief arrangements in the late 1930's.

The electoral system is another modern, and especially a capitalist, phenomenon. In a feudal or oligarchical polity, the poor could demonstrate their discontent only by begging, stealing, marching, burning, or rioting. These mass disturbances were a form of political action, a means by which the poor occasionally forced some degree of accommodation from their rulers. But civil disorder is far more costly and threatening in a highly organized and complex society, especially as urbanization and industrialization increase. To minimize disturbances, an elaborate mechanism has evolved in capitalist societies—slowly in England, more rapidly in the United States, unfettered by residual political traditions: namely, the universal franchise and the periodic election of political office holders. The votes of an enfranchised populace serve as a barometer of unrest, and the periodic contests for electoral office are intended to exert pressure on political leaders to deal with widespread discontent in the larger society.

To win and hold office, political leaders must weld together a majority made up of diverse groups. Here, as in England, majorities have been precarious. This means that the tenure of officeholders is intimately dependent on the stability of institutions in the larger society, especially economic institutions, for any breakdown in their functioning stirs unrest and conflict and causes disaffection and division among voters. Price inflation, housing shortages, rising local taxes, widespread unemployment, or demands for racial integration may lead to the threatened or actual disaffection of segments of the population from existing political leadership. Where in the past such disaffection was signaled primarily by disorder in the streets, the electoral system is designed to channel it into the voting booth. The electoral system is, moreover, sensitive to the outbreaks of disorder that do occur, for disorder generally leads large masses of voters to shift their votes to new leaders and parties.

Whether expressed in the streets or at the polls, the disaffection of any large segment of voters can wreak havoc with electoral majorities. Political incumbents try to use the power and resources of government to intervene in the institutional arrangements that breed dissension or to develop public programs intended to recapture the allegiance of disaffected blocs. If they fail, they may lose their office to contenders who promise to deal with the sources of unrest more effectively. During periods of electoral upset, in other words, political leaders proffer concessions to win the allegiance of disaffected voting blocs. It is this objective—the political "reintegration" of disaffected groups—that impels electoral leaders to expand relief programs at times of political crisis engendered by economic distress. Indeed, it was this objective that accounted for the initiation of a national public welfare system in the United States during the Great Depression. . . .

Notes

1. Many critics of capitalism have argued that the maintenance of a surplus of unemployed workers is not simply a by-product of market fluidity but a deliberately contrived condition, designed to ease the flow of labor and to lessen the bargaining power of workers in market transactions. The periodic intervention of government to increase the pool of unemployed by slowing the rate of economic growth and the use of government power to force men to work for any bidder lend credence to these views. . . .
2. Quoted in Ashley, Vol. II, 341. Emphasis added.
3. Webb and Webb, Part I, 31–32.
4. In 1531 the emperor elaborated his earlier edict in a scheme that prohibited vagrancy and begging under pain of prison and the lash, and commanded every city in the Netherlands to provide for its poor by putting the able-bodied to work while caring for indigent women and orphans (*ibid.*, 32; de Schweinitz, 33).
5. Ypres, in Flanders, initiated a scheme very similar to Lyons' in 1525. Bruges, Paris, and Rome also inaugurated relief systems at about the same time. We use Lyons only as an illustration of developments that were going forward in many places. For a detailed description of the circumstances leading to Lyons' welfare program, see Davis.
6. The hospital was in fact used to incarcerate some paupers as well as to care for the sick. Juan Luis Vivès, a humanitarian of the time, wrote in his plan for relief in Bruges, dated January 6, 1526: "I call 'hospitals' those places where the sick are fed and cared for, where a certain number of paupers is supported, where boys and girls are reared, where abandoned infants are nourished, where the insane are confined, and where the blind dwell. . . ." (11). Four centuries later, the almshouse or workhouse was performing roughly the same function in England and America.

7. More, 33, as quoted in de Schweinitz, 10.

8. Quoted in de Schweinitz, 9. Nor were the disorders merely idleness and decay. "When the sense of oppression became overwhelming, the popular feeling manifested itself in widespread organised tumults, disturbances and insurrections, from Wat Tyler's rebellion of 1381, and Jack Cade's march on London of 1460, to the Pilgrimage of Grace of 1536, and Kett's Norfolk rising of 1549—all of them successfully put down, but sometimes not without great struggle, by the forces which the Government could command. But vagrancy was not actually prevented; nor, as we shall presently describe, was the habit of making a living by wandering on the roads brought to an end" (Webb and Webb, Part I, 27–28).

9. de Schweinitz, 80.

10. In 1563, these contributions for relief were made compulsory (de Schweinitz, 25).

11. The Webbs suggest the motive for thus restricting the church: "Throughout the whole period . . . [up to 1597], the King, his Council and his Parliament, were enacting and carrying out laws relating to the poor of a character exactly opposite to that of the almsgiving of the mediaeval Church or to that of the benevolent institutions established by pious founders, Craft Guilds and municipal corporations. All these activities were derived from the obligation of the Christians to relieve the suffering of 'God's poor.' The King and his nobles were intent upon an altogether different object, namely, maintaining order—that is (as governments always understand it) the maintenance of the then-existing order, based on a social hierarchy of rulers and ruled, of landowners and those who belonged to the land" (Part I, 23).

12. Edward P. Cheyney, *History of England*, 1926, Vol. II, 36, as quoted in Webb and Webb, Part I, 62.

13. Webb and Webb, Part I, 44, n. 2.

14. *Ibid.*, 75–100. Trevelyan writes of the Privy Council during this period that it "had a real regard for the interests of the poor, with which the interests of public order were so closely involved" (170–171).

15. According to E. M. Leonard, there was more poor relief in England from 1631 to 1640 than ever before or since (266).

16. Enclosure was also encouraged by the high rentals paid by factories located in outlying areas, and especially by the prospects of coal-mining, from which the landed gentry drew great fortunes in royalties.

17. Hobsbawm and Rudé, 27. There were about four thousand parliamentary acts for enclosure during this hundred-year span, most of them in the 1760's and 1770's and during the war period of 1793–1816.

18. The loss of "gleaning rights" illustrates how the commercialization of farming affected the precarious margin of the laborers' existence. More efficient farming methods deprived them of the right to pick the fields clean after the harvest. The Hammonds estimate that such gleaning rights represented the equivalent of six or seven weeks' wages (1948, Vol. I, 103).

19. Hobsbawm and Rudé, 38–42.

20. Between 1701 and 1831, the population of the agricultural counties almost doubled, from 1,563,000 to 2,876,000. Moreover, after 1751, emigration fell off sharply, draining off only about 40 per cent of the natural increase (*ibid.*, 43).

21. The laborers' vulnerability was assured by laws prohibiting workers from combining for the purpose of exerting influence to reduce hours or raise wages. There were forty such laws on the books by 1800. New statutes in 1799 and 1800 effectively prohibited all joint action by the workers (Hammond and Hammond, 1917, 112–142).

22. The relief system was by no means the only solution. This was an era of brutal repression; indeed, in no other domestic matters was Parliament so active as in the elaboration of the criminal codes. At the same time, troops were spread across the country and quartered in barracks (rather than in the homes of citizens) to avoid the possibility that they would identify with the rebellious population (Hammond and Hammond, 1917, 37–94).

23. "At no other period in modern British history," writes Hobsbawm of this period, especially the decades between Waterloo and the 1840's, "have the common people been so persistently, profoundly, and often desperately dissatisfied. At no other period since the seventeenth century can we speak of large masses of them as revolutionary . . ." (Vol. II, 55). It should be said that agitation arose from both the middle and working classes. After Parliament extended the franchise to the middle classes in 1832, however, the workers' movement was effectively isolated and weakened.

24. Hammond and Hammond, 1948, Vol. I, 118.

25. Hobsbawm and Rudé (76).

26. Mantoux, 437; de Schweinitz, 114; Nicholls, Vol. II, 133, 438. During this period, expenditures under the poor law nearly equaled the entire peacetime cost of the English national government, excluding the army and navy (Webb and Webb, Part II, Vol. I, 2).

27. Hobsbawm, 70.

28. *The Report from His Majesty's Commissioners for Inquiring into the Administration and Practical Operation of the Poor Laws*, 1834, 271, as quoted in de Schweinitz, 123.

29. And terrorized is the right word, for workhouse conditions were terrifying even in an age when life for the laboring classes was always brutal. Conditions were such that a House of Commons investigation conducted in 1767 found that only 7 out of 100 infants born or received into workhouses had survived two years (de Schweinitz, 66).

30. Hobsbawm comments on the intent of the Poor Law: "The residuum of paupers could not, admittedly, be left actually to starve, but they ought not to be given more than the absolute minimum—provided it was less than the lowest wage offered in the market—and in the most

discouraging conditions. The Poor Law was not so much intended to help the unfortunate as to stigmatize the self-confessed failures of society" (69).

31. *The Report from His Majesty's Commissioners for Inquiring into the Administration and Practical Operation of the Poor Laws,* 1834, 228, as quoted in de Schweinitz, 123.

References

Ashley, W. J., *An Introduction to English Economic History and Theory,* Part II, *The End of the Middle Ages.* New York, G. P. Putnam's Sons, 1893.

Davis, Natalie Zemon, "Poor Relief, Humanism and Heresy." Paper given at the Newberry Library Renaissance Conference in Chicago, April 16, 1966 (mimeographed).

de Schweinitz, Karl, *England's Road to Social Security: From the Statute of Laborers in 1349 to the Beveridge Report of 1942.* Philadelphia, University of Pennsylvania Press, 1943.

Hammond, J. L., and Barbara, *The Town Labourer, 1760–1832: The New Civilisation.* London, Longmans, Green & Company, 1917.

Hammond, J. L., and Barbara, *The Village Labourer.* London, Longmans, Green & Company, 1948. 2 vols. (Guild Books Nos. 239 and 240.)

Hobsbawm, E. J. *Industry and Empire: The Making of Modern English Society.* Vol. II, *1750 to the Present Day.* New York, Pantheon Books, 1968.

Hobsbawm, E. J., and Rudé, George, *Captain Swing.* New York, Pantheon Books, 1968.

Leonard, E. M., *The Early History of English Poor Relief.* Cambridge, University Press, 1900.

Mantoux, Paul, *The Industrial Revolution in the Eighteenth Century: An Outline of the Beginnings of the Modern Factory System in England.* New York, Harper & Row, 1962.

More, Sir Thomas, *Utopia.* Cambridge, University Press, 1935.

Nicholls, Sir George, *A History of the English Poor Law, in Connection with the State of the Country and the Condition of the People,* Vol. II, *A.D. 1714 to 1853.* New York, G. P. Putnam's Sons, 1898.

Trevelyan, G. M., *English Social History: A Survey of Six Centuries, Chaucer to Queen Victoria.* London, Longmans, Green & Company, 1942.

Vivès, Juan-Luis, *Concerning the relief of the Poor or Concerning Human Need: A Letter Addressed to the Senate of Bruges, January 6, 1526,* trans. Margaret M. Sherwood. New York, New York School of Philanthropy (now Columbia University School of Social Work), 1917. (Studies in Social Work, No. 11.)

Webb, Sidney and Beatrice, *English Poor Law History.* Part I, *The Old Poor Law.* Hamden, Conn., Archon Books, 1963.

Webb, Sidney and Beatrice, *English Poor Law History.* Part II, *The Last Hundred Years.* London, Longmans, Green & Company, 1929. Vols. I and II (*English Local Government,* Vol. 8.)

WHO DESERVES HELP? WHO MUST PROVIDE?

LINDA GORDON

Most people in all cultures enjoy the feeling of helping others, and most cultures consider charity a community or religious duty or a measure of good character. But a distaste for freeloaders also characterizes many cultures. The violator may appear to not really need the help, or to use the help in a bad way, or to not work hard. The giver then feels taken in and may become hostile and resentful. But if the recipient is truly needy and unable to help himself or herself—a child, for example, or a handicapped person—the giver no longer feels exploited or concerned about freeloading. These mixed feelings about giving and sharing have surrounded aid to the needy for centuries in most cultures.

Human communities are, for better or for worse, moral communities. So helping others has often been conditional on approving their morals; a good moral reputation combined with genuine neediness creates deservingness. In the smaller communities that characterized most societies prior to a few centuries ago, people's need and morality were readily observable by others, and those who could help made their judgments with all the petty prejudices and partialities that characterize any community. When states developed large-scale welfare programs, they increasingly measured deservingness through formal supervision and bureaucratic tests, although not necessarily with more objectivity.

Responsibility for others has been imbedded in every human society, limited of course by an insider-outsider distinction. For whom are we responsible? The perimeter of the sphere of obligation varies, of course. We are usually expected to help family members, but the extent of that responsibility has drastically diminished in the past century: in the United States, for example, grown children are no longer legally responsible for their parents, or parents for their grown children, and siblings bear no legal responsibility for each other. A sense of obligation to help a neighbor is now the exception, not the rule, although many would help on the understanding that what they are doing is voluntary.

In the English colonies in North America, members of a township derived their entitlement to help from settlement, that is, continuing residence in a community. In the twentieth century, that community expanded so that residence in a state or nation is what matters. As governments developed programs such as public education, garbage collection, and water purification, it was settlement that created entitlement, while for other programs the standard was higher, and especially after migration became widespread, settlement was distinguished from citizenship. Many Europeans refer to entitlements to government programs promoting public welfare as "social citizenship." Benefits conceived in that way belong to the recipient as a right of citizenship. But in the United States, to a larger degree than elsewhere, some entitlements remain dependent on various tests of morality and neediness, that is, on deservingness.

Obligation, the other side of the exchange, can also derive from several positions: kinship, membership in a church, or membership in a fraternal order or a union. The obligation to help has shifted too in the last centuries, in some ways shrinking but in other ways expanding. Givers may ignore their neighbors' poverty but contribute generously to earthquake victims in Armenia or orphans in Rwanda. As states become democratized and citizens become increasingly unequal, demands for large-scale alleviation of poverty create state forms of provision, and these rely on taxation, an impersonal form of obligation. That form of obligation establishes no bond and engenders no joy of giving on the part of the taxpayer; the depersonalization of recipients deprives them of sympathy and makes them targets of resentment.

Two phenomena counteract this resentment. One is universal welfare programs, which are available to everyone. In the United States, for example, attending a public university (and thereby receiving valuable government assistance) is perfectly honorable; although some wealthier parents may choose to spend more on private schools. Discounts for the elderly are embarrassing only to those who wish to appear young. The second is the impression that poverty is not the poor person's fault. In agrarian societies, for example, poor harvests could be universal and were universally visible. Earthquakes, floods, and droughts remain in that category. The industrial equivalent of harvest failure—recessions, depressions, structural unemployment, deindustrialization—have been less perceptible because of market ideology. When nationwide catastrophes struck, for example, the Great Depression of the 1930s, poverty lost some of its stigma, and emergency federal government relief was popular and relatively uncontroversial. But in times that appear normal, work-ethic ideology, combined with ignorance about labor market opportunity, leads to blaming those who seek public assistance.

A major structural feature of the U.S. welfare state is that stratification in entitlement, justified by degrees of deservingness, creates public conceptions of deservingness and undeservingness. This is not an accidental but a conscious strategy. As one welfare administrator urged the Social Security Board in 1939, "'denial of benefits to [some] would, by furnishing a convenient contrast, make those who are covered somewhat more aware of their benefits, and would thereby strengthen the concept of a purchased right" ' (Gordon forthcoming). The most expensive U.S. transfer programs, like Social Security Old Age Insurance, were designed to appear to be earned and based on worker contributions, although they were not.[1] The Social Security Board operated a large public relations campaign to sell Old Age Insurance as an honored entitlement. As sociologist Theda Skocpol (1992) put it, "Through a clever and widely disseminated public metaphor, Americans were told that their 'contributions' insured that each wage earner would be entitled in old age to collect benefits that he or she had 'individually earned.' Actually, benefits are paid out of a common fund" (B1). By contrast, programs for the poor are stigmatized in numerous ways: surveillance of recipients for possible cheating throws suspicion on all recipients; surveillance of recipients for moral standards throws suspicion on all recipients; critics of welfare suggest that paying for it raises taxes substantially. In fact, the word "welfare" has metamorphosed in the last half century to become a unique and pejorative term for means-tested programs.

The Gender of Deservingness

Most standards of deservingness have been deeply gendered, expressing and reinforcing social norms about appropriate male and female behavior. Almost every category of means-tested (and some non-means-tested) benefits separates recipients by gender and treats them differently. Old Age Insurance, for example, requires that the recipient has been employed for 11 quarters in an eligible job; when the program was passed, the great majority of American women did not meet that condition because they were not employed, they worked in "casual," uncovered employment (hardly casual in the case of maids or farmworkers), or they worked for the government (including tens of thousands of schoolteachers). This gender difference was deliberate and explicit: women's employment was, as welfare designers ought to be, temporary because most women married and married women belonged at home. As historian Alice Kessler-Harris (1995) summed it up, the principles of welfare were "the dignity of men (defined as their capacity to provide)" and "the virtue of women (their willingness to remain dependent on men and to rear children" (95). But this principle of women's domesticity was always contradicted by a class double standard. While prosperous mothers were (and sometimes still are) expected to devote full-time to home and child care, poor and working class mothers were not; public assistance was meager, and administrators expected recipients to supplement it with wages.

The most fundamental gendering of social provision arises from the fact that women do most of the child-raising work, whether they have a partner or not. If a man's wages could rarely support a whole family, a woman's wages (about 50 percent of a man's in the early twentieth century) surely could not do so. Mothers without male support were often forced to surrender their children to orphanages.

The program called "welfare" in the United States was designed to care for these mothers and children who lacked male support (Gordon 1994). Aid to Dependent Children (ADC)—Title IV of the Social Security Act—sailed through Congress in 1935, absolutely without controversy or opposition, in contrast to the unemployment compensation or old-age insurance titles that provoked strong opposition.[2] Partly, this is because ADC was cheap: cheap because the cost of institutionalizing children was much greater than paying their mothers to raise them, and cheap because the designers radically underestimated the number of lone-mother families. In 1930, there were approximately 10.5 million people living in female-headed households, accounting for 8.6 percent of the population. The ADC planners, by contrast, estimated that they would be serving 288,000 families, or 0.9 of 1 percent of the population (Gordon and McLanahan 1991; Coll 1988). Their estimate was even lower than the number of female-headed families already receiving public assistance in 1934—358,000 (Committee on Economic Security 1937, 241). ADC was also popular because at the time lone mothers and children seemed the quintessentially deserving recipients. By devoting themselves to mothering, the female recipients were performing what God, nature, and society intended women to do and doing so, moreover, under difficult circumstances. Children were by definition deserving. Mother-children families certainly seemed as deserving of public support as the elderly.

Yet lone mothers, 70 years later, have become the most reviled of all welfare recipients. To understand this radical shift, we need to examine changing definitions of deservingness and obligation. At each stage, we will see that sympathetic, pitying notions of lone mothers could not successfully counteract apprehension about supporting female-headed households and thereby rendering women less dependent on men. In other words, lone mothers could not stay in the "deserving" category despite the lingering ideology that they should devote full-time to their children.

When the first campaign for public assistance began, in the 1890s, deserted wives were envisaged as the primary recipients (Gordon 1994).[3] Progressive reformers blamed male irresponsibility: "The bread-winner shifts his burdens for bachelor freedom. . . . If he is at all clever, he can in most cases escape punishment" (Eliot 1900, 346). Social workers set up desertion bureaus to track down the absconders and, just as today, urged punitive action to get nonsupporting fathers to provide child support, "making the deserter pay the piper" (Baldwin 1902; see also Zunser 1923). Reformers more conservative about gender provided justifications for deserting husbands. They described deserted wives as untidy, lazy, shiftless, neglectful of housework, intemperate, slovenly, having a "trying disposition," extravagant, and sexually immoral (Smith 1901, 41–42; Brandt 1905; Weyl 1908, 389). The premise here, of course, is that women who deviated from female virtue neither deserved help nor evoked any obligation among others. (Children were invisible in this discourse.)

Yet, in practice, woman-blaming analyses of the sources of desertion did not make things significantly worse for wives who seemed to behave badly. Even in the cases of wives deemed blameless, charity workers were reluctant to offer financial support for fear of encouraging desertion. They presumed that men who knew their families could receive support if they fled would lose their sense of responsibility (Gordon 1988). The result was that deserted wives themselves were made suspect by the stigma of the family form in which they functioned—single-mother families—no matter how blameless or blameworthy they were for landing in that situation.

Widows, who formed the majority of single mothers, came to dominate the discussion later, between 1910 and 1920. The shift did not result from an increase in widowhood; rather, welfare advocates redrew the picture of the single mother, erasing deserted wives and painting in widows, as a state-building strategy. By now they had stirred up enough public concern for unsupported mothers and children that they had a political chance to win public aid, but to do so, they believed, they needed to disarm those who charged that aid encouraged immorality. A chorus of sympathetic studies of the plight of widows emerged from among those who were campaigning for state and local mothers' aid laws (Commonwealth of Massachusetts 1913).

At first, the welfare advocates' new focus on quintessentially blameless widows seemed to succeed. The fervent sympathy widows engendered constituted an argument for public obligation. The widow had a "unique claim on the community" (New York State Commission 1914, 7). Between 1910 and 1920, 40 of the then 48 states instituted programs of public aid for widows. But the discursive strategy of the campaign produced contradictory consequences. Mothers' aid advocates praised widows' morality, forbearance, hard work, and good housekeeping. Of course, the same might have been said of deserted mothers and their children; the widow had become a synonym for the virtuous lone mother, while any woman whose marriage had come unstuck, whatever the circumstances, was suspect. Thus, the widow discourse worked to intensify the stigmatization of other lone mothers; the obvious implication of emphasis on the widow's innocence was, of course, the non-innocence of others.

But widows could not escape a stigma that spread to all lone-mother families. Even the staunchest supporters of public aid insisted on scrutinizing widows' domestic standards closely, examining their housekeeping, their children's cleanliness, whether they drank or had objectionable companions, and making sure they did not consort with men. Even widows were condemned if they did not actively seek employment, appeared inadequately grateful for their relief stipends, or appeared to take those stipends as an entitlement (Gordon 1994).

Unmarried mothers began to figure importantly in this discussion only in the 1920s, after the mothers' aid laws were passed. Progressive-era reformers avoided out-of-wedlock motherhood like a curse because they did not want to call attention to unchastity among potential beneficiaries. When public discussion of illegitimacy began, it was, of course, a moralistic discourse. Out-of-wedlock mothers in the nineteenth century were defined as "fallen women." Progressive-era feminists tried to make this moralistic discourse more sympathetic to women: emphasizing their youth, positioning them as victims rather than sinners, and offering them opportunities for reform, for a new start. Conservatives were more likely to treat them as problem girls, delinquents (Lundberg and Lenroot 1921; Kunzel 1988). But both sides engaged in biologistic explanations, substituting "feeble-mindedness" where once there had been "hereditary depravity" (Lowe 1927, 793). Even the most sympathetic explanations of illegitimate motherhood were often inaccurate because many out-of-wedlock mothers were formerly married women or married women unable to be divorced, now living in out-of-wedlock partnerships.

■ ■ ■ ■

Stigmatizing Welfare

[T]he very structure of ADC made its recipients seem undeserving. Local determination of eligibility resulted in inserting a "suitable home" requirement, which became the basis for a great deal of snooping into the private lives of welfare recipients: Did they have boyfriends? Were they buying clothes that were too "nice"? Was their housekeeping adequate? The humiliating and infantilizing surveillance not only forced recipients to be secretive but produced bad publicity that stigmatized welfare in general.

ADC was stigmatized not only by its means testing and morals checking but also by its contrast with programs defined as non-welfare, earned, and therefore free from surveillance. To this programmatic effect were added racist and misogynistic slurs, some coded and some explicit, that maligned welfare recipients as lazy, immoral, and dishonest. In the early 1960s, two nationally publicized welfare cutoffs—in Newburgh, New York, and in Louisiana—helped build antiwelfare sentiment by demonizing ADC recipients. Newburgh City manager Mitchell claimed that "trollops" and the "dregs of humanity" were migrating to his city from the South in order to collect welfare, and this discourse evoked widespread national support. In Louisiana, the legislature, at the request of the governor, expelled mothers of "illegitimate" children from the welfare rolls, thereby throwing 23,000 children, 95 percent of them black, off welfare. Both events featured rhetoric that vilified African American women in particular, and both events defined women as primary recipients in the public view, pushing children into the background (Levenstein 2000).

The repeal of Aid to Families with Dependent Children (AFDC, formerly ADC) in 1996, although promoted by a heavily funded conservative propaganda campaign against welfare, was conditioned on the structure of the welfare state itself. From the beginnings of public welfare programs in the United States, advocates sought political support through the manipulation of a presumably compassionate discourse about innocent, victimized, fragile, and morally pure women and children. That propaganda inadvertently rendered logical and acceptable the prototypical antiwelfare emphasis on immoral women and neglectful, self-centered mothers. In other words, both discourses shared the assumption not only that the state had the authority to hold women to an unrealistic, saintly standard of selflessness and submissiveness but also that the state should supervise and investigate to a degree that would not have been tolerated had the recipients been men. Both of these gendered discourses substituted for and contributed to preventing the grounding of entitlement in concepts of citizenship, collective responsibility, or even equal opportunity.

Moreover, the construction of deservingness emphasized the supposedly charitable nature of public assistance, thus distinguishing its recipients from taxpayers. Defining away the benefits that the welfare state provided to the nonpoor allowed taxpayers to think of themselves only as benefactors and not as beneficiaries, thus defining welfare recipients as parasites. Once deservingness had been the basis for assistance; now receipt of assistance itself became a marker of undeservingness.

True, the fundamental underpinning of antiwelfare sentiment is social structure rather than political structure. The deservingness and undeservingness of welfare recipients both rest on the fact that women raise children. Over time, the racialized nature of poverty in the United States radically escalated antiwelfare sentiment, associating the alleged immorality and parasitism of welfare recipients not only with their gender but also with their race. But the achievement of today's virtual consensus in the United States on the pejorative meanings of welfare dependency could not have been achieved without both the negative and the (allegedly) positive discourses about women and mothers that arose from political advocacy. The 1996 repeal of welfare could not have been achieved without this antidependency chorus, which has created even among decent and generous people the idea that reducing the welfare rolls by forcing women into independence—in reality, an independence characterized by dependence on low-wage labor and disappearance into a ghettoized poverty—represented an achievement.

The notions of deservingness and obligation that underlay the repeal of AFDC and its replacement by a nonmandatory, temporary aid program (Temporary Aid to Needy Families, or TANF) remain today structured by gender, race, and class ideologies so pervasive and hegemonic that they seem like realism or even common sense. Not only are they unsupported by evidence, but they actually defy widespread ethical values. The ethical premise for forcing poor mothers into independence, defined as reliance on wages, represents a repudiation of the value of the work most universally associated with women: parenting. More accurately, the new values represent a class double standard that esteems female parental labor among the prosperous but not among the poor, although the labor is far harder and requires more skill among the poor. Poor mothers who devote themselves to their children are now defined as undeserving.

This lack of deservingness ascribed to our poorest—women and children—serves simultaneously to negate a sense of public obligation to help those who do parenting labor or who lack the advantages to compete for living-wage jobs in the labor market. The denial rests on closely related and equally false ideologies: that there are living-wage jobs for all and that there is equal opportunity to gain the skills necessary for a living wage. As with earlier gendered notions, TANF's values represent in addition a specifically gendered ideology about the wage labor market, one that equally veils reality. The program requires poor mothers to shift their dependence to wage labor while ignoring the realities of women's lower wages and inferior jobs in relation to men, not to mention the realities of the demands of child raising, particularly among the poor.

Pointing out that these beliefs are ideological does not necessarily mean that wage labor is undesirable for poor mothers. Very few households—even those with two parents—can survive now without women's wages. Moreover, studies show repeatedly that most AFDC recipients *want* to support themselves with wages. Where ideology overcame realism is in the use of coercion to force mothers to take jobs rather than beginning by enabling those who wanted to do so to live and support children on these jobs.

Not one state has enacted a program that realistically assesses what is needed to support even one mother and one child and then provided it.

Our welfare policy rests on a contradiction—an official honoring of motherhood combined with distrust, disdain, even contempt, for women who do it. As a result, those who were once quintessentially deserving, and to whom the whole society felt obligated—mothers—are often now prime examples of undeservingness, with very little sense of social obligation to aid them in their child-raising work. In fact, this contradiction extends to our overall policy toward working women and all poor women, whether they are lone mothers or not. The politicized family values of the last three decades often rest on denial of the actual difficulties of simultaneously earning for and caring for children, difficulties particularly great for low-wage-earning women.

Notes

1. When the Social Security Act was passed in 1935, the phrase "social security" was understood to refer to all types of programs of government provision, including aid to the elderly, the handicapped, the unemployed, the poor, and so on. Over three or four decades, the label migrated to refer specifically to old-age pensions, but in the 1930s and 1940s pensions were referred to by specific program titles, including Old Age Insurance and Old Age Assistance.

2. ADC became AFDC, Aid to Families with Dependent Children, in 1962 when coverage was extended to two-parent families, and AFDC-UP in 1961 when coverage was extended to two-parent families with unemployed fathers. In 1996, the program was repealed. It was replaced with Temporary Aid to Needy Families, which provides no guarantee of help and limits recipients to a certain number of years of aid.

3. Today, we would call these separated women. To understand the then common notion of desertion, we must recall the nineteenth-century Christian family and gender system that, in theory at any rate, considered marriage as an eternal sacrament and women as inevitably the weaker sex. Very few Americans at this time approved of breaking a marriage covenant. In such sinful behavior, there was a sinner and a sinned against; marital separation was rarely conceived of as mutual, a concept that expresses a greater acceptance (characteristic of the late twentieth century) of separation as an honorable alternative and of marriage as a human, not a divine, institution. Moreover, both feminists and antifeminists as well as most people in between agreed that women were usually the victims of marital breakup because of their economic dependence on men and their social and political subordination.

References

Baldwin, William. 1902. Making the Deserter Pay the Piper. *Survey* 23(20 Nov.):249–52.

Brandt, Lilian. 1905. *Five Hundred and Seventy-Four Deserters and Their Families: A Descriptive Study of Their Characteristics and Circumstances.* Committee on Social Research, no. 1. New York: Charity Organization Society.

Coll, Blanche. 1988. Public Assistance: Reviving the Original Comprehensive Concept of Social Security. In *Social Security: The First Half Century*, ed. Gerald D. Nash, Noel H. Pugach, and Richard F. Romasson. Albuquerque: University of New Mexico Press.

Committee on Economic Security. 1937. *Social Security in America.* Social Security Board, no. 20. Washington, DC: Social Security Board.

Commonwealth of Massachusetts. 1913. *Report of the Commission on the Support of Dependent Minor Children of Widowed Mothers.* Boston: Wright & Potter.

Eliot, Ada. 1900. Deserted Wives. *Charities Review* 10(5):346–49.

Gordon, Colin. Forthcoming. *Dead on Arrival.* Princeton, NJ: Princeton University Press.

Gordon, Linda. 1988. *Heroes of Their Own Lives: The Politics and History of Family Violence.* New York: Viking/Penguin.

———. 1994. *Pitied but Not Entitled: Single Mothers and the History of Welfare.* New York: Free Press.

Gordon, Linda and Sara McLanahan. 1991. Single Parenthood in 1900. *Journal of Family History* 16(2):97–116.

Kessler-Harris, Alice. 1995. Designing Women and Old Fools: The Construction of the Social Security Amendments of 1939. In *U.S. History as Women's History*, ed. Linda K. Kerber, Alice Kessler-Harris, and Kathryn Kish Sklar. Chapel Hill: University of North Carolina Press.

Kunzel, Regina P. 1988. The Professionalization of Benevolence: Evangelicals and Social Workers in the Florence Crittenden Homes, 1915–1945. *Journal of Social History* 22(1):21–44.

Levenstein, Lisa. 2000. From Innocent Children to Unwanted Migrants and Unwed Moms: Two Chapters in the Public Discourse on Welfare in the United States, 1960–61. *Journal of Women's History* 11(Winter): 10–33.

Lowe, Charlotte. 1927. The Intelligence and Social background of the Unmarried Mother. *Mental Hygiene* 11(4):793.

Lundberg, Emma and Katharine F. Lenroot. 1921. *Illegitimacy as a Child-Welfare Problem.* U.S. Children's Bureau, no. 75. Dependent, Defective, and Delinquent Classes series, no. 10. Washington, DC: U.S. Department of Labor.

New York State Commission on Relief for Widowed Mothers. 1914. Final Report. New York: New York State Commission on Relief for Widowed Mothers.

Skocpol, Theda. 1992. The Narrow Vision of Today's Experts on Social Policy. *Chronicle of Higher Education,* 15 Apr:B1.

Smith, Zilpha. 1901. *Deserted Wives and Deserving Husbands: A Study of 234 Families.* Boston: Geo. H. Ellis.

Weyl, Walter E. 1908. The Deserter. *Charities and the Commons* 21(5 Dec.):389.

Zunser, Charles. 1923. The National Desertion Bureau. In *Proceedings.* New York: National Conference of Jewish Social Service.

WELFARE REFORM AS RACE POPULATION CONTROL

KENNETH J. NEUBECK AND NOEL A. CAZENAVE

As a social control process, racism changes not only its face but its entire socially structured body to meet the changing needs of its white beneficiaries. It is a shape shifter. When the building of individual and national fortunes was predicated on cheap or unpaid labor from abroad, racial state policies encouraged both the importation of such labor and, once it arrived, high fertility rates, so that first slave labor, and then immigrant labor, would reproduce itself. However, racial state policies shifted once the national infrastructure had been built, and technological and economic changes diminished the need for cheap labor from abroad. And as white needs have changed, so too has welfare racism.

The ability of racism to adapt to meet the changing labor and other needs of racialized societies helps to explain why, as the United States moves deeper into a new millenium, the color line persists. As this line is redrawn it increasingly takes the form of a boundary line which enforces the sentiment that certain types of people should not be here. That is, "those people"—the racialized Other—should not be allowed to come into the United States. Moreover, so goes the sentiment, poor people of color who are here, whether immigrants or native born, should be discouraged from reproducing.

Even a quick glance at the rationale and provisions of the Personal Responsibility and Work Opportunity Reconciliation Act of 1996 (PRWORA) suggests that one of its authors' major goals—in addition to other racial control functions like forcing indolent African-American mothers receiving welfare to take jobs—was *race population control.* As we will show, the act focused on two types: procreation-focused race population control and immigration-focused race population control.

■ ■ ■ ■

Welfare Reform as Immigration-Focused Race Population Control

The PRWORA and the Color Line at U.S. Borders

[I]n the 1990s many European Americans believed that AFDC was essentially a "black program." It is important to stress, however, that welfare racism is not simply a matter of black and white. Latino/a Americans and other people of color are subject to welfare racist stereotypes similar to those imposed on African Americans, albeit to different degrees.[1] The impact of welfare racism on Latino/a Americans, Asian Americans, and other people of color becomes evident when we examine the link between racism, immigration, and welfare reform built into certain eligibility provisions of the Personal Responsibility and Work Opportunity Reconciliation Act. Indeed, consistent with demographic changes in the United States, it has been suggested that the stereotypical face of the undeserving welfare recipient is changing from the African-American "welfare queen" to the "Hispanic immigrant."[2]

A major goal of the framers of the PRWORA was to eliminate what was considered to be the welfare inducement for immigration to the United States. . . . The PRWORA and other immigration-focused race population control efforts were initiated in the 1990s by political elites who were concerned with the threat to white supremacy posed by those coming into U.S. society.

To reduce the numbers of poor people of color migrating to the United States, the PRWORA made both legal and illegal "aliens" ineligible for most federal programs. Illegal aliens were declared ineligible for Temporary Assistance for Needy Families; legal aliens were deemed not eligible until five years after they entered the United States. It was also stipulated that the individual states and public housing agencies were to report names, addresses, and other pertinent information regarding noncitizen recipients to the U.S. Immigration and Naturalization Service. Clearly the act was intended to serve a major immigration control function.[3]

When it comes to race population control policies the avoidance of overtly racist language by racial state actors is necessary. The passage of legislation to implement such policies typically requires that the racial sentiment upon which they are based remain camouflaged or out of sight. Consequently, what are essentially racial arguments tend to be couched in cultural rather than biological terms.

Racializing "Foreign" Culture, Demonizing Dark-Skinned Immigrants

The racial state actors who framed the immigration provisions of the PRWORA treated certain immigrant groups as foreign "aliens" who threatened to undermine the core U.S. value of "self-sufficiency." The tone of the act, and the rhetoric surrounding it, implied that large numbers of racially different aliens were coming to the United States ill prepared or unwilling to work, expecting public assistance and other government benefits, and with the goal of being dependent on government and hardworking taxpayers.[4] As is the case in science fiction movies, "aliens" from abroad were clearly depicted as Other—creatures unlike the socially dominant "us."

Immigrants, however, tended not to be treated explicitly by racial state actors as a racial Other. This covert tactic is effective both as an offensive and defensive maneuver. That is, the "race card" can be simultaneously played and denied. The racial contours of welfare policies aimed at keeping "aliens" out of the country are clearly visible, however, in the writings of some conservative policy analysts. Nowhere was this racial sentiment communicated more clearly than in the writings of Peter Brimelow, author of *Alien Nation*,[5] a book extremely critical of U.S. immigration policy. In that book, Brimelow expresses concern that immigration is bringing about an unprecedented racial and ethnic transformation of U.S. society. His ultimate nightmare is, as he put it, "the fateful day when American whites actually cease to be a majority."[6] Brimelow expresses concern as well with what he sees as the tendency of recent immigrants of color to join the welfare rolls.

■ ■ ■ ■

Understanding racism as a process requires examining the emotions that fuel it. While recent immigration-focused race population control policies have typically been justified by carefully selected facts and arguments regarding the benefits to society of restricting "our" borders, they are ultimately based largely on white racist sentiment toward people of color. As applied to certain groups of "aliens," that sentiment can be summed up as follows: "We don't want them here!"

This kind of overt racial sentiment is usually difficult to find in most public policy analysis, which tends to be couched in the methods of social science. With its claim to value neutrality, social science is even more skillful at camouflaging racial sentiment than are political elites.[7] This is obvious in painstakingly dispassionate "scientific" studies with patently racial agendas, such as Herrnstein and Murray's *The Bell Curve.*

Immigration Control through Welfare Denial

After the PRWORA was passed in 1996, welfare benefits were denied to impoverished immigrant families who needed help in their struggle to gain an economic foothold in U.S. society. We do not believe it was any accident that this attack on immigrants occurred in an era when, as was documented in great detail in *Alien Nation*, a high proportion of those who were coming to the United States were people of color from Latin America, the Caribbean, and Asia. After all, the very same racial state actors who incorporated highly racialized, New Paternalism-style, mandatory work and reproductive control provisions into the PRWORA also voted in its immigration control provisions.[8]

As an expression of welfare racism, the immigration-focused race population control provisions of the PRWORA parallel the racially exclusionary policies by which many impoverished African-American families were kept off the welfare rolls for many years. African Americans were not driven out of the United

States in response to such expressions of welfare racism. Likewise, it is extremely doubtful that immigrants of color—legal or illegal—will avoid coming to the United States, or that many of those already here will leave because of being denied access to public assistance. After all, as with African Americans, there is no evidence that welfare motivates immigrants' decisions to come, remain, or go, despite the claims of Brimelow and other political conservatives.[9] Instead, immigrants of color will continue to come across U.S. borders, legally or illegally, and many will choose to stay. But without access to Temporary Assistance for Needy Families, those who arrive impoverished will be much more vulnerable to the kinds of labor exploitation by employers to which native-born people of color denied welfare have always been vulnerable. Moreover, as immigrants' desperation for work swells the pool of labor seeking low-wage jobs, this puts downward pressure on wages for all low-wage workers—including whites. It seems unlikely that racial state actors who framed the immigration provisions of the PRWORA did not know this. While Brimelow and others anguish and wring their hands over fear that the United States will cease being a "white nation," the federal racial state's denial of welfare to immigrants does serve the interests of European-American economic elites and other members of the dominant class who are looking for cheap domestic labor.

■ ■ ■ ■

Controlling African-American Reproduction through Welfare Racism

Welfare Reform as Procreation-Focused Race Population Control

Congressional discourse preceding the passage of the Personal Responsibility and Work Opportunity Reconciliation Act of 1996 largely reflected concern with young, single, inner-city mothers. The act's proponents argued that such mothers need the incentive of restricted welfare benefits and strict time limits on welfare eligibility in order to motivate them to avoid out-of-wedlock pregnancies and to encourage them to marry. People from varying political viewpoints have drawn attention to the goal of procreation control in connection with the PRWORA and other recent welfare reform.

From the political left:

> *Ensuring that poor women do not reproduce has become one of the most popular welfare reform proposals of the 1990s.*[10]
>
> SUSAN L. THOMAS, POLITICAL SCIENTIST, HOLLINS UNIVERSITY

From the political right:

> *Today everyone recognizes that dealing with births out of wedlock is the central issue of welfare reform.*[11]
>
> DOUGLAS BESHAROV, AMERICAN ENTERPRISE INSTITUTE

And from those stuck in the middle:

> *I think they trying to say, trying to tell us to stop having kids.*[12]
>
> AFRICAN-AMERICAN MOTHER RECEIVING WELFARE, BOSTON

A "natalist perspective," which examines the social locations of different views concerning who should and who should not reproduce, provides a powerful lens through which to view the intersection of "race," class, gender, and the state. We agree with Susan Thomas that there is ample evidence that recent welfare reform legislation has been used to promote racially and class driven fertility control. First, low-income African-American women are disproportionately affected by such racial state legislation. Second, childbearing by low-income African American women in the United States has long been both devalued and discouraged by European Americans, having lost its economic value to dominant-class whites with the abolition of slavery. This observation is supported by an abundance of historical evidence on involuntary sterilization. Third, contemporary welfare discourse seems to be driven by racist stereotypes and negative controlling images of African-American women that stress their supposed hypersexuality, promiscuity, and enormous fecundity (e.g., the welfare queen).[13]

White Political Backlash and Black Motherhood as a Social Problem

Expressions of welfare racism have changed shape as the racial state moved away from public assistance policies of racial exclusion. When, in the 1960s, impoverished African-American mothers and their children could no longer be legally denied access to the welfare rolls and eligibility rules loosened, the rolls progressively expanded and their racial composition became visibly darker. It was seemingly inevitable, as part of the white political backlash fueling welfare racism, that mainstream political elites and policy analysts would become concerned with how welfare policy could be used to contribute to procreation-focused race population control. The latter had been openly called for by white supremacists for many years.

Because of their relative intensity and overtness, periods of white backlash are especially instructive of how procreation-focused race population control works, even under ordinary circumstances. Examining the white backlash process offers important insights into the dynamics of shifts in the racial state and its welfare policy discourse. An important public policy discourse accompaniment to the white political backlash that emerged in the 1960s was a gender shift in who was blamed for the intergenerational reproduction of poverty among African Americans.[14]

Emblematic of the white backlash that commenced in the 1960s was the so-called Moynihan Report on the changing composition of African-American families.[15] In this 1965 report, social scientist Daniel Patrick Moynihan, then a top official of the U.S. Department of Labor, presented Census Bureau statistics that documented African Americans' high rates of: 1) marital dissolution, 2) out-of-wedlock births, and 3) female-headed families.[16] The data Moynihan presented were not, however, the major source of the widespread controversy that his report generated when it became public. Indeed, in the decades since that report was published, the statistical portrait of African-American family structures has if anything become grimmer. The major locus of controversy was not the data in the report but their interpretation.

As the civil rights movement became more militant, the white political backlash began to manifest itself. By the mid-1960s, at a time when the Johnson administration was searching for a way to back away from its verbalized commitments to civil rights and economic justice,[17] the 1965 Moynihan report conveniently concluded that "at the heart of the deterioration of the fabric of Negro society is the deterioration of the Negro family."[18] With this conclusion Moynihan provided members of the Johnson administration and other racial state actors with the social science-legitimated ideology that they needed to redirect the blame for the poverty status of many African Americans from white racism to the supposed pathology of their families.[19]

[I]n connection with negative controlling images of African-American women, the specific target of blame in the Moynihan Report was the assumed dysfunctionality of "black matriarchy."[20] As both a family structure and process, the black matriarchy was assumed to be dysfunctional because it was different from the two-parent nuclear family considered normative by most European Americans and was seen as incapable of providing proper socialization of and control over rebellious young African-American males.[21] By its targeting of supposedly overly assertive and independent African-American female family heads at a time when the feminist movement in the United States had begun an important resurgence, the Moynihan Report also served an important early gender backlash function.[22]

With the publication of the Moynihan Report, the social science notion of a "culture of poverty," which blamed poverty on the values of the poor, was racially re-gendered. The report shifted attention away from the supposedly deficient values of African-American men as the chief cause of black intergenerational poverty and social pathology[23] to the deficient values of the "culture of single motherhood."[24] This revised culture of poverty focus would come to dominate the thinking of New Paternalism advocates and helped to frame provisions of the PRWORA.

A key ingredient in the re-gendering of the culture of poverty was the slavery-rooted, gendered racist controlling image of sexually promiscuous and irresponsible African-American women. In this image, free of and unburdened by either sexual or marital controls, low-income African-American women were seen as constituting a threat to the entire society's normative order and moral character. Not surprisingly, the principal solutions that political elites developed for the problem of the culture of single motherhood were public policy—pressured birth control and marriage.[25]

■■■■

Examining the Discourse over Unwanted "Breeding"

Our brief discussion of the Moynihan Report and its significance reveals the importance of viewing welfare racism in the broader context of race relations during a given historical period. In any historical period, welfare racism, like other forms of racism, is a process of racial control.[26] Analyses of social structures and processes can be framed around two key questions posed by distant observers: 1) *Who is there?* and 2) *What are they doing?*

. . . "Who is there?," is relevant to analyzing policies aimed at procreation-focused race population control, as well as policies aimed at immigration-focused race population control. Underlying these forms of race population control and the welfare policies to which they give rise is the racist sentiment that certain people of color should not be in a certain place in society, should not reside within its borders, or should not exist at all. Immigration-focused race population control and procreation-focused race population control are opposite sides of the "Who is there?" control coin.

While often presented by their advocates as if they were ostensibly concerned with the issue of overpopulation, U.S. reproductive control policies have tended to be fashioned by white male elites who impose their ideas about who should not reproduce on women from groups judged to be inherently inferior and undesirable.[27] Unfortunately, like many other expressions of white racism, procreation-focused race population control initiatives are often barely visible as such. Racial state actors are skilled at camouflaging them. Consequently, the racial sentiment underlying policies that might prove controversial and be contested by racially subordinated groups can be difficult to detect, much less to analyze or to oppose.[28] How explicit procreation-focused race population control advocates are in their proposals varies with both the nature of race relations at a particular point in time and with how deeply the proposals penetrate the political policy formation process.[29]

In the early 1960s the white segregationist Louisiana legislature pushed procreation-focused race population control legislation as a part of a white political backlash against court orders to desegregate public schools. But as the civil rights movement grew in strength and spread nationally, overt mention of procreation-focused race population control faced quick and powerful responses. Such measures could not be proposed without considerable risk of a counterattack. With the emergence of white political backlash against the movement later in the 1960s, the climate for race population control discourse and initiatives changed again. By the early 1970s, as the backlash was blossoming nationally and after the Moynihan Report had recast the problem of widespread African-American poverty as a problem of single motherhood, physicians engaged in widespread involuntary sterilization of low-income African-American women.[30]

A revealing example of the raw racist sentiment and stereotypes around which procreation-focused race population control proposals are sometimes organized is J. Philippe Rushton's *Race, Evolution, and Behavior.* Published in 1995, only a year after Herrnstein and Murray's controversial *The Bell Curve,* Rushton's book likewise employed the methods of scientific racism to provide ideological justification for racially targeted human eugenics. Both of these books exploited one of the U.S. society's oldest and most powerful racist stereotypes, the low intelligence of African Americans.

What made Rushton's book so effective in stirring up white racist animus and as a justification of racist human eugenics was its pseudoscientific linking of the stereotype of low African-American intelligence to the stereotype of African-American hypersexuality and fecundity. From his statistical analysis of race data, Rushton concluded that Mongoloids (or Asians) and

Caucasoids (or "whites") had "the largest brains," while "Negroids" (or "blacks") had the greatest reproductive capability.[31] Consistent with popular welfare racist stereotypes of African-American mothers having at state expense large numbers of children that they do not properly care for, Rushton argued that because of genetics, different races employ divergent reproductive and caregiving strategies to ensure their survival. Those high in intelligence (Asians and whites) have fewer children and make a higher "parental investment" in the children that they do have. In contrast, less intelligent "blacks" have more children and make less parental investment in them.[32]

Rushton's ideas and research did not emerge in isolation. Like much racial human eugenics research in the United States, his work was funded by The Pioneer Fund, a nonprofit foundation more than six decades old that makes grants of about a million dollars each year to academicians. Most of the researchers receiving foundation funds have dedicated themselves to establishing that racial differences in intelligence and personality are genetically based. Academicians whom the foundation has funded include not only Rushton, but William Shockley, Arthur Jensen, and Michael Levin.[33] The racist beliefs of these "scholars" is often evident from their public pronouncements. For example, in an interview with a reporter for *Rolling Stone* magazine, Rushton made the following summation of his research findings in response to the charge that he is in fact arguing that whites are racially superior to black people: "It's a trade off: more brain or more penis. You can't have everything."[34]

The Pioneer Fund's grant recipients lobbied for changes in immigration-focused race population control as a form of racial human eugenics.[35] They have also been vocal in advocating procreation-focused race population control policies targeted against welfare recipients. Stanford University's William Shockley, a longtime advocate of the view that African Americans are genetically inferior in intelligence to whites, "proposed sterilizing welfare recipients." Shockley's "Bonus Sterilization Plan" of cash incentives for low-I.Q. welfare recipients provoked controversy in the 1970s and 1980s.[36] City College of New York's Michael Levin, who complained that "the country is being overrun by people who don't work and have illegitimate children," blamed African Americans for many of society's social problems. His solution to these problems was simply stated: "End welfare . . . End welfare." According to Levin, ending welfare, by "ceasing to subsidize them . . . would automatically have a very excellent demographic effect."[37]

We believe that, while seldom expressed so overtly and publicly, such racial sentiments lie not far beneath the surface of much of the mainstream political discourse that has surrounded welfare reform. Periodically, however, such sentiments rise to the surface among political elites. The year before the PRWORA was passed in 1996, New Jersey Governor Christine Todd Whitman told a London publication about the "jewels in the crown" game she said was played by young African-American males, in which they compete to see who can impregnate the most women.[38]

In 1996, as welfare reform legislation moved through Congress, the Reform Party founder and presidential candidate, Ross Perot, provided television celebrity David Frost with his imitation of how black men approach reproduction. Note the multiple racist stereotypes that Perot mobilized:

> I'm just kind of a dumb dude who never finished the fourth grade. I'm wandering around the streets with my baseball hat on backward and $150 tennis shoes I knocked another kid out to get. I'm looking for real trouble to prove that I am a man. Well, how do I define what a man is? I define what a man is from the rap music I hear. . . . A man is defined in that culture as a breeder who gets the woman pregnant and then she gets welfare.[39]

This kind of overt racist stereotyping of black sexuality has occasionally leaked out of the mouths of political elites in one or another context. For example, a few years later, commenting on the likelihood that George W. Bush would become the Republican presidential nominee for the 2000 election, Utah's Republican Senator Bob Bennett stated that "unless George W. steps in front of a bus or some black woman comes forward with an illegitimate child that he fathered within the last 18 months," he would be the Republican nominee.[40]

■ ■ ■ ■

What Are They Doing?

[W]e have thus far explored how recent welfare reform policy was informed by concerns with immigration-focused race population control and procreation-focused race population control. Both forms of control address the analytical question "Who is there?" However, the PRWORA was also concerned with the work effort of welfare recipients. In that instance, consistent with white racist stereotypes of lazy African-American welfare recipients, racial state actors and other political elites were concerned with the second question emanating from concerns with racial control: "What are they doing?"

This concern with work effort was also closely linked to conservative political elites' efforts to frame welfare receipt as welfare "dependency," which they often depicted as "enslaving" poor mothers. Their attacks on dependency led some members of Congress to draw Social Darwinian analogies between welfare recipients and animals, similar to the animal analogy suggested by references to welfare recipients' "breeding" at which procreative race population control policies were aimed.[41] During the House debate on the Republican-proposed Personal Responsibility Act of 1995, Florida Representative Dan Mica spoke in support of the need for mandatory work requirements by comparing welfare recipients to alligators:

> Mr. Chairman, I represent Florida where we have many lakes and natural reserves. If you visit these areas, you may see a sign like this that reads, "Do Not Feed the Alligators." We post these signs for several reasons. First, because if left in a natural state, alligators can fend for themselves. They work, gather food, and care for their young. Second, we post these warnings because unnatural feeding and artificial care creates dependency. When dependency sets in, these otherwise able-bodied alligators can no longer survive on their own.
>
> Now, I know people are not alligators, but I submit to you that with our current handout, nonwork welfare system, we have upset the natural order. We have failed to understand the simple warning signs. We have created a system of dependency.[42]

Throwing her support behind mandatory work requirements, Wyoming Republican Representative Barbara Cubin likened welfare recipients to wolves in the same House debate:

> My home state is Wyoming, and recently the Federal Government introduced wolves into the State of Wyoming, and they put them in pens and they brought elk and venison to them every day. This is what I call the wolf welfare program. The Federal Government introduced them and they have since provided shelter and they have provided food, they have provided everything that the wolves need for their existence. Guess what? They opened the gate to let the wolves out and now the wolves will not go. They are cutting the fence down to make the wolves go out and the wolves will not go. What has happened with the wolves, just like what happens with human beings, when you take away their incentives, when you take away their freedom, when you take away their dignity, they have to be provided for. The biologists are now giving incentives outside of the gates, trying to get them out.[43]

As Congress moved to approve mandatory work requirements as a condition for the receipt of welfare by allegedly indolent mothers, the racism and classism that helped to shape such provisions of the Personal Responsibility and Work Opportunity Reconciliation Act of 1996 also seemed to immobilize many affluent white feminists, who might have been expected to oppose such punitive requirements for their gender and racial control impact on impoverished mothers of color.

The image of the lazy and promiscuous "welfare queen" and other racist controlling images of African-American women worked very effectively in the political assault on AFDC. They worked so well that many affluent white feminists and other liberal opponents of the PRWORA accepted the mandatory work provisions, and were inclined to express outrage only over what they predicted would be the bill's harmful impact on poor children. On the other hand, the predicament of mothers forced to rely on Temporary Assistance for Needy Families was assumed to be self-inflicted. Their alleged work, family, and reproductive behaviors were thought to be indefensible. Consequently any concern expressed was often only for the innocent child victims of welfare reform, not for despicable welfare queens.[44]

Indeed, some opponents of welfare reform had so completely internalized or been caught up with such racist controlling images—either out of contempt for poor single mothers or fear of having the "legitimate" concerns of feminists tarnished, or both—that they failed to see mothers receiving welfare as women or welfare reform as a women's issue. Consequently, although the targets of punitive welfare reform were clearly impoverished mothers of color, many affluent white feminists failed to fight a piece of landmark welfare reform legislation which, in appearance at least, de-gendered the issue.

Notes

1. Lawrence Bobo and James M. Kluegel, "Modern American Prejudice: Stereotypes, Social Distance, and Perceptions of Discrimination toward Blacks, Hispanics, and Asians." Paper presented at the 1991 meetings of the American Sociological Association, Cincinnati.
2. Amy Ansell, *New Right, New Racism: Race and Reaction in the United States and Britain* (Washington Square: New York University, 1997), p. 230.
3. Personal Responsibility and Work Opportunity Reconciliation Act of 1996 (Enrolled bill sent to president) 104th Congress, at http://thomas.loc.gov.
4. Ibid.
5. Peter Brimelow, *Alien Nation: Common Sense about America's Immigration Disaster* (New York: Random House, 1995), p. xvii. We are not suggesting, however, that Peter Brimelow's works represent the views articulated by most conservatives who have addressed the issue. Some conservatives are in favor of the relatively open new immigration policies which they feel strengthen the economy and provide powerful evidence that with the proper motivation and work ethic anyone can achieve affluence in the United States, a land of extraordinary opportunity. Economic conservatives are likely to favor policies that encourage open immigration, whereas social conservatives are more likely to oppose such policies. For an example of a pro-immigration conservative view, see Ron K. Unz, "Immigration or the Welfare State: Which Is Our Enemy?" *Policy Review* (fall 1994): 33–38. Also see George Gilder's and Jack Kemp's comments in "Immigration: Where to Go from Here," *Wall Street Journal*, November 27, 1995.
6. Brimelow, *Alien Nation*, p. 65.
7. Nina Perales, "A Tangle of Pathology: Racial Myth and the New Jersey Family Development Act," in *Mothers in Law: Feminist Theory and the Legal Regulation of Motherhood*, ed. Martha Fineman and Isadore Karpin (New York: Columbia University Press, 1995), pp. 258–259. She also discusses a much more sophisticated expression of anti-immigration and antiwelfare sentiment. She cites a *New York Times* op-ed essay by a Nobel Prize–winning economist as "using the image of the immigrant on welfare to symbolize a racial threat to the country." In that October 14, 1992, essay Gary Becker argued that to keep immigrants from poor countries from coming to the United States in search of welfare benefits, immigration permits should be auctioned.
8. The conservative anti-immigrant sentiment in the Congress was not only reflected in the PRWORA. In 1996, the Republican-dominated Congress also passed the Illegal Immigrant Reform and Immigrant Responsibility Act. This act expanded the grounds for deportation of immigrants, drastically reduced their rights to appeal, and speeded up the deportation process. The result has been a sharp rise in deportations, particularly of recent immigrants. See Eric Rich, "Deportations Soar under Rigid Law," *Hartford Courant*, October 8, 2000, pp. A1, A8.
9. On debunking the myth that poor residents migrate within the United States to get better welfare benefits, see Sanford F. Schram, Lawrence Nitz, and Gary Krueger, "Welfare Migration as a Policy Rumor: A Statistical Accounting," in *Tales of the State: Narrative in Contemporary U.S. Politics and Public Policy*, ed. Sanford F. Schram and Philip T. Neisser (Lanham, MD: Rowman & Littlefeld, 1997), pp. 139–149.
10. Susan Thomas, "Race, Gender, and Welfare Reform: The Antinatalist Response," *Journal of Black Studies* 28 (March 1998): 420.
11. Quoted in Nancy Gibbs, "The Vicious Cycle," *Time*, June 1994, pp. 25–32.
12. Linda Burton et al., *What Welfare Recipients and the Fathers of Their Children Are Saying about Welfare Reform* (June 1998), p. 11. This is the first report from "Welfare Reform and Children: A Three-City Study," a project conducted in Baltimore, Boston, and Chicago. Available from www.jhu.edu/~welfare/.
13. Thomas, "Race, Gender, and Welfare Reform," p. 437. For more on racism and eugenics see Steven Selden, *Inheriting Shame: The Story of Eugenics and Racism in America* (New York: Teachers College Press, 1999). In a broadcast by popular radio talk-show host Bob Grant,

Grant was quoted mimicking the dialect of an African-American welfare recipient who laments, "I don't have no job, how'm I gonna feed my family?" In explaining what he saw as their great reproductive proclivities and the need for the "Bob Grant Mandatory Sterilization Act," Grant stated, "It's like maggots on a hot day. You look back one minute and there are so many there, and you look again and, wow, they've tripled!" Quoted in Dorothy Roberts, *Killing the Black Body: Race, Reproduction, and the Meaning of Liberty* (New York: Vintage Books, 1997), p. 18.
14. Thomas, pp. 420, 426.
15. Lee Rainwater and William L. Yancey, *The Moynihan Report and the Politics of Controversy* (Cambridge: MIT Press, 1967).
16. Ibid. See also Noel A. Cazenave, "Race, Class, Ideology and Changing Black Family Structures and Processes," in *Institutional Racism and Black America: Challenges, Choices, Change*, ed. Mfanya Donald Tryman (Lexington, MA: Ginn, 1985), p. 40.
17. Cazenave, "Race, Class, Ideology," p. 41.
18. Rainwater and Yancey, *The Moynihan Report*, p. 5.
19. Cazenave, "Race, Class, Ideology," p. 41.
20. Roberts, *Killing the Black Body*, p. 16.
21. Rainwater and Yancey, *The Moynihan Report.*
22. Thomas, "Race, Gender, and Welfare Reform."
23. For a critique of this view of the culture of poverty, see Elliot Liebow, *Tally's Corner: A Study of Negro Streetcorner Men* (Boston: Little Brown, 1967).
24. Thomas, "Race, Gender, and Welfare Reform," p. 426. See also Susan L. Thomas, "From the Culture of Poverty to the Culture of Single Motherhood: The New Poverty Paradigm," *Women & Politics* 14 (1994): 65–97.
25. Thomas, "Race, Gender, and Welfare Reform," pp. 419–420, 426.
26. Consistent with this approach, Thomas defines racism as "a process of systematic oppression directed against people who are defined as inferior, usually in pseudobiological terms such as skin color." Thomas, "Race, Gender, and Welfare Reform," p. 441, note 4.
27. Thomas M. Shapiro, *Population Control Politics: Women, Sterilization and Reproductive Choice* (Philadelphia: Temple University Press, 1985), pp. 9, 29. His analysis of population control efforts targeted at low-income women of color influenced our use of the term *race population control.*
28. Ibid., p. 23.
29. Shapiro makes the latter point. Ibid.
30. Ibid., p. 5. Shapiro cites a 1974 federal court ruling that found: "Over the last few years, an estimated 100,000 to 150,000 low-income persons have been sterilized annually under federally funded programs," and "an indefinite number of poor people have been improperly coerced into accepting a sterilization operation under the threat that various federally supported welfare benefits would be withdrawn" (p. 5). See also Roberts, *Killing the Black Body*, pp. 90–91.
31. J. Philippe Rushton, *Race, Evolution, and Behavior* (New Brunswick, NJ: Transaction Publications, 1995), p.4.
32. Ibid., p. xiii.
33. Adam Miller, "Professors of Hate," *Rolling Stone*, October 20, 1994, pp. 107–108, 110, 112–114.
34. Ibid., p. 112.
35. Ibid., pp. 107, 114.
36. Ibid., pp. 107, 113.
37. Ibid., p. 108.
38. Joseph F. Sullivan, "Whitman Apologizes for Remarks on Blacks," *New York Times*, April 14, 1995, p. B6; "New Jersey Gov. Christie Whitman Apologizes for Racial Slur," *Jet*, May 1, 1995, p. 6.
39. "News of the Weak in Review," *The Nation*, May 20, 1996, p. 7.
40. Paul Foy, "Bennett Apologizes to Black Leaders," Associated Press, August 24, 1999.
41. See Charles Derber, "The Politics of Triage: The Contract with America's Surplus Populations," *Tikkun*, 10 (May 1995): 40.
42. *Congressional Record*, U.S. House of Representatives, 104th Congress, March 24, 1995, p. H3766.
43. Ibid., p. H3772.
44. Gwendolyn Mink, *Welfare's End* (Ithaca, NY: Cornell University Press, 1998), pp. 1–2. Mink observed that while there were some feminist activist exceptions, for the most part "among policy makers, even the usual champions of gender equality erased mothers from the debate."

THE THREE WORLDS OF WELFARE CAPITALISM

GØSTA ESPING-ANDERSEN

Welfare-state studies have been motivated by theoretical concerns with other phenomena, such as power, industrialization, or capitalist contradictions; the welfare state itself has generally received scant conceptual attention. If welfare states differ, how do they differ? And when, indeed, is a state a welfare state? This turns attention straight back to the original question: what is the welfare state?

A common textbook definition is that it involves state responsibility for securing some basic modicum of welfare for its citizens. Such a definition skirts the issue of whether social policies are emancipatory or not; whether they help system legitimation or not; whether they contradict or aid the market process; and what, indeed, is meant by "basic"? Would it not be more appropriate to require of a welfare state that it satisfies more than our basic or minimal welfare needs?

■■■■

Rights and De-commodification

In pre-capitalist societies, few workers were properly commodities in the sense that their survival was contingent upon the sale of their labor power. It is as markets become universal and hegemonic that the welfare of individuals comes to depend entirely on the cash nexus. Stripping society of the institutional layers that guaranteed social reproduction outside the labor contract meant that people were commodified. In turn, the introduction of modern social rights implies a loosening of the pure commodity status. De-commodification occurs when a service is rendered as a matter of right, and when a person can maintain a livelihood without reliance on the market.

The mere presence of social assistance or insurance may not necessarily bring about significant de-commodification if they do not substantially emancipate individuals from market dependence. Means-tested poor relief will possibly offer a safety net of last resort. But if benefits are low and associated with social stigma, the relief system will compel all but the most desperate to participate in the market. This was precisely the intent of the nineteenth-century poor laws in most countries. Similarly, most of the early social-insurance programs were deliberately designed to maximize labor-market performance (Ogus, 1979).

There is no doubt that de-commodification has been a hugely contested issue in welfare state development. For labor, it has always been a priority. When workers are completely market-dependent, they are difficult to mobilize for solidaristic action. Since their resources mirror market inequalities, divisions emerge between the "ins" and the "outs", making labor-movement formation difficult. De-commodification strengthens the worker and weakens the absolute authority of the employer. It is for exactly this reason that employers have always opposed de-commodification.

De-commodified rights are differentially developed in contemporary welfare states. In social-assistance dominated welfare states, rights are not so much attached to work performance as to demonstrable need. Needs-tests and typically meager benefits, however, service to curtail the de-commodifying effect. Thus, in nations where this model is dominant (mainly in the Anglo-Saxon countries), the result is actually to strengthen the market since all but those who fail in the market will be encouraged to contract private-sector welfare.

A second dominant model espouses compulsory state social insurance with fairly strong entitlements. But again, this may not automatically secure substantial de-commodification, since this hinges very much on the fabric of eligibility and benefit rules. Germany was the pioneer of social insurance, but over most of the century can hardly be said to have brought about much in the way of de-commodification through its social programs. Benefits have depended almost entirely on contributions, and thus on work and employment. In other words, it is not the mere presence of a social right, but the corresponding rules and preconditions, which dictate the extent to which welfare programs offer genuine alternatives to market dependence.

The third dominant model of welfare may, at first glance, appear the most de-commodifying. It offers a basic, equal benefit to all, irrespective of prior earnings, contributions, or performance. It may indeed be a more solidaristic system, but not necessarily de-commodifying, since only rarely have such schemes been able to offer benefits of such a standard that they provide recipients with a genuine option to working.

De-commodifying welfare states are, in practice, of very recent date. A minimal definition must entail that citizens can freely, and without potential loss of job, income, or general welfare, opt out of work when they themselves consider it necessary. With this definition in mind, we would, for example, require of a sickness insurance that individuals be guaranteed benefits equal to normal earnings, and the right to absence with minimal proof of medical impairment and for the duration that the individual deems necessary. These conditions, it is worth noting, are those usually enjoyed by academics, civil servants, and higher-echelon white-collar employees. Similar requirements would be made of pensions, maternity leave, parental leave, educational leave, and unemployment insurance.

Some nations have moved towards this level of de-commodification, but only recently, and, in many cases, with significant exemptions. In almost all nations, benefits were upgraded to nearly equal normal wages in the late 1960s and early 1970s. But in some countries, for example, prompt medical certification in case of illness is still required; in others, entitlements depend on long waiting periods of up to two weeks; and in still others, the duration of entitlements is very short. . . . [T]he Scandinavian welfare states tend to be the most de-commodifying; the Anglo-Saxon the least.

The Welfare State as a System of Stratification

A more basic question, it seems, is what kind of stratification system is promoted by social policy. The welfare state is not just a mechanism that intervenes in, and possibly corrects, the structure of inequality; it is, in its own right, a system of stratification. It is an active force in the ordering of social relations.

Comparatively and historically, we can easily identify alternative systems of stratification embedded in welfare states. The poor-relief tradition, and its contemporary means-tested social-assistance offshoot, was conspicuously designed for purposes of stratification. By punishing and stigmatizing recipients, it promotes social dualisms and has therefore been a chief target of labor-movement attacks.

The social-insurance model promoted by conservative reformers such as Bismarck and von Taffe, was also explicitly a form of class politics. It sought, in fact, to achieve two simultaneous results in terms of stratification. The first was to consolidate divisions among wage-earners by legislating distinct programs for different class and status groups, each with its own conspicuously unique set of rights and privileges which was designed to accentuate the individual's appropriate station in life. The second objective was to tie the loyalties of the individual directly to the monarchy or the central state authority. This was Bismarck's motive when he promoted a direct state supplement to the pension benefit. This state-corporatist model was pursued mainly in nations such as Germany, Austria, Italy, and France, and often resulted in a labyrinth of status-specific insurance funds.

Of special importance in this corporatist tradition was the establishment of particularly privileged welfare provisions for the civil service. In part, this was a means of rewarding loyalty to the state, and in part it was a way of demarcating this group's uniquely exalted social status. The corporatist status-differentiated model springs mainly from the old guild tradition. The neo-absolutist autocrats, such as Bismarck, saw in this tradition a means to combat the rising labor movements.

The labor movements were as hostile to the corporatist model as they were to poor relief—in both cases for obvious reasons. Yet the alternatives first espoused by labor were no less problematic from the point of view of uniting the workers as one solidaristic class. Almost invariably, the model that labor first pursued was that of self-organized friendly societies or equivalent union- or party-sponsored fraternal welfare plans. This is not surprising. Workers were obviously suspicious of reforms sponsored by a hostile state, and saw their own organizations not only as bases of class mobilization, but also as embryos of an alternative world of solidarity and justice; as a microcosm of the socialist haven to come. Nonetheless, these micro-socialist societies often became problematic class ghettos that divided rather than united workers. Membership was typically restricted to the strongest strata of the working class, and the weakest—who most needed protection—were most likely excluded. In brief, the fraternal society model frustrated the goal of working-class mobilization.

The socialist "ghetto approach" was an additional obstacle when socialist parties found themselves forming governments and having to pass the social reforms they had so long demanded. For political reasons of coalition-building and broader solidarity, their welfare model had to be recast as welfare for "the people." Hence, the socialists came to espouse the principle of universalism; borrowing from the liberals, their program was, typically, designed along the lines of the democratic flat-rate, general revenue-financed model.

As an alternative to means-tested assistance and corporatist social insurance, the universalistic system promotes equality of status. All citizens are endowed with similar rights, irrespective of class or market position. In this sense, the system is meant to cultivate cross-class solidarity, a solidarity of the nation. But the solidarity of flat-rate universalism presumes a historically peculiar class structure, one in which the vast majority of the population are the "little people" for whom a modest, albeit egalitarian, benefit may be considered adequate. Where this no longer obtains, as occurs with growing working-class prosperity and the rise of the new middle classes, flat-rate universalism inadvertently promotes dualism because the better-off turn to private insurance and to fringe-benefit bargaining to supplement modest equality with what they have decided are accustomed standards of welfare. Where this process unfolds (as in Canada or Great Britain), the result is that the wonderfully egalitarian spirit of universalism turns into a dualism similar to that of the social-assistance state: the poor rely on the state, and the remainder on the market.

It is not only the universalist but, in fact, all historical welfare-state models which have faced the dilemma of changes in class structure. But the response to prosperity and middle-class growth has been varied, and so, therefore, has been the outcome in terms of stratification. The corporatist insurance tradition was, in a sense, best equipped to manage new and loftier welfare-state expectations since the existing system could technically be upgraded quite easily to distribute more adequate benefits. Adenauer's 1957 pension-reform in Germany was a pioneer in this respect. It avowed purpose was to restore status differences that had been eroded because of the old insurance system's incapacity to provide benefits tailored to expectations. This it did simply by moving from contribution- to earnings-graduated benefits without altering the framework of status-distinctiveness.

In nations with either a social-assistance or a universalistic-type system, the option was whether to allow the market or the state to furnish adequacy and satisfy middle-class aspirations. Two alternative models emerged from this political choice. The one typical of Great Britain and most of the Anglo-Saxon world was to preserve an essentially modest universalism in the state, and allow the market to reign for the growing social strata demanding superior welfare. Due to the political power of such groups, the dualism that emerges is not merely one between state and market, but also between forms of welfare-state transfers: in these nations, one of the fastest growing components of public expenditure is tax subsidies for so-called "private" welfare plans. And the typical political effect is the erosion of middle-class support for what is less and less a universalistic public-sector transfer system.

Yet another alternative has been to seek a synthesis of universalism and adequacy outside of the market. This road has been followed in countries where, by mandating or legislation, the state incorporates the new middle classes within a luxurious second-tier, universally inclusive, earnings-related insurance scheme on top of the flat-rate egalitarian one. Notable examples are Sweden and Norway. By guaranteeing benefits tailored to expectations, this solution reintroduces benefit inequalities, but effectively blocks off the market. It thus succeeds in retaining universalism and also, therefore, the degree of political consensus required to preserve broad and solidaristic support for the high taxes that such a welfare-state model demands.

Welfare-State Regimes

As we survey international variations in social rights and welfare-state stratification, we will find qualitatively different arrangements between state, market, and the family. The welfare-state variations we find are therefore not linearly distributed, but clustered by regime-types.

In one cluster we find the "liberal" welfare state, in which means-tested assistance, modest universal transfers, or modest social-insurance plans predominate. Benefits cater mainly to a clientele of low-income, usually working-class, state dependents. In this model, the progress of social reform has been severely circumscribed by traditional, liberal work-ethnic norms: it is one where the limits of welfare equal the marginal propensity to opt for welfare instead of work. Entitlement rules are therefore strict and often associated with stigma; benefits are typically modest. In turn, the state encourages the market, either passively—by guaranteeing only a minimum—or actively—by subsidizing private welfare schemes.

The consequence is that this type of regime minimizes de-commodification-effects, effectively contains the realm of social rights, and erects an order of stratification that is a blend of a relative equality of poverty among state-welfare recipients, market-differentiated welfare among the majorities, and a class-political dualism between the two. The archetypical examples of this model are the United States, Canada and Australia.

A second regime-type clusters nations such as Austria, France, Germany, and Italy. Here, the historical corporatist-statist legacy was upgraded to cater to the new "post-industrial" class structure. In these conservative and strongly "corporatist" welfare states, the liberal obsession with market efficiency and commodification was never preeminent and, as such, the granting of social rights was hardly ever a seriously contested issue. What predominated was the preservation of status differentials; rights, therefore, were attached to class and status. This corporatism was subsumed under a state edifice perfectly ready to displace the market as a provider of welfare; hence, private insurance and occupational fringe benefits play a truly marginal role. On the other hand, the state's emphasis on upholding status differences means that its redistributive impact is negligible.

But the corporatist regimes are also typically shaped by the Church, and hence strongly committed to the preservation of traditional familyhood. Social insurance typically excludes nonworking wives, and family benefits encourage motherhood. Day care, and similar family services, are conspicuously underdeveloped; the principle of "subsidiarity" serves to emphasize that the state will only interfere when the family's capacity to service its members is exhausted.

The third, and clearly smallest, regime-cluster is composed of those countries in which the principles of universalism and de-commodification of social rights were extended also to the new middle classes. We may call it the "social democratic" regime-type since, in these nations, social democracy was clearly the dominant force behind social reform. Rather than tolerate a dualism between state and market, between working class and middle class, the social democrats pursued a welfare state that would promote an equality of the highest standards, not an equality of minimal needs as was pursued elsewhere. This implied, first, that services and benefits be upgraded to levels commensurate with even the most discriminating tastes of the new middle classes; and, second, that equality be furnished by guaranteeing workers full participation in the quality of rights enjoyed by the better-off.

This formula translates into a mix of highly de-commodifying and universalistic programs that, nonetheless, are tailored to differentiated expectations. Thus, manual workers come to enjoy rights identical to those of salaried white-collar employees or civil servants; all strata are incorporated under one universal insurance system, yet benefits are graduated according to accustomed earnings. This model crowds out the market, and consequently constructs an essentially universal solidarity in favor of the welfare state. All benefit; all are dependent; and all will presumably feel obliged to pay.

The social democratic regime's policy of emancipation addresses both the market and the traditional family. In contrast to the corporatist-subsidiarity model, the principle is not to wait until the family's capacity to aid is exhausted, but to preemptively socialize the costs of familyhood. The ideal is not to maximize dependence on the family, but capacities for individual independence. In this sense, the model is a peculiar fusion of liberalism and socialism. The result is a welfare state that grants transfers directly to children, and takes direct responsibility of caring for children, the aged, and the helpless. It is, accordingly, committed to a heavy social-service burden, not only to service family needs but also to allow women to choose work rather than the household.

Perhaps the most salient characteristic of the social democratic regime is its fusions of welfare and work. It is at once genuinely committed to a full-employment guarantee, and entirely dependent on its attainment. On the one side, the right to work has equal status to the right of income protection. On the other side, the enormous costs of maintaining a solidaristic, universalistic, and de-commodifying welfare system means that it must minimize revenue income. This is obviously best done with most people working, and the fewest possible living off of social transfers.

Neither of the two alternative regime-types espouse full employment as an integral part of their welfare-state commitment. In the conservative tradition, of course, women are discouraged from working; in the liberal ideal, concerns of gender matter less than the sanctity of the market.

. . . [W]elfare states cluster, but we must recognize that there is no single pure cause. The Scandinavian countries may be predominantly social democratic, but they are not free of crucial liberal elements. Neither are the liberal regimes pure types. The American social-security system is redistributive, compulsory, and far from actuarial. At least in its early formulation, the New Deal was as social democratic as was contemporary Scandinavian social democracy. And European conservative regimes have incorporated both liberal and social democratic impulses. Over the decades, they have become less corporativist and less authoritarian.

Notwithstanding the lack of purity, if our essential criteria for defining welfare states have to do with the quality of social rights, social stratification, and the relationship between state, market, and family, the world is obviously composed of distinct regime-clusters. . . .

Reference

Ogus, A. 1979: Social insurance, legal development and legal history. In H. F. Zacher, (ed.), *Bedingungen fur die Entstehung von Sozialversicherung*. Berlin: Duncker und Humboldt.

SECTION V
MEDIA AND IDEOLOGY

Since the mid-1970s, the students, faculty, and staff at Sonoma State University in northern California have been putting together a very informative annual edition called *Censored* (Phillips 2003). Each year they list the top twenty-five censored news stories judged by a distinguished team of media specialists. What links these stories is that they expose unethical or criminal behavior by corporations and government institutions. Among the top twenty five stories in the latest edition we find:

- U.S. Illegally Removes Pages from Iraq U.N. Report
- The Effort to Make Unions Disappear
- Closing Access to Information Technology
- Treaty Busting by the United States
- In Afghanistan: Poverty, Women's Rights, and Civil Disruption Worse than Ever
- Africa Faces Threat of New Colonialism
- U.S. Military's War on the Earth
- Third World Austerity Policies: Coming Soon to a City Near You
- Welfare Reform Up for Reauthorization, But Still No Safety Net
- Convicted Corporations Receive Perks Instead of Punishment

While the mainstream media give time and space to conservative commentators who charge that the media are liberal, it is striking that none of the above stories received any coverage in a major urban daily paper anywhere in the United States (Alterman 2003). Nor were they broadcast on mainstream radio or television stations. Instead they appeared in the small alternative press, publications such as *The Asheville Global Report, The Texas Observer, Z Magazine, The Progressive, The Nation, Peacework, Mother Jones*, and others. The important question is why? Why is it that in a democracy where people need to have access to factual information about the important issues of the day to make informed political decisions, they are denied that information by the newspapers, magazines, and radio and television stations that most people read, listen to, and watch?

There are a number of factors that bear on this question, but the most important is that the media are commercialized big business, operating to generate profits through the sale of time and space to advertisers. In the first edition of his book *The Media Monopoly* in 1983, Ben Bagdikian reported that fifty firms dominated the mass media in the United States. By the time the sixth edition came out in the year 2000, Bagdikian reported that the number of dominant firms had been reduced to six. They are AOL/Time Warner, Disney, Viacom (an amalgam of CBS and Westinghouse), News Corporation, Bertelsmann, and General Electric. These six have more annual media revenues than the next twenty media corporations combined (Bagdikian 2000: x, xx; Phillips 2003: 171–79). These are vertically integrated firms that produce newspapers, magazines, books, movies, and radio and television programming. They also own broadcast and cable networks, and own or have interests in phone lines, cable systems, and satellite dishes (Bagdikian 2000: xvii).

The status of media corporations as giant economic enterprises means that they are linked through shared members of their boards of directors with hundreds of other large corporate enterprises. These media and nonmedia corporations broadly share the same class interests. They benefit from nonunion labor, cheaper labor, automated technologies, low taxes, accelerated depreciation on capital investments, subsidized and protected foreign investments, and growing concentrations of corporate wealth. This is reflected in the themes of their entertainment programs, what they decide is newsworthy, and how articles are written and where they are placed.

In the first selection, Robert Perrucci and Earl Wysong examine the content of the television and film industries. Although there are occasional exceptions, they argue that most of what is offered serves to divert people's attention from serious economic and political issues. Furthermore, when these issues are presented, it is done in a way that excludes any consideration of social classes and conflicting class interests. Perrucci and Wysong note that the terrorist attacks of September 11, 2001 did temporarily shift media attention from the infotainment themes and story lines. Yet this was done in a familiar context of focusing on individual human interest stories. The media otherwise lent themselves entirely to allowing official spokespersons, such as the president, define the events. Americans were told that the attacks were caused by other nations' jealousies over America's freedoms and living standards. As events unfolded into war against Afghanistan and later Iraq, there was a striking absence of dissenting views, presentations of policy alternatives, and discussions of the causes of anti-Americanism that would lead to 9/11. One of the reasons given for the invasion of Iraq was to seize and destroy Iraqi weapons of mass destruction. When no such weapons were found, the issue disappeared from the headlines. The media, in other words, and we believe this is typical, served less to inform the public than to shift public opinion in the direction of already decided upon policy options (Ali 2002; Kellner 2003; Rampton and Stauber 2003).

In the second selection, Edward S. Herman and Noam Chomsky further develop the themes introduced by Perrucci and Wysong by introducing their propaganda model of the media. Here they argue that "... among their other functions, the media serve, and propagandize on behalf of, the powerful social interests that control and finance them." In their book *Manufacturing Consent* (Herman and Chomsky 2002), the authors trace the trends in increasing media concentration and then examine the media's coverage of major foreign policy issues in Central America and Southeast Asia along with a number of domestic issues including international trade agreements, labor-management conflict, and chemical hazards in the environment. The selection reprinted here highlights recent media mergers and their impact on media coverage of globalization and its opponents.

Wars are always most popular at the beginning, before the human and social costs are brought home to people. By the early 1970s, the Vietnam War had become the most unpopular of America's foreign wars if one can judge by public opinion polling results and high levels of sustained protest over many years. The possibility of future antiwar protest, particularly one that linked civilian and GI concerns, as was the case during the Vietnam War (Hunt 2001), threatened the ability of corporate and governmental elites to engage in military actions abroad. Since those actions were considered essential to access raw materials, cheap labor, and markets, and to enforce free trade agreements, efforts were made to create a national mood more favorable to war. One prong of that effort was to divide civilians from the military and to portray antiwar movements as unpatriotic, and even treasonous. An important linchpin in this argument was to bury the history of military opposition to the Vietnam War and to create a myth of GI hatred by the anti-Vietnam War movement. Central to that effort was promoting the myth of antiwar protestors spitting on returning Vietnam War veterans. Once that myth was widely established in American culture, it could be argued that opposition to the war constituted a refusal to support American troops. In the last selection, Jerry Lembcke examines the media's role in promoting the myth of the spat-upon Vietnam War veteran combined with the yellow ribbon display to mobilize public support for the 1991 war with Iraq. Similar processes were repeated for the current Iraq war through the use of symbol and myth to manufacture support for war within a very narrow definition of patriotism.

Despite the considerable power of the mass media to shape public consciousness in the interests of the privileged, there still remains room for people and organizations to challenge mainstream media. This reinforces the point made by Gramsci earlier in Section I that hegemony is never absolute and always contains opportunities for resistance. The United States, for example, has a lively (though marginalized) alternative press (Phillips 2003). There are also growing challenges to media throughout the world by labor, peasant, feminist, environmental, and other progressive groups in an effort to create a media more responsive to public needs (McChesney and Nichols 2002).

References

Ali, Tariq. 2003. *The Clash of Fundamentalisms: Crusades, Jihads, and Modernity.* New York: Verso.

Alterman, Eric. 2003. *The Myth of the Liberal Media: The Truth About Bias in the News.* New York: Basic Books.

Bagdikian, Ben H. 2000. *The Media Monopoly.* Boston: Beacon Press.

Herman, Edward S. and Noam Chomsky. 2002. *Manufacturing Consent: The Political Economy of the Mass Media.* New York: Pantheon.

Hunt, Andrew E. 2001. *The Turning: A History of Vietnam Veterans Against the War.* New York: New York University Press.

Kellner, Doug. 2003. *From 9/11 to Terror War: Dangers of the Bush Legacy.* Lanham, MD: Roman & Littlefield.

McChesney, Robert W. and John Nichols. 2002. *Our Media, Not Theirs: The Democratic Struggle Against Corporate Media.* New York: Seven Stories Press.

Phillips, Peter, and Project Censored. 2003. *Censored 2004: The Top 25 Censored Stories.* New York: Seven Stories Press.

Rampton, Sheldon, and John Stauber. 2003. *Weapons of Mass Deception: The Uses of Propaganda in Bush's War on Iraq.* New York: Putnam Publishing Group.

THE PACIFICATION OF EVERYDAY LIFE

ROBERT PERRUCCI AND EARL WYSONG

The culture industry . . . encompasses far more than the dissemination of information. It is a complex enterprise composed of large multimedia firms that are increasingly interlocked with even larger industrial and service corporations, advertising agencies, and nominally nonprofit groups (such as the Public Broadcasting Service). The heart of this industry consists of large firms that produce and disseminate a wide range of entertainment, information, and advertising products through television, radio, recorded music, movies, books, newspapers, magazines, and the Internet. . . . [O]ur goal here is to present a brief overview of the scope and content of the electronic-media segment of the industry—especially television and films—to provide a sense of how it contributes to the pacification of everyday life.

The massive scope and everyday reach of the electronic media are evident in the huge distribution networks that disseminate culture-industry products such as TV and radio programming, sporting events, movies, videotapes, audio tapes and CDs, video games, and Internet website materials to thousands of communities and millions of homes and consumers. In the early 2000s, the "wiring of America" provided electronic links between various media firms and seven thousand hometown movie theaters (with 36,000 screens), the 98 percent of households with TVs (85 percent of TV households had VCRs), and 67 percent of TV households with TV cable or satellite service.[1] In 2001, several firms were providing online services to 82 percent of the 66 million U.S. households with personal computers (out of 107 million total U.S. households in 2001). Moreover, in 2001, the typical family spent $595 on communications services (Internet, wireless phones, pagers), which was more than triple the $175 spent in 1995.[2] One result of this extensive penetration of communities and homes by media networks has been that Americans are spending more and more time as passive consumers of electronic media products.

Time spent by individuals on noncommercial activities such as informal socializing or critical reflection and writing produces no benefits for culture-industry profits. Only time devoted to the consumption of products generated by culture-industry firms (TV programming, movies, software, commercial websites, videogames, etc.) juices market shares, sales, and profits. The industry has an interest in channeling more and more consumer time into its commercial products. And it is succeeding. In 1988, the average American spent 1,751 hours consuming various electronic media products (TV was no. 1, at 1,490 hours, followed by recorded music, home videos, and theater movies), with a total of 3,310 hours devoted to all forms of media consumption (including newspapers, magazines, and books).[3] By 2003, total American media consumption is projected to increase to 3,587 hours per person, with 3,261 of those hours devoted to all forms of electronic media. This includes TV (still no. 1, 1,610 hours), followed by radio (192 hours), recorded music (319 hours), online Internet access (192 hours), home video games (67 hours), home videos (66 hours), and theater movies (15 hours).[4] This means Americans—for a variety of reasons—are devoting more and more discretionary time to media consumption, and especially to electronic media consumption.

The Colonization of Consciousness

To the extent that the awareness and limited free time of nonprivileged-class members are dominated by ideas, programs, activities, and events created by the superclass-owned and credentialed-class-managed culture industry, it means that their consciousness is, in a sense, captured or colonized—by an outside force. This privileged-class-directed "media force" is driven by class interests that are quite different from those of nonprivileged consumers. For us, then, the colonization of consciousness refers to the ongoing invasion by the culture industry—especially through electronic mass media entertainment and advertising content—of ever larger shares of peoples' time, interests, and imagination. This process is driven by many techniques, including the electronic media firms' constant tracking, creating, and linking of popular cultural trends with media content.[5] It also involves the media's use of compelling imagery (in TV programming, movies, advertising, video games, web search-engine graphics) and its constant barrage of cleverly produced ads emphasizing the prestige and novelty features of mass, niche, and (upscale and downscale) consumer products.[6] Although this process results in a number of consequences, including increases in culture-industry profits, from our perspective the reduction in time available to individuals for all other activities outside of media consumption is among the most important. Of particular importance in this regard is how the colonization of consciousness contributes to the marginalization of class-related issues and interests in individuals' everyday thoughts and discussions as more time and "thought space" are devoted to media products.

Although we may live in a "24–7" world (twenty four hours a day, seven days a week), each of us can claim only about sixteen waking hours a day—or about 5,800 hours per year. If we subtract the time devoted to work (about 2,000 hours per year), family and personal obligations, and the 3,261 hours spent on electronic media consumption, we find very little time remains each year for nonprivileged-class members to read, think, or talk about public issues—including class inequalities. Moreover, given the taboo nature of class in America and the interests of superclass culture-industry owners, we would not expect to find class-based themes, issues, or interests routinely included in the movie and television content "inserted" in consumers' minds as the colonization of consciousness process unfolds.

Movies: Class-Free Content?

Class-related issues and themes are rarely presented in movies, as revealed by a content analysis we conducted of large samples of dramas (699), science-fiction films (750), and documentaries (263) drawn from the *1995 Movie/Video Guide*. In this study we found that only about 5 percent of the films in each category (thirty-five dramas, forty science-fiction films, fifteen documentaries) included story lines or themes that could be interpreted as critiques of elite-class power or as providing sympathetic portrayals of working-class individuals or organizations (e.g., labor unions).[7] Our short list of thirty-five critical dramas that addressed working-class interests and grievances or critiqued elite-class-dominated institutions included "classics" (from the 1940s on) as well as recent films.

In many respects the findings from our study parallel what movie historian Steven J. Ross found in his review of class themes in the movies. With a focus primarily upon silent films, Ross found that a substantial number of films sympathetic to working-class interests were produced in the United States prior to World War I. However, he points out, the advent of talkies led to the demise of such movies. In a brief discussion of the contemporary period, he notes that class-critical films with "labor-capital" themes have virtually disappeared from the American cinema—reinforcing what we found in our study.[8]

The *Grapes of Wrath* (1940), starring Henry Fonda, was a high-profile, classic film from our list that we viewed as important because it helped establish and legitimate a kind of critical, sympathetic movie treatment of class underdogs in the contemporary era. Bringing the Steinbeck novel of the same title to the screen exposed millions of Americans who had not read the book to its heartbreaking portrayal of the Joad family. Tracing the family's experiences as it migrated from the Dust Bowl during the Great Depression, the movie provides a compelling and sympathetic account of how the Joads and people from similar working-class families were brutalized by the American economic and class structures of the 1930s.

Very few high-profile dramas from the recent past have followed in the class-critique, sympathy-for-the-class-underdog film tradition and also featured well-known Hollywood stars. Five recent titles illustrate as well as virtually exhaust the list of recent films with both qualities.

1. *Norma Rae:* This 1979 film starring Sally Field compassionately portrays the title character's transformation from passive worker to union activist in a southern textile plant.
2. *Reds:* Warren Beatty and Diane Keaton star in this 1981 film that presents a sympathetic account of American radical journalist Jack Reed's career, including his reporting on the Russian Revolution.
3. *Remains of the Day:* This 1993 film starring Anthony Hopkins powerfully depicts how the British class system of the 1930s stunted and distorted servants, masters, and human relationships.
4. *Bulworth:* Warren Beatty produced and starred in this 1998 "political farce" that, although flawed in many respects, includes scenes that voice powerful critiques of current American class and race inequities.
5. *Erin Brockovich:* Julia Roberts starred in and won an academy award for best actress in director Steven Soderbergh's adaptation of a true story (2000). Brockovich, a poor single mother, lands a job as a legal aide for a small law firm. In a toxic tort case she wins the trust of working-class families, documents their health problems linked to environmental toxins, and gathers evidence on toxic chemical releases by a large utility firm. In the end, the plaintiffs receive a limited measure of justice in a legal battle pitting working-class interests against those of the privileged class. The film provides a sympathetic view of workers' interests and portrays Brockovich as a kind of working-class hero—albeit one who becomes a millionaire in the end.

A smaller number of less well known recent dramas have also followed in the class-critique, sympathy-for-the-class-underdog tradition, but with much less star power. Two examples include *Matewan* and *The Killing Floor.* The former is a 1987 film directed by John Sayles that sympathetically depicts the union side of the West Virginia "coal wars" of the 1920s. The latter title is a 1993 film that presents a historically informed account of how Chicago meatpacking firms in the early 1900s resisted unionization by exploiting racial and ethnic divisions and tensions among the workers.

Although more titles could be added to the examples listed, the entire group of class-critique dramas identified in our study makes for a very short list. Few movies in the genres we reviewed provided critiques of elite-class power or sympathetic accounts of the economic, political, social, and personal grievances of the working class. Dramas reflecting the class-critique tradition as well as science-fiction films including overt critiques of ruling-class power (such as *They Live!*) are infrequently made, narrowly promoted, and seldom viewed by mass audiences. Moreover, they are notable exceptions to the non-class-based, escapist themes and action story lines routinely depicted in most mainstream American films. In fact, we are likely to see even more escapist action movies in the future as global film-going audiences' tastes become more American-like and as the foreign market for U.S. films continues to grow—to the point where U.S. films often generate more revenue overseas than in the domestic market.[9] Moreover, it has been well documented that "violent action fare is the genre that crosses borders most easily and makes the most commercial sense."[10]

As action films and those in other escapist genres become ever more common, class themes are likely to appear even less often in movies than in the past. The film formula of the future seems to be more action equals more distraction. Speaking to the effects of movie content on culture and class consciousness, film historian Ross maintains that "American filmmakers have helped create a culture whose citizens either no longer view class as an important part of their lives or define the middle class so broadly that class no longer seems to matter."[11]

TV and ABC

So what's on TV? For openers, try advertising. A typical thirty-minute TV-network program includes at least seven minutes of advertising. Local programs have even more. American television networks now broadcast six thousand commercials per week, up 50 percent since 1983.[12] Moreover, advertisers have increased their spending on all forms of television advertising (broadcast and cable) from $29 billion in 1990 to $51 billion in 1999.[13] This nearly doubling of TV ad expenditures reflects not only the increase in broadcast time devoted to advertising but also advertisers' faith in the power of TV to sell more stuff.

What kinds of programming do the ads support? Or what else besides ads do we find on TV? The really short answer is ABC: Anything but Class. If we set aside TV news as being part of the information industry, we find TV advertising supports a wide range of programming that for the most part ignores class issues and tends heavily toward distraction. A tour of *TV Guide*'s daytime and evening listings for the 2001 fall season reveals recurring programming patterns, particularly for network TV. Mornings are devoted mainly to newsmagazine and talk shows. Afternoons bring soap operas and more talk shows. Evening programming is more diverse and includes paranormal *X-Files*-like series (e.g., *Buffy the Vampire Slayer*—moved from WB to UPN, *Dark Angel*, and *Freakylinks* [FOX]), "reality-based" crime shows (e.g., *Cops* [FOX]), "reality" programs (e.g., *The Amazing Race* [CBS]), sporting events, comedy series staples (e.g., *Frasier* [NBC]), Gen-X nighttime soap-like shows (e.g., *Friends* [NBC], *Pasadena* [FOX]), dramas (e.g., *West Wing* [NBC]), more newsmagazine shows, and more talk shows. Cable, satellite, PBS, syndicated programs, and movies add diversity to daily programming, but studies of TV content reveal a striking absence of programs that depict the lives or concerns of working-class Americans or that deal with class-based inequalities in ways that might promote critical reflection among viewers.

One study of the four decades of TV entertainment (from 1946 to 1990) found that of 262 domestic situation comedies, only 11 percent featured blue-collar, clerical, or service workers as heads of households. By contrast, the vast majority of the series, 70.4 percent, portrayed "middle-class" families with incomes and lifestyles that were more affluent than those of most middle-income American families. In fact, in 44.5 percent of the comedy series studied, the head of the household was a professional.[14]

Another study of thirteen TV situation comedies from the 1990s found the issue of social mobility across class lines is sometimes used as a source of comic tension and moral instruction. On the rare occasions when characters in the series studied aspired to or encountered upward mobility, the outcomes reminded viewers that "achieving inter-class mobility is rare, and the rewards of any substantial social movement will likely be bittersweet." The study concluded that TV situation comedies send mixed and paradoxical messages where social mobility is concerned. On one hand, these programs typically reinforce the myth of America as a land of opportunity where hard work and persistence pay off. On the other hand, on the rare occasions when characters actually encounter social mobility, their experiences tend to be portrayed as disruptive and often undesirable.[15] The net result is the subtle reinforcement of existing class divisions, structures, and locations as normal, natural, and preferred—to the disruptive effects of social mobility.

During the 2001–2002 television season, only two prime-time network series (FOX) occasionally portrayed working-class characters, families, issues, or problems in sympathetic or positive terms. Both were animated comedies and both aired on Sunday nights: *The Simpsons* (created by cartoonist Matt Groening), and *King of the Hill* (devised by Beavis and Butthead creators Mike Judge and Greg Daniels—formerly of *The Simpsons*).[16] In contrast to the occasional sympathetic treatment of working-class concerns by these series, TV newsmagazines such as *60 Minutes, 60 Minutes II, Dateline,* and *20/20* almost never report on working-class issues or concerns—except to "expose" an occasional "bad apple" business guilty of abusing working-class consumers. The syndicated tabloid-style TV "newsmagazines" totally avoid working-class issues. The mission of these programs (e.g., *Access Hollywood, Entertainment Tonight, Inside Edition,* and *Extra!*) is to traffic in high-energy celebrity profiles and gossip about the stars—especially reports concerning sex, drugs, deviance, and opulent lifestyles. Such titillating stories appear designed to deliberately appeal to nonelite viewers by providing vicarious thrills and voyeuristic gratification. They seem to say, Maybe you can't afford it or do it or would never do it yourself, but you can watch glamorous stars own it and do it—Right here! Right now!

The themes of titillation and distraction are also staples of most daytime TV talk shows. The 2001–2002 season saw the following sampling of shows and topics: Jerry Springer on prostitution and transsexuality, Jenny Jones on people who think they're celebrity look-alikes and their friends who disagree, and Montel Williams on tough love for troubled teens.[17] Other, more "prestigious," daytime TV talk shows have adopted formats that frequently mix viewer concerns involving personal or family problems with celebrity interviews (usually TV, movie, or sports stars or the suddenly famous or infamous promoting their movies, books, or careers). A typical month of Oprah Winfrey (August 2001) included shows on how to heal a broken heart, how to age gracefully, messy home makeovers, and what kids really need.[18] Meanwhile, Rosie O'Donnell hosted an "Everybody Loves Raymond" hour including Ray Romano. Other shows included interviews with Tim Robbins, Amy Brenneman, Britney Spears, and Sarah Ferguson.[19] The pattern of TV talk show hosts interviewing celebrities also extends to nighttime TV talk shows—with talk show hosts often interviewing the celebrity hosts of other TV talk shows![20]

ABC and the Oprahfication of the Mind

In situation comedies, talk shows, newsmagazines, and other programming formats, ABC—Anything but Class—is what's on TV. "ABC" is an important factor contributing to the colonization of consciousness; and the "ABC" focus and content of most TV programming—especially talk shows and newsmagazines—contribute to another phenomenon involved in the pacification process: the Oprahfication of the mind. This term refers to how the electronic media—especially television "infotainment" (superficial information presented in "information" or "news" formats but whose primary value is as entertainment)—contributes to the demise of critical thinking about current and past social, cultural, and political events and issues.

High-profile media stars (e.g., Oprah Winfrey) projected through powerful TV media platforms help establish a pop-culture conceptual framework that blends current events, celebrity, and social issues into short, seamless entertainment packages. As a result, working-class TV viewers are encouraged to concentrate on only the most dramatic or high-profile current events or the most glamorous or sensationalized personalities and issues. The September 11, 2001 terrorist attacks on the United States temporarily interrupted talk show attention to infotainment themes and story lines. For awhile, hosts shifted their focus to heroic, tragic, and touching human stories associated with the attacks. Themes of horror, heroism, the face of evil (Osama bin Laden), and the quest for justice (or vengeance), were also woven into many talk show programs—for a time.

The transient dose of reality-based content that talk show hosts delivered to TV viewers in the autumn of 2001 may well have promoted national unity and even informed viewers. But in at least one respect it was similar to the more typical content of such programs: It deflected critical attention from any consideration of class inequality issues. In fact, the wave of talk show programming devoted to the attacks and the aftermath, like the typical fare delivered to these programs, was soon depleted of novel and compelling story lines, shock value, and ratings utility. As the September 11 story lines faded, waiting in the wings were new angles on familiar infotainment topics: breathless reports on pop-culture icons (movie stars, Michael Jordan, Bill Gates, the Kennedys—our royal family, and Jackie O, Marilyn Monroe, or Lady Di—forever), breaking stories on British royalty, new serial killers, the latest movie trailers, hot new fashions, and the long-running Wall Street drama. Through such programming, American TV viewers are coached to conceptualize and think about most news and talk show topics at the most immediate, superficial, and individualized level of detail. Any sense of how social-class inequalities or wider historical or cultural contexts may be linked to current themes is lost to Oprahfication.

American TV viewers are also encouraged to think about social, political, and economic issues through a superficial popular cultural lens that brings into dazzling focus "SGP" (shock, glamour and the perverse) topics while blurring the field of vision where serious issues like working-class interests, grievances, or inequalities are concerned. As our review of TV talk show content suggests, the SGP focus of these shows (and many TV newsmagazines) may sometimes be interrupted by serious events—like the September 11 attacks—but even those are channeled through and mined by the insatiable media appetite for novelty. More routinely, the SGP programming profile ranges across predictable topics with shock and novelty value such as twisted sexual practices, abuse, body piercing, satanic rituals, tattoos, racial strife, and gender bending, along with the latest medical, movie, fashion, hairstyle, and other pop-culture trends.

The SGP focus is reinforced by increasingly common "socialization to novelty" experiences among TV viewers and consumers of popular culture generally. Mass media advertising often encourages consumers to devalue stability and continuity in products, packaging, entertainment, and lifestyle trends. Much of the content and many of the commercials in the electronic media reinforce the idea that routine is boring and changes—especially fast-paced novel changes—are good. Viewers are encouraged to think that "been there, done that" experiences equal boring repetition and are to be avoided. Consumers are encouraged to pursue and prefer novel products, experiences, and activities because novelty is presented as the source of fulfillment and fun.[21] Preferences for novel products, images, and activities are driven by the mass media's recognition that speed, action, color, change, and novelty juice viewer interests as well as TV and merchandise-marketing profits.

SGP programming and accelerated socialization to novelty experiences are key factors leading to the Oprahfication of the mind. Oprahfication is a kind of truncated and compartmentalized cognitive style that not only erodes peoples' capacity for critical thinking but also diminishes even the legitimacy of critical thought. Oprahfication reduces (1) the likelihood that people will think of social issues or current events in terms of class analysis (too boring!); (2) peoples' ability to think in such terms (they have too little practice or experience); and (3) peoples' ability to understand or appreciate a class-based analysis of problematic social conditions if it is presented to them (too confusing!). Colonization and Oprahfication are major elements in the pacification of everyday life through the culture industry.

Pacification and Provocation: Two Sides of Everyday Life

> *Question: If men in power and younger women were all it took to fascinate media, wouldn't we see wall-to-wall coverage of the sweatshop industry?*
> —"SOUNDBITES," *EXTRA!* SEPTEMBER–OCTOBER 2001

As we have shown, the pacification of everyday life is a pervasive, complex, and powerful process. The illustrations presented suggest that it promotes privileged-class interests through a variety of institutionalized routines and practices that for the most part legitimate and reproduce existing class inequalities and at the same time distract working-class members from these issues. However, it is also important to recognize that pacification does not proceed as an unopposed process, nor is it a seamless, one-dimensional force without internal contradictions.

. . . [A]lternative class-power networks essentially operate in ways that call attention to, challenge, and contest the pacification process. The provocation efforts of these networks typically operate outside the organizations and structures that dominate the pacification process—but not always. Some branches or substructures of mainstream organizations that drive the pacification process sometimes deliberately include people and ideas from the alternative power networks. For example, public (and on occasion commercial) radio and television broadcasters sometimes include members of the alternative power network on some programs, typically as a means of legitimating their image as providers of "open forums" for discussions of public issues. Whatever the motives of gatekeepers controlling privileged-class-dominated organizations, whenever labor leaders, consumer advocates, or elite-power critics (e.g., AFL-CIO President John Sweeney, Ralph Nader, Gore Vidal) testify at congressional hearings or appear on TV or radio talk shows and newsmagazines, their messages challenging the pacification process are heard and seen by the working class.

Perhaps more important than token mainstream appearances by members of the alternative power networks are the effects that occur as a result of internal contradictions arising from institutional imperatives associated with the routine practices of the organizations that drive the pacification process. At the same time that privileged-class-dominated organizations produce pacifying "products" such as the policies, programs, and entertainment described in this chapter, some features of some products also result in paradoxical effects. That is, some products produced in the routine course of the pacification process may highlight or even challenge class inequalities rather than legitimate them. When this occurs, these features of the pacification process may actually contribute to contradictory outcomes—such as increased class tensions and resentment or even heightened class consciousness.

One illustration of how class provocation and pacification can occur at the same time as a result of routine organizational imperatives and practices can be found in the political arena. Candidates for office are largely financed by superclass-provided funds. However, candidates must also appeal to working-class voters. The latter reality can sometimes lead even superclass-funded candidates to take public positions on some issues that appear to reinforce working-class interests at the expense of the privileged class, for example, . . . Al Gore's flirtation with populist rhetoric in the 2000 presidential election. . . . Green Party candidate Ralph Nader went even further. His speeches denouncing corporate greed, NAFTA, the loss of American jobs, and the growth of economic insecurity among American workers led to accusations by mainstream media pundits that he was promoting "class war." The emergence of populist and even progressive messages in national political campaigns illustrate that the routine operation of a political system that generally reinforces the pacification process has the potential to generate contradictory messages—at least temporarily and episodically.

The electronic media also illustrate how institutional imperatives can produce contradictions in pacification products. Although most media products help to distract public attention from class issues and serve to legitimate class inequalities, mass media firms are fundamentally money-making businesses. Because TV and movie corporations are driven by profit-maximization concerns, they must deliver a constant stream of novel products to attract viewer attention so as to increase sales and profits. In the absence of explicit censorship and in the routine course of producing creative and marketable products, some movies and TV programs are produced that include content critical of class inequalities or privileged-class interests.

As noted earlier, some movies include story lines that portray working-class characters and interests in sympathetic terms. Thus, studios which typically traffic in pacification products do sometimes produce provocative films that call attention to class inequalities. When viewers identify with or share the concerns of the working-class characters portrayed in such films, the stories can resonate powerfully with audiences, help legitimate class grievances, generate large box-office revenues, and even produce critical acclaim. We know movie studios are not in the business of delivering progressive political messages or stimulating class consciousness. However, if movies with such story lines generate strong profits, then they will be delivered—at least from time to time. Recent movies with big-name stars illustrating this reality include *A Civil Action* (1999, starring John Travolta) and *Erin Brockovich* (2000, starring Julia Roberts). Both films were based on factual events concerning the negative health effects of toxic waste products released into the environment by seemingly callous corporations. And while both films are flawed and send mixed class messages (e.g., rogue firms are to blame, not the larger economic system; workers need elite-class advocates; class justice is finally rendered, etc.), they do legitimate working-class grievances and expose class-based injustices.

It's clear that few movies focus on class inequalities. However, the ones that do often encourage viewers to empathize with exploited working-class underdogs or to be outraged by exposés of elite-class arrogance and power abuses. These themes are included in classic hits like *Grapes of Wrath*, and they are woven into more recent films critical of elites, such as the two just noted and others such as *Bulworth, They Live!* and *The Big One.*[22] Although we would agree that most movies are much more likely to have pacifying rather than provocative effects where class issues are concerned, the routine operation of the pacification process still produces some films that inject critical class-based themes and ideas into popular culture.

Like the movies, television is also most closely associated with pacifying effects. However, even routine television products can produce paradoxical outcomes. For example, some TV newsmagazines and talk show forums have reported on topics that do not necessarily serve privileged-class interests, such as soaring CEO pay levels, plant closings, sweatshops, campaign finance reform, capital gains tax cuts for the rich, and ethical lapses among professionals (e.g., physicians and attorneys). Such programming has the potential to fuel class tensions and resentment, increase public cynicism about mainstream institutions (especially corporations and government), and even increase class consciousness. Growing awareness of class-divergent interests is, in part, revealed by recent public opinion polls. In a 1995 Gallup poll, 58 percent of Americans said major corporations have "too much power," and 76 percent agreed "the government is pretty much run by a few big interests looking out for themselves."[23] More recently, in a 1999 Gallup Poll, 67 percent of Americans reported having only some or very little confidence in major corporations.[24]

Sometimes regularly scheduled TV programs include content that heightens some forms of class consciousness among nonprivileged-class viewers. During the 1994 (NBC) and 1995 (FOX) summer seasons, Michael Moore's *TV Nation* garnered high ratings and won awards while often featuring entertaining reports that were critical of class inequalities and privileged-class interests.[25] The series was canceled, but Moore was able to return in 1999 and 2000 with a new show, *The Awful Truth.* Shown on the Bravo cable channel, the program was similar in style and content to *TV Nation,* but it too disappeared after two seasons.*

The fate of Moore's programs reveals the difficulties faced by producers and writers of progressive media products in getting and keeping their work on the air. As might be expected, progressive television programming critical of elite-class interests and sympathetic to working-class concerns is infrequently produced and aired. Even so, such TV programming does on occasion get written, produced, and aired even in a medium where pacification products, themes, and story lines dominate the airwaves.

The parade of examples illustrating the flip side of the pacification process could go on and on, but the point is that there is another side. The everyday, routine functioning of mainstream social institutions like local newspapers, drug education programs, movies, and TV programs does, for the most part, serve to distract nonprivileged groups from class issues, defuse class tensions, and legitimate class inequalities. But at the same time, the daily routines and practices of mainstream institutions occasionally can and do subvert the pacification process. On those infrequent occasions, chunks from the dark mass of conflicting interests from beneath the waterline of the class iceberg churn to the surface and produce transient episodes of inconvenience, embarrassment, and even anger for privileged-class members. Fortunately for them, such "provocations" are usually isolated and quickly smoothed over by the powerful and predictable privileged-class-controlled institutional routines that on a daily basis reinforce the pacification of everyday life.

*See editors' note at end of reading.

Notes

*Editors' note: Moore's 2004 film *Fahrenheit 9/11* was seen in many parts of the U.S. and Canada by large audiences. The film, which presents a powerful critique of the Bush administration for its "war on terrorism" and invasion of Iraq, is equally critical of the news media's failure to examine these policies in a critical, independent manner. While Moore ultimately succeeded in finding a distributor for the film after its original distributor, Disney, backed out, the major news media have been active in seeking to discredit Moore's film. In other words, in those unusual instances where the corporate media do produce an alternative vision, that same media will react quickly to close that small, brief window of difference. As Eric Alterman points out, "If the president's speeches to the nation about his decision to go to war had received a significant fraction of the journalistic attention that Moore's film has, it's a good bet 5,600 American soldiers would still be enjoying their release from the military—rather than being called back to duty to carry out an increasingly chaotic and counterproductive occupation." *(http//www.americanprogress.org/site/pp.asp?c=biJRJ8OVF&b=106595)*

1. "2000 U.S. Economic Review: U.S. Theaters," Motion Picture Association of America, on the Internet at http://www.mpaa.org/useconomicreview/2000 Economic/slide.asp?ref=24. Also see U.S. Department of Commerce, Bureau of the Census, Statistical Abstract of

the United States (Washington, D.C.: U.S. Government Printing Office, 2000), 567.

2. Rick Lyman, "A Partly Cloudy Forecast for Theater Owners," *New York Times*, March 12, 2001, C12; Tony Pugh, "Massive Immigration Steers Population Reapportionment," *Indianapolis Star*, December 29, 2000, A1, A21; Associated Press, "Americans Are Wired into New Bills," *Indianapolis Star*, July 7, 2001, A1.

3. U.S. Department of Commerce, Bureau of the Census, *Statistical Abstract of the United States* (Washington, D.C.: U.S. Government Printing Office, 1995), 572.

4. U.S. Department of Commerce, *Statistical Abstract of the United States* (2000), 566.

5. Tom Frank, "Let Them Eat Lifestyle," *Utne Reader*, November–December 1997, 43–47. Also see *The Merchants of Cool*, PBS *Frontline* TV Documentary, narrated by Douglas Rushkoff, 2001.

6. David Leonhardt, "Two-Tier Marketing," *Business Week*, March 17, 1997, 82–90.

7. Earl Wysong, "Class in the Movies," unpublished paper, 1996; Mick Martins and Mick Porter, *1995 Video Movie Guide* (New York: Ballantine Books, 1994).

8. Steven J. Ross, *Working-Class Hollywood: Silent Film and the Shaping of Class in America* (Princeton: Princeton University Press, 1998).

9. Robert W. McChesney, *Rich Media, Poor Democracy: Communication Politics in Dubious Times* (Chicago: University of Illinois Press, 1999), 109.

10. Ibid.

11. Ross, *Working-Class Hollywood*, 255.

12. Jerold M. Starr, *Air Wars: The Fight to Reclaim Public Broadcasting* (Boston: Beacon Press, 2000), 16.

13. U.S. Department of Commerce, *Statistical Abstract of the United States* (2000), 579.

14. Richard Butsch, "Class and Gender in Four Decades of Television Situation Comedy: Plus ça Change . . . ," *Critical Studies in Mass Communication* 9 (1992): 387–99.

15. Lewis Freeman, "Social Mobility in Television Comedies," *Critical Studies in Mass Communications* 9 (1992): 400–406; quote, 405.

16. "Returning Favorites," *TV Guide*, September 8, 2001, 4.

17. *TV Guide*, 2001, June 16–22, 145; August 4–10, 123; August 18–24, 93.

18. *The Oprah Show*, "Show Archive, August 2001," on the Internet at http://www.oprah.com/tows/pastshows/tows past20108.jhtml (visited October 1, 2001).

19. *TV Guide*, 2001, September 10, 128; September 25, 140.

20. Sam Husseini, "Talking about Talk," *EXTRA!* May–June 1996, 20.

21. Ronald Dahl, "Burned Out and Bored," *Newsweek*, December 15, 1997, 18.

22. Jeremy Smith, "Intellectual Snobs versus Political Snobs," *Dollars and Sense*, May–June 1998, 38–39.

23. Michael Golay and Carl Rollyson, *Where America Stands, 1996* (New York: Wiley, 1996), 137, 173.

24. "Confidence in Institutions," Gallup Poll News Service, June 8–10, 2001, on the Internet at http://www.gallup.com/pol/indicators/indconfidence.asp (visited October 6, 2001).

25. Miranda Spencer, "TV Nation: A Show for 'The Rest of Us,' " *EXTRA!* November–December 1995, 24–25.

MANUFACTURING CONSENT

EDWARD S. HERMAN AND NOAM CHOMSKY

It is our view that, among their other functions, the media serve, and propagandize on behalf of, the powerful societal interests that control and finance them. The representatives of these interests have important agendas and principles that they want to advance, and they are well positioned to shape and constrain media policy. This is normally not accomplished by crude intervention, but by the selection of right-thinking personnel and by the editors' and working journalists' internalization of priorities and definitions of newsworthiness that conform to the institution's policy.

Structural factors are those such as ownership and control, dependence on other major funding sources (notably, advertisers), and mutual interests and relationships between the media and those who make the news and have the power to define it and explain what it means. The propaganda model also incorporates other closely related factors such as the ability to complain about the media's treatment of news (that is, produce "flak"), to provide "experts" to confirm the official slant on the news, and to fix the basic principles and ideologies that are taken for granted by media personnel and the elite, but are often resisted by the general population.[1] In our view, the same underlying power sources that own the media and fund them as advertisers, that serve as primary definers of the news, and that produce flak and proper-thinking experts, also play a key role in fixing basic principles and the dominant ideologies. We believe that what journalists do, what they see as newsworthy, and what they take for granted as premises of their work are frequently well explained by the incentives, pressures, and constraints incorporated into such a structural analysis.

These structural factors that dominate media operations are not all-controlling and do not always produce simple and homogeneous results. It is well recognized, and may even be said to constitute a part of an institutional critique such as we present . . ., that the various parts of media organizations have some limited autonomy, that individual and professional values influence media work, that policy is imperfectly enforced, and that media policy itself may allow some measure of dissent and reporting that calls into question the accepted viewpoint. These considerations all work to assure some dissent and coverage of inconvenient facts.[2] The beauty of the system, however, is that such dissent and inconvenient information are kept within bounds and at the margins, so that while their presence shows that the system is not monolithic, they are not large enough to interfere unduly with the domination of the official agenda.

■ ■ ■ ■

Updating the Propaganda Model

The propaganda model . . . explains the broad sweep of the mainstream media's behavior and performance by their corporate character and integration into the political economy of the dominant economic system. For this reason, we focus heavily on the rise in scale of media enterprise, the media's gradual centralization and concentration, the growth of media conglomerates that control many different kinds of media (motion picture studios, TV networks, cable channels, magazines, and book publishing houses), and the spread of the media across borders in a globalization process. We also noted the gradual displacement of family control by professional managers serving a wider array of owners and more closely subject to market discipline.

All of these trends, and greater competition for advertising across media boundaries, have continued and strengthened over the past dozen years, making for an intensified bottom-line orientation. Thus, centralization of the media in a shrinking number of very large firms has accelerated, virtually unopposed by Republican and Democratic administrations and regulatory authority.

Since 1990, a wave of massive deals and rapid globalization have left the media industries further centralized in nine transnational conglomerates—Disney, AOL Time Warner, Viacom (owner of CBS), News Corporation, Bertelsmann, General Electric (owner of NBC), Sony, AT&T–Liberty Media, and Vivendi Universal. These giants own all the world's major film studios, TV networks, and music companies, and a sizable fraction of the most important cable channels, cable systems, magazines, major-market TV stations, and book publishers. The largest, the recently merged AOL Time Warner, has integrated the leading Internet portal into the traditional media system. Another fifteen firms round out the system, meaning that two dozen firms control nearly the entirety of media experienced by most U.S. citizens. [Ben] Bagdikian concludes that "it is the overwhelming collective power of these firms, with their corporate interlocks and unified cultural and political values, that raises troubling questions about the individual's role in the American democracy."[3]

Important branches of the media such as movies and books have had substantial global markets for many years, but only in the past two decades has a global media system come into being that is having major effects on national media systems, culture, and politics.[4] It has been fueled by the globalization of business more generally, the associated rapid growth of global advertising, and improved communications technology that has facilitated cross-border operations and control. It has also been helped along by government policy and the consolidation of neoliberal ideology. The United States and other Western governments have pressed the interests of their home-country firms eager to expand abroad, and the International Monetary Fund (IMF) and World Bank have done the same, striving with considerable success to enlarge transnational corporate access to media markets across the globe. Neoliberal ideology has provided the intellectual rationale for policies that have opened up the ownership of broadcasting stations and cable and satellite systems to private transnational investors.

The culture and ideology fostered in this globalization process relate largely to "lifestyle" themes and goods and their acquisition; and they tend to weaken any sense of community helpful to civic life. Robert McChesney notes that "the hallmark of the global media system is its relentless, ubiquitous commercialism."[5] Shopping channels, "infomercials," and product placement are booming in the global media system. McChesney adds that "it should come as no surprise that account after account in the late 1990s documents the fascination, even the obsession, of the world's middle class youth with consumer brands and products."[6] The global media's "news" attention in recent years, aside from reporting on crusades such as "Operation Allied Force" (the NATO war against Yugoslavia) and on national elections, has been inordinately directed to sensationalism, as in their obsessive focus on the O. J. Simpson trial, the Lewinsky scandal, and the deaths of two of the West's supercelebrities, Princess Diana and John F. Kennedy, Jr.

Globalization, along with deregulation and national budgetary pressures, has also helped reduce the importance of noncommercial media in country after country. This has been especially important in Europe and Asia, where public broadcasting systems were dominant (in contrast with the United States and Latin America). The financial pressures on public broadcasters has forced them to shrink or emulate the commercial systems in fund-raising and programming, and some have been fully commercialized by policy change or privatization. The global balance of power has shifted decisively toward commercial systems. James Ledbetter points out that in the United States, under incessant right-wing political pressure and financial stringency, "the 90s have seen a tidal wave of commercialism overtake public broadcasting," with public broadcasters "rushing as fast as they can to merge their services with those offered by commercial networks."[7] And in the process of what Ledbetter calls the "malling" of public broadcasting, its already modest differences from the commercial networks have almost disappeared. Most important, in their programming "they share either the avoidance or the defanging of contemporary political controversy, the kind that would bring trouble from powerful patrons."[8]

Some argue that the Internet and the new communications technologies are breaking the corporate stranglehold on journalism and opening an unprecedented era of interactive democratic media. And it is true and important that the Internet has increased the efficiency and scope of individual and group networking. This has enabled people to escape the mainstream media's constraints in many and diverse cases. Japanese women have been able to tap newly created Web sites devoted to their problems, where they can talk and share experiences and information with their peers and obtain expert advice on business, financial, and personal matters.[9] Chiapas resisters against abuse by the Mexican army and government were able to mobilize an international support base in 1995 to help them publicize their grievances and put pressure on the Mexican government to change its policies in the region.[10] The enlarged ability of Bolivian peasants protesting against World Bank privatization programs and user fees for water in 2000, and Indonesian students taking to the streets against the Suharto dictatorship in Indonesia in 1998, to communicate through the Internet produced a level of publicity and global attention that had important consequences: Bechtel Corporation, owner of the newly privatized water system in Bolivia that had quickly doubled water rates, backed off and the privatization sale was rescinded; the protests and associated publicity, along with the 1998 financial crisis, helped drive Suharto from office.[11]

Broader protest movements have also benefited from Internet-based communication. When the leading members of the World Trade Organization (WTO) attempted in 1998 to push through in secret a Multilateral Agreement on Investment that would have protected further the rights of international investors as against the rights of democratic bodies within states, the Internet was extremely valuable in alerting opposition forces to the threat and helping mobilize an opposition that prevented acceptance of this agreement.[12] Similarly, in the protest actions against the WTO meetings in Seattle in November 1999 and the IMF and World Bank annual gatherings in Washington, D.C., in April 2000, communication via the Internet played an important role both in organizing the protests and in disseminating information on the events themselves that countered the mainstream media's hostile portrayal of these protests.[13]

However, although the Internet has been a valuable addition to the communications arsenal of dissidents and protesters, it has limitations as a critical tool. For one thing, those whose information needs are most acute are not well served by the Internet—many lack access, its databases are not designed to meet their needs, and the use of databases (and effective use of the Internet in general) presupposed knowledge and organization. The Internet is not an instrument of mass communication for those lacking brand names, an already existing large audience, and/or large resources. Only sizable commercial organizations have been able to make large numbers aware of the existence of their Internet offerings. The privatization of the Internet's hardware, the rapid commercialization and concentration of Internet portals and servers and their integration into non-Internet conglomerates—the AOL–Time Warner merger was a giant step in that direction—and the private and concentrated control of the new broadband technology, together threaten to limit any future prospects of the Internet as a democratic media vehicle.

The past few years have witnessed a rapid penetration of the Internet by the leading newspapers and media conglomerates, all fearful of being outflanked by small pioneer users of the new technology, and willing (and able) to accept losses for years while testing out these new waters. Anxious to reduce these losses, however, and with advertisers leery of the value of spending in a medium characterized by excessive audience control and rapid surfing, the large media entrants into the Internet have gravitated to making familiar compromises—more attention to selling goods, cutting back on news, and providing features immediately attractive to audiences and advertisers. The *Boston Globe* (a subsidiary of the *New York Times*) and the *Washington Post* are offering e-commerce goods and services; and Ledbetter notes that "it's troubling that none of the newspaper portals feels that quality journalism is at the center of its strategy . . . because journalism doesn't help you sell things."[14] Former *New York Times* editor Max Frankel says that the more newspapers pursue Internet audiences, "the more will sex, sports, violence, and comedy appear on their menus, slighting, if not altogether ignoring, the news of foreign wars or welfare reform."[15]

New technologies are mainly introduced to meet corporate needs, and those of recent years have permitted media firms to shrink staff even as they achieve greater outputs, and they have made possible global distribution systems that reduce the number of media entities. The audience "interaction" facilitated by advancing interactive capabilities mainly help audience members to shop, but they also allow media firms to collect detailed information on their audiences, and thus to fine-tune program features and ads to individual characteristics as well as to sell by a click during programs. Along with reducing privacy, this should intensify commercialization.

In short, the changes in politics and communication over the past dozen years have tended on balance to enhance the applicability of the propaganda model. The increase in corporate power and global reach, the mergers and further centralization of the media, and the decline of public broadcasting, have made bottom-line considerations more influential both in the United States and abroad. The competition for advertising has become more intense and the boundaries between editorial and advertising departments have weakened further. Newsrooms have been more thoroughly incorporated into transnational corporate empires, with budget cuts and a further diminution of management enthusiasm for investigative journalism that would challenge the structures of power.

Over the past dozen years, sourcing and flak have also strengthened as mechanisms of elite influence. Media centralization and the reduction in the resources devoted to journalism have made the media more dependent than ever on the primary definers who both make the news and subsidize the media by providing accessible and cheap copy. They now have greater leverage over the media, and the public relations firms working for these and other powerful interests also bulk larger as media sources. . . . Studies of news sources reveal that a significant proportion of news originates in public relations releases.[16] There are, by one count, 20,000 more public relations agents working to doctor the news today than there are journalists writing it.[17]

The force of anti-communist ideology has possibly weakened with the collapse of the Soviet Union and the virtual disappearance of socialist movements across the globe, but this is easily offset by the greater ideological force of the belief in the "miracle of the market" (Reagan). The triumph of capitalism and the increasing power of those with an interest in privatization and market rule have strengthened the grip of market ideology, at least among the elite, so that regardless of evidence, markets are assumed to be benevolent and even democratic ("market populism" in Thomas Frank's phrase) and nonmarket mechanisms are suspect, although exceptions are allowed when private firms need subsidies, bailouts, and government help in doing business abroad. When the Soviet economy stagnated in the 1980s, it was attributed to the absence of markets; when capitalist Russia disintegrated in the 1990s, this was blamed not on the now ruling market but on politicians' and workers' failure to let markets work their magic.[18] Journalism has internalized this ideology. Adding it to the residual power of anticommunism in a world in which the global power of market institutions makes nonmarket options seem utopian gives us an ideological package of immense strength.

These changes, which have strengthened the applicability of the propaganda model, have seriously weakened the "public sphere," which refers to the array of places and forums in which matters important to a democratic community are debated and information relevant to intelligent citizen participation is provided. The steady advance, and cultural power, of marketing and advertising has caused "the displacement of a political public sphere by a depoliticized consumer culture."[19] And it has had the effect of creating a world of virtual communities built by advertisers and based on demographics and taste differences of consumers. These consumption- and style-based clusters are at odds with physical communities that share a social life and common concerns and which participate in a democratic order.[20] These virtual communities are organized to buy and sell goods, not to create or service a public sphere.

Advertisers don't like the public sphere, where audiences are relatively small, upsetting controversy takes place, and the settings are not ideal for selling goods. Their preference for entertainment underlies the gradual erosion of the public sphere under systems of commercial media, well exemplified in the history of broadcasting in the United States over the past seventy-five years.[21] But entertainment has the merit not only of being better suited to helping sell goods; it is an effective vehicle for hidden ideological messages.[22] Furthermore, in a system of high and growing inequality, entertainment is the contemporary equivalent of the Roman "games of the circus" that diverts the public from politics and generates a political apathy that is helpful to preservation of the status quo.

It would be a mistake to conclude from the fact that the public buys and watches the offerings of the increasingly commercialized media that the gradual erosion of the public sphere reflects the preferences and free choices of the public either as citizens or consumers. The citizenry was never given the opportunity to approve or disapprove the wholesale transfer of broadcasting rights to commercial interests back in 1934,[23] and the pledge made by those interests, and subsequently by the Federal Communications Commission (FCC) itself, that public service offerings would never be buried in favor of the entertainment preferred by advertisers, was never fulfilled.[24] The public is not sovereign over the media—the owners and managers, seeking ads, decide what is to be offered, and the public must choose among these. People watch and read in good part on the basis of what is readily available and intensively promoted. Polls regularly show that the public would like more news, documentaries, and other information, and less sex, violence, and other entertainment, even as they do listen to and watch the latter. There is little reason to believe that they would not like to understand why they are working harder with stagnant or declining incomes, have inadequate medical care at high costs, and what is being done in their name all over the world. If they are not getting much information on these topics, the propaganda model can explain why: the sovereigns who control the media choose not to offer such material.

■ ■ ■ ■

Applications

In his book *Golden Rule*, political scientist Thomas Ferguson argues that where the major investors in political parties and elections agree on an issue, the parties will not compete on that issue, no matter how strongly the public might want an alternative. He contends that for ordinary voters to influence electoral choices they would have to have "strong channels that directly facilitate mass deliberation and expression."[25] These would include unions and other intermediate organizations that might, through their collective power, cause the interests of ordinary voters to be given greater weight in the political system.

. . . For example, polls regularly indicate that, except in periods of war and intense war propaganda, the public wants a smaller defense budget and favors a spending shift from defense to education and other civil functions.[26] But because the major investors agree that a large defense budget is desirable, the two dominant parties compete only on whether the one or other is stinting on military expenditures, with both promising to enlarge it (as both George W. Bush and Al Gore did in the presidential election campaign of 2000). And the mainstream media do the same, limiting debate to the terms defined by the two parties and excluding deliberation and expression of the position that large cuts are desirable. The alternative presidential candidate, Ralph Nader, called for such cuts, but the media denied him a voice on the issues, some of them explicitly defending his exclusion from the presidential debates on the grounds that the options afforded by the two parties sufficed.[27]

The U.S. corporate community has favored an immense defense budget—currently more than five times the size of that of a steadily weakening Russia, the second biggest spender—because of the great benefits its members derive from military spending. These include weapons and other contracting business, direct and indirect subsidies in research,[28] and the role played by military power in supporting the global economic expansion in which many U.S. transnational corporations are active participants and beneficiaries. Business also benefits from the market-opening actions of trade agreements and from the supportive operations of the WTO, the World Bank, and the IMF. But these trade agreements and the activities of the international financial institutions have generated controversy and political struggle, because while their benefits to business are clear, their costs are borne heavily by workers forced to compete in a global job market. Furthermore, globalization and trade agreements strengthen the political as well as the economic power of the corporate community, in part because they shift decision-making authority from democratic polities to bankers and technocrats who more reliably serve the transnational corporate interest. Here also, as in the case of defense-versus civilian-oriented budgets, polls show a sharp dichotomy between corporate and public preferences, with the latter generally hostile to the agreements and institutional arrangements favored by business.[29]

The propaganda model fits well the media's treatment of this range of issues. Consider, for example, their coverage of the passage of the North American Free Trade Agreement (NAFTA) and the subsequent Mexican financial crisis and meltdown of 1994–95. Polls taken before its enactment consistently showed substantial majorities opposed to NAFTA—and later to the bailout of investors in Mexican securities—but the elite in favor. Media editorials, news coverage, and selection of "experts" in opinion columns were heavily skewed toward the elite preference; their judgment was that the benefits of NAFTA were obvious, were agreed to by all qualified authorities, and that only demagogues and "special interests" were opposed.[30] The "special interests" who might be the "losers" included women, minorities, and a majority of the workforce.[31] The media dealt with the awkward fact that polls showed steady majority opposition to the agreement mainly by ignoring it, but occasionally they suggested that the public was uninformed and didn't recognize its own true interests.[32] The effort of labor to influence the outcome of the NAFTA debates was sharply attacked in both the *New York Times* and the *Washington Post*, with no comparable criticism of corporate or governmental (U.S. or Mexican) lobbying and propaganda. And while labor was attacked for its alleged position on these issues, the press refused to allow the actual position to be expressed.[33]

■ ■ ■ ■

. . . [W]hen the growing global opposition to the policies of the WTO, the IMF, and the World Bank led to mass protests at the WTO conference in Seattle in November and December 1999, and then at the annual meeting of the IMF and the World Bank in Washington, D.C., in April 2000, media coverage of these events was derisive and hostile to the protesters and almost uniformly failed to deal with the substantive issues that drove the protests. The media portrayed the Seattle protesters as "all-purpose agitators" (*U.S. News & World Report*), "terminally aggrieved" (*Philadelphia Inquirer*), simply "against world trade" (ABC News), and making "much ado about nothing" (CNN), but the bases of the protesters' grievances were almost entirely unexplored.[34] Similarly, in the case of the Washington, D.C., protests, the media repeatedly reported on activists' attire, looks, body odors, fadism, and claimed a lack of "anything that can coherently be called a cause" (Michael Kelly, journalist, *Washington Post*), and they continued their refusal to address issues.[35] There were many informed protesters with coherent agendas at Seattle and Washington—including reputable economists, social theorists, and veteran organizers from around the world[36]—but the media did not seek them out, preferring to stereotype antiglobalization activists as ignorant troublemakers. On op-ed pages, there was a major imbalance hostile to the protestors. TV bias was at least as great, and often misleading on the facts. In his November 29, 1999, backgrounder on the WTO, Dan Rather explained that the organization had ruled on many environmental issues, implying that those rulings were protective of the environment when in fact they generally privileged trade rights over environmental needs.

Another notable feature of media reporting on both the Seattle and Washington, D.C., protests, and a throwback to their biased treatment of the protests of the Vietnam War era (1965–75),[37] was their exaggeration of protester violence, their downplaying of police provocations and violence, and their complaisance at illegal police tactics designed to limit all protestor actions, peaceable or otherwise.[38] Although the Seattle police resorted to force and used chemical agents against many nonviolent protesters well before a handful of individuals began breaking windows, both then and later the media reversed this chronology, stating that the police violence was a response to protester violence. In fact, the vandals were largely ignored by the police, while peaceful protesters were targeted for beatings, tear gas, torture with pepper spray, and arrest.[39] One *New York Times* article went so far as to claim that the Seattle protesters had thrown excrement, rocks, and Molotov cocktails at delegates and police officers; the *Times* later issued a correction acknowledging that these claims were false.[40] Dan Rather, who had falsely alleged that the protesters had "brought on today's crackdown" at Seattle, later suggested that the Washington protesters were possibly "hoping for a replay of last year's violence in Seattle," setting this off against "those charged with keeping the peace" who "have other ideas."[41]

In their eighty-seven-page report, *Out of Control: Seattle's Flawed Response to Protests Against the World Trade Organization*, the American Civil Liberties Union (ACLU) stated that "demonstrators [in Seattle] were overwhelmingly peaceful. Not so the police." The response of the Seattle police to the protests was characterized by "draconian" violations of civil liberties, including widespread use of "chemical weapons, rubber bullets and clubs against peaceful protesters and bystanders alike." But NBC, ABC, CBS, CNN, and the *New York Times* and *Washington Post* all ignored the release of the ACLU's findings, which ran counter to their own uniformly pro-police and anti-protester line.

The media's reversal of chronology and inflation of the threat of activist violence, and their low-keyed treatment of numerous illegal police actions designed to instill fear in those wanting to protest peaceably,[42] provided the enabling ground for both police violence and serious restrictions on free speech. . . .

Notes

1. On a number of issues, such as trade agreements, health care, and the appropriate size of the military budget, there is a sharp division between media personnel and the elite on the one hand and the general population on the other hand.

2. This was even true in the Soviet Union, where the media's disclosure of inconvenient facts on the Afghan war caused the Soviet defense minister to denounce the press as unpatriotic; see Bill Keller, "Soviet Official Says Press Harms Army," *New York Times*, January 21, 1988.

3. Ben Bagdikian, *The Media Monopoly*, 6th ed. (Boston: Beacon Press, 2000), p. xxi.

4. Edward S. Herman and Robert McChesney, *The Global Media* (London: Cassell, 1997).

5. Robert McChesney, *Rich Media, Poor Democracy* (Urbana: University of Illinois Press, 2000), p. 108.

6. Ibid., p. 109.

7. James Ledbetter, "Public Broadcasting Sells; (Out?)," *The Nation*, December 1, 1997.

8. Ibid.

9. Stephanie Strom, "Japanese Sites for Women Aim for Empowerment," *New York Times*, December 25, 2000.

10. Mark Fineman, "Military Can't Outflank Rebels in War of Words," *Los Angeles Times*, February 21, 1995; Leonard Doyle, "Rebels Try to Advance via Internet," *The Independent*, March 7, 1995.

11. Jim Shultz, "Bolivia's Water War Victory," *Earth Island Journal*, September 22, 2000; "Bolivia—The Last Word," April 13, 2000, *JShultz@democracyctr.org*; "How the Internet Helped Activists," *Straits Times* (Singapore), May 25, 1998; Marshall Clark, "Cleansing the Earth," *Inside Indonesia* (October–December 1998).

12. Madelaine Drohan, "How the Net Killed the MAI," *Globe and Mail*, April 29, 1998.

13. Kayte Van Scoy, "How Green Was My Silicon Valley," *PC/Computing*, March 1, 2000; Keith Perine, "Power to the (Web-Enabled) People," *Industry Standard*, April 10, 2000.

14. James Ledbetter, "Some Pitfalls in Portals," *Columbia Journalism Review* (November–December 1999).

15. Quoted in ibid.

16. Alex Carey, *Taking the Risk out of Democracy* (Urbana: University of Illinois Press, 1997); John Stauber and Sheldon Rampton, *Toxic Sludge Is Good for You!* (Monroe, Maine: Common Courage Press, 1995); Stuart Ewen, *PR! A Social History of Spin* (New York: Basic Books, 1996).

17. Mark Dowie, "Introduction," Stauber and Rampton, *Toxic Sludge*.

18. See Stephen Cohen, *Failed Crusade: America and the Tragedy of Post-Communist Russia* (New York: Norton, 2000). See also Thomas Frank, *One Market Under God* (New York: Doubleday, 2000).

19. Kevin Robins and Frank Webster, *Times of the Technoculture* (London: Routledge, 1999), p. 127.

20. Patricia Aufderheide, "Journalism and Public Life Seen Through the 'Net,'" in Aufderheide, *The Daily Planet* (Minneapolis: University of Minnesota Press, 2000); Joseph Turow, *Breaking Up America* (Chicago: University of Chicago Press, 1997).

21. Herman and McChesney, *Global Media*, chapter 5.

22. On the ideological messages borne in commercials, see Erik Barnouw, *The Sponsor* (New York: Oxford University Press, 1978), part 2, chapter 1.

23. See Robert McChesney, *Telecommunications, Mass Media, and Democracy* (New York: Oxford, 1993).

24. See Edward S. Herman, *Myth of the Liberal Media*, (New York: Peter Lang, 1999), pp. 32–33.

25. Thomas Ferguson, *Golden Rule* (Chicago: University of Chicago Press, 1995), pp. 28–29.

26. For a major study, see Steven Kull, "Americans on Defense Spending: A Study of U.S. Public Attitudes," *Report of Findings*, Center for Study of Public Attitudes, January 19, 1996. On public opposition to excessive defense spending even during the Reagan era, see Thomas Ferguson and Joel Rogers, *Right Turn* (New York: Hill & Wang, 1986), pp. 19–24.

27. The two major parties offer voters "a clear-cut choice," so there is "no driving logic for a third-party candidacy

this year," according to the editors of the *New York Times*: "Mr. Nader's Misguided Crusade," June 10, 2000.
28. Especially after World War II, the military budget, and therefore the taxpayer, financed a very large fraction of the basic science that underpinned advances in the aircraft, computer, and electronics industries, the Internet economy, most of the biotech industry, and many others.
29. On the public opposition to the NAFTA agreement, see Herman, *Myth of the Liberal Media*, pp. 185–86. A *Business Week*/Harris poll in early 2000 revealed that only 10 percent of those polled called themselves "free traders"; 51 percent called themselves "fair traders" and 37 percent "protectionists." "Harris Poll: Globalization: What Americans Are Worried About," *Business Week*, April 24, 2000.
30. For more extended accounts, see Herman, *Myth of the Liberal Media*, chapter 14; Thea Lee, "False Prophets: The Selling of NAFTA," Briefing Paper, Economic Policy Institute, 1995; John McArthur, *The Selling of "Free Trade"* (New York: Hill & Wang, 2000).
31. Thomas Lueck, "The Free Trade Accord: The New York Region," *New York Times*, November 18, 1993.
32. Editorial, "NAFTA's True Importance," *New York Times*, November 14, 1993.
33. On the refusal of the administration to allow any labor inputs in arriving at the NAFTA agreement, contrary to law, and the media's disinterest in this as well as any other undemocratic features of the creation of this and other trade agreements, see Noam Chomsky, *World Orders Old and New* (New York: Columbia University Press, 1994), pp. 164–78.
34. Citations from Seth Ackerman, "Prattle in Seattle: WTO coverage Misrepresented Issues, Protests," *EXTRA!* (January–February 2000), pp. 13–17.
35. Rachel Coen, "For Press, Magenta Hair and Nose Rings Defined Protests," *EXTRA!* (July–August 2000). An exception at the time of the Washington meetings and protests was Eric Pooley's "IMF: Dr. Death?" *Time*, April 24, 2000.
36. See Walden Bello, "Why Reform of the WTO Is the Wrong Agenda" (Global Exchange; 2000).
37. Edward P. Morgan, "From Virtual Community to Virtual History: Mass Media and the American Antiwar Movement in the 1960s," *Radical History Review* (Fall 2000); Todd Gitlin, *The Whole World Is Watching* (Berkeley: University of California Press, 1980).
38. Rachel Coen, "Whitewash in Washington: Media Provide Cover as Police Militarizes D.C.," *EXTRA!* (July–August 2000); Ackerman, "Prattle in Seattle"; Neil deMause, "Pepper Spray Gets in Their Eyes: Media Missed Militarization of Police Work in Seattle," *EXTRA!* (March–April 2000).
39. Coen, Ackerman, and deMause items cited in note 38.
40. Nichole Christian, "Police Brace for Protests in Windsor and Detroit," *New York Times*, June 3, 2000.
41. *CBS Evening News* Report, April 6, 2000.
42. Zachary Wolfe, National Lawyers Guild legal observer coordinator, concluded that "police sought to create an atmosphere of palpable fear," and that anyone even trying to hear dissident views ran a risk of police violence "just for being in the area where speech was taking place." Quote in Coen, "Whitewash in Washington."

YELLOW RIBBONS AND SPAT-UPON VETERANS

Making Soldiers the Means and Ends of War

JERRY LEMBCKE

In early January 1991 the U.S. Congress authorized President George Bush to use armed force to expel Iraq from Kuwait. But for thousands of Americans, including the anonymous soldier interviewed by *New York Times* reporter James LeMoyne (1990b), the reasons for the war in the Persian Gulf had more to do with support for the American men and women already stationed there than it did with Iraq or Kuwait. By the time the United States went to war on January 16, the U.S. soldiers in the Gulf had become the primary reason for the war.

An analysis of news stories gleaned from the press accounts of fall 1990 reveals that the administration had put forth one reason after another for U.S. involvement, to the point that nobody could reason about the rightness or wrongness of the war. With the ends always changing, reasoning within a means-ends framework became paralyzed. At that point, public decision-making defaulted to levels of emotion, symbolism, and myth.

Reasoning about the War

On August 1, 1990, Iraq sent troops into Kuwait in a dispute over boundary and oil rights. A week later the United States began airlifting 200,000 troops to the Persian Gulf. By the end of the year double that number would be in the region as momentum built for a military conflict between Iraq and the United States.

As the number of soldiers dispatched for war grew during the fall of 1990, so too did the list of reasons offered by the Bush administration for the buildup. In all, the administration put forth six reasons for U.S. involvement in the war: the defense of Saudi Arabia; putting military teeth in the economic blockade of Iraq; freeing the hostages; the liberation of Kuwait; the removal of Saddam Hussein; and jobs. The six appeared more or less sequentially between August and December of 1990, although they sometimes overlapped with one another thematically and were often conjoined in administrative press statements in packages of two or three.

At the time, the United States alleged that Iraq's movement of troops into Kuwait was a prelude to an attack on Saudi Arabia. On August 6, U.S. Defense Secretary Dick Cheney arrived in Riyadh, the capital of Saudi Arabia, to persuade the cautious Saudis to open their naval bases and airport installations to the Americans. This framing of the initial U.S. troop deployment had a formative effect on how people in the United States would interpret the events that were to unfold over the next months, and it virtually insured that debate over increased military involvement would take place within a discourse of "defense."

The framing of the initial U.S. troop deployments as a defensive measure kept opposition to administration actions frozen during the first week of August. But no sooner was the defense of Saudi Arabia established in the public's mind as the reason for the troops having been sent to the Gulf than the reason changed. On August 9, the United States dispatched an armada of fifty major ships to the Persian Gulf with the stated intention of enforcing the economic sanctions the United Nations had imposed on Iraq three days earlier. The naval blockade created a nonmilitary rationale—the enforcement of economic and diplomatic tactics—for U.S. military forces in the Gulf. It also began weaving the fig leaf of "internationalism" behind which the Bush administration would walk throughout the course of the war and reframed the issue so that it was less a question about the use of military means than about nonmilitary objectives, a maneuver that stymied opposition for most of the month (Kifner 1990).

The third reason for the military buildup, and the keystone of the Bush administration's strategy to muster domestic support for the Gulf War, involved the creation of a hostage issue. On the lead end of the crisis, the hostage issue connected with the defense motif about U.S. intentions in the Gulf: the Iraqis were the aggressors and the United States was the defender of innocent lives. On the other end, as Washington's intentions became more openly offensive, the hostage issue was an important element of the U.S. effort to demonize Iraq's leader, Saddam Hussein.

The hostage issue was also a transitional issue that allowed the Bush administration to begin recasting the crisis from "this is about them"—the defense of Saudi Arabia and the liberation of Kuwait—to "this is about us." In that sense, it was a prelude to fuller discussions of what U.S. "vital interests" were at stake in the region. Moreover, by writing the role of hostage into the script, any Americans who were in the Gulf, including military personnel, could be cast in the role and used as a justification for U.S. military intervention. The hostage issue, in other words, paved the way for means and ends to be conflated and, ultimately, for the troops in the Gulf to be both the reasons for the war and the means of war.

Headlining of the hostage issue began on August 18, coincident with Bush's decision to call up military reservists. Iraq viewed the administration's call-up as further evidence that the United States was moving toward war. Iraq's response was to declare, on August 18, that foreigners in Iraq would endure the same hardships of the economic blockade and war as the Iraqi people. Foreigners, including Americans, would be accommodated in facilities operated by the ministries of Oil and Military Industrialization and the armed forces.

Headlines declaring that Saddam Hussein was taking hostages dominated the news of the war for the next several days. The hostage stories were combined with stories about troops in the Gulf in ways that, at times, conveyed the impression that it was U.S. troops who were the hostages. George Bush abetted the comingling of images by choosing the Veterans of Foreign Wars (VFW) convention on August 21 as the occasion on which to declare the beginning of the "hostage crisis." Other than making the declaration and saying that he would hold the Iraqis responsible for the safety of Americans in Iraq, Bush was noncommittal with regard to the so-called hostages. His speech, which was excerpted in the *New York Times*, moved seamlessly from hostages to troops, to whom he also pledged his support. Then, in a manner that echoed the news media's profiling of civilian individuals and families trapped in Iraq, Bush read family profiles of U.S. soldiers already in the Gulf. This was very personal and moving, but was this supposed to be a speech about civilian hostages or military troops?

On the surface, of course, it was a speech about hostages but the president had said nothing of substance, leaving the symbolism of the occasion to speak volumes. The message was in the medium and the medium was the venue: by declaring the hostage crisis at the VFW convention and conflating the national anxieties about hostages and soldiers, the association between soldiers, veterans, and hostages was forged. The American people could now be asked to go to war to free civilian hostages or to free the troops in harm's way.

The ultimate comingling of hostage and troop-support symbolism was in the use of yellow ribbons—the quintessential hostage/prisoner symbol—for a support-the-troops symbol. Still, it was not a given that Americans would transfer their emotional support for individuals to support for policy. Someone would have to *say* that the two were linked—or that they were *not* linked. Either would do as a means to create a storm of controversy over support for troops versus support for the war. The Democratic National Committee took the latter tack.[1]

On September 16, the DNC expressed support for the American troops in the Persian Gulf while criticizing the Republican administration that put them there (Toner 1990). This support-the-troops-but-not-the-policy statement signaled to the public that there was a debatable issue while evading the important question of how one could oppose the policy without opposing the troops. Therein was the rub. On the surface, the statement legitimized opposition to the U.S. military role. But it did so in the context of hysteria over hostages and troops-as-hostages that was several weeks in the making and already had a grip on the emotions of the American people. Could opponents of the policy voice their opposition without appearing to be attacking the troops? Not likely. Nor was it likely that the yellow-ribbon campaigners would translate their support for the troops into opposition to the war and demand that the troops be brought home. In reality, the DNC had constructed a one-sided discourse that mobilized the pro-war sentiments of the American people.

In mid September the administration began weaving Kuwait into its hostage narrative. Many of the news stories—including the widely reported story about Iraqi soldiers dumping 312 Kuwaiti babies out of hospital incubators—we now know were concocted by a Washington public relations firm, Hill and Knowlton, headed by Craig Fuller, a former chief of staff for then Vice President Bush. For five straight days, from September 25 to September 30, the liberation of Kuwait was the headline story of the Gulf crisis, and then it faded, like the others, to be periodically returned to prominence as events and administrative needs dictated (MacArthur 1992; Kellner 1992).

Reason five was Saddam Hussein himself. The demonization of Saddam Hussein was a logical extension of the hostage issue. If there were hostages to be liberated, they would have to be liberated from someone. The press began the vilification of Hussein by running personal profiles contrasting the Iraqi leader and the emir of Kuwait. Hussein was called a socialist, an assassin, and the head of a ruling clique, while the emir was characterized as the head of a family and a benevolent patriarch. Expediting the propaganda campaign, the press constructed the one comparison that no one would mistake: Hussein was a modern Hitler (Safire 1990). President Bush added the Hitler-Hussein analogy to his narrative in October and wove the phony incubator story into it. At a Dallas fund-raising event, he spoke of "newborn babies thrown out of incubators" and, in his signature clipped syntax, added:

> Every day now, new word filters out about the ghastly atrocities perpetrated by Saddam's forces. Eyewitness accounts of the cruel and senseless suffering endured by the people of Kuwait; of a systematic assault on the soul of a nation. Summary executions, routine torture. Hitler revisited. ("Bush Talks of Atrocities," 1990)

Reason six was jobs. Presumably, the Bush administration thought that the working people who would not fight for Texaco might fight to protect the oil on which their jobs depended. Although many Americans then and now believed the war was about oil, Secretary of State James Baker's November 14 attempt to equate oil with jobs and thereby sell a war for the oil companies as something that was in workers' interest did not work. The oil crisis that some expected to result from the Iraq-Kuwait dispute never materialized. On January 10, the eve of the first U.S. bombing of Iraq, the *New York Times* editorially shot down the oil-as-a-vital-interest reason for war (see also Friedman 1990).

Reason Abandoned: Toward War with Iraq

On the surface, the administration's resort to "jobs" as a reason for military intervention appeared to be an act of desperation. The administration had, after all, frantically constructed one reason after another for its military buildup in the Gulf. Yet, none of those reasons had convinced the American people that war was necessary. The administration had failed.

Or had it? In the end, the proffering of one reason after another functioned to paralyze rational discourse. No one could make sense of what this looming conflict was all about. And that was the point. The administration had succeeded in making it impossible to reason about the rightness and wrongness of this war. With reason having been neutralized, opinion about the war drew upon emotion, symbolism, and myth. It was the myth of the spat-upon Vietnam veteran that galvanized the sentiments of the American people sufficiently to discredit peace activists and give George Bush his war.

During the previous August and September there had been only scattered reports of active opposition to military intervention, but by early October mainstream religious groups were voicing their disagreement with the administration's policy. Church opposition was based on the principle of the just war. Just-war theorists involved the public in a carefully reasoned debate about whether war was justified in this case. The problem for the administration was that its policy did not pass the test. While some church leaders found "just cause" in the need to expel Iraq from Kuwait, few were satisfied that war was the last remaining resort (Steinfels 1990).[2]

After the November 8 announcement of increased troop deployment, opposition grew. By early December, reports of organizing by students and anti-war groups began to mount. The most troublesome voices from the administration's point of view, however, were coming from within the military. Within a week after the announcement, reports began to trickle out about soldiers resisting service in the Gulf. During the next few weeks, a large number of active-duty soldiers and National Guardsmen sought conscientious objector status. And not all of the in-service dissent was stateside. When Secretary of State James Baker and Chairman of the Joint Chiefs of Staff Gen. Colin Powell visited troops in the Gulf in November, they faced discontent bordering on hostility. Later, when President Bush made his Thanksgiving tour of the troops, special security measures were taken, and soldiers "were carefully selected and briefed on how to conduct themselves with him." The appearance that the commander in chief had to be protected from his own troops was very embarrassing for the administration.[3]

Then, on December 6, Saddam Hussein delivered what could have been a lethal blow to George Bush's domestic propaganda campaign. Announcing that all Westerners were free to leave Iraq and Kuwait, Hussein took away the most emotionally potent reason for U.S. military intervention: the hostages. The announcement came just at the time, three weeks before Christmas, when the administration could have used real hostages to exploit the separation anxieties of the nation. Moreover, with no American civilians in either Kuwait or Iraq (except those who were clearly there by their own choice) to use as an excuse for military intervention, Bush was on a shorter leash. The hostages issue, finally, had been a large blind hiding the offensive posture of the administration and that, symbolically, had provided a sure means for rallying pro-war public opinion when necessary. With its position uncovered, the administration now had either to abandon its aggressive stance or to confront, more candidly, the growing opposition.

Against the Coalition against the War

As we know, George Bush stayed the course to war and successfully transferred much of the sentiment that had been mobilized around hostages to soldiers. In effect, soldiers became the new hostages that needed to be rescued—by other soldiers, of course. Soldiers thus became the ends and the means of George Bush's war. The fledgling movement against the war, dubbed the "Coalition Against the U.S." in the *National Review* (Horowitz 1991), would have to be engaged.[4]

As the Senate Armed Services and Foreign Relations committees opened hearings on the policy in September, Bush began to complain that critics threatened the success of what was then still called Operation Desert Shield. Bush's strategy was to turn the tables on his opponents by using their anti-war position against them. Implicit in this strategy, previously employed by the Nixon administration in the closing years of the Vietnam War, was the assumption that peace could best be achieved through strength: those who were against the war in Vietnam were undermining the strength of America and thus prolonging the war. Applied to the Gulf War, the reasoning went that those who were opposed to the administration's policies were, objectively speaking, pro-war and by extension would have to be held accountable for the deaths of American soldiers in the Gulf (Lewis 1990).

A conservative group calling itself the Coalition for America at Risk began running a series of paid television commercials and newspaper advertisements that made the soldiers themselves the reason for the war. The full-page ads in such major papers as the *New York Times* and *Wall Street Journal* featured a large photograph of barren ground with a curvy line running across it. Beneath the picture, in mid-sized type justified to the left margin, was the caption: "It's not just a 'line in the sand' . . . it's . . . " Then, in large block type beneath the caption and centered on the page, was the single word: PEOPLE. The bottom half of the page addressed itself to "all the men and women participating in Operation Desert Shield" with the words, "We are behind you and support you 100%!" Reading down, the ad passed along a "special hello from home" to sixty-three nicknamed soldiers—Slick, Max, Rooster, Elvis, Bilbo, Badfinger, Fuzzy, the Dakota Kid, etc.—in a unit identified as HMLA-367 (Tolchin 1990).[5]

In no sense, however, was this a greetings message to the troops in the Gulf. The audience for this ad was not the troops but the American people. The construction of the ad asked us to make a distinction between the material and the human reasons for the war. It gave us, the readers, permission to choose, but not simply what the war was about. It instructed us about *how* to make choices about support or nonsupport for the war. To choose the "line in the sand" as a reason for what "it" was about was to choose a materialist framework within which logical propositions about the ends and means related to the defense of national boundaries could be debated and adjudicated. It was in effect a choice to make one's decision within the mode of discourse chosen, up to that point, by both the Bush administration and the anti-war theologians. To choose "people," on the other hand, was to choose to make decisions about the war on different, largely emotional, grounds. But which people was this war about? Who were the people in this ad? Not Kuwaitis. Not Saudis. This war was about Fuzzy and Bilbo, the boys from down the block. The war was about the American soldiers who had been sent to fight it.

In other words, the ad conflated the objectives of war with those who had been sent to fight the war. By thus dissolving the distinction between ends and means, the framework within which people could reason about the war was destroyed. In place of a discourse of reason, the ad gave us a discourse of emotion and identity: we were not to *think* about what this war was about, we were to *feel* what it was about. Henceforth, the campaign for the war was framed by symbols, emotion, and myth.

What we were to feel was mediated by the symbols mobilized for the occasion. Most visible, of course, was the yellow ribbon. During December, the yellow ribbon became a symbol of opposition to the anti-war movement. The yellow ribbon campaign dovetailed neatly with two issues from the Vietnam era about which the American people felt great emotion: the prisoner of war/missing in action (POW/MIA) issue and the issue of spat-upon Vietnam veterans. The POW/MIA issue was a natural, but it was the image of the spat-upon Vietnam veteran that figured most prominently in the rhetoric of those supporting the Gulf War. In that image, soldiers were the scapegoats against whom those who had opposed the war directed their hostility. Allegedly, members of the anti-war movement spat on soldiers just returned from Vietnam; the acts of spitting were said to have been accompanied by cries of "Baby Killer!" and "Murderer!"

That image had been cultivated mostly by the makers of such movies as the Rambo series during the 1980s. Those movies were very popular, so the issue of how Vietnam veterans had been treated was undoubtedly a concern shared by many Americans in 1990. But the link between that Vietnam-era issue and support for the Gulf War did not come about spontaneously. In fact, the link was first suggested by members of Congress, themselves Vietnam veterans, who were interviewed for a story that appeared in the *New York Times* on September 16. The story was accompanied by linked photographs: Sen. John Kerry sitting in his office, paired with a photo of the boat he commanded in Vietnam; Sen. John McCain in his office, paired with a photo of himself as a POW hospitalized in North Vietnam.

The story itself framed the linkage between the Vietnam War and the Gulf War in such a way that the treatment of soldiers and veterans became *the* issue. Rep. John Murtha, for example, who had served as a marine in Vietnam, said that on a recent visit to the Gulf "troops repeatedly asked [him] whether 'the folks back home' supported them. 'The aura of Vietnam hangs over these kids,' the Pennsylvania Democrat said. 'Their parents were in it. They've seen all these movies. They worry, they wonder'" (Apple 1990).

The "aura of Vietnam." It was not the loss of the war, not the massive destruction of Vietnam itself, not the death of 58,000 Americans and 1,900,000 Vietnamese, not any of the myriad other things the war was more evidently about that was at issue. The aura of Vietnam as framed in this story—what the war in Vietnam was about—was the level of support that soldiers and veterans had received from the American people. To make sure that nobody missed the point, the *Times* linked the package—Vietnam veterans, the Gulf War, and hostility for the anti-war movement—with reports from the Gulf like the following:

> One soldier asked that his name not be used and also asked that an officer step away to permit the soldier to speak freely to a reporter. . . . "When we deployed here, people cheered and waved flags," he [said], "but if I go back home like the Vietnam vets did and somebody spits on

> me, I swear to God I'll kill them." (LeMoyne 1990b)

These sentiments, brought to the surface during the middle weeks of the Gulf War buildup, were then played upon by Operation Yellow Ribbon in December. Operation Yellow Ribbon carried out its campaign through such state and local organizations as "Operation Eagle," headquartered in the Boston suburb of Shrewsbury, Massachusetts.[6]

Claiming the support of the U.S. Army, Navy, and Air Force, the Marine Corps, and Coast Guard Reserve units, Operation Eagle functioned on three levels. One level involved the collection of items that Operation Eagle leaders claimed were needed by soldiers in the Gulf. Using the stationery of the Third Marine Division Association, Operation Eagle solicited donations of reading material, board games, videos, sports equipment, and personal items such as lip balm and sunglasses. The solicitation listed a "hotline" number for further information without revealing that the number belonged to the Defense Logistics Agency in the Department of Defense.[7]

Additionally, Operation Eagle/Yellow Ribbon carried out a propaganda campaign in the public schools. The program sent Operation Eagle leaders and military personnel into schools and got students involved in writing letters to soldiers in the Gulf. Students who wrote letters were given red, white, and blue Operation Eagle hats.

The school campaign gave Operation Eagle enormous visibility and, through the thousands of children directly touched by military personnel who went into the schools, indirect access to the hearts and minds of thousands more adults. Most important, however, the political fallout from Operation Eagle's appearances in the schools created a pretext for attacks on the anti-war movement. When parents and interested citizens objected to Operation Eagle's self-evidently propagandistic project, the press and grassroots conservatives construed their objections as anti-soldier.

Operation Eagle's war against the anti-war movement was the third, and most important, level at which it operated. When a Worcester, Massachusetts mother objected to the presence of Operation Eagle in her son's school, the local press ridiculed her in an editorial. Two days later, the paper ran a large cartoon showing a soldier with an envelope addressed to "Any Soldier, Desert Shield," the generic address that Operation Eagle had been telling school children to use. The soldier was tipping the envelope so that a large amount of what looked like tiny scraps of paper were pouring out of it. The cartoon has him saying, "Some grade school kids from Worcester mailed us . . . CONFETTI?!?" A second soldier is shown saying, "Nope . . . those are kids LETTERS . . . edited by some protest group."

Within days, the paper was flooded with letters that parroted the themes of soldiers, hostages, Vietnam, and the anti-war movement that the Bush administration had so ably stirred together during the previous weeks. One writer said war opponents were causing him flashbacks to the 1960s. "I hope and pray," he said," Gulf war veterans will never return to the unfriendly and unsupportive country my generation returned to." Another letter claimed that anti-war activists had broken the hearts of thousands of Vietnam veterans. Still another asked if the peace activists opposing the Gulf War were "the same people that spit on the GIs when they came home from Vietnam." A supporter of Operation Yellow Ribbon, when asked why she was at a rally to protest the war, told an interviewer:

> The first reason, the first time I came out, the reason was, is, because of what happened to the Vietnam vets. I felt that they were treated so badly and they fought for their country and they were treated so bad that I tried to make up for it in this way. . . .
>
> I heard *they* [motions to peace vigil] were going to be here. And I didn't know anybody else was going to be here but I came down to protest the protesters. That's the only reason I came. Was to protest the protesters. I want the boys over there to know that there *are* people over here who are behind them and they're not gonna have to come home ashamed of their uniform; they're not gonna be having to take their uniform off at the airport so they can sneak into their own country and not be called murderers and everything. (Porter 1991)

Across the country, the role played by Operation Eagle in Massachusetts was played by other affiliates of Operation Yellow Ribbon. One that drew national attention was in the Chicago suburb of Schaumburg where efforts to block an Operation Yellow Ribbon group from entering Dooley Elementary School drew a response from President Bush. That story, carried in the pages of major newspapers across the country, reinforced the feeling that the real line of conflict in the Gulf War was drawn between those who supported and those who opposed the troops (Mills 1991).

But the yellow ribbon was only a symbol. The "real" thing was the image of the Vietnam veteran abused by the anti-war movement. That image was invoked countless times during the Gulf War period, sometimes in news accounts intended to be sympathetic to the war protesters:

> Vietnam-era protests often were directed at the soldiers themselves, revealing an ugly streak of elitism at best; this year's demonstrators see the GIs as victims. "You won't see protesters spitting on soldiers as they come off the plane," predicted Greg Sommers, director of the Fayetteville, NC branch of Quaker House, a pacifist organization. (Adler 1991)

The not infrequent invocation of the spat-upon veteran image by those who had been active opponents of the Vietnam War, and were now opposed to the Gulf War, may have been opportunism on the part of some, as suggested by David Horowitz (1991).[8] More likely, though, the self-incriminating statements of anti-war activists testified to the hegemony that the image of the defiled Vietnam veteran had acquired through the medium of popular culture and the power of the news media to keep the image in the faces of the American people during the period of the Gulf War buildup.

Fighting the Vietnam Syndrome

The dispatching of troops to the Gulf was an exercise in what is sometimes called "armed propaganda," a way of persuading through action. A substantial component of the propaganda campaign was directed at the American people. Armed propaganda substitutes for reason and rational argument through its appeals to the emotions. It communicates through a discourse of military symbolism, not words and logical propositions. Once the Bush administration had paralyzed the ends-means discourse, the armed propaganda technique enabled it to reduce public opinion on the war to the levels of emotion and symbolism.[9] The image of the spat-upon veteran functioned during the Gulf War as a "perfecting myth." Perfecting myths, explains Virginia Carmichael in her book *Framing History*, provide a justification for the world while simultaneously reinforcing the relationship between individuals and the state. They insure, she argues, "individuals' voluntary acquiescence to, support for, and daily investment in a specific history not of their choosing."[10]

By this reading, the Gulf War was a kind of necessary shock therapy to jolt the American people out of their reluctance to go to war, a reluctance that, allegedly, was a hangover from the defeat in Vietnam. The Gulf War was to be a demonstration of military prowess so awesome that positive identification with it would be irresistible. Opposition to the war, by the same token, would look so hopeless that the few pathetic souls who dared would be automatically subjected to devastating scorn and belittlement (Cloud 1991).

■ ■ ■ ■

The Gulf War brought scholars to a new level to appreciation for the audacity of governmental power at the turn of the twenty-first century. As economist Andre Gunder Frank (1992) observed in his analysis of Gulf War propaganda, the capacity of today's high-tech news management to brainwash a global population makes fascist mind control of the World War II era look like child's play.

Most of the historical analysis of the Gulf War has focused on the media and the ability of the government to censor the press.[11] The analysis made here is more in keeping with that of Neil Postman, who points out in his book *Amusing Ourselves to Death* that control over *how* we know is more important than control over *what* we know. While it is true that the government controlled the content of news during the Gulf War, it is more important to understand how it was able to influence significantly the way the American people thought about—or did not think about—the war. Its control was more Huxleian than Orwellian, its problematic more epistemological than empirical.

Few analyses, moreover, have had sufficient historical depth to recognize the foreshadowing of the Bush administration's tactics in the way in which the Nixon-Agnew administration prolonged the Vietnam War. From the mobilization of paramilitary patriots for pro-war rallies through the disparagement of anti-war activists and the exploitation of soldiers already in Vietnam as a reason to keep the war going, the Nixon-Agnew administration did it first.

The historical orientation . . . does not deny the ongoing relevance of the spat-upon veteran imagery. In his study of political apathy on today's college campuses, Paul Loeb (1994) found that the image of the spitting anti-war activists of the 1960s is an icon of 1990s conservative ideology and is used to intimidate would-be activists. Many of today's students prefer to remain inactive out of fear that activism will lead others to associate them with the 1960s' types who spat on the veterans. It is not surprising then, that as U.S. soldiers were dispatched to Bosnia late in the fall of 1995, a leaflet circulated on the campus of Holy Cross College in Worcester, Massachusetts, expressing opposition to the mission but support for the troops and the "hope that no student today will repeat the mistakes of the generation that proceeded us—by spitting on Marines" (Thompson 1995).

To get beyond this syndrome—a "Vietnam syndrome" of America's political culture—the real story of solidarity between the anti-war movement and Vietnam veterans has to be told, and the image of the spat-upon veteran has to be debunked and its mythical dimensions exposed.

Notes

1. "Operation Yellow Ribbon" was founded in the fall of 1990 by Gaye Jacobson, a manager for a Silicon Valley, California, defense contractor. Later incorporated in the state of California, Operation Yellow Ribbon eventually grew to twenty-seven chapters with five thousand members in six states. Jacobson, who had a son in the Gulf, initially volunteered her time to the organization but her board of directors eventually voted her $4,000 a month in salary. In April 1991, she founded another organization, the American Awareness Foundation ("Gaye Jacobson" 1991).

2. See the statement of Archbishop Daniel Pilarczyk, the president of the National Conference of Catholic Bishops, in Goldman 1990.

While the question of "proportionality" was a hypothetical one in the fall of 1990, it was clear within a few weeks after the bombing of Iraq began in January 1991 that the United States was inflicting massive civilian casualties on the country and generally engaging in gross overkill.

3. The first reports were about Sgt. Michael R. Ange's lawsuit over the constitutionality of the orders that he be transferred with his unit to the Gulf. The same story told of marine corporal Jefferey A. Patterson's court-martial for refusing to be shipped to the Gulf. By November 26, the War Resisters League, a pacifist group, was reporting "several hundred" applications for conscientious objector status by in-service soldiers while the Pentagon gave a lower number (Gonzalez 1990; LeMoyne 1990a).

4. On December 9, Bush claimed in a speech that his "alliance" was firm on the need for war against Iraq even though there were no longer hostages and even if Iraq pulled out of Kuwait (Dowd 1990a).

5. See the *New York Times*, December 17, 1990, p. B14, for an example of the advertisement.

6. Operation Eagle was founded during the fall of 1990 by two retired marines, Paul F. Roughan and Ray M. Kelley although it was not incorporated in Massachusetts until February 25, 1991. Articles of incorporation for Operation Eagle were obtained from the Commonwealth of Massachusetts.

7. Most of the information on Operation Eagle comes from copies of its own literature and a collection of newspaper stories kept on file at the Catholic Worker House in Worcester, Massachusetts.

8. Horowitz wrote, "To disarm their critics, [Gulf War protesters] volunteer their past 'mistakes,' like spitting on U.S. soldiers returning from Vietnam." Given that the press was trying to frame the opposition to the Gulf War with narrative of anti-war movement hostility toward war veterans, it is also possible that Vietnam-era activists were misquoted or had their words taken out of context.

9. Until memoirs are written, we might not know how consciously the Bush administration pursued the tactic of switching from one reason to another in order to make nonsense out of any effort to figure out what the war was about. In a moment of rare incisiveness, however, the *New York Times* suggested on November 1, 1990, that the tactic was rehearsed. Referring to the way the administration had handled Congress during the just-completed struggle over the budget, the *Times* wrote, "In an eerie replay of the budget ordeal, the President and his advisers are talking in different voices, sending different messages and moving back and forth between opposing positions—sometimes at the same moment." The *Times'* suggestion, however, that the resulting "confusion" was functioning to "redirect the public's attention in the week before elections away from the budget battle" seems superficial. Rather than redirecting

the public's attention, the shuffling of narratives was rendering attention to the Gulf War, in any cognitive sense, nearly impossible. See Dowd 1990b.

10. This is Virginia Carmichael's explication of how perfecting myths perform (1990, 1–7). She attributes the notion of perfecting myth to Kenneth Burke (1969, 240–41).

11. The best of such analyses are MacArthur 1992, and Kellner 1992.

References

Adler, Jerry. 1991. "Prayers and Protest." *Newsweek,* January 28, p. 37.

Apple, R. W. 1990. "Views on the Gulf: Lawmakers Versed in Vietnam." *New York Times,* September 16, p. I18.

Burke, Kenneth. 1969. *A Rhetoric of Motives.* Los Angeles: University of California Press.

"Bush Talks of Atrocities." 1990. *New York Times,* October 16, p. A19.

Carmichael, Virginia. 1990. *Framing History: The Rosenberg Story and the Cold War.* Minneapolis: University of Minnesota Press.

Cloud, Stanley W. 1991. "Exorcising an Old Demon: A Stunning Military Triumph Gives Americans Something to Cheer About—and Shatters Vietnam's Legacy of Self Doubt and Divisiveness." *Time,* March 11, pp. 52–53.

Dowd, Maureen. 1990a. "Bush Denies 'Payback' on Embassy." *New York Times,* December 9, p. I14.

———. 1990b. "Bush Intensifies a War of Words against the Iraqis." *New York Times,* November 1, p. A1.

Frank, Andre Gunder. 1992. "A Third World War: A Political Economy of the Persian Gulf War and the New World Order." In *Triumph and the Image: The Media's War in the Persian Gulf—A Global Perspective,* edited by Hamid Mowlana, George Gerbner, and Herbert Schiller. Boulder, Col.: Westview.

Friedman, Thomas L. 1990. "U.S. Gulf Policy: Vague 'Vital Interests.' " *New York Times,* August 12, p. A24.

"Gaye Jacobson." 1991. Spring/Summer. *People,* p. 44.

Goldman, Aril L. 1990. "Council of Churches Condemns U.S. Policy in Gulf." *New York Times,* November 16, p. A13.

Gonzalez, David. 1990. "Some in the Military Are Now Resisting Combat." *New York Times,* November 26, p. A13

Horowitz, David. 1991. "Coalition against the U.S." *National Review,* February 25, 36–38.

Kellner, Douglas K. 1992. *The Persian Gulf TV War.* Boulder, Col.: Westview.

Kifner, John. 1990. "Iraq Proclaims Kuwait's Annexation." *New York Times,* August 9, p. A1.

LeMoyne, James. 1990a. "President and the G.I.s: He Will Get Respect."*New York Times,* November 22, p. A23.

———. 1990b. "Troops in Gulf Talk of War, and of Vietnam and Respect." *New York Times,* September 30, p. I1.

Lewis, Anthony. 1990. "Democracy in the Way?" *New York Times,* November 26, p. A19.

Loeb, Paul. 1994. *Generation at the Crossroads.* New Brunswick, N.J.: Rutgers University Press.

MacArthur, John R. 1992. *Second Front: Censorship and Propaganda in the Gulf War.* New York: Hill and Wang.

Mills, M. 1991. "School's Ribbon Policy Draws Bush Response." *Chicago Tribune,* February 26, p. C2.

Porter, Janice. 1991. February. Interview with Carolyn Howe, Audio recording, author's possession.

Safire, William J. 1990. "The Hitler Analogy." *New York Times,* August 24, p. A29.

Steinfels, Peter. 1990. "Church Leaders Voice Doubts on U.S. Gulf Policy." *New York Times,* October 12, p. A1.

Thompson, John. 1995. "Bay of the Wolf: The Feral Howl." Worcester, Mass.:" Self-published Newsletter at Holy Cross College.

Tolchin, Martin. 1990. "TV Ads Seek U.S. Support on Gulf Stand." *New York Times,* December 17, p. A12.

Toner, Robin. 1990. *New York Times,* September 16, p. I27.

SECTION VI

THE NATION-STATE AND THE GLOBAL ECONOMY

Over the past thirty years, corporations have taken advantage of developments in communications and transportation technology to decentralize their operations. Key investment, design, and marketing functions tend to remain concentrated in particular cities (New York, London, Tokyo, etc.), while production has been dispersed; this has produced what has been called the "deindustrialization" of the United States, a steady decline in domestic manufacturing that began in the early 1970s. This and the increasing internationalization of services and the quickening pace with which financial capital can be moved and traded have been identified as signs that the national economies once characteristic of capitalism have been replaced by a truly global market (Barnet and Cavanagh 1994). Others argue that nationally specific resources are still central to economic activity; for example, the great bulk of foreign investment remains within the most advanced capitalist economies, and multinational corporations still remain tied to specific host countries (Hirst and Thompson 1996). This would suggest that the argument that national economies have been superseded by a global economy is incorrect, or at best premature.

The debate over the extent and consequences of globalization raises important questions for social scientists studying power. We have already seen throughout this book how the distribution of social resources serves as both a resource for and an expression of power. The class nature of political power becomes magnified at the global level. Of the fifty largest economic entities in the world, only fifteen of these are national economies, while the rest are corporations (Sklair 2002). These corporations obviously are able to wield extraordinary power, but the more significant question is what happens to the nation-state in the context of this global economic power. In asking this question, we must be clear that the history of capitalism from its origins has been characterized by the subordination of political institutions in the periphery of global capitalism to the economic needs of the dominant, core countries (Spain, Portugal, Holland, Great Britain, France, Belgium, Germany, and the United States have all taken on this role at various points in modern history). Indigenous political institutions were destroyed and replaced with more compliant colonial regimes. More recently, when governments in poorer countries have challenged this relationship of subordination and dependency, they have been subjected to various forms of subversion (assassination, military coups, invasion, psychological warfare), sponsored and supported, either directly or indirectly, by core countries (Blum 1985; Parenti 1989). Thus, the question of what the impact of global capitalism has been on the nation-state must be seen as directed toward the nation-states of the core countries themselves.

James Petras and Henry Veltmeyer argue that the nation-state continues to play a major role in global capitalism. They reject the argument that contemporary global capitalism represents a fundamentally new stage of development, and instead argue that what is today called "globalization" is really a contemporary version of imperialism. Although the dominant economic powers do not occupy colonies as in earlier forms of imperialism, they continue to exploit poorer regions of the global economy through military domination, political enforcement of structural adjustment programs that include privatization of public services and cuts in wages and social spending, and economic extraction of wealth through enforcement of low wages and the crushing burden of debt.

Although they acknowledge that nation-states have seen some of their authority shift to multilateral institutions such as the World Bank, the International Monetary Fund, and the World Trade Organization, Petras and Veltmeyer argue that the nation-state remains a major agent in the creation of global capitalism rather than its victim. As such, the nation-state continues to be a central institution of global capitalism.

The article by Robert O'Brien, Anne Marie Goetz, Jan Art Scholte, and Marc Williams provides an analysis of one of the multilateral institutions discussed by Petras and Veltmeyer: the World Bank. The World Bank provides loans for development projects in poorer countries, but because it is governed by contributor countries, it has had a history of imposing Western definitions of "development" with little sensitivity to local conditions or cultures. In recent years, numerous social movements, including environmental and women's movements, have challenged the World Bank to revise its criteria for lending to take greater account of social issues. In their study of the impact of women's movement organizations on the Bank, the authors indicate that while they have had some success in getting the Bank to support some women-oriented development projects, they have not been able to temper the dominance of market-based criteria in its decision making with feminist concerns for more socially oriented development that addresses the gender division of labor.

The ideology of global capitalism is examined in Steger's article. He is less interested in whether a global economy has actually emerged to displace the significance of national economies, and more interested in how a particular narrative about the global economy ("globalism") has been constructed to win popular support for global capitalism. In doing so, he is presenting a Gramscian argument that state institutions and multinational corporations cannot simply impose global capitalism through political or economic coercion, but instead must win support for it through cultural education and negotiation. The narrative of globalism, which is more commonly referred to as neoliberalism (Tabb 2001), presents the case that globalization can mean only one thing: the unlimited power of free markets. Globalization is presented as an inevitable, uncontrollable process in which market values are superior to all else, and in which any effort by the state to regulate the market to ensure socially desirable outcomes (for example, social equality, protection of the environment, etc.) must give way to deregulation and privatization of public services. The result, according to the narrative, is that everyone will benefit. Not only does such a narrative make it easier to sell global capitalism to the world's population, it also, in its claim of inevitability, seeks to demobilize resistance to global capitalism.

The ideology of globalism is in apparent contradiction with an expansion of nationalism across the world; on its face, the former unites the world in the pursuit of profit, while the latter fragments the world into specific cultural communities. While both Bogdan Denitch and Tom Nairn recognize this apparent contradiction, they offer competing interpretations of it. Denitch argues that nationalism defines an "imagined community" in which members are identified by certain subjective traits such as race, ethnicity, or religion. In doing so, nationalism simultaneously constructs nonmembers of this imagined community as an alien "other." The result of this process can be found in the war that destroyed Yugoslavia in the 1990s, in the long-standing conflict between Palestine and Israel, and in the genocide of Tutsis by the Hutus in Rwanda in 1994, to name but a few examples. For Denitch, nationalism represents a fundamental threat to democracy. Nairn, on the other hand, sees the critique of nationalism as a tired cliché. Nairn argues that nationalism has played an important role in social development; rather than being backward-looking, nationalism has been necessary to protect people from the power of the dominant, core countries. As such, any hope for global democracy must acknowledge the positive role played by nationalism.

The continued relevance of national identity, either as an obstacle to or resource for social development, speaks to an important limitation in the reach of globalism as a hegemonic project. The appeal of nationalism, for good or for bad, can be seen as a form of resistance to a global capitalism. People experience tension between the unifying claims of globalism and the alienated reality of their daily existence in a global capitalism that has exacerbated social inequalities and increased economic insecurity. From Denitch's perspective, nationalist claims of a glorified past and its scapegoating of the alien "other" offer an easy explanation for people's discomfort and the promise of a better life; we will see later that this is an important element in right-wing populist social movements. For Nairn, nationalism offers a resource for constructing space in which people can exercise some control over social development. Either way, globalism and the global capitalism that it is trying to sell are revealed to be more tenuous than its advocates imagine.

References

Barnet, Richard J., and John Cavanagh. 1994. *Global Dreams: Imperial Corporations and the New World Order.* New York: Simon & Schuster.

Blum, William. 1985. *Killing Hope.* Monroe, ME: Common Courage Press.

Hirst, Paul and Grahame Thompson. 1996. *Globalization in Question.* Cambridge: Polity Press.

McMichael, Philip. 2000. *Development and Social Change: A Global Perspective.* Thousand Oaks, CA: Pine Forge Press.

Parenti, Michael. 1989. *The Sword and the Dollar.* New York: St. Martin's Press.

Sklair, Leslie. 2002. *Globalization: Capitalism and Its Alternatives.* New York: Oxford University Press.

Tabb, William K. 2001. *The Amoral Elephant: Globalization and the Struggle for Social Justice in the Twenty-First Century.* New York: Monthly Review Press.

"GLOBALIZATION" OR "IMPERIALISM"?

JAMES PETRAS AND HENRY VELTMEYER

Globalization is at the centre of diverse intellectual and political agendas, raising crucial questions about what is widely considered to be the fundamental dynamic of our time—an epoch-defining set of changes that is radically transforming social and economic relations and institutions in the 21st century.

Globalization is both a description and a prescription, and as such it serves as both an explanation—a poor one, it has to be said—and an ideology that currently dominates thinking, policy-making and political practice. As a *description*, "globalization" refers to the widening and deepening of the international flows of trade, capital, technology and information within a single integrated global market. Like terms such as "the global village," it identifies a complex of changes produced by the dynamics of capitalist development as well as the diffusion of values and cultural practices associated with this development (UNRISD 1995; Watkins 1995; WCCD 1995). In this context, reference is often made to changes in the capitalist organization of production and society, extensions of a process of capital accumulation hitherto played out largely at the national level and restricted to the confines (and regulatory powers) of the state. As a *prescription*, "globalization" involves the liberalization of national and global markets in the belief that free flows of trade, capital and information will produce the best outcome for growth and human welfare (UNDP 1992). When the term "globalization" is used, whether to describe or prescribe, it is usually presented with an air of inevitability and overwhelming conviction, betraying its ideological roots.

How the before-mentioned epoch-defining developments and changes are interpreted depends in part on how "globalization" is conceived. Most scholars see it as a set of interrelated processes inscribed within the structures of the operating system based on capitalist modes of global production. Others, however, conceive of it not in structural terms but as the outcome of a consciously pursued strategy, the political project of a transnational capitalist class, and formed on the basis of an institutional structure set up to serve and advance the interests of this class.

We have here a major divide in analysis and theoretical perspective. On the one hand, those who view globalization as a set of interrelated processes tend to see it as inevitable, something to which necessary adjustments can and should be made. . . . From the inevitability-of-globalization perspective, the issue is how a particular country, or group of countries, can adjust to changes in the world economy and insert themselves into the globalization process under the most favourable conditions. . . .

On the other hand, those who view globalization as a class project rather than as an inevitable process tend to see the changes associated with it differently. In the first place, "globalization" is regarded as not a particularly useful term for describing the dynamics of the project. It is seen, rather, as we do—as in ideological tool used for prescription rather than accurate description. In this context it can be counterposed with a term that has considerably greater descriptive value and explanatory power: *imperialism.*

Using this concept, the network of institutions that define the structure of the new global economic system is viewed not in structural terms, but as intentional and contingent, subject to the control of individuals who represent and seek to advance the interests of a new international capitalist class. This class, it is argued, is formed on the basis of institutions that include a complex of some 37,000 transnational corporations (TNCs), the operating units of global capitalism, the bearers of capital and technology and the major agents of the new imperial order. These TNCs are not the only organizational bases of this order, which also include the World Bank, the International Monetary Fund (IMF) and other international financial institutions (IFIs) that constitute the self-styled "international financial community," or what Barnet and Cavanagh (1994) prefer to call "the global financial network." In addition, the New World Order is made up of a host of global strategic planning and policy forums such as the Group of Seven (G-7), the Trilateral Commission (TC) and the World Economic Forum (WEF); and the state apparatuses in countries at the centre of the system that have been restructured so as to serve and respond to the interests of global capital. All of these institutions form an integral part of the new imperialism—the new system of "global governance."

From this alternative perspective, "globalization" is neither inevitable nor necessary. Like the projects of capitalist development that preceded it—modernization, industrialization, colonialism and development—the new imperialism is fraught with contradictions that generate forces of opposition and resistance that can, and under certain conditions will, undermine the capital accumulation process as well as the system on which it depends. The recent crisis of the Asian economies (of Indonesia, South Korea, Thailand, Malaysia, etc.) was deeply rooted in their integration into the world's financial markets and the highly volatile movement of international capital.

Globalists emphasize the constraints placed on government policy or the action of social groups, the strategies pursued by diverse social organizations and the possibility of significant or substantial (systemic) change. Critics of globalization, on the other hand, emphasize the opportunities and emergence of social forces for change provoked by the social contradictions of the imperialist system—developments that chronically disrupt all areas of life under capitalism. At issue in this controversy are the conflicting interests at play, the forces of opposition and resistance generated, and the practical political possibilities for mobilizing these forces.

The "inevitability" of globalization is a critical issue. But a more critical issue, perhaps, is what the discourse on globalization is designed to hide and obfuscate: the form taken by imperialism in the current, increasingly worldwide capitalist system of organizing economic production and society. . . .

The Dynamics of Change: World Capitalism Today

There is little question that capitalism has undergone profound changes in its national and global forms of development in the post–World War II period. This is particularly obvious in view of the deep systemic crisis that beset the system in the late 1960s. Nor is there much argument about the capitalist nature of the organization that has been put into place. That this organization has increasingly taken a global form is also not disputed. In fact, this is the defining characteristic of the epochal shift that has occurred. What is disputed, however, is the significance and meaning of these changes, and the question of whether globalization represents a qualitatively new phenomenon or yet another phase in a long historical process of imperialist expansion.

Whatever view is taken on this point—and it is hotly disputed—it is possible to identify within the history of capitalist development a series of long waves, each of which is associated with a protracted period of crisis in the conditions of capital accumulation and a subsequent restructuring of the whole system. The last of these waves extended roughly from the 1920s to the 1970s. By drawing on diverse perspectives on this development, we can identify some key structures of the system put into place.

1. The concentration and centralization of capital that ensued in the last decades of the 19th century, in the context of a system-wide crisis in the late 1870s, resulted in the merging of large industrial and financial forms of capital, the growth of corporate monopolies, the territorial division of the world into colonies, the export of capital, and the worldwide extension of the market based on a division of labour between countries specializing in the production of manufactured goods and those oriented towards the production of raw materials and commodities.

2. The adoption of a Fordist regime of accumulation and mode of regulation resulted in a system of mass production and scientific management of labour at the point of production within diverse formations of the nation-state.

3. Under pressure from labour unions and Left parties, a series of state-led economic and social reforms created the political conditions for

a capital-labour accord on the share of labour in productivity gains, the social redistribution of market-generated income, and the legitimacy of a capitalist state based on the provision of social programs (welfare, health and education) and the guarantee of full employment. In the pre–World War II context, these reforms were designed to save the capitalist system from its contradictory features and its propensity towards crisis. In addition, the representatives of the capitalist class accepted welfare reforms to compete with the new Communist welfare states for the allegiance and loyalties of the working class in Europe, Asia and the rest of the Third World. These welfare reforms did not put an end to the class struggle but did push it into reformist channels. These reforms, which in effect responded to the demands made by Marx in the *Communist Manifesto,* resulted in what Patel (1993) has termed "the taming of capitalism." In the post-war context, the deepening of social reforms temporarily instituted a social democratic form of state capitalism, a state-led capitalist development that expanded production on both a national and global scale.

4. In the post–World War II context of an East-West division of the world, the hegemony of the U.S. within the world economic system, a major decolonization process and the resolve (at Bretton Woods) to impose a liberal world economic order created the framework for twenty-five to thirty years of continuously rapid rates of economic growth and capitalist development—the "Golden Age of Capitalism" (Marglin and Schor 1990). Within the institutional framework and economic structure of this world order, and through the agency of the nation-state, a large part of the developing world—countries organized as the Group of 77 within the United Nations system—were incorporated into the development process, initiating what Patel (1992) has termed the "Golden Age of the South," characterized by high rates of economic growth and major advances in social development.

5. The state in many instances was converted into the major agency for national development, implementing an economic model based on nationalism, industrialization and modernization, the protection of domestic industry, and the deepening and extension of the domestic market to incorporate sectors of the working class and direct producers.

By the end of the 1960s this system experienced cracks in its foundations and began to fall apart under conditions of stagnant production, declining productivity, and intensified class conflict over higher wages, greater social benefits and better working conditions. These conditions created a profit-crunch on invested capital (Davis 1984). In this context, two schools of political economy emerged, one emphasizing the inherent tendency of capitalism towards crisis and the social contradictions that chronically disrupt all areas of capitalist life, the other laying stress and focusing on various forms and levels of response to systemic crisis. It is possible to identify several strategic responses:

1. *Diverse efforts of the U.S. administration to offset world market pressures on its production apparatus that had been reflected in a rapid deterioration in its trade balance and the loss of market share to the economies of Germany and Japan.* These efforts took a number of forms, including the unilateral abrogation of the Bretton Woods agreement on the value and exchange rate of the U.S. dollar (with a fixed gold standard) and the manipulation by the Federal Reserve Board of exchange and interest rates. (Aglietta 1982).

2. *Relocation by TNCs of their labour-intensive industrial operations in the search for cheaper labour.* In the process, there emerged a new international division of labour (NIDOL) characterized by the growth of a new global production system based on the operations of the TNCs and their affiliates, now estimated by the United Nations Conference on Trade and Development (UNCTAD 1994) to number some 206,000. By 1980 the world's top five hundred TNCs had an annual turnover exceeding $3 trillion (U.S. dollars), equivalent to almost 30 percent of gross world production and an estimated 70 percent of international trade (UNCTAD 1994: 93). According to UNCTAD, 50 percent of these operations, in terms of their market value, did not involve the world market but consisted of intra-firm transfers.

3. *The internationalization of capital in both productive forms (investment to extend trade and expand production) and unproductive or speculative forms.* The driving force behind this process was a policy of liberalization and deregulation. This strategy was designed and fostered by economists associated with the IFIs and was adopted all over the world by governments that were either dominated by

transnational capital or subject to its dictates. The first form of capital to be internationalized and to escape the regulatory powers of the state involved the formation of offshore capital markets based on portfolio investments centered on speculation on foreign currency exchange rates. From the mid-1970s to the early 1990s the daily turnover of the foreign-exchange markets climbed from $1 billion to $1.2 trillion a day, close to twenty times the value of daily trade in goods and services (UNCTAD 1994; McMichael 1996). Joel Kurtzman, editor of the *Harvard Business Review*, estimates that for every U.S. dollar circulating in the real economy, $25–50 circulates in the world of pure finance (Sau 1996). Less than five percent of circulating capital has any productive function whatsoever (*Third World Guide* 95/96: 48).

On the heels of these globalizing and ballooning money markets, defined by the United Nations Conference on Trade and Development (UNCTAD 1994: 83) as "less visible but infinitely more powerful" than other capital flows, a number of banks in the 1970s began to internationalize their operations, resulting in a large-scale debt financing of government operations and development projects in countries all over the developing world. This was particularly the case for Mexico, Argentina and Brazil, countries that collectively received by volume over 50 percent of all such loans. In 1972 the estimated value of the overseas loans extended by these banks was $2 billion (Strange 1994: 112). The value of such loans peaked in 1981 at $90 billion ($58 billion for Latin America), falling to $50 billion in 1995 in the wake of a major region-wide debt crisis.

In the late 1980s, these forms of capital, used to finance government operations or development projects, increasingly gave way to foreign direct investment (FDI). This has become the capital of choice, estimated to represent up to 60 percent of the new capital extended to the developing world in the 1990s (UNIDO 1996). In 1990 the flow of FDI to Latin America and Asia, the two regions of the world that consumed the bulk of development finance or investment capital, was valued at only $2.6 billion, less than a twentieth of the international loans made that year. By 1995 the flow of FDI to Latin America had increased to $20.9 billion, more than 25 percent of the total loans extended to these two regions and close to one-half of all official transfers. Though most FDI goes to the Organization for Economic Co-operation and Development (OECD) countries, the higher rates of return on productive and speculative investments in developing countries and the opening up of privatization programs to the TNCs have resulted in a rapid expansion of FDI in this direction (UNCTAD 1994). By 1993, according to UNCTAD, developing countries attracted a record $80 billion in FDI, double the flow of 1991 and equal to the total level of FDI in the world in 1986. As a result, the share of these countries in the global flow of FDI, the largest component of new resource transfers to developing countries, grew from 20 percent in the mid-1980s to 40 percent by 1993 (UNCTAD 1994: xix, 3). One of the major consequences of developing countries' dependency on foreign financing is the growing vulnerability and volatility of their economies and financial markets as evidenced by the Mexican crash of 1994/95 and the near collapse of the economies of South Korea, Indonesia and Thailand in 1997. Massive foreign financing provides an immediate spur to growth, followed by a resounding economic crisis of overaccumulation, huge debt payments and collapse.

4. *The creation and growth of an integrated production system based on a new international division of labour, the global operations and strategies of the TNCs, a new enabling policy framework and new technologies.* These factors have dramatically shortened and lowered the costs of the transportation and communication circuits of capital in the production process and revolutionized the internal structure of production (see UNCTAD 1994: 123). By the end of the 1980s, entire lines of production and industries were technologically converted, and transformed in the process, dramatically raising the productivity of labour and shedding large numbers of workers and employees. This trend towards technological conversion and transformation has been associated with a shift in the structure of production and generated profound changes in labour markets and class structures all over the world.

5. *The adoption of new, flexible production methods based on a post-Fordist regime of accumulation and mode (or social structure) of regulation of both capital and labour.* These production methods were predicated on what has been termed a new "social structure of accumulation," a structure that

requires a radical change in the relation of capital to labour. The conditions for such a change have been generated in different contexts through a protracted political process based on an ongoing struggle between capital and labour which, according to Robinson (1996), has taken on the dimensions of another world war. The campaigns and battles in this war can be traced out at the national and the global level in political terms, and structurally in the reduced share of labour (wages) in the benefits of economic growth (income). Since the widespread implementation of neoliberal programs of structural adjustment in the 1980s, the share of labour in national income has been drastically reduced—from 48 percent to 38 percent in Chile, 41 percent to 25 percent in Argentina and 38 percent to 27 percent in Mexico (Veltmeyer 1999). In terms of a tendency towards wage dispersal (deviation from the average), the fall in the real value of wages and the share of wages in value added to production, the situation is even worse. In Latin America, conditions of structural adjustment have exaggerated disparities in income and wealth that were already the worst in the world.

6. *In the 1980s and 1990s, capital launched a direct assault on labour in terms of its wages, conditions and benefits, as well as its capacity to organize and negotiate contracts.* This offensive has taken numerous forms and is reflected in empirical evidence of a reduced capacity and level of labour organization, the compression and polarized spread of wages, the fall of wages as a share of national income, widely observed changes in the structure of labour markets all over the world and associated conditions of employment and unemployment (Veltmeyer 1999).

The International Labour Organization (ILO) (1996) argues that this system-wide decline in the value of wages and the dramatic expansion of jobs at the low end of the wage spectrum result in part from changes in the structure of production (the shift towards services, etc.), the introduction of new technologies and changes in the global economy. However, it adds, with reference to the U.S., that at least 20 percent of the variance can be attributed directly to a weakening of labour's capacity to negotiate collective agreements, which is directly associated with declines in organizational capacity and level of unionization and with the decentralization of negotiations (from the sectoral to the firm level)—all consequences of a protracted political struggle with capital.

It is evident that labour has borne the brunt of the restructuring and adjustment process. In the global context it is estimated by UNCTAD (*Third World Guide* 95/96: 28) that up to 120 million workers are now officially unemployed (35 million in the European Community alone) and another 700 million are seriously underemployed, separated from their means of production and eking out a bare existence in what the ILO defines as the unstructured or informal sector, accounting for over 50 percent of the developing world's labour force (ILO 1996; McMichael 1996). In addition to this reservoir of surplus labour, it is estimated by the authors that a mobile labour force of 80 million expatriate labourers has formed to constitute a new world labour market.

7. *The creation of a New World Order found expression in the founding of the IMF and the World Bank, which established an institutional framework for a process of capitalist development and free international trade.* Initially, in the 1940s, protectionist forces in the U.S. prevented the institution of a third element of this world economic order, namely the International Trade Organization (ITO). In a compromise solution, the institution of the General Agreement on Tariffs and Trade (GATT), a forum designed to liberalize trade through various rounds of negotiation, cleared the way for a world market with low tariffs and the elimination of other barriers to free trade in goods and services. It was not until 1994, fifty years later, that the original design was completed in the form of the World Trade Organization (WTO), instituted as part of an ongoing effort to renovate the existing world economic order and establish what ex-president Bush and the Heritage Foundation, a Washington-based right-wing policy forum, termed the "New World Order."

The pursuit of the New World Order and the widespread adoption of structural adjustment programs (SAPs) led to a new enabling policy framework for a global free trade regime and the constitution of a new imperial economy. Its one missing element was a general agreement governing the free flow of investment capital. It is to this end that the political representatives of imperial capital designed the Multilateral

Agreement on Investment (MAI), at first behind the closed doors of the OECD, the club of the world's richest and most powerful nations, and then the World Trade Organization, its latest and one of its most effective institutional weapons. The MAI and GATT, as well as the WTO itself have been criticized by, *inter alia*, the South Commission (South Centre 1997). The Commission argued that the imperial arrangements pressed for by the GATT and to be facilitated by the MAI were not in the interest of the South. For one thing, "a fully liberalized regime . . . would not necessarily promote widespread growth and development or take account of developing countries' preoccupations" (1997: 2). On the contrary, the Commission notes, the worldwide implementation of liberalization, deregulation and privatization measures since the mid-1980s has resulted in a significant deterioration of socio-economic conditions for a large part of the world's population and a widening of the North-South gap in market-generated wealth and income. In addition, these measures have seriously eroded the capacity of developing countries to pursue and advance their national interests, not to mention to control their own destiny. Echoing the conclusions of the UNDP, a recent statement by the South Commission was that "[globalization] is proceeding largely for the benefit of the dynamic and powerful countries" (1997: 82).

The UNDP's conclusion was derived from its analysis of the anticipated results of a process unleashed by the implementation of agreements negotiated at the GATT Uruguay Round. At the time, the UNDP (1992) calculated that these agreements would lead to an increase of $212–510 billion in global income—anticipated gains from greater efficiency, higher rates of return on capital, and expansion of trade. But the least developed countries, it argued, as a group would lose up to $60 million a year. Sub-Sahara Africa, containing a group of countries that could least afford losses and their associated social costs, would lose $1.2 billion a year (UNDP 1992: 82).

The loss for the least developed countries that would result from the GATT-induced growth in global incomes—and from their unequal access to trade, labour and capital—was estimated by the UNDP at $500 billion a year, ten times what they received annually in the form of foreign assistance (1992: 87). In this context, the UNDP added, the notion that the benefits of increased free trade on a global scale would necessarily trickle down to the poorest "seem far-fetched" to say the least. Subsequent developments have confirmed this worst-case scenario.

8. *The restructuring of the capitalist state to serve the imperial project.* For Aglietta (1982) and other regulationists, the world economy is theorized as a system of intersecting national social formations, which is to say, nation-states that have been able to resist what Petras and Brill (1985) have termed "the tyranny of Globalization." As Lipietz (1987: 24–25), a companion-in-theory of Aglietta, has put it: "A system must not be seen as an intentional structure or inevitable destiny [simply] because of its coherence. . . . Its coherence is simply the effect of the interaction between several relatively autonomous processes, of the provisionally stabilized complementarity and antagonism that exists between various national regimes of accumulation." These regimes, Lipietz (1987: 14) notes, are identifiable at the level of the nation-state and are designed to secure "the long term stabilization of the allocation of social production between consumption and accumulation." The same applies to the corresponding "mode of regulation," which "describes a set of internalized rules and social procedures for ensuring the unity of a given regime of accumulation" (Lipietz 1987: 14). In this view, the nation-state remains the major agency of the capital accumulation process even under conditions of its globalization.

Notwithstanding considerable evidence of the state's continued prominence and agency within the global development process, it is just as clear that under the present widespread structural and political conditions, the powers of the nation-state have been significantly eroded, giving way to the influence of international institutions. A closer look at these IFIs (the World Bank, IMF, Inter-American Development Bank [IDB], etc.) reveals that within their internal composition and mode of selection of key policymakers and beneficiaries, a distinct set of nation-states are dominant, namely the advanced capitalist, or imperialist, states of North America, Europe and Asia. This was already well recognized in the 1970s when the sheer size and economic clout of the biggest TNCs, as well as their relative international mobility, was seen as a major pressure on national sovereignty—on the capacity of the state to regulate the operations of capital or make national policy. In the 1980s, under the conditions of the New World Order, the powers of the state have been drastically reduced relative to those of TNCs and other global organizations. Political economists such as Manfred Bienefeld (1995), formed in an earlier mould, deplore this fact and search for conditions that might restore to the nation-state its sovereign powers or policy-making capacity. Others, Keith Griffin (1995) among them, argue that globalization and reduced power for the state are inevitable. From this perspective, the view and efforts of scholars such as Bienefeld, who is oriented towards a Keynesian welfare state or a strong developmentalist state able to determine national policy over vital areas of economic and social life, are somewhat quixotic and highly anachronistic.

Cutting across this debate is a view of the new role of the state in a context of globalization, whereby the real issue is seen to be not the reduction of the size and powers of the state, the loss of national sovereignty or the hollowing out of state responsibilities and functions, but the realignment of the state towards the interests of the transnational capitalist class.

The Economic Benefits of Globalization and Their Distribution

Another major issue is whether world inequalities and the North-South gap in the distribution of economic resources and income is growing, as supporters of the imperialism thesis argue, or as globalization theorists argue, conditions are maturing for a reduction of these disparities. This issue would seem to be easily settled by examination of relevant facts and statistics. However, the question is by no means clear or settled. It has been widely recognized or conceded that market-led or market-friendly developments associated with globalization have exacerbated existing global inequalities or generated new ones. Social inequalities in the distribution of economic or productive resources, and income, are widely seen to be on the increase. Many studies along these lines take a critical approach towards neoliberal capitalism and global development. However, even a number of advocates and apologists for globalization have come to the same view. The UNDP, for example, in its 1992 *Human Development* report determined that from 1960 to 1989 those countries with the richest 20 percent of the world's population saw their share of global output (income) rise from 70.2 percent to 82.7 percent while the share of those with the poorest 20 percent shrank from 2.3 percent to 1.4 percent. The United Nations Industrial Development Organization (UNIDO 1997) has argued the same point on the basis of more recent data.

Similarly, the World Bank and the international Monetary Fund have acknowledged that a large number of countries have regressed in the conditions of their development, in many cases to levels achieved in 1980 or even 1970. These countries have clearly failed to share in the fruits of recent development or to participate in what is seen by the World Bank (1995: 9) as a "trend towards prosperity." In the case of sub-Saharan Africa, it is estimated by the World Bank (2000) that per capita incomes since 1987 have fallen by 25 percent. The World Bank explains this failure in terms of wrong-headedness or policy mistakes, to an inability or unwillingness of certain countries to draw the necessary lessons from the development record or consistently pursue prescribed policies and adopt the institutional changes required. The Bank takes the position that, on the basis of correct policies, the gap in global incomes can be closed and more and more countries can share in the "trend towards prosperity."

Advocates of globalization have not been especially concerned about the identified increase in global social inequalities. With reference to a theory that has been converted into a doctrine, growing inequalities are generally taken to be the inevitable *short-term* effect of the market-led growth process, based as it is on an increase in the national savings rate and an increased propensity to invest these savings. The reason for this is that necessary conditions for an increase in the rate of savings and investment include a larger share of capital in national income and, ergo, a decline in the share of income available for consumption, that is, distributed in the form of wages or salaries. A trend in this direction has been identified at the national level in diverse contexts, particularly in Latin America, but it also exists at the global level. Indeed, global disparities in income have reached such a point that some scholars are drawing attention to them as a problem that could reach crisis proportions. The political dimensions of these global social inequalities have been subject to considerable analysis and, at the national level, to corrective policy. The problem is that the social discontent generated by these inequalities is liable to be mobilized into movements of opposition and resistance, giving the adjustment process the potential to destabilize political regimes committed to them. . . .

Despite broad agreement among advocates and opponents of globalization that global inequalities in economic resources and income can be assumed or shown to be on the increase since the mid-1980s, there are some who argue the contrary—that the North-South gap is closing. Interestingly (or oddly) enough, this point has been made by, *inter alia*, Griffin (1995), a recognized opponent of market-led development and an advocate of state regulation of the operations of capital in the market. As Griffin sees it, and argues in a heated debate with Bienefeld, the empirical evidence clearly suggests that the North-South income gap is closing rather than growing. Griffin also argues that global income inequality has begun to diminish in recent years. There has occurred, he notes, "a remarkable change in the distribution of the world's income," with average global incomes rising, resulting in many of the poor becoming less poor.

Is this an empirical or conceptual issue? How can Griffin's view be reconciled with the argument advanced by Bienefeld and many others that the North-South gap in wealth and income has been growing and has accelerated under conditions of structural adjustment and globalization? The UNDP, for example, has documented a dramatic worsening of the disparity in income distribution between the richest and poorest segments of the world's population along North-South lines. According to the UNDP (1992), since 1980, the disparity between the poorest and richest 20 percent of the world's population has increased from 11:1 to 17:1. UNIDO, which makes reference to an earlier study by Griffin and Khan (1992), makes the same point in different terms, citing the obvious fact (also noted by the UNDP) that globalization has clear winners and losers, and that the developing countries are clearly the losers. A part of the discrepancy in viewpoint and analysis lies in the assumption made by Griffin and others that with the rise of average global incomes the poor are relatively better off. However, as Bienefeld (1995) points out, most of the world's poor do not have access to income-generating productive resources. And with the explosive growth of the world's informal sectors and low-income activities or forms of employment, as well as the sharp decline of real wages and wage incomes in many parts of the world, a significant part of the world's population is worse off today than in the mid-1980s. Quite apart from the growth of average incomes at the global level, this deterioration in socio-economic conditions is reflected in the persistent growth in numbers of those in poverty, whether measured in absolute numbers or as a percentage of population.

The dynamics of this process might take the form of structural forces (or that is how they appear to many economists), but they relate to actions by organizations and capitalist enterprises clearly taken in their own interests. This was the point—one not well understood, or ignored by many economists—made by the prime minister of Malaysia in his critical remarks on a global economic system that allows "traders [to] take billions of dollars of profits and pay absolutely no taxes to the countries they impoverish" (South Centre 1997: 7). Michel Chossudovsky (1997) documents the working of this process on a global scale. He views the process in the same way as did the delegates at the April 2000 Conference of the Group of 77 (now 133)—as the globalization of poverty.

The "globalist view" that describes the world market as made up of integrated and interdependent national economies was totally demolished by the events leading to and following the collapse of the Asian economies, when insolvent loans led to massive bankruptcies among of banks and enterprises. Asian regimes putting out the begging bowl to the big banks of Europe, North America and Japan highlighted the nature of imperial relations in the so-called globalized economy. U.S. and European TNC buyouts of large Asian corporations for a fraction of their previous value, under the dictates by U.S. and European leaders of the terms of refinancing, further highlight the imperial nature of interstate relations in the world economy. The outcome of the Asian and Latin American crises in which the former lose and the imperial financiers win describes not "integration" and interdependence but rather subordination and imperialism. The inequalities and exploitation that define the interstate system illustrate the utility of the imperial over the globalist conceptual framework.

The Political Dimension of Globalization: The Question of Governance

One of the political arguments of globalization theorists has been that a diffusion of democratic institutions or the democratization of existing institutions accompanies the growth of "free markets." This process has unfolded at various levels. One has been a widespread trend towards decentralization of government that for the most part can be traced back to initiatives "from above and within" the state apparatus. In theory, if not in practice, this process has created some of the mechanisms and conditions (local power) for popular participation in public decision-making (Veltmeyer 1999). However, the critics of "decentralization" point to the lack of control by local authorities over the allocation of funds and the design of macroeconomic policy, and to the undemocratic nature of the selection of local officials. Another dimension of the "(re)democratization" process has been a shift away from military regimes and unconstitutional governments and towards civilian regimes formed within the institutional framework of liberal democracy. . . .

These trends have been so pervasive and concomitant with the institution of market-friendly economic reforms and structural adjustment policies that they have revived notions of a necessary link between economic and political forms of liberalization. Whereas the orthodox view of liberal scholars and politicians has been, and for many corporate CEOs still is, that authoritarian regimes are more likely to institute free-market neoliberal reforms and create the political conditions for rapid economic growth, the "new" ideology is that political liberalization (the institution of liberal democracy) either is the necessary precondition for or the inevitable result of the prescribed market-oriented reforms. In this context, the U.S. and international institutions such as the World Bank have turned against the dictatorships and authoritarian regimes they once nurtured or supported. In the name of democracy and as its self-appointed guardians, they now promote the institution of liberal democracy and even require it as a condition of access to aid, loans or investment capital (on this point see the World Bank's 1997 *World Development Report*).

Needless to say, this issue remains unsettled. What is clear is that the democracy now called for by the U.S. involves what Robert Dahl, *inter alia*, has termed "polyarchy," an elite-led form of liberal democracy. Not only is there no effective form of popular participation or substantive democracy in this institution, but under conditions of globalization, effective decision-making on key policy issues, including the regulation of capital, have been shifted towards international institutions, such as the IMF, the World Bank and the G-7 forum, that are notoriously undemocratic in their political processes.

At issue here is the capture of the state by global capital, or its reorientation towards the interests vested in the globalization process. In this context, the role of the new neoliberal state can be defined in terms of three critical functions: (1) to adopt fiscal and monetary policies that ensure macroeconomic stability; (2) to provide the basic infrastructure necessary for global economic activity; and (3) to provide social control, order and stability. The role of the neoliberal state prescribed by these functions has been to facilitate accumulation on a global scale and, it would seem, to regulate labour, which for some reason is less mobile today than it was in an earlier era of globalization from 1870 to the First World War. To assume this role, the state has been generally downsized, decentralized and modernized, and has had its regulatory and policy-making capacities hollowed out.

Another matter of particular concern to global capital is the question of governance, or the capacity to govern. The problem is posed by Ethan Kapstein (1996), Director of the U.S.

Council on Foreign Relations, in terms of the growing social inequalities in the global distribution of incomes which, he argues, exceed the level at which the forces of opposition and resistance can be contained. At issue is an emerging and potentially explosive level of social discontent which could all too easily be mobilized into political movements of opposition and resistance. The forces generated and mobilized by these movements, Kapstein fears, are likely to undermine and destabilize newly formed democratic regimes committed to market-oriented or friendly economic reforms. As a result these regimes are unlikely to stay the course, underlining the political will needed to fully implement the prescribed medicine of structural adjustment. The governability of the whole process, he concludes, is at risk, threatened by mounting forces of opposition and resistance.

Labour in the World Economy

The brunt of the capitalist globalization process has been borne by labour, the restructuring of which in effect has been the major mechanism of structural adjustment. This process has two major dimensions *vis-à-vis* labour. On the one hand, the capitalist development process has separated large numbers of direct producers from their means of production, converting them into a proletariat and creating a labour force which at the global level was estimated to encompass 1.9 billion workers and employees in 1980, 2.3 billion in 1990 and close to 3 billion by 1995 (ILO 1996). On the other hand, the demand for labour has grown more slowly than its supply. The process of technological change and economic reconversion endemic to capitalist development has generated an enormous and growing pool of surplus labour, an industrial reserve army that is estimated at one-third of the total global labour force. An estimated 50 percent of the enormous proletariat generated by capitalist development is either unemployed or underemployed, eking out a bare existence in the growing informal sector of the Third World's burgeoning urban centres or on the margins of the capitalist economy.

Our prognosis for the first decade of the 21st century is that the deepening crisis in Asia and the continuing crisis in Latin America will lead to an enormous growth of informal workers with incomes at or below the level of subsistence; large-scale movements of impoverished workers and peasants back and forth between urban and rural economies; the cheapening of industrial production and a decline in well-paid jobs in the advanced capitalist countries; the growth of poorly paid service jobs; and a worldwide crisis of living standards for labour.

Technological innovations, largely related to the processing of information, will lead to the growth of a relatively small elite of well-paid software engineers and executives and a mass of poorly paid "information processors"—the new proletariat. The outsourcing of labour-intensive computer work to low-wage areas is already a growing social phenomenon. Thus, the centrality of wage labour—contrary to the prognosis of the globalization theorists who talk about the "disappearance of wage labour"—will greatly increase even as it is impoverished. Insofar as the new information systems are linked to the vast movement of speculative capital, they can be seen as an integral technical instrument in the assault on productive capital and the living standards of wage workers.

The social and political implications of this change are momentous. For one thing, it will generate a radically different social structure and system of class relations. For another, it highlights the strategic position of labour. Combined with the growth of a huge industrial reserve army (mainly informal and contingent in form) and its depressant effect on the wages of the employed, the change wrought in the labour force and the social structure of society will undermine and weaken the capacity of capital to discipline labour and to stimulate the accumulation process.

Forces of Opposition and Resistance

For the sake of analysis, the economy and society are often portrayed as a system, which is to say, a set of interconnected structures, the conditions of which are objective in their effects and whose operation (on people, classes and nations) can be theorized by reference to "laws of development." The problem with this systems perspective is that it is all too easy to confuse an analytical tool—in this case a theoretical model—with reality. In this confusion structures are reified and their conditions are attributed an objectivity they do not have. As a result the structure of economic and social relations that people enter into is viewed as a mould into which they must pour their behaviour. And the institutionalized practices that make up the structure of the system appear as a prison from which there is no escape, subjecting individuals and entire nations to forces that are beyond their ability to control, let alone understand. Needless to say, this view breeds complacence and resignation—and notions of inevitability. Globalization appears as an immanent and intelligible process to which adjustments must be made.

The reality, however, is otherwise. In fact, the system, if it exists (and for the sake of analysis we too assume that it does), is fraught with contradictions that generate forces of opposition and resistance—of social change. However, as a matter of principle, for the sake of both analysis and political action, we argue that there is nothing inevitable about globalization viewed either as a process or a project. Like the underlying system, it is instituted by an identifiable class of individuals—transnational capitalists—and advanced in their collective or individual interests related to the accumulation of capital.

References

Aglietta, M. (1982). "World Capitalism in the 1980s." *New Left Review* 136 (Nov.–Dec.): 5–41.

Barnet, Richard, and John Cavanagh (1994). *Global Dreams: Imperial Corporations and the New World Order.* New York: Simon & Schuster.

Bienefeld, Manfred (1995). "Assessing Current Development Trends: Reflections on Keith Griffin's 'Global Prospects for Development and Human Security.'" *Canadian Journal of Development Studies* 16 (3).

Chossudovsky, Michel(1997). *The Globalization of Poverty.* London: Zed, Penang: Third World Network.

Dahl, Robert A. (1971). *Polyarchy.* New Haven: Yale University Press.

Davis, Mike (1984). "The Political Economy of Late-Imperial America." *New Left Review* 143 (Jan.–Feb.).

Griffin, Keith (1995). "Global Prospects for Development and Human Security." *Canadian Journal of Development Studies* 16 (3).

Griffin, Keith, and Rahman Khan (1992). *Globalization and the Developing World.* Geneva: UNRISD.

International Labour Organization (ILO) (1996). *World Employment, 1996.* Geneva: ILO.

Kapstein, Ethan (1996). "Workers and the World Economy." *Foreign Affairs* 75, (3).

Lipietz, Alain (1987). *Mirages and Miracles: The Crisis of Global Fordism.* London: Verso.

Marglin, Stephen, and Juliet Schor (1990). *The Golden Age of Capitalism: Reinterpreting the Postwar Experience.* Oxford: Clarendon Press.

McMichael, Philip (1996). *Development and Change: A Global Perspective.* Thousand Oaks, Calif: Pine Forge Press.

Patel, Surendra (1993). "Taming of Capitalism: The Historic Compromise," S. V. Desai Memorial Lecture, Ahmedabad. *Mainstream.* New Delhi.

——— (1992). "In Tribute to the Golden Age of the South's Development." *World Development* 20 (5).

Petras, James, and Howard Brill (1985). "The Tyranny of Globalism." IDS working paper no. 85-3. Halifax: Saint Mary's University.

Robinson, William (1996). "Globalization: Nine Theses on our Epoch." *Montelibre Monthly* March/April.

Sau, Ranjit (1996). "On the Making of the Next Century." *Economic and Political Weekly* 31 (April 6): 14.

South Centre (1997). *Foreign Direct Investment, Development and the New Global Economic Policy.* Geneva.

Strange, Susan (1994). *States and Markets.* London/New York: Pinter.

Third World Guide 95/96 (1996). Montevideo: Instituto del Tercer Mundo.

UNCTAD (1994, 1997, 1998). *World Investment Report.* New York and Geneva: U.N.

UNDP (1992). *Human Development: Reports 1992.* New York: Oxford University Press.

UNIDO (1997). *Industry and Development Global Report, 1996.* Chapter one ("Globalization: Its Challenges and Opportunities for Industrial Development") in *Economia Política: Trayectorias y Perspectives* (Universidad Autónoma de Zacatecas), 12 (Marzo–Abril 1997).

UNRISD (1995). *States of Disarray: The Social Effects of Globalization.* Geneva: UNRISD.

Veltmeyer, Henry (1999) "Labour and the World Economy." *Canadian Journal of Development Studies* 20, special issue.

Watkins, Kevin (1995). *Oxfam Poverty Report.* Oxford: Oxfam.

World Bank (2000). *World Development Report 2000/2001: Attacking Poverty.* New York: Oxford University Press.

——— (1988, 1990, 1991, 1993, 1995, 1997). *World Development Report.* Oxford: Oxford University Press.

——— (1995). *World Development Report 1995: Workers in an Integrating World.* New York: Oxford University Press.

World Commission on Culture and Development (WCCD) (1995). *Our Creative Diversity.* Paris: UNESCO.

THE WORLD BANK AND WOMEN'S MOVEMENTS

ROBERT O'BRIEN, ANNE MARIE GOETZ,
JAN AART SCHOLTE, MARC WILLIAMS

The World Bank is the world's biggest development bank, providing finance, research and policy advice to developing countries, with an annual turnover in new loan commitments to developing nations of over $20 billion.[1] Up to the 1980s Bank loans were primarily for specific development projects, but in response to national crises in economic management in the 1980s it embarked on the more controversial course of policy-based lending, attaching conditions on loan disbursement which resembled the IMF's economic austerity conditions.[2] This influence over how loans are spent gives the Bank an important position in setting the terms of development policy discourses, which is why the Bank's policies are of such great interest to global social movements and alternative development practitioners.

The Bank's operations are divided across four main institutions: the International Development Authority (IDA) for concessional lending to the poorest countries, the International Bank for Reconstruction and Development (IBRD) for regular loans, the International Finance Corporation (IFC) for private sector commercial lending, and the Multilateral Investment Guarantee Agency (MIGA) to insure private foreign direct investors against "political risks" in developing countries. IDA loans are funded by regular voluntary contributions by developed countries ("Part I" countries in Bank terminology), and increasingly from IDA repayments and IBRD profits. IBRD loans are funded through the sale of Bank bonds on international capital markets ($15 billion a year compared to $6 billion a year for IDA). The operations of the IFC and the MIGA are the least subject to conditionalities and quality controls, but are just as much of concern to gender equity advocates. The Bank's support to the private sector through the IFC and the MIGA is the fastest growing component of Bank lending, and it has a "multiplier" effect, in that Bank activity in the private sector of a given country acts as a green light to other commercial investors. Bank critics therefore target Bank activities in the private sector as an arena in which labour and environmental standards, and gender equity concerns, could be modelled as standards for the commercial sector.

The World Bank is not a monolithic or monological institution, for all it may seem so to its critics. It has always been somewhat torn between two competing identities. On the one hand, it is a bank, an institution driven by a "disbursement imperative for capital-driven growth-oriented lending" (Nelson 1995: 171). On the other, it is a development organisation with a stated objective of poverty reduction through economic growth. These two identities can clash, when new development ideas diverge from financial management requirements. The tension between the two identities actually creates space within the Bank for pockets of resistance and the development of alternatives to dominant neoliberal economic development paradigms. This tension is also productive of the periodic sea-changes in the Bank's approach to its development mandate. In the 1950s and 1960s the Bank promoted strong state-led investment in developing economies and poverty reduction programmes. From the late 1970s this approach was virtually reversed with a new neoliberal economic orthodoxy prescribing state withdrawal from markets. By the late 1980s as the human costs of structural adjustment programmes emerged, the Bank recommitted itself to its poverty reduction mission, and although it has not deviated from its neoliberal policies on market liberalisation, it is devoting more attention to human capital development and social development more generally. Since 1990, and very markedly since President James Wolfensohn took office in June 1995, there has been a shift, at least in the Bank's rhetoric, to promoting "participatory development." One of Wolfensohn's first acts in office was to launch a report by the Bank's "Learning Group on Participatory Development," thus enormously validating the importance of participation in policy and project development, giving a fillip to the efforts of NGOs to make the Bank's work more transparent and accessible to those most affected by it (World Bank 1994f: 1). A partner to this agenda is the Bank's new concern with promoting good governance, and although its Articles of Agreement forbid any explicit promotion of political change—such as transitions to democracy—its approach to good governance aims to encourage greater participation in national institutions of governance, and to improve the accountability of these institutions, all of which should encourage a deepening of democracy in some contexts.

Formal power at the Bank rests with its owners—its member states. These are represented on the Board of Governors, a body which meets just twice a year and delegates decision making to the Bank's twenty-four-member Executive Board, which meets twice a week to review, approve, or reject Bank project proposals, as well as to review Bank policy. The president of the Bank chairs the Executive Board on which he has the casting vote in the event of a tie. The five largest shareholders in the Bank (the USA, Japan, Germany, United Kingdom and France) each appoint an Executive Director; the remainder of the Board is elected by the other member governments every two years. The Board operates on a weighted voting basis but most decisions are based on consensus. There is an obvious North–South power division between the rich, non-borrowing countries on the Executive Board who make the capital contributions which support the IDA, and the poor, borrowing countries. Within Part I countries the US Treasury exercises the most power, as it controls the biggest single-country contribution to the IDA. As a result the most effective way of influencing the Bank from the outside is by lobbying Congress to threaten funds released through the US Treasury to the Bank; precisely the strategy used to great effect by environmental groups in the mid-1980s. Another effective strategy is to lobby Executive Directors and the national legislatures to which they report to act as advocates for certain issues when scrutinising Bank policy.

The Executive Board is not the only site of power in the institution. Another important locus of power in the Bank in terms of setting policy priorities is the Bank's president and top management team. As Williams (1994: 107) points out, the ability of the management and staff of the bank to shape policies and decisions—and indeed, to enjoy a high degree of autonomy in relation to its Board of Directors, arises from a combination of the Bank's relatively "independent financial base, the impressive technical and intellectual reputation of its staff, its pre-eminent position among multilateral lending agencies and the activities of successive presidents to develop and preserve organisational autonomy." This relative autonomy extends to the rank and file of economists and other specialists working in the operational and technical divisions of the Bank in the sense that they have some room for manoeuvre in pursuing new ideas. This facilitated, for instance, the creation in 1990 of a Bank-wide learning Group on Participatory Development—on the face of it a rather counter-cultural subject for the Bank. This kind of elasticity in the Bank's institutional culture has been very important to the relative successes of advocates of gender equity in development.

Bank–NGO Relations

No formal place existed in the Bank's original institutional structure for the representation of the interests of non-state actors such as social movements. Since 1982, however, there has been an increasing degree of dialogue and cooperation between the Bank and development NGOs. The 1990s have seen increasing reference to the importance of "dialogue" with "stakeholders" and "civil society" in the Bank's discourse. Such sentiments appear in particular in the Bank's new governance documents (World Bank 1994a) and in its discussion papers on participatory development and development partnership (World Bank 1998).[3] "Civil society" is very broadly defined in these kinds of documents, as are the range of actors which are embraced by the notion of "stakeholders" in any particular set of economic reform policies or sectoral investment programmes. These might include trade unions, business associations, social movements and so on, but in the Bank's actual engagement with non-state actors, this has boiled down to NGOs involved in development.

Outreach to and incorporation of NGOs is prompted by two concerns. First, there is increasing recognition of the "comparative advantage" exercised by NGOs over state bureaucracies in delivering development resources to the poor—and thereby in enhancing development effectiveness. Second, there is a growing recognition of the effectiveness of NGOs in determining the climate of public opinion, particularly in the North, about the Bank's work—and thereby threatening some of the Bank's operating funds, let alone the environment of good will for its work. There is also recognition of their role in developing countries in channelling and expressing popular frustrations with the sometimes painful social impact of economic reform policies, a role which can contribute to an often already weak national sense of ownership of these policies. Developing a partnership with NGOs is seen as helpful in enhancing the social sustainability of the Bank's work.

■ ■ ■ ■

Pursuing Women's Interests in the International Arena

Multilateral organisations concerned with global governance, peacekeeping and human rights have proven important arenas in which women have been able to legitimise their rights claims and develop transnational networks. Indeed, women's movements have had much more success in securing recognition (although not enforcement) of their rights in the UN's social institutions than in multilateral economic institutions. This owes in part to the differing cognitive frameworks and official ideologies of the different institutions. International organisations set up to enhance cross-national dialogue espouse values of tolerance and respect for human rights which women's movements can call upon when seeking equal respect for women's concerns. In contrast, multilateral economic institutions monitoring and supporting stability in national budgets, such as the World Bank and the IMF, or promoting the interests of transnational capital, such as the WTO, are governed by a set of values drawn from neoliberal economics, within which women's concerns with social justice can sometimes be seen as attempts to impose market distortions.

■ ■ ■ ■

Women's Movements and Alternative Economics

Until recently, economic development policy has been a policy arena fairly closed to feminist critiques, with its technical language and its impervious international institutions maintaining high entrance barriers to the participation of women (let alone feminists). Western feminist critiques of economic development processes initially did not challenge the conceptual framework of economics; rather, the "Woman in Development" (WID) critique which developed out of the work of feminist development practitioners in Northern bilaterals in the early 1970s saw the problem as the exclusion of women from access to new development resources and opportunities (Tinker 1990).

A rather different critique of the development process itself (as opposed to women's apparent exclusion from it) had been emerging from feminist anthropologists, and socialist feminists, including women in developing countries, often developing out of critiques of colonial exploitation, post-colonial neo-imperialism, and consequent dependency. This critique was expanded by a new international network of women researchers from the economic South: Development Alternatives with Women for a New Era (DAWN), founded in 1984 on the eve of the NGO and official conferences marking the end of the UN Decade for Women. Their starting point was to establish that the problem of women's disprivilege was not caused by exclusion from the development process, but by their inclusion in a process which relies upon gendered divisions of labour and power (as well as systems of class and national inequality) to fuel processes of growth (Sen and Grown 1987). As Peggy Antrobus, one of DAWN's General Coordinators, noted with reference to current neoliberal economic development policies: "The problem with structural adjustment policies is not that they assume women are outside of development and need to be brought in, but that they are actually grounded in a gender ideology which is deeply and fundamentally exploitative of women's time, work, and sexuality" (Antrobus 1988).[4]

Feminist critiques of economic development have proceeded from this point, exposing the unacknowledged assumptions made in economic theory about the low or zero value of women's labour. Economists such as Diane Elson (1991), Gita Sen (Sen and Grown 1987), and Nancy Folbre (1986) have elaborated principles of feminist economics which begin from new perspectives on household economic behaviour to endow women's work with value in spite of being unpaid, and which recognise that relations of power between women and men (and people of different age groups or life-cycle stages) within the household mean that members of households do not share equally in economic opportunities and wealth. This critique is a strong challenge to assumptions made by economic planners because it demonstrates that people will not respond to economic or market signals in a "free," rational way unencumbered by social relations. The fact that gender relations ascribe female labour to domestic tasks means that this female labour is immobilised in activities which are not responsive to market signals. Thus price signals, so key to neoliberal economic planning, will not necessarily change the way a household allocates its labour. The non-attribution of economic value or cost to household work leads planners mistakenly to assume that women's time has a zero opportunity cost, and that women can therefore be called upon to expand their labour input to paid production or voluntary community activity with no negative impact on human reproductive activity—on the well-being of children, for example, or on the stability of the household.

In the context of the structural adjustment policies promoted by the World Bank and IMF since the late 1970s, these feminist economic principles explain the unequal impact of economic reform on women and men. Adjustment policies have sought to stabilise economies and reduce balance of payments deficits by devaluing the currency, reducing government expenditures, increasing interest rates and controlling credit expansion, reducing the role of the state, privatising national industries, liberalising markets and removing government subsidies and minimum wages. A measure which has an immediate impact on women is the reduction of state expenditures on social services, with women expected to expand their domestic responsibilities to compensate for decreasing state investment in children's education or health. The introduction of charges to recover costs of social services can exacerbate gender biases in household decisions about which children to educate or bring to the clinic, with girls often losing out. In some cultures, gendered expectations about appropriate responsibilities for the sexes can mean that it is women's incomes which are expected to cover social service costs, not men's.[5] In effect, women are expected to bear the "invisible" costs of adjustment:

> there is the risk that what is perceived in conventional economic analysis as efficiency improvements may in fact be a shift in costs from the visible (predominantly male) to the invisible (predominantly female) economy . . . Gender bias (or "neutrality") in the underlying concepts and tools of economics has led to invisibility of women's economic and non-economic work and to an incomplete picture of total economic activity. (World Bank 1994c)

However, it is the positive growth programme proposed in neoliberal economic reform policies which have had more profoundly negative impacts upon women's well-being and household survival. Adjustment measures in productive sectors aim to encourage production for the market and for export. Price signals sent out by liberalised markets encourage this shift. But the capacity of producers to respond to these signals is affected by gender relations. Women's labour may be subject to the control of men, and in addition, their unequal rights and obligations mean they have differential access to and control over economically productive resources (such as land, labour, credit, extension services, transport infrastructure). In many parts of Sub-Saharan Africa, where women dominate agricultural production, these constraints have led to a much lower response than expected to economic incentives. . . . Alternatively, men have demanded increased inputs of women's labour on crops sold for cash and export, which has detracted from women's investment in food crops, undermining the food security of their families (Floro 1994; World Bank 1990). Some of the consequences of the strains which economic reform has put on women's time are becoming evident in family breakdown and increasing female household headship in urban areas of Latin America and Asia (Dayal and Mukhopadhyay 1995: 18), in women's deteriorating health and in girls' withdrawal from school to support mothers with household work (Sparr 1994).

■ ■ ■ ■

Gender Issues in the Bank's Work

It has been extremely difficult for women's movements to gain direct access to the Bank. Its Washington offices are inaccessible to most women's associations around the world unless they are represented by powerful Washington-based NGOs with an established relationship with the Bank. The Bank's economistic policy language is highly technical and can seem deliberately arcane and indecipherable to many women critics. In any case, its policy documents such as the important Country Assistance Strategy papers have been, until very recently, inaccessible to readers in civil society, protected by a comprehensive embargo on outside scrutiny. Above all, the Bank does not recognise women's movements as legitimate interlocutors in economic policy making; until very recently its policy dialogue process has been conducted exclusively between the Bank and the borrowing country.

The Bank has been markedly slow in its response to the concerns of women's movements. Most development agencies such as bilaterals and regional development banks were spurred into an institutional and policy response to the gender issue by the series of UN Conferences on Women. Most began putting in place institutional infrastructure to house Women in Development concerns after the Mexico City conference in 1975. Most had a policy directive to promote gender equity in development planning by the end-of-decade conference in Nairobi; those which did not issued policy statements shortly afterwards. At the World Bank, although the idea of developing a gender equity policy statement was first mooted in 1975, a Policy Paper: *Enhancing Women's Involvement in Economic Development,* was not issued until 1994.

In the mid-1970s, the Bank was criticised by women's movements for failing to include women in its development projects. And indeed, from FY 67 to FY 86 only 7 per cent of Bank projects included "gender-related activities" (World Bank 1994d: 37). These activities formed a relatively small part of project objectives, and were also hardly oriented towards achieving gender equity; they tended merely to target women's reproductive roles, often just by providing contraceptives in family planning projects (World Bank 1994d: 37). Since FY 86 there has been a greater proportion of Bank projects with "gender-related actions"; up to almost 30 per cent of Bank operations in 1995, although as we will see, women's groups question the quality of these actions. During the 1980s, the focus of critiques by women's movements shifted to a condemnation of the negative impact of Bank structural adjustment measures on women's livelihoods and on gender relations. Feminist critics charged that the Bank ignores gender issues in its important Economic and Sector Work (ESW) which includes the Bank's macroeconomic policy analysis and its research on development sectors such as finance, industry, agriculture, and infrastructure, as well as cross-cutting concerns such as poverty and the environment (Women's Eyes on the World Bank 1997).

Institutionally, the Bank has found it difficult to find a home for the gender equity concern. A lone woman advisor on Women in Development was appointed in 1977, who, lacking resources to develop policy or to monitor gender equity concerns in Bank projects, focused on defending the Bank's work to outside critics (Kardam 1991: 77). There was certainly no question of endowing this position with powers of influence over the Bank's work—such as a veto over inappropriate policies. This problem of inadequate resources for the gender equity concern within the Bank, and a lack of effective powers over Bank policies and processes, has plagued subsequent efforts to "mainstream" a Women in Development focus in the Bank's work (Kardam 1991; Razavi and Miller 1995). In 1986, a three-person WID office was established, and the following year placed within the Population and Human Resources Department. By 1988 the WID office had become a division with eight staff. In 1990 each region was given funding to establish a full-time WID Coordinator post. This was an important step towards bringing WID issues into the operational part of the Bank, but rather pales in comparison to the expansion occurring simultaneously in another area related to the quality of Bank loans: the environment. Between 1983 and 1987 professional staff assigned to monitor environmental concerns multiplied from six to sixty; there were environmental divisions in the regional departments, and a full department for the environment in the technical support services of the Bank (Rich 1994).

In the 1990s, particularly since the UN Conference on Women in Beijing, the pace of change and enhanced commitment to gender equity concerns at the Bank has been accelerating. In 1993 after a Bank-wide reorganisation, a Gender Analysis and Policy (GAP) thematic group was set up in the Education and Social Policy Department of the new vice-presidency for Human Resources Development and Operations Policy. In 1995, the Bank's new president, James Wolfensohn, attended the Beijing conference, the first time a World Bank president had done so. The nature of his participation, in which he consulted with women's civil society groups at the NGO linkage Caucus on Economic Justice, and accepted a petition from the Women's Eyes on the Bank Campaign for policy reform at the Bank, signalled an important new opening to global women's movements. Wolfensohn, who is noted for his concern with the social impact of economic reform, responded to the Women's Eyes on the Bank campaign by setting up an External Gender Consultative Group (EGCG) composed of fourteen women who are members of women's movements around the world. Top management at the Bank has consulted with this group on an annual basis since Beijing. In spite of tremendous obstacles to regular communication among members, or to the development of a common strategy or set of concerns, the EGCG has taken steps in areas which are relatively new for the feminist critique of the Bank. For instance, it has pressed the Bank to apply its principles on gender equity to its work in private sector development. Wolfensohn also demanded regional gender action plans of all Bank regional operations (most had been completed by mid-1997), asked the Bank to produce annual reports on progress in addressing gender issues in development, launched gender flagship projects,[6] and included gender equity in the institutional change process at the Bank which is intended to produce a new mission for the Bank based on fostering social as well as economic development. As part of a general effort to open up civil society participation in the design and implementation of some programmes, a commitment has been made to consult women in the Bank's economic and sector work, particularly the Country Assistance Strategy process.

In 1997, after yet another massive reorganisation, a Gender Sector Board was set up in one of the four new Technical Networks which represent restructured thematic support services to country-level operations. The Gender Sector Board is intended to operate as a family of gender specialists across the Bank, anchored by a core group in the Poverty Reduction and Economic Management Technical Network, whose other concerns include public sector management and poverty.[7] Locating the gender equity interest in this Technical Network is a coup for the internal Bank gender advocates who lobbied for this. It signals that gender equity is not considered a "soft" sector issue related mainly to reproductive concerns. However, there has been no change to the fact that the gender unit at the Bank has little command over the incentive system and cannot therefore enforce compliance with gender equity goals in Bank lending. Indeed, outside observers suggest that the new system may make it even more difficult to impose a whole range of quality-related concerns on Bank project design, including social assessments, poverty reduction and participation. The new system is demand-driven, which means that gender specialists will have to rely upon project designers, or "task team managers" in country departments, to call upon their services, but these managers will be under no strict obligation to do so (Bread for the World Institute 1996: 20). This puts the onus on gender specialists to "sell" their services in ways which will attract project designers—and in a neoliberal economic environment this means stressing the business case for gender equity, not the social justice case, which has tended to be the stronger suit of gender advocates.

On the surface, the Bank appears to have taken gender equity concerns seriously. Many feminist critics, however, are sceptical about the Bank's commitment to these measures. A post-Beijing assessment of gender equity at the World Bank by the US chapter of the Women's Eyes on the Bank campaign lists a range of shortcomings in the Bank's approach to gender equity concerns. It charges that the Bank's 1994 gender policy is not actionable, because "Bank gender initiatives have yet to translate into concrete actions that address gender inequalities and break down gender barriers in a majority of its policies" (Women's Eyes on the World Bank 1997: 2). It charges that the Bank has failed to recognise gender-specific constraints on the participation of women from civil society in Bank policy dialogues, pointing out that it makes no allowance for the greater time needed for "participation" where vast differences of power exist and where women's groups may be unfamiliar with economic planning languages. What is more, the Bank is accused of disingenuousness, of claiming credit for a greater degree of sensitivity to gender issues than it actually reflects in practice. For example, the Bank is satisfied that its economic and sector work addresses gender issues when its documents merely make mention of women or gender, rather than incorporate a gender-sensitive perspective into economic analyses. For instance, a Country Assistance Strategy for Indonesia was cited by the Bank as addressing gender issues, on the rather shallow basis that it mentions "women" three times and "gender" once, yet lacks either a gender analysis or strategies to address gender inequalities. The same problem applies to projects which are said to contain "gender-related actions"; by and large, these actions do not challenge inequities in gender relations (Women's Eyes on the World Bank 1997: 3). The Bank is charged with persistently refusing to entertain a gendered critique of its macroeconomic policy framework; and with failing to alter its approach to structural adjustment to minimise its negative impact on poor women. The Bank has been described as "conspicuously noncommittal" in response to pressure from the External Gender Consultative Group to bring gender issues into its more commercial arms. . . .

The Bank's opening to consultation with women's movements through the External Gender Consultative Group has also attracted criticism. The legitimacy of the EGCG is challenged by some women's groups on the grounds that as a body it is neither representative nor accountable—a very similar criticism as that levelled by many NGOs at the NGO–World Bank Committee when it was set up in 1982. Neither the criteria for nor process of selecting members was transparent, with only a narrow stratum of women's groups consulted for advice on suitable candidates. Very few of the fourteen members come from associations involved in day-to-day Bank monitoring and some are therefore not sufficiently familiar with Bank procedures to provide the kind of recommendations and advice which could result in real changes in the Bank. It has no resources and no clear mandate, nor are members certain about their expected term of tenure in the group. Not all members have extensive links with women's movements. It was not until June 1998 that a secretariat for the EGCG was created (based at the NGO Tools for Transition in Netherlands), with funds from the World Bank. The Women's Eyes on the Bank campaign has questioned the group's legitimacy, particularly as it is assumed to represent global women's movements. It has been described by one feminist activist in Washington DC as "just a bone which Wolfensohn threw them [women's movements],"[8] and by a gender advocate within the Bank as "Bank defined, managed, and implemented. Low-level and low-brow [. . .] and handled like a damage limitation measure."[9]

■ ■ ■ ■

However promising recent developments may seem, the gender equity issue has had a troubled time at the Bank. In order to explain this it is important to understand aspects of the Bank's cognitive framework and its power structure. The Bank's cognitive framework affects the ways new development concerns like gender equity have been entertained by its staff, and determines the arguments used by external critics to plead their case. Its power structure affects its sensitivity to external critique and determines lines of entry or attack by outsiders.

The World Bank's Cognitive Framework: The 'Business Case for Gender Equity'

The Bank's cognitive universe—its framework for understanding human behaviour—is neoclassical economics. As the political scientist Yusuf Bangura notes: "Perhaps the greatest barrier to the institutionalisation of gendered development is the inflexible nature of the dominant neo-liberal discourse [. . .] wide gaps exist between the fundamental premises, values and goals of neo-liberalism and the broad gender discourse" (Bangura 1997: 20).

The two policy discourses could not be more different. Neoliberal economics pitches its analyses at the level of the macro economy, whereas feminist economics begins in the microeconomics and politics of decision making between women and men in the household. The driving concern of neoliberal economics is to improve market efficiency, which, optimally, will lead to fairness in the allocation of resources and rewards. To create market efficiency, measures such as limited state intervention, private ownership of assets, trade liberalisation, and unregulated competition are encouraged. In contrast, the driving concern of feminist economics is gender justice, righting the wrongs experienced by women because of their sex, including the derogation of the value of their work, the limits on their rights to property ownership, unequal access to education, employment, or positions of public power, and even the denial of women's rights to control their bodies and sexuality. This approach relies upon interventions to assign value to women's work and to mitigate distortions caused by gendered ideologies in institutions such as households, markets and state bureaucracies. There is some premium on the interventionist role of the state as an agent to challenge some of the tyrannies of private-sphere patriarchy. Neoliberal economists base their predictions of people's responses to economic signals on assumptions about the rationality of individuals keen to maximise personal advantage, with society simply the aggregate of these choices. Feminist economists are trying to find ways of working the politics of gender relations into economics so as to acknowledge the constraints on individual choices created by social structure, belief systems and ideologies.[10]

In interactions between gender equity advocates and the Bank, the terms of discourse are set by the Bank, as the more powerful interlocutor, obliging feminists critics to work within the framework of the neoliberal concern with efficiency. At the May 1997 meeting between the Bank and the EGCG, Minh Chau Nguyen, the acting head of the Bank's Gender Sector Board, described this as putting the onus on gender equity advocates to "make the business case for gender and sell it to staff" (World Bank 1997a: 4). At this same meeting, phrases such as "the business case for gender," as well as "the economic rationale for investing in gender" were reiterated frequently by a series of senior Bank managers, including the president. This is nothing new, and gender equity advocates have become adept at demonstrating women's productive efficiency, which has resulted in a highly instrumental perspective on women's contribution to development, rather than the contribution of development to women's empowerment.

The case for the efficacy of investing in women has been made most effectively in the arena of human capital development. Research has demonstrated higher social pay-offs (or "social externalities") to investing in women's rather than men's health and education; the results are lower fertility rates, higher life expectancy, better nutrition levels and overall education levels. This evidence has persuaded the Bank to increase its investments in girls' education and women's health. Over the last twenty-five years, of the 615 Bank projects (out of 5,000) which included "gender-related components,"[11] 46 per cent were in the health, population and education sectors (Alexander 1996: 5; also ODA/ICRW 1995). These are relatively non-controversial areas in which to invest; they support women's reproductive roles[12] and do not overtly challenge gender roles. As an independent assessment of the Bank's record on gender equity explains, "Development thinking has more easily embraced women's reproductive roles because . . . an emphasis on motherhood validates widely held beliefs about women's role in society" (Razavi and Miller 1995: 2).

Gender equity advocates have had much less success in challenging the framework of the Bank's economic and sector work. Gender equity concerns have tended to receive scant mention in investment strategies for "hard" sectors like agricultural or industrial planning, or industry, energy and transport which absorb the bulk of Bank sectoral loans, where women's differential resources and options as producers and homemakers are ignored.[13] Gender equity concerns do not even penetrate very deeply into the Bank's work on poverty reduction; its country-specific Poverty Assessments (PAs) by and large fail to disaggregate the experience of poverty by gender.[14] The important exception is the Bank's new programme of loans and grants to institutions offering micro-credit to the very poor: the Consultative Group to Assist the Poorest (C-GAP). The majority of borrowers in many of these micro-credit programmes are women. Investing in women's access to micro-credit coheres comfortably with efficiency and poverty-reduction agendas without raising issues of social change because of the very individualised and home-based nature of micro-enterprise activities.

Two problems hold back the potential impact of the feminist critique on the bank's economic and sectoral work. The most fundamental is the clash in the two cognitive frameworks. Forced to make the business case for investing in women's economic productivity, the feminist case has floundered somewhat. It is perfectly plausible to argue that women's productivity could be increased tremendously by enhancing women's human capital endowments and rights to factors of production and inputs (Saito 1992). Indeed, the Bank is prepared to support the project of "investing in and releasing the economic potential of women" to enhance their contribution to economic development.[15] But this argument seems to be suggesting that gender inequalities would be eradicated if market imperfections were removed, and ignores the persistence of gendered power inequities whichcan keep women from controlling the fruits of their increased productivity. In addition, any increase in women's productivity in income-generating work represents a loss of their time for work within the home. In a policy environment which refuses to legitimate or to finance the costs of compensating for the loss of women's investment [in] household reproduction, women will be expected to work harder in "productive" and "reproductive" arenas, depleting their productivity in both. Thus the arguments sometimes offered by gender equity advocates that "investing in women's productivity is economically efficient," or that "economic growth requires women's participation" are a little unconvincing.[16] One does not have to be a great cynic to note that economic growth in the West took place without rewarding women's participation, and indeed, probably profited from the unpaid subsidy provided by women's work.

The second problem has to do with the ethics and ideologies surrounding judgements about what is "unfair" in gender relations. Gender relations are seen as cultural matters, and the condemnation of inequities in gender relations is assumed to reflect a narrow, highly ideological, Western feminist perspective. The Bank therefore demurs on assessing justice in gender relations because this is seen as cultural interference. Its Operational Directive to all staff to integrate gender equity concerns into their work carries an important let out clause: staff are enjoined to pay "due regard to cultural sensitivity" (World Bank 1994a). No similar delicacy is expected of staff when dealing with other subjects which can interfere with cultural matters, such as population policy, privatisation, poverty reduction measures, policies to educate girls and so on. Nor does the Bank acknowledge the highly ideological nature of its own cognitive framework. As William Claussen, Bank president from 1981 to 1986, said: "the Bank is not a political organisation, the only altar we worship at is pragmatic economics" (Razavi and Miller 1995: 31).

Power Systems at the World Bank: Few Points of Access or Influence

. . . [T]he Executive Board is locus of formal decision making at the Bank, and as such it has been a very important channel for the expression of the concerns of global women's movements, depending on their success at lobbying certain member country governments. Nordic governments have been particularly critical in introducing "social conscience" themes to the Bank, including poverty reduction, social sector lending, debt management reform, and gender equity, even though they have a weak position on the Executive Board in terms of their voting power. The UK, Canada, and the Netherlands have also been particularly sympathetic on gender equity matters. It was criticism from the Executive Board that triggered renewed efforts in the Bank in 1990 to institutionalise the gender and development interest.

■ ■ ■ ■

Not all Executive Board members represent this kind of constructive lobbying resource for the feminist case in macroeconomic planning. Some Executive Directors find even the Bank's cautious approach to gender equity issues to be too radical; at the same 1994 meeting, the Executive Director for Korea asked that the policy paper be "toned down," and both he and the Executive Director for Saudi Arabia implied that an interest in reducing gender disparities was a Western concern which violated their countries' cultural sensitivities. This familiar "cultural" objection to gender equity concerns gives the Bank a defence for its caution on the gender issue. Ambivalence from some Executive Directors over gender equity issues reflects either the weakness of domestic women's movements in influencing their governments, or it can reflect a lack of democracy in state–civil society relationships, which may be obstructing the expression of women's interests in national politics. This makes it important for women's movements to have access to international NGOs that can represent their views to the World Bank, an issue to which we return in a moment.

Women's movements have not attempted the most powerful lobbying manoeuvre in relation to the governance and financing of the World Bank, which is to lobby the more wealthy countries' Treasuries to withhold replenishment funding for the IDA in the way the environmental movement has done. Women's movements tend to have a much narrower base of support than environmental movements and hence cannot exercise the same degree of political leverage. Most importantly, the gender and development concern has not been taken up by the US women's movement in a strong enough way to support an assault on the Bank's funds through Congress. The US environmental movement was central to the success of campaigns by global environmental movements because it is well resourced, has a wide base of domestic support and is familiar with the legislative and lobbying dynamic in Washington. But in the case of the US women's movement, even though it is the largest and most powerful women's movement in the world, its focus is squarely domestic, not international. It has not put its weight and political resources behind gender and development concerns. In addition, there is a great reluctance to tamper with US government funds for development since most women's groups in the USA which are involved in development issues rely heavily upon USAID for funds, and have no wish to threaten its Congress allocation, something which could occur as a side-effect of challenging the quality of World Bank spending of Congress allocations.

■ ■ ■ ■

However, it is difficult to reform any institution, particularly one with such a solidly homogeneous culture of economic rationality, professionalism, exclusiveness, and excellence, as well as a history of secrecy in its intellectual processes and products, with many policy documents embargoed from public scrutiny. From this perspective considerable power rests in the hands of the Bank's professional staff in Operations, the six regional departments and the individual country management units where the loans and sectoral projects are designed, negotiated and supervised. At the heart of this work are the task team managers, who have "the principle operational role of the Bank, the role that does the work that justifies the existence of the organisation: preparing loans or making studies" (Wade 1997: 29).

As noted above, issues which concern the actual quality of the Bank's work are located in the less powerful Technical Networks, "which have large staffs and small budgets," in comparison with the country management units in Operations "which have large budgets and small staffs" (Bread for the World 1997: 6). Staff in the Technical Networks are meant to supply their expertise to task team managers on demand. These support services are weakly placed in the Bank's incentive system, which centres on pressure on staff to move money, to make and recover loans.[17] There is less pressure to ensure compliance with Bank standards such as environment, resettlement, information disclosure or gender equity. Directives do exist to set out Bank policies on best practice in these and many other areas. However, there are over 150 mandatory actions or procedures spelled out in these directives—it is difficult to comply with all of them.[18] Inclusion of social concerns in project preparation therefore depends upon the commitment of the individual task team manager. Although issues of gender equity and social justice may interest many staff members, they sit uneasily in the Bank's culture as "value-laden and subjective" concerns (Kardam 1991: 72).

This puts the onus on internal gender equity advocates or "policy entrepreneurs" to promote the merits of sensitivity to gender issues in the work of their Country departments. . . .

Internal gender specialists are in a difficult position. Careers in the Bank are not made by arguing the case for what is seen as a marginal interest. They, and other staff who are feminists or are sympathetic to gender equity positions, are in a minority position both by virtue of their sex (though some are men of course), and by virtue of the fact that whether they are economists or not, their feminist convictions mean they are in a counter-cultural position in relation to the Bank's dominant cognitive framework. The vast majority of the Bank's staff are economists, and they are also mostly men,[19] two facts which are not immaterial in terms of creating an organisational culture resistant to feminist concerns.[20]

■ ■ ■ ■

Conclusion

Over the last thirty years, women's movements have developed increasingly sophisticated and politically credible critiques of economic development, and have targeted their concerns at multilateral economic institutions, most particularly the World Bank. . . .

The Bank's attitude to gender issues has definitely become less dismissive than when these issues first came up in the 1970s. The Bank has installed an internal machinery to promote gender equity in its work, setting up standards of best practice in this area, and expanding the resources it targets to women, such as lending programmes for girls' education and women's reproductive health, and grants to institutions providing micro-credit to poor women borrowers. It has been much slower to review its structural adjustment policies from the point of view of their impact on women, and has made little serious effort to entertain feminist critiques of macroeconomics in its economic and sectoral work.

Notes

1. However, the importance of Bank lending has diminished with increased private capital flows—e.g. in the Latin American region public capital flows have dropped from 50 per cent to 20 per cent of total capital flows in the last five years. In the last seven years, the flow of private sector funds to developing countries has increased fivefold (World Bank 1997a: 7, 13).
2. The Bank's adjustment loans are actually only a small proportion of its loans. In 1995, it made 130 adjustment loans (average size $140 million) and 1,612 project investment loans (average size $80 million) (Alexander 1996).
3. Note that the notion of partnership is intended mainly to apply to more effective partnerships with borrowing country governments, as a step towards establishing more effective in-country ownership and management of economic reform processes. This, it is hoped, will overcome the tendency of borrowing countries to see economic reform agendas as an external imposition.
4. Also cited in Dayal and Mukhopadhyay (1995).
5. This problem is discussed in the context of poverty in Uganda in Goetz, Maxwell and Maniyire (1994).
6. These are sectoral investment programmes which are intended to be particularly productive in terms of enhancing women's or girls' development, such as the Tanzania Girls' Secondary Education Support Project, or the Zimbabwe Health Sector Projects.
7. The other three Technical Networks are: Human Development (population, health, nutrition, education); Private Sector and Infrastructure (small and medium-sized businesses, banking and capital markets, telecoms, transportation, sanitation, energy); Environment, Rural and Social Development (participation, NGOs and post-conflict work).
8. Interview, NGO, Washington DC, 9 September 1997.

9. Interview, World Bank, Washington DC, 11 September 1997.
10. This comparison of the two approaches to economic analysis is summarised from Bangura (1997: 20–21).
11. By the Bank's own admission, the rating system which identifies projects as having "gender-related components" is insensitive to the quality and "depth" of those components, not differentiating between whether the project addresses gender equity issues in a substantive or superficial way. See the Bank's two progress reports to date (World Bank 1996, 1997b). Note that for all regions except for the Middle East, over half of these "gender-related" projects were approved only very recently, between 1989 and 1993. Before then, "gender-related components" in Bank projects were very scarce. The Bank's Operations and Evaluations Division estimated that between FY 79 and FY 84, the height of the UN Decade for Women, only 7 per cent of the investment portfolio could be said to relate to gender equity concerns (World Bank 1994e).
12. Quite literally. The bulk of the Bank's early research on women was preoccupied with establishing the determinants of fertility, underlining the strong association between women and biological reproduction. See Razavi and Miller (1995: 35).
13. "Hard" sector loans totalled $18 billion in 1995 compared with $4 billion loaned to the social sectors (Alexander 1996: 7).
14. Important exceptions are the PAs for Cameroon, Kenya, and Uganda. See the study of the World Bank's Poverty Assessments in IDS (1994).
15. The quoted phrase is the subtitle of a special Bank memorandum for the Fourth UN Conference on Women (World Bank 1994b).
16. Although research by the Bank and others has convincingly demonstrated the high returns to investing in women's education and health, according to the Bank, efforts to show that countries which invested heavily in women experienced more rapid economic growth has not been done in a "rigorous and convincing" manner (Razavi and Miller 1995: 73).
17. Late in 1997 the Bank introduced new products which are designed to modify the "moving money" incentives with new concerns to enhance the quality and success rate of loans. These products include Adaptable Programme Loans and Learning and Innovation Loans. The first is a loan with a phased-in implementation process to enable borrowers to pilot test solutions with small amounts without risking large amounts and exposing the Bank. At the same time, the borrower retains the Bank's commitment to supporting the development sector in question. The Learning and Innovation Loans are a smaller version of the Adaptable Programme Loans and are intended to foster iterative learning and solution testing (Bread for the World 1997: 9–10).
18. Interview, NGO, Washington DC, 9 September 1997. These directives had been rationalised down from 400 "operational policies," examples of "best practice" or "good practice," and they have less force than they had before. This may not make much of a difference for some directives which had previously been respected mostly in the breach. One NGO interviewee suspected that this is the Bank's way of defending itself from charges that it is not respecting its own policies, weakening procedures that should be mandatory like resettlement, indigenous peoples, [and] gender policy.
19. The composition of Bank staff in terms of professional training and gender has been changing gradually, with growing numbers of sociologists and anthropologists being hired, and with more women being appointed (Razavi and Miller 1995: 31).
20. A growing body of feminist organisational analysis is demonstrating that the balance of genders in an organisation's staff, and a range of other features of organisations such as the tolerance of justice and equity concerns in intellectual and ideological frameworks, the openness of decision making, the rigidity of calibrations in status hierarchies, and so on, can create gendered organisational cultures which profoundly affect the impact of an organisation's work on women and men, as well as the experience of women and men within organisations (Kardam 1991; Razavi and Miller 1995). For general expositions of approaches to feminist analyses of development bureaucracies see Goetz (1997) and Staudt (1997).

References

Alexander, Nancy, 1996. *Gender Justice and the World Bank*, Silver Spring, Md: Bread for the World Institute (September).

Antrobus, Peggy, 1988. *The Impact of Structural Adjustment Policies on Women: The Experience of Caribbean Countries*, Santo Domingo: INSTRAW.

Bangura, Yusuf, 1997. "Policy Dialogue and Gendered Development: Institutional and Ideological Constraints," Discussion Paper 87, Geneva: UNRISD.

Bread for the World, 1996. "Downsizing the World Bank," *News and Notices for World Bank Watchers*, 15 (November) (Silver Spring, Md: Bread for the World Institute).

——— 1997. *News and Notices for World Bank Watchers*, 19 (December) (Silver Spring, Md: Bread for the World Institute).

Dayal, Ashvin and Maitrayee Mukhopadhyay, 1995. "Econonic Liberalisation and Women: An Overview of Assumptions, Theory, and Experience," *AGRA South 1995: Gender and Structural Adjustment*, Oxford: Oxfam.

Elson, Diane, 1991. "Male Bias in Macro Economics: The Case of Structural Adjustment," in Diane Elson (ed.), *Male Bias in the Development Process*, Manchester: Manchester University Press.

Floro, M.S., 1994. "The Dynamics of Economic Change and Gender Roles, Export Cropping in the Philippines," in Sparr (ed.), pp. 116–33.

Folbre, Nancy, 1986. "Hearts and Spades: Paradigms of Household Economics," *World Development*, 14 (2): 245–55.

Goetz, Anne Marie (ed.), 1997. *Getting Institutions Right for Women in Development*, London: Zed Books.

Goetz, Anne Marie, Simon Maxwell and Henry Maniyire, 1994. *Poverty Assessment and Public Expenditure: Country Field Study—Uganda*, Brighton: Institute of Development Studies.

IDS, 1994. *Poverty Assessment and Public Expenditure Study for the SPA Working Group on Poverty and Social Policy*, Brighton: Institute of Development Studies for the ODA and SIDA (July).

Kardam, Nuket, 1991. *Bringing Women In: Women's Issues in International Development Programs*, Boulder: Lynn Reinner.

Nelson, Paul, 1995. *The World Bank and Non-Governmental Organisations*, London: Macmillan.

ODA/ICRW, 1995. *Women's Issues in World Bank Lending: A Preliminary Summary of Findings*, draft report (August), Washington DC: Overseas Development Council/ International Center for Research on Women.

Razavi, Shahra and Carol Miller, 1995. "Gender Mainstreaming: A Study of Efforts by the UNDP, the World Bank and the ILO to Institutionalise Gender Issues," Occasional Paper 4 (August), Geneva: UNRISD.

Rich, Bruce, 1994. *Mortgaging the Earth: The World Bank, Environmental Impoverishment and the Crisis of Development*, London: Earthscan.

Saito, Katrine, 1992. *Raising the Productivity of Women Farmers in Sub-Saharan Africa*, Overview Report, Washington, DC: World Bank, Women in Development Division, Population and Human Resources Department.

Sen, Gita and Caren Crown, 1987. *Development, Crises, and Alternative Visions: Third World Women's Perspectives*, New York: Monthly Review Press.

Sparr, Pamela (ed.), 1994. *Mortgaging Women's Lives: Feminist Critiques of Structural Adjustment*, London: Zed Books.

Staudt, Kathleen, 1997. *Women, International Development, and Politics: The Bureaucratic Mire*, Philadelphia: Temple University Press.

Tinker, Irene, 1990. "The Making of a Field: Advocates, Practitioners, and Scholars," in Irene Tinker (ed.), *Persistent Inequalities: Women and World Development*, Oxford: Oxford University Press.

Wade, Robert, 1997. "Development and Environment: Marital Difficulties at the World Bank," Global Economic Institutions Working Paper Series, ERSC, 29 (July), London.

Williams, Marc, 1994. *International Economic Institutions and the Third World*, Hemel Hempstead: Wheatsheaf.

Women's Eyes on the World Bank (US Chapter), 1997. "Gender Equality and the World Bank Group: A Post-Beijing Assessment," Executive Summary (May), Washington DC: Oxfam America.

World Bank, 1990. *Analysis Plan for Understanding the Social Dimensions of Adjustment*, Washington, DC: World Bank Africa Region.

——— 1994a. "The Gender Dimension of Development," Operational Directive 4.20, *The World bank Operational Manual: Operational Policies* (April), Washington, DC: World Bank.

——— 1994b. *Closing the Gender Gap: Investing in and Releasing the Economic Potential of Women* (June), Washington, DC: Revised Initiating Memorandum.

——— 1994c. "Gender and Economic Adjustment in Sub-Saharan Africa," *Findings* (June), Washington, DC: World Bank; Africa Technical Department.

——— 1994d. *Gender Issues in Bank Lending: An Overview*, Report 13246 (June), Washington, DC: World Bank Operations and Evaluation Division.

——— 1994e. *Gender Issues in Bank Lending: An Overview* (30 June), Washington, DC: Operations Evaluation Department.

——— 1994f. *The World Bank and Participation* (September), Washington, DC: World Bank Operations Policy Department.

——— 1996. *Implementing the World Bank's Gender Policies*, Washington, DC: World Bank, Gender Analysis and Policy.

——— 1997a. *World Development Report 1997: The State in a Changing World*, Oxford: Oxford University Press.

——— 1997b. *Implementing the World Bank's Gender Policies*, Progress Report No. 2 (June), Washington, DC: World Bank.

——— 1998. *Partnerships for Development: A New World Bank Appraisal*, Washington, DC: World Bank.

FIVE CENTRAL CLAIMS OF GLOBALISM

MANFRED B. STEGER

Neoliberal market ideology serves a concrete political purpose. It presents globalization in such a way as to advance the material and ideal interests of those groups in society who benefit the most from the liberalization of the economy, the privatization of ownership, a minimal regulatory role for government, efficient returns on capital, and the devolution of power to the private sector. Like all ideologists, globalists engage continuously in acts of simplification, distortion, legitimation, and integration in order to cultivate in the public mind the uncritical attitude that globalization is a "good thing." When people accept the claims of globalism, they simultaneously accept as authority large parts of the comprehensive political, economic, and intellectual framework of neoliberalism. Thus the ideological reach of globalism goes far beyond the task of providing the public with a narrow explanation of the meaning of globalization. Most importantly, globalism is a compelling story that sells an overarching neoliberal worldview, thereby creating collective meanings and shaping personal and collective identities.

Protected by this powerful discursive regime, the marketization tendencies in the world have grown stronger than at any point in history. Globalism has become what some social and political thinkers call a "strong discourse." Such a hegemonic discourse is notoriously difficult to resist and repel because it has on its side powerful social forces that have already preselected what counts as "real" and, therefore, shape the world accordingly. As American social philosopher Judith Butler notes, the constant repetition, public recitation, and "performance" of an ideology's central claims and slogans frequently have the capacity to produce what they name.[1] As more neoliberal policies are enacted, the claims of globalism become even more firmly planted in the public mind. They solidify into what French social philosopher Michel Foucault calls a solid "ground of thinking."[2] The political realization of the neoliberal agenda, in turn, leads to the further weakening of those political and social institutions that subject market forces to public control. Neoliberal policies are made to appear as the most rational response to inevitable, but efficient, market forces. Growing global disparities in wealth and well-being are shrugged off as mere temporary dislocations on the sure path to a brighter future.

This chapter analyzes significant passages in the utterances, speeches, and writings of influential advocates of globalism. These persons usually reside in wealthy Northern countries and include corporate managers, executives of large transnational corporations, corporate lobbyists, journalists and public-relations specialists, intellectuals writing to a large public audience, state bureaucrats, and politicians. Putting before the public a globalist agenda of things to discuss, questions to ask, and claims to make, this powerful phalanx of neoliberal forces seeks to imbue the concept of globalization with values, beliefs, and meanings that support the global realization of societies based on free-market principles. This perspective is being promoted on a daily basis to the U.S. public and lawmakers alike by the spokespersons of major corporations and corporate associations.

After introducing the reader to what I consider to be five central globalist claims, I subject these assertions to critical examination. . . .

■ ■ ■ ■

My critical examination of the five central claims of globalism suggests that the neoliberal language about globalization is ideological in the sense that it is politically motivated and contributes toward the construction of popular beliefs and values. Exposed to a shifting context of political competition, rivalry, and conflict, the claims of globalism seek to fix a particular meaning of globalization in order to preserve and stabilize existing asymmetrical power relations. Although these meanings undergo ceaseless contestation and redefinition in the public arena, the dominant party of this struggle enjoys the advantage of turning its ideological claims into the foundation of a widely shared framework of understanding. Thus the claims of globalism become an important source of collective and individual identity.[3]

■ ■ ■ ■

Claim No. 1: Globalization Is about the Liberalization and Global Integration of Markets

The first claim of globalism is anchored in the neoliberal ideal of the self-regulating market as the normative basis for a future global order. According to this perspective, the vital functions of the free market—its rationality and efficiency, as well as its alleged ability to bring about greater social integration and material progress—can only be realized in a democratic society that values and protects individual freedom. For Friedrich Hayck and his neoliberal followers, the free market represents a state of liberty, because it is "a state in which each can use his knowledge for his own purpose."[4] Thus the preservation of individual freedom depends on the state's willingness to refrain from interfering with the private sphere of the market. Liberals refer to this limitation on governmental interference as "negative liberty." This term refers to the protection of a private area of life within which one "is or should be left to do or be what he is able to do or be, without interference by other persons."[5] Since neoliberals allege that the free market relies on a set of rules applying equally to all members of society, they consider it both just and meritocratic. While the existence of the market depends on human action, its resulting benefits and burdens are not products of human design.[6] In other words, the concrete outcomes of market interactions are neither intended nor foreseen, but are the result of the workings of the "invisible hand."

Opposing the expansion of governmental intervention in the economy that occurred in Western industrialized nations during the first three-quarters of the twentieth century, globalists call for the "liberalization of markets"; that is, the deregulation of the national economies. In their view, such neoliberal measures would not only lead to the emergence of an integrated global market, but they would also result in greater political freedom for all citizens of the world. As Milton Friedman notes: "The kind of economic organization that provides economic freedom directly, namely competitive capitalism, also promotes political freedom because it separates economic power from political power and in this way enables the one to offset the other."[7] This citation highlights the crucial neoliberal assumption that politics and economics are separate realms. The latter constitutes a fundamentally unpolitical, private sphere that must remain sheltered from the imposition of political power. Governments ought to be limited to providing an appropriate legal and institutional framework for the fulfillment of voluntary agreements reflected in contractual arrangements.

Globalist voices present globalization as a natural economic phenomenon reflected in the liberalization and integration of global markets and the reduction of governmental interference in the economy. Privatization, free trade, and unfettered capital movements are portrayed as the best and most natural way for realizing individual liberty and material progress in the world.

Perhaps the most eloquent exposition of the neoliberal claim that globalization is about the liberalization and global integration of markets can be found in Thomas Friedman's recent bestseller, *The Lexus and the Olive Tree: Understanding Globalization.* Indeed, many commentators have emphasized that Friedman's book provides the "official narrative of globalization" in the United States today.[8] Although the award-winning *New York Times* correspondent claims that he does not want to be considered as "a salesman of globalization," he eagerly admonishes his readers to acknowledge the factuality of new global realities and "think like globalists."[9] For Friedman, this means that people ought to accept the following "truth" about globalization:

> The driving idea behind globalization is free-market capitalism—the more you let market forces rule and the more you open

> your economy to free trade and competition, the more efficient your economy will be. Globalization means the spread of free-market capitalism to virtually every country in the world. Therefore, globalization also has its own set of economic rules—rules that revolve around opening, deregulating and privatizing your economy, in order to make it more competitive and attractive to foreign investment.[10]

Asserting that, for the first time in history, "virtually every country in the world has the same basic hardware—free-market capitalism," Friedman predicts that globalization will result in the creation of a single global marketplace. He informs his readers that this feat will be achieved by means of the "Golden Straitjacket"—the "defining political–economic garment of this globalization era."[11] Stitched together by Anglo-American neoliberal politicians and business leaders, the Golden Straitjacket forces every country in the world to adopt the same economic rules:

> [M]aking the private sector the primary engine of its economic growth, maintaining a low rate of inflation and price stability, shrinking the size of its state bureaucracy, maintaining as close to a balanced budget as possible, if not a surplus, eliminating and lowering tariffs on imported goods, removing restrictions on foreign investment, getting rid of quotas and domestic monopolies, increasing exports, privatizing state-owned industries and utilities, deregulating capital markets, making its currency convertible, opening its industries, deregulating its economy to promote as much domestic competition as possible, eliminating government corruption, subsidies and kickbacks as much as possible, opening its banking and telecommunications systems to private ownership and competition and allowing its citizens to choose from an array of competing pension options and foreign-run pension and mutual funds. When you stitch all of these pieces together you have the Golden Straitjacket.[12]

Friedman concludes his pitch for the liberalization and global integration of markets by pointing out that today's global market system is the result of "large historical forces" that gave birth to a new power source in the world—the "Electronic Herd." Made up of millions of faceless stock, bond, and currency traders sitting behind computer screens all over the globe, the Electronic Herd also includes the executive officers of large TNCs who shift their production sites to the most efficient, low-cost producers. In order to succeed in the new era of globalization, countries not only have to put on the Golden Straitjacket, but they also have to please the Electronic Herd. Friedman explains:

> The Electronic Herd loves the Golden Straitjacket, because it embodies all the liberal, free-market rules the herd wants to see in a country. Those countries that put on the Golden Straitjacket are rewarded by the herd with investment capital. Those that don't want to put it on are disciplined by the herd—either by the herd avoiding or withdrawing its money from that country.[13]

A critical discourse analysis of the globalist claim that globalization is about the liberalization and global integration of markets must begin by contrasting the neoliberal rhetoric of liberty with Friedman's depiction of globalization proceeding by means of the Golden Straitjacket. . . . In selling their will as the general will, globalists disregard local ways of organizing the economy. Their project of "opening up economies" is advocated as an endeavor of universal applicability, for it supposedly reflects the dictates of human freedom in general. Thus it must be applied to all countries, regardless of the political and cultural preferences expressed by local citizens. As former U.S. Undersecretary Stuart Eizenstat put it: "All nations—developed or developing—must maintain a solidly pro-growth, open-market orientation which supports trade liberalization."[14] However, such efforts to stitch together a neoliberal economic straitjacket—one size fits all countries—are hardly compatible with a process of globalization that is alleged to contribute to the spread of freedom, choice, and openness in the world.

Secondly, as Friedman concedes, the globalist message of liberalizing and integrating markets is only realizable through the *political* project of engineering free markets. In order to advance their enterprise, globalists must be prepared to utilize the powers of government to weaken and eliminate those social policies and institutions that curtail the market. Since only strong governments are up to this ambitious task of transforming existing social arrangements, the successful liberalization of markets depends upon the *intervention* and *interference* by centralized state power.

Globalists expect governments to play an extremely active role in implementing their political agenda. The activist characters of neoliberal administrations in the United States, the United Kingdom, Australia, and New Zealand during the 1980s and 1990s attests to the importance of strong governmental action in engineering free markets.[15] Indeed, promarket governments serve as indispensable catalysts of what Richard Falk calls "globalization from above." In their pursuit of market liberalization and integration, neoliberal political and economic elites violate their own principles of decentralization, limited government, and negative liberty.

Finally, the neoliberal claim that globalization is about the liberalization and global integration of markets serves to solidify as "fact" what is actually a contingent political initiative. Globalists have been successful because they have persuaded the public that their neoliberal account of globalization represents an objective or at least neutral diagnosis rather than a contributor to the emergence of the very conditions it purports to analyze. To be sure, neoliberals may indeed be able to offer some "empirical evidence" for the "liberalization" of markets. But does the spread of market principles really happen because there exists an intrinsic, metaphysical connection between globalization and the expansion of markets? Or does it occur because globalists have the political and discursive power to shape the world largely according to their ideological formula:

LIBERALIZATION + INTEGRATION OF MARKETS = GLOBALIZATION?

Moreover, this economistic-objectivist representation of globalization detracts from the multidimensional character of the phenomenon. Ecological, cultural, and political dimensions of globalization are discussed only as subordinate processes dependent on the movements of global markets. Even if one were to accept the central role of the economic dimension of globalization, there is no reason to believe that these processes must necessarily be connected to the deregulation of markets. An alternative view might instead suggest linking globalization to the creation of a global regulatory framework that would make markets accountable to international political institutions.

In either case, the setting of a successful political agenda always occurs simultaneously with concerted efforts to sell to the public the general desirability of a particular system of ideas. Globalism is no exception. Like all ideologies, its values and beliefs are conveyed through a number of justificatory claims, usually starting with one that establishes what the phenomenon is all about. As international-relations expert Edward Luttwak points out, there is a good reason why the spectacular advance of "turbo-capitalism" in the world is accompanied by so much talk about globalization in the public arena. For business interests, the presentation of globalization as an enterprise that liberates and integrates global markets as well as emancipates individuals from governmental control is the best way of enlisting the public in their struggle against those laws and institutions they find most restrictive.[16] As long as globalists succeed in selling their neoliberal understanding of globalization to large segments of the population, they will be able to maintain a social order favorable to their own interests. By engineering popular consent, globalists are only rarely forced to resort to open forms of coercion. The Golden Straitjacket will do splendidly to keep the global South in line. For those who remain skeptical, globalists have another claim up their sleeves: Why doubt a process that proceeds with historical inevitability?

Claim No. 2: Globalization Is Inevitable and Irreversible

According to the globalist perspective, globalization reflects the spread of irreversible market forces driven by technological innovations that make the global integration of national economies inevitable. In fact, globalism is almost always intertwined with the deep belief in the ability of markets to use new technologies to solve social problems far better than any alternative course.[17] When, years ago, British Prime Minister Margaret Thatcher famously pronounced that "there is no alternative," she meant that there existed no longer a theoretical and practical alternative to the expansionist logic of the market. In fact, she accused those nonconformists who still dared to pose alternatives as foolishly relying on anachronistic, socialist fantasies that betrayed their inability to cope with empirical reality. Governments, political parties, and social movements had no choice but to "adjust" to the inevitability of globalization. Their sole remaining task was to facilitate the integration of national economies in the new global market. States and interstate systems should, therefore, serve to ensure the smooth working of market logic.[18]

Journalist Friedman comes to a similar conclusion: "Globalization is very difficult to reverse because it is driven both by powerful human aspiration for higher standards of living and by enormously powerful technologies which are integrating us more and more every day, whether we like it or not."[19] But Friedman simply argues by asserting that there is something inherent in technology that requires a neoliberal system. He never considers that, for example, new digital-communication technologies could just as easily be used to enhance public-service media as it can be utilized in commercial, profit-making enterprises. The choice depends on the nature of the political will exerted in a particular social order.

■ ■ ■ ■

The neoliberal portrayal of globalization as some sort of natural force, like the weather or gravity, makes it easier for globalists to convince people that they must adapt to the discipline of the market if they are to survive and prosper. Hence, the globalist claim of inevitability serves a number of important political functions. For one, it neutralizes the challenges of antiglobalist opponents by depoliticizing the public discourse about globalization: Neoliberal policies are above politics, because they simply carry out what is ordained by nature. This view implies that, instead of acting according to a set of choices, people merely fulfill world-market laws that demand the elimination of government controls. There is nothing that can be done about the natural movement of economic and technological forces; political groups ought to acquiesce and make the best of an unalterable situation. Since the emergence of a world based on the primacy of market values reflects the dictates of history, resistance would be unnatural, irrational, and dangerous.

The narrative of inevitability also helps globalists to justify the creation and execution of governmental austerity measures. Following Paul Ricoeur's understanding of ideology functioning as legitimation, this globalist claim legitimizes public-policy choices directed at the dismantling of the welfare state and the deregulation of the economy. It allows globalists to portray these measures as a rational response to objective historical pressures rather than the self-interested agenda of particular political interests. The idea of inevitability also supports the excuse often utilized by neoliberal politicians: "It is the market that made us cut social programs." As German President Roman Herzog put it in a nationally televised appeal, the "irresistable pressure of global forces" demands that "everyone will have to make sacrifices."[20] To be sure, President Herzog never spelled out what kinds of sacrifices will await large shareholders and corporate executives. In fact, historical evidence suggests that it is much more likely that sacrifices will have to be borne disproportionately by those workers and employees who lose their jobs or social benefits as a result of neoliberal trade policies or profit-maximizing practices of "corporate downsizing."

By turning the market into a natural force, globalists suggest that human beings are at the mercy of external imperatives they cannot control. . . . The strategy seems to be working. Even prolabor voices such as David Smith, AFL-CIO Director of Public Policy, have accepted the globalist claims of inevitability and irreversibility: "Globalization is a fact. . . . We're not going to turn these tides back. We shouldn't want to turn these tides back; even if we wanted to, we couldn't."[21]

■ ■ ■ ■

. . . Conversely, market infidels and agnostics . . . argue that the market is neither an ahistorical nor an asocial manifestation of blind natural forces working behind people's backs. Markets are the creation of human interactions; they do not dictate policy. Global economic integration is not a natural process. Rather, it is driven by decisions of governments that have removed barriers to cross-border movements of capital and goods. People who are organized in powerful social groups facilitate the process of neoliberal globalization. They demand—in the name of "The Market"—the implementation of economic policies favorable to their interests.

Finally, the claim that globalization is inevitable and irresistable is inscribed within a larger evolutionary discourse that assigns a privileged position to those nations that are in the forefront of "liberating" markets from political control.

Francis Fukuyama represents an extreme perspective on this issue. He insists that globalization is really a euphemism that stands for the irreversible Americanization of the world: "I think it has to be Americanization because, in some respects, America is the most advanced capitalist society in the world today, and so its institutions represent the logical development of market forces. Therefore, if market forces are what drives globalization, it is inevitable that Americanization will accompany globalization."[22] Thomas Friedman, too, ends his book on globalization with a celebration of America's unique role in a globalizing world.

> And that's why America, at its best, is not just a country. It's a spiritual value and role model. . . . And that's why I believe so strongly that for globalization to be sustainable America must be at its best—today, tomorrow, all the time. It not only can be, it must be, a beacon for the whole world.[23]

These statements reveal the existence of a strong link between the globalist claim of inevitability and the American pursuit of global cultural hegemony. As John Gray observes, neoliberal forces have successfully "appropriated America's self-image as the model for a universal civilization in the service of a global free market."[24] History looks kindly upon the "shining city on the hill," because it has been listening to the voice of the market. As a reward, objective market forces have chosen the United States to point all other nations in the right direction. In what appears to be the globalist version of the old American theme of manifest destiny, U.S. political and business leaders proclaim to the rest of the world: Adopt our neoliberal policies and you, too, can become "America."

By activating what Paul Ricoeur calls the ideological function of integration, globalists favor the creation of an American-style market identity that is designed to eclipse most other components of personal, group, or class identity. As Steven Kline points out, global marketing efforts particularly attempt to provide young people with the identity of the consuming global teenager. Coca-Cola, Levi-Strauss, McDonald's, and Disney "have become the source of endless campaigns to enfranchise youth in the globalizing democracy of the market."[25] Why should mere consumers be interested in strengthening civic ties and work for global justice if such endeavors aren't profitable? Why show moral restraint and solidarity if "we," the consumers, are incessantly told that we can have it all? As Benjamin Barber emphasizes, by broadly endorsing happiness that comes with shopping and consuming, this market identity takes on distinct cultural features, because "America" and "American culture" are best-selling commodities in the global marketplace. American films, American television, American software, American music, American fast-food chains, American cars and motorcycles, American apparel, and American sports—to name but a few of those cultural commodities—are pervading the world to such an extent that even ordinary Indonesians have become convinced that they also can become "cool" by drinking Coke instead of tea. In Budapest, people are breathlessly watching *The Cosby Show* on reruns, and the Russian version of *Wheel of Fortune* offers lucky winners Sony VCRs into which they can load their pirated versions of wildly popular American films.[26]

And so it appears that globalist forces have been resurrecting the nineteenth-century paradigm of Anglo-American vanguardism propagated by Herbert Spencer and William Graham

Sumner. The main ingredients of classical market liberalism are all present in globalism. We find inexorable laws of nature favoring Western civilization, the self-regulating economic model of perfect competition, the virtues of free enterprise, the vices of state interference, the principle of *laissez-faire*, and the irreversible, evolutionary process leading up to the survival of the fittest. Indeed, globalism merely provides new verbiage for these old liberal themes. . . . [G]lobalists look forward to the final realization of their free-market utopia. They are confident that history will end on a positive note—in spite of some undeniable risks and conflicts inherent in the process of globalization.

Claim No. 3: Nobody Is in Charge of Globalization

Globalism's deterministic language offers another rhetorical advantage. If the natural laws of "The Market" have indeed preordained a neoliberal course of history, then globalization does not reflect the arbitrary agenda of a particular social class or group. In other words, globalists merely carry out the unalterable imperatives of a transcendental force much larger than narrow partisan interests. People are not in charge of globalization; markets and technology are. Certain human actions might accelerate or retard globalization, but in the last instance . . . the invisible hand of the market will always assert its superior wisdom.

In the early part of *The Lexus and the Olive Tree*, Thomas Friedman imagines himself engaged in a spirited debate with the prime minister of Malaysia, who had accused Western powers of manipulating markets and currencies during the 1997–1998 Asian crisis in order to destroy the vibrant economies of their overseas competitors. Friedman tells his readers how he would respond to Prime Minister Mahatir Mohamad's charge:

> Ah, excuse me, Mahatir, but what planet are you living on? You talk about participating in globalization as if it were a choice you had. Globalization isn't a choice. It's a reality. . . . And the most basic truth about globalization is this: *No one is in charge*. . . . We all want to believe that someone is in charge and responsible. But the global marketplace today is an Electronic Herd of often anonymous stock, bond and currency traders and multinational investors, connected by screens and networks.[27]

Of course, Friedman is right in a formal sense. There is no conscious conspiracy orchestrated by a single evil force to disempower Asian nations. But does this mean that nobody is in charge of globalization? Is it really true that the liberalization and integration of global markets proceeds outside the realm of human choice? Does globalization, therefore, absolve businesses and corporations from social responsibility? A critical discourse analysis of Friedman's statement reveals how he utilizes a realist narrative to sell to his audience a neoliberal version of globalization. He implies that anyone who thinks that globalization involves human choice is either hopelessly naïve or outright dangerous. Such persons might as well apply for permanent residency on Prime Minister Mohamad's alien planet.

For Friedman, the real player in the global marketplace is the Electronic Herd. But he never offers his readers a clear picture of the Herd's identity. Throughout his book, he portrays the Herd as a faceless crowd of individual profit-maximizers whose human identity remains hidden behind dim computer screens. Apparently, these traders and investors are solely interested in moneymaking; they don't seem to be part of any politically or culturally identifiable group. Although they wield tremendous power, they are not in charge of globalization. Ah, excuse me, Tom, but where is the "realism" in your description?

Social thinkers Michael Hardt and Antonio Negri remind their readers that it is important to be aware of the two extreme conceptions of global authority that reside on the opposite ends of the ideological spectrum. One is the globalist notion that nobody is in charge, because globalization somehow rises up spontaneously out of the natural workings of the hidden hand of the world market. The other is the antiglobalist idea that a single evil power dictates to the world its design of globalization according to a conscious and all-seeing conspiratorial plan. Both conceptions are distortions.[28]

Still, even some neoliberal commentators concede that the globalist initiative to integrate and deregulate markets around the world is sustained by asymmetrical power relations. Backed by powerful states in the North, international institutions such as the WTO, the IMF, and the World Bank enjoy the privileged position of making and enforcing the rules of the global economy. In return for supplying much-needed loans to developing countries, the IMF and the World Bank demand from their creditors the implementation of neoliberal policies that further the material interests of the First World. Unleashed on developing countries in the 1990s, these policies are often referred to as [the] "Washington Consensus." It consists of a ten-point program that was originally devised and codified by John Williamson, formerly an IMF adviser in the 1970s. The program was mostly directed at countries with large remaining foreign debts from the 1970s and 1980s. Its purpose was to reform the internal economic mechanisms of debtor countries in the developing world so that they would be in a better position to repay the debts they had incurred. In practice, the terms of the program spelled out a new form of colonialism. The ten areas of the Washington Consensus, as defined by Williamson, required Third World governments to enforce the following reforms:

1. A guarantee of fiscal discipline, and a curb to budget deficits.
2. A reduction of public expenditure, particularly in the military and public administration.
3. Tax reform, aiming at the creation of a system with a broad base and with effective enforcement.
4. Financial liberalization, with interest rates determined by the market.
5. Competitive exchange rates, to assist export-led growth.
6. Trade liberalization, coupled with the abolition of import licensing and a reduction of tariffs.
7. Promotion of foreign direct investment.
8. Privatization of state enterprises, leading to efficient management and improved performance.
9. Deregulation of the economy.
10. Protection of property rights.[29]

To call this program [the] "Washington Consensus" is no coincidence. The United States is by far the most dominant economic power in the world, and the largest transnational corporations are based in the United States. Both the substance and direction of economic globalization are, indeed, to a significant degree shaped by American foreign and domestic policy.

Substantiation of this claim comes from no less an observer than Thomas Friedman, who, in later passages of his book, surprisingly contradicts his previous account of a leaderless, anonymous Electronic Herd. Speaking in glowing terms about the global leadership of the United States, he suddenly acknowledges the existence of a captain at the helm of the global ship:

> The Golden Straitjacket was made in America and Great Britain. The Electronic Herd is led by American Wall Street Bulls. The most powerful agent pressuring other countries to open their markets for free trade and free investments is Uncle Sam, and America's global armed forces keep these markets and sea lanes open for this era of globalization, just as the British navy did for the era of globalization in the nineteenth century.[30]

Toward the end of his book, the *New York Times* journalist becomes even more explicit:

> Indeed, McDonald's cannot flourish without McDonnell Douglas, the designer of the U.S. Air Force F-15. And the hidden fist that keeps the world safe for Silicon Valley's technologies to flourish is called the U.S. Army, Air Force, Navy, and Marine Corps. And these fighting forces and institutions are paid for by American taxpayer dollars.[31]

In other words, global neoliberalism does not rely blindly on a hidden hand of the self-regulating market. When the chips are down, globalism seems to prefer the not-so-hidden fist of U.S. militarism.

The claim of a leaderless globalization process does not reflect social reality. Rather, the idea that nobody is in charge serves the neoliberal political agenda of defending and expanding American global hegemony. Like the globalist rhetoric of historical inevitability, the portrayal of globalization as a leaderless process seeks to both depoliticize the public debate on the subject and demobilize antiglobalist movements. The deterministic language of a technological progress driven by uncontrollable market laws turns political issues into scientific problems of administration. Once large segments of the population have accepted the globalist image of a self-directed juggernaut that simply runs its course, it becomes extremely difficult for antiglobalists to challenge what Antonio Gramsci calls the "power of the hegemonic bloc." As ordinary people cease to believe in the possibility of choosing alternative social arrangements, globalism gains strength in its ability to construct passive consumer identities. This tendency is further enhanced by globalist assurances that globalization will bring prosperity to all parts of the world.

Claim No. 4: Globalization Benefits Everyone

This claim lies at the very core of globalism because it provides an affirmative answer to the crucial normative question of whether globalization represents a "good" or a "bad" phenomenon. Globalists frequently connect their arguments in favor of the integration of global markets to the alleged benefits resulting from the liberalization and expansion of world trade. At the 1996 G7 Summit in Lyon, France, the heads of state and government of the seven major industrialized democracies issued a joint communiqué that contains the following passage:

> Economic growth and progress in today's interdependent world is bound up with the process of globalization. Globalization provides great opportunities for the future, not only for our countries, but for all others too. Its many positive aspects include an unprecedented expansion of investment and trade; the opening up to international trade of the world's most populous regions and opportunities for more developing countries to improve their standards of living; the increasingly rapid dissemination of information, technological innovation, and the proliferation of skilled jobs. These characteristics of globalization have led to a considerable expansion of wealth and prosperity in the world. Hence we are convinced that the process of globalization is a source of hope for the future.[32]

The public discourse on globalization reverberates with such generalizations. Here are some examples. Former U.S. Secretary of the Treasury Robert Rubin asserts that free trade and open markets provide "the best prospect for creating jobs, spurring economic growth, and raising living standards in the United States and around the world."[33] Alan Greenspan, chairman of the U.S. Federal Reserve Board, insists that "there can be little doubt that the extraordinary changes in global finance on balance have been beneficial in facilitating significant improvements in economic structures and living standards throughout the world."[34]

[A]ntiglobalist forces have offered solid evidence that income disparities between nations are actually widening at a quicker pace than ever before in recent history. . . .

There are many indications that the global hunt for profits actually makes it more difficult for poor people to enjoy the benefits of technology and scientific innovations. Consider the following story. A group of scientists in the United States recently warned the public that economic globalization may now be the greatest threat to preventing the spread of parasitic diseases in sub-Saharan Africa. They pointed out that U.S.-based pharmaceutical companies are stopping production of many antiparasitic drugs because developing countries cannot afford to buy them. For example, the U.S. manufacturer for a drug to treat bilharzia, a parasitic disease that causes severe liver damage, has stopped production because of declining profits—even though the disease is thought to affect over 200 million people worldwide. Another drug used to combat damage caused by liver flukes has not been produced since 1979, because the "customer base" in the Third World does not wield enough "buying power."[35]

While globalists typically acknowledge the existence of unequal global-distribution patterns, they nonetheless insist that the market itself will eventually correct these "irregularities." As John Meehan, chairman of the U.S. Public Securities Association, puts it, while such "episodic dislocations" are "necessary" in the short run, they will eventually give way to "quantum leaps in productivity."[36]

■■■■

In fact, globalists such as Thomas Friedman even pretend to know beyond the shadow of a doubt that the poor in developing countries are itching to assume the identity of Western consumers: "[L]et me share a little secret I've learned from talking to all these folks [in the Third World]: With all due respect to revolutionary theorists, the 'wretched of the earth' want to go to Disney World—not the barricades. They want the Magic Kingdom, not *Les Misérables*."[37]

In short, globalists do their best to convince their audiences that the liberalization of trade and the integration of global markets serve the interests of everyone. . . .

■■■■

Claim No. 5: Globalization Furthers the Spread of Democracy in the World

This globalist claim is anchored in the neoliberal assertion that *free markets* and *democracy* are synonymous terms. Persistently affirmed as common sense, the compatibility of these concepts often goes unchallenged in the public discourse. The most obvious strategy by which neoliberals generate popular support for the equation of democracy and the market is through a discreditation of traditionalism and socialism. The contest with both precapitalist and anticapitalist forms of traditionalism such as feudalism has been won rather easily because the political principles of popular sovereignty and individual rights have been enshrined as the crucial catalyst for the technological and scientific achievements of modern market economies. The battle with socialism turned out to be a much tougher case. As late as the 1970s, socialist thinkers provided a powerful critique of the elitist, class-based character of liberal democracy, which, in their view, revealed that a substantive form of democracy had not been achieved in capitalist societies. Since the collapse of communism in Eastern Europe, however, the ideological edge has shifted decisively to the defenders of a neoliberal perspective who emphasize the relationship between economic liberalization and the emergence of democratic political regimes.

Francis Fukuyama, for example, asserts that there exists a clear correlation between a country's level of economic development and successful democracy. While globalization and capital development do not automatically produce democracies, "the level of economic development resulting from globalization is conducive to the creation of complex civil societies with a powerful middle class. It is this class and societal structure that facilitates democracy."[38] Praising the economic transitions towards capitalism in Eastern Europe, U.S. Senator Hillary Rodham Clinton told her Polish audience that the emergence of new businesses and shopping centers in former communist countries should be seen as the "backbone of democracy." Clinton insisted that

> choosing the path of democracy, free markets, and freedom required great vision, courage, and moral leadership. Ten years ago it was not the obvious choice, nor was it easy. But today in so many of your countries, there is no question that the path of free markets and democracy is the right choice.[39]

Fukuyama and Clinton agree that the globalization process strengthens the existing affinity between democracy and the free market. Their argument hinges on a limited definition of democracy that emphasizes formal procedures such as voting at the expense of the direct participation of broad majorities in political and economic decision-making. This "thin" definition of democracy is part of what William I. Robinson has identified as the Anglo-American neoliberal project of "promoting polyarchy" in the developing world. For Robinson, the concept of polyarchy differs from the concept of "popular democracy" in that the latter posits democracy as both a process and a means to an end—a tool for devolving political and economic power from the hands of elite minorities to the masses. Polyarchy, on the other hand, represents an elitist and regimented model of "low intensity" or "formal" market democracy. Polyarchies not only limit democratic participation to voting in elections, but also require that those elected be insulated from popular pressures, so that they may "effectively govern."[40]

This focus on the act of voting—in which equality prevails only in the formal sense—helps to obscure the conditions of inequality reflected in existing asymmetrical power relations in society. Formal elections provide the important function of legitimating the rule of dominant elites, thus making it more difficult for popular movements to challenge the rule of elites. The claim that globalization furthers the spread of democracy in the world is largely based on a narrow, formal-procedural understanding of "democracy." Neoliberal economic globalization and the strategic promotion of polyarchic regimes in the Third World are, therefore, two sides of the same ideological coin. They represent the systemic prerequisites for the legitimation of a full-blown world market. The promotion of polyarchy provides globalists with the ideological opportunity to advance their neoliberal projects of economic restructuring in a language that ostensibly supports the "democratization" of the world.

Friedman's discussion of the democratic potential of globalization represents another clear example of such ideological maneuvers. Assuring his readers that globalization tends to impose democratic standards (like voting) on undemocratic countries, he argues that the integration of countries such as Indonesia and China into the global capitalist system has shown that the global market forces upon authoritarian regimes the rules-based business practices and legal standards they cannot generate internally. Friedman coins the term "globalution" to refer to today's "revolutionary process" by which the powerful Electronic Herd contributes to building the "foundation stones of democracy":

> The Electronic Herd will intensify pressures for democratization generally, for three very critical reasons—flexibility, legitimacy, and sustainability. Here's how: The faster and bigger the herd gets, the more greased and open the global economy becomes, the more flexibility you need to get the most out of the herd and protect yourself from it. While one can always find exceptions, I still believe that as a general rule the more democratic, accountable, and open your governance, the less likely it is that your financial system will be exposed to surprises.[41]

It is not difficult to notice the instrumentalist tone of Friedman's argument. Devoid of any moral and civic substance, democracy represents for Friedman merely the best shell for the imperatives of the market. His use of the term "accountability" hardly resonates with the democratic idea of civic participation. Rather, he equates accountability with the creation of social and economic structures conducive to the business interests of the Electronic Herd. Moreover, he uses "flexibility" as a code word for deregulatory measures and privatization efforts that benefit capitalist elites but threaten the economic security of ordinary citizens. Granted, the "flexibility" of labor markets may well be an important factor in attracting foreign investment, but it is hardly synonymous with the successful creation of popular-democratic institutions in developing nations.

Friedman's claim that globalization furthers the spread of democracy in the world stands in stark contrast to the results of empirical research, most of which point in a rather different direction. Even media outlets that faithfully spread the gospel of globalism occasionally concede that large TNCs often prefer to invest in developing countries that are not considered "free" according to generally accepted political rights and civil liberties standards. For example, the *Chicago Tribune* recently cited a report released by the New Economic Information Service that suggests that democratic countries are losing out in the race for American export markets and American foreign investments. In 1989, democratic countries accounted for more than half of all U.S. imports from the Third World. Ten years later, with more democracies to choose from, democratic countries supplied barely one-third of U.S. imports from the Third

World: "And the trend is growing. As more of the world's countries adopt democracy, more American businesses appear to prefer dictatorships." These findings raise the important question of whether foreign purchasing and investment decisions by U.S. corporations are actually undermining the chances for the survival of fragile democracies. Why are powerful investors in the rich Northern countries making these business decisions? For one, wages tend to be lower in authoritarian regimes than in democracies, giving businesses in dictatorships a monetary advantage in selling exports abroad. In addition, lower wages, bans on labor unions, and relaxed environmental laws give authoritarian regimes an edge in attracting foreign investment.[42]

Toward the end of his chapter on democratization, Friedman seems to be less clear on the role of globalization in creating open societies. While he still emphasizes that the Electronic Herd and the influential financial "Supermarkets" in New York, London, and Frankfurt will be important contributors to democratization, he also concedes that they might also create the opposite effect. As he puts it, "they will contribute to a widespread feeling, particularly within democracies, that even if people have a democracy at home they have lost control over their lives, because even their elected representatives have to bow now to unelected market dictators." In fact, Friedman even acknowledges that "the biggest challenge for political theory in this globalization era is how to give citizens a sense that they can exercise their will, not only over their own governments but over at least some of the global forces shaping their lives." Regrettably, however, the *New York Times* journalist shies away from suggesting a solution to this problem. Instead, he ends his discussion of the postulated link between democracy and globalization with another troubling question: "How do we deal with a world where the Electronic Herd gets to vote in all kinds of countries every day, but those countries don't get to vote on the herd's behavior in such a direct and immediate manner?"[43]

This question raises the important issues of what kind of democratic governing mechanisms can be attached to economic globalization. Globalists have consistently suggested that globalization can be harnessed to democratic processes by utilizing existing global and regional institutions such as the World Trade Organization (WTO). In their view, globalization promotes democratic forms of international cooperation while at the same time combating virulent forms of ethnonationalism. For example, Mike Moore, Director-General of the WTO, emphasizes that his organization is a "member-driven organization" that encourages the representatives of all member states to express their opinions freely on all matters of international trade. According to Moore, the WTO can be characterized by "democratic transparency," because its decision-making process is based on the "consensus principle." In other words, consensus is "at the heart of the WTO" because it represents a "fundamental democratic guarantee."[44]

However, Moore's representation of the "consensus principle" leaves out important information. Consensus, in the WTO, is typically managed by a handful of powerful nations led by the United States, Japan, the European Union, and Canada. Decisions are arrived at informally via oligarchical caucuses convoked by the big trading powers in the organization's corridors and in "green-room" negotiations during the WTO ministerial meetings. The formal plenary sessions, which in representative democracies are the central arena for decision-making, are reserved for prescripted speeches. Consensus usually functions as a cloak to render nontransparent a process where smaller, weaker countries are pressured to conform to decisions made in advance by powerful countries.

During the raucous 1999 WTO meeting in Seattle, the vast majority of the developing countries were shut out of the negotiation process. They were not even informed which meetings were held or what the topics for discussion were. Confronted with assurances that a "consensus" was being worked on, many delegates from the Third World reacted with open defiance. For example, the African ministers issued a strong statement that there was "no transparency" in the meetings, and African countries had been systematically excluded from the process: "Under the present circumstances, we will not be able to join the consensus required to meet the objectives of this Ministerial Conference." Similar statements were issued by the Caribbean

Community ministers and by some Latin American countries.[45]

Given the WTO's continued efforts to expand the neoliberal economic order, the prospect for genuine international cooperation on the basis of democratic principles appears to be slim. It seems that the inequalities resulting from the rapid globalization of markets can only be tackled by a commensurable globalization of political and civic institutions that are committed to "thick" participatory forms of democracy.

Conclusion

. . . [G]lobalism is sufficiently comprehensive and systematic to count as a new ideology. As capitalism has been restructuring itself in the last decade, it has largely drawn on the central ideas of nineteenth-century free-market philosophers. It is the ability of globalists to connect these old arguments to the twenty-first-century framework of globality that bestows new currency upon their antiquated vision. Thus it appears that the Anglo-American framers of globalism have grasped the political advantage of utilizing the concept of "globalization" as a vehicle for the solidification and further expansion of their market paradigm. Presented to the public as a leaderless, inevitable juggernaut that will ultimately produce benefits for everyone, globalism has emerged as the dominant ideological vision of our time. It provides much of the conceptual and cultural glue that sustains the social and political power of neoliberal elites throughout the world. Its well-publicized promises of material well-being and social mobility often sustain consensual arrangements of rule, thus providing the foundation of what Antonio Gramsci has called "hegemony."

However, to argue that globalism has become a hegemonic discourse does not mean that it enjoys undisputed ideological dominance. There exists a multiplicity of stories about globalization that aim to provide authoritative accounts of what the phenomenon is all about. Globalism's claims are increasingly contested by nationalist-protectionist forces of the political Right and egalitarian-communitarian cohorts of the political Left. . . .

Notes

1. Judith Butler, "Gender as Performance," in *A Critical Sense: Interviews with Intellectuals*, ed. Peter Osborne (London: Routledge, 1996), 112.
2. Michel Foucault, *The Archeology of Knowledge* (New York: Pantheon, 1972), 59–68.
3. Andrew Chadwick, "Studying Political Ideas: A Public Political Discourse Approach," *Political Studies* 48 (2000):290–292.
4. Friedrich Hayek, *Law, Legislation, and Liberty*, 3 vols. (London: Routledge & Kegan Paul, 1979), 1:55.
5. Isaiah Berlin, "Two Concepts of Liberty," in *Four Essays on Liberty* (London: Oxford University Press, 1969), 121–22.
6. For an apt summary of the market principles of economic liberalism, see Timothy J. Gaffaney, "Citizens of the Market: The Un-Political Theory of the New Right," *Polity* 32(*2*) (winter 1999):181–84.
7. Milton Friedman, *Capitalism and Freedom* (Chicago: University of Chicago Press, 1962), 9.
8. See, for example, William Bole, "Tales of Globalization," *America* 181, no. 18 (December 4, 1999):14–16.
9. Thomas Friedman, *The Lexus and the Olive Tree: Understanding Globalization*, New York) Farrar, Straus and Giroux, 200), xii, 23–24.
10. Ibid., 9.
11. Ibid., 104, 152.
12. Ibid., 105.
13. Ibid., 109–10.
14. Stuart Eizenstat, "The U.S. Perspective on Globalization," April 1999 <http://www.odc.org/com mentary/vpapr.html>.
15. For a detailed discussion of these neoliberal policy initiatives, see John Micklethwait and Adrian Woolridge, *A Future Perfect: The Challenge and Hidden Promise of Globalization* (New York: Crown Publishers, 2000), 22–54.
16. Edward Luttwak, *Turbo-Capitalism: Winners and Losers in the Global Economy* (New York: HarperCollins 1999), 152.
17. See Robert W. McChesney, "Global Media, Neoliberalism, and Imperialism," *Monthly Review* (March 2001) <http://www.monthlyreview.org/301rwm.html>.
18. For a critical assessment of Thatcher's experiment, see John Gray, *False Dawn: The Delusions of Global Capitalism*, Capitalism (New York: New Press, 1998), 24–34.
19. Friedman, *The Lexus and the Olive Tree*, 407.
20. Roman Herzog cited in Hans-Peter Martin and Harold Schumann, *The Global Trap: Globalization and the Assault on Democracy and Prosperity* (London: Zed Books, 1997), 6.
21. David Smith, "Putting a Human Face on the Global Economy: Seeking Common Ground on Trade," 1999 DLC Annual Conference, Washington, DC, October 14, 1999 <http://www.dlcppi.org/speeches/99conference/99conf_panel1.html>.
22. "Economic Globalization and Culture: A Discussion with Dr. Francis Fukuyama" <http://www.ml.com/woml/forum/global2.html>.

23. Friedman, *The Lexus and the Olive Tree*, 474–75. See also Friedman's remark on page 294: "Today, for better or worse, globalization is a means for spreading the fantasy of America around the world. . . . Globalization is Americanization."
24. Gray, *False Dawn*, 131.
25. Steven Kline, "The Play of the Market: On the Internationalization of Children's Culture," *Theory, Culture and Society* 12 (1995):110.
26. Benjamin R. Barber, *Jihad vs. McWorld* (New York: Ballantine Books, 1996), 119–151.
27. Friedman, *The Lexus and the Olive Tree*, 112–13.
28. Michael Hardt and Antonio Negri, *Empire* (Cambridge, MA: Harvard University Press, 2000), 3.
29. Cited in Richard Gott, *In the Shadow of the Liberator: Hugo Chávez and the Transformation of Venezuela* (London: Verso, 2000), 52–53.
30. Friedman, *The Lexus and the Olive Tree*, 381.
31. Ibid., 464.
32. Economic Communiqué, Lyon G7 Summit, June 28, 1996 <http://library.utoronto.ca/www/g7/96ecopre.html>.
33. Robert Rubin, "Reform of the International Financial Architecture," *Vital Speeches* 65, no. 15 (1999): 455.
34. Alan Greenspan, "The Globalization of Finance," October 14, 1997 <http://cato.org/pubs/journal/cj17n3-1.html>.
35. "Tropical Disease Drugs Withdrawn," *BBC News*, October 31, 2000.
36. John J. Meehan, Chairman of the Public Securities Association, "Globalization and Technology at Work in the Bond Markets," speech given in Phoenix, March 1, 1997 <http://www.bondmarkets.com/news/Meehanspeechfinal.shtml>.
37. Friedman, *The Lexus and the Olive Tree*, 364.
38. "Economic Globalization and Culture: A Discussion with Dr. Francis Fukuyama" <http://www.ml.com/woml/forum/global2.html>.
39. Hillary Rodham Clinton, "Growth of Democracy in Eastern Europe," Warsaw, October 5, 1999 <http:/www.whitehouse.gov/WH/EOP/First Lady/html/generalspeeches/1999/19991005.html>.
40. William I. Robinson, *Promoting Polyarchy: Globalization, U.S. Intervention, and Hegemony* (Cambridge: Cambridge University Press, 1996).
41. Friedman, *The Lexus and the Olive Tree*, 187.
42. R. C. Longworth, "Democracies Are Paying the Price," *Chicago Tribune*, November 19, 1999.
43. Friedman, *The Lexus and the Olive Tree*, 191–92.
44. Mike Moore, "Address to the Development Committee of the European Parliament," February 21, 2000 <http://www.wto.org/wto/speeches/mm25.html>.
45. Martin Khor, "Seattle Debacle: Revolt of the Developing Nations," in Danaher and Burbach, *Globalize This!*, 50–51.

ETHNIC NATIONALISM AS IT REALLY EXISTS

BOGDAN DENITCH

Those of us who are by origin from the general area of the Balkans (that is, Balkanites) are often irritated when the historical divides between Europe and Byzantium or between Catholicism and Islam are invoked by "Western" commentators to explain the crimes, furies, and carnage released by ethnic nationalism in Bosnia or the atrocities committed during the conflict in Croatia. That is an easy and irresponsible way to blame the victims of the scandalous role that the European Community and the United States have played in the death of Yugoslavia and the murder of Bosnia. Some of us even consider ourselves to be more Western, in terms of political and cultural values, than these commentators. And we believe ourselves to be more Western in that specific sense than, let us say, the National Fronters in England, Basque ETAers, IRA and Protestant extremist killers in Ulster, and neo-Nazis and racists in the United States, not to mention various chauvinist, quasi-fascist nationalist parties, movements, and grouplets in Western Europe and the United States. It all depends on what one considers to be the genuine values of Western political culture in this day and age. The West, indeed, has an ambiguous history and tradition in this respect.

Ethnic Chauvinism: Not an East European Product

One could easily argue that racism and ethnic chauvinism have historical roots in the Western tradition. That rootage is one of the major reasons (reflexive anti-Communism being the other) there was so much understanding and tolerance for the vicious chauvinism of the anti-Communist, right-wing exiles and for the nationalist, post-Communist regimes that arose in the ruins of former Yugoslavia and the former Soviet Union.

"Scientific" (or better, "scientistic") racism and ethnic chauvinism are genuine Western European products and a part of the major current of the development of social and political ideas. Racial or ethnic theories of nationalism are relatively recent. . . . *Nationalism,* as distinct from patriotism, has its roots in the nineteenth century and did not really become a major force until the end of that century. One can argue that its course of development parallels and interacts with that of the mass socialist movement.

Nationalism, as Benedict Anderson argues, posits the centrality of *imagined communities,*[1] or rather, as he cogently put it, "imagined political community—and imagined as both inherently limited and sovereign."[2] His point, which is similar to the one made by Ernest Gellner and others, stresses that the national community in question is subjectively imagined in ways that have little to do with objective history or real attributes. Such an imagined community, again following Anderson, is *limited* because outside that community lie other nations; it is *sovereign* because it strives for the freedom of the nation to be realized in a sovereign state. But this makes nationalism a modern category, no older than the notion of the sovereignty of a people as distinct from the legitimacy of hereditary dynastic rule. After all, dynastic rule was more often than not nonnational, as was the feudal system itself. Nationalism, when ethnically defined, ascribes boundaries that designate who is and who is not a member of the *political* nation, the political community to which sovereignty belongs. Once it does so it *may* also define broader or narrower rights for those who are not members of that national community but who reside within the borders of the national state belonging to the political nation. Such rights for resident foreigners have a long and varied history, but one thing is clear: they cannot be equal with those of the citizens who are members of the political nation.

Racism and ethnic chauvinism in the history of political thought in the United States and Western Europe are well documented (books on

American racism have been a minor industry for decades). It takes little effort to dig up endless quotations, laws, and works that reveal that in the not very distant past this racism and ethnic chauvinism were even quite "politically correct" in the United States and Western Europe. Racism and ethnic chauvinism were also found on the left: Jack London left the Socialist party because it objected to his explicit notion that socialism was for the white workingman only. He was not alone: many trade unions were openly racist; most supported racist, anti-Chinese laws at the beginning of this century; many remain racially exclusionary to this day. It is hardly necessary to emphasize here that Hitler came to power in Germany, a nation celebrated for its contributions to Western culture.

Racial chauvinism was quite explicit in both Theodore Roosevelt's neo-Darwinian imperialism and Woodrow Wilson's treatment of African Americans. Under the former, the last African-American fighting unit of the U.S. Army was ignominiously dissolved. Under the latter, racial segregation in the nation's capital reached new lows. More to the point, there was no outcry in either case from an outraged public. A public holding truly democratic and ethnically egalitarian principles hardly existed at all and was rare even on the left. Most social scientists and the educated public took it for granted that mass intelligence testing of U.S. Army draftees during the First World War *proved*, scientifically no less, that Italians, Greeks, Latin Americans, East Europeans, and Jews were intellectually inferior to Americans from northwestern Europe. The inferiority of African Americans was simply assumed. In New England, French speakers and Portuguese were numerous enough to constitute an ethnic "other" and were also widely defined as stupid, dirty, and unreliable. Ethnic chauvinism played an explicit role in the sentencing of Sacco and Vanzetti—the sentencing judge even said so, using a vulgar chauvinist epithet. Ironically enough, today theories of racial and ethnic specificity or "mentalities" are openly propounded by "essentialists" in African-American studies.

Mass violence and brutality against others do not, however, have to be based on notions of ethnic nationalism or historical grievances. The outsider can be defined in other than ethnic ways. There is little evidence, for instance, that the images Serbs, Croats, and Muslim Slavs have of each other attribute racial or ethnic inferiority to those whom they are fighting or persecuting. After all, they are all of the same ethnic origin and use the same language. No one denies that the ancestors of the Muslim Slavs were either Serbs or Croats before they converted to Islam. Ethnic chauvinism is no more or less present among groups of British soccer fans fighting one another than it is in Croatia, Bosnia, or Serbia. In fact, the first armed paramilitary groups formed in the Yugoslav states were recruited from the soccer fans who already had a history of fighting all and sundry, not too different from the British soccer club fans. The difference was that in former Yugoslavia the new political elites (post-Communist former Communists) who chose to mobilize support with nationalist legitimation *armed* their thugs. Most of these were as little "historically shaped" as most individual British soccer gang members, whom they matched in loutish illiteracy. Intellectuals, or at least semi-intellectuals, particularly those local historians, ethnographers, journalists, novelists, and poets whose turf was defined by the boundaries of their national language or a specific local variant of a language, were generally the real believers and spreaders of the nationalist myths. Such beliefs are hardly uppermost for the combatants in the civil wars, who are often quite open about their own motives for fighting, which are similar to those of postdisaster looters. That is, their motives are greed, settling real or imagined accounts, and wielding, for once in their alienated lives, some visible and frightening power over unarmed, helpless others.

No Winners in Former Yugoslavia

Rebecca West's flawed masterpiece, *Black Lamb and Grey Falcon*, seems to continue to fascinate a host of Western authors writing about the present-day Yugoslav tragedy. But West wrote from a point of view that was almost completely pro-Serbian and strongly pro Yugoslav. That is, her guide, "Constantine," was Vinaver, a brilliant Serbian nationalist of Jewish origin who managed to convince her that Islam had been an unalloyed catastrophe in the Balkans. He also helped convince her that the Croats were hopelessly corrupted by years of culturally shallow and morally bankrupt Austrian rule, and that only the Serbs, rooted in a vibrant Byzantine and pristine national tradition, could save a Yugoslavia that would represent a barrier to the pernicious eastward march of Germanic culture, commerce, and power. This march presumably threatened the Western European liberal democracies and had to be opposed.[3] (Echoes of this idea are heard among lovers of conspiracy theories even today.) This notion of the Serbs as a bulwark against such threats was what made saving Yugoslavia important for some people. It was also dangerous nonsense, for it was Serbian hard-fisted domination of the first Yugoslav state that made it an all-too-ready victim of Nazi Germany and fascist Italy.

Serbian centralist rule also helped foster a vicious, defensive Croatian chauvinism and native fascism that make the creation of a democratic Croatian state today so difficult. Tom Nairn and others to the contrary, a large majority of Serbs in Croatia today do not live anywhere near the old military frontier (the Kraina). They are, therefore, quite sensibly frightened of becoming second-class citizens in a Croatian state run by right-wing nationalists and leavened by returned fascist exiles and young semieducated ultras who combine body building and skinhead viciousness with a nostalgia for a distorted Ustaše past. For the Serbs in Croatia, then, there are only three possible solutions: immigration into a desperately poor and increasingly less hospitable Serbia; moving to a Kraina that is run by political thugs and whose political future is very much in doubt; or the victory of nonnationalist democratic forces in Croatia.

The first two are *personal* solutions, and they are enthusiastically encouraged by Croatian right-wingers because the result would be a Croatia ethnically cleansed of Serbs. The last solution requires the self-mobilization of Croatian non-nationalist democrats on the basis that it is in their own interest to live in a decent country that can call on the patriotism of all of its citizens irrespective of ethnic origin. In such a civic state both individual and collective human rights would be protected, including broad cultural autonomy for those members of the minorities who seek it. But that most desirable outcome is one to which Serbs in Croatia can contribute in only a minor way, for such an outcome depends on the problematic prospects of democracy in Croatia.

Contemporary ethnic chauvinism insists that individual citizens are not responsible for solely their own actions; rather, individual citizens are seen as existing essentially as members of "real"—that is to say, "ethnic"—national communities and thus share in collective responsibility for the actions of the leaders or sections of that community.[4] Therefore, it becomes completely logical for some Croats to persecute peaceful Serbian citizens of Croatia for what their rebellious fellow nationals have done to other Croats. This was even explicitly stated by the *zupan* (governor) of Zupania, an eastern Croatian district. "It is intolerable that there are Serbs who are living quite normally in Croatia today," he pronounced. Presumably he believes something should be done about that intolerable situation, and many superpatriotic Croat nationalists will presumably see to it. But this local politician was not alone. Alas, he is all too typical of the new little men whom the post-Communist nationalist wave has tossed into power. His type will be found throughout the states that have emerged from the wreckage of Yugoslavia, and for that matter throughout the former Soviet Union.

The Croatian people are clearly major losers in the destruction of Yugoslavia. This is a taboo topic in Croatia because the gain of national independence (a "thousand-year dream") is supposed to be so great an achievement that it is unpatriotic to question the price. The price, however, has been paid on many levels. In terms of economics, the way independence was achieved and the war that inevitably followed created a financial catastrophe for all but a small band of speculators, black marketeers, and people with political connections to the ruling party and the right-wing émigré community. Incomes have dropped to a fraction (perhaps a quarter) of what they were before the war. An immense amount of industrial and tourist capacity was destroyed by the war of aggression of the Yugoslav army, and probably even more was destroyed by the criminal process of "privatization" that shamelessly robbed Croatia of much of its industrial wealth. To compound the trouble, hundreds of thousands of refugees, who will never be able to return home because their homes no longer exist, will be a massive burden on the economy for decades. They will also be an irredentist factor skewing Croatian politics to the right for a long time. In terms of politics, independence has relegitimated fascist and near-fascist political forces reveling in nostalgia and symbols of the 1941–45 period. This permeates and corrupts political and cultural life and is so uncontrolled that it has resulted in Croatia losing almost all the international sympathy it had earned as the victim of the savage destruction of Vukovar and the bombing of Dubrovnik. The barbarism of Croatian troops in Bosnia, the destruction of Mostar, concentration camps, and ethnic cleansing have equated the Croat political establishment in Croatia and above all in Bosnia with the much more massive crimes committed by the Serbian regime and its Bosnian surrogate. It will take decades before Croatia recovers from the poison fruits of independence obtained within the framework of an ethnically national state. There was nothing whatsoever inevitable about this. This is a catastrophe created by human beings, and the first Croatian president, Franjo Tudjman, will not be treated kindly by future Croatian historians.

As I have said above, there is no question but that Yugoslavia, particularly the Yugoslavia of the almost confederal constitution of 1974, had been a much lesser evil. That semiconfederal Yugoslavia, however, was no longer on offer by 1988–89 because of the destructive mobilization of massive Serbian chauvinism by Serbia's president, Slobodan Milošević.

Milošević will go down as a highly successful and cunning politician who brought untold misery and destruction to the Croats, repression to the Albanians in Kosovo, and near genocide to the Bosnian Muslims. He did all this while destroying Yugoslavia. It is already clear, however, that the greatest damage he has done has been to the Serbs themselves. The Serbs in Serbia and in the other states of former Yugoslavia will be paying for decades for their murderous nationalist and chauvinist celebration and disgraceful love affair with Milošević and fascist killers and war criminals like Vojislav Šešelj, Arkan, and the Bosnian Serbian junta. Both the innocent and guilty will be paying, but the innocent will be paying more because many of the guilty have looted all there was to loot in Serbia and Bosnia and have prepared retreats in friendly places like Greece and Cyprus. Under Milošević the Serbian economy became a basket case. Per capita wages and pensions dropped from some place around DM 4000 to DM 120! Tens of thousands of talented young people have left the universities, institutes, and research centers and will probably never return. The reputation of Serbia as the center of liberal and democratic thinking in old Titoist Yugoslavia has been completely obliterated by an unprecedented level of conformist compliance with the nationalist celebration of primitive xenophobic fantasies. The Serbian intelligentsia proved unable to organize even a minimally effective opposition to the repression in Kosovo and mass slaughter and rape in Bosnia. The shame for the failure of the opposition has driven most intellectuals out of politics completely and will poison political life in Serbia for decades, making the work of those few courageous enough to attempt to build a decent antinationalist opposition even harder.

Milošević has succeeded in impoverishing his nation and making it the pariah of Europe and the world community. The tragedy did not result, however, simply because Milošević was more skilled than his opponents in the brutal game of Balkan politics and deceit. This skill of his has, indeed, been a curse for Serbia, and it will not recover for generations. And yet, others are also at fault: this tragedy could have been prevented with early and energetic intervention from the European Community and the United States.

Most contemporary Bosnians are urbanites on whom the primacy of national identity was forced by a bankrupt political class, first Communist and then post-Communist. By voting for the social-democratic reformists or for the former Communists, 28 percent of Bosnians voted against all nationalist parties. The reformists won the elections in Tuzla and the center of Sarajevo. They still hold power in Tuzla. More than 25 percent did not vote at all, and a substantial number who did vote for the Serbian, Croatian, and Muslim parties did not expect their vote to result in either a partition or a civil war. Huge demonstrations for peace took place in Sarajevo just before the Serbian aggression began the war. A few Serbian sniper mercenaries shot at the demonstrators.

Why on earth, then, do so many—like U.S. Secretary of State Warren Christopher, the spokespersons for the UN, and Vance, Owen, and Stoltenberg—keep insisting that the various ethnic nationalist leaders represent a majority of the Bosnian population? There is absolutely no hard evidence to prove that proposition. A great deal of evidence exists to the contrary. Could it be that the existence of a substantial body of citizens who did not fit neatly into the three tribal flocks would be inconvenient because they would make the partition of Bosnia an obvious outrage? This is, indeed, the very outrage that the entire international community, led by the United States, seems bound and determined to impose on the hapless citizens and government of Bosnia. Presumably this plan is supposed to make the world forget the genocide of the Muslim Slavs as a viable community. Of course that is a delusion—the problem will not be that easily disposed of. Not only will over three million of these miserable refugees haunt Western Europe and the world community, but almost certainly a bitter terrorist war of revenge will keep the Bosnian issue alive well into the twenty-first century. At a time when there appears to be some hope that the Palestinian problem might move toward a solution in the Middle East, Europe and the United States have helped create a similar problem right in the Middle of Europe.

No group will come out of the Bosnian catastrophe with its honor intact. The mass murderers of the Serbian and Yugoslav government and armed forces, their Croatian accomplices, and the local Bosnian surrogates of Belgrade and Zagreb are obvious culprits. Their policies of mass murder, "ethnic cleansing," and rape have been documented all too well. By 1993, reports of Croats massacring Muslims and driving them into concentration camps made it clear that morally there was little to choose from between the Serbian and Croatian aggressors, in Bosnia at least. The Bosnian government contributed its little bit through its incompetence and lack of clear goals, but it was obviously primarily the victim. What are we to say about a U.S. policy, in both the Bush and Clinton administrations, that, on the one hand, encouraged the Bosnians to keep fighting and dying, dangling promises of aid, and, on the other hand, cravenly escaped taking any steps that might actually have stopped the carnage? How about the European Community that piously kept insisting that every means, short of force, should be used to get food, fuel, and medicine to cities suffering medieval siege in the heart of Europe?

By November 1993, Senator Robert Dole was calling for an investigation of the increasingly well-documented claim that UN food and fuel aid was being manipulated to pressure the Bosnian government to accept a partition of Bosnia, a scenario in which the results of Serbian and Croatian aggression would be recognized not only by the world community, but also by the victims.[5] In particular, the charge was that the UN was deliberately not stockpiling food, medicine, and fuel in Sarajevo and other Bosnian cities, this in order to make it clear to the Bosnian forces that they could not survive another winter of sieges without catastrophic casualties. The UN thus became an accomplice in the murder of Bosnia. Most of the food was provided by the United States, yet U.S. officials not only did not protest UN efforts to prevent the Bosnian government from stockpiling food and other supplies for the winter; those officials also classified the relevant documents to provide a cover-up. Further, Fikret Abdic's rebels, who are fighting against the Bosnian government in the Bihac area, were supplied with fuel and food.[6] The French troops within the UN forces even built a pipeline to ensure delivery of such supplies. All this to pressure the Bosnian government to sign its own death warrant.

The UN—which gave its peace-keeping forces an impossibly limited mandate that prevented them for shooting back when shot at and forbade them to defend the civilian victims of mass rape and murder—did not cover itself with honor in this mission. This failure to develop an effective UN role in Bosnia and Croatia, despite the great cost involved, will set back the development of genuine international peace-keeping forces for decades.

There were many alternative policies that the UN, the United States, and the European Community could have pursued. And here we must remind ourselves that the limitation of the powers of the UN forces is mostly the result of U.S. and West European policies, just as the passivity of the European Community and NATO is in good part, although not exclusively, the result of the absence of an energetic and clear

U.S. policy. Arms could have been made available to the legitimate government of Bosnia to enable it to fight against the aggressors. There could have been air attacks on the Serbian artillery positions from which Sarajevo has been shelled for almost two years. Even if all the positions had not been taken out, the air attacks still would have been a clear message to both the aggressors and victims. Croatia could have been threatened with sanctions if it did not stop carving an independent state of "Herzeg-Bosna" out of Bosnia. Above all, the United States could have mobilized its own powers and those of its West European allies to stop the war. That would have been a message to all—and there are many—who want to use the Bosnian "method" to deal with inconvenient demographic facts.[7]

Nationalism: Delusions and Realities

Many Western liberal or even leftist analysts seem still to believe that nationalism (*their* decent and democratic nationalism to be sure—not the existing, ugly, bloody, soiled, and real-life thing) represents authentic democracy. They have not gotten over their sentimental and uncritical love affair with national liberation movements in the Third World or the nationalists of the "submerged" nations of Western Europe.[8] This spurs them to write all manner of god-awful stuff. For instance, in an article entitled "We Are All Bosnians Now," Thomas Nairn writes: "Democracy is people power. And in this region people are primarily communities, the democratic impulse is strong but also collective, ethnic rather than individual or abstract."[9] But democracy, as we should know by now, must be more than the untrammeled rule of a mob. It must, certainly, include the right of individuals to organize collectively along class or national lines. But it must also include individual rights and the right to choose not to be a part of a collectivity; and, in particular, it must include the right of individuals and minorities not to be a part of the national collectivity, particularly the national collectivity as defined by the momentary nationalist leaders. Individual freedom and rights of minorities are threatened even further when national and religious identities are combined, as secularists in Ireland and Israel know all too well. In the case of Israel, the religious establishment defines who is and is not a Jew and thus who is and is not a full citizen of the state. This should be intolerable in a democracy and in a situation where in reality a large proportion of the Jews are secular. The minority has in this case been allowed to tyrannize the majority.

It is the failure to understand this principle that has made a settlement in Northern Ireland so difficult. Does being Irish necessarily have to mean being Catholic or subject to explicitly Catholic laws on matters like divorce, abortion, and the place of religion in schools? Can one today be a full *citizen* of Croatia and not be a Croat? Can a non-Muslim be an equal citizen in an Islamic state? How about someone who is an atheist but is of Muslim origin? Can non-Serbs (who constitute over 30 percent of the population of Serbia) be equal citizens with Serbs in a state that defines itself as the national state of the Serbs and uses the exclusive, emotion-laden symbols of Serbian history (often a version concocted by the nationalists themselves) and the Serbian Orthodox church in public institutions and schools? Those types of issues, not in the least bit specific to former Yugoslavia, make the revival of ethnic nationalism as a major factor in mass politics so problematic and dangerous to democracy today.

Further, there is the problem of defining present-day, really existing nationalism. It will not do to invoke Mazzini and the liberal nationalism of the nineteenth century[10] or for that matter the nationalism of the national liberation movements. Those movements in the Third World also had problems with concepts of democracy, but those problems were of a different sort. Present-day nationalism, particularly in Eastern Europe and the former Soviet Union, stresses the centrality of the imagined national community to political mobilization and action. It is not about cultural autonomy, the right to a national identity, or equal rights. More often than not it is about imposing a view, very often a minority view, of what the proper national (or religious) identity and language of all citizens living in a given territory must be. The imposition can be done administratively or even by force and terror. The IRA and Basque ETA are good examples of the latter. So are Muslim fundamentalists in many countries today.

In a world in which more and more people must live and work in countries where they were not born and where they constitute a national or ethnic minority, this new ethnic nationalism is an obvious threat to democracy. For one thing, it defines the citizens of the polity *ethnically* and therefore drives all others to become second-class citizens, or at best to assimilate. In most, though not all, cases, new ethnic nationalists do not permit just anyone to become a part of the politically dominant nation. Membership is open only to those who are born into it. Clearly this is incompatible with any notion of democracy that includes personal rights and freedom. But I will not cheat: it is not on those extreme examples that I base my basic argument that *today*, in an increasingly integrated and cosmopolitan world, ethnic nationalism is hostile to democracy and pluralist societies. Contemporary ethnic nationalism represents, in Benjamin Barber's phrase, a "jihad against McWorld." It is antimodern and antidemocratic in its basic impulse, and that is why it is attractive to the present postmodernist academic obscurantists. Decent democrats do not really belong in that company.

Ethnic nationalism today is the form of communitarian politics that is explicitly opposed to liberal-democratic concepts of *individual* rights. The ethnic community is defined as the only relevant unit when it comes to rights, grievances that need to be addressed, and representation. The ethnic group (sometimes a religious community), in counterposition to *intentional associations* (that is, communities that individuals associate with voluntarily, such as social and political movements, which make up the base of a civil society), is defined as the most relevant community, certainly the most *politically* relevant community. Therefore, modern nationalism in the form that it actually (not ideally) takes in most countries today represents a problem for democratic politics in a great number of places beside the post-Communist societies.

Confronting the Realities of Present-Day Nationalisms

There are many who would claim that the above cases represent perversions of true nationalism and that *their* nationalism is a far better and nobler thing. That sort of caveat reminds me of Leszek Kolakowski's bitter prose poem *What Is Socialism?* (written when Kolakowski was still a socialist), which begins: "We will tell you what socialism is. But first we must tell you what socialism is not. . . ." After listing all that socialism is not, he ends: "That was the first part. But now listen attentively, we will tell you what socialism is: Well, then, socialism is a good thing."[11] Such was Kolakowski's way of adding to the debate on socialism.

In the United States today, there is widespread debate about the politics of cultural pluralism. On the left of that debate, there are many advocates of nationalism and politics of ethnic identity who are unaware of the real-life history and role of the concept of national identity. Too many go around saying that "their" nationalism—or at least the nationalism of oppressed groups—is a good thing. Like Kolakowski and "his" socialism, they are ready to explain what "their" nationalism is not. Their nationalism, of course, is not the nasty, real-life stuff practiced by new national states that have emerged out of the debris of late Communism; it is not the nationalism of the Croat regime that represses all independent press and massively denies citizenship to non-Croats; it is not the nationalism of the Latvian regime, or the Estonian regime, or the Georgian, Armenian, and Azerbaijanian regimes, all of which yearn for ethnically pure—or at least much purer—homelands and set about obtaining them by hook or by crook, bureaucratic repression or violence. The list—at each step undermining abstract notions of a good and pure nationalism—continues.

We have Russian and Serbian nationalisms, which are even more dangerous because they have more subject peoples and because the Russians and Serbs are far stronger militarily than their neighbors. The nationalists of both larger and smaller nations demand the right to deal with their own minorities the way they consider just. A grim reality here is that many of these "minorities" were only relatively recently transformed into minorities in lands where their ancestors have lived for centuries; these transformations have been accomplished administratively through the creation of new national states or by new policies adopted by the dominant national group. This is the case with Russians in the Ukraine, particularly in Crimea (which never was a part of the Ukraine until Khrushchev generously "gave" it to the Ukraine in the early 1960s); with Serbs in Croatia; with Muslims in Bulgaria; with various Transcaucasian peoples who found themselves on the wrong side of a previously "soft" frontier; with Russian and Ukrainian speakers born in Latvia and Estonia; and so on.

The right of self-determination in real life poses many complicated questions about national rights and the rights of fragments of nations distributed among many states. An example is the long-suffering Roms (Gypsies). Then, of course, there is the not so minor issue that the right of self-determination in sub-Saharan Africa could create dozens and dozens of new "nation-states," all of which would also have historical grievances, often against other peoples living among them.

The memory of the fate of Asians in East Africa, who for the most part had no other national home, should sober some of the advocates of unlimited self-determination for all. Then we have the nasty fact that India, Sri Lanka, Pakistan, Afghanistan, and Burma all have the potential for endless fragmentation into the many ethno-national groups of which they now consist. There is no possible consensus about frontiers or mutual responsibility for infrastructural assets that were jointly built. Do we favor the breakup of these states into new *imagined* national states? I write "imagined" because many are too small to survive except as some kind of Bantustan, and many are hopelessly ethnically mixed, no matter what their nationalists claim.

There are at least two additional problems. One is when the claim is for territories that used to be populated by the people in question but that have in recent times changed demographically. This applies, for example, to the Native American claims for parts of the United States; to Basque claims for territories that are held by Spanish-speaking peoples; to claims of Baltic nationalists against descendants of Russian post-1945 settlers; to the clashing claims for Palestine; and to the "historical" claims of Serb, Hungarian, Croatian, German, and Polish nationalists. A second problem—seemingly somewhat eclipsed for the moment—has to do with "submerged" nationalisms. In the 1960s it was fashionable to back these nationalisms—that is, nationalisms that probably no longer had the support of the majority of the people involved but were nevertheless passionately advocated (sometimes violently) by romantic minorities, often including poets, linguists, and historians. Maoists had a weakness for that sort of thing. These nationalisms may not be as much to the forefront as they once were, but they continue to loom as problems.

Nationalism Jettisoning Democracy

In some of the richer regions of national—or multiethnic—states, there is a "nationalism" based on resentments that "we" are being unfairly taxed for "them," who usually breed too much and work too little. An excellent example is the case of the Lombard Leagues, which want to stop paying for the south of Italy and use an increasingly racist and nationalist language to insist on the differences between the north and the south. There was a good bit of that sort of thing in the language of the right-wing nationalist separatists in Slovenia and Croatia. I nevertheless believe that what really broke up Yugoslavia was the aggressive national populism of Slobodan Milošević's Serbian regime with the help of the federal army. I believe that until Milošević began his nationalist rampage in 1987, no national group was repressed or exploited as a national group, except the Albanians.

Today, after two aggressive wars—one waged against Croatia and the other against Bosnia—Yugoslavia is effectively dead. However, it is not at all clear why a fight for separate states was more logical than a fight for a democratic, multiethnic confederation that might have avoided the worst of the carnage *and* provided a sounder base for future development. The problem is that the separatist minorities that took over Slovenia and Croatia wanted separate national states no matter what, and were not too concerned with democratic practices or legitimacy.[12] This poses a question: What if tomorrow, or ten years from now, a new narrow majority voted to reunite with other Yugoslav states? Why would that be a less legitimate decision? But clearly one cannot build and break up states at each election; therefore, one is constrained to ask: Should not constitutions make the act of separation a weighty and serious act that requires, let us say, two-thirds of the vote? But nothing of the sort happened in either the violent breakup of Yugoslavia or the non-violent breakup of Czechoslovakia. In the latter case it was clear that large *majorities* on both sides of the new national divide were against breaking up the unified state, and yet an irresponsible political establishment was able to force the breakup. In what sense was this an advance for democracy?

Nationalism of Internal Oppressed Minorities

Another type of nationalist language and grievance is advanced by internal minorities like the African Americans, Native Americans, and Latin Americans in the United States. Some people on the left seem to assume automatically that this process is unquestionably good and involves sound demands leading to effective tactics. I think otherwise. I believe that broad civic solidarity—involving support by the majority of the population—is necessary in order to bring about the massive economic transformation necessary to establish minimal economic equality. To achieve that the most powerful claim is that of common citizenship in a common polity, that which we have in common, not that which separates us. Without massive economic transfers and full-employment policies, which cannot be won without the support of majorities, competing ethnic claims become a deadly zero-sum game that the weaker and less numerous will almost always lose. And if for some reason they do not lose, a massive backlash of resentments can do long-range damage to any possibility of building majority-minority coalitions capable of maintaining economic justice.

The notion of historical grievances—often harbored by internal, oppressed minorities—leads us back to the post-Communist scenarios. There, the dangers of concentrating on historical grievances are pronounced. . . . [O]ne of the first effects of Gorbachev's glasnost was that for the first time in decades the expression of pent-up, age-old hatreds and grievances was permitted. These grievances were nursed by dissident intellectuals who were catapulted into power with the unanticipatedly rapid collapse of Communism. They represented the only non-Communist elites, and as such they had a totally disproportionate influence on the media and public opinion in the first post-Communist years. These intellectuals legitimated a renewed or reinvented ethnic nationalism and revived its traditional language of historical grievances. Because past wrongs cannot be righted, what has remained is vengeance.

Transcending Nationalism

■ ■ ■ ■

Historically, the left and nationalists competed for the same voters and supporters. But the left is today wounded and in a moral crisis. The tribes are mobilizing, and this is not a process that seems limited to any particular area of the globe. It is now at its most acute stage in Eastern Europe and the former Soviet Union. This mobilization is a dangerous and hollow substitute for democracy. It is also extremely dangerous for regional peace.

In order to fight this danger effectively it is essential to develop new notions of community: the community must be understood as being constituted by all citizens within the polity, and these citizens must be bound by some concept of common good. This kind of community cannot be created and maintained if a society is flooded with messages that stress a ruthless struggle for personal advancement and enrichment regardless of social costs. It cannot be created and maintained in a society in which social and economic differences are expanded and in which an increasing number of citizens are destined for permanent unemployment or marginal employment that keeps them below the poverty level, no matter how defined. It cannot be created and maintained in a society in which ever-larger numbers of the homeless become nonpersons, as we are told that it is not possible for the state to do anything for these fellow citizens in desperate need, and that to try to do something will only make things worse. In short, neo-Darwinian "cold" values stressing market egoism militate against building a democratic community of equal citizens. One cannot create a community bound by common universalist values if the stress is on consumerist values that define an ever-growing portion of the society as surplus outsiders. For an effective community to exist, some minimal notions of social equality are necessary. That means not only abolishing all discrimination based on socially defined ascribed characteristics, such a gender, race, or ethnicity, but also minimizing the social distance created by excessive differences in wealth and opportunity. Thus just as modern nationalism and socialism developed simultaneously and in interaction with each other, overcoming the imagined exclusive national communities requires creating an alternate voluntary community based on democracy and social justice. That remains the supreme democratic project for the twenty-first century.

Notes

1. Benedict Anderson, *Imagined Communities*, 2d ed. (London: Verso, 1993). This is one of the absolutely indispensable books about modern nationalism. Others are: Ernest Gellner, *Thought and Change* (London: Weidenfeld and Nicolson, n.d.); Hans Kohn, *The Age of Nationalism* (New York: Harper and Row, 1962); and Hugh Seton-Watson, *Nations and States: An Enquiry into the Origins of Nations and the Politics of Nationalism* (Boulder, Colo.: Westview, 1977).

2. Anderson, *Imagined Communities*, 6.

3. Germany's clumsy diplomatic strong-arming of its West European partners for early recognition of Croatia seemed to confirm this long-lived conspiracy theory.

4. This is not at all limited to Eastern Europe. Nor is it limited to majorities in multiethnic societies. The assumption by many African-American nationalists that *all* whites are racists or that they are *all* responsible for racism is an illustration of this view. Clearly, "gender" exclusivists who argue that all males are sexists who long to rape are of a piece with that stereotyping mind-set. Catherine MacKinnon is a good example of the latter.

5. *News from Bob Dole, U.S. Senator from Kansas, Senate Republican Leader*, bulletin dated 4 November 1993.

6. See *Christian Science Monitor*, 8 October 1993.

7. An example is the Abkhasian "independence movement," which claims territories in Georgia, where the Abkhasians are only 17 percent of the population. The members of the movement apparently intend to "correct" this demographic inconvenience through "ethnic cleansing," Bosnian-Serb style.

8. The left had a great deal of uncritical sympathy for the Welsh, Scots, Breton, Occidant, Basque, Irish, and Catalan nationalisms in the 1960s. Some of that is still around. The assumption was that these nationalisms represented the wishes of the local peoples; however, that assumption often had no foundation in fact. In that case, we were told that the people suffered from a false consciousness imposed on them by their colonizers.

9. Thomas Nairn, "We Are All Bosnians Now," *Dissent* (fall 1993).

10. This was a state-building, nonethnic nationalism, that was mostly secular. This is why Jews could and did play such a major role in the national unification of Italy and why the Vatican opposed that unification.

11. Leszek Kolakowski, *What Is Socialism?* (n.p., 1956).

12. All opinion polls had shown that a minority was for secession in both Slovenia and Croatia before the war began. Even after the war, the ruling party in Croatia had only a plurality. It is an open question how much support the nationalists would have if peace were signed and they no longer had a monopoly of the media.

DEMONISING NATIONALITY

Tom Nairn

Two and a half years ago *Time* magazine published a special exposé about the future of the world.[1] "Being on the cover of *Time*" has always been an American honour (something like a knighthood) and on this occasion *Time* did not let readers down. The cover of 6 August 1990 obliged with a portrait of . . . Nationalism.

An elementary tombstone-shaped visage of plasticine, or possibly mud, glowers out from an equally rudimentary map of central Europe. One primitive, soulless eye is located near Vilnius. Beneath the emergent snout a hideous, gash-like mouth splits the continent open from Munich to Kiev before dribbling its venom down across Yugoslavia and Romania. No semiotic subtlety is needed to decode the image, since closer perusal shows the teeth inside the gash read simply 'Nationalism.' But in case anyone failed to register that, the whole image was crowned with a title in 72-point scarlet lettering: "OLD DEMON."

This was two and a half years ago. Hardly an in-depth retrospect, therefore, more an early, apprehensive glance during the first round of the ex-Soviet and post-Yugoslav tumult. It was, in fact, what most Western or metropolitan opinion really expected, on the basis of these early stirrings. Some time before either the Baltic peoples, the Ukrainians or the Georgians had actually established their independence, when virtually all Western diplomacy was still devoted to shoring up Gorbachev and Yugoslavia, there already lurked a pervasive sense of doom in the North Atlantic mind. It was summed up in a *Guardian* leader of the same vintage: "Don't Put Out More Flags!" This editorial did become famous enough to endure mild mockery but only because it was characteristically over the top, exaggerating what most readers instinctively felt.

What they felt was that if enough new national flags were put out the Old Demon would, unless severely dealt with, wreak havoc with the New World Order. The second springtime of nations was, in this glum perspective, already turning to winter, and a bad one at that.

Now, anyone could see from the outset that there were at least three principal strands in the gigantic upheaval against Communism. There was a popular, democratic rebellion against one-party autocracy and state terror. There was an economic revulsion against the anti-capitalist command economies which for forty years had imposed forced-march development on the East. And thirdly there was the national mould into which these revolts were somehow inevitably flowing—the new salience of the ethnic, or (as in Bosnia) of the ethnic-religious in post-communist society.

The *Time–Guardian* perspective on this triad is that the third element will most likely end by confining, endangering or even aborting the first two. And I suppose what I am primarily objecting to is that perspective itself—the instinctive notion that number 3 on the list is somehow an atavistic revenant, there by unfortunate accident, the bad news which has resurfaced alongside the good, an Old Adam who refuses to let the Angel of Progress get on with it.

The conclusion to the *Time* article by John Borrell accompanying the front cover puts this point as well as anyone else, in terms which, since then, have been echoed thousands of times in tones of mounting hysteria: "Not since Franz Ferdinand's assassination have conditions been so favourable for enduring new order to replace the empires of the past. With a unified Germany locked in the embrace of democratic Europe, and the Soviet Union re-examining its fundamental values, the way is open for an era of peace and liberty—but only so long as the old demons do not escape again."

But escape they did, alas, notably in what used to be Yugoslavia and especially—as if some truly profound irony of history was working itself out—in and around the very town where Franz Ferdinand perished in 1914. The general view or new received wisdom soon became set in concrete: nationalism is upsetting everything. It has ruined the End of History, in Fukuyama's sense. History has come back like some evil shade, mainly in order to ruin the State Department's triumphal victory celebrations.

There were always serious difficulties in store in the East for both democracy and capitalism, of course, and no serious commentator has ignored them. But what has made these insoluble is the return and dominance of the third force—the atavistic, incalculable force of the ethnic revival, compelling peoples to place blood before reasonable progress and individual rights. Three years ago it already felt as if this might be the story: mysterious unfinished business of Eastern nationality wrecks any "enduring new order." And so it has proved. We (in the West) now face a prospect of interminable Balkan and post-Soviet disorder, where forms of demented chauvinism and intolerance risk arresting progress altogether. Putting out too many new flags, having too many liberated nations, leads only to *etnicko ciscenje*, "ethnic cleansing."[2]

Unless civilization intervenes, they may end up by replacing naissant democracy with forms of nationalist dictatorship like those prefigured in Gamsakurdia's Georgia or the Serbia of Slobodan Milosevic. As for economics the consequences can hardly be anything but intensified backwardness.

Old Stories

You are all over-familiar with this dreary tale. . . . What "civilised" news coverage of Eastern folly perceives is primarily a re-emergence of archaism. It rarely occurs to the editorialists or reporters concerned that this enlightened, liberal perspective on the great change may itself be archaic.

Yet I believe it is. Whether or not old demons are returning to haunt anyone in Bosnia and Ngorny-Karabakh, there can be no doubt that old theories the conventional wisdom of the day before yesterday—have come back to haunt and distort Western interpretations of what is happening. This wisdom is easily dated. One need only turn to the nearest available library shelf groaning beneath a copy of *Encyclopaedia Britannica.* Turn to "Socio-Economic Doctrines and Reform Movements" (vol. 27, pp. 467–71), and the signature, "H. K."—Hans Kohn, a prominent and prolific writer on the political history of nationalism in the 1940s.

The thesis which Kohn argued at that time rested mainly upon a distinction between Western and Eastern nationalism. The former was original, institutional, liberal and good. The latter was reactive, envious, ethnic, racist and generally bad. Undeniably, Western-model nation-states like Britain, France and America had invented political nationalism. But Kohn argued that these societies had also limited and qualified it, linking it to certain broader, more universal ideals. Nationalism may have been a child of Western Enlightenment. But that very fact enabled the original enlightened countries to at least partially transcend it—to confine and then pass beyond the demon's potency (as it were). As time passed, in spite of various imperialist adventures, a measure of tolerance and internationalism came to compensate for such original sin, and to moderate the crudity of Anglo-French nationality.

Not so in the East. By the "East" I think Kohn really meant the rest of the world, but typified by Central and Eastern Europe. He was talking about all those other societies which from the eighteenth century onwards have suffered the impact of the West, and been compelled to react against it. That reaction bred a different kind of national spirit—resentful, backward-looking, detesting the Western bourgeoisie even while trying to imitate it, the sour and vengeful philosophy of the second- or third-born. It was this situation (he claimed) which generated genuinely narrow nationalism.

Countries were hurled into the developmental race without time to mature the requisite institutions and cadres. Hence they were forced to mobilise in other ways. The intellectuals and soldiers who took charge there needed an adrenaline-rich ideology to realise their goals, and found it in a shorthand version of the Western national spirit. This was of course blood-based nationality, a heroic and exclusive cult of people and state founded upon custom, speech, faith, colour, cuisine and whatever else was found available for packaging.

Though originally drawn to the West, the Germans had ended by succumbing to an

Eastern-style package. Developed into a form of eugenic insanity, it was their blood cult which threatened to drown the Enlightenment inheritance altogether after 1933. This was mercifully (though only just) defeated in 1945. However, out of it came the experience which stamped a lasting impression of nationalism's meaning upon both the Western and the communist mind. Nazism may in truth have been a form of genetic imperialism—in its bizarre, pseudo-scientific fashion universal (or at least would-be universal) in sense—but its nationalist origins were undeniable, as well as keenly felt by all the victims. So its sins were inevitably visited upon nationality politics as such. Since the largest, most important ethnos in Europe had gone mad in that particular way then the ethnic as such must remain forever suspect.

Such is the mentality which the post-1989 events have brought again to the surface. Instead of prompting a new search for theories to account for this extraordinary transformation of the world, these events have by and large resurrected the old ones. There are some important exceptions here . . . but on the whole it seems to me that theory has contributed astonishingly little to understanding of the New World Order (or the New World Disorder as—like nearly everybody else—Ken Jowitt calls it in his interesting if eccentric 1991 study[3]). The greatest revolution in global affairs since the epoch of world war is currently being explained almost wholly in terms of *Time* magazine's Old Demons. Somehow a new age seems to have been born without any new ogres: all we have are the old ones, the Old Adam of atavistic Eastern-style nationalism thawed out from the Cold War icebox and on the rampage once more.

World of Nations

■ ■ ■ ■

These creaky old ideological vehicles trundled out to cope with the post-Soviet and Balkan upheavals explain nothing whatever about their subjects. Their gore-laden pictures of ethnic anarchy, of the Abyss and the Doom to come start off by obscuring what is, surely, so far easily the most significant feature of the new world disorder.

Since 1988 the post-communist convulsions have drawn in about forty different nationalities and a population of well over three hundred million in an area comprising about one-fifth of the world. Thanks to the holding operation in Tienanmen Square they did not embrace an actual majority of the world's population (but it's surely reasonable to think that they will still end by doing so).

Now, when this scale and those numbers are kept in mind, the most impressive fact is surely not how much the transformation has cost in terms of either life or social and economic destruction. It is how astoundingly, how unbelievably little damage has been done. In one of the few efforts made at countering conventional hysteria the *Economist* did try last September to estimate loss of life in the ex-Soviet empire, and published a map showing that probably about 3,000 plus had perished, mostly in Georgia, Tajikistan and the war between Armenia and Azerbaijan.* "Fewer than most people think," it concluded, and far less serious than what was happening in one small part of the Balkans. Social and economic disaster had been brought about by the collapse of the old Soviet-style economies, but though aggravated by the political breakaways and national disputes these were certainly not the cause.

This impression must be reinforced if any concrete time-scale or historical memory is brought into the picture. The Old Demon mythology is essentially timeless—a dark or counter-millennium of re-emergent sin. In actual time the reflorescence of ethnic nationhood has followed a forty-year period during which humanity cowered in the effective shadow of imminent extinction. The demonologies of that epoch (anti-capitalism and anti-communism) at least rested on something real, in the sense of an array of missiles and other hardware which any serious clash between the empires—or even any sufficiently serious accident—could have activated, with the genuinely apocalyptic results everyone now seems (understandably enough) to have exiled from recollection.

But the old frozen mentality did not vanish with the missiles. Instead it has found the temporary surrogate—Devil of Nationalism. Another End of the World has been located—Armageddon

*See editors' note at end of reading.

has been replaced by the ethnic Abyss. A pretty feeble substitute, in fact, in the obvious sense that, even if some worst-possible-case scenario were to unfold—a prolonged "Third Balkan War" in Misha Glenny's phrase, a Russo-Ukrainian war over the Crimea, the break-up of the Indian state, and so on—the consequences would not, by the standards of 1948 to 1988, be all that serious. Nobody would have to worry about taking refuge on another planet.

Anarchy and Method

Almost by definition there is a great deal of anarchy in the New Disorder, and no sign of its coming to an end. But there is . . . no abyss save the ideological one in metropolitan craniums. As Ben Anderson says in another of the more critical contributions to the debate (also entitled "The New World Disorder") the key misconception is that what's going on is essentially,

> "fragmentation" and "disintegration"—with all the menacing, pathological connotations these words bring with them. This language makes us forget the decades or centuries of violence out of which Frankensteinian 'integrated states' such as the United Kingdom of 1900, which included all of Ireland, were constructed . . . Behind the language of 'fragmentation' lies always a Panglossian conservatism that likes to imagine that every status quo is nicely normal.[4]

But as Anderson and anyone else making this kind of objection knows all too well, the immediate result is bitter recrimination. One is at once accused of apologising for savagery, or of indifference to the escalating Balkan wars. An appeal to Western governments and the Secretary-General of the United Nations was published in last week's *New York Review*, demanding that the world take action to stop the Yugoslav wars: "If democracies acquiesce in violations of human rights on such a massive scale they will undermine their ability to protect these rights anywhere in the post-cold war world. And then, when, as has happened many times before, an armed hoodlum kicks our own doors ajar, there will be no one to lift a finger in our defence or to raise a voice."[5]

In this climate, to suggest that on the whole the nationalist course of history after 1989 may be preferable to what went before, and may not be treatable by any recourse to the old multinational or internationalist recipes, is to risk virtual excommunication. One must be lining up with the armed hoodlums. One is either a dupe of Demons like Tudjman and Karadzic or some sort of narrow nationalist oneself (I'm not clear which of these is considered worse).

Well, no: it does not follow, and the point at issue is a really a methodological one. Though obvious, it usually gets ignored in the new fury of the ideological times. Both anti-nationalism and pro-nationalism are extremely broad attitudes or principles—the kind of important yet very general rules which are needed as signposts or reference points. But signposts do not map out or explain the journey which they indicate. Although by no means empty or meaningless, attitudes on this plane of historical generality are bound to have—indeed, to demand—hosts of qualifications or exceptions. . . .

This was blatantly true of anti-nationalism. Both in its standard liberal or Western form and in the socialist or Leninist versions which used to hold court in the East, it was always acknowledged that occasionally, reluctantly, a few more flags had to be run up. This was permitted in cases of hallmarked national oppression. Emphatically colonial or imperialist dominance gave legitimacy to nationalism, at least for a time. "Great-power chauvinism" could morally underwrite small-country national liberation, though only up to the point of independence, when universal values were supposed at once to reassert themselves.

So, the very least a pro-nationalist can say is that he or she is as entitled to exceptions as *that.* That political and economic nationalism is, very generally, a good thing does not mean there are no blots, excrescences or failures on the increasingly nationalised map of the world. Recognition that only a broadly nationalist solution will be found for the succession to the Soviet Union, Yugoslavia and Czechoslovakia does not entail apologising for the bombardment of Dubrovnik or the political rape of Muslim women in Bosnia. Insistence that the small battalions are likely to be "on the whole" better than the large—particularly the multi national large—does not imply there can be no pathology of the ethnic, or no cases where nationalists are wrong.

I must say too that it seems to me that since 1989 the pro-nationalist is justified in a measure of sarcasm. He or she can also observe that, however many pustules and warts there turn out to be in the new world of nations, the small-battalion principle is unlikely to end up consisting of nothing but exceptions. Such has of course been internationalism's fate since 1989. The seamless garment always had to make room for occasional, supposedly temporary, tears and patches; but after 1989 it come to consist of almost nothing except empty holes, which no amount of lamentation or wish-fulfilment will repair.

For the first time in human history, the globe has been effectively unified into a single economic order under a common democratic-state model—surely the ideal, dreamt-of conditions for liberal or proletarian internationalism. Actually, these conditions have caused it almost immediately to fold up into a previously unimaginable and still escalating number of different ethno-political units.

■ ■ ■ ■

Grander Theory

This returns us to that larger plane of theory I alluded to before, and on which I would like to conclude. To understand the difference, to retain and cultivate a wider, more balanced perspective on the post-1989 transformation must be the task for serious theorists in this new world. Why has the End of History carried us forward into a more nationalist world? Why is a more united globe also—and almost at once—far more ethnically aware, and more liable to political division?

In mentioning theories of nationalism before, I hope I didn't give the impression of nothing having been done in the field. Far from it—the years before 1989 were actually ones where very significant advances were made in both the history and the sociology of nationalism. The central weakness of Kohn and liberal theory had been its neglect of economics, its failure to place the rise of ethnic politics within a more substantial framework of development. This failure was remedied by the important work of Ernest Gellner,[6] Anthony D. Smith and others from the 1960s to the 1980s.

They showed, to my mind conclusively, that nationalism was inseparable from the deeper processes of industrialisation and socio-economic modernity. Far from being an irrational obstacle to development, it was for most societies the only feasible way into the developmental race—the only way in which they could compete without being either colonised or annihilated. If they turned to the past (figuratively to "the blood") in these modernisation struggles, it was essentially in order to stay intact as they levered themselves into the future. Staying intact, or obtaining a new degree of social and cultural cohesion, was made necessary by industrialisation—even (as in so many cases) by the distant hope, the advancing shadow of industrialisation. And *ethnos* offered the only way of ensuring such cohesion and common purpose.

The strategy was indeed high-risk, both in the sense that the blood might take over and drown them, and because they might never really catch up. However, that risk was itself unavoidable. It arose from the conditions of generally and chronically uneven development—the only kind which capitalism allows. The only kind, and the kind which has finally, definitively established itself since 1989 as the sole matrix of further evolution.

In this more rational but insufficiently appreciated perspective, nationalism is therefore as much a native of modernity as democracy and the capitalist motor of development. It is as inseparable from progress as they are. In his earlier work Gellner in particular stressed how vital was the function of nationalism in resisting over-centralised and monolithic development. Without "fragmentation and disintegration" some type of Empire would long ago have appropriated industrialisation to its own political purpose.

Earlier on I mentioned the standard triad of categories used to read the post-1989 changes: democracy, capitalism and nationalism, the third representing some kind of ghost or retreat from reason, an upsurge of atavism interfering with the other two—with the reasonable adaptation of the East to modernity. This is itself a piece of superstition. But unfortunately a superstition which has grown so popular that today it has come partly to define (or redefine) the task of nationalist theory. It seems to me that anti-demonism is the prerequisite of getting anywhere with a debate about ethnic issues and their future.

Notes

*Editors' note: By the end of the 1990s, these modest mortality figures had increased to 5,000 for Georgia, 40,000 for Tajikistan, and 25,000 for the war between Armenia and Azerbaijan.

1. First appeared in *London Review of Books*, vol. 9, no. 4 (1993).
2. The infamous phrase was first coined by an unfortunate UN representative, José-Maria Mendiluce, as recounted in Laura Silber and Allan Little, *The Death of Yugoslavia*, London, 1995, ch. 16, pp. 245–8.
3. Ken Jowitt, *New World Disorder: The Leninist Extinction*, Berkeley, 1991.
4. *New Left Review*, May–June 1992.
5. Signatories include Timothy Garton Ash, Norberto Bobbio, Pierre Bourdieu, Anthony Giddens, Simon Schama, Arthur Miller, and Jonathan Fanton, Director of the New School for Social Research in New York (where the Appeal was launched).
6. Some of Gellner's recent contributions include: "Nationalism and Politics in Eastern Europe," *Le Débat*, Jan–Feb, 1991 and *New Left Review*, Sept.–Oct. 1991; Introduction to *The Soviet Empire: Its Nations Speak Out: The First Congress of People's Deputies, Moscow, 25 May to 10 June 1989*, ed. O. Glebov and J. Crowfoot, Yverdon, 1989. Other interesting essays include Branka Magas, "Response to Ernest Gellner," *New Left Review*, Nov.–Dec. 1991; and Slavoj Zizek, "Republics of Gilead", *New Left Review*, Sept.–Oct. 1990.

SECTION VII

WAR, GENOCIDE, AND REPRESSION

War, genocide, and repression are three forms of violence carried out by agents of the state such as armies and police forces or by irregular forces such as militias and vigilantes that the state supports or tolerates. The most direct victims are targeted civilian populations, members of the armed forces, and in ways large and small, the social fabric of society. Highly militarized societies claim large percentages of the wealth created through people's labor either in the form of high taxes or neglect of social services. There may also be widespread censorship of information, the absence of fully open discussion and debate in education, the erosion of civil and personal liberties, indifference to the human pain and suffering of officially defined enemies, and skewed conceptions of gender roles, particularly in prevailing definitions of manhood (Herman and Chomsky 2002; Loewen 1995).

In "War Making and State Making as Organized Crime," Charles Tilly examines the role of war in European nation-state formation from 1500 to 1800. Tilly argues that war allowed rulers to consolidate power by expanding territories, weakening rivals, and offering protection to weaker allies, and in the process acquiring the political power to tax, conscript, and otherwise amass the resources to carry out these activities. There is a striking resemblance between Tilly's analysis of war as racketeering during the early modern period and contemporary U.S. foreign and military policy. After the Second World War, the United States organized a permanent war economy with large-scale military mobilization during peace and war alike and frequent wars and interventions so that the country has been at war as often as it has been at peace. Instilling fear of enemies such as communism and, more recently, terrorism and "weapons of mass destruction" and then offering protection from them has been basic to this policy and is consistent with Tilly's analysis.

Gabriel Kolko examines war and U.S. foreign policy post-1945. Based on his study of war in the twentieth century, Kolko argues that political leaders frequently make miscalculations concerning war (Kolko 1994). They typically underestimate the enemy, overestimate their own prospects, and ignore very important political dimensions of war, including its long-term consequences. Analyzing U.S. foreign policy in the post-war years, Kolko sees a pattern of blunders based on the mistaken beliefs that superior military technology guarantees victories and that communism, terrorism, and Islamic fundamentalism are causes of conflict rather than responses to Third World poverty and immiseration.

Tilly and Kolko imply that state power includes the power to frame, control, and direct public discourse about war by demonizing enemies, controlling the flow of information, and denying critics access to the public. This recalls Gramsci's earlier discussion of the state as an "educator," and the media section where it is argued that the media often serve as a pipeline for the delivery of official viewpoints. As such, these readings provide a clear illustration of how coercive, ideological, and economic power are interrelated.

Genocide, the mass murder of a people, has a very long history (Chalk and Jonassohn 1990). Genocides frequently accompany wars, although they can occur independently of them. In ancient and medieval times genocide often took the form of massacres of military and civilian populations of conquered city states and empires. Beginning with the sixteenth century, genocide accompanied the expansion of developing capitalist nations in Europe and their conquest of Third World continents (Smith 1999).

The twentieth century has been called the century of genocide. The century's first genocide was probably the mass killings of the Hereros and Namas in Namibia by German military forces (1904–7) (Bridgman 1981; Drechsler 1980; Silvester and Gewald 2003). This was a genocide of the colonial type. Most twentieth century genocides, however, have been of a different caste (Smith 1999). The Ottoman Turkish genocide of the Armenian people during World War I was followed by the genocide of European Jewish and Roma people by the Nazis.[1] The last quarter of the twentieth century delivered genocides in Cambodia, East Timor, Bosnia, and Rwanda. These victims were neither conquered nor unexploitable colonized peoples. They were long-established residents of countries, usually ethnic, religious, linguistic, racial, or political minorities defined as a scapegoat for larger political problems and targeted for mass death.

Genocide is now a crime under international law. The United Nations Convention on the Prevention and Punishment of Genocide was passed by the U.N. General Assembly in 1948, and it has since been ratified by nearly all of the world's nations, including the United States. U.S. ratification, however, was delayed for nearly four decades into the mid-1980s. Ward Churchill presents a detailed analysis of the Genocide Convention in the context of American politics and the peculiar and controversial circumstances under which it was approved.

Repression is best considered an aspect of the broader problem of social control that faces rulers in societies based on the exploitation of the many by the few. Societies' rulers are always radically outnumbered by everybody else, and this presents the problem of how to get the many to agree to the rules established by the few. The many "solutions" to this problem fall into two broad categories. The first is force. This includes unrestricted police and military force, elimination of civil and personal liberties, torture, political assassination, and murder to create a climate of terror. These techniques can be effective, even for lengthy periods of time, in controlling the behavior of all but a very small number willing to be martyred.

The problem posed by a heavy reliance on force as a mechanism of control is that the nature of the political system becomes obvious to all who are familiar with it. A far more effective system of control, as the readings in this book have demonstrated, is one in which power is not obvious to society's members. Why then do governments such as the United States employ force? The main answer to this complex question is that indirect means are not always effective. Some people, especially poor people, members of minority groups, the unemployed, and debtors, may receive so few rewards from the system that their loyalty to it is weak or nonexistent. In other cases, people may be forced to organize around issues of concern to them, for example, workers in unions, and these activities place them in direct conflict with employers and possibly police forces and hired goons (Huberman 1939; Smith 2003). Another possibility is that people will protest government- and corporate-initiated environmental degradation, racism, gender oppression, or war.

Repression manifests itself in the daily workings of a criminal justice system that targets poor and minority communities (Human Rights Watch 2000). Few writers are more acutely aware of this than Mike Davis in his analysis of greater Los Angeles. He finds a tragic cycle of more affluent voters consistently favoring tax cutting, which results in the neglect of poorer areas, leading to urban decay, high unemployment, and street crime to which the majority responds with gated communities and a draconian prison system.

The broad outlines of Davis's analysis of southern California can be applied to the country as a whole. In the United States, there are over 2 million people in prisons and jails. This is the highest rate of incarceration among industrial nations. Those imprisoned are overwhelmingly lower income whites and members of minority groups. The political nature of prison demographics becomes clear when we ask what would be the class makeup of prisoners if the war on drugs were eliminated and a war on tax fraud were instituted. Tax fraud is commonplace, and its perpetrators tend to be well educated, affluent, and white. With lots of federal government money, armies of tax police infiltrating affluent communities, politicians vowing to crack down on tax cheats, radio commentators attacking tax cheaters for destroying the moral fabric of America, and a compliant media, we would quickly have a very different kind of prison population. This will not happen, of course, because tax cheats have the political resources to prevent it whereas low-level drug criminals are powerless and easily targeted (Winslow 1999; Reiman 1995; Miller 1996).

Combined with mandatory sentencing, the war on drugs has served as a tool of repression with major political consequences.[2] Imprisonment generally deprives citizens of the right to vote. In the 2000 presidential election nearly 4 million Americans could not vote because they were serving a felony sentence or were previously convicted felons. This affects 2 percent of the population and 13 percent of African American males (Mauer and Chesney-Lind 2002: 51). In addition, a dozen states impose a lifetime loss of voting rights on convicted felons, a practice nonexistent in any other country in the world (Fellner and Mauer 1998). As a result, the racialized electoral system that Guinier spoke of earlier in the book, in which African Americans are effectively denied political representation in a winner-take-all electoral system, is reinforced by the racialized system of criminal justice in the United States.

Although Davis was writing prior to the September 11 attack, his observations on surveillance and social control are applicable to the "war on terrorism" (Cole and Dempsey 2002). The USA Patriot Act, for example, introduces unprecedented levels of government secrecy, weakens judicial oversight of the executive branch, and allows for extensive wiretapping, searches, sophisticated access to private records (banking, health, education, library, bookstore, etc.), and secret arrest and detention solely on the basis of country of origin, race, religion, and ethnicity (Foerstel and Kranich 2003). The racialized nature of social control noted by Davis, in which African Americans have been targeted as the enemy, has been extended much more broadly to potentially include anyone who is not defined as "white."

Notes

1. There were no successful war crimes tribunals for Turkish perpetrators of the Armenian Genocide. No less a figure than Adolf Hitler drew the logical conclusion in his August 22, 1939 speech to his officer corps on the eve of the German invasion of Poland:

> I have issued the command . . . that our war aim does not consist in reaching certain lines, but in the physical destruction of the enemy. Accordingly, I have placed my death-head formations in readiness—for the present only in the East—with orders to them to send to death mercilessly and without compassion, men, women, and children of Polish derivation and language. Only thus shall we gain the living space which we need. Who, after all, speaks today of the annihilation of the Armenians? (Bardakjian 1985: 43).

2. The impact of the war on drugs and heavier policing of minority neighborhoods looking for drug offenders can be seen in the racial composition of federal prisons. In 1926 the prison population was 79 percent white, 21 percent African American, and 1 percent other. By 1993 it had changed to 27 percent white, 55 percent African American, and 18 percent other (Miller 1996: 54–55).

References

Bardakjian, K. B. 1985. *Hitler and the Armenian Genocide.* Cambridge, MA: The Zoryan Institute.

Bridgman, Jon. 1981. *The Revolt of the Hereros.* Berkeley: University of California Press.

Chalk, Frank, and Kurt Jonassohn. 1990. *The History and Sociology of Genocide.* New Haven: Yale University Press.

Cole, David, and James X. Dempsey. 2002. *Terrorism and the Constitution: Sacrificing Civil Liberties in the Name of National Security.* New York: The New Press.

Drechsler, Horst. 1980. *Let Us Die Fighting: The Struggle of the Herero and Nama Against German Imperialism.* London: Zed Books.

Fellner, Jamie, and Marc Mauer. 1998. "Losing the Vote: The Impact of Felony Disenfranchisement Laws in the United States." New York: Human Rights Watch and the Sentencing Project.

Foerstel, Herb, and Nancy Kranich. 2003. "The USA Patriot Act: Uncensored." In *Censored 2004*, eds. Peter Phillips and Project Censored. New York: Seven Stories Press, 265–81.

Herman, Edward S., and Noam Chomsky. 2002. *Manufacturing Consent: The Political Economy of the Mass Media.* New York: Pantheon Books.

Huberman, Leo. 1939. *The Labor Spy Racket.* New York: Modern Age Books.

Human Rights Watch. 2000. "United States, Punishment and Prejudice: Racial Disparities in the War on Drugs." New York: Human Rights Watch.

Kolko, Gabriel. 1994. *Century of War: Politics, Conflicts, and Society since 1914.* New York: The New Press.

Loewen, James. 1995. *Lies My Teacher Told Me: Everything Your American History Teacher Got Wrong.* New York: The New Press.

Mauer, Mark, and Meda Chesney-Lind. 2002. *Invisible Punishment: The Collateral Consequences of Mass Imprisonment.* New York: The New Press.

Miller, Jerome. 1996. *Search and Destroy: African-American Males in the Criminal Justice System.* Cambridge: Cambridge University Press.

Reiman, Jeffrey. 1995. *The Rich Get Richer and the Poor Get Prison.* Needham Heights, MA: Allyn & Bacon.

Silvester, Jeremy, and Jan-Bart Gewald. 2003. *Words Cannot Be Found: German Colonial Rule in Namibia, An Annotated Report of the 1918 Blue Book.* Leiden: Brill.

Smith, Robert Michael. 2003. *From Blackjacks to Briefcases: A History of Commercialized Strikebreaking and Unionbusting in the United States.* Athens: Ohio University Press.

Smith, Roger W. 1999. "State Power and Genocidal Intent: On the Uses of Genocide in the Twentieth Century." In *Studies in Comparative Genocide,* eds. Levon Chorbajian and George Shirinian. New York: St. Martin's Press, 3–14.

Winslow, George. 1999. *Capital Crimes.* New York: Monthly Review Press.

WAR MAKING AND STATE MAKING AS ORGANIZED CRIME

CHARLES TILLY

If protection rackets represent organized crime at its smoothest, then war making and state making—quintessential protection rackets with the advantage of legitimacy—qualify as our largest examples of organized crime. Without branding all generals and statesmen as murderers or thieves, I want to urge the value of that analogy. At least for the European experience of the past few centuries, a portrait of war makers and state makers as coercive and self-seeking entrepreneurs bears a far greater resemblance to the facts than do its chief alternatives: the idea of a social contract, the idea of an open market in which operators of armies and states offer services to willing consumers, the idea of a society whose shared norms and expectations call forth a certain kind of government.

The reflections that follow merely illustrate the analogy of war making and state making with organized crime from a few hundred years of European experience and offer tentative arguments concerning principles of change and variation underlying the experience. My reflections grow from contemporary concerns: worries about the increasing destructiveness of war, the expanding role of great powers as suppliers of arms and military organization to poor countries, and the growing importance of military rule in those same countries. They spring from the hope that the European experience, properly understood, will help us to grasp what is happening today, perhaps even to do something about it.

. . . It will show us that coercive exploitation played a large part in the creation of the European states. It will show us that popular resistance to coercive exploitation forced would-be power holders to concede protection and constraints on their own action. It will therefore help us to eliminate faulty implicit comparisons between today's Third World and yesterday's Europe. That clarification will make it easier to understand exactly how today's world is different and what we therefore have to explain. It may even help us to explain the current looming presence of military organization and action throughout the world. Although that result would delight me, I do not promise anything so grand.

This essay, then, concerns the place of organized means of violence in the growth and change of those peculiar forms of government we call national states: relatively centralized, differentiated organizations the officials of which more or less successfully claim control over the chief concentrated means of violence within a population inhabiting a large, contiguous territory. . . .

. . . The . . . argument stresses the interdependence of war making and state making and the analogy between both of those processes and what, when less successful and smaller in scale, we call organized crime. War makes states, I shall claim. Banditry, piracy, gangland rivalry, policing, and war making all belong on the same continuum—that I shall claim as well. For the historically limited period in which national states were becoming the dominant organizations in Western countries, I shall also claim that mercantile capitalism and state making reinforced each other.

Double-Edged Protection

In contemporary American parlance, the word "protection" sounds two contrasting tones. One is comforting, the other ominous. With one tone, "protection" calls up images of the shelter against danger provided by a powerful friend, a large insurance policy, or a sturdy roof. With the other, it evokes the racket in which a local strong man forces merchants to pay tribute in order to avoid damage—damage the strong man himself threatens to deliver. The difference, to be sure, is a matter of degree: A hell-and-damnation priest is likely to collect contributions from his parishioners only to the extent that they believe his predictions of brimstone for infidels; our neighborhood mobster may actually be, as he claims to be, a brothel's best guarantee of operation free of police interference.

Which image the word "protection" brings to mind depends mainly on our assessment of the reality and externality of the threat. Someone who produces both the danger and, at a price, the shield against it is a racketeer. Someone who provides a needed shield but has little control over the danger's appearance qualifies as a legitimate protector, especially if his price is no higher than his competitors'. Someone who supplies reliable, low-priced shielding both from local racketeers and from outside marauders makes the best offer of all.

Apologists for particular governments and for government in general commonly argue, precisely, that they offer protection from local and external violence. They claim that the prices they charge barely cover the costs of protection. They call people who complain about the price of protection "anarchists," "subversives," or both at once. But consider the definition of a racketeer as someone who creates a threat and then charges for its reduction. Governments' provision of protection, by this standard, often qualifies as racketeering. To the extent that the threats against which a given government protects its citizens are imaginary or are consequences of its own activities, the government has organized a protection racket. Since governments themselves commonly simulate, stimulate, or even fabricate threats of external war and since the repressive and extractive activities of governments often constitute the latest current threats to the livelihoods of their own citizens, many governments operate in essentially the same ways as racketeers. There is, of course, a difference: Racketeers, by the conventional definition, operate without the sanctity of governments.

How do racketeer governments themselves acquire authority? As a question of fact and of ethics, that is one of the oldest conundrums of political analysis. Back to Machiavelli and Hobbes, nevertheless, political observers have recognized that, whatever else they do, governments organize and, wherever possible, monopolize violence. It matters little whether we take violence in a narrow sense, such as damage to persons and objects, or in a broad sense, such as violation of people's desires and interests; by either criterion, governments stand out from other organizations by their tendency to monopolize the concentrated means of violence. The distinction between "legitimate" and "illegitimate" force, furthermore, makes no difference to the fact. If we take legitimacy to depend on conformity to an abstract principle or on the assent of the governed (or both at once), these conditions may serve to justify, perhaps even to explain, the tendency to monopolize force; they do not contradict the fact.

In any case, Arthur Stinchcombe's agreeably cynical treatment of legitimacy serves the purposes of political analysis much more efficiently. Legitimacy, according to Stinchcombe, depends rather little on abstract principle or assent of the governed: "The person *over whom power is exercised* is not usually as important as *other power-holders*."[1] Legitimacy is the probability that other authorities will act to confirm the decisions of a given authority. Other authorities, I would add, are much more likely to confirm the decisions of a challenged authority that controls substantial force; not only fear of retaliation, but also desire to maintain a stable environment recommend that general rule. The rule underscores the importance of the authority's monopoly of force. A tendency to monopolize the means of violence makes a government's claim to provide protection, in either the comforting or the ominous sense of the word, more credible and more difficult to resist.

Frank recognition of the central place of force in governmental activity does not require us to believe that governmental authority rests "only" or "ultimately" on the threat of violence. Nor does it entail the assumption that a government's only service is protection. Even when a government's use of force imposes a large cost, some people may well decide that the government's other services outbalance the costs of acceding to its monopoly of violence. Recognition of the centrality of force opens the way to an understanding of the growth and change of governmental forms.

Here is a preview of the most general argument: Power holders' pursuit of war involved them willy-nilly in the extraction of resources for war making from the populations over which they had control and in the promotion of capital accumulation by those who could help them borrow and buy. War making, extraction, and capital accumulation interacted to shape European state making. Power holders did not undertake those three momentous activities with the intention of creating national states—centralized, differentiated, autonomous, extensive political organizations. Nor did they ordinarily foresee that national states would emerge from war making, extraction, and capital accumulation.

Instead, the people who controlled European states and states in the making warred in order to check or overcome their competitors and thus to enjoy the advantages of power within a secure or expanding territory. To make more effective war, they attempted to locate more capital. In the short run, they might acquire that capital by conquest, by selling off their assets, or by coercing or dispossessing accumulators of capital. In the long run, the quest inevitably involved them in establishing regular access to capitalists who could supply and arrange credit and in imposing one form of regular taxation or another on the people and activities within their spheres of control.

As the process continued, state makers developed a durable interest in promoting the accumulation of capital, sometimes in the guise of direct return to their own enterprises. Variations in the difficulty of collecting taxes, in the expense of the particular kind of armed force adopted, in the amount of war making required to hold off competitors, and so on resulted in the principal variations in the forms of European states. It all began with the effort to monopolize the means of violence within a delimited territory adjacent to a power holder's base.

Violence and Government

What distinguished the violence produced by states from the violence delivered by anyone else? In the long run, enough to make the division between "legitimate" and "illegitimate" force credible. Eventually, the personnel of states purveyed violence on a larger scale, more effectively, more efficiently, with wider assent from their subject populations, and with readier collaboration from neighboring authorities than did the personnel of other organizations. But it took a long time for that series of distinctions to become established. Early in the state-making process, many parties shared the right to use violence, the practice of using it routinely to accomplish their ends, or both at once. The continuum ran from bandits and pirates to kings via tax collectors, regional power holders, and professional soldiers.

The uncertain, elastic line between "legitimate" and "illegitimate" violence appeared in the upper reaches of power. Early in the state-making process, many parties shared the right to use violence, its actual employment, or both at once. The long love–hate affair between aspiring state makers and pirates or bandits illustrates the division. "Behind piracy on the seas acted cities and city states," writes Fernand Braudel of the sixteenth century. "Behind banditry, that terrestrial piracy, appeared the continual aid of lords."[2] In times of war, indeed, the managers of full-fledged states often commissioned privateers, hired sometime bandits to raid their enemies, and encouraged their regular troops to take booty. In royal service, soldiers and sailors were often expected to provide for themselves by preying on the civilian population: commandeering, raping, looting, taking prizes. When demobilized, they commonly continued the same practices, but without the same royal protection; demobilized ships became pirate vessels, demobilized troops bandits.

It also worked the other way: A king's best source of armed supporters was sometimes the world of outlaws. Robin Hood's conversion to royal archer may be a myth, but the myth records a practice. The distinctions between "legitimate" and "illegitimate" users of violence came clear only very slowly, in the process during which the state's armed forces became relatively unified and permanent.

Up to that point, as Braudel says, maritime cities and terrestrial lords commonly offered protection, or even sponsorship, to freebooters. Many lords who did not pretend to be kings, furthermore, successfully claimed the right to levy troops and maintain their own armed retainers. Without calling on some of those lords to bring their armies with them, no king could fight a war; yet the same armed lords constituted the king's rivals and opponents, his enemies' potential allies. For that reason, before the seventeenth century, regencies for child sovereigns reliably produced civil wars. For the same reason, disarming the great stood high on the agenda of every would-be state maker.

■ ■ ■ ■

By the later eighteenth century, through most of Europe, monarchs controlled permanent, professional military forces that rivaled those of their neighbors and far exceeded any other organized armed force within their own territories. The state's monopoly of large-scale violence was turning from theory to reality.

The elimination of local rivals, however, posed a serious problem. Beyond the scale of a small city-state, no monarch could govern a population with his armed force alone, nor could any monarch afford to create a professional staff large and strong enough to reach from him to the ordinary citizen. Before quite recently, no European government approached the completeness of articulation from top to bottom achieved by imperial China. Even the Roman Empire did not come close. In one way or another, every European government before the French Revolution relied on indirect rule via local magnates. The magnates collaborated with the government without becoming officials in any strong sense of the term, had some access to government-backed force, and exercised wide discretion within their own territories: junkers, justices of the peace, lords. Yet the same magnates were potential rivals, possible allies of a rebellious people.

Eventually, European governments reduced their reliance on indirect rule by means of two expensive but effective strategies: (*a*) extending their officialdom to the local community and (*b*) encouraging the creation of police forces that were subordinate to the government rather than to individual patrons, distinct from war-making forces, and therefore less useful as the tools of dissident magnates. In between, however, the builders of national power all played a mixed strategy: eliminating, subjugating, dividing, conquering, cajoling, buying as the occasions presented themselves. The buying manifested itself in exemptions from taxation, creations of honorific offices, the establishment of claims on the national treasury, and a variety of other devices that made a magnate's welfare dependent on the maintenance of the existing structure of power. In the long run, it all came down to massive pacification and monopolization of the means of coercion.

■ ■ ■ ■

What Do States Do?

. . . Under the general heading of organized violence, the agents of states characteristically carry on four different activities:

1. War making: Eliminating or neutralizing their own rivals outside the territories in which they have clear and continuous priority as wielders of force
2. State making: Eliminating or neutralizing their rivals inside those territories
3. Protection: Eliminating or neutralizing the enemies of their clients
4. Extraction: Acquiring the means of carrying out the first three activities—war making, state making, and protection

■ ■ ■ ■

War making, state making, protection, and extraction each take a number of forms. Extraction, for instance, ranges from outright plunder to regular tribute to bureaucratized taxation. Yet all four depend on the state's tendency to monopolize the concentrated means of coercion. From the perspectives of those who dominate the state, each of them—if carried on effectively—generally reinforces the others. Thus, a state that successfully eradicates its internal rivals strengthens its ability to extract resources, to wage war, and to protect its chief supporters. In the earlier European experience, broadly speaking, those supporters were typically landlords, armed retainers of the monarch, and churchmen.

Each of the major uses of violence produced characteristic forms of organization. War making yielded armies, navies, and supporting services. State making produced durable instruments of surveillance and control within the territory. Protection relied on the organization of war making and state making but added to it an apparatus by which the protected called forth the protection that was their due, notably through courts and representative assemblies. Extraction brought fiscal and accounting structures into being. The organization and deployment of violence themselves account for much of the characteristic structure of European states.

The general rule seems to have operated like this: The more costly the activity, all other things being equal, the greater was the organizational residue. To the extent, for example, that a given government invested in large standing armies—a very costly, if effective, means of war making—the bureaucracy created to service the army was likely to become bulky. Furthermore, a government building a standing army while controlling a small population was likely to incur greater costs, and therefore to build a bulkier structure, than a government within a populous country. Brandenburg–Prussia was the classic case of high cost for available resources. The Prussian effort to build an army matching those of its larger Continental neighbors created an immense structure; it militarized and bureaucratized much of German social life.

In the case of extraction, the smaller the pool of resources and the less commercialized the economy, other things being equal, the more difficult was the work of extracting resources to sustain war and other governmental activities; hence, the more extensive was the fiscal apparatus. England illustrated the corollary of that proposition, with a relatively large and commercialized pool of resources drawn on by a relatively small fiscal apparatus. As Gabriel Ardant has argued, the choice of fiscal strategy probably made an additional difference. On the whole, taxes on land were expensive to collect as compared with taxes on trade, especially large flows of trade past easily controlled checkpoints. Its position astride the entrance to the Baltic gave Denmark an extraordinary opportunity to profit from customs revenues.

With respect to state making (in the narrow sense of eliminating or neutralizing the local rivals of the people who controlled the state), a territory populated by great landlords or by distinct religious groups generally imposed larger costs on a conqueror than one of fragmented power or homogeneous culture. This time, fragmented and homogeneous Sweden, with its relatively small but effective apparatus of control, illustrates the corollary.

Finally, the cost of protection (in the sense of eliminating or neutralizing the enemies of the state makers' clients) mounted with the range over which that protection extended. Portugal's effort to bar the Mediterranean to its merchants' competitors in the spice trade provides a textbook case of an unsuccessful protection effort that nonetheless built up a massive structure.

Thus, the sheer size of the government varied directly with the effort devoted to extraction, state making, protection, and, especially, war making but inversely with the commercialization of the economy and the extent of the resource base. What is more, the relative bulk of different features of the government varied with the cost/resource ratios of extraction, state making, protection, and war making. . . .

■ ■ ■ ■

Clearly, war making, extraction, state making, and protection were interdependent. . . . In an idealized sequence, a great lord made war so effectively as to become dominant in a substantial territory, but that war making led to increased extraction of the means of war—men, arms, food, lodging, transportation, supplies, and/or the money to buy them—from the population within that territory. The building up of war-making capacity likewise increased the capacity to extract. The very activity of extraction, if successful, entailed the elimination, neutralization, or cooptation of the great lord's local rivals; thus, it led to state making. As a byproduct, it created organization in the form of tax-collection agencies, police forces, courts, exchequers, account keepers; thus it again led to state making. To a lesser extent, war making likewise led to state making through the expansion of military organization itself, as a standing army, war industries, supporting bureaucracies, and (rather later) schools grew up within the state apparatus. All of these structures checked potential rivals and opponents. In the course of making war, extracting resources, and building up the state apparatus, the managers of states formed alliances with specific social classes. The members of those classes loaned resources, provided technical services, or helped ensure the compliance of the rest of the population, all in return for a measure of protection against their own rivals and enemies. As a result of these multiple strategic choices, a distinctive state apparatus grew up within each major section of Europe.

How States Formed

This analysis, if correct, has two strong implications for the development of national states. First, popular resistance to war making and state making made a difference. When ordinary people resisted vigorously, authorities made concessions: guarantees of rights, representative institutions, courts of appeal. Those concessions, in their turn, constrained the later paths of war making and state making. To be sure, alliances with fragments of the ruling class greatly increased the effects of popular action; the broad mobilization of gentry against Charles I helped give the English Revolution of 1640 a far greater impact on political institutions than did any of the multiple rebellions during the Tudor era.

Second, the relative balance among war making, protection, extraction, and state making significantly affected the organization of the states that emerged from the four activities. To the extent that war making went on with relatively little extraction, protection, and state making, for example, military forces ended up playing a larger and more autonomous part in national politics. Spain is perhaps the best European example. To the extent that protection, as in Venice or Holland, prevailed over war making, extraction, and state making, oligarchies of the protected classes tended to dominate subsequent national politics. From the relative predominance of state making sprang the disproportionate elaboration of policing and surveillance; the Papal States illustrate that extreme. Before the twentieth century, the range of viable imbalances was fairly small. Any state that failed, to put considerable effort into war making was likely to disappear. As the twentieth century wore on, however, it became increasingly common for one state to lend, give, or sell war-making means to another; in those cases, the recipient state could put a disproportionate effort into extraction, protection, and/or state making and yet survive. In our own time, clients of the United States and the Soviet Union provide numerous examples.

This simplified model, however, neglects the external relations that shaped every national state. Early in the process, the distinction between "internal" and "external" remained as unclear as the distinction between state power and the power accruing to lords allied with the state. Later, three interlocking influences connected any given national state to the European network of states. First, there were the flows of resources in the form of loans and supplies, especially loans and supplies devoted to war making. Second, there was the competition among states for hegemony in disputed territories, which stimulated war making and temporarily erased the distinctions among war making, state making, and extraction. Third, there was the intermittent creation of coalitions of states that temporarily combined their efforts to force a given state into a certain form and position within the international network. The war-making coalition is one example, but the peace-making coalition played an even more crucial part: From 1648, if not before, at the ends of wars all effective European states coalesced temporarily to bargain over the boundaries and rulers of the recent belligerents. From that point on, periods of major reorganization of the European state system came in spurts, at the settlement of widespread wars. From each large war, in general, emerged fewer national states than had entered it.

War as International Relations

In these circumstances, war became the normal condition of the international system of states and the normal means of defending or enhancing a position within the system. Why war? No simple answer will do; war as a potent means served more than one end. But surely part of the answer goes back to the central mechanisms of state making: The very logic by which a local lord extended or defended the perimeter within which he monopolized the means of violence, and thereby increased his return from tribute, continued on a larger scale into the logic of war. Early in the process, external and internal rivals overlapped to a large degree. Only the establishment of large perimeters of control within which great lords had checked their rivals sharpened the line between internal and external. . . .

■ ■ ■ ■

If we allow that fragile distinction between "internal" and "external" state-making processes, then we might schematize the history of European state making as three stages (*a*) The differential success of some power holders in "external" struggles establishes the difference between an "internal" and an "external" arena for the deployment of force; (*b*) "external" competition generates "internal" state making; (*c*) "external" compacts among states influence the form and locus of particular states ever more powerfully. In this perspective, state-certifying organizations such as the League of Nations and the United Nations simply extended the European-based process to the world as a whole. Whether forced or voluntary, bloody or peaceful, decolonization simply completed that process by which existing states leagued to create new ones.

The extension of the Europe-based state-making process to the rest of the world, however, did not result in the creation of states in the strict European image. Broadly speaking, internal struggles such as the checking of great regional lords and the imposition of taxation on peasant villages produced important organizational features of European states: the relative subordination of military power to civilian control, the extensive bureaucracy of fiscal surveillance, the representation of wronged interests via petition and parliament. On the whole, states elsewhere developed differently. The most telling feature of that difference appears in military organization. European states built up their military apparatuses through sustained struggles with their subject populations and by means of selective extension of protection to different classes within those populations. The agreements on protection constrained the rulers themselves making them vulnerable to courts, to assemblies, to withdrawals of credit services, and expertise.

To a larger degree, states that have come into being recently through decolonization or through reallocations of territory by dominant states have acquired their military organization from outside, without the same internal forging of mutual constraints between rulers and ruled. To the extent that outside states continue to supply military goods and expertise in return for commodities, military alliance or both, the new states harbor powerful, unconstrained organizations that easily overshadow all other organizations within their territories. To the extent that outside states guarantee their boundaries, the managers of those military organizations exercise extraordinary power within them. The advantages of military power become enormous, the incentives to seize power over the state as a whole by means of that advantage very strong. Despite the great place that war making occupied in the making of European states, the old national states of Europe almost never experienced the great disproportion between military organization and all other forms of organization that seems the fate of client states throughout the contemporary world. A century ago, Europeans might have congratulated themselves on the spread of civil government throughout the world. In our own time, the analogy between war making and state making, on the one hand, and organized crime, on the other, is becoming tragically apt.

Notes

1. Arthur L. Stinchcombe, *Constructing Social Theories* (New York: Harcourt, Brace & World, 1968), p. 150; italics in the original.
2. Fernand Braudel, *La Méditerranée et le monde méditerranéen à l'époque de Philippe II* (Paris: Armand Colin, 1966), vol. 2, pp. 88–89.

THE MAKING OF AMERICAN FOREIGN POLICY: SUCCESSES, AND FAILURES

GABRIEL KOLKO

The more ambitious wars are, the greater the likelihood that they will go awry. Wars usually become nightmares that last far longer than expected, and their ultimate consequences can rarely be predicted. These monumental legacies of failure have shaped the past century profoundly and have altered decisively the existence of countless millions: destroyed their lives, driven them into exile, or traumatized what might have been the joys and cares of normal existence. Innumerable nations that embarked on vainglorious missions to use their military power to attain political goals inflicted unimaginable suffering on other countries but also on their own people, thereby condemning their own destinies: some to social and political disorder or even to revolutions, to the decline of power and prestige, and to fates that were far worse than had they done nothing. Empires have risen, but they have also fallen. The strongest argument against one nation interfering with another does not have to be deduced from any doctrine, moral or otherwise; it is found by looking honestly at the history of the past centuries.[1]

False Expectations: The Illusions of War

At the inception of the twenty-first century, even as inherited conventional wisdom has guided U.S. foreign policy, the horrors of the past are being reenacted. The same policies that in varying degrees have produced disasters for the United States are still considered the only way to relate to the continuous and growing problems of a world that was already far too complex for it to manage fifty years ago. With the rapid diffusion of ever deadlier weapons over the past decade, America is today even less able to control events; and rather than producing greater stability, the disintegration of the Communist orbit has led to a proliferation of new and usually unmanageable crises both within and between dozens of nations.

At the end of the nineteenth century there were many causes of militarism, above all in those nations that started wars, but various forms of jingoism and nationalism permeated all of the states that went to war in 1914 and again in 1939. Intellectualized doctrines of power and Darwinian biological theory were the rule rather than the exception, used to justify the colonialism of Great Britain, France, the United States, Japan, and other nations that made their foreign policies their preoccupation. Men of power everywhere, ranging from Theodore Roosevelt in the United States to most of Japan's and Germany's leaders, shared the belief that destiny had ordained them for the noble calling of armed combat. A romantic cult of action and physical fitness produced an aristocratic warrior ethos, and such notions were transnational, with morale—bravery—alleged to be the decisive element in warfare. All the political and military leaders of the belligerent nations in 1914 had read with great respect the writings of Carl von Clausewitz, a German whose pseudo-scientific theories of strategy and war gave warriors a rationale for their power; Charles Darwin, an Englishman whose notions of the survival of the fittest reinforced their ambitions; and the American Alfred Thayer Mahan, the leading theorist of naval expansion and the acquisition of foreign bases. Such romanticism was surely less important than geopolitics, domestic politics, or economics, but it persisted after 1918, when the Italians and Japanese especially shared this military consensus. What they also all held in common was the conviction that wars would be brief and fought in a strategically convenient fashion that conformed to their equipment, budgets, and priorities. In its own way, war was supposed to be rational, not catastrophic.

This persistent illusion was a grave error, but scarcely the only one. The criterion of rationality for evaluating policies that lead to war is ultimately socially conditioned, and in most nations both generals and civilians share it and produce predictably common optimistic prognoses. In every country, only a finite range of views receive a hearing in policy-making circles, and ambitious individuals fully understand the boundaries of permissible analyses. Indeed, with the growing importance of simulated war games and strategic doctrines, civilian intellectuals have often been more bellicose than officers. It is precisely because of the growing disparity between the increasingly complex realities of modern warfare and strategic estimates, and the decision-making structures that produce them, that wars increasingly create unanticipated shocks, not just military but especially political. Since the beginning of the last century, only wars have tested to their very foundations the stability of existing social systems, and communism, fascism, and Nazism would certainly not have triumphed without the events of 1914–18 to foster them.

It was precisely the optimistic illusion of wars as relatively short, even clinical events that made possible the widespread conviction that a nation's "credibility" was at stake if it refused to fight or come to the defense of its alliance members. For the nations that went to war in 1914, this readiness to use force was an article of faith; credibility was crucial to Washington's repeatedly escalating the war in Vietnam. Since such alliances have flourished, the destiny of major powers has frequently depended on the behavior and role of often fragile allied states. Coalition diplomacy and the logic of credibility have together led to wars. After 1947 the United States created the Truman Doctrine and amplified credibility to add the "domino theory" to its strategic doctrines, believing that its refusal to become involved in a relatively minor nation would lead to a succession of other and larger defeats in a region. This viewpoint was crucial in leading it into the war in Vietnam.

There have been significant differences in the ways that nations have responded to foreign policy crises, but they have also shared astonishingly similar premises and perceptions. These common assumptions made it possible for states to embark on wars, oblivious of the costs in blood, time, and property that their astonishingly adventurist and often casual policies would demand. Those whose decisions shape the world have learned very little—indeed virtually nothing—from the past century of myopia and repeated failures. We live, as never before, with the risk of yet more wars, perhaps for a hundred years, as Pentagon intellectuals have predicted.

All wars in the past century began with the men who initiated them substituting their delusions, in which domestic political interests and personal ambitions often played a great part, for realistic evaluations of the titanic demands and consequences that modern warfare invariably imposes. They had neither the analytic clarity nor the honesty for such realism, and as careerists they often rejected pessimistic assessments of the risks that their intelligence organizations frequently produced. There were, obviously, many differences among these leaders, but with the possible exception of the Japanese in 1941, the men who led the major nations all shared a common consensus that they would emerge victorious from military conflicts. In a purely narrow technical sense, in the case of the Second World War, Roosevelt and Churchill were correct, and Nazism and Japanese imperialism were destroyed. But like those who so blithely entered the First World War, they refused to calculate the ultimate material and political costs that wars impose on themselves, their allies, or their enemies, and the spread of communism to Eastern Europe and a large part of Asia meant that politically the war was a disaster for them too. Military struggles have continuously turned out very differently than leaders imagined. They have been oblivious of surprises and have harbored false expectations; wars almost never conform to the convenient assumptions about how long conflicts will last and their decisive political consequences. The result was a twentieth century in which political upheavals were dominant: communism, fascism in various forms, and authoritarianism.

This persistent refusal to face reality's challenges and adjust foreign and military policies to them, to admit frankly that conventional wisdom and policies undermined the nation's security and long-term interests, has been virtually universal. Those who become the leaders of states are ultimately conformists on most crucial issues, and individuals who evaluate information in a rational manner—and therefore frequently criticize traditional premises—are weeded out early in their careers. The socialization process in most, even all nations eliminates such people, and ambitious ones comprehend full well the analytic and political boundaries upon which their future careers depend. Every large nation will have bureaucratic differences on implementing policies, but there is consensus on the policies themselves—a consensus that makes repeated errors increasingly likely. Leaders in every nation expect loyalty from potential decision makers, and except in rare cases, they get it. Political systems are not constructed to obtain and confront unpleasant facts, and they have few safeguards against irrational behavior. This myopia is increasingly dangerous.

The Roots of American Failure

Until the successful Soviet development of an atomic bomb in August 1949, the United States had complete confidence in its technology and its ability to maintain a relatively modest military budget of about $15 billion annually. The Truman administration believed, for good reason, that a war with the USSR was highly unlikely because Stalin's military and economic power was still feeble. But when the U.S. monopoly on the atomic bomb ended, the administration embarked on a far-reaching review of U.S. military power, and in April 1950 it decided to build a hydrogen bomb and to increase military spending to three to four times the fiscal 1949 outlay. What it could not predict was wars beginning in places that Moscow did not control. In 1949 the Communists took power in China, which was purely the consequence of the profound impact of Japan and the Second World War on that country. Stalin mistrusted Mao Tse-tung from the inception, and China was to prove—as Titoism had in Yugoslavia in 1948—that world communism was inherently a fissiparous, divided movement, united in little more than name. Washington over the next decade partially accepted this obvious reality, but it suited its propaganda for most of the 1950s to describe communism as entirely Moscow-controlled.

But while America's priorities strongly emphasized Europe, it also declared in January 1950 that Communist governments could not come to power in the remainder of Asia. This meant a much more active role in the Philippines, where a relatively small Communist insurgency was in progress. It also meant helping the French with arms and money to defeat the much more formidable Communist forces in Indochina—a decision whose ultimate consequences were far greater than American decision makers could imagine. When the North Korean army crossed the thirty-eighth parallel at the end of June 1950 the United States was already becoming involved in Asia even though it had no desire to sacrifice its Europe-first priorities and its emphasis on developing military power suited for warfare against modern concentrated military and urban targets. What it never acknowledged was that the outbreak of conflict anywhere in the world frequently imposed priorities upon it. In this fundamental sense, the United States has never been in full control of its foreign policy. But it has neither acknowledged nor admitted this fact.

America's leaders utterly failed to comprehend the Korean War's potential military costs or its political and economic repercussions at home. From its inception it relied on air power and artillery—the intensive use of munitions. While much of the North's infrastructure was destroyed, the war ended in mid-1953 very close to the thirty-eighth parallel. The lavish use of firepower—three million tons, 43 percent of the tonnage the United States utilized in all of World War II—did not produce military victory. The North Koreans, joined by the Chinese at the end of 1950, adjusted their tactics to neutralize incredibly destructive and expensive technology and firepower. Roughly two million civilians died and half the southern population lost their homes or became refugees; killed and wounded soldiers on both sides were also about two million. The war ended in a stalemate, and the Republicans came to power in 1953 largely on a pledge to end the war.

The United States could easily get into wars, but its weaponry was all too fallible. Its military and political premises were gravely unrealistic. Its ally in the South, Syngman Rhee, was completely uncontrollable—at one point Washington even considered assassinating him. The credibility of its military power and technology was very much in doubt because it could not defeat enemies who decentralized their forces and utilized the weather and time to foil it; there was a cheap equivalent to its firepower. A war that the Americans intended to be short and limited lasted almost as long as World War II, only to end inconclusively. The United States still could not acknowledge the obvious reality, or the limits of high technology. It also depended on client regimes, which greatly complicated its efforts, and after its initial jingoism the American public tired of the war and proved inconstant, which in politics is fatal.

The Eisenhower administration and its successors were acutely aware of the potential inflationary impact of excessive military budgets, since inflation was one of the Korean War's many consequences. To a critical extent, its desire to restrain spending colored profoundly its definition of the challenges it confronted and the responses they demanded. Massive nuclear retaliation became the answer to Soviet power, but after the Korean experience it also realized that wars outside of Europe might absorb too large a proportion of American forces and that it needed a "flexible response" to Communist insurgencies and threats elsewhere. This took various forms. Military aid and training under the Eisenhower administration was quadrupled and the Southeast Asia Treaty Organization (SEATO) was created. In effect, the United States chose to respond to the Korean debacle by depending on proxies to do most of the fighting, tying its credibility to their destinies in ways whose implications it scarcely appreciated at the time. Under the Truman administration the CIA's clandestine services had expanded twenty times, to about six thousand people. Under Eisenhower another two thousand were added to it. The CIA became one of the decisive instruments of American foreign policy, especially in the Third World. Covert warfare was much less onerous, and Washington now had what it termed "plausible deniability" in its attempts to shape the future of hapless nations. Above all, it had flexibility and alternatives to using conventional force in confronting political developments of which it disapproved.[2]

Covert warfare and similar adaptations seemed to produce great successes, first in Iran in 1953 and in Guatemala in 1954, and then in numerous other places. It seemed to be an uncomplicated and inexpensive way for the United States to replace regimes and control the destinies of nations. After 1955 the United States also began to intimidate those it disapproved of by "showing the flag" much more frequently, sending its boats and manpower to various nations to make certain that local political and military instability did not produce outcomes Washington deemed dangerous. There were 215 such instances of "force without war" during 1946–75. Some were minor, but others were major and potentially dangerous, and the United States exhibited its power virtually everywhere.[3] Lebanon in 1958, the Dominican Republic in 1961–66, Jordan in 1970, and yet other examples I deal with later: these victories restored the confidence that America's leaders had lost after the Korean stalemate. By and large, such interventions guaranteed that the Third World's political evolution would not clash with U.S. interests, tip ping the balance not merely away from communism but in favor of conservative and often reactionary regimes both unable and unwilling to meet their peoples' material and political needs. A large number of them violated their citizens' human rights, ranging from torture and imprisonment to press censorship, and many were recipients of U.S. arms and police and military training missions, which became ubiquitous after the early 1950s. To a critical extent, successive Washington administrations made state-sponsored terrorism possible.

The United States after 1947 attempted to guide and control a very large part of the change that occurred throughout the world, and a significant part of what is wrong with it today is the result of America's interventions. Others have paid for their consequences, and now the United States too must pay.

The Korean War also intensified the United States' dependence on imports of raw materials, primarily from the Third World. All its leaders were conscious of the importance of these imports, an awareness that constantly influenced foreign policy decisions. Only 5 percent of its total consumption of metals, excluding gold and iron, was imported in the 1920s, but 38 percent was imported from 1940–49, and 48 percent in the following decade. America's growth was linked to access to absolutely essential imports, the Western Hemisphere being its single largest supplier of vital metals, but the Middle East was crucial for petroleum.

What began as part of an effort to make its military responses both cheaper and more flexible, to resolve the limits and contradictions of its strategic doctrines, also made it possible for the United States to involve itself in many more potentially dangerous situations. It thereby became far more dependent on the wisdom and fate of its proxies, such as Ngo Dinh Diem in South Vietnam after 1954 and the shah in Iran from 1953 to 1979. But the dictators' soldiers and guns could not stabilize the politics of these and innumerable other places. What were intended to be small decisions in fact often became incremental errors that pushed Washington in unanticipated and unintended directions, and they were eventually to prove decisive to America's preoccupations and interests—in Southeast Asia and ultimately also in the Middle East. The result was that the United States lost more control over its military and foreign policy. There were many successes for it, some of which we know little about because they were covert; but the failures eventually led it to escalate its involvement in various nations to avert the appearance of impotence.

Today we live under the shadow of these failures.

The Vietnam War and America's Strategic Dilemma[4]

Vietnam was to become the ultimate example of how infinitely complex social realities in the Third World had become, and of the danger to the United States in its fatal dependence on venal rulers. It exposed the fragility of the foundations on which American foreign policy was based. Initially Washington responded to the events in Vietnam in the larger context of its ongoing search for a decisive strategy relevant for the entire Third World. The efficacy of limited war, its new weapons technology, its credibility, the domino theory, political rivalries and ambitions, and much else became tangled in a skein of interrelated causes. It was virtually preordained that the United States would somewhere attempt to confirm its credibility after the crucial failures it had suffered in Korea, Cuba, and elsewhere. Vietnam was to become the epitome of the postwar crisis in American power and ambition, a testimony to its inability to articulate a successful military and political basis for establishing a global socioeconomic environment congenial to its interests and desires.

The causal elements of the crisis that existed in Vietnam existed in many other countries, and still do. There was a grossly inequitable land distribution, and a corrupt leader whom the United States selected and who ruled with an iron hand. After nine years with Diem the CIA aided in his assassination, but there was no alternative to repeated American military escalation, and in the end approximately two million U.S. military personnel served there. The cycle of corruption and instability, the massive use of fifteen million tons of munitions, and the conflict's intensity and length, produced the longest war and the most important defeat in American history. High mobility and firepower, the latest military concepts, virtually unlimited expenses—all were in vain. There were approximately one million deaths, at least half of the people were driven from their homes, and far more military aid—sophisticated aviation and equipment—was given to its proxies than they knew how to utilize. By 1968 the CIA and other official experts warned policy makers in Washington that the war was going badly and victory might elude them. The American public grew weary and critical of the war, Congress eventually responded to this mood, and the soldiers they sent were demoralized to an extent that had no precedent. In April 1975 the war ended in a total, ignominious disaster for the United States, largely because it had depended on politically shrewd but venal, corrupt proxies.

The crisis in America's foreign and military strategy that the Vietnam War created was matched by the grave divisions in the Communist world and the ultimate demise of most of these regimes. But while the fall of communism gave a momentary breathing spell to the United States, in the end it ushered in a far more complex and unstable world, the grave consequences of which we are now experiencing. The CIA had repeatedly argued that the Soviet leaders feared an American nuclear attack (many British leaders also thought a preemptive American strike a very real possibility), and that while they were developing a modern arsenal only as a deterrent, the Soviet leaders believed that they would prevail by nonmilitary means or not at all. As Marxists they were certain that the ineluctable march of history was on their side. But their power over China—which America's leaders for well over a decade argued publicly was absolute—was far more nominal than real, and by the early 1960s they were deadly enemies. In Eastern Europe the Soviet influence withered away more gradually, save for the open break with Yugoslavia in 1948. The USSR simply could not afford to both build a modern army and shower economic and military aid abroad. Moscow wasted immense sums in nations where it had very little, if any, political influence. And while Soviet power was disintegrating, significant parts of the Third World were being economically and demographically traumatized. The single most important cause for this shock was that export-oriented, capital-intensive agriculture drove peasants off the land and into cities. The political reaction to it took many forms, but, especially in Central America, they were leftist only in the broad sense of that term.

In brief, large parts of the Third World were being destabilized economically even as communism was disintegrating and eventually disappearing as a historical force. The United States chose to respond to the inevitable social and political consequences of such objective trends as growing challenges, but it also intervened actively elsewhere for a variety of reasons certain to win it enemies. It supported Pakistan in its confrontation with India over the Bangladesh secession only because it was an old ally employing American weapons; in fact, American leaders also believed the secessionists had good reasons for wanting independence. Nixon supported Ferdinand Marcos's declaration of martial law in the Philippines in the fall of 1972. In Angola in 1975 Kissinger ignored the advice of his advisers, and the CIA supported movements about which it knew very little because he felt that after the Vietnam humiliation it was more essential than ever to show that the United States still had power—its "credibility" required action for its own sake. To this day Angola remains war-torn. The deaths and injuries since the conflict began run well over a hundred thousand, and over one-third of the population has been displaced at some time and become refugees. There were innumerable other instances where the United States sought only to confirm the credibility of its power, intervening everywhere but especially giving its support and loyalty to Third World tyrants and corruptionists who acted as faithful proxies. This fixation—and blindness in estimating the long-term consequences of its actions—grew as Soviet power, which had inhibited America in some places, was weakening gravely.

The Structural Causes of Third World Crises

Poverty is one of the crucial root causes of every form of political instability, from religious fundamentalism to revolutionary movements, that pose challenges to the United States' goal of reorganizing the world to suit its own definitions—and interests. This was true a century ago, and it is just as valid today. The United States has been amazingly successful, working through the International Monetary Fund (IMF), the World Bank, and its own corporations as well as those in Europe and Japan who share America's desire to see the world "globalized," in opening key countries to private investors and businesses, and in restructuring the world in what it alleges is its own image. The entire former Soviet bloc, China, and Vietnam have also accepted the "Washington consensus" and are attempting to impose the "globalization" model on their now capitalist economies. This very broad and essentially vague consensus—which attributes a mystical efficiency and rationality to the market and competition—among those who guide the economic affairs of nations is both astounding and virtually universal. But it also ignores history entirely, for the United States has always behaved very differently, defending its farmers, steel producers, and countless other business constituencies with subsidies, antidumping quotas, and the like. The gap between the theory of "globalization" and the actual practice of the states that urge others to implement it is enormous. To the United States it means free mobility of every form of capital, but to Japan and East Asia it means unfettered exports—and every nation, including America, implements it to suit its own interests and exceptions.

But the dilemma facing the Americans and all those who share their faith is that poverty—and the instability that it aggravates—have remained in the midst of prosperity for some. The failure to eliminate or even significantly reduce poverty leaves them with a structural legacy in which desperation thrives. Sooner or later they will have to pay the unknown but frequently substantial political and social price that structural inequities such as these create. The wars in Afghanistan for the past quarter century have a variety of sources, but poverty and the conditions it produces—above all illiteracy and the religious and ethnic fanaticism that it nourishes—have certainly been important.

Statistics on poverty are only rough estimates and keep changing, but poverty has untold human—and often political—consequences, and it has persisted. Even before much of the full impact of the 1997 East Asia turmoil could be felt elsewhere, the number of people in the Third World (excluding China) living below the World Bank's meager poverty standard of $1.79 per day (in 1993 purchasing power) had increased 15 percent from 1987 to 1998—to 1.4 billion people. Eastern and central Europe, Latin America, and sub-Saharan Africa—regions where the IMF was most influential—experienced a higher incidence of poverty from 1980 to 1997, while poverty declined in booming East and South Asia, the Middle East, and North Africa. But the financial crisis in East Asia that began in the summer of 1997 caused the real 1998 per capita household income to decline 20 percent in South Korea, 12 percent in the Philippines, and 24 percent in Indonesia. And by late 1999 the crisis had pushed from 15 million to 75 million people below the poverty line. Most lived in Asia, whose integration in the "globalized" world economy was trumpeted as the source of their prosperity. They have now been subjected to globalization's many inherent instabilities.

Increasingly unequal income distribution in much of the Third World explains part of this persistence, and grossly inadequate economic growth explains much of the remainder. In Russia and Eastern Europe this inequality, stagnant and declining economies, and the abolition of virtually all forms of social protection have added greatly to the world's poverty and human and social problems. IMF insistence on balancing budgets has caused many poor countries to reduce the proportion of their gross domestic product allocated to health and education. But education, health, and transfer programs in developing nations did not reverse growing income inequality, and in many nations they benefited mainly upper-income groups. Latin America fared especially badly, with utterly inadequate social safety nets, and in some nations there was a reversal during the 1990s of gains made in preceding decades. Argentina, which took the IMF's guidance on virtually all economic matters and accumulated enormous debts, is the best-known example of nations now in serious decline. But in fact it is quite typical of the way many nations have managed their economic policies.[5]

Such nuances in economic, social, and political transformations have made instability and great changes inherent in the modern historical experience. This chronic disorder, in turn, has left the United States floundering for an effective strategic synthesis. The self-confident optimism that characterized its efforts after the mid-1950s is now largely gone. Counter-insurgency and a reliance on massive firepower failed in Vietnam, and while the Pentagon has had plenty of theorists who could concoct assorted doctrines, in fact America's policies since then have been ad hoc and incremental, ranging from barely concealed covert aid of arms and advisers to the contras in Nicaragua and the mujahideen in Afghanistan during the 1980s, to the outright use of American troops in Grenada in 1983, to the Iranian hostage rescue debacle in April 1980. Both in theory and financially, the Reagan administration after 1981 favored a massive arms buildup. Doctrinally, in November 1984 it articulated the "Weinberger Doctrine" to warn that it would utilize its military power massively should it fight again. The threat was sufficiently vague to frighten the Russians with visions of America using its nuclear weapons in a first strike, but it also caused many in the CIA and Washington to share the Russians' deep anxieties.

In practice, however, America's responses to military challenges have never been consistent or coherent, and the Weinberger Doctrine became just one of many ideas that Washington has concocted—and usually forgotten. The United States has persisted in its futile search for a doctrinally logical justification for employing its massive military power, but even the domino theory remained conventional wisdom on how political change occurred in the Third World. Above all, whether Republicans or Democrats, America's leaders failed to comprehend the negative long-term political, economic, and ideological consequences of its policies in much of the world. This was their calamitous oversight, because the world is far more complicated than weaponry can cope with. Countless U.S. interventions have done great harm while solving few problems; they have been counterproductive by every criterion.

The United States has almost always succeeded in its military efforts, whether covert or open. It has won, at least in the short run, most of its interventions. In Cuba it failed because its proxies were venal and its efforts were incompetent. There was, in many regards, a basis for its overweening self-confidence, but these victories failed to take into account the long-term political and ideological consequences of what seemed to be successes. Moreover, America's losses in Vietnam and Korea were crucial because they revealed how finite was its military power when it confronted able enemies ready to make the most of the terrain and space, enemies able to neutralize its firepower and concentrated forces. Few, if any, in Washington seriously analyzed these defeats. But they have eventually proved to be decisive, and they are today more crucial than nominal military victories.

The breakup of the Soviet Union only intensified the official U.S. confusion, since no one could any longer explain why problems arise by referring to some nefarious forces in Moscow. Indeed, as the Soviets no longer played their inhibiting and essentially conservative role, the world became less safe and more unstable than ever. Even worse, the Pentagon's strategy and military equipment were heavily oriented to Soviet targets and Eastern European conditions, and now these were irrelevant. An obvious and visible enemy had been very useful for Washington's leaders after 1946, if only because they could often convince an occasionally reticent Congress and American public that more arms spending was justified. Communist parties no longer existed but change still occurred, indeed more rapidly than ever, and political groups of all other ideological persuasions were just as active. Washington refused to acknowledge the role that the Soviets played after 1947 in discouraging radicalism throughout the world, and that the Western European parties most under their control were often docile members of ruling political coalitions. In China, especially, they urged the Communists to pursue a much more moderate line, laying the basis for the subsequent break with Mao Tse-tung. But today the original justification for the United States' virtually hegemonic global leadership pretensions—with its bases and massive military hardware almost everywhere—is now gone.

The dissolution of the Soviet Union has left the United States feeling stronger than ever, but in reality it is also more vulnerable, and it has only increased the risks it is now taking with the welfare and security of its own people.

Notes

1. I take up these questions in my *Century of War: Politics, Conflicts, and Society Since 1914* (New York, 1994), and, with Joyce Kolko, *The Limits of Power: The World and United States Foreign Policy, 1945–1954* (New York, 1972).

2. See my *Confronting the Third World* (New York, 1988), pp. 51–52.

3. Barry M. Blechman and Stephen S. Kaplan. *Force Without War: U.S. Armed Forces as a Political Instrument* (Washington, 1978), pp. 33, 556.

4. I discuss the Vietnam War in extensive detail in my *Anatomy of a War: Vietnam, the United States, and the Modern Historical Experience* (New York, 1994).

5. There is a large substantiating literature. See, for example, Gabriel Kolko, "Ravaging the Poor: The International Monetary Fund Indicted by Its Own Data," *Multinational Monitor*, June 1998, pp. 20–23; James C. Knowles et al., "Social Consequences of the Financial Crisis in Asia: The Deeper Crisis," *Manila Social Forum* (Asian Development Bank, November 9–12, 1999, conference); Martin Ravallion, "Growth, Inequality and Poverty: Looking Beyond Averages," World Bank Working Paper 2558, February 26, 2001, p. 21.

THE UNITED STATES AND THE GENOCIDE CONVENTION

A Half-Century of Obfuscation and Obstruction

WARD CHURCHILL

It is clear that the Genocide Convention is a moral document. It is a call for a higher standard of human conduct. It is not a panacea for injustice, [but it is] an important step toward civilizing the affairs of nations.

—SENATOR WILLIAM PROXMIRE

One of the earliest matters taken up by the United Nations after its 1945 founding convention in San Francisco was the sponsoring of an international legal instrument to punish and prevent the crime of genocide.[1] In General Assembly Resolution 96(1), passed unanimously and without debate on December 11, 1946, the U.N. made it clear that, although it may have been prompted to act with urgency because of what had been revealed during the recently concluded trials of the major nazi war criminals at Nuremberg, it was more broadly motivated in pursuing the issue: "*Many* instances of such crimes of genocide have occurred when racial, religious, political, and other groups have been destroyed, entirely or in part (emphasis added)."[2] The body's Economic and Social Council (ECOSOC) was mandated by the resolution to produce a draft of the desired convention for consideration at the next annual session of the General Assembly.[3]

ECOSOC immediately turned to the U.N. Secretariat for support in retaining several international legal consultants, including Dr. Raphaël Lemkin, an exiled Polish–Jewish jurist who had coined the term "genocide" in 1944, and who was thus considered a leading expert on the topic.[4] The initial draft, authored primarily by Lemkin, was duly submitted to the Council on the Progressive Development of International Law and Its Codification in June 1947.[5] In July, however, the General Assembly, noting "important philosophical disagreements" among some member states with elements of the draft document, declined to put the matter to a vote. Instead, through Resolution 180(II), the assembly instructed ECOSOC to prepare another draft instrument for consideration the following year.[6]

An ad hoc committee, consisting of representatives of China, France, Lebanon, Poland, the United States, the U.S.S.R., and Venezuela, was then organized by the council to make the necessary revisions.[7] The new document was passed along to ECOSOC's Sixth (Legal) Committee, which made minor alterations, before submitting it to the General Assembly, which unanimously adopted it without further modification on December 9, 1948.[8] By January 12, 1951, a sufficient number of countries had ratified the Convention on Prevention and Punishment of the Crime of Genocide to afford it the status of binding international law (of both "customary" and "black letter" varieties).[9] As of 1990, more than a hundred United Nations member states had tendered valid ratifications.[10] The only significant exception was the United States of America.

The situation remains unchanged today, despite a pretense of ratification made at the behest of the Reagan administration in 1988, *forty years* after the convention first passed muster with the civilized countries of the world.[11] How and why this came to be are questions of no small significance, insofar as they shed a penetrating light on the true character and priorities of this "nation of laws," the self-professed "most humane and enlightened nation in the history of humanity."[12] They are no less important in that the United States, as the planet's only remaining superpower, is now in an unparalleled position to visit its version of "humanitarianism" upon virtually any sector of the species it chooses.[13]

Gutting the Convention

The United States assumed a leading role in formulating the application of international legal principle under which the nazi leadership was tried at Nuremberg, especially with regard to the somewhat nebulous category of "Crimes Against Humanity" under which the regime's most blatantly genocidal policies and practices were prosecuted.[14] Similarly, while engineering establishment of the United Nations in 1945—ostensibly as a barrier against the sort of "excesses" evidenced by nazism—it did much to promote the idea that each element of customary human rights law, including implicit prohibitions against genocide, should be codified as a "black letter" international legal instrument, formally embraced through a process of treaty ratifications by member states.[15]

When it came time for the drafting of an actual genocide convention, however, the United States conducted itself in what can only be described as a thoroughly subversive fashion. This began with its response to the initial draft instrument, a document which sought to frame the crime in a manner consistent with accepted definition.

> The draft aimed to protect "racial, national, linguistic, religious, or political groups." In sweeping terms it branded as criminal many physical and biological acts aimed at the destruction of such groups in whole or in part, or of "preventing [their] preservation or development." It specified that acts would be punishable, including attempt to commit genocide, participation in genocide, conspiracy to commit genocide, and engaging in a number of "preparatory" acts such as developing techniques of genocide and setting up installations. It called for punishment of "all forms of public propaganda tending by their systematic and hateful character to promote genocide, or tending to make it appear as a necessary, legitimate, or excusable act." It called for the creation of an international court to try offenders in cases when states were unwilling either to try them or extradite them to another country for trial.[16]

As the Saudi Arabian delegation observed at the time, the draft clearly articulated the nature of genocide as consisting not only in the systematic killing of members of a targeted population, but also in policies devoted to bringing about the "planned disintegration of the political, social, or economic structure of a group or nation" and/or the "systematic moral debasement of a group, people, or nation."[17] Things seemed to be moving in the right direction until U.S. representatives, often working through third parties such as Canada and Venezuela, went to work to scuttle what became known as the "Secretariat's Draft" on the grounds that its "net was cast much too wide[ly]" and, if approved as law, might therefore serve to "impair the sovereignty" of signatory states.[18]

The previously mentioned ad hoc committee, chaired by U.S. delegate John Maktos, was then assembled to produce a new draft, with attention focused on "the political as well as the legal dimensions" of the issue.[19] In short order, a *quid pro quo* was effected in which the Soviets were allowed to strike socioeconomic aggregates of the very sort they had been steadily obliterating since the early 1930s from the list of entities to receive protection under the law.[20] In exchange, the United States was able to remove an entire article delineating the criteria of cultural rather than physical or biological genocide, a maneuver serving to exempt a range of its own dirty linen from scrutiny.

> The secretariat's draft [had gone] to considerable lengths to detail the specific conditions of the three forms of genocide. In the category of *physical,* it outlined mass extermination and "slow death" measures (i.e., subjection to conditions of life which, owing to lack of proper housing, clothing, food, hygiene and medical care or excessive work or physical exertion are likely to result in the debilitation or death of individuals; mutilations and biological experiments imposed for other than curative purposes; deprivation of all means of livelihood by confiscation of property; looting, curtailment of work, and the denial of housing and supplies otherwise available to the other inhabitants of the territory concerned) . . . The secretariat's draft took *biological* genocide to mean the restricting of births in the group. It named the methods of sterilization or compulsory abortion, segregation of the sexes and obstacles to marriage . . . *Cultural* genocide was defined as the destruction of the specific characteristics of the group. Among the acts specified: forced transfer of children to another

human group; forced and systematic exile of individuals representing the culture of a group; the prohibition of the use of the national language, or religious works, or the prohibition of new publications; systematic destruction of historical or religious monuments, or their diversion to alien uses; destruction or dispersion of documents and objects of historical, artistic, or religious value and of objects used in religious worship.*

In the Secretariat's Draft, one crime—genocide—was thus defined as having three distinct but often interactive modes of perpetration. No effort was "made to distinguish the relative seriousness of the modes which are left to stand on par," with the deliberate eradication of cultural existence being treated with as much legal gravity as programs of outright physical annihilation.[21] By the time the United States had completed its overhaul of the text, over the heated objections of the Lebanese delegate, all that remained of the concept of cultural genocide was a provision prohibiting the forced transfer of children. Even the secretariat's proscription of genocidally oriented propaganda—a concept deployed by the United States in its prosecution of Julius Streicher at Nuremberg—had been scrapped in favor of a much more restrictive clause prohibiting "direct and public incitement."[22] In its final form, the key ingredients of the draft finally presented to the General Assembly had been reduced to the following:

> *Article II.* In the present Convention, genocide means any of the following acts committed to destroy, in whole or in part, a national, ethnical, racial or religious group, as such:
>
> (a) Killing members of the group;
>
> (b) Causing serious bodily or mental harm to members of the group;
>
> (c) Deliberately inflicting on members of the group conditions of life calculated to bring about its physical destruction in whole or in part;

*Robert Davis and Mark Zannis, *The Genocide Machine in Canada: The Pacification of the North* (Montreal: Black Rose Books, 1973), pp. 19–20. The provision on cultural genocide, as well as Lemkin's original definition of the crime, would have taken in the virtual entirety of U.S. Indian policy from the 1880s onwards. Officially entitled "Assimilation," the goal of the policy was, according to Commissioner of Indian Affairs Francis Leupp, to systematically "kill the Indian, but spare the man" in every native person in the United States, thus creating a "great engine to grind down the tribal mass"; Francis Leupp, *The Indian and His Problem* (New York: Scribner's, 1910), p. 93. The express intent was to bring about the total disappearance of indigenous cultures—as such—as rapidly as possible; Henry E. Fritz, *The Movement for Indian Assimilation, 1860–1890* (Philadelphia: University of Pennsylvania Press, 1963). To this end, the practice of native spiritual traditions were universally forbidden under penalty of law in 1897; Oliver Knight, *Following the Indian Wars* (Norman: University of Oklahoma Press, 1960). A comprehensive and compulsory "educational" system was put in place to "free [American Indian] children from the language and habits of their untutored and often savage parents" while indoctrinating them not only in the language but in the religion and cultural mores of Euroamerican society; U.S. Department of Interior, Bureau of Indian Affairs, *Annual Report of the Commissioner of Indian Affairs to the Secretary of Interior* (Washington, D.C.: U.S. Government Printing Office, 1886), p. xxiv. This was accomplished through a complex of federally run boarding schools which removed native students from any and all contact with their families, communities and cultures for years on end; David Wallace Adams, *Education for Extinction: American Indians and the Boarding School Experience: 1875–1928* (Lawrence: University Press of Kansas, 1995). The structure of indigenous property relations was meanwhile forcibly dissolved under provision of the 1887 General Allotment Act, the populations of all indigenous nations encapsulated by the United States were unilaterally declared to be its subjects via the 1924 Indian Citizenship Act, and traditional forms of native governance were unilaterally dissolved, supplanted by governing council structures designed and implemented by the United States through the 1934 Indian Reorganization Act; Vine Deloria, Jr., and Clifford M. Lytle, *The Nations Within: The Past and Future of American Indian Sovereignty* (New York: Pantheon, 1984). By the late 1950s, entire indigenous nations—109 in all—were being declared "extinct" by unilateral decree of the federal government, through a series of "Termination Acts" passed pursuant to House Resolution 108 (August 1, 1953). Simultaneously, a process was initiated under Public Law 959, the Relocation Act, through which more than half the entire native population was dispersed from its own landbase into urban localities where it was mostly subsumed within "mainstream" society by the 1980s; Donald L. Fixico, *Termination and Relocation: Federal Indian Policy, 1945–1960* (Albuquerque: University of New Mexico Press, 1986). As to the disposition of American Indian religious shrines, one need only consider the creation of the Mt. Rushmore National Monument and a correspondingly vast tourist industry in the Black Hills—the most sacred geography of the Lakotas, Cheyennes, and other peoples—to get the idea.

(d) Imposing measures intended to prevent births within the group;

(e) Forcibly transferring children of the group to another group.

Article III. The following acts shall be punishable:

(a) Genocide;

(b) Conspiracy to commit genocide;

(c) Direct and public incitement to commit genocide;

(d) Attempt to commit genocide;

(e) Complicity in genocide.

It was this U.S.-designed and highly truncated instrument, not just diluting but effectively gutting Lemkin's original conception of genocide and the draft convention which arose from it, which was ultimately approved by the General Assembly. From there, it was an easy slide down the slippery slope of definitional erosion into a generalized misunderstanding that genocide occurs *only* within peculiarly focused incidents or processes of mass murder (à la Auschwitz and Babi Yar). For all practical intents and purposes, then, the United States had attained a diplomatic triumph of sorts, managing to void the very meaning of the crime in question while simultaneously appearing to stand at the forefront of those opposing it.

Nonratification

It appeared for a time that America might be able to have its cake and eat it too, at least on matters of international legality. At home, this liberal accomplishment—not only subversion of the Genocide Convention, but the forging of a position of primacy for the United States within the U.N. itself had been masterminded by Truman-era State Department holdovers from the previous administration of Franklin Delano Roosevelt—foundered on the shoals of extreme right-wing reaction.[23]

■ ■ ■ ■

The State Department was a particular target of the Right during the entire period [of the Cold War]. . . .

One purpose of the whole charade was to discredit the "communistic" notion of creating a workable system of international problem resolution through nonmilitary means, embodied in the U.N.'s mandate to establish standards of comportment by progressively codifying and gaining universal ratification of the laws of nations. . . .

While such forces never managed to fulfill their original objective of bringing about an actual U.S. withdrawal from the United Nations—after Korea, even the more thoughtful right-wingers could see the utility of remaining within the organization—they were able to neutralize much of what they found most objectionable about it by crafting an American posture of refusing to ratify its promulgation of international legal instruments they perceived as constraining the latitude of U.S. policy options. Among the more important elements of evolving human rights law which the United States still refuses to accept are the International Covenant on Civil and Political Rights (1966); the Covenant on Economic, Social and Cultural Rights (1966); the Convention on the Elimination of All Forms of Racial Discrimination (1966); and the American Convention on Human Rights (1965).[24] The same holds true concerning the Laws or War, specifically the Declaration on the Prohibition of the Use of Thermo-Nuclear Weapons (1961); the Resolution Regarding Weapons of Mass Destruction in Outer Space (1964); the Resolution on the Non-Use of Force in International Relations and Permanent Ban on the Use of Nuclear Weapons (1972); the Resolution on the Definition of Aggression (1974); Protocols Additional to the 1949 Geneva Convention (1977); and the Declaration on the Prohibition of Chemical Weapons (1989).[25]

By and large, the arguments advanced in the Senate against ratification of the treaties accepting each of these legal instruments has been that to do so would "impair U.S. sovereignty" by conceding that there was some body of law "standing at a level higher than that of our own constitution."[26] This follows precisely the logic embodied in a cornerstone of the nazis' Nuremberg defense: insofar as the German government of which the defendants had been a part had never accepted most of the international laws at issue, they had not been required to abide by them.* Rather, the defense contended, they were legally bound only to adhere to the legal code of the sovereign German state under which authority they asserted legitimation of their various actions.[27] The tribunal rejected this line of reasoning out of hand, countering that the defendants—indeed, the members of *all* governments—were bound under pain of criminal prosecution to conform to "higher laws" than those evidenced in their own domestic constitutions and statutory codes.[28] The U.N. member states, including the United States, went on to affirm this position in December 1946.[29]

Nonetheless, after conducting hearings on the matter in 1950—during which it became clear that many of its members were "profoundly skeptical about, and even hostile to, the notion of assuming an international legal obligation on genocide"[30]—the Senate Committee on Foreign Relations [rejected] the Genocide Convention. . . .

■ ■ ■ ■

Deeper Motives

Beneath the transparently invalid gloss of constitutional argument with which the Senate coated its rejection of the Genocide Convention lay deeper and more important motives.† These devolved upon the understanding that certain ongoing U.S. policies and practices abridged the meaning of the Convention, even in its most highly diluted form. In testimony brought before the Foreign Relations Committee, this was expressed in terms of the implications of the treatment accorded racial minorities in light of the Convention's provision that intent to destroy a target group "in part" was sufficient to predicate a charge of genocidal conduct.[31] Witness the following exchange between ABA representative [Alfred] Schweppe and the subcommittee chair, Connecticut Senator Brien McMahon, during the 1950 hearings:

> SCHWEPPE: The point is that the intent does not need to exist to destroy the whole group. It needs only to exist to destroy part of the group. Now whether we say part of the group could mean one person or whether we say a substantial part again requires us to inquire into the facts, as you often do in these cases, what is the group and how many were there?
>
> MCMAHON: Part of the group—but because he is part of the group. Now let's take lynching for example. Let's assume that there is a lynching and a colored man is murdered in this fashion. Is it your contention that that could be construed as being within the confines of the definition; namely, with intent to destroy him as part of a group?
>
> SCHWEPPE: Well, Mr. Chairman, I don't want to answer that categorically . . . Certainly, it

*The reference was to black letter instruments such as the 1928 Kellogg-Briand Pact (45 Stat. 2343, T.S. No. 796, 2 Bevans 732, L.N.T.S. 57)—to which Germany was not a signatory—outlawing aggressive wars for purposes of seizing territory. As concerned much of what fell under the rubric of "Crimes Against Humanity," it had never been codified in black letter form. The defense therefore argued that no body of law existed prohibiting certain offenses at the time the defendants allegedly committed them, and that—under injunctions against application of *ex post facto* law—they could not thus be legitimately prosecuted; Herbert Wechsler, "The Issues of the Nuremberg Trial," *Political Science Quarterly*, No. 62, Mar. 1947. Some U.S. politicians, of course, agreed with the nazis; see, e.g., Sen. Robert A. Taft, "Equal Justice Under the Law: The Heritage of English-Speaking Peoples and Their Responsibility," *Vital Speeches*, Vol. 13, No. 2, Nov. 1, 1946.

†Not least of these was entrenched racism/antisemitism and nativism. This was abundantly evident in the treatment accorded Raphaël Lemkin, who, despite the misgivings he must have felt concerning the U.S./Soviet dilution of the Secretariat's Draft, did his best to lobby the 1948 Convention through the Senate. In response, the subcommittee declined to call him as a witness in its hearings on the matter. According to New Jersey's Republican Senator H. Alexander Smith, this was because he and his colleagues were "irritated no end" by the idea that "a Jew . . . who comes from a foreign country [and] speaks broken English" should be the Convention's "biggest propagandist." Liberals like Brien McMahon (D–Connecticut) and Theodore Francis Green (D–Rhode Island) appear to have substantially agreed, describing Lemkin's conspicuous Jewishness as "the biggest minus quality" of the entire ratification effort; quoted in Lawrence J. LaBlanc, *The United States and the Genocide Convention* (Durham: Duke University Press, 1991), p. 20.

> doesn't mean if I want to drive five Chinamen out of town . . . that I must have the intent to destroy all the 400,000,000 Chinese in the world or the 250,000 within the United States. It is part of a racial group, and if it is a group of 5, a group of 10, a group of 15, and I proceed after them with guns in some community solely because they belong to some racial group that the dictators don't like, I think you have a got a serious question. That's what bothers me.[32]

What was bothering both McMahon and Schweppe was not only the gratuitous violence habitually visited upon Chinese immigrants to the United States during the twentieth century, but the history of the lynchings of at least 2,505 black men and women in ten southern states between 1882 and 1930. That comes to an average of one such act of racially explicit lethal mob violence directed against African Americans each week for the entire 48-year period, in an area encompassing only one-fifth of the country.[33] When the remaining 80 percent of the United States is added in, the actual number was probably about double—more than 5,000—a racial murder rate markedly higher than that evidenced in Germany against Jews and Gypsies combined prior to 1939.[34]

> As staggering as the lynching toll was, it vastly understates the total volume of violence aimed toward African-American citizens . . . [The] lynching inventory does not count casualties of the urban race riots that erupted during those years, nor does it embrace victims of a single killer or pairs of assassins. Neither does it include the all-too-frequent beatings, whippings, verbal humiliations, threats, harangues, and other countless indignities suffered by the Black population [in much the same manner as they were undergone by target populations in Germany].[35]

The lynching of African Americans had not ended in 1930, of course. Indeed, with 21 reported fatalities in that year, it represented a high point for the period reported. In 1932, however, there were 22 documented lynchings of blacks in the South, another 18 in 1933.[36] While the level of such violence would abate somewhat after 1935, it could hardly be said to have disappeared by 1950, and it would rise again sharply during the latter part of the decade and on through the mid-'60s.[37] There was, after all, a rather prominent organization, the Ku Klux Klan, which had been openly advocating not only the sort of atrocities at issue, but the sordid racial doctrines underlying them. Not only had authorities at all levels declined to take decisive action to quell Klan-style activity, they had in many cases encouraged it, and in more than a few, could be shown to have actively participated in it.[38]

Unquestionably, such a pattern could be argued as falling within the categories of state-sanctioned behavior prohibited by the Genocide Convention. It is therefore instructive that the immediate response of conservatives like Schweppe and McMahon was *not* to embrace the law as a potentially powerful tool which might be useful in an official drive to end the rampant and sustained racist violence plaguing the United States. Instead, it was the opposite: they denounced the Convention on the bizarre premise that such atrocities were somehow or another "constitutionally protected" under the mantle of U.S. sovereignty. Even more revealing in many ways is the fact that liberals agreed, albeit rather than rejecting the Convention outright, they sought to apply finesse by pretending it meant something other than what it said. Consider the following exchange between McMahon and then-Deputy Under Secretary of State Dean Rusk:

> RUSK: Genocide, as defined in Article II of the Convention, consists of the commission of certain specified acts, such as killing or causing serious bodily harm to individuals who are members of a national, ethnical, racial or religious group, with the intent to destroy that group. The legislative history of Article II shows that the United Nations negotiators felt that it should not be necessary that an entire human group be destroyed to constitute the crime of genocide, but rather that genocide meant the partial destruction of such a group with the intent to destroy the entire group concerned.

MCMAHON: That is important. They must have the intent to destroy the entire group.

RUSK: That is correct.

MCMAHON: In other words, an action leveled against one or two of a race or religion would not be, as I understand it, the crime of genocide. They must have the intent to go through and kill them all.

RUSK: That is correct. The Convention does not aim at the violent expression of prejudice which is directed against individual members of groups.[39]

This, to be sure, was nonsense, as Schweppe later emphatically—and quite correctly—pointed out to the committee.

> [Rusk] has undertaken in a gloss to say that basic to any charge of genocide must be the intent to destroy the entire group. Now that is an exact negation of the text which is to be construed not only by [the Senate] but . . . by the International Court of Justice. Now, the International Court of Justice is not going to say intent to destroy a group in whole or in part means only to destroy a whole group . . . The Convention says you only need the intent to destroy part of a group; so there is a contradiction, gentlemen . . . which I suggest you very seriously consider.[40]

If the circumstances attending the lynching of blacks smacked of genocide, their targeting for involuntary sterilization was even worse. Already in 1950 there was considerable discussion in the African American community about this, and in December 1951, a 240-page petition, written by black attorney William L. Patterson for the American Civil Rights Congress (CRC) and entitled "We Charge Genocide," was deposited with the U.N. Secretariat in New York.[41] Although U.S. diplomats were able to prevent the document—which provided copious details on sterilization programs to which the Afroamerican community had been subjected—from being taken up by the U.N.'s Commission on Human Rights, the submission sent lingering shock waves throughout the federal hierarchy.*

By 1970, when an updated version of the CRC petition was deposited with the secretariat, the situation was even more "sensitive." At that point, the government was not only continuing its "birth control efforts" with regard to poor blacks, it had secretly launched similar programs targeting American Indians and Puerto Ricans which eventually resulted in upwards of 30 percent of the women of childbearing age in each group undergoing involuntary—and in many instances completely unwitting—sterilization.†

*It seems U.S. delegates successfully argued that whatever was being done to poor blacks was being done to them as an economic aggregate rather than as a racial group. Hence, the victims were not subject to protection under the Genocide Convention—thanks to the *quid pro quo* these same delegates had effected with the Soviets during the ad hoc committee process in 1947—and any review of petitions in their behalf claiming otherwise would be "inappropriate." Meanwhile, right-wing senators and expert witnesses like the ABA's Alfred Schweppe were busily rejecting the convention, partly because political and economic aggregates hadn't been retained among the protected groups, thereby "letting the Communists off the hook" for the genocidal aspects of Stalinist and Maoist collectivization policies; U.S. Senate, *Hearings on the Genocide Convention Before a Subcommittee of the Senate Committee on Foreign Relations* (Washington, D.C.: 81st Cong., 2d Sess., U.S. Government Printing Office, 1950); U.S. Senate, *Hearings on the Genocide Convention Before a Subcommittee of the Senate Committee on Foreign Relations* (Washington, D.C.: 92d Cong., 1st Sess., U.S. Government Printing Office, 1971).

†As concerns American Indian women, it was determined in 1976 that up to 42 percent were involuntarily sterilized in clinics run by the Indian Health Service, a component of the Interior Department's Bureau of Indian Affairs, between 1970 and 1975. In perhaps a quarter of these cases, the women had not only not consented, they had never been informed that a sterilization had been performed; Brint Dillingham, "Indian Women and IHS Sterilization Practices," *American Indian Journal*, Vol. 3, No. 1, Jan. 1977; Janet Larsen, "And Then There Were None," *Christian Century*, Jan. 26, 1977; Women of All Red Nations, *American Indian Women* (New York: International Indian Treaty Council, 1978); Robin Jarrell, "Women and Children First: The Forced Sterilization of American Indian Women" (undergraduate thesis, Wellesley College, 1978). With respect to Puertorriqueñas, the data were one-third of the women of childbearing age on the island of Puerto Rico, 44 percent of the same target population in New Haven and 51 percent in Hartford, Connecticut; Committee for Abortion Rights and Against Sterilization Abuse, *Women Under Attack: Abortion, Sterilization Abuse, and Reproductive Freedom* (New York: CARASA, 1979); Margarita Ostalaza, *Política Sexual y Socializatcón Política de la Mujer Puertorriqueña la Consolidación del Bloque Historico Colonial de Puerto Rico* (Río Piedras, PR: Ediciones Huracán, 1989).

The only question in this regard which seemed to concern Idaho's liberal Senator Frank Church during testimony provided by Assistant Attorney General (and future Chief Justice of the Supreme Court) William Rehnquist in hearings conducted the same year, was whether responsible officials could be "safeguarded" from meaningful prosecution, perchance charges were ever brought against them under the Genocide Convention.

> CHURCH: Another extreme criticism leveled at the Convention is that it would make birth control efforts among the poor blacks an act of genocide. How would you answer this allegation?
>
> REHNQUIST: I think that any birth control effort that might reasonably be contemplated in this country would certainly be a voluntary one, and would likewise be directed towards all individuals rather than any particular race. I think it inconceivable that any sort of birth control effort that would ever receive public approval in this country would violate the provisions of this treaty.
>
> CHURCH: Is it true that if any such effort were to be made, based upon some compulsory method and directed toward some particular group, that the protections of the Constitution would be fully applicable whether or not the United States had ratified and become party to the Genocide Convention?
>
> REHNQUIST: Certainly.[42]

Other aspects of U.S. domestic policy were coming into similar focus at about the same time. There were, for instance, potential ramifications to the maintenance of the apartheid structure of Jim Crow segregation throughout much of the nation for more than a hundred years.[43] As ABA representative Eberhard Deutsch put it in his testimony before the subcommittee in 1971, such a systematic pattern of statutory racial discrimination could, at least in part, be seen as a violation of even the most rigorous interpretation of the Convention's injunction against visiting mental harm upon members of a target group.

> In *Brown v. Board of Education*, the leading desegregation case . . . the Supreme Court of the United States . . . held expressly that separation of Negro children . . . from others of similar age and qualifications solely because of their race, generates a feeling of inferiority as to their status in the community that affects their hearts and minds in a way unlikely ever to be undone . . . and has a tendency to retard their education and mental development . . . In light of this holding by the Supreme Court, such an understanding as this committee has proposed . . . that mental harm is to be construed "to mean permanent impairment of mental faculties," would hardly deter any tribunal from determining that any form of local segregation is within the definition of the international crime of genocide under the Convention.[44]

At no point during the subcommission's hearings was there serious discussion of the implications of the Convention's prohibition against the forced transfer of children in light of U.S. policy.[45] The reasons for this are readily apparent. To have done so would have been to expose the entire system of compulsory boarding schools long imposed by the government upon American Indians to the kind of scrutiny it could ill afford. Any such attention to Indian affairs would, moreover, all but inevitably raise the specter of the extermination campaigns waged against America's indigenous peoples in previous centuries.[46] From there, discussion would have led unerringly into the very sphere of consideration the United States had sought to evade when it arranged for deletion of the third article of the Secretariat's Draft: the broad range of culturally genocidal practices through which the Indians' final extinction was still being relentlessly pursued as a matter of policy. Rather, these genies were left in their bottles altogether, and the subjects of Indians and Indian policy never came up.[47]

Be that as it may, it is unquestionably a matter of record that it was with full knowledge that many of its own undertakings and positions were genocidal by legal definition—and with the stated intention of maintaining its own imagined "sovereign discretion" to continue in exactly the same vein—that the Senate of the United States, cheered on by the country's most representative body of jurists and attorneys, openly rejected the Genocide Convention for fully two generations. . . .

■ ■ ■ ■

"Ratification"

It was not until 1985, after the first signs of significant deterioration in the Soviet system signaled the potential for a decisive and potentially permanent shift in global power back to the United States, that a genuine senatorial interest in ratifying the Genocide Convention finally emerged.[48] By then, the Reagan administration had restored a certain "luster and authority" to America's martial image through the conquest of tiny Grenada, endorsement of Israel's invasion and partial occupation of neighboring Lebanon, support for Iraq's bloody attritional contest with Iran, initiation of a pair of substantial low-intensity wars in Nicaragua and El Salvador, and the repeated provocation of lopsided aerial combat over Libya's Gulf of Sidra, among numerous other things.[49] Moreover, the administration was in the process of repudiating the jurisdiction of the World Court to require U.S. adherence to even those relatively few standards of international legality it had formally embraced.*

Given that these developments dictated an increasing "unenforcability" of the Convention against the United States (to quote Reagan), it was decided that the time was finally ripe for America to reap whatever propaganda benefits might accrue from the "humanitarian gesture" of signing on to what had long since become customary law.[50] It was also discerned by more perceptive officials that, with the United States effectively self-exempted from abiding by provisions of this or any other element of international legality it might find inconvenient, endorsement of the relevant instruments might serve to forge useful new weapons for concrete rather than rhetorical utilization against America's enemies on certain occasions. A team of leading senatorial conservatives—Indiana's Richard Lugar, Orrin Hatch of Utah, and Jesse Helms—were therefore assembled to sell ratification to the Right.†

Together, the three crafted what they described as a "Sovereignty Package" containing two "reservations" and five "understandings" upon which U.S. "acceptance" of the Genocide Convention would be conditioned. These "clarifications" served to preclude any possibility that its provisions might actually be applied to America by reaffirming U.S. repudiation of the jurisdiction of international courts, asserting the primacy of the United States Constitution over international law, . . . rejecting extradition of U.S. nationals for violation of the Convention (rather than the U.S. "interpretation" of it), and specifically absolving the effects of discriminatory domestic policies and external military actions from being classified as genocidal other than in cases where genocide was a stated intent.‡ As the package read in its final form:

Resolution of Ratification (Lugar-Helms-Hatch Sovereignty Package) Adopted February 19, 1986

Resolved (two-thirds of the Senators present concurring therein), That the Senate advise and consent to the ratification of the International Convention on the Prevention and Punishment of the Crime of Genocide, adopted unanimously by the General Assembly of the United Nations in

*The action—renouncing America's voluntary 1946 acceptance of jurisdiction by the International Court of Justice (ICJ or "World Court")—was taken in response to the ICJ's October 1985 decision in the *Nicaragua v. United States* case, finding the covert U.S. war against the former country to be in violation of international law; "U.S. Terminates Acceptance of ICJ Compulsory Jurisdiction," *Department of State Bulletin,* No. 86, Jan. 1986.

†The three were apparently selected for this task, not simply on the basis of their individual credibility with various sectors of the Right, but because each had been prominent in opposing ratification on one or another grounds. Lugar and Hatch also chaired key bodies, the Foreign Affairs Committee and the Subcommittee on the Constitution of the Committee on the Judiciary; respectively; Ben Whitaker, *Revised and Updated Report on the Punishment and Prevention of the Crime of Genocide,* U.N. Doc. E/CN.4/Sub.2/1985/6, pp. 42–4.

‡As further indication that the United States waited until the global balance of power shifted emphatically in its favor, thus effectively precluding the possibility that the Genocide Convention might be enforced against it, before ratifying the instrument, it should be noted that all the ingredients that eventually went into the Lugar-Helms-Hatch package had been placed on the table at least as early as 1971; *Hearings on the Genocide Convention (1971), op. cit.*

Paris on December 9, 1948 (Executive O, Eighty-first Congress, first session), *Provided that*:

I. The Senate's advise and consent is subject to the following reservations:

(1) That with reference to Article IX of the Convention, before any dispute to which the United States is a party may be submitted to the International Court of Justice under this article, the specific consent of the United States is required in each case.

(2) That nothing in the Convention requires or authorizes legislation or other action by the United States prohibited by the Constitution of the United States as interpreted by the United States.

II. The Senate's advise and consent is subject to the following understandings, which shall apply to the obligations of the United States under this Convention:

(1) That the term "intent to destroy, in whole or in part, a national, ethnical, racial, or religious group as such" appearing in Article II means the *specific* intent to destroy, in whole or in *substantial* part, a national, ethnical, racial, or religious group as such by the acts specified in Article II (emphasis added).

(2) That the term "mental harm" in Article II(b) means the permanent impairment of mental faculties through drugs, torture, or similar measures.

(3) That the pledge to grant extradition in accordance with a state's laws and treaties in force found in Article VII extends only to acts which are criminal under the laws of both the requesting and requested state and nothing in Article VII affects the right of any state to bring trial before its own tribunals any of its nationals for acts committed outside a state.

(4) That acts in the course of armed conflicts committed without the *specific* intent required by Article II are not sufficient to constitute genocide as defined by the Convention (emphasis added).

(5) That with regard to the reference to an international tribunal in Article VI of the Convention, the United States declares that it reserves the right to effect its participation in any such tribunal only by a treaty entered into specifically for that purpose with the advise and consent of the Senate.

III. The Senate's advise and consent is subject to the following declaration: That the President will not deposit the instrument of ratification until after the implementing legislation referred to in Article V has been enacted.*

With the force and implications of the instrument thus thoroughly negated, this "ratification" was affirmed by congressional passage of the Genocide Convention Implementation Act—also called the "Proxmire Act," a rather ironic reference to the senator who had been most prominent in advocating adoption of the law in its undiluted form—in October 1988.[51] The resulting documents, including the Lugar-Helms-Hatch package, were deposited by the Reagan administration with the United Nations a month later.[52] The Convention, in its congressionally approved form, became "binding" upon the United States in February 1989.

Long before the process was completed, however, some senators, like Connecticut Democrat Christopher Dodd and Charles Mathias, a Maryland Republican, were warning that the U.S. claim to have ratified the Convention in this fashion would likely be

*U.S. Senate, *Senate Executive Report No. 2* (Washington, D.C.: 99th Cong., 1st Sess., U.S. Government Printing Office, 1985), pp. 26–7. It should be noted that at p. 23, mental harm accruing from the imposition of systematic discrimination against racial groups is specifically exempted from the American definition of genocide: "Psychological harm resulting from living conditions, differential treatment by government authorities and the like is excluded." No other country has ever tried to assert such a qualification. Similarly, no signatory has ever belabored the notion of specific intent in the manner evident in the Lugar-Helms-Hatch package. Nor has any country sought to require the destruction of a "substantial" part of a target group—whatever that means: 10 percent? one-quarter? half? three-quarters? almost all?—as a qualification of genocide (apparently for the explicit purpose of removing the onus from the arbitrary destruction of some smaller portion of the group targeted): LaBlanc, *U.S. and the Genocide Convention, op. cit.*, pp. 52–3.

rebuffed by the international community on grounds that the U.S. rejection of Article IX "would completely undermine the [law's] effectiveness."[53] Dodd and Mathias were joined by several others when they argued that the *a priori* exoneration entered with respect to military action might have equally adverse effects.

> [A] question arises as to what the United States is really trying to accomplish by attaching this understanding. The language suggests the United States has something to hide. Moreover, the relatively imprecise definition of "armed conflict" in international law is an invitation to problems and will almost certainly draw adverse comments from other nations trying to figure out what the language is intended to do. To call attention to our fears of being brought to account for acts committed in armed conflicts is really an embarrassment to the United States and should have no place in our ratification of the Genocide Convention.[54]

As analyst Lawrence J. LaBlanc has observed, "There is much to commend this viewpoint, though it could be carried further . . . [Other] provisions—for example, the understandings regarding intent and the meaning of mental harm—seem to carve out exceptions for the United States . . . [They] could be understood by other parties as being reservations that are incompatible with the object and purpose of the Convention. The considerations that gave rise to these understandings—mainly domestic racial considerations—lend credibility to the viewpoint of those who object.[55]

LaBlanc's assessment is borne out in the fact that, by December 1989, nine European countries—Denmark, Finland, Ireland, Italy, the Netherlands, Norway, Spain, Sweden, and the United Kingdom—had entered formal objections to the "constitutional provision" of the U.S. Sovereignty Package with the U.N. Secretariat, describing it as a violation of international treaty law.[56] The United Kingdom and the Netherlands, joined by Australia, also objected to America's repudiation of World Court jurisdiction.[57] The Netherlands flatly declined to recognize U.S. ratification of the Convention as being valid until such time as these "problems" are corrected.[58] The other objecting governments were not so explicit in this regard, although the legal and diplomatic implications of their filing of objections is the same.[59] Hence, all pretensions to the contrary not withstanding, the United States remains—quite conspicuously—an outlaw state.

Costs and Consequences

. . . The U.S. refusal to ratify even the ludicrously abbreviated conception of genocide it had itself engineered, in effect undermined any attempt to apply the Convention to prevent or punish perpetrators of the global proliferation of systematic mass murder programs which have been documented after 1945.

■ ■ ■ ■

In *none* of the "episodes" occurring prior to 1990—encompassing processes of such magnitude as the U.S.-sponsored 1965 Indonesian extermination of perhaps a half-million "communists,"* to the holocausts in Burundi and Bangladesh in 1972[60]—was the Genocide Convention invoked by the United Nations.[61] Indeed, with the notable exception of the Khmer Rouge "autogenocide" in Cambodia/Kampuchea—which was showcased in the most propagandistic fashion, as a post hoc justification for U.S. aggression there—none were ever described as being genocidal by mainstream journalists and commentators. It was not until the pretended U.S. ratification of the Convention had gone into effect that it became permissible for the U.N. to employ the term in serious fashion, and then only with respect to *some* perpetrators in *certain* instances.

The most salient illustrations of this concern the recent establishment of international tribunals—the first such since Nuremberg—to prosecute a few of those responsible for bloodbaths in Bosnia-Herzegovina and Rwanda on

*America provided crucial political, economic, and military assistance—including the training of the bulk of the officers corps—to the Indonesian army, which perpetrated the vast slaughter in the interests of the kind of "regional stability" demanded by U.S. policy; Deirdre Griswold, *The Bloodbath That Was* (New York: World View Publishers, 1975).

charges of genocide and other crimes.[62] While this seems at first glance to be a positive development, suggesting that the belated U.S. pretense of ratification, however illegitimate it may have been, is nonetheless serving constructive purposes, closer scrutiny reveals a rather different picture.* Those slated to be hauled into the defendants' dock are composed entirely of those who are at most marginal to U.S. policy interests, and whose actions have offered the prospect of disrupting the planetary order that policy is intended to impose.†

To all appearances, the United States, now that it has finally signed on to the Convention, has embarked upon a course of "claiming moral high ground" by instigating show trials on charges of genocide against those it considers essentially irrelevant—as it will undoubtedly do against outright enemies whenever opportunity knocks—the better to immunize itself and governments it deems useful from precisely the same charge. . . .

The upshot is that after a half-century of blocking implementation of the Genocide Convention, the United States has moved decisively to domesticate it, harnessing international law entirely to the needs and dictates of American policy.‡ Universal condemnation of the crime of genocide is thus being coopted to a point at which condemnation accrues only to genocides which, whether in form or in function, have failed to receive the sanction of the United States. Those which have not, are to be punished. Those which have are to be reinforced, rewarded, defined as anything but what they are, even to the extent of describing them as "democratic."§

*This is by no means to argue that the tribunals are in themselves inappropriate, or that those suspected of genocide in Africa and the Balkans should not be brought to trial. They should. The principle of equal justice before the law should, however, apply as much to this level of jurisprudence as to any other. Thus, more than a few U.S. friends—Pol Pot, for example, there being no statute of limitations on the crime of genocide—should by rights be seated right alongside the Serbian and Rwandan defendants. For that matter, there is still time to try a number of prominent American officials—from Robert McNamara to Ronald Wilson Reagan, George Herbert Walker Bush and William Jefferson Clinton—for their multitudinous war crimes and implementation of genocidal policies at home and abroad.

†No clearer indication of the marginality of the players involved is possible than that offered by U.S. State Department adviser (and former Democratic Senator from Colorado) Tim Wirth when—after State Department official Peter Tarnoff admitted on April 28, 1993, that what was happening in Bosnia-Herzegovina amounted to genocide, and that the U.S. was therefore legally/morally obligated to intervene by all means necessary to stop it—he observed that such a move would be unpopular because America had "no vital interest" in the Balkans. Intervention stood to erode support for the Clinton administration among American citizens, Wirth argued, and "the survival of the fragile liberal [*sic*] coalition represented by this Presidency" was more important than putting a stop to mere genocide; Francis Anthony Boyle, *The Bosnian People Charge Genocide* (Northampton, MA: Aletheia, 1996), p. xix. The administration's performance vis-á-vis the slaughter in Rwanda was even more lackluster. It was only after the killing had run its course in both instances, and the perpetrators selected for prosecution were safely out of power, that the administration discovered the "resolve" to "do something"; for further details, see David Rieff, *Slaughterhouse: Bosnia and the Failure of the West* (New York: Touchstone, 1995).

‡American demands that the codification of elements of international law be undertaken in conformity with the provisions of the U.S. Constitution (as interpreted by the U.S. Supreme Court)—thereby converting international law into little more than a global adjunct to the federal statutory code—have become endemic. The latest example is the assertion of the U.S. Department of State that it would block a Draft Declaration of the Rights of Indigenous Peoples unless the instrument was written to such specifications. This maneuver, which would have enshrined the denial of the right to self-determination to native peoples as a matter of international as well as U.S. domestic law, precipitated a mass walkout by indigenous delegates from a meeting of the United Nations Working Group on Indigenous Populations on October 22, 1996.

§Witness the example of Guatemala, which has slaughtered hundreds of thousands of indigenous Mayans since a CIA-sponsored coup in 1954, all the while being described as a "democratizing country" by the U.S. State Department; Robert M. Carmack, ed., *Harvest of Violence: The Mayan Indians and the Guatemala Crisis* (Norman: University of Oklahoma Press, 1988). Another good illustration is Colombia; Javier Giraldo, S.J., *Colombia: The Genocidal Democracy* (Monroe, ME: Common Courage Press, 1996). For a broader overview, see Noam Chomsky, *Deterring Democracy,* (New York: Hill & Wang,1992); Noam Chomsky and Edward S. Herman, *The Political Economy of Human Rights, Vol. 1: The Washington Connection and Third World Fascism* (Boston: South End Press, 1979).

Notes

1. The United Nations Charter (59 Stat. 1031, T.S., No. 993, 3 Bevans 1153, 1976 Y.B.U.N. 1043) was done at San Francisco on June 26, 1945, and entered into force on October 24; Burns H. Weston, Richard A. Falk and

Anthony D'Amato, *Basic Documents in International Law and World Order* (St. Paul, MN: West, 2nd ed., 1990) p. 16.

2. Quoted in Lawrence J. LaBlanc, *The United States and the Genocide Convention* (Durham, NC: Duke University Press, 1991) p. 23. On the fact that there was no operant definition of genocide involved in the Nuremberg proceedings, see Bradley F. Smith, *Reaching Judgment at Nuremberg* (New York: Basic Books, 1977).

3. Ibid. Also see M. Lippmann, "The Drafting of the 1948 Convention on the Punishment and Prevention of Genocide," *Boston University International Law Journal*, No. 3., 1984.

4. For Lemkin's original definition of genocide, see his *Axis Rule in Occupied Europe: Laws of Occupation, Analysis of Government, Proposals for Redress* (Washington, D.C.: Carnegie Endowment for International Peace, 1944), pp. 79–94. ECOSOC's request to the Secretariat was made via Resolution 47(IV), March 28, 1947.

5. U.N. Doc. A/362, June 14, 1947.

6. Nehemiah Robinson, *The Genocide Convention: A Commentary* (New York: Institute for Jewish Affairs, 1960) pp. 18–9.

7. *Report of the Ad Hoc Committee on Genocide*, 3 U.N. ESCOR Supp. 6, U.N. Doc. E/794 (1948).

8. Convention on the Punishment and Prevention of Genocide (U.S.T. _____, T.I.A.S. _____, 78 U.N.T.S. 277); done in New York, Dec. 9, 1948; entered into force, Jan. 12, 1951.

9. International Court of Justice, *Reports of Judgments, Advisory Opinions and Orders: Reservations to the Convention on Punishment and Prevention of the Crime of Genocide* (The Hague, 1951) pp. 15–69.

10. *Multilateral Treaties Deposited with the Secretary General: Status as of 31 December 1989*, St/Leg/Ser. E/8 97–98 (1990).

11. LaBlanc, *U.S. and the Genocide Convention, op. cit.*, p. 2.

12. Statement by President Ronald Reagan, as shown on CNN, March 14, 1981.

13. For a good sample of U.S. practice in this regard, see Noam Chomsky, *Deterring Democracy* (New York: Hill & Wang, 1992); Cynthia Peters, ed., *Collateral Damage: The "New World Order" At Home and Abroad* (Boston: South End Press, 1992).

14. Bradley F. Smith, *The Road to Nuremberg* (New York: Basic Books, 1981). The same principles were employed in prosecuting the Japanese leadership a bit later; see Arnold C. Brackman, *The Other Nuremberg: The Untold Story of the Tokyo War Crimes Trials* (New York: William Morrow, 1987).

15. Edwin Tetlow, *The United Nations: The First 25 Years* (New York: Peter Owen, 1970).

16. LaBlanc, *U.S. and the Genocide Convention, op. cit.*, pp. 26–7.

17. Quoted in Robert Davis and Mark Zannis, *The Genocide Machine in Canada: The Pacification of the North* (Montréal: Black Rose Books, 1973) p. 19.

18. 3 U.N. ESCOR, Doc. E/447–623 (1948), esp. pp. 139–47.

19. See, e.g., the Brazilian intervention; ibid., p. 143.

20. On the Soviet policies at issue, see, e.g., Nikolai Dekker and Andrei Lebed, eds., *Genocide in the U.S.S.R.: Studies in Group Destruction* (New York: Scarecrow Press, 1958); Robert Conquest, *The Nation Killers: The Soviet Deportation of Nationalities* (New York: Macmillan, 1970). The compromise was effected by Ernest Gross, U.S. delegate to ECOSOC's Sixth (Legal) Committee; 3 U.N. GAOR C.6 (49th mtg) at 407 (1948).

21. Davis and Zannis, *Genocide Machine, op. cit.*, p. 19.

22. On the Streicher prosecution, see Smith, *Reaching Judgment at Nuremberg, op. cit.*, pp. 200–3.

23. A good analysis, both of the composition of the U.S. diplomatic cadre at the U.N. and the duplicity imbedded in their agenda, is offered in Lloyd Garner's *Architects of Illusion: Men and Ideas in American Foreign Policy, 1941–49* (Chicago: Quadrangle, 1970). Also see Thomas M. Campbell, *Masquerade Peace: America's U.N. Policy, 1944–1945* (Tallahassee: Florida State University Press, 1973).

24. For texts, see Weston, Falk and D'Amato, *Basic Documents in International Law, op. cit.*; also see Ian Brownlie, ed., *Basic Documents on Human Rights* (Oxford: Clarendon Press, 3rd ed. 1992).

25. For texts, see Weston, Falk and D'Amato, *Basic Documents in International Law, op. cit.*; also see Adam Roberts and Richard Guelff, eds., *Documents on the Laws of War* (Oxford: Clarendon Press, 1984).

26. See, e.g., the remarks of Iowa Republican Bourke B. Hickenlooper during the 1950 Senate hearings: "[We] are in effect, in this Genocide Convention [and other elements of international law] dealing with the question of a certain area of the sovereignty of the United States which amounts to a surrender of that sovereignty"; U.S. Senate, *Hearings on the Genocide Convention Before a Subcommittee of the Senate Committee on Foreign Relations* (Washington, D.C.: 81st Cong., 2d Sess., U.S. Government Printing Office, 1950) p. 36. The Supreme Court sought a way out of this bind in *Reid v. Covert* (354 U.S. 1, 1957) by holding that "any treaty provision that is inconsistent with the United States Constitution would simply be invalid under national law." Article 27 of the Vienna Convention on the Law of Treaties (U.N. Doc. A/CONF.39/27 at 289 (1969)) overrules this opinion, however, by stipulating that no party may "invoke the provisions of its internal law as justification for its failure to perform a treaty" obligation; see generally, Sir Ian Sinclair, *The Vienna Convention on the Law of Treaties* (Manchester: Manchester University Press, 2nd ed., 1984).

27. This position was actually perfectly in keeping with the formulations of German political philosophy, widely admired before the war; see e.g., Carl Schmidt, *Political Theology: Four Chapters on the Concept of Sovereignty* (Cambridge, MA: MIT Press, 1985 trans. of 1922 original).

28. Quincy Wright, "The Law of the Nuremberg Trial," *American Journal of International Law*, No. 41, Jan. 1947.

For interpretation and application, see Richard Falk, *Human Rights and State Sovereignty* (New York: Holmes & Meier, 1981).

29. Affirmation of the Principles of International Law Recognized by the Charter of the Nuremberg Tribunal, adopted by the U.N. General Assembly, Dec. 11, 1946 (U.N.G.A. Res. 95(1), U.N. Doc. A/236 (1946) at 1144); for text, see Weston, Falk and D'Amato, *Basic Documents in International Law, op. cit.*, p. 140. The Charter itself (59 Stat. 1544, 82 U.N.T.S. 279 (Sept. 10, 1945)) appears at pp. 138–9.

30. LaBlanc, *U.S. and the Genocide Convention, op. cit.*, p. 20.

31. For a sampling of violence directed against one Asian American target group, see Charles J. McClain, *In Search of Equality: The Chinese Struggle Against Discrimination in the Nineteenth Century* (Berkeley: University of California Press, 1994) pp. 173–90.

32. *Hearings on the Genocide Convention, (1950), op. cit.*, p. 205.

33. Stewart E. Tolnay and E.M. Beck, *A Festival of Violence: An Analysis of Southern Lynchings, 1882–1930* (Urbana: University of Illinois Press, 1995) p. 1.

34. For what may be the best survey of comparable prewar violence in Germany; see Raul Hilberg, *The Destruction of the European Jews*, 3 vols. (New York: Holmes & Meier, rev. ed., 1985).

35. Tolnay and Beck, *Festival of Violence, op. cit.* A more detailed examination of lynching in a given subregion will be found in W. Fitzhugh Brundage, *Lynching in the New South, 1880–1930* (Urbana: University of Illinois Press, 1993).

36. Arthur F. Raper, *The Tragedy of Lynching* (Chapel Hill: University of North Carolina Press, 1933) pp. 469–72.

37. For case studies, see James Forman, *Sammy Younge, Jr.* (New York: Grove Press, 1968); Howard Smead, *Blood Justice: The Lynching of Charles Mack Parker* (New York: Oxford University Press, 1986).

38. See e.g., Leon Friedman, ed., *Southern Justice* (New York: Pantheon, 1965); Robert Sherrill, *Gothic Politics in the Deep South: Stars of the New Confederacy* (New York: Grossman, 1968).

39. *Hearings on the Genocide Convention (1950), op. cit.*, p. 27.

40. U.S. Senate, *Hearings on the Genocide Convention Before a Subcommittee of the Senate Committee on Foreign Relations* (Washington, D.C.: 92d Cong., 1st Sess., U.S. Government Printing Office, 1971) p. 189.

41. William L. Patterson, *The Man Who Cried Genocide: An Autobiography* (New York: International, 1971).

42. U.S. Senate, *Hearings on the Genocide Convention Before a Subcommittee of the Committee on Foreign Relations* (Washington, D.C.: 91st Cong. 2d Sess., U.S. Government Printing Office, 1970) pp. 148–9.

43. See generally, C. Vann Woodward, *The Strange Career of Jim Crow* (New York: Oxford University Press, 3rd rev. ed., 1974).

44. *Hearings on the Genocide Convention (1971), op. cit.*, pp. 18–9. Deutsch was undoubtedly correct in his understanding, a matter which could have made the Convention a powerful weapon in any serious effort to abolish institutionalized racial/ethnical discrimination in the U.S. (a goal to which the ABA proclaimed itself "philosophically" committed). As with the earlier-discussed question of lynching however, it was this very potential effectiveness of the Convention in combating systemic discrimination which seems to have prompted the ABA to oppose its ratification.

45. Indeed, the only reference to the issue devolved upon an absurd query by segregationists as to whether the busing of school children to achieve integration in educational institutions might not qualify as "genocide"; *Hearings on the Genocide Convention (1970), op. cit.*, pp. 138–9, note 11.

46. Although most of it is carefully framed in terms other than genocide, there is a vast literature on these historical processes of extermination. Two excellent works which call things by their right names are David Svaldi's *Sand Creek and the Rhetoric of Extermination: A Case Study in Indian-White Relations* (Washington, D.C.: University Press of America, 1989) and David E. Stannard's *American Holocaust: Columbus and the Conquest of the New World* (New York: Oxford University Press, 1992).

47. There is, for example, not a single reference to "American Indians" or "Native Americans" in the index of LaBlanc's reasonably thorough study.

48. This followed Reagan's sudden endorsement of the Convention in a speech to the B'nai B'rith during his 1984 reelection campaign. The possibility of ratification was foreclosed that year through a filibuster by Jesse Helms; LaBlanc, *U.S. and the Genocide Convention, op. cit.*, pp. 142, 146.

49. As the editors of the *Wall Street Journal* were to put it on January 19, 1989, Reagan "restored the efficiency, and morale of the armed forces [and] demonstrated the will to use force in Grenada and Libya." For a thoroughly glorified account of the first of these travesties, see Major Mark Adkin, *Urgent Fury: The Battle for Grenada* (Lexington, MA: D.C. Heath, 1989). On the bloodbath in Lebanon, see Noam Chomsky, *The Fateful Triangle: The U.S., Israel and the Palestinians* (Boston: South End Press, 1983). On U.S. support to Iraq, see Rabab Hadi, "The Gulf Crisis: How We Got There," in Greg Bates, ed., *Mobilizing Democracy: Changing the U.S. Role in the Middle East* (Monroe: ME: Common Courage Press, 1991). On Nicaragua and El Salvador, see Holly Sklar, *Washington's War on Nicaragua* (Boston: South End Press, 1988). On Libya, see Jonathan Bearman, *Qadhafi's Libya* (London: Zed Books, 1986); Noam Chomsky, *Pirates and Emperors: International Terrorism in the Real World* (New York: Claremont, 1986) pp. 138–46. More broadly, see Michael T. Klare, *Beyond the "Vietnam Syndrome": U.S. Interventionism in the 1980s* (Washington, D.C.: Institute for Policy

Studies, 1981); Michael T. Klare and Peter Kornbluh, eds., *Low Intensity Warfare: Counterinsurgency, Proinsurgency and Antiterrorism in the Eighties* (New York: Pantheon, 1989); Chomsky, *Deterring Democracy, op. cit.*

50. As Reagan described the situation, for the United States, the Convention had been reduced to a "mere symbol of opposition to genocide"; U.S. Senate, *Executive Report No. 2* (Washington, D.C.: 99th Cong. 1st Sess., 1985) p. 4.

51. The act was passed by voice vote—thus preventing a record of how many and which representatives voted for and against it—in the House on April 25, 1988; U.S. Senate, *Senate Report No. 333* (Washington, D.C.: 100th Cong. 2d Sess., U.S. Government Printing Office, 1988) pp. 1–3. The same method was adopted in the Senate on October 14; *Congressional Record*, No. 134, Oct. 14, 1988, S16107–17, S16266–9.

52. *Multilateral Treaties Deposited with the Secretary-General, op. cit.*, p. 101, n. 2.

53. U.S. Senate, Hearings on the Genocide Convention Before a Subcommittee of the Committee on Foreign Relations (Washington, D.C.: 99th Cong., 1st Sess., U.S. Government Printing Office (1985)) pp. 24–5.

54. Aside from Dodd and Mathias, the signatories to the statement from which the quoted passage is excerpted were Claiborne Pell (D-Rhode Island), Joseph Biden, Jr. (D-Delaware), Paul Sarbanes (D-Maryland), Alan Cranston (D-California), Thomas Eagleton (D-Missouri) and John Kerry (D-Massachusetts); *Senate Executive Report No. 2, op. cit.*, p. 32.

55. LaBlanc, *U.S. and the Genocide Convention, op. cit.*, pp. 98, 240.

56. *Multilateral Treaties Deposited with the Secretary-General, op. cit.*, pp. 102–4.

57. This result was entirely predictable, given that the same three countries had already entered objections to attempts to avoid ICJ jurisdiction by Bulgaria, Poland and Romania; U.S. Senate, *Hearing on the Genocide Convention Before the Senate Committee on Foreign Relations* (Washington, D.C.: 98th Cong., 2d. Sess., U.S. Government Printing Office, 1984) p. 63.

58. LaBlanc, *U.S. and the Genocide Convention, op. cit.*, p. 12.

59. International Court of Justice, *Reports of Judgments, Advisory Opinions and Orders: Reservations to the Convention on the Prevention and Punishment of the Crime of Genocide* (The Hague: International Court of Justice) pp. 15–69. Also see Sinclair, *Vienna Convention, op. cit.* pp. 47–69; J. Kohn, "Reservations to Multilateral Treaties: How International Legal Doctrine Reflects World Vision," *Harvard International Law Journal*, No. 71, 1982.

60. The respective death tolls were about three million in Bangladesh, some 100,000 in Burundi; Kalyan Chaudhuri, *Genocide in Bangladesh* (Bombay: Orient Longman, 1972); Réné Lemarchand and David Martin, *Selective Genocide in Burundi* (London: Minority Rights Group Report No. 20, 1974).

61. E.g., the "United Nations [refused] even to discuss the case" of Bangladesh. Similarly, "the United States never publicly rebuked the Burundi government"; Chalk and Jonassohn, *History and Sociology of Genocide* (New Haven: Yale University Press, 1990) pp. 397, 391.

62. For examination of the groundwork upon which creation of the first of these tribunals was based, see Francis A. Boyle, *The Bosnian People Charge Genocide: Proceedings at the International Court of Justice Concerning* Bosnia v. Serbia *on the Prevention and Punishment of the Crime of Genocide* (Northampton, MA: Alethia Press, 1996).

ECOLOGY OF FEAR

MIKE DAVIS

In my 1990 book, *City of Quartz*, I explored various tendencies toward the militarization of the Southern California landscape. Events since the 1992 riots—including a four-year-long recession, a sharp decline in factory jobs, deep cuts in welfare and public employment, a backlash against immigrant workers, the failure of police reform, and an unprecedented exodus of middle-class families—have only reinforced spatial apartheid in greater Los Angeles. . . .

■ ■ ■ ■

Scanscape

Is there any need to explain *why* fear eats the soul of Los Angeles? Only the middle-class dread of progressive taxation exceeds the current obsession with personal safety and social insulation. In the face of intractable urban poverty and homelessness, and despite one of the greatest expansions in American business history, a bipartisan consensus insists that any and all budgets must be balanced and entitlements reduced. With no hope for further public investment in the remediation of underlying social conditions, we are forced instead to make increasing public and private investments in physical security. The rhetoric of urban reform persists, but the substance is extinct. "Rebuilding L.A." simply means padding the bunker.

As city life grows more feral, the various social milieux adopt security strategies and technologies according to their means. . . . To the extent that these security measures are reactions to urban unrest, it is possible to speak about a "riot tectonics" that episodically convulses and reshapes urban space. After the 1965 Watts rebellion, for instance, downtown Los Angeles's leading landowners organized a secretive "Committee of 25" to deal with perceived threats to redevelopment efforts.[1] Warned by the LAPD that a black "inundation" of the central city was imminent, the committee abandoned efforts to revitalize the city's aging financial and retail core. Instead, it persuaded city hall to subsidize the transplanting of banks and corporate front offices to a new financial district atop Bunker Hill, a few blocks to the west. The city's redevelopment agency, acting as a private planner, bailed out the committee's lost investments in the old business district by offering discounts far below real market value on parcels of land within the new core.

The key to the success of this strategy, celebrated as Downtown's "renaissance," was the physical segregation of the new core and its land values behind a rampart of regraded palisades, concrete pillars, and freeway walls. Traditional pedestrian connections between Bunker Hill and the old core were removed, and foot traffic was elevated above the street on "pedways" . . . access to which was controlled by the security systems of individual skyscrapers. This radical privatization of Downtown public space, with its ominous racial overtones, occurred without significant public debate.

The 1992 riots vindicated the foresight of Fortress Downtown's designers. While windows were being smashed throughout the old business district, Bunker Hill lived up to its name. By flicking a few switches on their command consoles, the security staffs of the great bank towers were able to cut off all access to their expensive real estate. Bullet-proof steel doors rolled down over street-level entrances, escalators instantly froze, and electronic locks sealed off pedestrian passageways. As the *Los Angeles Business Journal* pointed out, the riot-tested success of corporate Downtown's defenses has only stimulated demand for new and higher levels of physical security.[2]

One consequence of this demand has been the continuing erosion of the boundary between architecture and law enforcement. The LAPD have become central players in the Downtown design process. No major project now breaks ground without their participation. Police representatives have exerted effective pressure against the provision of public toilets ("crime scenes" in their opinion) and the toleration of street vending ("lookouts for drug dealers"). The riots also provided suburban police departments with a pretext for enhancing their involvement in planning and design issues. In affluent Thousand Oaks, for example, the sheriff's liaison to the planning commission persuaded the city to outlaw alleys as a "crime prevention priority."[3]

Video monitoring of Downtown's redeveloped zones, meanwhile, has been extended to parking structures, private sidewalks, and plazas. This comprehensive surveillance constitutes a virtual *scanscape*—a space of protective visibility that increasingly defines where white-collar office workers and middle-class tourists feel safe downtown. . . .

A premier platform for the new surveillance technology will be that anachronism of the nineteenth century: the skyscraper. Tall buildings are becoming increasingly sentient and packed with deadly firepower. The skyscraper with a mainframe brain in *Die Hard* (actually F. Scott Johnson's Fox-Pereira Tower in Century City) anticipates a new generation of architectural antiheroes as intelligent buildings alternately battle evil or become its pawns. The sensory systems of many of Los Angeles's new office towers already include panopticon vision, smell, sensitivity to temperature and humidity, motion detection, and, in a few cases, hearing. Some architects now predict that the day is coming when a building's own artificial intelligent computers will be able to automatically screen and identify its human population, and even respond to their emotional states, especially fear or panic. Without dispatching security personnel, the building itself will be able to manage crises both minor (like ordering street people out of the building or preventing them from using toilets) and major (like trapping burglars in an elevator).

The Invisible Riot

Friday, 5 May 1992. The armored personnel carrier squats on the corner like *un gran sapo feo*—a "big ugly toad"—according to nine-year-old Emerio. His parents talk anxiously, almost in a whisper, about the *desparecidos*: Raul from Tepic, big Mario, the younger Flores girl, and the cousin from Ahuachapan. Like all Salvadorans, they know about those who "disappear"; they remember the headless corpses and the man whose tongue had been pulled through the hole in his throat like a necktie. That is why they came here—to zip code 90057, Los Angeles, California.[4]

Their neighborhood, on the edge of MacArthur Park, is part of the large halo of older, high-density housing surrounding the scanscape of the fortified core. These tenement districts perform the classic functions of Burgess's "zone in transition": providing urban ports of entry for the city's poorest and most recent immigrants—in this case from Mexico, Guatemala, and El Salvador rather than Ireland and Bohemia—who work in Downtown hotels and garment factories. But the normally bustling streets are now eerily quiet. Emerio's parents are counting their friends and neighbors, Salvadoran and Mexican, who are suddenly gone.

Some are in the county jail on Bauchet Street, little more than brown grains of sand lost among the 17,000 other alleged *saqueadores* (looters) and *incendarios* (arsonists) detained after the most violent American civil disturbance since enraged Irish immigrants burned Manhattan in 1863. Those without papers are probably already back in Tijuana, broke and disconsolate, cut off from their families and new lives. Violating city policy, the police fed hundreds of hapless undocumented *saqueadores* to the INS for deportation before the ACLU or immigrant rights groups had even realized that they had been arrested.

For many days the television talked only of the "South Central riot," "Black rage," and the "Crips and Bloods." Truly, the Rodney King case was a watershed in national race relations, a test of the very meaning of the citizenship for which African-Americans have struggled for four hundred years. It was also the fuse on an explosive accumulation of local grievances among young blacks, ranging from Chief Gates's infamous mass detentions ("Operation Hammer") to the murder of 15-year-old Latasha Harlins by a Korean grocer in 1991. But the 1992 upheaval was far more complex than the 1965 Watts rebellion, although some issues, especially police abuse, remained the same. While most of the news media remained trapped in the black-and-white world of 1965, the second Los Angeles riot burst emphatically into technicolor.

. . . Despite the tabloid media's obsession with black violence, only 36 percent of the riot arrestees were African-American, while 52 percent had Spanish surnames and 10 percent were white. Moreover, the greatest density of riot-related "incidents" occurred north of the Santa Monica Freeway in predominantly Latino and Asian areas. Indeed, nearly as many suspects were booked by the LAPD's Ramparts station, which polices Emerio's neighborhood, as by all four stations which make up the department's South Bureau in South Central Los Angeles. Even the Hollywood station made twice as many arrests as the 77th Street station, which patrolled the supposed riot epicenter—where truck driver Reginald Denny was nearly beaten to death—at the intersection of Florence and Normandie Avenues.[5]

This invisible Mid-City riot, conflated by most news reports with events in majority-black areas,* was driven primarily by empty bellies and broken dreams, not by outrage over the acquittal of the cops who beat Rodney King. It was the culmination of a decade of declining economic opportunity and rising poverty followed by two years of recession that tripled unemployment in Los Angeles's immigrant neighborhoods. Academic studies since the riot have shown that Mexican and Central American immigrants arriving after 1980 had less hope than their predecessors of finding stable, entry-level positions in a regional economy that had become supersaturated with unskilled labor. "Massively growing numbers of Mexican immigrants," according to UCLA sociologist Vilma Ortiz, "have been packed into a relatively narrow tier of occupations."[7] Already by 1980, starting wages for new arrivals had fallen by 13 percent compared to 1970, and in the decade that followed, the portion of the Los Angeles population falling below the poverty line grew by a full percentage point or more each year.[8]

Then, 1990: cutbacks in defense spending and the bursting of the Japanese financial bubble (source of massive "super-yen" investments in Los Angeles real estate during the 1980s) converged to plunge the Southern California economy into its worst recession since 1938. An incredible 27 percent of national job loss was concentrated in the Los Angeles metropolitan region. In Los Angeles county this translated into a catastrophic 30 percent decline in manufacturing employment that savaged light industry, where Mexican immigrants make up the majority of workers, as well as aerospace and military electronics.[9] The impact of the recession, moreover, was intensified by simultaneous cutbacks in AFDC and MediCal benefits as well as deep slashes in local school budgets. Tens of thousands of families lost their tenuous economic footholds, while the number of children living in poverty increased by a third during the course of the recession.[10]

For anyone who cared to pay attention there were dramatic social storm warnings in the months before the spring 1992 riots. Indeed, no image revealed the mixed origins of the upheaval more clearly than the photograph published in the *Los Angeles Times* three days before Christmas 1991. It showed part of the throng of 20,000 women and children, predominantly recent Latino immigrants, waiting outside skid row's Fred Jordan Mission for the handout of a chicken, a dozen corn tortillas, three small toys, and a blanket. According to the *Times*, "Eight blocks were cordoned off around 5th Street and Towne Avenue to accommodate the crush of people. Some in the five-hour line said they were willing to brave the gritty streets for what one woman described as her 'only possibility' for a Christmas dinner.[11] Human distress on so broad a scale had not been photographed in California since the famous depression-era documentaries of Margaret Bourke-White and Dorothea Lange.

Nineteen-thirties-type misery was no surprise, however, to food bank volunteers, who had been warning city officials about the ominous decline in emergency food resources, or to public health workers, who were reporting classic symptoms of malnutrition—anemia and stunted growth—in nearly a quarter of the poor children passing through a county screening program.[12] Other visible barometers of the crisis included the rapidly growing colonies of unemployed busboys, gardeners, and construction laborers living on the desolate flanks of Crown Hill across from

*The "independent" press was as fixated as the mainstream on exclusively black-and-white images of the riots. The Institute for Alternative Journalism's *Inside the L.A. Riots*, for example, contains 70 dramatic photographs, only one of which clearly depicts a Latino (a small boy).[6]

Downtown or in the concrete bed of the Los Angeles River, where the homeless are forced to use sewage outflow for bathing and cooking.

Emerio's parents and their neighbors spoke of a gathering sense of desperation in early 1992, a perception of a future already looted of opportunity. The riot arrived like a magic dispensation. In Mid-City neighborhoods people were initially shocked by the violence, then mesmerized by the televised images of black and Latino crowds in South Central Los Angeles helping themselves to mountains of desirable goods without interference from the police. On the second day of unrest, 30 April, the authorities blundered twice: first by suspending school and releasing the kids into the street, second by announcing that the National Guard was on the way to help enforce a dusk-to-dawn curfew.

Thousands immediately interpreted this as a last call to participate in the general redistribution of wealth in progress. Looting exploded through the majority-immigrant neighborhoods of Mid-City, as well as Echo Park, Van Nuys, and Huntington Park. Although arsonists struck wantonly and almost at random, the looting crowds were governed by a visible moral economy. As one middle-aged lady explained to me, "Stealing is a sin, but this is more like a television game show where everyone wins." In contrast to the looters on Hollywood Boulevard who stole Madonna's underwear from Frederick's, the masses of Mid-City concentrated on the prosaic necessities of life like cockroach spray and Pampers.

■ ■ ■ ■

> Since most of the liquor stores and markets in this area greatly overcharge the customers for poor quality merchandise, there is great resentment. My students told me that when some of them saw Viva Market, on Hoover and Olympic, being looted as they watched television, their parents immediately left the apartment only to return an hour later with food and other items. They didn't see this as a "riot," just an opportunity to get even with the "exploiters."
>
> There was no coordination or planning by the people north of the Santa Monica Freeway, other than that provided by the roadmap shown on television. . . . I do not think that Korean stores were attacked for exclusively ethnic reasons. If Korean-owned liquor stores were burned, Korean travel agencies and beauty-shops were not touched. The uprising was directed against the police and rip-off merchants in general. It was driven by economic desperation and class resentment, not race.[13]

The official reaction to this postmodern bread riot was the biggest multiagency law enforcement operation in history. For weeks afterward, elite LAPD Metro Squad units, supported by the National Guard, swept through the tenements in search of stolen goods, while Border Patrolmen from as far away as Texas trawled the streets for undocumented residents. Meanwhile, thousands of *saqueadores*, many of them pathetic scavengers captured in the charred ruins the day after the looting, languished for weeks in the county jail, unable to meet absurdly high bails. One man, apprehended with a packet of sunflower seeds and two cartons of milk, was held on $15,000 bond. Some curfew violators received 30-day jail sentences, despite the fact that they were either homeless or spoke no English. Angry suburban politicians, meanwhile, outbid one another with demands to deport immigrants and strip their U.S.-born children of citizenship.

■ ■ ■ ■

Free-Fire Zone

By mid-May 1992, the National Guard, together with the army and the marines, had withdrawn from the inner city neighborhoods of Los Angeles. Flags folded and rifles stacked, thousands of citizen-soldiers returned to their ordinary suburban lives. As the humvees and trucks moved out, another army, the Eighteenth Street gang, immediately resumed its occupation of Los Angeles's Mid-City area. Some members taunted departing guardsmen with the boastful chant that weary neighbors had been hearing for years: "Soy Eighteen with a bullet / I got my finger on the trigger / I'm gonna pull it."

■ ■ ■ ■

By their own admission, the overwhelmed inner city detachments of the LAPD have been unable to keep track of all the bodies on the street, much less deal with common burglaries, car thefts, and gang-organized protection rackets.[14] . . . [T]he present-day occupants of the transition zone are left to fend for themselves. Lacking the resources or political clout of more affluent neighborhoods, they have turned to Mr. Smith and Mr. Wesson, whose names follow "protected by . . ." on hand-made signs decorating humble homes all over South Central and Mid-City Los Angeles.

Slumlords, meanwhile, are conducting their own private reign of terror against drug dealers, petty criminals, and deadbeat tenants. Faced with "zero tolerance" laws authorizing the seizure or destruction of properties used for drug sales, they are hiring their own goon squads and armed mercenaries to "exterminate" crime on their premises. Shortly after the 1992 riots, *Times* reporter Richard Colvin accompanied one of these crews on a swashbuckling rampage through the Westlake, Venice, and Panorama City districts.

Led by a six-foot-three, 280-pound "soldier of fortune" named David Roybal, this security squad was renowned among landlords for its efficient brutality. Suspected drug dealers and their customers, along with rent-in-arrears tenants and other landlord irritants, were physically driven from buildings at gunpoint. Those who resisted or even complained were beaten without mercy. In a Panorama City raid a few years earlier, "Roybal and his crew collared so many residents and squatters for drugs that they converted a recreation room into a holding tank and handcuffed arrestees to a blood-spattered wall." The LAPD knew about this private jail but ignored residents' protests. An envious police officer told Colvin, "If we could do what these security guards do, we'd get rid of the crime problem, just like that."[15]

■ ■ ■ ■

In addition to these rent-a-thugs, the inner ring has also spawned a vast cottage industry manufacturing wrought-iron bars and grates for home protection. An estimated 100,000 inner city homes, like cages in a human zoo, have "burglar bars" bolted over all their doors and windows. As in a George Romero movie, working-class families now lock themselves in every night from the zombified city outside. . . . Yet such security may be a cruel illusion. The Los Angeles Fire Department estimates that at least half of the city's barred homes lack the legally required quick-release mechanisms that allow residents to escape in an emergency. The result has been a recent epidemic of horrific fires in which entire trapped families have been immolated in their bungalows or apartments.[16]

The prison cell finds many other architectural resonances in the postriot inner city. Even before the Rodney King uprising, most liquor and convenience stores, taking the lead from pawnshops, had completely caged in their cash register counters, sometimes with lifesize cardboard cutouts of policemen placed near the window. Even local greasy spoons had begun to exchange hamburgers for money through bulletproof acrylic turnstiles. Now the same design—call it the "Brinks" aesthetic—has been extended to social service offices and hospitals. In light of recent cutbacks in welfare programs and medical services, along with all-day waits in welfare lines or for emergency medical treatment,[17] the county has sought to protect employees from public rage through the comprehensive installation of metal detectors, video monitors, convex surveillance mirrors, panic buttons, chairs bolted to the floor, and "interview booths divided by thick, shatterproof glass partitions." Not surprisingly, advocates for the poor have denounced this paranoid environment in which welfare mothers are treated like dangerous inmates in a high-security prison.[18]

Schools also have become more like prisons. Even as per capita education spending has plummeted in many local school districts, scarce resources are being absorbed in fortifying school grounds and hiring more armed security police. Teenagers complain bitterly about overcrowded classrooms and demoralized teachers, about decaying campuses that have become little more than daytime detention centers for an abandoned generation. Many students are literally locked in during school hours, while new daytime curfew laws—the violation of which carries stiff penalties for parents—allow police to treat truancy as a criminal offense. In some Southern California communities, the police have direct access to computerized school records. In the

Los Angeles Unified School District kids who become informers on fellow students' drug habits are rewarded with concert tickets, CDs, and new clothes, and if Mayor Riordan gets his way, the LAPD may even gain its very own high school: a "junior police academy" magnet school that would be a national first.[19]

The school yard, meanwhile, has become a killing field. Scores of students since 1985 have been wounded or killed during school hours. As a result, high school students in Los Angeles are now checked for weapons by metal detectors as they enter school each morning. At Long Beach's Lindbergh Junior High School, frequently raked by gunfire, administrators built a 900-foot-long, 10-foot-high wall "to deflect bullets" fired from a neighboring public housing project. At a Santa Monica elementary school, little kids regularly practice "drive-by drills." Just as their parents once learned to cower under desks in case of a nuclear attack, so are today's students "taught to drop at a teacher's signal in case of another drive-by shooting—and stay there until they receive an all-clear signal."[20]

Federally subsidized housing and public housing projects, for their part, are coming to resemble the "strategic hamlets" that were used to incarcerate the rural population of Vietnam. Although no Los Angeles housing project is yet as militarized as those in San Juan, Puerto Rico, where the National Guard was sent in by the governor, or as technologically sophisticated as Chicago's Cabrini-Green, where retinal scans (as in the opening sequence of *Blade Runner*) are used to check IDs, the housing authority police exercise absolute control over residents' freedom of movement.[21]

In a city with the nation's worst housing shortage, project tenants, fearful of eviction, are reluctant to claim any constitutional protection against unlawful search or seizure. Like peasants in a rebel countryside, they are routinely stopped and searched without probable cause, while their homes are broken into without court warrants. In several projects, public access is restricted by guard posts, and residents must submit lists of frequent visitors. And, as in other big cities, federal "one strike and you're out" regulations allow managers to evict otherwise innocent tenants of federally subsidized housing for crimes committed by their relatives or guests: a policy of collective punishment similar to that long practiced by Israelis on the West Bank.*

■ ■ ■ ■

Half-Moons of Repression

. . . In contemporary metropolitan Los Angeles, new species of enclaves are emerging in sympathy with the militarization of the landscape. For want of any generally accepted name, we might call them "social control districts." They merge the sanctions of the criminal or civil code with landuse planning to create what Michel Foucault would undoubtedly have recognized as a yet higher stage in the evolution of the "disciplinary order" of the modern city. Growing like weeds in a constitutional no man's land, Southern California's social control districts can be distinguished according to their specific juridical modes of imposing spatial "discipline."

Abatement districts, currently enforced against graffiti and prostitution in signposted neighborhoods of Los Angeles and West Hollywood, extend the traditional police power over nuisance (the legal fount of all zoning) from noxious industry to noxious behavior. Financed by fines collected (on prostitution offenses) or special sales taxes levied (on spray paints, for example), they devote additional law enforcement resources to specific social problems. Going a step further, business leaders in Little Tokyo and Hollywood have proposed the establishment of self-taxing "improvement districts" which would be able to hire private security guards to supplement the police. Needless to say, this would further erode the already fuzzy boundary between public and private policing in Los Angeles.

Since the 1992 riots, moreover, the LAPD has buttressed abatement programs by interventions in the zoning process. Using computer software to identify hot spots of prostitution, petty crime, and drug use, the police now routinely veto building and operating permits for "crime

*In November 1997, three mothers from a housing project in Venice, aided by the ACLU, challenged the constitutionality of the "one strike" policy in a major lawsuit against the federal government.[22]

magnet" businesses. "Most commanding officers don't want new bars in their area, or new liquor locations or new dance halls," a police spokesperson explained to the *Los Angeles Times.* "What you have is an increased police interest in using zoning laws as vehicles to stop these businesses when they have problems." The LAPD considers this a logical extension of "community-based policing," but some Latino community leaders have complained that it really constitutes discrimination against Spanish-speaking mom-and-pop businesses like meat markets and *tiendas* (corner grocery stores) that need liquor sales to break even. Drinkers simply shop at supermarkets instead.[23]

Enhancement districts, represented all over Southern California by the "drug-free zones" and "gun-free zones" surrounding public schools, add extra federal or state penalties ("enhancements") to crimes committed within a specified radius of public institutions. In other cases, new laws, targeted at specific groups and locations, criminalize otherwise legal behavior. As a condition of probation, for example, prostitutes are now given maps demarcating areas, including parts of Hollywood, South Central, and the San Fernando Valley, where they can be arrested simply for walking down the street. In Costa Mesa (Orange County) prostitutes are further humiliated by having their clothes confiscated after arrest. They are released from jail wearing flimsy white paper jumpsuits.[24]

From the circumscription of a group's otherwise legal behavior, it is a short step to *containment* districts designed to quarantine potentially epidemic social problems or, more usually, social types. In Southern California these undesirables run the gamut from that insect illegal immigrant, the Mediterranean fruit fly, to homeless people. Since the early 1980s, the city of Los Angeles has tried to prevent the spillover of cardboard "condos" into surrounding council districts or into the more upscale precincts of Downtown by keeping homeless people "contained" (the official term) within the 50-square-block area of skid row. In 1996, the city council formalized the status quo by declaring a portion of skid row's sidewalks an official "sleeping zone." As soup kitchens and skid row missions brace themselves for a new wave of homelessness in the wake of recent state and federal welfare reforms, the LAPD maintains its traditional policy of keeping street people herded within the boundaries of the nation's largest outdoor poorhouse.

Obverse to containment is the formal *exclusion* of pariah groups from public space or even the city limits. The tactics are sometimes ingenious. In Anaheim, for instance, a city-supported citizens' group ("Operation Steer Clear") dumped tons of steer manure in local parks in the hope that the stench would drive away drug dealers and gang members. "Anticamping" ordinances, likewise, have been passed by a spate of Southland cities, including the "Peoples' Republic" of Santa Monica, with the goal of banishing the homeless from sight. Since such exclusion ordinances merely sweep a stigmatized social group onto the next community's doorstep, each city, in a chain reaction, adopts comparable legislation in order to avoid becoming the regional equivalent of a human landfill.

Similarly, Los Angeles and a score of smaller cities have used sweeping civil injunctions—whose constitutionality was upheld by the California Supreme Court in January 1997—to prevent gangs from congregating in parks or on street corners. Although one high-ranking LAPD official has complained that these "gang-free zones" merely push gang activity into adjoining neighborhoods, they are highly popular with vote-conscious district attorneys and city council members who love the image that the injunctions broadcast of decisive action and comprehensive deterrence.[25] In a typical example, a Los Angeles judge banned Eighteenth Street homeboys in one neighborhood from "associating in public view" in groups larger than two, even in their own front yards. He also imposed an 8 P.M. curfew on juvenile gang members and banned the use of cellular phones and pagers. In addition, his injunction prohibited Eighteenth Street members from whistling in public—a form of signaling, the city attorney alleged, used by lookouts for drug dealers.[26]

As civil libertarians have pointed out, the social control district strategy penalizes individuals, even in the absence of a criminal act, merely for group membership. "Status criminalization," moreover, feeds off middle-class fantasies about the nature of the dangerous classes. And fearful fantasies have been growing in hothouse fashion.

In the mid-1980s, for example, the ghost of Cotton Mather suddenly appeared in suburban Southern California. Allegations that local day-care centers were actually covens of satanic perversion wrenched courtrooms back to the seventeenth century. In the course of the McMartin Preschool molestation trial—the longest and most expensive such ordeal in American history—children testified about molester-teachers who flew around on broomsticks and other manifestations of the Evil One.

The creation by the little city of San Dimas of the nation's first "child-molestation exclusion zone" was one legacy of the accompanying collective hysteria, which undoubtedly mined huge veins of displaced parental guilt. This Twin Peaks–like suburb in the eastern San Gabriel Valley was signposted from stem to stern with the warning: "Hands Off Our Kids! We I.D. and Fingerprint Our Kids for Safety." It is unclear whether the armies of lurking pedophiles in the mountains above San Dimas were deterred by these warnings, but any post-Burgess mapping of urban space must acknowledge the power that bad dreams now wield over the public landscape.

■ ■ ■ ■

The Neighbors Are Watching

The Neighborhood Watch program—comprising more than 5,500 crime surveillance block clubs—is the LAPD's most important contribution to urban policing. . . . [A] huge network of watchful neighbors provides a security system midway between the besieged, gun-toting homeowners of the transition zone and the private police forces of more affluent, gated suburbs. The brainchild of former police chief Ed Davis, the Neighborhood Watch concept has been emulated in hundreds of North American and European cities from Seattle to London. In the aftermath of the 1965–71 cycle of unrest in South Central and East Los Angeles, Davis envisaged the program as the anchor for a "basic car" policing strategy designed to rebuild community support for the LAPD. He wanted to reestablish a strong territorial identity between patrol units and individual neighborhoods. Although his successor Daryl Gates preferred the commando bravado of SWAT units to the public-relations-oriented basic car patrols, Neighborhood Watch continued to flourish throughout the 1980s.

According to LAPD spokesperson Sgt. Christopher West, "Neighborhood Watch clubs are intended to increase local solidarity and self-confidence in the face of crime. Spurred by their block captains, residents become vigilant in the protection of each other's property and well-being. Suspicious behavior is immediately reported and homeowners regularly meet with patrol officers to plan crime-prevention tactics." An off-duty cop in a Winchell's Donut Shop in Silver Lake was more picturesque. "Neighborhood Watch is like the wagon train in an old-fashioned cowboy movie. The neighbors are the settlers and the goal is to teach them to circle their wagons and fight off the Indians until the cavalry—the LAPD—can ride to their rescue."[27]

Needless to say, this Wild West analogy has its sinister side. Who, after all, gets to decide what behavior is "suspicious" or who looks like an "Indian"? The obvious danger in any program that conscripts thousands of citizens as police informers under the official slogan "Be on the Look Out for Strangers" is that it inevitably stigmatizes innocent groups. Inner city teenagers are especially vulnerable to flagrant stereotyping and harassment.

At one Neighborhood Watch meeting I attended in Echo Park, an elderly white woman asked a young policeman how to identify hard-core gang members. His answer was stupefyingly succinct: "Gang-bangers wear expensive athletic shoes and clean, starched tee-shirts." The woman nodded her appreciation of this "expert" advice, while others in the audience squirmed in their seats at the thought of the youth in the neighborhood who would eventually be stopped and searched simply because they were well groomed.

Critics also worry that Neighborhood Watch does double duty as a captive constituency for police interests. As Sgt. West acknowledged, "Block captains are appointed by patrol officers and the program does obviously tend to attract the most law-and-order conscious members of the community." These pro-police residents, moreover, tend to be unrepresentative of their neighborhoods. In poor, youthful Latino areas,

Watch captains are frequently elderly, residual Anglos. In areas where renters are a majority, the Watch activists are typically homeowners or landlords. Although official regulations are supposed to keep the program apolitical, block captains have long been regarded as the LAPD's precinct workers. In a bitter 1986 election, for example, the police union routinely used Neighborhood Watch meetings to campaign for the recall of the liberal majority, led by Rose Bird, on the California Supreme Court.

The "community policing advisory boards" established in the wake of the Rodney King beating have been hardly more independent. Although a reform commission headed by Warren Christopher criticized the LAPD's refusal to respond to citizen complaints, it failed to provide for elected advisory boards. As with Watch groups, board members serve strictly at the pleasure of local police commanders. When the Venice advisory board endorsed a spring 1992 ballot measure crafted by the Christopher Commission but opposed by the police union, they were summarily fired by the captain in charge of the Pacific Division.[28]

Since the 1992 riots some Neighborhood Watch groups have, with police encouragement, engaged in forms of surveillance that verge on vigilantism. In the San Fernando Valley, for example, volunteers from the white, upper-income neighborhoods of Porter Ranch and Granada Hills have been informally deputized as stealth auxiliaries in the police war against black and Latino gang youth. Clad in black ninja gear, they "perch in the dark on rooftops or crouch in vacant apartments, peering through shrouded windows," in hopes of photographing or videotaping graffiti taggers and drug peddlers. In a twist on the Rodney King affair, the videos are then used by the police as evidence in court.[29]

Several law-and-order pundits believe that Los Angeles needs to go even further and like Israel "flood the streets . . . every bus, shop and public space" with armed auxiliaries trained at police firing ranges and recruited from the respectable classes ("over forty and with a clean criminal record").[30] As a first approximation to this ideal "vigilantopolis," the LAPD has turned a blind eye on openly armed and menacing groups of homeowners and businessmen. In the Mid-City area, the ethnic enclave of "Koreatown" bristles with automatic weapons and informal militias composed of veterans of the Korean military who promise "punishment in kind" in the event of another attack on the businesses. Similarly in Hollywood, a member of the county Republican Central Committee claims that she has organized a gun-toting posse—"old West style"—to render summary justice to looters in the next riot:

> Civilians can deal with crime more easily because we are not hampered by constitutional restrictions like the police. We can slam and jam. People were nice in the last riot. Next time we will shoot looters first and ask questions later. A lot of blood will be spilled.[31]

■ ■ ■ ■

The Gulag Rim

The road from Mecca follows the Southern Pacific tracks past Bombay Beach to Niland, then turns due south through a green maze of marshes and irrigated fields. The bad future of Southern California rises, with little melodrama, in the middle distance between the skeleton of last year's cotton crop and the aerial bombing range in the Chocolate Mountains. From a mile away, the slate-gray structures resemble warehouses or perhaps a factory. An unassuming road sign announces "Calipatria State Prison." This is the outer rim of Los Angeles's ecology of fear. . . .[32]

Calipatria, which opened in 1993, is a "level 4," maximum security prison that currently houses 10 percent of California's convicted murderers, 1,200 men. Yet the guard booth at the main gate is unmanned, as are 10 of its 12 perimeter gun towers. If the startling absence of traditional surveillance looks negligent, it is deliberate policy. As Daniel Paramo, the prison's energetic public relations officer, explains, "The warden doesn't trust the human-error factor in the gun towers; he puts his faith, instead, in Southern California Edison."[33]

Paramo is standing in front of an ominous 13-foot electric fence, sandwiched between two ordinary chain-link fences. Each of the 15 individual strands of wire bristles with 5,000 volts of

Parker Dam power—about 10 times the recognized lethal dosage. The electrical contractors guarantee instantaneous death. (An admiring guard in the background mutters: "Yeah, toast. . . .")

The original bill authorizing the high-voltage "escape-proof" fence sailed through the legislature with barely a murmur. Cost-conscious politicians had few scruples about an electric bill that saved $2 million in labor costs each year. And when the warden quietly threw the main switch in November 1993, there was general satisfaction that the corrections system was moving ahead, with little controversy, toward its high-tech future. "But," Paramo adds ruefully, "we had neglected to factor the animal-rights people into the equation."

The prison is just east of the Salton Sea—a major wintering habitat for waterfowl—and the gently purring high-voltage fence immediately became an erotic beacon to passing birds. Local bird-watchers soon found out about the body count ("a gull, two owls, a finch and a scissor-tailed flycatcher") and alerted the Audubon Society. By January, Calipatria's "death fence" was an international environmental scandal. When a CNN crew pulled into the prison parking lot, the Department of Corrections threw in the towel and hired an ornithologist to help them redesign the fence.

The result is the world's only birdproof, ecologically responsible death fence. Paramo has some difficulty maintaining a straight face as he points out $150,000 in innovations: "a warning wire for curious rodents, anti-perching deflectors for wildfowl, and tiny passageways for burrowing owls." Calipatria has also built an attractive pond for visiting geese and ducks.

Although the prison system is now at peace with bird lovers, the imbroglio roused the powerful California Correctional Peace Officers' Association (CCPOA) to question management's right to "automate" the jobs of the 30 sharpshooters (three shifts per tower) replaced by the fence. To proceed with his plan to lethally electrify all the state's medium and maximum security prisons (23 of 29 facilities) in the coming years, Director of Corrections Joe Gomez may have to negotiate a compromise with the CCPOA that preserves more of the "featherbed" gun tower jobs.

Calipatria's four thousand inmates, most of them from the tough ghettos and barrios of Los Angeles County, shed few tears for either the ducks or the guards. Their lives are entirely absorbed in the daily struggle to survive soul-destroying claustrophobia and ever threatening racial violence. Like the rest of the system, Calipatria operates at almost double its design capacity. In the state's medium security facilities, squalid tiers of bunk beds have been crowded into converted auditoriums and day rooms much as in overflowing county jails. In "upscale" level-4 institutions like Calipatria, on the other hand, a second inmate has simply been shoehorned into each of the tiny, six-by-ten-foot one-man cells.

When "double-celling" was first introduced into the system a decade ago, it helped fuel a wave of inmate violence and suicide. Civil liberties advocates denounced the practice as "cruel and unusual punishment," but a federal judge upheld its constitutionality. Now inmates can routinely expect to spend decades or even lifetimes (40 percent of Calipatria's population are lifers) locked in unnatural, and often unbearable, intimacy with another person. The psychological stress is amplified by a shortage of prison jobs that condemns nearly half the inmate population to serve their sentences idly in their cells watching infinities of television. As behavioral psychologists have testified in court, rats confined in such circumstances invariably go berserk and eat each other.

The abolition of privacy, together with the suppression of inmate counterculture, are explicit objectives of "new generation" prisons like Calipatria. Each of its 20 housing units is designed like a two-story horseshoe with a guard station opposite. Yet another variation on Jeremy Bentham's celebrated eighteenth-century panopticon prison, this "270 plan" (referring to the guards' field of vision) is intended to ensure continuous surveillance of all inmate behavior. Official blurbs boast of a "more safe and humane incarceration" and an end to the "fear-hate syndrome" associated with prisons that tolerate zones of unsupervised inmate interaction.

In practice, however, panopticonism has been compromised by construction shortcuts and chronic understaffing. Although toilets sit nakedly in the middle of the recreational yards as symbols of institutional omniscience, there are still plenty of blind spots—behind tier stairs or in unsurveilled kitchen areas—where inmates can take revenge on staff or one another. As Paramo warns visitors when they sign the grim waiver acknowledging California's policy of refusing to negotiate for hostages, "The war is on."

For a quarter of a century, California prisons have institutionalized episodic violence between inmate guerrilla armies. The original order of battle, after the death of Black Panther leader George Jackson in 1971, allied the Black Guerrilla Family and La Nuestra Familia (mainly Northern California Latinos) against the Aryan Brotherhood and the East L.A.–based Mexican Mafia (or EME). Today there are also rising Asian and Central American gangs, but the carnage has been centralized into a merciless struggle for power between blacks and the EME.

■ ■ ■ ■

To deal with such explosions, California's higher level prisons have introduced new and extreme sanctions. Each institution, for example, now has its own internal SWAT unit—or Special Emergency Response Team—capable of countering outbreaks with staggering amounts of firepower and paramilitary expertise. These elite units have been widely praised for preventing inmate-upon-inmate slaughters like that in the New Mexico State Penitentiary in 1984. The price of such prevention, however, seems to be an extraordinary toleration of official violence. Over the last decade, trigger-happy guards have killed 38 inmates in California institutions (including three in Calipatria)—more than triple the *total* of the six other leading prison population states and the federal penitentiary system combined.[34]

Staff at Calipatria speak with measured awe of CCPOA president Don Novey, a former Folsom prison guard, who has made the Correctional Officers the most powerful union in the state. Under his leadership, the CCPOA has been transformed from a small, reactive craft union into the major player shaping criminal justice legislation and, thereby, the future of the California penal system. Part of the secret of Novey's success has been his willingness to pay the highest price for political allies. In 1990, for example, Novey contributed nearly $1 million to Pete Wilson's gubernatorial campaign, and CCPOA now operates the second most generous PAC in Sacramento.[35]

Novey has also leveraged CCPOA's influence through his sponsorship of the so-called victims' rights movement. Crime Victims United, for example, is a satellite PAC receiving 95 percent of its funding from CCPOA. Through such high-profile front groups, and in alliance with other law enforcement lobbies, Novey has been able to keep Sacramento in a permanent state of law-and-order hysteria. Legislators of both parties trample each other in the rush to put their names at the top of new, tougher anticrime measures, while ignoring the progressive imbalance between the number of felons sentenced to prison and the existing capacity of Department of Corrections facilities.[36]

This cynical competition has had staggering consequences. Rand Corporation researcher Joan Petersilia found that "more than 1,000 bills changing felony and misdemeanor statutes" had been enacted by the legislature between 1984 and 1992. Taken together, they are utterly incoherent as criminal justice policy, but wonderful as a stimulus to the kind of carceral Keynesianism that has tripled both the membership and the average salary of the CCPOA since 1980. While California's colleges and universities were shedding 8,000 jobs, the Department of Corrections hired 26,000 new employees to guard 112,000 new inmates. As a result, California is now the proud owner of the third largest penal system in the world (after China and the United States as a whole).[37]

A host of critics, including an official blue ribbon commission, have tried to wean the legislature from its reckless gulagism. They have produced study after study showing that superincarceration has had a negligible impact on the overall crime rate, and that a majority of new inmates are either nonviolent drug offenders (including parolees flunking mandatory urinalysis) or the mentally ill (28,000 inmates by official estimate). They have also repeatedly warned that a day of reckoning will come when the state will have to trade higher education, literally brick by brick, to continue to build prisons.[38]

Politicians do not dispute that this day is now close at hand. When one education leader in testimony before the legislature pointed to the inverse relationship between the college and prison budgets, state senator Frank Hill (R-Whittier) acidly retorted: "If push came to shove, the average voter is going to be more supportive of prisons than of the University of California."[39] Although it costs taxpayers more than twice as much to send an 18-year-old to prison as to university, politicians reap greater rewards from lobbyists and conservative voters for building cells than for building classrooms.

It was not surprising, therefore, that the legislature instead of hitting the brakes went full throttle in 1994 with a "three strikes" law (subsequently enshrined in the state constitution by a referendum in 1994) which doubles sentences for second felonies and mandates 25 years to life for three-time losers.[40] As a direct result, Department of Corrections planners predict a 262 percent increase in the penal population (to 341,420) by 2005 (as contrasted to 22,500 inmates in 1980). Commenting on these projections, a spokesman for Governor Wilson simply shrugged his shoulders: "If these additional costs have to be absorbed, I guess we'll have to reduce other services. We'll have to change our priorities."[41]

It is sobering to recall that the Department of Corrections with 29 major "campuses" is already more expensive than the University of California system, and that young black men in Los Angeles and Oakland are twice as likely to end up in prison as in college. The three strikes law, moreover, is widening racial disparities in sentencing. According to data from Los Angeles County public defenders, African-Americans made up 57 percent of the early three strikes filings, although they are only 10 percent of the population. This is 17 times the rate of whites, although other studies have shown that white men commit at least 60 percent of rapes, robberies, and assaults.[42] The majority-suburban legislature, however, has been unfazed by studies demonstrating the profound racial inequities of recent criminal legislation.

Initial hopes that Cruz Bustamante—the Fresno Democrat who in 1997 became the first modern Latino Assembly Speaker—would restore some sanity to crime-and-punishment debates were quickly dashed when Bustamante tried to outflank Governor Wilson on the subject of capital punishment for minors. When Wilson suggested death sentences for criminals as young as 14 (the current minimum age is 18), Bustamante responded that he might "with a tear in my eye, cast a vote to execute 'hardened criminals' as young as 13." (Thanks to bipartisan legislation in 1996, 14-year-olds in California can already be tried as adults and receive life imprisonment for serious felonies.)[43]

To Tom Hayden—one of the few members of the legislature to publicly denounce the three strikes legislation—such bravado about executing children is more proof that California is sinking to a "moral quagmire . . . reminiscent of Vietnam." "State politics has been handcuffed by the law enforcement lobby. Voters have no real idea of what they are getting into. They have not been told the truth about the trade-off between schools and prisons, or the economic disaster that will inevitably result. We dehumanize criminals and the poor in exactly the same way we did with so-called gooks in Vietnam. We just put them in hell and turn up the heat."[44]

Notes

1. Mike Davis, "The Infinite Game: Redeveloping Downtown L.A.," in Diane Ghirardo (ed.), *Out of Site: A Social Criticism of Architecture* (Seattle, 1991).
2. Jim Hathcock, "Security Firms Overwhelmed by Sudden Demand for Riot Protection," *Los Angeles Business Journal* 27 July 1992.
3. *LAT* 6 August 1993 (Ventura County edition).
4. This is based on my first-hand reportage of the Los Angeles riot, "In L.A., Burning All Illusions," *Nation*, 1 June 1992. For an extended discussion of the riot's origins and immediate aftermath, see my "Who Killed Los Angeles?" *New Left Review* 197 (January–February 1993) and 199 (May–June 1993).
5. Riot incident and arrest figures from William Webster, special advisor to the Board of Police Commissioners, *The City in Crisis: Appendices* (Los Angeles, 21 October 1992).
6. Institute for Alternative Journalism, *Inside the L.A. Riots: What Really Happened—and Why It Will Happen Again*, ed. Don Hazen (New York, 1992).
7. Vilma Ortiz, "The Mexican-Origin Population: Permanent Working Class or Emerging Middle Class?," in Roger Waldinger and Mehdi Bozorgmehr (eds.), *Ethnic Los Angeles* (New York: 1996), p. 257.
8. The seminal study is Paul Ong, project director of the Research Group on the Los Angeles Economy, *The Widening Divide: Income Inequality and Poverty in Los Angeles*, report, Graduate School of Architecture and Urban Planning (UCLA, 1989), p. 101 and passim.
9. Cf. Stephen Cohen, "L.A. Is the Hole in the Bucket," *LAT* 8 March 1993; Benjamin Cole, "Industrial Study Long on Problems, Short on Remedies," *Los Angeles*

Business Journal 14 November 1994, p. 22; and DRI/McGraw Hill, *Gateway Cities Economic Strategy Initiative* (Downey, 1996), p. ii (executive summary).

10. Jennifer Wolch and Heidi Sommer, *Los Angeles in an Era of Welfare Reform: Implications for Poor People and Community Well-Being* (Los Angeles, 9 April 1997), pp. iv, 8, 11, 71.

11. Photograph by Jim Mendenhall, *LAT* 22 December 1991.

12. Wolch and Sommer, *Los Angeles*, p. 96.

13. Letter from Mike Dreebin, 28 March 1993.

14. Repeated LAPD attempts "to take back the park," involving horse patrols, barricades, and 80-officer sweeps, usually end up trawling dozens of harmless but illegal street vendors. The gangs and crack dealers return as soon as the police leave.

15. *LAT* 19 October 1992.

16. *LAT* 20 July 1986.

17. In 1991, doctors at County-USC Medical Center told state officials that patients were dying because operating rooms were full and they were prematurely moved from ventilators. "We are being required to ration health care and at times to perform what amounts to passive euthanasia" (see *LAT* 18 December 1981).

18. *LAT* 27 January 1994.

19. *LAT* 9 February 1995.

20. Cf. Mary Jordan, "I Will Not Fire Guns in School. I Will Not Fire Guns in School," *Washington Post National Weekly Edition* 5–11 July 1993; and Kathleen Lund-Seeden, "Schools Step Up Security," *Outlook* (Santa Monica), 24 March 1992.

21. The Puerto Rican case—"the first time U.S. military units have been pressed into routine crime-fighting service with the police"—is an ominous precedent little appreciated on the mainland ("Puerto Rico Uses Troops to Occupy Housing Project," AP wire story, 2 October 1993).

22. *LAT* 22 November 1997.

23. *LAT* 26 September 1993.

24. *LAT* 4 May 1994 and 11 October 1995.

25. For the critical views of the LAPD deputy chief Michael Bostic, see *LAT* 23 November 1997.

26. *LAT* 22 May 1997.

27. What follows is based on interviews with the LAPD used in my article, "Vigilancia Policial Comunitaria: Ventajas y Desventajas," *La Opinion* (Los Angeles) 17 May 1992.

28. *LAT* 15 April 1992.

29. *LAT* 17 March and 2 June 1993.

30. *LAT* 3 May 1993.

31. Interview with E. Michael, July 1992.

32. What follows is based on formal interviews of prison staff at Calipatria State Prison in November 1994. In January 1995 I also spoke to several families of inmates, as well as one (anonymous) guard.

33. All statistics double-checked with Department of Corrections, "Institutional Population Characteristics" (Sacramento, August 1994).

34. *LAT* 27 October 1994.

35. Cf. *LAT* 6 February 1994; Joe Dominick, "Who's Guarding the Guards?" *Los Angeles Weekly* 2 September 1994; and Vincent Schiraldi, "The Undue Influence of California's Prison Guards' Union," *In Brief* (Center on Juvenile and Criminal Justice, San Francisco), October 1994.

36. Ibid.

37. Joan Petersilia, "Crime and Punishment in California," in James Steinberg et al. (eds.), *Urban America: Policy Choices for Los Angeles and the Nation* (Santa Monica, 1992).

38. Blue Ribbon Commission on Inmate Population Management, *Final Report* (Sacramento, January 1990).

39. *San Francisco Chronicle* 26 April 1993.

40. Cf. *LAT* 1 March 1994.

41. Cf. James Gomez, director of Department of Corrections, "Memorandum: Impact of '*Three Strikes*' on Occupancy Level and Future Bed Needs," 4 March 1994; Department of Corrections, *Statewide Emergency Housing Information* (Sacramento, 6 January 1995); and Department of Corrections, *1996–2001 Five-year Facilities Master Plan* (Sacramento, June 1996).

42. Vincent Schiraldi and Michael Godfrey, "Racial Disparities in the Charging of Los Angeles County's Third 'Strike' Cases," *In Brief*, October 1994.

43. *LAT* 11 April 1997.

44. Interview with Tom Hayden, January 1995.

SECTION VIII
REVOLUTION

Given the central role played by class and the state in modern society, it should be no surprise that the history of modernity has been a history of revolution. Revolutions are "major political and social transformations . . . involving mass participation and the aspiration to establish a radically different society" (Halliday 1999: 21). Modern revolutions have been major forces in the creation of contemporary society. Whether they occurred in France, Russia, or China (just to name a few examples), revolutions swept away the old social order characterized by tradition and replaced it with a new social order based on reason. This transition expressed a fundamental social truth that came to be one of the central tenets of sociology: that people create their social worlds. Traditional, prerevolutionary societies offered a vision of the world as being outside of human control; God was said to have created the world, along with its divisions between rich and poor, and so who were people to question God's divine plan? More specifically, to the extent that rulers claimed some kind of divine authority as the basis of their rule, social inequality and political oppression appeared to be inevitable and unchangeable. The very act of rising up against their rulers demonstrated the fallacy of this idea. Revolutions offered the promise that people could construct a society based on principles of reason and equality, and this promise came in large part to define the modern world.

At the same time that revolutions were central to the creation of modern society, they presented a fundamental challenge to that society. The separation of the public and private that was the central theme in Phillips's analysis of gender early on in this book was a defining feature of modern society, and the major revolutions of modern history challenged this dichotomy. They sought not only the replacement of specific political authorities or even types of political institutions, but the complete transformation of society. In addition to changing political institutions, these revolutions sought to create new forms of property and economic relations (socialism) and new ways of measuring time and space (for example, the new revolutionary calendar in France), and to subordinate existing institutions (such as religion and the family) to the public. At least in theory, social revolutions suggested that people could not be legally equal as citizens yet unequal in terms of the distribution of social resources. The other major feature of modern society called into question by revolutions was its division into nationally defined territories. In contrast to the centrality of nation-states in modern history, revolutions have always been international in scope (Halliday 1999). The American Revolution provided a demonstration effect for the French revolutionaries, who did the same for the Haitians who overthrew (ironically) French rule. The Soviet Union, China, and Cuba served as important influences for African, Asian, and Latin American revolutionaries. More recently, the Islamic revolution in Iran that began in 1979 has stimulated fundamentalist revolutionaries in Africa, the Middle East, and Asia. Although revolutions take place within specific territories, in their promise of a better world, however it is defined, they are fundamentally internationalist events.

The articles in this section provide critical evaluations of past revolutions as well as appraisals of the future of revolution. Stephen A. Resnick and Richard D. Wolff reject the commonsense view that the demise of the Soviet Union reflected a transition from communism to capitalism. The Soviet Union, they argue, was defined by a variety of class structures, the most significant of which were state capitalist rather than communist. That is, the Soviet Union did not become a society, as envisioned by its creators, in which socially owned property was managed democratically by workers for the benefit of all. Instead, the state came to replace the private capitalist as the agent that claimed the surplus value produced by workers. Thus, the alienation that Marx saw in capitalism as a result of commodity fetishism was expressed in relation to the state in the Soviet Union. When confronted by economic stagnation that began (as it did throughout the rest of the world) during the 1970s, as well as the increased contact with Western consumption patterns that came with the establishment of détente, the state's claim to legitimacy began to be exhausted. The elimination of genuinely communist class structures as Stalinism consolidated its hold over the Soviet Union during the 1930s had the effect of eliminating the only major alternative to capitalist or statist economic systems. This meant that efforts to restructure Soviet socialism (*perestroika*) in response to economic crisis ultimately were seen as inadequate and hollow, leaving those class structures that were clearly non-state (that is, capitalist institutions) as the most desirable option for change.

Giovanni Arrighi, Terence K. Hopkins, and Immanuel Wallerstein examine the uneasy relationship between socialism and national liberation movements during the twentieth century. For most of the national liberation movements in Africa, Latin America, and Asia, a commitment to socialist principles reflected a recognition that freedom from colonial rule simultaneously meant ensuring that a nation's resources could be protected from capitalist exploitation and instead be used to benefit the nation. At the same time, however, the focus on national liberation required cross-class alliances of workers, peasants, educated professionals, and small business owners, not all of whom shared a commitment to a socialist redistribution of wealth. The authors argue that although national liberation movements were successful in winning freedom from colonial rule, they were less successful in achieving their stated class goals of creating a socialist society. This was the result not only of internal class conflict within the newly liberated nations, but also because of their location in the international state system. The Western powers, particularly the United States, did their best to undermine efforts at socialist economic development, and the Soviet Union was just as likely to demand that these efforts be subordinate to its own political interests in its conflict with the West. Even with the end of the Cold War, the global context in which national liberation movements come to power continues to constrain their ability to act; the clearest example of this is the rejection by the African National Congress (ANC), once it came to power in South Africa in 1994, of its Freedom Charter commitments to the nationalization of industry and natural resources and to a socialist economic system. In the absence of a global alternative that could provide resources and support, the ANC-led government has accepted neoliberalism's concern for private property and the market (Desai 2002).

The twentieth century experience of revolution also stimulated what Mark Neocleous calls a "revolution against revolution." Fascism emerged as a revolutionary movement on the right in Italy and Germany during the 1920s and 1930s to restore social order in the face of threats of socialist revolution. Class conflict was "resolved" by appealing to a national identity that unified members of all classes within the state, but this unity in fact maintained class inequality. Workers and capitalists were brought together to work for "the people" under the leadership of the state, but without challenging the fundamental social relations of private property. Although fascism contained a critique of elites that serve as "parasites" on society (particularly financial capital), fascism was fundamentally a political system that defended capitalism. This explains the ambiguous position taken by the Western powers toward fascism prior to the Second World War; while seeing fascism as an authoritarian political system, political elites saw it as a useful defense against the potential spread of communism (Leibovitz and Finkel 1998).

John Foran argues that revolution, despite the collapse of the Soviet Union and the exhaustion of post-war national liberation movements, remains a relevant social force into the twenty-first century. Twentieth-century revolutions failed to achieve their goals of social equality and participatory democracy, largely for two major reasons. First, revolutionary movements, once in power, found it difficult to defend themselves from direct or indirect military attack and political hostility and from the constraints of the world capitalist system; and second, revolutionary movements foundered in their efforts to create participatory democratic institutions. The end of the Cold War and the breakup of the Soviet Union, however, make it more likely that revolutions could achieve their goals of social equality and democracy. Freed from the constraints of being forced to take sides in the Cold War, revolutionary movements are likely to have more space to develop on their own. This space is also likely to grow as the worldwide movement challenging capitalist globalization continues to expand (see Section VI on the nation-state in the global economy, as well as Moody's article on international labor solidarity in Section IX, the social movements section). In addition, Foran sees in the Zapatista rebellion in Mexico a model of a revolutionary culture that offers hope of maintaining revolution's focus on social equality and participatory democracy.

Foran's article captures quite eloquently the creative potential that people have to build a just world. As we saw in our discussion of the global economy, we live in a period in which we are expected to accept without question the goals and institutions of global capitalism. It is worth quoting Foran here: "The proper response to the pessimists of the dispirited acronym TINA—'There is no alternative'—of course is TATA: 'There are thousands of alternatives!'"

References

Desai, Ashwin. 2002. *We Are The Poors: Community Struggles in Post-Apartheid South Africa.* New York: Monthly Review Press.

Halliday, Fred. 1999. *Revolution and World Politics: The Rise and Fall of the Sixth Great Power.* Durham: Duke University Press.

Leibovitz, Clement, and Alvin Finkel. 1998. *In Our Time: The Chamberlain-Hitler Collusion.* New York: Monthly Review Press.

CLASS CONTRADICTIONS AND THE COLLAPSE OF THE SOVIET UNION

STEPHEN A. RESNICK AND RICHARD D. WOLFF

The USSR was born out of class contradictions similar to those in which it died. In 1917, Russian private capitalism and its social context—especially the distribution of private property, markets, and the czarist state—had either collapsed or reached such extremes as to undermine confidence and support. Socialist critics of the ultimate unworkability and unacceptability of private capitalism responded vigorously to growing sympathy for their arguments and programs. The crisis of 1917 provoked the USSR's birth in a transition chiefly from private to state capitalism. In the 1980s, it was the state capitalism and its social context—especially collective property, state planning, and the Communist Party—that were in critical decay. This crisis reversed the direction of 1917: this transition went from state back to private capitalism.

In class terms, no crash happened at the end of the 1980s. It was rather certain nonclass aspects of Soviet society that changed dramatically. Their impact on Soviet class structures was marginal and limited. The demise of the USSR was not a collapse of communist class structures in favor of the capitalist alternative. The USSR as a nation and the social position of the Communist Party collapsed. In contrast, the USSR's class structures marginally adjusted.

■ ■ ■ ■

In class terms, the postwar USSR differed only slightly from the prewar USSR. Both were fragile complexes of class structures caught up in contradictory relationships precariously balanced. For its first fifty years a remarkable set of circumstances combined to hold together the fragile Soviet class configurations as their composition changed. Internal catastrophes, actual and anticipated foreign attacks, forced march preparations for and recoveries from both catastrophes and attacks, and socialist fervor combined to produce historically unprecedented social development and to prevent the contradictions of the USSR's class structures from exploding. The euphoria and consolidation of the revolution drove the first decade. Completing the revolution by spreading it from industry to agriculture—collectivization—drove the second. Forced march industrialization arose across the first two decades to become the spirit of the third. Winning and recovering from World War Two defined the fourth and fifth decades.

Soviet history includes the awesome, unprecedented fifty-year achievement of not only sustained unity but industrialization and superpower status alongside the United States. All this happened despite the devastation of two world wars, a civil war (which included foreign invasions), agricultural collectivization (almost another civil war), and continuously dangerous encirclements and containments. Yet, not the least irony of Soviet history is that this achievement proved to be as well its undoing. When finally the USSR could stalemate its enemies, arrange a detente with the United States, and open its borders toward more regular political, cultural, and economic interactions, it could not find a new driving spirit for these new circumstances that could hold together the contradictions of its ever-fragile class composition.

Beginning in the 1970s, postwar nonclass changes altered the balance among contradictory Soviet class structures: mutual support gave way to mutual weakening. Dissatisfaction, resentment, corruption, and conflict deepened. Initially Soviet leaders searched for particular solutions to what they saw then as the particular problems of state industries, state farms, collective farms, and households. As these proved ineffective, there arose instead a society-wide sense of a need for some more fundamental, sweeping reorganization of the entire system. This set the stage for the collapse of the late 1980s.

■ ■ ■ ■

No transcendent or intrinsic inevitability attaches to postwar Soviet history and the remarkable differences between the changes in its class and nonclass aspects. The response to social deterioration after the mid-1970s might have been different and successful in reversing the collapse. A radical change of class structures—for example, a serious, society-wide experiment with communist class structures in industry; a return to and reform of communist class structures in agriculture; a renewed interest in and experiment with communist class structures in households—is one alternative that might have been attempted. Had Marxian class consciousness and debates over the class analysis of the USSR been major features of Soviet life, that alternative might have received more attention or even become official policy.

In class terms, two basic questions confronted the postwar USSR. First, would the surpluses appropriated from state capitalist industries and farms, the value flows from terms of trade manipulations and taxes at the expense of collectives, and the turnover taxes on workers suffice for the state to fund the USSR's program of heavy industrial capital accumulation, its superpower costs (military and political), its state and party expenses, and a growing allocation to raise collective consumption (housing, medical care, etc.)?[1] Second, would the Soviet state and the Party be able to manage the economic, political, and cultural (nonclass) processes needed to allow the USSR's fragile structure of classes to survive? . . .

Postwar Culture

■ ■ ■ ■

One complex of cultural changes after the war is associated with the establishment of detente with the West, slowly and in fits and starts from the 1950s to the 1970s (Riasanovsky 1984, 558–562). The rhetoric and realities of that Cold War period coincided with (and often contradicted) the concerted Soviet effort to construct agreements and relationships around the concept of a peaceful coexistence or detente. In turn, as detente emerged, it enabled and provoked a set of significant shifts in how Soviet citizens felt about their lives. The siege mentality dissipated gradually, although occasionally revived by moments of Cold War intensification. Public and private decisions were less often reached or justified under the pressures of actual or impending social dangers or catastrophes. Finally, after so many years of forced march preparations for and recoveries from social cataclysms, individual lives could begin to be viewed as occurring in peace—not only in the sense of the absence of war but in the sense of a relatively stable normalcy of daily life. Perhaps for the first time since 1917, for many of those who more or less supported the official goals and values of the USSR, the absence of acute social crisis meant that personal needs and desires could become legitimate individual priorities.

A certain detachment from feelings of immersion in vast social projects of industrial production, collectivization, constructing a new socialist civilization, war preparation, hysterical purges, and recovery from war became widespread. Stalin's death, the ensuing weakening of Stalinism as a cultural as well as political and economic condition, and detente encouraged this shift toward the personal or "private" spheres of life.[2] These developments had practical and also symbolic consequences in addition to legitimating the relaxation of the hitherto relentless crisis environment. Detente especially promoted the shift to private life by facilitating all sorts of contacts, communications, and exchanges with Western societies. In the latter, the spheres of private life were officially much more valued than those of public life, and no comparable tradition of siege mentality existed. . . .

The shift of Soviet feeling and focus from the larger society to the individual concerns of relationship and personal life had several class consequences. A deepened alienation from politics spilled over into a parallel alienation from what might be termed "social" production. Even before detente, the turbulence of party struggles and the legacy of Stalin's purges had turned many Soviet citizens away from participation in or even engagement with the dangerous domain of politics. But total commitment to the urgent goals of production had been much less affected. With detente, the relaxation of Soviet citizens' public and social foci and activities withdrew energy not only from their relationships with the state and the Party, but also from their work in the enterprises identified with the state and the Party (Shlapentokh 1989, 153–163).

Reduced commitments to work in state capitalist enterprises and in private capitalist and communist collective farms took various forms. Earlier patriotic and/or party-driven surges of extra (and unpaid) labor and campaigns to reduce waste of productive resources occurred less often and less effectively. Many individual Soviet laborers worked less intensely and with less commitment. For them, work became more a job for pay than a social mission, crusade, or project of national salvation. Unlike the 1930s, work intensity and labor productivity declined. Thus, in class terms, one effect of the postwar cultural changes associated with detente entailed such workers producing less surplus labor than before.[3] . . .

While the cultural shift into private concerns thus undercut the capitalist class structures of state enterprises and the capitalist and communist class structures of collective farms, it strengthened other class structures in the USSR. Chief among these were the ancient class structures on the private farm plots of individuals and families. They were the more "private" class structures: individuals or family groups labored alone rather than collectively with many other people. The widely recognized enthusiasm of Soviet workers for their private farm plots and their remarkable productive efficiency there contrasted ever more sharply with waning labor enthusiasm and troubled labor productivity in capitalist and communist class-structured enterprises.[4]

■ ■ ■ ■

Official state policy from the mid-1970s on not only celebrated the private plots but also welcomed more or less free markets for much of the produce from them. In this way, many Soviet citizens began, more or less consciously, positively to associate private concerns, market relations, and, in our terms, ancient class structures as components of economic and social progress. A cultural shift had contributed to a class shift that reacted back upon and so further developed the cultural shift. The direction of this interaction, in subtle and different ways, undermined both capitalist and communist class structures. Nor did Soviet leaders stop this undermining; they did not think in such class terms, nor envision any practicable alternative to accommodating private plots, nor could they blame some external or internal enemy for it. Thus it proceeded relatively unchecked.

The growth of ancient class structures and markets in their products was not limited to private plot farming. There is evidence (sketchy, of course) that across the postwar period increasing numbers of Soviet citizens supplemented their state jobs with semilegal and illegal productions of service commodities. Most of these seem to have been organized in individual, ancient class structural forms. Examples include the repair of apartments, automobiles, shoes, and appliances; the provision of transportation; the manufacture of selected consumer goods such as T-shirts; the tutoring of children and adults; and the private practice of medicine and dentistry (Shlapentokh 1989, 192–196). Millions of Soviet state employees participated. They worked in such ancient class structures in addition to working within the state's capitalist class structures. This no doubt provoked them to make comparisons just at an historical moment when the latter were experiencing increasing problems and difficulties while the former found increasing acceptance and success.

The significance of these cultural changes interacting with the shifting balance of class structures within Soviet society emerged in the 1980s. Then the accumulated difficulties of state capitalism—a result in part of the growing attachments to other noncapitalist class structures—provoked a crisis mentality throughout the USSR. As problems mounted, millions of Soviet citizens began to generalize from their personal histories. As they had shifted personally from reliance chiefly on state capitalist employment to an increasing reliance as well on significant amounts of "private" ancient self-employment, they began to see or accept a parallel social solution for the USSR. However, absent the class terms deployed here, they utilized instead the dominant concepts and languages of their time and place. They reasoned and spoke about the need to solve the problems of socialism by freeing (from the state and from collective activity) private/individual initiative and private/individual labor. At first this took the modest form of advocating such new freedoms merely as accompaniments to the state capitalism they called socialism. Later, as the problems deepened, more militant arguments demanded the replacement of socialism with such "private initiatives."

■ ■ ■ ■

In sum, the cultural turn from public, social concerns toward more private, personal foci had effects that included changing the balance among the USSR's class structures. On the one hand, the ancient class structure was favored at the expense of both the capitalist and communist class structures. On the other hand, the general turn toward things private served to legitimate a general, rising valuation of private over social organizations of production. The theoretical class blindness of virtually all observers precluded their inquiring about or debating such private enterprises' class structures. Likewise, their class blindness precluded examining how each of these would differently influence Soviet development generally, its socialist character, or its communist future in particular. Because both Soviet intellectuals and leaders wrote and spoke in terms of public versus private rather than in class-qua-surplus-labor terms, they contributed to the general invisibility of the class changes underway. Hence no policy debates or actions emerged explicitly to address those changes. In their absence, we can understand the remarkable postwar convergence in the class blindness with which both Soviet intellectuals and leaders and their western counterparts reasoned about economic and social development generally. Thus, what differentiated "capitalist thought" in the West from "socialist thought" in the East was not the absence versus the presence of class analysis in terms of surplus labor. Rather, both kinds of thought utilized the state-versus-private juxtaposition; they differed only (and decreasingly) on which was considered positive and which negative for economic and social progress.

■ ■ ■ ■

A parallel post-Khrushchev theoretical blindness characterized the endless criticisms of Stalin and Stalinism within the USSR and beyond. These critiques blamed bureaucracy (and its ultimate "cult of personality" form), careerism, and corruptions of "socialist legality and morality" located in some deep Russian traits or else in the Bolshevik distortions of them.[5] In contrast, Louis Althusser sharply lamented the dominant critiques of Stalinism in the USSR and elsewhere precisely because even the Marxists among them did not ask how the class structures of Soviet society contributed to the rise and survival of Stalinism. He suggested forcefully that by failing to do so, the criticisms had failed to defeat Stalinism within the Marxian tradition (1976, 92). High culture in the postwar USSR, in both its social celebratory and social critical formulations, elided anything approaching a class analysis....

The criticisms that were voiced focused especially on injustices, venalities, and inefficiencies attributed to unbridled bureaucratic power and not (even partly) to the social organization of surplus labor. Hence, the chief objects of attack were the largest and most bureaucratized social institutions: the state and the state capitalist enterprises in industry and agriculture. Their problems and failings, it was argued, flowed from their bureaucracies. Such arguments affirmed some inherent nature of bureaucracy per se (thwarting individual initiative, responsibility, and reward) and/or claimed that the still insufficiently socialized nature of the Soviet citizenry produced a largely passive general population in the face of a bureaucratic despotism (Hochschild 1994, 118).

One effect of such criticisms was a growing tendency after Stalin, sometimes conscious but usually inadvertent, to celebrate and thereby encourage transfers of admiration, loyalty, and effort to enterprises with less or no bureaucracy. These were, of course, the smaller, private enterprises whose class structures were capitalist, communist, or ancient. These enterprises came to be viewed increasingly as sites of less bureaucracy and hence less of the careerism and corruption that kept the large, bureaucratized state industries from making the Soviet economy more productive. Soviet high culture's criticisms along these lines thus contributed to the Gorbachev-Yeltsin-Putin approach to solving the USSR's perceived crisis: policies enhancing the conditions of existence of private enterprises (of whatever class structure) at the expense of the state capitalist class structures in the USSR.[6]

In still another way, postwar Soviet high culture helped to shape its class structures. To the degree that it adopted and repeated the dogma of top state and party officials that dichotomized society into a "proletarian" positivity struggling against a "bourgeois" negativity, high culture reinforced the dialectical potential of such dichotomies. If ever the vaunted positivity encountered a serious crisis that undermined popular loyalties, then people would know of nowhere else to look but to the one "other." If the Soviet people came to view the "proletarian way" as mired in intractable problems that could not credibly be blamed on "bourgeois" agents, foreign or domestic, the way would have been prepared for increasing numbers of people, entrapped within the dualism, to reverse its valuation. The "time" might then arrive to try the only conceivable other way (bourgeois) instead of the one in place ("proletarian") that had become exhausted and intolerable. The crescendo of economic and political problems of the 1970s and 1980s combined with detente and the nearly universal cultural dualism of proletarian versus bourgeois to produce such reverse valuations in many people. Since "proletarian" had long been associated with the supposedly socialist state and collective enterprises, collective property, and economic planning, the reverse valuation exalted instead their opposites: private enterprises, individual property, and markets.

■ ■ ■ ■

One of the greater ironies of the twentieth century was a society that endlessly proclaimed and celebrated its communist revolutionary origins and commitments while being anything but communist revolutionary in its own class structures. The blindness of supporters and critics alike to Marxian surplus-labor concepts of class precluded their revealing and debating the USSR's fundamentally conservative stance toward class. Partly because it could not recognize the contradiction between revolutionary rhetoric and goals and the underlying conservatism of its class structures, Soviet postwar culture sank into a kind of resignation in relation to politics and economics. Progress toward communism became ever more elusive, distant, and vague. Mass mobilizations and campaigns struck ever more Soviet leaders and citizens as unnecessary or irrelevant. Actual or proposed mass mobilizations became instead objects of ridicule or jokes or else were viewed as cruel hoaxes attributed to distrusted leaders pursuing ulterior motives. The distrust further deepened a profound conservatism that many observers have noted and studied (Cohen 1985, 145–157). It also contributed to a disengagement from the entire ideological contest of official Marxism-Leninism that had been so pronounced a feature of prewar thought, speech, and public action. The post-Khrushchev era, 1964 on, was widely experienced as "an ideological vacuum in the Soviet Union" (Leonhard 1984, 56).

After World War Two, much Soviet culture turned inward to private concerns and away from the storms of public (collective) life. The hope was that the storms would become fewer and shorter. Resignation to the apparent impossibility of real change settled deeply into the national psyche. At the same time, these poets, novelists, journalists, filmmakers, painters, and others who did not resign themselves and did dare social criticism lacked concepts of the class organization of surplus labor to integrate into their work. Thus they vented their critical genius only on nonclass aspects of Soviet society—the arrogance of the state power, bureaucracy, economic inefficiencies, corruption, alienated intimacy, and so on. They could not link those to any imagining of a revolutionary project aimed at a communist class alternative to the present Soviet society.

Those aspects of postwar Soviet culture that we have discussed illustrate certain of its contradictions: how it partly contributed to a maintenance of the state capitalist Soviet status quo while it also reinforced or encouraged private capitalist, ancient, and feudal class structures in small enterprises and households respectively. The celebration of private life and the general conservative aversion to any more campaigns for social transformation displayed similarly contradictory class effects. In addition, the class-blind theoretical climate in which the *only* conceivable alternative economic arrangements were either state property with planning or private property with markets was pregnant with yet another eventual class effect. If and when Soviet state capitalism lost the confidence of the Soviet people, the only conceivable resolution would be more or less transition to the only conceivable alternative: the kinds of private capitalism associated with European social democracies and the United States.

Postwar Politics

■ ■ ■ ■

We first consider external political conditions impinging upon the USSR in the first decade after 1945. The combination of Cold War encirclement, nuclear confrontation, and the defeat or decline of communist parties and movements in many Western countries created a new form of the siege mentality that had inspired previous surges of Soviet economic growth. Social mobilization to recover from the world war's devastation could still win popular support when combined with the simultaneous march toward the superpower status needed for defense. Maintaining the strong central state apparatus to manage all this seemed a self-evident social need. . . .

Such an international political climate supported the impressive, albeit uneven, growth of state capitalist industry in the USSR during the three decades after the war. The state gave first priority to that growth; technical advances in military production were sometimes diffused to enhance nonmilitary industrial expansion; and Cold War alliances sometimes provided important industrial inputs under more advantageous terms than would otherwise have been possible. On the other hand, that same international climate also posed major new problems for Soviet state capitalism. The Cold War arms race with the United States required the Soviet state to distribute to the military and to industries producing military products growing portions of the revenues gathered in its coffers (the surpluses appropriated in state capitalist enterprises, those collected by the state from other surplus appropriators, and nonsurplus sources of state revenue). This left less of the state's revenues to distribute to nonmilitary industrial expansion, agricultural growth, social infrastructure (collective consumption), and so on.

While the Cold War climate perhaps stimulated Soviet workers to labor more intensely and productively and promoted technical change, thereby yielding the state some more surpluses from its state capitalist industries, that climate simultaneously absorbed more of those surpluses into the costly production of rapidly obsolescent weapons systems (Gaddy 1996, 9–46).[7] If future developments slowed the growth of surpluses produced in state capitalist industries or the growth of state revenues from other sources while political considerations increased state expenditures on the military, a crisis of insufficient state revenues might quickly mature, unless, of course, the state could sufficiently reduce nonmilitary expenditures. However, reducing the latter undermined the survival of state capitalism's class structures as well as the private communist, capitalist, ancient, and feudal class structures outside the state. . . .

The international political climate also confronted the USSR with a single hegemonic superpower, the United States. Not only U.S. foreign policies but also its internal laws, political practices, and prevalent political theories came to define the challenging "other" against which the USSR measured as well as articulated much of its own political life. The remarkable economic prosperity of the United States after 1945, its military buildup, hegemony over its allies, and the relative ease with which all of these survived its few political reverses (especially China in 1949, Cuba in 1959, and Vietnam in 1970) steadily reinforced this situation. In the West, official pronouncements, mass media, and countless academic formulations explained these U.S. successes as consequences of private property, markets, and the political freedoms of voting, nonstate mass media, and civil liberties. The whole was summarized most often in a morally inflected celebration of "decentralized democracy" as against "totalitarianism."[8] . . .

■ ■ ■ ■

International politics made the United States a major touchstone for Soviet thinking about their own society. The model of the U.S. economy that systematically attributed economic and military success to its political institutions (especially laws securing private property and limiting state activity) proved subtly persuasive to supporters as well as critics of postwar Soviet society. The latter saw in Soviet economic and social problems the effects of this or that quality of U.S. society that was regrettably absent from the USSR. The former saw in the United States the great threat—militarily, politically, and economically. They aimed to learn from (and eventually outperform) the United States technically, to mobilize the world's workers so as to outmaneuver the United States politically, and to stalemate it militarily.

The political impact of the United States upon the USSR worked profoundly and on many levels. The image of the United States—as a society in which the state apparatus was far less centralized and much less socially intrusive than in the USSR—supported those inside the USSR who connected U.S. successes and Soviet failures to just that difference. Soviet citizens with all sorts of grievances against the state could and did take comfort from the United States as a model of where, more of less, to direct the political transformation of Soviet society. A general reinforcement of antistate attitudes and social theories inside the USSR flowed from the U.S.-USSR global confrontation. This happened alongside and in contradiction to the strengthening of the state required and justified as necessary to mobilize the Soviet people to defend against "U.S. imperialism" in all its manifestations. People influenced more by the antistatism than the defensism inculcated after the war might, therefore, have looked less favorably on state capitalist enterprises than on private capitalist and ancient enterprises. As we noted earlier, such shifts in attitude could have negative effects on the labor intensities and productivities of labor in state capitalist enterprises and hence on their profitability. This would further problematize the surpluses available to Soviet state planners just as increasing demands were placed upon such surpluses. In addition, growing antistatist attitudes prompted Soviet workers to devote more labor and hope to existing and prospective private capitalist and ancient enterprises.

The great U.S.–USSR detente declared by Nixon and Brezhnev in the early 1970s shifted the balance of antistate and defensist attitudes and hence their contradictory effects on surplus available to the Soviet state. On the one hand, detente, viewed as the achievement of Soviet military might, legitimated the mobilizations and sacrifices it had required. On the other hand, detente itself worked against any further mobilizations and sacrifices, legitimated the cultural turning inward toward more private concerns discussed above, and enabled more questioning of and opposition to the power of the Soviet state. The political process of detente, by reinforcing antistatist tendencies already developing inside the USSR, also further weakened the capacity of the Soviet state to appropriate surplus within its state capitalist enterprises.

Detente also accelerated the post-Stalin relaxation of political obstacles to the flows of tourism, professional and mass media exchange programs, and so on between the USSR and other countries including the United States. The consequences of this relaxation went beyond greater Soviet awareness and appreciation of the United States as a less statist society. As Soviet citizens grasped the difference between Soviet levels of individual consumption and those in the wealthy Western countries, many reacted by questioning the legitimacy of Soviet political institutions. . . .

It was not only a matter of comparing U.S. and Soviet consumption quantitatively but also qualitatively. Detente revealed above all the much higher levels of private or individual consumption of U.S. workers, especially their private consumption of housing, clothing, automobiles, meat, and appliances.[9] Supporters of the USSR responded by stressing the collective consumption provided by the state to Soviet workers, especially subsidized medical care, education, transport, childcare, and so on. A contestation emerged over the relative merits of private/individual versus state/collective kinds of consumption. However, such a contestation worked against the USSR, precisely because it coincided historically with the turning inward, private focus, and antistatism that were increasingly pervasive across Soviet culture. It was private consumables which just then seemed the most important. Detente allowed the United States to represent itself as the realization of a level of private consumption that Soviet citizens could only yearn for.

Moreover, in the USSR private consumption seemed closely linked to private ancient class structures. The goods most prized for private consumption (goods beyond the basics) emerged from them. In private ancient class structures the connection between personal labor effort and rewards in the form of heightened personal consumption seemed most direct. If work in and for state capitalist enterprises and private capitalist and communist collective farms could not generate the promised levels of private, individual consumption, then that work was not worthwhile. Workers would be somehow justified in either shirking labor in those enterprises and farms or else shifting their enthusiasm to private, ancient class structural production sites, or both.

Alongside the effects of international politics and especially the interactions with the United States, political changes inside the USSR also participated in the overdetermination of its class structures. Most of the "economic" reforms after Stalin were in fact political: they shifted the power to make managerial decisions to relatively more decentralized levels of the state apparatus. For the reasons discussed earlier in this chapter, postwar Soviet thinking increasingly linked decentralization of managerial power to greater economic growth and development. The reform shift culminated in the Law on State Enterprises passed in 1987. It mandated that managers and directors would be elected by workers' collectives (although they would not be workers themselves and would still be controlled by state officials). In the years leading up to passage of this law, the celebratory climate of decentralization expanded the informal, "out of plan" contacts, exchanges, and mutual assistance among local enterprise managers and directors (Ellman and Kontorovich 1998, 145–146). As a result of these political changes in the social location of effective managerial power, the central plan became less important relative to the ad hoc arrangements of local enterprise managers in shaping the Soviet economy and the broader society.[10]

In this way a step was taken that could, under certain conditions, function as an intermediate stage in moving from state to private capitalism. Some insiders in the upper reaches of the Soviet political apparatus understood the political decentralization in approximately such terms (Ellman and Kontorovich 1998, 16). The increasing managerial powers of local state officials in charge of individual enterprises or groups of enterprises brought them nearer to possibly also functioning as appropriators and distributors of the surpluses generated in those enterprises. Indeed, Soviet industrial development did evolve before 1990 from (1) centralized state capitalist appropriation of surplus and centralized management to (2) centralized state capitalist appropriation and decentralized management to (3) decentralized state capitalist appropriation and decentralized management. In the dramatically altered political landscape after 1990, the next evolutionary step, achieved with remarkably little social upheaval, entailed decentralized private capitalist appropriation with decentralized management. In the specific political conjuncture of the postwar USSR, the decentralization of managerial power did contribute to a class transition from state to private capitalism.[11]

■■■■

The results of the decentralization reforms of the Soviet economy undertaken periodically after Stalin's death have been summarized by Janos Kornai.[12] He believes that the "coherence" of the "classical system of socialist economy" was destroyed by the reforms (1992, 377–379). They worsened the "irrationalities" of the Soviet planning system as ministries, regions, industries and enterprises increasingly secured their own situations by circumventing central plans. Decentralized economic planning introduced greater uncertainties (than had centralized planning) into the flows of material and financial inputs needed by enterprises to fulfill their plan targets. At the same time, decentralization further enabled enterprises—singly or in various groupings—to evade the targets or else to achieve them by hoarding inputs and/or reaching separate, "private" exchange agreements with one another outside of the central plan. As the well-being of these enterprises and enterprise groupings came increasingly to depend upon such circumventing of central plans, the effectiveness of the plans declined. For Kornai, the economic "inefficiencies" he believed to flow from one essential source—decentralized state planning—warranted only one conceivably "rational" response, namely further decentralization to an economy that was chiefly "free market coordinated."[13]

We need to add that decentralization of management need not necessarily undermine (centralized or decentralized) state capitalist appropriation of surplus labor. When confronted with the inefficiencies of centralized state planning in the 1930s, local managers had taken on a variety of schemes—outside of the central plans—to acquire needed but often delayed or never delivered promised resources, including food for the workers at the local enterprise level. Such an unintended decentralization of management helped to secure Stalinism's centralized surplus appropriation of surplus labor. However, in the different context of the years after Stalin's death and very much unlike the social environment of the 1930s, such enterprising efforts of managers—whether unintended or intended under the reforms—likely undermined first centralized and then decentralized state capitalist appropriation. The difference was in the attitudes of managers who, like many others in the USSR, increasingly saw themselves coping with economic disorganization flowing from reforms, struggling to secure their own positions, and less caught up in a larger social movement or campaign.

Officially, the Party believed that its expanded social role would function as the antidote for the economic problems associated with the decentralization reforms. But that did not happen. Instead, party leaders and many members were increasingly integrated into the routines for circumventing the economic plans. Enterprises determined to operate outside of central plans had to secure the Party's approval or at least its disinterest. The party did not rise to this economic challenge. Instead, local, regional, and industrial managers (themselves often party members) persuaded party officials to condone the necessity of their semi- and illegal maneuvers in the new, reformed economic circumstances.[14] Where and when that proved difficult, the extraordinary (and "off-the-books") gains from working around economic plans enabled financial inducements (bribes) to supervising party authorities. Management "corruption" in coping with the problems of reformed economic planning spread to corruption of the Party itself. The decentralizing economy had transformed the Party more than the Party had been able to control it.[15]

Political "corruption" of the Party—in the sense of a growing, systemic dereliction of its economic control duties—evolved into the individual corruption that drew increasing popular anger and derision. Economic bureaucrats and party officers and members formed interlocking directorates that often went beyond maneuvering around central economic plans to secure privileges that elevated their individual standards of living and power positions even further above those of average Soviet workers (Keep 1995, 212–216).[16] Their alienation from the general population thus deepened, as did popular resentment of the controls exercised by a privileged Communist Party in the name of Soviet society as a whole.

For the mass of Soviet citizens, this system provided certain benefits, notwithstanding how distasteful it became especially in the 1970s and 1980s. War seemed ever less a threat to Soviet society—a victory widely attributed, at least in part, to the state's diplomacy. Levels of mass consumption, collective and private, grew, albeit at declining rates. Cultural freedoms and the space for private, individual life expanded. And perhaps most important, a kind of entitlement to obtain and keep one's job settled in as a virtually absolute political commitment of the state and Communist Party to Soviet workers.[17] Hence the famous workers' joke aimed squarely at the post-1975 enterprise-Party directorate: "They pretend to pay us properly, and we pretend to work properly." Better than most treatises, this joke summarized many of the economic, cultural, and political dilemmas into which the postwar USSR had descended.

The growth and corruption of the Party had contradictory class consequences. On the one hand, its presence and control functions within nearly all enterprises and labor unions likely raised the intensity and productivity of labor. In this way, party activities expanded the surplus and thereby the state's revenue. However, as noted above (party facilitation of out-of-plan arrangements, corruption, etc.), its activities also likely undermined labor productivity (and hence surplus production in individual enterprises), siphoning appropriated surpluses to non-plan distributions or personal use, or both. Another contradictory effect was the Party's own costs of operation that were covered by state expenditures. A rapidly expanding Communist Party absorbed more of the state's revenues. That left less revenue for the state's other priority objectives: industrial growth, military preparedness, provision of public services for mass, collective consumption, and so on.

To maintain or, better still, to increase the surpluses that the state could appropriate in its capitalist enterprises, party policy also often aimed to justify restraints on productive workers' wages there. Party pressure worked likewise to limit the portions of state capitalist surpluses (subsumed class payments) that were spent on the unproductive laborers (the wages and budgets of clerks, managers, and so on) in those enterprises. At the same time, the unofficial activities of the Party enriched their leaders and many of their activists. Popular opinion increasingly defined them as an unjustifiably privileged group, whose intrusions into social life were then all the more unwelcome. Resisting or avoiding hard work became, in part, a form of protest against the Party's policies and pressures. This situation also fostered shifts of workers' productive efforts from state enterprises toward private ancient class structures where the Party intruded much less. Productive laborers in state capitalist enterprises worked less intensely, broke more tools, and produced low-quality outputs and/or ever fewer outputs per hour. This happened partly to vent dissatisfaction with party policies or personnel and partly because workers were tired, having spent increasing time and energy elsewhere on private plots and second-economy undertakings.

Widespread distaste for the Party combined with envy at its privileges (especially after detente revealed western standards of individual consumption) to reinforce, if not promote, apparently large and rising levels of pilfering especially in the 1980s (Shlapentokh 1989, 214–216). In class terms, if outputs were pilfered, they represented a portion of the surplus produced by productive workers but diverted from surplus appropriators (in the state capitalist industries or in private capitalist and communist collective farms). If means of production were pilfered, they represented corresponding declines in labor productivity: a day's labor yielded less output and thus less surplus than would have been the case without such pilfering. Pilfering supplemented the perpetrators' incomes and so perhaps eased the tensions and contradictions of the ancient and feudal class structures of Soviet households. However, the pilfering directly and indirectly reduced the quantities of surplus appropriated in and by the USSR's state capitalist, private capitalist, and private communist enterprises.

It is impossible to quantify the enlarged Communist Party's net effects on surplus production and appropriation in the USSR during the 1970s and 1980s. However, the broad literature suggests to us that the unintended negative results outweighed—perhaps by a wide margin—the intended positive goals. To the extent that Soviet leaders had hoped to manage the postwar reform movement (decentralization of state planning and power, and reduced social intrusion by the state) by enlarging the centralized Communist Party's social role, that plan failed. The Party's evolution in the circumstances proved wholly inadequate to the task. The vast turning inward to private and individual and away from state and social concerns that characterized Soviet postwar culture came to include a turning away in resentment and anger from the Party as well as from the state. Central to this development was a growing gap between the surpluses produced and available to the state and the state expenditures necessary to sustain the multiple demands of the USSR's postwar global position.

■ ■ ■ ■

The 1990s displayed the consequences of the diverging conditions of U.S. private capitalism and Soviet state capitalism in the 1970s and 1980s. The United States entered upon an unprecedented peacetime explosion of private corporate surplus appropriation (reflected in its stock market boom) that encouraged (and financed) a euphoric global celebration of the neoliberal "perfection" of private property and markets. The Soviet state could neither appropriate enough surplus in state capitalist enterprises nor siphon enough surplus away from other class structures nor find other revenues sufficient to secure its own survival even to the end of the 1980s. It was increasingly unable simultaneously to finance industrial expansion, military preparedness, global superpower status, and a rising standard of living for its masses. A population increasingly able and determined to compare the Soviet state's troubles with Western private capitalism's economic boom and political and cultural openness became ever more disaffected as citizens and unproductive as workers. The state and Party collapsed.

Soviet history starkly exemplifies a global pattern of the twentieth century. The century's first half displays tendencies of transition from private to state capitalisms. The second half moves in the reverse direction. The specific problems of the private capitalisms inherited from the nineteenth century included their growing difficulties in appropriating enough surplus to secure their nonclass conditions of existence. These problems eventuated in crises that were resolved by solutions that ranged from state-regulated to state-managed to state-owned-and-operated capitalisms. The rightist versions in Nazi Germany, fascist Italy, and imperial Japan focused on military aggression. On the left, the post-1917 USSR was the longest sustained and most globally influential of these statist solutions. In the reverse movements provoked by the 1970s crises of state-regulated, state-managed and state-run capitalisms, the solutions entailed returns to various forms of more private capitalism. The post-Soviet return to private capitalism has been the starkest example.

■ ■ ■ ■

The Collapse

The historically quite rapid economic, political, and cultural changes of the later 1970s and 1980s broke upon Soviet society (and most outside observers) as rather mysterious and overwhelming. Many ignored them in the belief they were minor or temporary. Others revived or refurbished versions of past reforms and campaigns of exhortation on the presumption that they would again reverse the flow of events. Rapidly intensifying conflicts erupted across Soviet society in which the two alternatives that the different sides could imagine were debated. At first, the old positions resurfaced: more versus less centralized "socialisms." Then debate swirled around alternative socialisms allowing more or less private property and markets, more or less political pluralism, and so on. But rather quickly this time a new willingness and even eagerness to discuss the two alternatives as "socialism" and "capitalism" overtook their designation as alternative kinds of socialism.

However, the basic polarity—common to all the different ways of describing the alternatives—was familiar because, in one form or another, it had long haunted Soviet society as its dominant conceptualization of the two alternative paths. One side tended to favor more private property, multiparty parliamentarism, cultural freedom, and private markets; the other side supported more state (or collective) property, state-administered (planned) markets, and Communist Party political and cultural hegemony. With all the positions mixing only various degrees of the classic two alternatives, the old dichotomy resurfaced repeatedly as reformers or liberals confronted bureaucrats or conservatives.

Because economic growth slowed drastically, because the Afghanistan disaster marked a decline in Soviet superpower status, because detente made the comparison of Soviet and U.S. living standards (cultural and political as well as economic) socially subversive, the early 1970s peaking of the USSR turned into a cumulative and unstoppable slide into disaster. The Soviet leaders too recognized the exhaustion of their "system" and so moved from the one polar alternative toward the other. They partly made and partly allowed a relatively bloodless transition from state property to private property, from state planning to private markets, from Communist Party monopoly to multiparty politics, from state and party cultural controls to a largely private cultural life. The Soviet system "collapsed."

What the Soviet leaders could not see—because they lacked the concepts—were the class dimensions of what had led to their impasse, what was happening to them, and what they were doing. They could not grasp that they were preserving the capitalist class structure of industry and only changing the form of capitalist exploitation from state to private. They did dimly grasp that they were undermining rural communism in collective farms (to the extent that it still existed) by fostering ancient and capitalist class structures there instead. They had neither understood nor directly treated the class crises of industrial and agricultural Soviet state capitalist enterprises; they had likewise failed in relation to the collective farms' communist and capitalist class structures. Trapped within the same paradigmatic polarity of state and private that informed their critics at home and abroad, they collapsed into the other side of that polarity. Thus, while we arrive there via a very different theoretical route, we share other commentators' rejection of "the fashionable theory that the Soviet system was toppled by the Party and state officials in order to turn their power into private wealth" (Ellman and Kontorovich 1998, 27). No doubt, such motives guided some and perhaps many officials (Kotz 1997), but our analysis has sought to explain how the class contradictions of Soviet development helped to shape such motives, swell the numbers so motivated, and enable them to prevail.

As much as the Soviet people and leadership brought down state capitalism and the Communist Party's political hegemony, they preserved and indeed strengthened capitalism as the prevalent form of surplus labor organization in both industrial and agricultural production. Gorbachev and Yeltsin saved capitalism by removing the state and the Party from their social roles, replacing a discredited state capitalism by its private counterpart. The historical parallel might be Franklin Roosevelt saving capitalism in the United States by the reverse movement, bringing the state into a much greater role as regulator, employer, and even commodity producer to correct and compensate for a discredited private capitalism. While many nonclass dimensions of life "collapsed" in and with the USSR, its capitalist class structures survived and grew in their new, private forms.

The death of the Soviet experiment thus shares something with its birth. At both points, a class-blind theory informing the agents of change combined with the social circumstances constraining them to preclude any basic class transformation beyond capitalism. In 1917 and thereafter these agents made no society-wide transition from capitalism to communism; in 1989 and thereafter they made no society-wide transition from communism to capitalism.

The Soviet revolution certainly did make momentous changes in economics, politics, and culture, but—except for some years in agriculture—not changes in the social organization of surplus labor from capitalist to communist. The Bolsheviks socialized productive property, established central planning, and deprived most private capitalists, feudal landed gentry, orthodox clergy, czarist state officials, merchants, bankers, and so on of their fundamental and subsumed class positions respectively. These latter groups lost the political, economic, and cultural hegemony they had wielded before 1917. The Bolsheviks dramatically bolstered the ancient class structure in agriculture and established a vast new state capitalist class structure in industry and then extended it to agriculture in state farms. At the end of the 1920s and over the 1930s, they also established private communist class structures in collective farms, allowed a transition of some collective farms to private capitalist class structures, and then after the war actively encouraged the growth of state capitalist farms alongside the collective farms. In this way, successive Soviet leaderships transferred political, economic, and cultural hegemony from the old fundamental and subsumed classes who had held it before 1917 to a new group. The members of this new group included the few who were members of the Council of Ministers, leaders of the Communist Party, the chief managers of state capitalist (industrial and farm) enterprises and of collective farms, and top state officials (planners, technocrats, and police enforcers), academics, journalists, and so on.[18] Since these individuals came from families that had occupied the lowest class positions before 1917, the USSR worked a genuinely remarkable transformation of life for many millions of its citizens.

Yet the Bolsheviks could not get beyond the transition from private to state capitalism. They achieved stunning economic growth, global political power, and rising standards of living despite the setbacks of two world wars, a foreign invasion, two civil wars, and nearly continuous encirclement by hostile powers. Given their class-blind social theories, they understood and celebrated those achievements as themselves signs or markers that the USSR had superseded capitalism, achieved socialism, and was progressing successfully toward communism.

Gorbachev, Yeltsin, and Putin, like the Bolsheviks from whom they descended and absorbed class-blind theory, have also made momentous changes, often precisely in directions opposite to the Bolsheviks'. Over the past twenty years, they have been dismantling the state capitalist enterprises and much of the state bureaucracy, replacing them with private capitalist enterprises and markets. Privatization and other related policies are displacing the relatively few communist class structures left in agriculture in favor of ancient and capitalist class structures. Having destroyed the Communist Party's political monopoly and cultural control apparatus, they are presiding over the rapid development of a multiparty parliamentary system, private media enterprises, universities dependent on business enterprises, and the other components of the group that typically dominates civil society in western societies. Given their class-blind social theories, the followers of Gorbachev, Yeltsin, and Putin understand and celebrate these achievements as signs or markers that the nations of the former USSR have broken fundamentally with and superseded the Soviet economic and social system.

Like most of their Bolshevik ancestors, Gorbachev, Yeltsin, and Putin cannot recognize their roles as agents of oscillations between state and private capitalism. They take themselves rather as agents of far more fundamental changes. Lenin at least glimpsed the possibility of communist class structures radically different from those of capitalism. He wanted and strived to be, even while recognizing that he could not yet be, more than an agent of an oscillation from one to another form of capitalism. With Stalin's ascendancy, what Lenin had glimpsed as a future possibility was transformed instead to something already achieved. Official Marxian theory now held that the establishment of Soviet power simply equalled the abolition of classes. The heroic sacrifices of mobilized militants that had made the revolution, won the civil war, constructed a hegemonic state industry and marketing apparatus, and established the Communist Party in full power had thereby abolished classes. It remained only to do likewise in agriculture, which collectivization did, in the official view. Thus capitalism, classes, and class struggles had been vanquished and socialism established in the USSR. Neither Stalin nor the hegemonic groups within Soviet society thereafter could admit, to themselves or anyone else, that their vast struggles, achievements, sacrifices, and losses from 1917 to 1989 could have gotten them no further—in class terms—than an oscillation from private to state capitalism.

Gorbachev, Yeltsin, and Putin likewise cannot admit (or imagine) the possibility that their social role has been no more than to enable yet another oscillation of capitalism from a state to a private form. They and their supporters worldwide need to theorize their actions as entailing rather the defeat of communism and a victory for capitalism, democracy, civil liberties, freedom, and prosperity. They strive to convince themselves that what they are establishing will look more like Sweden, Germany, or France, than Turkey, Mexico, or India. They need to believe that mass corruption is limited to a transitional "mafia" rather then becoming the normal mode of social life. In short, they strain to shape how the people of the former USSR construct their deepening disappointment with the gap between the promised benefits of their "revolution" against Soviet socialism and what the renewed private capitalism actually delivers. They lack, so far, any political organization comparable to the Communist Party to accomplish such a consciousness-shaping project. So their recourse is to media-driven persuasion, to an endless drumbeat of argument that the problems are only temporary (and the fault of the former USSR), progress is happening everywhere, the future is bright, and the return to the past unthinkable (while tarring all social critics as proponents of such a return).

Once again, no conceptualizations of classes in the surplus labor sense are current. Absent them, it takes no great foresight to suggest how post-Soviet society will likely understand and respond when the first great crisis hits its private capitalist economy. On the one hand, many will then demand a "fundamental" change of the sort that might enable a Russian FDR to lead the pendulum swing back to a liberal or leftist state-managed private capitalism or maybe even further to a state capitalism. On the other hand, many may well demand something more like a rightist state-managed or even a fascist state capitalism. Either way, a transition from private back toward state capitalism will be conceived instead as a fundamental change from one social system to another.

The USSR was not the first, nor will it be the last effort of people suffering a social crisis to find fault with and rise against the mix of class structures in which they live and especially against the capitalist class structures within that mix. This has happened and will happen whether or not class structures are explicitly theorized in surplus labor terms. For us, the abiding questions therefore are these: What will happen in future revolts against societies in which capitalist class structures (state or private) prevail? What will their people have learned from the experience of the USSR? Where those revolts occur against state capitalisms, will their thinking and strategies be limited to an oscillation back to private capitalism? Where revolts materialize against private capitalisms, will a shift to state capitalism be the limiting horizon of their activists?

Or might the sort of class analysis of the USSR undertaken here contribute to the realization that communist class structures can and should be tried and tested on a social scale as an alternative to all forms of capitalism? For us, that realization is the answer to the question: "What is to be done?"

Notes

1. The urgency of postwar reconstruction combined with the focus on state industrial capital accumulation inherited from before the war to keep the state's priority on heavy industrial growth. That priority was credited with enabling the defeat of Hitler's invasion. The USSR's emergence as the Cold War nuclear archrival of the United States induced an even greater emphasis on military development that further reinforced the priority of heavy industry. The Cold War also sharpened the pressures on the Soviet state to raise workers' consumption levels—especially of industrial products—relative to those boasted by Western Europe and the United States. State capitalist industrial capital accumulation including accumulation in wage-good industries was thus the overwhelming priority.

2. Hochschild (1994, 115–127) eloquently explores how and why, despite denunciations of Stalin and Stalinism, the latter's multiple layers unevenly and yet doggedly held a grip on the consciousness of Soviet citizens throughout the postwar period.

3. Reduced work intensity meant that less value was added by a day's labor than had previously been the case. Worker's wages, in value terms, were already too low to be any further reduced; in other words, the value of wages that had to be paid out to workers was fixed by the circumstances. Hence the reduction in value added by workers meant an equivalent reduction in the surplus value portion that could be appropriated. In addition, workers became less productive in the sense of generating fewer use-values of output per hour of abstract labor (i.e., each use-value therefore embodied more labor). In Marxian value theory terms, this meant that the consumer goods that workers required to reproduce their labor power embodied more labor per unit than they had before. Thus the value of their labor power had risen (assuming again no further reduction in the already meager basket of consumer goods given to workers). Given the length of the Soviet working day, if the value of labor power rises, then the remaining surplus labor portion of the working day must correspondingly fall.

4. Shlapentokh writes that one third of the urban Soviet population, as well as most of the rural population, engaged in private plot (or "garden plot") farming. He also cites several reports suggesting there was far greater labor productivity on private plots than on state and collective farms (1989, 191).

5. Stephen Cohen has presented a critical evaluation of such critiques (1977).

6. The association of collective property ownership with "socialism" and hence with the Soviet state tarred it with bureaucracy as well. Thus, antibureaucratic social criticism tended not to support communist class structures such as those within some collective farms; this left the small private capitalist and ancient enterprises as those most free of "bureaucratic distortions."

7. Gaddy (1996, 44–45) stresses the immense costs of the Soviet commitment to "extensive development" in this regard. Old weapons systems and the economic resources devoted to producing them were maintained alongside the new systems and the labor and means of production allocated to them.

8. Of course, the political practices and discourses in the United States were likewise shaped by those in the USSR; the influences were dialectically interactive. Thus the prevalent forms of U.S. politics defined and justified themselves often against those asserted to prevail in the USSR.

9. The comparisons of consumption levels stimulated by detente became weapons in official propaganda battles and in intense academic and public media debates (themselves often deeply influenced by official propaganda). Problems inherent in determining and gathering the relevant data and in its statistical organization guaranteed that all comparisons would be deeply colored by the broader interests of those offering the comparisons. However, the United States possessed far more developed industries of information dissemination—above all,

advertising. Thus it could easily best the USSR, which lacked anything comparable, in spreading its spin on such comparisons across the world and into the USSR. To this day, it remains remarkable how well citizens of the former USSR grasp the existence and extent of high levels of individual consumption in the West and how poorly they recognize the extent of low levels of collective consumption there.

10. It is worth noting that decentralization of enterprise management likely operated as both effect and cause of the economic slowdown in the USSR that began in the 1970s. While the slowdown no doubt strengthened the social forces favoring decentralization, decentralization also contributed to the slowdown, as even Kornai (1992) admits. Only those committed to equating decentralization with exclusively positive economic effects regardless of context need to deny that it can ever have negative economic effects and that centralization can ever have positive economic effects.

11. We attach no historical necessity or inevitability to the stages of class transition sketched here for the postwar USSR. Only the specific, historical conditions then in place, internationally and domestically, overdetermined that political decentralization of Soviet enterprise management would serve as a step in that class transition. Had those highly unstable conditions changed or been otherwise, a different pattern of stages would have occurred.

12. Kornai claims a "positive" rather than a "normative" approach (1992, 577). This represents an epistemological naiveté (a positivism advanced as if none of the many, complex critiques of it existed and as if no defense of it was even passingly necessary). The naiveté is coupled with an absolutist apology for one set of theories (those that link private property and markets with economic "success"). Just like the Soviet theorists he abhors, Kornai believes his theoretical approach to be scientific and realistic—it gets (absolutely) at how the socialist economy really worked—while others' are wrong and/or evil. He writes without awareness let alone critique of the possibility that alternative perspectives reach alternative understandings and judgments—different understandings based on different criteria and methods of analysis: difference rather than absolutes of right and wrong.

13. A return to more centralized planning, perhaps very different from what had existed earlier, seems not to have figured even as a possibility in Kornai's work (1992).

14. Cohen has stressed in this connection the devastating effects of Stalin's late 1930s terror against the Party (1985, 63–66). The repeated decimation of the "old Bolshevik" party leaders undermined many of the qualities (independence, principled courage, etc.) that might have made the next party generation able to perform rather than betray the enhanced watchdog role assigned to it under the later reforms.

15. This conclusion is consistent with the evidence from "insiders" in the Soviet political apparatus: namely that "The withdrawal of the Party from economic management made the economy ungovernable in the old ways" (Ellman and Kontorovich 1998, 27). In our view, "the old ways" refers to party control over the Council of Ministers, Gosplan, and other central levers of surplus appropriation and economic management. The new way—the Party's assignment to more microlevel controls—could not compensate for the demise of the old control system.

16. Recent calculations suggest that when taking into account earnings outside of officially sanctioned activities (in the "second economy"), income in the USSR became more unequally distributed during the 1980s (Gregory and Stuart 1998, 157). The higher incomes were correlated with higher educational attainments and party members were increasingly better educated than the Soviet population at large (Kerblay 1983, 249). A reasonable inference is that at least after the mid-1970s, party members were located in the higher reaches of the income distribution.

17. To view the Soviet system's full employment commitments as guaranteeing each worker that he/she can keep the *same* job entails a logical error. State-planned full employment is compatible with all sorts of reallocations and retraining of workers (from declining industries to growing industries) who remain employed throughout the process of shifting from one job to another.

18. These members comprise what others often describe as a "ruling elite." In this sense, Mawdsley and White (2000) offer a history of members of the Party's Central Committee from 1917 to 1991. In our class terms, these were individuals who occupied state capitalist subsumed class positions as members of the Central Committee and in many cases also occupied state capitalist fundamental class positions as members of the Council of Ministers. Of course, in addition to one or both of these class positions, they could and did occupy still other state capitalist subsumed class positions in the military, union, police, industrial, financial, or administrative bureaucracy. Mawdsley and White provide glimpses into the multiple class positions occupied by these individuals.

References

Althusser, Louis. 1976. *Essays in Self-Criticism*, trans. by Grahame Lock. London: New Left Books.

Cohen, Stephen F. 1977. "Bolshevism and Stalinsim." In *Stalinism*, ed. by Robert C. Tucker. New York: W. W. Norton, 3–29.

———. 1985. *Rethinking the Soviet Experience: Politics and History Since 1917*. New York: Oxford University Press.

Ellman, Michael, and Vladimir Kontorovich, eds. 1998. *The Destruction of the Soviet Economic System: An Insider's View*. Armonk and London: M. E. Sharpe.

Gaddy, Clifford G. 1996. *The Price of the Past: Russia's Struggle with the Legacy of a Militarized Economy*. Washington: Brookings Institution Press.

Gregory, Paul, and Robert C. Stuart. 1998. *Russian and Soviet Economic Performance and Structure*, 6th ed. Reading: Addison-Wesley.

Hoschschild, Adam. 1994. *The Unquiet Ghost: Russians Remember Stalin*. New York: Viking.

Keep, John L. H. 1995. *Last of the Empires: A History of the Soviet Union, 1945–1991*. Oxford: Oxford University Press.

Kerblay, Basile. 1983. *Modern Soviet Society*, trans. by Rupert Swyer. New York: Pantheon.

Kornai, Janos. 1992. *The Socialist System: The Political Economy of Communism*. Princeton: Princeton University Press.

Kotz, David M. 1997. *Revolution from Above: The Demise of the Soviet System*. New York and London: Routledge.

Leonhard, Wolfgang. 1984. *The Kremlin and the West: A Realistic Approach*, trans. by H. E. Chehabi. New York: W. W. Norton.

Mawdsley, Evan, and Stephen White. 2000. *The Soviet Elite from Lenin to Gorbachev*. Oxford: Oxford University Press.

Riasanovsky, Nicholas V. 1984. *A History of Russia*. 4th ed. New York: Oxford University Press.

Shlapentokh, Vladimir. 1989. *Public and Private Life of the Soviet People: Changing Values in Post–Stalin Russia*. New York: Oxford University Press.

THE LIBERATION OF CLASS STRUGGLE?

GIOVANNI ARRIGHI, TERENCE K. HOPKINS
AND IMMANUEL WALLERSTEIN

The struggle for national liberation as we have come to know it has a long history. National liberation from what? Obviously, the answer is national liberation from the unequal relations among different zones of the modern world-system. This system has taken, as we know, the form of a capitalist world-economy, which has expanded in space over time, incorporated zones previously external to it, subordinated them (economically, politically, and culturally), and held them tightly within an integrated whole.

One of the fundamental ideological themes of all modern nationalism has been the struggle for equality—both the hypothetical equality of all members of the "nation" and the demand for equality with "outside" oppressor states/groups. (Of course, this was only one of the themes. There has also been the theme of "uniqueness" which, under certain conditions, could be translated into a justification for the oppression of others.)

Egalitarian demands in the guise of nationalism are already in evidence in the nineteenth, even the late eighteenth, centuries. The struggle of White colonists for independence in the Americas, the Haitian revolution, the Spanish resistance to Napoleon, Mehemet Ali's effort to "modernize" Egypt, the "Springtime of the Nations" in 1848, Garibaldi and Kossuth, the founding of the Indian National Congress were all reflections of this global thrust.

But it is only in the twentieth century that we can see national-liberation movements as a major organizational phenomenon of the world-system. Even before the First World War, the political "revolutions" in Mexico, the Ottoman Empire, Persia, and China made it clear that, no sooner had the "expansion of Europe" reached its apogee (the last two decades of the nineteenth century), than the counterpressures immediately began to be significant.

The Russian Revolution of October 1917 was no doubt a turning point in the political history of the modern world-system. The Bolsheviks presented themselves as the protagonist of the working-class struggle for Communism, the outgrowth of the nineteenth-century "social movement" (at that time largely a European movement) of the proletariat against the bourgeoisie. This was no doubt the case. But from the outset, everyone remarked on the fact that this "first proletarian revolution" had taken place not in the most "advanced" capitalist country or countries (where the theory had predicted it would happen) but in a relatively "backward" zone.

Although much of the support for the revolution came from "proletarians" struggling against "bourgeois," surely one element of support for the Bolsheviks took the form of a drive for "national liberation." That this latter "nationalist" element was involved and was not always compatible with the other "class" element in the Bolshevik agenda was most poignantly and significantly reflected in the stormy career and eventual elimination of Sultan Galiev who called upon Bolshevik leaders to redirect their strategy from a concentration on Europe to a concentration on the "East." Lenin himself did try to bring together the world's "socialist" movements and the world's "national-liberation" movements in the Congress of Baku. Ever since, the cohabitation of these two "antisystemic" forces has remained both very real and very uneasy. In the last fifty years it has become more and more difficult to separate the two rhetorics (socialism and national liberation), and even to keep them organizationally separate (as the political histories of China and Vietnam both illustrate very well). This combination has been very efficacious. Nonetheless, the cohabitation of these two rhetorics, tendencies, forces, has been at best uneasy, at worst deeply obscuring of social reality.

At one level, since 1945, national-liberation movements have been magnificently successful. Almost all parts of the world that in 1945 were colonies of "metropolitan" states are today independent sovereign states, equal members of the United Nations. The process by which this occurred was threefold. On the one hand, in a certain number of states, there was a significant amount of organized armed struggle, which culminated in the coming to political power in the state of the movement that had led this armed struggle. In other states, merely the potential for such armed struggle by a movement, given the world context of the many armed struggles going on elsewhere, was enough to enable the movement to achieve power (usually by "electoral" means). Finally, in a third set of states, precisely in order to head off such movements, the metropolitan power arranged a transfer to power of some so-called moderate indigenous group (what the French called an "*indépendance octroyée*").

No doubt there are many instances in which the story falls in the interstices of this model. And no doubt, too, a few such struggles for the "transfer of power" are still going on, particularly in states that are already "sovereign." . . . However, the bulk of the struggles for what might be called "formal" national liberation are now over. We are now able to look back upon what they have accomplished.

On the one hand, these struggles have accomplished very much. The arrogant and self-confident global racism involved in colonialism has disappeared or at least gone underground. The role of indigenous persons in the political decisions affecting the less powerful states of the world is considerably greater today than it was in 1945. The actual state policies of such countries have tended to reflect this "indigenization" of political decision-making.

On the other hand, the changes certainly have not been as the national-liberation movements had anticipated as of, say, 1945. There are two kinds of explanation for this. One is that the control of the state machinery of a state (any state) in the interstate system affords less real power in practice than it does in theory. The second is that there are internal class struggles going on in the states who have already known "national liberation." These two factors are linked, but it would be clearer to begin the analysis by provisionally keeping them analytically separate.

The analytical question: "How much power does one have when one has state power?" is relatively simple to explicate, once one distinguishes ideology from reality. One of the ideological principles of the modern interstate system is the totality of sovereignty. Sovereignty, or the independent juridical status of a "state" as recognized by the other state members of the interstate system, means in theory the right of the government of that state to make laws and administer its "internal" affairs without any constraints other than those that are self-imposed by the state's constitutional structure. In plain English, every government is supposed to be able to do whatever it deems wise within its borders. However, this is in fact not the case. . . .

The restraints on the power of sovereign states are many. First, there are those restraints that exist but are "illegitimate." For example, one restraint is the *de facto* power of outside forces to subvert openly or to seek to modify *sub rosa* the policies of a given state by some form of "interference" in that state's "internal" affairs. This is a familiar story. Ultimately, such an activity can involve actual military intrusion. Although in some formal sense such practices are "illegitimate" in terms of "international law," they are in fact engaged in with such frequency that any government must take cognizance of these possibilities if it intends to remain in power. Hence the threat of such illegitimate interference in practice compels a certain "prudence" on sovereign states.

Since the interstate system is normally the arena of known rivalries . . . , it is often thought that a sovereign state can "escape" the threat of interference by one strong state if it links itself politically with that state's principal rival. This is to some extent true, of course. To be sure, it then risks "interference" by the state to which it has linked itself, but it may consider this prospect less immediate and less threatening. The real question is not in this prospect. The real question lies in the realm of what might be called the "legitimate" constraints on the powers of sovereign states.

What are these "legitimate" constraints? They are those that *all* the major powers of the interstate system agree *de facto* to impose not only on the weaker states but on themselves. They are those that maintain the existence of an interstate system. These constraints are more numerous than we ordinarily recognize, primarily because they are seldom codified and are somewhat amorphous and variable in their details. They include what is sometimes called "civilized behavior" among states. For example, diplomatic immunity is a quite sacred principle, rarely violated. The social pressure to maintain this system is so strong that states often restrain themselves on matters about which they feel very strongly in order to fulfill their obligations under this principle.

A second imposed restraint has to do with trans-state property rights. The *de facto* principle is that all states may exercise eminent domain on foreign-owned property within their frontiers *up to a point.* That point is somewhat unclear. But it has not been historically true that any state could in fact nationalize without *any* compensation. Many have tried, but the counterpressures have been such that they have *all* retreated in part. A rapid look at the practices of the government of the USSR vis-à-vis foreign-property rights will make this eminently clear. . . .

A third imposed restraint has to do with the support of oppositional movements in other countries. All states (or almost all states) engage in such supportive actions. Sometimes they do it intensively. Yet they all do it only *up to a point.* There seems regularly to intrude some limit to comradely assistance. Once again the limit is unclear. But the reality is there.

If one asks how these imposed "legitimate" restraints on sovereignty really operate, often even in wartime, the answer has to be that there are implied threats of force against the violators of the norms, which are efficacious because they are supported by an exceptionally strong consensus of the world's states. Regimes that flaunt such a strong consensus rarely survive very long. When, therefore, in the early years of a "revolutionary" government, after the coming to power of a "national-liberation movement" there is a faction talking about "realism," what this faction is arguing is the need to take cognizance of these mechanisms of the interstate system. When some other movement accuses a regime that has decided to be "realistic" of being "revisionist," the accusation rings true. But the "revisionism" is structural, not volitional. Let us be very clear. We are not preaching the virtues of "realism" or "revisionism." We are merely trying to explain its repeated occurrence in states where national-liberation movements have come to power.

But this is of course not the whole story. There is also the factor of the class struggle. As long as we live in a capitalist world-economy, there is class struggle, and it continues to exist within all states located within the world-system, no matter what its political coloration. Statements of regimes that there does not exist, or there no longer exists, a class struggle within the boundaries of their state, are ideological statements devoid of analytical substance. The underlying social reality of the class struggle continues within all existing states, including those where national-liberation movements have come to power. The question is, what is the role of this national-liberation movement in relation to this class struggle in the period after it has come to power, or perhaps we should invert the question and ask what is the role of class struggle in relation to other kinds of struggle that typically characterize the capitalist world-economy, the struggle between competing "elites," that is, intra-bourgeois struggles.

There are two varieties of such intra-bourgeois struggles. One is the struggle for state power or political command. Its protagonists compete with each other (within and outside of parliaments, parties, state bureaucracies, and so on) in an attempt to seize the "commanding heights" of state apparatuses (that already exist or are being created *ex novo*) and, once in control, to enforce the sovereignty of the state. This enforcement involves struggles against other states . . . but also struggle against the state's own subjects.

The outcomes of the struggle among such competing political elites for state power on these three fronts (control over the state apparatus, sovereignty in the interstate system, and authority over the state's subjects) are obviously closely interrelated. In turn they are strongly influenced by the other kind of intra-elite struggle that must also be clearly distinguished from the class struggle: the struggle for the appropriation of wealth or economic command.

The protagonists of this economic struggle compete with each other (within and outside of markets and economic organizations) to obtain as large a share as possible of the wealth produced in the world-economy. The larger the share actually obtained, the larger the resources that can be mobilized in future struggles. Since "wealth" can be accumulated more easily than "state power," economic command has a cumulative character that is wanting in political command. . . . [T]he difference is one of degree and . . . the reproduction of economic command also involves a permanent struggle on many fronts.

At the global level, the essential characteristic of the economic struggle is that each actor (normally but not necessarily a capitalist enterprise) tries to force competition upon the other actors while simultaneously creating for itself a relatively protected niche from which a rent or a quasi-rent (natural, positional, technological, organizational, and so on) can be reaped. This struggle continually structures and restructures economic activities into core activities (those that afford the appropriation of a rent or a quasi-rent) and peripheral activities (those that afford no such appropriation). Core niches are never secure for long. As soon as they are created, they invite the direct or indirect counter-attack of other economic elites that have been forced by that very creation into less competitive niches. And as the counterattack unfolds, previously core activities are peripheralized and with it the locales and the organizations that hang on to them.

It follows that mobility (as among activities, locales, organizational forms, and so on) is an essential requirement for the survival/reproduction of economic elites, and this requirement often tends to bring them into conflict with political elites; despite the fact that, at the individual level, many persons move back and forth between a political role and an economic one. To be sure, the interests of political and economic elites overlap on many grounds. The very reproduction of economic elites requires the backing of political command, if for no other reason than to enforce property rights and contractual obligations; and whenever they can, economic elites are all too keen to exploit or use political command to back up or create for themselves rent and quasi-rent positions.

Conversely, political elites cannot succeed in their multifaceted struggle for state power without the backing of the economic command wielded by economic elites. This is particularly true in view of the fact mentioned earlier that wealth or economic command accumulates more easily than political command. The implication of this difference is that success and failure in the struggle for state power is increasingly related to the actors capability to bring (cumulating) economic command to bear upon (noncumulating) political command.

Economic and political elites are thus under considerable pressure to share/exchange the economic and political command they respectively wield. As we shall see presently, the pressure to do so originates not only in the competitive struggles for state power and wealth, but also and especially in the class struggle. When all is said and done, however, it remains true, first, that the logic of the struggle for political command is different from that of the struggle for economic command; and, second, that this difference is a source of conflict and struggle between (as well as among) political and economic elites.

For one thing, conflicts are bound to arise over the "terms of exchange" between political and economic command. The fact that both types of elite benefit from the exchange does not in and of itself determine the terms at which the two parties will agree to carry out the exchange. A more or less wide zone of indeterminacy remains, and both types of elite will be under the pressure of their respective competitive struggles to strike the best possible bargain and, if pressed too hard, to transform the bargaining process into open conflict.

What makes this transformation likely is the fact that political command is typically "territorial" (in the sense that it is bound to a given territory) while economic command is very often, and particularly for major actors, "transterritorial" (in the sense that it operates across territories). In this case too, the difference between the two types of command is one of degree. Yet it is real enough, and it leads to a permanent struggle between political and economic elites over the "transterritoriality" of the latter, that is, their ability to move in and out of state jurisdictions rather than being permanently and completely subjected to any one of them.

All these inter- and intra-elite struggles are often confusingly discussed as though they were part of the class struggle. In our view, it is more useful to restrict the concept of class struggle to vertical conflicts that counterpose groups and individuals in situations differently related to the means of production. Inter- and intra-elite conflicts, in contrast, are typically horizontal conflicts that counterpose groups and individuals related in similar ways to the means of production or to the means of legitimate violence. As such, they are better referred to as competitive struggles and labeled as either economic or political intra-elite struggles depending on whether the primary object of the competition is wealth or state power.

Strictly speaking, in order to be able to speak of the existence of class struggle, three conditions must be fulfilled. First, there is an identifiable pattern of collective or generalized protest. Second, the objectives or the forms of the protest are such that the struggle is traceable to a class situation (that is, a given relationship to the means of production) of the participants in the protest. Third, the struggle derives from, or creates a counterposition between, groups differently related to the means of production.

According to these criteria some struggles (strikes and other forms of collective or generalized workplace protest by wage workers, the withholding of agricultural surpluses or the cutting down of cultivation by peasants or farmers, the seizure of land by landless peasants, food riots by the urban unemployed, and so on) have a strong likelihood of qualifying as episodes of class struggle. In other cases (demonstrations, urban and rural guerrilla warfare, acts of terrorism, and so on), whether or not the acts of protest qualify as episodes of the class struggle depends, among other things, on their context, protagonists, objectives, and so on. The problem in these latter instances is that the form of struggle is more frequently associated with a competitive struggle among political elites than it is with a class struggle in the sense we have defined it.

The two types of struggle can of course intersect and overlap, and they normally do. Quite often, the class struggle generates demands for leadership and organization that are supplied either by new political elites that emerge out of the class struggle itself or by previously existing elites. In either case the class struggle "flows out" into a competitive struggle for state power. As this occurs, the political elites that provide social classes with leadership and organization (even if they sincerely consider themselves "instruments" of the class struggle) usually find that they have to play by the rules of that competition and therefore must attempt to subordinate the class struggle to those rules in order to survive as competitors for state power. Conversely, it often happens that the inter- and intra-elite struggles over political and economic command wittingly or unwittingly stir up the class struggle. In this case, a particular class struggle that emerges initially as an "instrument" of intra- and inter-elite competition may very well subsequently develop its own momentum. In both instances the class struggle intersects and overlaps with the struggle over political command but remains or becomes a distinct process. *Mutatis mutandis*, the same could be said of the relationship between the class struggle and the struggle over economic command.

The Russian Revolution of 1917 was the outcome of a very special conjuncture of these three types of struggle, namely the convergence and fusion of particularly acute horizontal and vertical conflicts over world political and economic command within and across national locales. The Bolsheviks, skillfully exploiting this conjuncture, seized the commanding heights of the Russian Empire in the name of the working class. They were thereby faced with the dilemma of whether to use this newly-conquered power to sustain the class struggle within and outside their state boundaries or to consolidate their power within a restructured but tendentially stable interstate system. Although the eventual solution of the dilemma in the direction of the second vector was already foreshadowed at Kronstadt, the outcome was the result of long inter- and intra-elite struggles in which the rhetorical identification of the political interest of the Bolshevik Party and the state with the class interests of world labor played a major role in influencing and constraining the behavior of all involved.

This subordination of the class struggle in the USSR to other considerations . . . had two consequences. It . . . tended to de-legitimize the class struggle when waged against the interests of the Soviet political leadership and its more or less temporary allies. And it . . . promoted an ideological polarization in the interstate system that could be, and has been, exploited by national-liberation movements and the political elites that have emerged out of them. The combined effect of these two tendencies has been the continuing ambiguous relationship between the political leadership of national liberation movements and the class struggle.

In the phase of actual struggle for national liberation, that is; in the process of formation of new formally sovereign states, the political elites leading the struggles have used a double standard toward the class struggle. The legitimacy of genuine episodes of class struggles, as defined above, was upheld or denied according to whether they strengthened or weakened the elites' hand in the pursuit of Political Kingdom. For example, whether a strike was supported/organized or not often depended on whether it was directed against the colonial authorities and sectors of capital hostile to independence, or against sectors of capital favorable to independence. This double standard was more strictly enforced when the leaderships of national-liberation movements depicted themselves as instruments or agents of the class struggle in the interstate system.

Once national independence was attained, the use of this double standard meant a further narrowing of the legitimacy of the class struggle in the new national locales. This tendency has two quite distinct roots. On the one hand, we have regimes that have attempted to consolidate their power through an alliance with the political and economic elites of core zones. In this case, the class struggle was de-legitimized as part of the political exchange between core and peripheral elites, whereby the former respect/protect the formal sovereignty of the latter in exchange for the latter's creation within their national boundaries of an environment favorable to core capital. On the other hand, we have regimes that have attempted to consolidate their power through the opposite route of struggle against core elites. In this case, the class struggle within the country was de-legitimized as an obstacle to the former struggle, which was itself defined as class struggle at a higher level.

The fact that opposite strategies of consolidation of power led to similar outcomes from the point of view of the legitimacy of class struggle in the Third World can only be understood in the light of the peripheral position of most Third World states. This position implies little or no command over world surplus, and this, in turn, has two implications for the class struggle: (1) from the point of view of its protagonists (social classes) there is not much to be gained from it, so that actual episodes of class struggle are likely to engender frustration rather than class consciousness; (2) under these circumstances, peripheral elites competing for political command do not normally find social classes upon which to constitute reliable bases of power and hence have resorted to one of the two strategies mentioned above.

Our conception of class struggle as the pivotal process of the capitalist world-economy is thus unremarkably conventional. As struggle, it is conceived to be a struggle over the development and organization or productive forces; hence over the directional control of means of production and means of livelihood; hence over the social relations factually effecting that control. As historical process, it is conceived to be a process that continually forms and reforms the relational classes it joins in conflict. In turn, of course, their structuring, consciousness, organization, and development vary immensely, among and within the time-space structural zones of the world-scale accumulation process, owing, as was said in another context, to a "historical and moral element." As a result, the process of class struggle and the relational character of the classes formed therein continually occur historically in culturally, organizationally, and civilizationally distinctive versions, each as it were with its own authenticity and originality, which mark the scope of its historical presence. Moreover, the ongoing changes which the class struggle effects in the social structuring of the accumulation process themselves transform in locationally distinctive ways the circumstances in and through which the class struggle as historical process operates. It is as if the game and the players—there are no spectators—were always the same but the rules, officials, and boundaries of the playing field were novel on each and every occasion—and not at all that knowable until seen in retrospect.

We know from the sketch in Part I of the *Communist Manifesto* how Marx and Engels saw that class struggle formed the two great classes during the period when the ramifying social division of labor that marked industrialization of the core at that time was occurring. We know too from the European writers of the interwar period—Gramsci, Lukács, Reich, Korsch, for example—how deeply state encapsulation of the projected development of the proletariat contradicted the uniting of the workers of the world. It deflected the formative revolutionary tendencies into national and international organs, that is, into organs that work through, and so reinforce and depend upon, one of the fundamental structures and planes of operation of the capitalist economy, namely, the relational network we call its interstate system. And we know the counterpart movement: in the phrasing of E. H. Carr,

> When the cause of revolution, having proved barren in the west, flourished in the fertile soil of Asia, the shape of things to come radically changed. . . . The [Russian] revolution could now be seen not only as a revolt against bourgeois capitalism in the most backward western country, but as a revolt against western imperialism in the most advanced eastern country (1969: 30–31).

. . . Samir Amin drew the necessary inference for theoretical work, in remarking on the amazing power of Eurocentrism. "The vision of the 'advanced' proletariat of the West bringing socialism as a 'gift' to the 'backward' masses of the periphery is not 'intolerable'—it is merely refuted by history" (1974: 603).

With the reestablishment of hegemony in the world-system under the aegis of the United States as hegemonic power, there developed in thought—Eastern and Western, Northern and Southern—an effort to bring class struggle and national liberation, as conceptions of transformation, into more definite *theoretical* (not merely historical) relations. We pass over here the kinds of effort we earlier called ideological in character, those where the leadership of national-liberation struggles was seen as acting in the cause of, and by some in the name of, the world proletariat's historical mission. Not many students of the capitalist world-economy today work with this sort of version, or vision, or the relation between the two constructs.

What we called the political form of the relation, however—in which the common element of struggle for state power provides the ground for considering the two, the national struggle and the class struggle, as historically alternative precursors to socialist revolution—does require brief comment. Many of us have moved theoretically in this direction if not embracing the formulation explicitly. An influential statement of the theoretical development was by Lin Biao in "The International Significance of Comrade Mao Tse-tung's Theory of People's War." There it will be recalled he first notes that "the proletarian revolutionary movement [i.e., class struggle] has for various reasons been temporarily held back in the North American and West European capitalist countries . . . " He subsequently asserts that the "national-democratic revolution is the necessary preparation for the socialist revolution, *and* the socialist revolution is the inevitable sequel to the national-democratic revolution." The national-democratic struggle has of course the form of a united front: "The revolution embraces in its ranks not only the workers, peasants, and the urban petty bourgeoisie, but also the national bourgeoisie and other patriotic and anti-imperialist democrats" (1967: 352–3 [emphasis added]).

This is not a *theoretical* understanding of the relations between national liberation and class struggle with which we can concur, as our reflections above probably suggest. There may indeed be theoretical virtue, when arraying the historical alternatives (here, futures) to which national-liberation struggles could lead (might have led, might yet lead), in the drawing of an analogy between them and the world-historical class struggle and the revolutionary transformation the conception entails. There is, however, no theoretical virtue in, and much confusion produced by, the drawing of an analogy between, (1) national-liberation struggles and the historical alternatives their attainments define and, (2) class struggle on a world scale and the historical alternatives it conceptually entails. National liberation in segments of the capitalist world-economy, and the transformations it has effected in relations of rule and other social relations, have altered the social structuring of the world-historical accumulation process. That much is historically evident and therefore theoretically to be taken into account. But it has not eliminated the relational conditions through which the accumulation process operates. And precisely that world-historical elimination, of the relational conditions through which accumulation of capital occurs, is what is entailed in the idea of the class struggle as the pivotal process in the transformation of the capitalist world-economy into a socialist world order.

Nor theoretically, in our view, could national-liberation movements, any more than core-zone social-democratic movements—given their common historical focus on securing and exercising power *within* the interstate system—have effected much more by way of change than they have done. If, however, we cease to accord strategic primacy to acquiring such state power within the interstate system, far more becomes historically possible and thereby, within the domain of historically realistic alternatives, theoretically possible. It would seem a dubious *theoretical* tenet to assert that national liberation, in its successive occurrences, is in any way a necessary condition of the revolutionary transformation of the world-economy. It is surely indefensible to claim it as a sufficient condition.

References

Amin, Samir (1974). *Accumulation on a World Scale.* New York: Monthly Review Press.

Carr, E. H. (1969). *The October Revolution, Before and After.* New York: Knopf.

Lin Biao (1967). "Mao Tse-tung's Theory of People's War," in F. Schurmann & O. Schell, eds., *The China Reader: III, Communist China, Revolutionary Reconstruction and International Confrontation, 1949 to the Present.* New York: Vintage Books, 347–59.

FASCISM: REVOLUTION AGAINST THE REVOLUTION

Mark Neocleous

. . . Fascism styles itself as anti-Marxist and anti-Bolshevik, yet insists, for a variety of reasons, that it contains a commitment to socialism. The nature of "fascist socialism" or "national socialism" therefore needs to be addressed. To do this I shall be rather old fashioned, which these days can only mean one thing: I shall be discussing capitalism and revolution. I shall argue that fascism appropriates socialist language, slogans and, occasionally, arguments, but by incorporating them into a broader ideological framework with nationalist, elitist and conservative intentions it dissolves socialism's key premises into a politics of reaction and, building on the work of the conservative revolutionaries, reveals itself as a counter-revolutionary phenomenon in defence of capitalism.

The argument is developed at a critical distance from the frequent claim that fascism and Marxism share common ground. A. James Gregor's account of the "intellectual origins of fascism" rests on the belief that fascism is a *variant* of Marxism and that both are illustrative of the "fascist persuasion" in radical politics; a similar claim is made by Noël O'Sullivan. Even Zeev Sternhell, in his far more subtle work on the "birth of fascist ideology," claims that fascism is a *revision* of Marxism.[1] . . . But there are a number of reasons why such an approach should be rejected. First, as soon as one incorporates German fascism into this picture it becomes difficult to sustain the exclusive focus on the revision of Marxism, given the widespread violent opposition to Marxism within the German context. Second, as a movement fascism defines itself categorically as anti-communist and anti-Marxist. Third, the term "revision" has an ambiguity which obscures more than it reveals. The entire history of Marxism since Marx's death can in some ways be read as a series of "revisions" of Marx in the light of theoretical critique and historical change. Can one distinguish between revisions of Marxism that remain Marxist and revisions which leave the Marxist fold? If terms such as "Marxism" and "fascism" (and, for that matter, liberalism, conservatism, and so on) are to retain any meaning the answer must be in the affirmative. That Marxism and fascism may share some features—an anti-parliamentarianism and commitment to radical change, for example—is less significant than the features which set them apart and place them on opposite sides of historical struggle. At the heart of this opposition lies the issue of class.

A Mongrel of Lies: National Socialism

Despite the fact that only the Nazis included in the title of their party the designation "National Socialist," fascism generally presents itself as socialist. . . . [F]ascism has the same aim as socialism and communism—the representation of the people—yet unlike communism it does not intend to abolish property. Instead property is to be utilized in a national framework which will harness all social forces—especially those on opposite sides of the class divide—into a national synthesis providing the basis for social justice. In this "social nationalism" or "national socialism," in which "nationalism + socialism = fascism" the state is to belong to all classes and will unite the nation with socialism.[2] For Hitler, the chief crime of Marxism is its internationalism. The way to avoid Marxists using the working class to destroy the nation is to integrate the class into the nation through the nationalization of the masses. The national socialist state will thus have no classes since classes will be united into a common framework of national unity. National prosperity will be achieved through people being bound together by a common pride and joy.[3]

What the shift to nationalism does more than anything else is to obliterate the class struggle in ideological terms. Instead of the end of class struggle through the victory of the working class and the production of a genuinely classless society, fascism ends class struggle in *this* society, that is, in class society, by dissolving the question of class *per se*. In other words, the shift in the concept of the oppressed group enables fascism to "resolve" the question of class by assuming the classlessness of class society. As Marcuse puts it:

> The whole that it [totalitarian universalism] presents is not the unification achieved by the domination of *one* class within the framework of class society, but rather a unity that combines *all* classes, that is supposed to overcome the reality of class struggle and thus of classes themselves. . . . A classless society, in other words, is the goal, but a classless society on the basis of and within the framework of—the existing class society.

The purpose of this is the prevention of communism through a socialism for the nation. In practice, this is to take the form of nationalization, the direct opposite of socialization.[4] The fascist "resolution" of the problem of class is thus a mystification; it deals with class on an ideological rather than material level. In this sense fascism reveals itself as ideology: since the fascist considers conceptions, thoughts, ideas—all the products of consciousness—as the real human chains they need fight only against these illusions of consciousness. This demand to change consciousness amounts to a demand to interpret reality in another way, that is, to recognize it by means of another interpretation.[5]

The nation is thus a concept for a new interpretation of reality, a class-ridden reality reinterpreted as classless unity. This is true of all nationalism. In fascism, however, the same is true of other key concepts such as race and state. In the case of fascist racism, for example, it is by positing fundamental differences between races and then arranging them hierarchically that the working class can be (re)presented as part of a higher race. By positing racial struggle as the driving force of history, and by pointing to the aristocratic principle in nature, the working class can be conceptualized as part of this aristocracy and part of the driving force of history. For Hitler, it is

> because of the Communists, if for no other reason, that Germany is no longer able to fight beyond its borders . . . For the nation is paralysed by class divisions. My aim is to lead the many millions of workers back to the idea of the *Volk*. That will only happen when they sincerely believe in the ideal.[6]

The message to the worker then, is: why identify with an oppressed class when you can identify with the (racial) aristocracy? Racism is thus a substitute for the class struggle, the racial other being the new enemy for the newly unified people's community. By subsuming class under a racial form the question of class struggle and the possibility of communism are obliterated. Satisfied with his own blood, the worker gives up the struggle for greater social riches.[7] The whole purpose behind *völkisch* thought is that it presents a mechanism for not only *incorporating* the working class but also *subduing* it. The working class is dangerous because, as a product of the rise of capitalism, this class more than any other embodies modern rootlessness and restlessness; as such the workers threaten the social order. If this class is given a standing in the *Volk*, the worker loses his status as an alienated proletarian and recaptures the unity of the past by being part of a new harmonious social totality; this would simultaneously be an end to social antagonism.[8] Incorporation into the *Volk* can do this because the *Volk* is the universal and spiritual unity of the German people.

In other forms of fascism the idea of the corporate state plays an almost identical role. In declaring it the *people's* state, fascism presents the state as above classes, that is, no longer under the control of one class. But it simultaneously declares that there can be nothing outside the state; that is, nothing opposed to the state. Fascism is *opposed* to socialism, claim Mussolini and Gentile, because socialism "confines the movement of history within the class struggle and ignores the unity of classes established in one economic and morality in the State." Fascism recognizes that divergent and opposed interests have existed, but "wishes to bring them under the control of the State and give them a purpose within the corporate system of interests reconciled within the unity of the State." And yet fascism also *assists* the cause of socialism by stopping it drifting down the path of communism and focusing on class struggle.[9] . . .

In its focus on class Marxism conceptualizes society as fragmented and subject to internal struggle. By thinking of society as constituted as one state and one race the illusion of unity is created. Through either *Volk* or state, fascism presents its own version of totality, rooted in the nation-state. Within this totality all forms of particularity are overcome—the atomization of individuals along with separation of classes. Fascism "liberates" the working class by identifying it as part of the universal state or transcendent *Volk*. As such the place of the working class in history is guaranteed, but guaranteed as part of another totality; there is no need for it to struggle as a class *for itself*. To achieve this "liberation" all forms of fascism present themselves as a form of socialism; the socialist image, however, is always undermined by the nature of the racial or statist totality being offered. For at the heart of fascism is not the material emancipation of the working class but the taming of the masses.[10]

Fascism accepts one of Marx's insights into the nature of capitalism: by being the class with a material investment in the overthrow of capitalism, the working class constitutes *the* revolutionary threat to capitalism. Fascism mobilizes this revolutionary energy while simultaneously taming the force behind it. As Walter Benjamin puts it:

> Fascism attempts to organize the newly created proletarian masses without affecting the property structure which the masses strive to eliminate. Fascism sees its salvation in giving these masses not their right, but instead a chance to express themselves. The masses have a right to change property relations; fascism seeks to give them an expression while preserving property.[11]

. . . [D]espite its self-designation as socialist and its appropriation of some of the language, slogans and liturgy of the left, fascism established itself historically as a defence of capitalism and thus a *reaction* against working-class revolutionary potential. This will show that the film-maker Sergei Eisenstein's description of "national socialism" as a 'mongrel of lies' is an apt description of all fascist "socialism."[12]

Fascism sits comfortably in the tradition of reactionary thought which identifies money and finance capital rather than capitalist commodity production as the "enemy." The goal in this tradition is not a classless society and the abolition of exploitation but a "people's community" in which the excesses of the money-based modern society are curbed. Fascist attacks on "capital" are always attacks on finance or banking capital rather than capitalist production. Despite operating under the label "socialist," such attacks are always the hallmark of pseudo-socialist movements, that is, movements which steer clear of tackling the foundations of capitalist society. (It is precisely this kind of socialism which Marx and Engels attack in *The Communist Manifesto.*) Those who attack finance and banking capital play into the hands of industrial capital. Far from being anti-capitalist, fascism's attack on finance, banking and money capital constitutes a capitulation to fascist capitalist production.[13] Admittedly, distinguishing between "creative" and "parasitic" capital appeals to workers—by creating a mystique of socialist intentions—but, crucially, in its attack on "parasitical" banking or finance capital this distinction also appeals to capitalists. Thus, far from being established in opposition to private property, fascism establishes itself as private property's saviour. Mussolini made the point that as far as economics went he was a Manchester liberal, Hitler never tired of stating that one of the symptoms of decay was the slow disappearance of the right of private property, and the policy of the Parti Populaire Française was for profit to remain the motor of production, even in "fascist socialism."

Historically this meant that fascism faced the problem of defending private property while retaining a "socialist" façade and mobilizing the masses behind it. The practical outcome of this was to defend private property against the working class by either eliminating workers' organizations or turning them into instruments for the furtherance of national unity. In both Italy and Germany the result was the institutional emasculation of the working-class movement. . . .

The corporate state in Italy provided the foundation for the incorporation of capital and labour. Intended as a third way between liberalism and communism, Italian corporatism sought to unify the nation by invoking the image of unity gleaned from medieval corporations.

Instead of workers and capitalists on opposite sides of the class divide, all were to be thought of as "producers" contributing to the success of the nation.[14] For this reason organizations with only workers' interests were replaced by those obeying the demand for fascist national unity. The socialist General Confederation of Labour was abolished, to be replaced by the Fascist Labour Confederation, given an extra stamp of approval with the Vidoni Pact of October 1925 in which the Confederation and the industrialists' Confederazione Generale dell'Industria Italiana (CGII) officially recognized each other as representatives of labour and capital, respectively. . . .

■ ■ ■ ■

. . . But while organized capital continued to be represented by its own spokesmen in the CGII, labour found itself "represented" by fascist party bureaucrats, as formalized by the Vidoni agreement (and usefully assisted by the fact that the original leaders and representatives of labour were either in prison or underground). The juridicial form appeared to overcome the traditional confrontation between capital and labour in the formerly "private" sphere, but whereas capital still had a great deal of autonomy and freedom, labour was a subjugated force. The CGII was "nominally subject to the same government controls that applied to other syndicated associations but, unlike them, it was strong enough to resist the demands of government officials and Fascist radicals."[15] Organized industry was *in* the state but not *of* the state; organized labour, on the other hand, was "free" only to the extent that it was *of* the state. A corporate system forms a mystified veil behind which the process of capital accumulation continues unhindered. By incorporating the working class, fascism nullifies the potential political action of that class and, in turn, facilitates the extraction of surplus value.

Two features of the Nazis' anti-capitalist rhetoric are important. First, the Nazi attack on unproductive or finance capital was equally an attack on Jewish capital. And, second, the Nazis also consistently attacked communism, Marxism, and demands for workers' autonomy and the heightening of the class struggle. These two features were combined in Nazi ideology through the insistence that there existed a Jewish–Bolshevik world conspiracy which was simultaneously a mechanism for the domination of finance capitalism. The Nazis presented themselves as the saviours of socialism through their fight against the Jewish–Bolshevik domination. Goebbels was to declare that "socialism can be achieved only in opposition to the Jews, and it is because we want socialism that we are anti-Semitic," and in *Mein Kampf* Hitler openly professed that the Jew, like the Marxist, encourages contempt for the worker and seeks to shatter the national economy.[16] . . .

The Nazis began by encouraging the trade unions to dissolve their links with the Social Democratic Party, winning the unions over by declaring 1 May a national holiday—a "Day of National Labour." In front of some 1 million people, in a celebration of the 'communal workers' state' and in honour of the "productive workers of all classes," Hitler spoke out against the Marxist misunderstanding of manual labour and its presentation of society as torn apart by social class conflict. Like the Jew, the Marxist is said to denigrate manual labour. The Nazis, in contrast, would praise the work and industry of the people and end the isolation of classes and ranks. The following day, independent trade unionism was crushed. . . .

■ ■ ■ ■

. . . Following Hitler's thoughts on trade unions in *Mein Kampf*, where he had argued that the problem was the *Marxist* use of trade unions to foment class divisions and thus undermine national unity rather than trade unions themselves, the Nazi regime slashed trade unions thought to be under the control of communists or containing workers who were communist sympathizers; other unions continued to exist after 1933.[17]

■ ■ ■ ■

At the level of the firm one of the earliest pieces of legislation seeking a solution to the "problem" of the working class was the Law on the Organization of National Labour (*Arbeitsordnungsgesetz*, or AOG). All institutions previously concerned with labour relations—from mass organizations to arbitration authorities—were to be replaced by the "factory community" (*Betriebsgemeinschaft*) which, in turn, was to be the "cell" of the national community (*Volksgemeinschaft*), a model of society which Hitler described as a "process of coming together" of the "artificial classes" in the nation. The employer as head of the workforce was to be the mirror image of a *Führer*; workers, to be known as his "followers," were to swear "fealty and obedience" to him, while he was to be concerned with the welfare of his workers. This would help develop the workers' inner commitment to the firm, loyalty to the leader, integration in the factory community and thus into the national community. Although the Trustees of Labour (from May 1933) stood above the "community of the firm" to protect the interests of the state, such protection meant as little interference as possible as the responsibility for day-to-day problems was to remain with the cells of the social organism. A new system of "social honour courts" was introduced in which "offences against social honour" would be punished. Such offences included an employer overexploiting his workforce and a worker threatening the industrial peace.[18] The effects of these changes are obvious: emasculate the working-class movement by obliterating its institutional basis while simultaneously increasing the authority and power of the factory "leaders" to dominate the workforce.

This domination operated alongside both the more overt repression of the workers and their representatives—the presence of the Gestapo at strikes and, from 1938, its terroristic surveillance over workers, including the use of miniature concentration camps attached to major industrial firms (of which there were 165 up to the middle of the war)—and the appropriation of the language and iconography of socialism. Not content with crushing the working-class movement, torturing and killing socialists, fascism also steals the jewellery from the corpse: the colour red, the street, the flag, May Day, socialist film-making, all adopted for the ideology of the nation and state power rather than world revolution.[19]

The different practices of the Italian and German fascist regimes are, on the one hand, a reflection of their very different ideological mechanisms for the subsumption of class struggle: in the Italian case the incorporation of the working class through a juridicial and statist corporate form, in the German case through the organization of the factory as a community, in turn being the cell of the national community. . . .

. . . [T]hese divergent ideological mechanisms possess an underlying unity of a twofold kind. First, the grounds for the taming of the working class were the presupposition of the necessity for national unity over class conflict. The different means for achieving this—incorporation or obliteration through organization—rested nonetheless on the unity of the nation and authoritarian state power. What fascism understands by "unity," then, is a nation-state in which oppressing and oppressed classes are forced together under a structure of domination.[20] 'Unity' here refers less to harmony than to class and state domination, with all forms of resistance and opposition effectively crushed. Second, these divergent mechanisms had a common core—a return to a mythic past, in which such unity was present. Italian corporations were an attempt to invoke the unity achieved by the medieval corporations, a revival of medieval form stuffed full of modern content (capitalism), and the organic form for factory communities in Germany was an attempt to redeem the lost unity of the medieval world. Both were reactions to modernity and its core political components of Marxism and liberalism, with their insistence that bourgeois society is divided on class lines or is merely a collection of atomized individuals. . . .

■ ■ ■ ■

To the extent that fascism facilitates capital accumulation and crushes workers' organizations it reveals itself, regardless of its revolutionary rhetoric, as an essentially conservative political phenomenon in defence of capitalism, a political attempt to revive flagging capitalist economies by overcoming the political weaknesses of liberal democratic regimes. Fascism thus reveals the truth of capitalism. . . . Industrial capital can come to terms with any political regime so long as that regime does not actually expropriate it, and will willingly and happily come to terms with any regime which solves economic depression, ends political chaos, destroys the revolutionary communist and socialist movement, eliminates workers' institutions, and commits itself to industrial (capitalist) modernization. Attempts to describe fascism under categories such as totalitarianism, state capitalism and bureaucratic collectivism fail to address this; indeed, they mask it over. Horkheimer's comment, that whoever is not willing to talk about capitalism should also keep quiet about fascism, is thus well made, despite arguments to the contrary made by historians of the opposite political persuasion.[21] But if fascism reveals the truth of capitalism, its defence of capitalism also reveals the truth of fascism.

One of the reasons why this issue has been downplayed in some of the recent literature on fascism is the primacy of politics found in fascist theory and practice. For fascism, the crucial feature of modern order is the political, the very sphere which Marxists and liberals are said to denigrate. For fascism, Marxism treats the political as an epiphenomenon of the economic, while liberalism treats it as mere night-watchman, overseeing a self-regulating civil society. The fascist response is to emphasize the political over the economic, to work, in effect, with a strong concept of the political, collapsing the state–civil society distinction and subsuming civil society under the state—nothing outside of the state. The ideological effect of this is that fascism works without an economic doctrine to speak of. The practical effect is a fairly *laissez-faire* attitude to capital accumulation. Its solution to the economic contradictions and crises of capitalism is ever more authoritarian state power. For this reason commentators have tended to focus their analyses here, on the political. But the stress on the primacy of politics obscures the continuation of structures of *social* domination.

■ ■ ■ ■

The Politics of Revolution

■ ■ ■ ■

. . . Fascism undoubtedly does present itself as a revolutionary doctrine and its seizure of power as a revolution. Mussolini and Gentile continually insisted that fascism was revolutionary,[22] and leading Nazis referred to their movement as revolutionary and the regime itself as constituting a national or national socialist revolution.[23] Many commentators have taken these claims at face value and, by pointing to the supposedly revolutionary changes that the fascist regimes brought about, take the fascist claim one step further. First mooted by Hermann Rauschning in his description of Nazism as a "revolution of nihilism," the claim has been extended to incorporate arguments that Hitler did achieve a genuine social revolution or that the revolution was one of destruction, paving the way for the modernization of German society. Similar claims are made for Italy.[24] In whatever shape they come, such claims are generally intended as a riposte to Marxist arguments that fascism is by definition a counter-revolutionary and reactionary movement.

One of the difficulties faced by anyone dealing with the question of the "revolutionary" nature of fascism is that they enter what has been called a "semantic minefield,"[25] with associated concepts such as "counter-revolutionary" and "reactionary" only adding to the dangers. The minefield is made more hazardous by fascist ideology itself: as much as the fascists present themselves as revolutionary, and may sincerely think of themselves as such, they also think of themselves as counter-revolutionary and reactionary. Mussolini describes fascism in *any* language he finds useful. In regarding itself as somehow beyond all intellectual systems fascism freely borrows from them all; by being anti-systematic and anti-intellectual it does not matter whether this borrowing renders fascism unintelligible. The fact that fascism is, for Mussolini, some kind of glorious synthesis of opposites means that fascists can be "aristocrats and democrats, revolutionaries and reactionaries, proletarians and anti-proletarians, pacifists and anti-pacifists."[26] Hitler notoriously declared himself a revolutionary against the revolution.

One of the reasons why so many have lost intellectual limbs in this minefield is the careless use of the concept of revolution and, where it is not being used carelessly, the widely divergent meanings attached to the word: in some cases it refers to the demands made in fascist ideology, in others it refers to the seizure of power, while in yet others it is taken to refer to a social revolution said to have occurred in Italy and Germany once power had been seized. The confusion here is one handed down to us by the English and

French revolutions (and, to a lesser extent, the Bolshevik one). But the confusion does not require us to jettison the concept of revolution (and, relatedly, counter-revolution) as some suggest.[27] One way to use the concept of revolution is to distinguish between political and social revolution, where the former represents a transformation of political power relations and the latter a transformation in the socio-economic relations of production. Revolution can be thought of as both process and moment, where a process of revolutionary social transformation is accompanied by moments of revolutionary political change. This is the kind of distinction Marx operates with. Although for Marx 1640 and 1789 are revolutionary *moments,* the general thrust of his concern is the long term *process* by which capitalist relations of production come to dominate. It is for this reason that he points to an "era of social revolution." The strength of this lies in being able to distinguish between the long, slow and often "silent" process by which a particular mode of production and its concomitant property relations place their stamp on human relations, and the moments of political rupture or crisis in which relations of political power and authority undergo substantial alteration. . . .

■ ■ ■ ■

Crucially, revolutionary political moments need not necessarily contribute to a longer process of social revolution.

Clearly the seizures of power by the fascists in both Germany and Italy were reactions to the perceived crises of the state and threat of communist revolution. In Germany the failure of the political elites and institutions of the Weimar Republic to overcome the economic crises created an opening for an authoritarian intervention. In providing this intervention the Nazis obliterated the Weimar constitution and thus liberal democracy in Germany. Whether this constituted a *political* revolution is at least questionable: the old political elites continued to exist alongside the new Nazi elites, and key institutions such as the civil service and the army retained a large degree of autonomy.[28] That it did not constitute a *social* revolution is clear: the class structure remained more or less intact. In the case of Italy one may wish to describe the seizure of power as a revolutionary political moment, but thereafter the regime had no long-term revolutionary effect on the nature of the social structure. The fascist regime emerged as a new authoritarian political defence of the increasingly capitalist social order. As a centralized and authoritarian regime it could carry out some degree of social transformation—it managed to usurp Mafia power bases, for example—but it at no point sought to undermine the real class structure then in existence.[29]

■ ■ ■ ■

Fascism sets itself against the possibility of a communist—that is, social—revolution. The fascist political revolution is the *alternative* to social revolution; as such it is equally counter-revolutionary.[30] Hitler's description of himself as a revolutionary against the revolution thus reveals much about fascism. The double meaning of the description—on the one hand it was a revolution against the revolution of 1918 (and thus also the October revolution of the previous year), and on the other hand it was a revolution to block any future communist revolution—reveals that the fascist revolution has an essentially conservative nature. It is for this reason that liberal democracies were happy with the fascist regimes. (For example, in 1937 Lord Halifax told Hitler that he and other government colleagues "were fully aware that the Führer had not only achieved a great deal inside Germany herself, but that, by destroying communism in his country, he had barred its road to Western Europe and that Germany therefore could rightly be regarded as a bulwark of the West against Bolshevism."[31] Fascism's politically revolutionary effect—the imposition of an authoritarian regime as an illiberal solution to crises—reveals its socially conservative and counter-revolutionary essence. For this reason we can describe fascism as the culmination of the *conservative revolutionary* tradition.

■ ■ ■ ■

Fascism appropriated the central themes articulated by the conservative revolutionaries, radicalized them and put them into practice. And this applies to fascism generally: even before the march on Rome, Mussolini was claiming that one could be both revolutionary and conservative.[32]

This reading of fascism . . . undermines the attempt to present it as a 'third way' between capitalism and communism or as "neither right nor left." Supposedly the synthesis of all oppositions, fascism freely claims that it also overcomes the artificial right–left distinction. . . .

■ ■ ■ ■

If "the right" is associated with the defence of private property then fascism, given its supposed ideological opposition to capitalism, has to declare itself to be not of the right. But because of the integral links between Marxism, revolutionary anti-capitalism and "the left," fascism also has to differentiate itself from the left generally. This leaves fascism in an apparent no man's land in the battleground of political thought, which it reinterprets positively as the transcendence of false dichotomies. But the fact that fascism's opposition to capitalism is an attack on parasitical finance capital but not capitalism *per se* means that fascism is never a third way between capitalism and communism, whatever its own ideologies might say. . . .

Moreover, fascists know full well that their enemy is on the left: it is, after all, left-wing and not right-wing activists who fill the cells of fascist prisons. Conservative elites may be boring, flabby, impotent and decrepit, but they do not constitute the same kind of danger to fascism as socialism and communism. If fascism is revolutionary, then, it is a particular form of conservative revolution, and thus a revolution from the right.

Notes

1. A. James Gregor, *The Fascist Persuasion in Radical Politics* (Princeton, NJ: Princeton University Press, 1974); Gregor, *Young Mussolini and the Intellectual Origins of Fascism* (Berkeley: University of California Press, 1979); Noel O'Sullivan, *Fascism* (London: J.M. Dent & Sons, 1983); Zeev Sternhell, with Mario Sznajder and Maia Asheri, *The Birth of Fascist Ideology: From Cultural Rebellion to Political Revolution*, trans. David Maisel (Princeton, NJ: Princeton University Press, 1994).

2. George Valois, "Empty Portfolios" (1926), in Roger Griffen (ed.), *Fascism* (Oxford: Oxford University Press, 1995), pp. 197–8; Zeev Sternhell, *Neither Right Nor Left: Fascist Ideology in France*, trans. David Maisel (Berkeley: University of California Press, 1986), pp. 105–6. On Drieu and Barrès, see Robert Soucy, *Fascist Intellectual: Drieu La Rochelle* (Berkeley: University of California Press, 1979), and *Fascism in France: The Case of Maurice Barrès* (Berkeley: University of California Press, 1972).

3. Adolph Hitler, *Mein Kampf* (1925), trans. Ralph Manheim (Boston: Houghton Mifflin Co., 1943), pp. 155, 168, 209, 333, 336, 427, 600–1, 679.

4. Herbert Marcuse, "The Struggle against Liberalism in the Totalitarian View of the State" (1934), in *Negations: Essays in Critical Theory*, trans. Jeremy Shapiro (Harmondsworth: Penguin, 1968), p. 21. Max Horkheimer, "The Jews and Europe," in Stephen Eric Bronner and Douglas MacKay Kellner (eds), *Critical Theory and Society: A Reader* (London: Routledge, 1989), p. 85.

5. See Karl Marx and Frederick Engels, *The German Ideology*, ed. Chris Arthur (London: Lawrence and Wishart, 1970), p. 41.

6. Hitler, Speech in December 1930, cited in Tim Mason, *Social Policy in the Third Reich: The Working Class and the "National Community,"* trans. John Broadwin (Oxford: Berg, 1993), p. 25.

7. Franz Neumann, *Behemoth: The Structure and Practice of National Socialism* (London: Victor Gollancz, 1942), p. 107. Ernst Bloch, *Heritage of Our Times*, trans. Neville and Stephen Plaice (Cambridge: Polity, 1991), p. 44.

8. See George Mosse, *The Crisis of German Ideology: Intellectual Origins of the Third Reich* (London: Weidenfeld & Nicolson, 1966), pp. 21–22.

9. Benito Mussolini, "The Doctrine of Fascism," in Adrian Lyttelton (ed.), *Italian Fascisms: From Pareto to Gentile* (London: Jonathan Cape, 1973), p. 42. Giovanni Gentile, "The Philosophic Basis of Fascism," *Foreign Affairs*, vol. 6, 1928, pp. 290–304, claims that corporatism is expected to unite as a productive force the whole of society. Ernst Nolte, *Three Faces of Fascism: Action Française, Italian Fascism, National Socialism*, trans. Leila Vennewitz (New York: Mentor, 1969), p. 264.

10. Nolte, *Three Faces of Fascism*, p. 269; George Mosse, "Mass Politics and the Political Liturgy of Nationalism," in Eugene Kamenka (ed.), *Nationalism: The Nature and Evolution of an Idea* (London: Edward Arnold, 1976), p. 40.

11. Walter Benjamin, "The Work of Art in the Age of Mechanical Reproduction," in Benjamin, *Illuminations*, trans. Harry Zohn (London: Fontana, 1973), p. 243.

12. Sergei Eisenstein, "On Fascism, German Cinema and Real Life. Open Letter to the German Minister of Propaganda, Dr. Goebbels," in Richard Taylor (ed. and trans.) *Sergei Eisenstein: Selected Works Vol. I, Writings 1922–1934* (London: British Film Institute, 1988), p. 283.

13. Neumann, *Behemoth*, p. 264. "whenever the outcry against the sovereignty of banking capital is injected into a popular movement, it is the surest sign that fascism is on its way."

14. After the First World War the *Popolo d'Italia* was given the new subtitle "The Newspaper of Combatants and Producers"; its previous subtitle had been "Socialist Daily." Mussolini, "Doctrine of Fascism," p. 45.

15. Roland Sarti, *Fascism and the Industrial Leadership in Italy, 1919–1940: A Study of the Expansion of Private Power under Fascism* (Los Angeles: University of California Press, 1971), p. 76.
16. Goebbels, *Der Nazi-Sozi* (1931), cited in Daniel Guerin, *Fascism and Big Business* (New York: Pathfinder Press, 1973), p. 81. Hitler, *Mein Kampf*, pp. 51, 63, 65, 323.
17. Hitler, *Mein Kampf*, pp. 323, 339. He adds that trade unions are in fact crucial for national life, but they need to become national socialist and thus relinquish their role as organs of class struggle imposed on them by Marxists (pp. 598–600). John Hiden and John Farquharson, *Explaining Hitler's Germany: Historians and the Third Reich* (London: Batsford, 1983), p. 103.
18. Neumann, *Behemoth*, pp. 187, 338, 340; Martin Broszat, *The Hitler State: The Foundation and Development of the Internal Structure of the Third Reich*, trans. John Hiden (Harlow: Longman, 1981), pp. 145–6; Tim Mason, "The Law on the Organization of National Labour of 20 January 1934. An Investigation into the Relationship between 'Archaic' and 'Modern' Elements in Recent German History," in Jane Caplan (ed.) *Nazism, Fascism and the Working Class: Essays by Tim Mason* (Cambridge: Cambridge University Press, 1995), pp. 80–2; and Mason, *Social Policy in the Third Reich*, pp. 104, 164.
19. Tim Mason, "The Containment of the Working Class in Nazi Germany," in Caplan, *Nazism, Fascism and the Working Class*, p. 239. Bloch, *Heritage of Our Times*, pp. 64–8, 117–8, 141.
20. Klaus Theweleit, *Male Fantasies, Vol. 2: Male Bodies: Psychoanalyzing the White Terror*, trans. Chris Turner and Erica Carter (Cambridge: Polity Press, 1989), p. 87.
21. See Henry Turner, *German Big Business and the Rise of Hitler* (Oxford: Oxford University Press, 1985), p. 358. "He [Horkheimer] and the others who had applied that formula had been mistaken about the nature of Nazism at the time, but most learned nothing from their defeat. Nor have their disciples, who continue to subordinate the study of Nazism to a crusade against capitalism."
22. See Gentile, "Philosophic Basis of Fascism," p. 299.
23. See, for example, Alfred Rosenberg, "Totaler Staat?" (1934), in Robert Pois (ed.) *Alfred Rosenberg: Selected Writings* (London: Jonathan Cape, 1970), p. 191; Adolf Hitler, "The Nationalist Socialist Revolution" (30 January 1937), in Bruce Mazlish, Arthur D. Kaledin and David B. Ralston (eds), *Revolution: A Reader* (New York: Macmillian, 1971), pp. 470–85. See Hans Mommsen, *From Weimar to Auschwitz: Essays in German History*, trans. Philip O'Connor (Cambridge: Polity Press, 1991), p. 152, for similar comments by Goebbels.
24. Hermann Rauschning, *The Revolution of Nihilism: Warning to the West*, trans. E.W. Dickes (New York: Alliance Book Corporation, 1939). On Germany in particular, see David Schoenbaum, *Hitler's Social Revolution: Class and Status in Nazi Germany 1933–1939* (London: Weidenfeld & Nicolson. 1967); Ralf Dahrendorf, *Society and Democracy in Germany* (London: Weidenfeld & Nicolson, 1967), pp. 402–18; and Daniel Jonah Goldhagen, *Hitler's Willing Executioners: Ordinary Germans and the Holocaust* (London: Little, Brown and Co., 1996), pp. 173, 455–63. On revolution and fascism generally, see O'Sullivan, *Fascism*, p. 39; Roger Griffen, *The Nature of Fascism* (London: Routledge, 1993), p. 48; George Mosse, "Introduction: Towards a General Theory of Fascism," in Mosse (ed.), *International Fascism: New Thoughts and New Approaches* (London: Sage, 1979), pp. 5, 36.
25. Jeremy Noakes, "Nazism and Revolution," in Noel O'Sullivan (ed.), *Revolutionary Theory and Political Reality* (Brighton: Wheatsheaf, 1983), p. 73; Ian Kershaw, *The Nazi Dictatorship: Problems and Perspectives of Interpretation*, 2nd edn. (London: Edward Arnold, 1989), p. 132.
26. Cited in Neumann, *Behemoth*, p. 378, from Mussolini's "Relativismo e Fascismo," emphasis added. Mussolini goes on to add that "it is sufficient to have a single fixed point: the nation." See also Mussolini, "Doctrine of Fascism," pp. 40, 42.
27. See, for example, Eugen Weber, "Revolution? Counter-Revolution? What Revolution?" in Walter Laqueur (ed.), *Fascism: A Reader's Guide* (Harmondsworth: Penguin, 1979), pp. 488–531.
28. Neumann, *Behemoth*; Noakes, "Nazism and Revolution," p. 84; Kershaw, *The Nazi Dictatorship*, p. 143.
29. Eric Hobsbawm, *The Age of Extremes: The Short Twentieth Century, 1914–1991.* (Harmondsworth: Penguin, 1994), p. 128.
30. See Arno J. Mayer, *Dynamics of Counterrevolution in Europe, 1870–1956: An Analytic Framework* (New York: Harper Torchbooks, 1971).
31. Cited in Lionel Kochan, *The Struggle for Germany, 1914–1945* (Edinburgh: Edinburgh University Press, 1963), p. 64. Kochan adds that while many nuances of response to Nazism existed, none was such as to go beyond accepting Germany as a partner in the struggle against communism.
32. Cited in Weber, "Revolution? Counter-revolution? What Revolution?," p. 523. See also the passages cited in note 26 above. For an account of how the work of one conservative revolutionary, Carl Schmitt, is developed partly from an understanding of Italian fascism and then used to legitimize Nazism, see Mark Neocleous, "Friend or Enemy? Reading Schmitt Politically," *Radical Philosophy*, 79, 1996, pp. 13–23.

MAGICAL REALISM: HOW MIGHT THE REVOLUTIONS OF THE FUTURE HAVE BETTER END(ING)S?

JOHN FORAN

. . . I foresee revolutions occurring well into the future and arising in the not-so-distant future, at that. This chapter therefore asks the question: How might the revolutions of the future—whatever form they take—have better outcomes? That is, what have we learned from the revolutionary record to date that might be of use to revolutionaries in the near to middle-run future (say, the next half-century)? This is perhaps an even trickier field to enter. It begs questions such as: Why would a supposedly neutral scholar try to assist revolutionaries? Why would revolutionaries listen to a First World ivory tower (OK, concrete block) self-styled intellectual? Isn't this an exercise in revolutionary romanticism or—worse—exoticism? And the ominous one: Couldn't states use this information against revolutionaries? I will return to these matters in the conclusion. For now, let us survey the record of twentieth-century revolutions to see what their lessons might include.

The Angel of History and the Lessons of the Past

The twentieth century we depart has been the age of revolutions, in Skocpol's sense of "rapid, basic transformations of a society's state and class structures . . . accompanied and in part carried through by class-based revolts from below" (1979: 4; in my view still the most useful definition or revolution). From the Russian events of 1917 that so profoundly shook the world, to the great Third World social revolutions in Cuba and China (and the lesser ones—in transformational terms—in Nicaragua and Iran, among many other places) and the anti-colonial revolutions in Algeria, Vietnam and southern Africa; from the shorter-lived but no less remarkable democratic revolutions in Chile under Allende and May 1968 in France and the more enduring revolutions of 1989 in Eastern Europe, to the current struggle in Chiapas, the historical record is rich in dramatic experiences of ordinary people undertaking extraordinary collective acts.

In previous work I have argued that five interrelated causal factors must combine in a given conjuncture to produce a social revolution: (1) dependent development; (2) a repressive, exclusionary, personalist state; (3) the elaboration of effective and powerful political cultures of resistance; and a revolutionary crisis consisting of (4) an economic downturn and (5) a world-systemic opening (a let-up of external controls). The coming together in a single place of all five factors leads to the formation of broad revolutionary coalitions which have typically succeeded in gaining power—in Mexico, China, Cuba, Iran, Nicaragua, as well as in Algeria, Vietnam, Zimbabwe, Angola and Mozambique, and revolutions that were ultimately reversed in Guatemala, Bolivia, Chile and Grenada.[1]

What are some of the lessons we might cull from the revolutionary record in light of this theory of causes? Let me try stating a few in propositional terms:

- Revolutions have typically been directed against two types of states at opposite ends of the democratic spectrum: exclusionary, personalist dictators or colonial regimes, and—more paradoxically—truly open societies where a critical left had a fair chance in elections.
- They have usually been driven by economic and social inequalities caused by both the short-term and the medium-run consequences of "dependent development"—a process of aggregate growth by which a handful of the privileged have prospered, leaving the majority of the population to their hardships (each group relative to its social location).

- They have had a significant cultural component in the sense that no revolution has been made and sustained without a vibrant set of political cultures of resistance and opposition that found significant common ground, at least for a time.
- They have occurred when the moment was favorable on the world scene—that is, when powers that would oppose revolution have been distracted, confused, or ineffective in preventing them.
- Finally, they have always involved broad, cross-class alliances of subaltern groups, middle classes and elites; to an increasing extent women as well as men; and to a lesser degree racial or ethnic minorities as well as majorities.

Once in power, a series of related difficulties have typically arisen, which result from the continued significance of the patterns above for revolutionary transformation:

- Truly democratic structures have been difficult to construct following revolutions against dictators, while democratically chosen revolutionaries have been vulnerable to non-democratic opponents, internal and external.
- Dependent development has deep historical roots that are recalcitrant to sustained reversal, however much the material situation of the majority can be improved in the short and medium run.
- The challenge of forging a revolutionary political culture to construct a new society has generally foundered rapidly on the diversity of subcurrents that contributed to the initial victory, compounded by the structural obstacles all revolutions have faced.
- Few revolutions have been able to withstand the renewed counter-revolutionary attention of dominant outside powers and their regional allies.
- Given the above, the broad coalitions that have been so effective in making revolutions are notoriously difficult to keep together, due to divergent visions of how to remake society and unequal capacities to make their vision prevail; meanwhile women and ethnic minorities have consistently seen at best limited reversal of patriarchy and racism after revolutions.

The reader will be able to fill in many of the concrete examples that underlie the above propositions (as well as thinking of counter-examples and other propositions, no doubt).

In addition to these linked causal and outcome issues, there seem to be recurrent trade-offs or contradictions in the revolutionary record as well. For example, the participation of massive numbers runs up against the leadership's need to take decisive measures to deal with all kinds of problems once in power; this in part explains the often bloody narrowing of substantively democratic spaces even as so many previously disenfranchised members of society are gaining new rights and opportunities. When movements have been radically democratic, as in France in 1968 and Chile in the early 1970s, they have had troubles articulating a program acceptable to all parties at the debates, and withstanding illegal subversion from the right. Similarly, a series of economic trade-offs are associated with many revolutions, particularly in the Third World: impressive gains in employment, wages, health, housing and education have after short periods been eroded by internal economic contradictions (demand-driven inflation, limited human and material resources, labor imbalances) and powerful international counter-thrusts (boycotts and embargoes on trade, equipment, loans). As if these political and economic contradictions are not daunting enough, massive external violence has often also been applied, whether covert or openly military in nature, further undermining prospects for democracy and development.

These patterned realities have produced disappointing outcomes, including authoritarian, relatively poor socialisms in Russia, China, Cuba and Vietnam (the only revolutions to last much longer than a generation, except for Iran, where the degree of economic change has been limited); violent overthrows of revolutionaries in Guatemala, Chile and Grenada; slow strangling of change leading to political reversals in Mexico (by 1940), Bolivia (by 1960), Manley's Jamaica and Sandinista Nicaragua; and blocking the path to power altogether in France 1968, El Salvador in the 1980s, China in 1989 and Iraq in 1991, among many other places. This is not to mention the containment of social revolution in the form of far more limited political revolutions in places like the Philippines in 1986, Zaire in 1996 and, in a different and complex way, in the Eastern European reformist capitalist revolutions and the spectacular overthrow of apartheid in the 1990s. No revolutionary movement of the twentieth century has come close to delivering on the common dreams of so many of its makers: a more inclusive, participatory form of political rule; a more egalitarian, humane economic system; and a cultural atmosphere where individuals and local communities may not only reach full self-creative expression but thereby contribute unexpected solutions to the dilemmas faced by society. In this sense Benjamin's image of the angel of history being swept forward by the storm of progress willy-nilly into the future, its face turned to the catastrophic debris of the past, appears an apt one. Yet the past may hold other messages for the future, if we know how to read them.

Magical Realism: How Might the Future Be Different?

What, then, is to be done? In the knowledge that a definitive answer to such a question would be presumptuous (even were it possible), I would like to suggest what I see as some alternatives to the comparative-historical record to date. Insofar as these observations recall aspects of the actual historical record and introduce some emerging practices—notably from Chiapas—they are grounded in a collective creative process, open to all to extend and continue.

The Magic of Political Cultures

In the post–1989–91 conjuncture, it is a truism that there exists a crisis of the left. At the same time, as Forrest Colburn has argued sensibly and hopefully, it is only *after* 1989 that "A new revolutionary political culture may emerge, one that may prove more capable of fulfilling its promises" (1994: 17). The Zapatistas have offered some radically new ways of doing politics to the revolutionaries of the future. Javier Eloriaga, a member of the National Coordinating Commission of the FZLN (the unarmed, civil-society political wing of the Zapatista movement), notes that "they say we are dreamers or fanatics. The institutional left continues to regard politics as the art of the possible. And Zapatismo doesn't. We have to do politics in a new way. You can't accept only what is possible because it will bring you into the hands of the system. This is a very difficult struggle. It is very, very difficult" (quoted in Zugman 2001: 113; this section on the Zapatistas' own views draws primarily on this remarkable work).

Sergio Rodriguez, founding member of the FZLN (and before that, a leader in the Trotskyist Partido Revolucionario de Trabajadores), raises the issue of whether this new form of political action can be harnessed and organized (even as he speaks eloquently of its transformative power):

> When the Zapatistas came to Mexico City [at the time of the National Consultation of 1999] and traveled all over the country, I remember being in the Zocalo where people were saying goodbye to the Zapatistas. There were these mothers with young people and children who accompanied the Zapatistas to the vans. I realize that there, in that moment, something was being created. I don't know what to call it. I don't know how you could organize it. I don't know how it would be expressed politically. But this relationship is more than thousands of speeches and discourse and propaganda. This is a life relationship. They lived together. They talked and spent time together. Two different communities lived together. There was a chemistry there that is impossible to break down. I think that someone would have to be totally blind or have a lot of bitterness not to see this. Luis Hernandez once said that Zapatismo is a state of being. In the beginning of the century, when the socialists and the anarchists organized clubs and strikes they said that socialism was a way of life. Zapatismo is like that too. It is a way of expressing yourself. It isn't just economic or social or political or cultural. It is that and more. Organizing it is very difficult, maybe impossible. I say that it is there. It is an underground relationship between communities. And it

> creates a very powerful force. . . . In very few countries is there a force that is so strong. It isn't what we dreamed of in the sixties. It isn't pure and orthodox. But I think that it is better the way that it is. (quoted in Zugman 2001: 124)

Core Zapatista principles include: *mandar obedeciendo* ("to rule, obeying"—that leaders serve at the pleasure of the community and its struggle, not vice versa); *para todos todo, nada para nosotros* ("for everyone, everything, nothing for ourselves"); "walking at a slower pace" (i.e. the recognition that change is a long and slow process, not secured with the mere seizure of power or electoral victories); and, indeed, "not aspiring to take political power." This last raises an intriguing question for us to ponder. As the second declaration of the Lacandón jungle put it in 1994: "This revolution will not end in a new class, fraction or group in power, but in a free and democratic space of political struggle" (EZLN 1994, quoted in Zugman 2001: 74; the quotation can also be found in Vazquez Montalban 2000). But what does this mean and how is it to be done? For Subcomandante Marcos, "This democratic space will have three fundamental premises that are already historically inseparable: the democratic right of determining the dominant social project, the freedom to subscribe to one project or another, and the requirement that all projects must point the way to justice" (Marcos 1995: 85). The dethroning of the ruling PRI, Mexico's seventy-year-old "perfect dictatorship," in the July 2000 elections contains many lessons, no doubt, of which one is the success of the Zapatistas in altering the political landscape of Mexico. Though too many observers see their role in this historic event as minimal, it would be hard to imagine the collapse of authoritarianism without the insurgency in Chiapas undermining the government's legitimacy. The new government of Vicente Fox immediately offered to resume negotiations, which the Zapatistas equally quickly accepted; talks soon broke down again as Mexico's two dominant conservative parties, the PRI and Fox's PAN, proved recalcitrant. The rebels now face new challenges, but seem to me all the more well-positioned to meet them in a more democratic, or at least more fluid, political climate (see Ross 2000, 2000a; Weiner 2000).

One innovative Zapatista practice is embodied in the phrase *dar su palabra* (literally to have one's say). This refers to a dialogue in which everyone present participates, in which the value of the unique vantage point of each member of a community and the insights this affords is appreciated. It usually means taking far longer to arrive at a collective decision, but it also ensures that decisions arrived at have maximum input from the community they will affect, and (hopefully) a stronger consensus (or at least a more open sense of disagreements) behind them. As the Zapatistas put it, the goal is to build "a world where many worlds fit" (Zugman 2001: 110). Meanwhile, Mexican artist and scholar Manuel De Landa may have provided the beginnings of an answer to the daunting organizational question, again from observing Zapatista practices: he uses the term 'meshworks' for self-organizing, non-hierarchical and heterogeneous networks (De Landa 1997; a remarkable book brought to my attention by Escobar and Harcourt 2002). This is a lead worth pursuing, and it has taken shape in the United States around the anti-WTO and G8 demonstrations in Seattle and Washington, DC, in November–December 1999 and April 2000, respectively, soon followed in the fall of 2000 in Prague and Melbourne and the summer of 2001 in Genoa (this list will grow). The combination of "having one's say" and organizing meshworks has an important US antecedent, the direct action movements of the 1980s that fought nuclear weapons, US involvement in Central America, and the prison industrial complex, among other issues. Their tactics of nonviolence, consensus decision-making and fluid leadership, so effective at the local level in the initial phases of radical mobilization, ran into complex difficulties when the time came to build a national-level movement encompassing diverse groups, and led to tensions at the local level within groups between old and new activists, producing leadership burnout and membership dropout (Borgers 2000, citing Epstein 1988).

These limitations must be confronted in the future, if revolutions are to succeed. Revolutionaries may be well positioned to negotiate the problem of *levels* of struggle, as they straddle the boundary between grassroots and global conflict. This raises the question of the supposedly declining significance of the nation-state in the new global conjuncture: while its powers and competencies have certainly come under strong pressure from global financial institutions and the transnationals, it yet remains one of the most likely sites for revolutionary activity, as the terrain on which political democracy, economic development and oppositional alliances meet and play themselves out. The new communications technologies are another contested arena linking levels, strikingly evidenced by the Zapatistas' use of both fax and Internet. The anti-globalization protests in Washington, DC, in April 2000 were in part organized by a website maintained by the group A16, for several months prior to the mobilization.[2] Whatever their potential for enhancing the repressive powers of states and corporations, such technologies also represent tools for the education of and communication among social forces from below to foster meshworks of what we might call "netizens" (a term coined in Hauben and Hauben 1997). Deep and clear thinking about all these matters is required work for would-be revolutionaries.

Finally, under the heading of magical cultures, we arrive at the frontier of emotions to ask, what do we know about the social psychology of liberation? Here, four US women, cultural producers and activists, have insights that recognize the power of this dimension of social change better than most theorists. Photographer Paula Allen and playwright Eve Ensler, in *The Feminist Memoir Project,* celebrate the strength that can be drawn from this source: "Being an activist means being aware of what's happening around you as well as being in touch with your feelings about it—your rage, your sadness, your excitement, your curiosity, your feeling of helplessness, and your refusal to surrender. Being an activist means owning your desire" (Allen and Ensler 1998: 425). Alice Walker writes in *Anything We Love Can Be Saved: A Writer's Activism*:

> There is always a moment in any kind of struggle when one feels in full bloom. Vivid. Alive. One might be blown to bits in such a moment and still be at peace. Martin Luther King, Jr., at the mountaintop. Gandhi dying with the name of God on his lips. Sojourner Truth baring her breasts at a women's rights convention in 1851. . . . To be such a person or to witness anyone at this moment of transcendent presence is to know that what is human is linked, by a daring compassion, to what is divine. During my years of being close to people engaged in changing the world I have seen fear turn into courage. Sorrow into joy. Funerals into celebrations. Because whatever the consequences, people, standing side by side, have expressed who they really are, and that ultimately they believe in the love of the world and each other enough *to be that*—which is the foundation of activism. (1997: xxiii)

Poet Adrienne Rich cautions that this power, arising in individuals, must become a social, interpersonal force to realize its potential to shake the world:

> When we do and think and feel certain things privately and in secret, even when thousands of people are doing, thinking, whispering these things privately and in secret, there is still no general, collective understanding from which to move. Each takes her or his own risks in isolation. We may think of ourselves as individual rebels, and individual rebels can be easily shot down. The relationship among so many feelings remains unclear. But these thoughts and feelings, suppressed and stored-up and whispered, have an incendiary component. You cannot tell where or how they will connect, spreading underground from rootlet to rootlet till every grass blade is afire from every other. This is that "spontaneity" that party "leaders," secret governments, and closed systems dread.[3]

The revolutionaries of the past and present have been enormously creative and expressive at critical junctures, as celebrated in the May '68 slogan "Power to the imagination!" While we are thankfully far from some new hegemonic reigning oppositional culture, the revolutionaries of the future will likely forge multiple new amalgams of old and new ideas, ideals and ideologies in the best sense. I have argued that love and dreams need to be woven into the fabric of such globalized political cultures of resistance (Foran 2002).

The "Realities" of the Political Economic

Articulating an economic alternative to neoliberalism seems a fool's quest these days. Yet tapping the magical possibilities of a political culture of liberation might help make progress on this. One principle for such a political economy might be called, simply, the economics of "social justice." Recalling the principle of *para todos todo, nada para nosotros*, a woman who is active in the FZLN notes:

> in the Zapatista movement, people are working for something much broader than themselves . . . for a change that will benefit everyone. I mean the Zapatistas don't have anything to hand out to people. There is no housing or powerful political positions to obtain. This isn't for your own benefit. It is a benefit for the whole country. It is for all the people who have been fucked over like the indigenous people. (FZLN member interviewed by Zugman 2001: 126)

Social justice has been the foundation of the economic side of revolutionary political cultures the world over, assuming many local expressions—"Land and Liberty" in Mexico in the 1910s; "Bread, Land and Peace" in 1917 Russia; "Equality," from 1789 France to 1990s South Africa; "Socialism with a Human Face" in 1968 Czechoslovakia; "Dignity" in Chiapas; "Fair Trade" and "Democracy" in Seattle. Thus, defining what it means must be specific to particular times and places. Inventorying these and assessing what common meanings social justice has had across cases is a project of some urgency for activists and scholars of revolution, an important task for others to pursue.

A second need is that of protecting revolutions in a hostile world-system. The impact of the new global conjuncture is difficult to grasp fully, but it is far from uniformly dampening. The end of the cold war may in fact have opened up opportunities for revolutionaries to operate if the other four factors are in place, precisely because the countries in question can no longer be treated as pawns in a larger geopolitical struggle between the United States and the Soviet Union. Democratic revolutionaries and nonviolent movements in particular may find new spaces in which to maneuver. The United States also lost something with the end of the cold war: no longer (or not yet) certain of the bases of its global political–economic strategic vision, it may also be loath to intervene in conflicts in certain parts of the Third World, at least with overwhelming military force. The US under Clinton sought to expand corporate power with free trade agreements and aid to foreign militaries to fight "drug wars" (aimed at guerrillas in Colombia and elsewhere), a "strategic vision" of sorts. The post–2001 Bush–Cheney administration with realpolitiker Condoleezza Rice as national security advisor and throwback cold warrior Donald Rumsfeld as secretary of defense, and only Colin Powell as secretary of state to moderate them, surely *wishes* to be more aggressive militarily, but will it carry the needed weight, locally or internationally, to target democratic, nonviolent challengers to the global logic of economic injustice? (for early analyses of the ambiguous (if ominous) direction of US global strategy, see Perlez 2001; Lemann 2001). I should note that this chapter was completed well before the events of 11 September 2001; the logic and analysis of this section still seem accurate to me, as the Taliban do not fill the requirements of being democratic, nonviolent *or* revolutionary. The danger, of course, is that in the new counterrevolutionary discourse of US power, the term "terrorist" will become a proxy for "communist" in a new post–cold war world, and aimed at the real targets—national (and now global) revolutionaries.

The US pursuit of an obscenely expensive and chimerical space missile "defense" system suggests that the imperial grand intent remains intact, but at the same time alienates allies as well as would-be adversaries, and may indicate a greater willingness for easy symbolic expressions of global power than any real ability to halt local rebellions effectively as they arise. The disarray of all leading First World nations in the face of imaginative anti-globalization protests since 1999 may also portend the limits of US power. This claim, too, needs updating, as the WTO's decision to hold its November 2001 meetings in Qatar made on-site protest impossible. But the movement's imagination will surely catch up with this ploy, and even with it the continued relevance of the WTO was just barely accomplished by the delegates, who understood that failure to agree on further discussions would mean the organization's end. The meaning and legacy of the Battle of Seattle were also clearly at stake, as the US representative claimed that the meeting had "removed the stain of Seattle." Even the *New York Times* questioned this, notably with its headline "Measuring Success: At Least the Talks Didn't Collapse" and comment that "Seattle, and subsequent protests at other international gatherings, have shown the potency and the breadth of opposition to free trade and the concept of globalization" (15 November 2001). Of course, I may well be wrong to discern openings here. The revolutionaries of the near-term future may themselves soon enough provide clues to the answer; my point is that their actions will surely influence the degree and type of interventions they face.

One way forward would be to build on the lessons of the radically democratic revolutions of the past. In counterpoint to Jeff Goodwin's insight that "The ballot box is the coffin of revolutionaries" (1998: 8), democracy in its many forms may become one of the best weapons of the revolutionaries of the future. Though May '68, Allende, Tiananmen, Mussadeq, Arbenz and Manley all experienced defeat, they gave us a form that the radical reformers and revolutionaries of today in Chiapas, Iran, Uruguay, Brazil, South Africa, Seattle and beyond are already imaginatively appropriating and trying to deepen.[4] Among these movements are to be found new goals, tactics and coalitional possibilities as well as anti-hierarchical and creative political cultures, a sort of message to the future. As Alain Touraine said of it: "The May Movement was a thunderbolt announcing the social struggles of the future. It dispelled the illusion that improvement in production and consumption result in a society in which tensions replace conflicts, quarrels replace disruptions, and negotiations replace revolution" (Touraine 1971: 79–80, quoted in Poster 1975: 371). All such democratic revolutionary movements can yield valuable lessons in fighting a *structure*, though this is harder than overthrowing a dictator. Out of the ashes of past failures may yet grow the seeds of future gains.

By Way of Concluding Thoughts (for Now)

"Magical realism," then, is a poetic way of referring to and relying on the immense creative potential of people the world over to construct what Perry Anderson once called a "concrete utopianism" (in Elliott 1998: 168), or what David Harvey has recently named a "dialectical utopianism" (2000) and Daniel Singer a "realistic utopianism" (1999).[5] That this must be more socially inclusive than it ever has been in the past seems crucial, as FMLN representative and former guerrilla Lorena Peña puts it in the Salvadoran context: "A proposal of the left that doesn't integrate the elements of class, gender and race, is not viable or objective, and it doesn't go to the root of our problems" (quoted in Polakoff 1996: 22). That it must somehow also prove capable of forging strong and imaginative consensus agreements around complex, cross-cutting issues makes the task even more formidable. The proper response to the pessimists of the dispirited acronym TINA—"There is no alternative"—of course is TATA: "There are thousands of alternatives!"[6] It appears to me that only a radically deepened, participatory process can unite these several dimensions, informing magical political cultures, making visible an economics of social justice, and (just maybe) disarming the US and other global interventionist forces.

We end, then, with a new set of paradoxes and challenges:

- to find a language capable of uniting diverse forces and allowing their not necessarily mutually compatible desires full expression;
- to find organizational forms capable of nurturing this expression and debate as well as enabling decisive action when needed, both locally and across borders;
- to articulate an economic alternative to neoliberalism and capitalism that can sustain itself against the systemic weight of the past and the pervasive and hostile reach of the present global economic system;
- and to make all this happen, in many places and at different levels (local, national, "global") over time, working with both the

> deep strengths and frailties of the experiences and emotions of human liberation.

In negotiating the contradictory currents of the future, we must somehow be magical as well as realistic, finding a path marked by pleasures as well as perils.

As for the right of academics to intervene in the transformation of the world, I stand with John Dewey, who felt that our task is not just to map out patterns of causal regularity in social processes but to exercise more intelligent control over them—that is, to help solve problems.[7] It seems well beside the point to be overly concerned with leaving behind one's objectivity, worrying about romanticizing revolutionary violence, or being reluctant to share one's ideas with like-minded others. Nor do I fear that any of this talk could fall into the wrong hands; a greater and more realistic fear is that it will not fall into the right ones. In any case, as Marx urged exactly 150 years ago in 1852 (another epoch in which few saw a bright future for revolutions), let us "find once more the spirit of revolution, not make its ghost walk again" (Marx 1972 [1852]: 438). As usual, Marx was at least half right: both spirits and ghosts will be needed tomorrow.

Notes

1. The fullest elaboration of this argument to date is my 1997 essay. The strange functional equivalence of dictatorships and democracies to explain the cases of Guatemala under Arbenz and Arévalo, Chile under Allende, and Jamaica under Manley is discussed there.
2. I learned this from one of my students, Sarah Macdonald, at Smith College in the fall of 2000. Among many websites, see www.a16.org.
3. I found this quotation by Adrienne Rich, significantly enough, as the epigraph to a book on the Zapatistas: Katzenberger 1995.
4. The intense struggle for democracy in Iran is worth following closely, as are the electoral fortunes of the Frente Amplio–Progressive Encounter alliance in Uruguay: see Moghadam 1999, as well as other essays published in the same special issue of the *Journal of Iranian Research and Analysis* on the former, and Zibechi 2000 on the latter. Another key case is the left-led municipal government of Porto Alegre, Brazil.
5. One is strongly tempted to contrast unfavorably Anderson's pessimistic turn by the year 2000—"The only starting-point for a realistic Left [note term] today is a lucid registration of historical defeat" (Anderson 2000: 16)—with the conclusion to Harvey's book, a playfully imaginative vision of a post-capitalist utopia named "Edilia" (2000: 257–81).
6. I first heard the term used by Robert Ware at the Marxism 2000 conference at Amherst, Massachusetts, in September 2000, who was quick to point out that he hadn't coined this wonderful rejoinder.
7. This notion of Dewey's was conveyed to me by Mustafa Emirbayer (2000).

Bibliography

Allen, P. and E. Ensler (1998) "An activist love story," in R. Blau DuPlessis and A. Snitow (eds) *The Feminist Memoir Project: Voices From Women's Liberation*, New York: Three Rivers Press, pp. 413–25.

Anderson, L. (2000) "Dynasts and nationalists: why monarchies survive," in J. Kostiner (ed.) *Middle East Monarchies: The Challenge of Modernity*, Boulder: Lynne Rienner, p. 53–69.

Anderson, P. (2000) "Renewals," *New Left Review*, second series, 1 (January–February): 5–24.

Borgers, F. (2000) "War of the flea, war of the swarm: reflections on the anti-globalization movement and its future," *Voice* (University of Massachusetts, Amherst) XIV (ii): 18–9.

Colburn, F. D. (1994) *The Vogue of Revolution in Poor Countries*, Princeton: Princeton University Press.

De Landa, M. (1997) *A Thousand Years of Nonlinear History*, New York: Zone Books.

Elliott, G. (1998) *Perry Anderson: The Merciless Laboratory of History*, Minneapolis: University of Minnesota Press.

Emirbayer, M. (2000) "Mechanisms of fantasy, mechanisms of passion: the role of emotions in political life," talk at the University of California, Santa Barbara, 17 May.

Epstein, B. (1988) "The politics of prefigurative community: the non-violent direct action movement," in M. Davis and M. Sprinker (eds) *Reshaping the US Left: Popular Struggles in the 1980s*, London: Verso, pp. 63–92.

Escobar, A. and W. Harcourt (2002) "Conversations towards feminist futures," in K. -K. Bhavnani, J. Foran and P. Kurian (eds) *Feminist Futures: Re-imagining Women, Culture and Development*, London: Zed Books.

EZLN (1994) "Segunda declaración de la selva lacandona," EZLN communiqué of 10 June 1994.

Foran, J. (1997) "The comparative-historical sociology of Third World social revolutions: why a few succeed, why most fail," in J. Foran (ed.) *Theorizing Revolutions*, London: Routledge, pp. 227–67.

——— (2002) "Alternatives to development of love, dreams and revolution," in K. -K. Bhavnani, J. Foran and P. Kurian (eds) *Feminist Futures: Re-imagining Women, Culture and Development*, London: Zed Books.

Goodwin, J. (1998) "Is the age of revolution over?" paper presented at the meetings of the International Studies Association Meetings, Minneapolis (March).

Harvey, D. (2000) *Spaces of Hope*, Berkeley and Edinburgh: University of California Press and Edinburgh University Press.

Hauben, M. and Hauben, R. (1997) *Netizens: On the History and Impact of Usenet and the Internet*, Los Alamitos: IEEE Computer Society Press.

Katzenberger, E. (ed.) (1995) *First World, Ha Ha Ha! The Zapatista Challenge*, San Francisco: City Lights.

Lemann, N. (2001) "The quiet man: Dick Cheney's direct rise to unprecedented power," *New Yorker*, 7 May: 56–71.

Marcos, Subcomandante (1995) *Shadows of Tender Fury: The Letters and Communiqués of Subcomandante Marcos and the Zapatista Army of National Liberation*, trans. F. Bardacke, L. López and the Watsonville, California, Human Rights Committee, New York: Monthly Review Press.

Marx, K. (1972) [1852] "The eighteenth Brumaire of Louis Bonaparte," in R. C. Tucker (ed.) *The Marx-Engels Reader*, New York: Norton, pp. 436–525.

Moghadam, V. M. (1999) "The student protests and the social movement for reform in Iran," *Journal of Iranian Research and Analysis* 15 (2) (November): 97–105.

Perlez, J. (2001) "Bush's team's counsel is divided on foreign policy," *New York Times*, 27 March.

Polakoff, E. (1996) "Gender and the Latin American left," *Z Magazine* (November): 20–3.

Poster, M. (1975) *Existential Marxism in Postwar France: From Sartre to Althusser*, Princeton: Princeton University Press.

Ross, J. (2000) "Voters reject PRI," *Latinamerica Press*, 10 July: 3.

——— (2000a) "Are the Zapatistas history?" *Latinamerica Press*, November: 2.

Singer, D. (1999) *Whose Millennium? Theirs or Ours?* New York: Monthly Review Press.

Skocpol, T. (1979) *States and Social Revolutions: A Comparative Analysis of France, Russia, and China*, Cambridge: Cambridge University Press.

Touraine, A. (1971) *The May Movement; Revolt and Reform: May 1968—The Student Rebellion and Workers' Strikes—The Birth of a Social Movement*, trans. L. F. X. Mayhew, New York: Random House.

Vazquez Montalban, M. (2000) *Marcos: el hombre de los espejos*, Mexico City: Aguilar.

Walker, A. (1997) *Anything We Love Can Be Saved: A Writer's Activism*, New York: Random House.

Weiner, T. (2000) "Mexico's new leader swiftly seeks peace in Chiapas," *New York Times*, 4 December.

Zibechi, R. (2000) "The growth of the Uruguayan left," *NACLA Report on the Americas* XXXIII (4) (January–February): 1.

Zugman, K. (2001) "Mexican awakening in postcolonial America: Zapatistas in urban spaces in Mexico City," Ph.D. dissertation, Department of Sociology, University of California, Santa Barbara.

SECTION IX
SOCIAL MOVEMENTS

At the beginning of this book, we used Steven Lukes's concept of "three-dimensional power" as the major theme in our readings on power. The most fundamental form of power, Lukes argued, is that which is not readily apparent because it is taken for granted; from this perspective, power is so thoroughly embedded in the patterns of our everyday lives that we cannot see how it shapes us. If this is the case, then what is to be done? How can we rebel against power if we are not aware of its presence in our lives? All of the writers on power that we examined earlier would agree that, despite the thoroughness with which social institutions organize power in the interests of dominant groups, power is never absolute. Marx, for example, saw social phenomena as inherently contradictory, always containing elements of opposition that carried the potential to undermine the existing social order and construct a new one. Gramsci's understanding of hegemony as a negotiated form of power suggested the transformative potential of subordinate groups withholding their consent. Foucault's argument that power is dispersed throughout society simultaneously disperses the sites of struggle between subordinate and dominant groups. From whatever perspective, the critical approach to power suggests that divisions emerge from within the power elite on particular issues, and economic or political crises call into question, if only momentarily, established patterns of power. There are always contradictions found in social institutions, and these contradictions provide opportunities for people to challenge institutionalized power. The process of racial segregation in the South, for example, produced a cohesive African American community that possessed the leadership and material resources to organize a social movement for civil rights that eventually destroyed legal segregation. Indeed, to take this example further, the use of nonviolent civil disobedience by civil rights activists used the legal institutions that enforced segregation to so raise the material and moral cost of maintaining segregation that political authorities were forced to acknowledge that it could no longer be accepted. These contradictions provide necessary structural opportunities for social change, but by themselves they are not sufficient to make such change. People must be ready to take advantage of these opportunities.

The primary way in which people challenge power is through social movements. Social movements are "collective challenges by people with common purposes and solidarity in sustained interaction with elites, opponents, and authorities" (Tarrow 1994: 3–4). It is notable that all of the readings in Section I on power (as well as many of the articles in the other sections of the book), which provided the theoretical foundation for the rest of the book, were written in the context of movements for social change: Marx and nineteenth-century revolutionary movements, Marcuse and the New Left of the 1960s, Gramsci and the revolutionary movements following the First World War, Lipsitz and anti-racist movements, Phillips and the women's movement, and Foucault and movements for sexual liberation. Social movements call into question the taken-for-granted patterns of institutional power that these theorists discussed. They do so by engaging in sustained disruption of these taken-for-granted patterns in pursuit of shared goals held by people with a collective identity. United States history can be seen as a series of attempts by people, who at various times and for various reasons were excluded from or marginalized by the political process, to make real the promise of democracy. Every advance in democracy and equality in history has been the result of conflict, of mobilization by marginalized, oppressed, and exploited social groups that challenged the legitimacy of existing social institutions. The readings in this section address some important issues in social movement organization as well as some important case studies of social movements.

The article by Frances Fox Piven and Richard A. Cloward, taken from their study of "poor people's movements" (movements of the unemployed, the labor movement, the civil rights movement, and the welfare rights movement), conveys a sense of the power that social movements have to make change. At the same time, however, they are critical of social movement organizations' inability to maintain their oppositional politics in the face of institutional resistance and co-optation. Popular insurgency may succeed in stimulating elite concessions, but these concessions are designed to absorb movement energies into acceptable channels. As a result, movement organizations face the choice of reining in insurgency in return for concessions or, should they seek more radical change, running the risk of being marginalized. Piven and Cloward conclude that the institutional framework in which social movement organizations operate, rather than internal factors such as resources or leadership, are most important for understanding the potential of social movement organizations.

In contrast, Suzanne Staggenborg argues that even if a social movement organization "fails" to achieve its stated goals and even if it "fails" to survive as an organization, it can still be seen as successful. Her discussion of the women's movement finds that social movement organizations can have important cultural outcomes that go beyond whatever limited public policy impact a short-lived organization might have. The women's movement has created alternative institutions, models of participatory collective action, and cultural/ideological interpretive meanings that have outlived the specific organizations from which they emerged originally. Indeed, women who join movement organizations are likely to continue to be activists after the collapse of their particular organization, and so organizations help to create a pool of activists who go on to form new organizations. Thus, a movement organization that "fails" in a conventional sense (due to the external institutional forces identified by Piven and Cloward) can have important results in generating resources for further social movement activism.

With its focus on the external forces in which social movements operate, Piven and Cloward's article is a good example of the political process model of social movements, while Staggenborg's article is a good illustration of the resource mobilization model (see McAdam and Snow 1997). Chip Berlet and Matthew N. Lyons's article on right-wing populist movements is significant for expanding our understanding of social movements beyond those whose goal is the reduction of social inequality. Right-wing populist movements have emerged in response to the successes of more traditionally defined social movements. In identifying the major interpretive themes of these organizations—such as a concern with "producers" over "unproductive" elites and subordinate groups, the use of scapegoating, and an apocalyptic narrative—Berlet and Lyons focus on the cultural resources that allow right-wing populist movements to advocate an anti-elitist politics that simultaneously maintains existing social inequalities. In their most extreme forms, right-wing populist movements become the organizational expression of fascism as discussed in the earlier article by Neocleous.

Robert D. Bullard's article on the environmental justice movement is critical of the mainstream environmental movement for ignoring how race shapes the chances people have to be exposed to pollution and toxic chemicals, as well as how social movements led by people of color have sought to address the environmental concerns they face. One of the benefits that whites receive from what Lipsitz calls their "possessive investment in whiteness" is a greater likelihood of not being exposed to the potentially harmful consequences of ecological degradation. Bullard examines how activists have organized themselves to challenge government and corporate officials who have ignored the unequal impact of pollution on communities of color or have more actively sought to locate polluting industries and waste treatment sites in those communities. These movement organizations have been important advocates of making a safe and healthy environment a right that must be available to everyone.

Kim Moody examines efforts to develop an international labor solidarity that emphasizes greater worker control over production and the reduction of class as well as gender and racial inequality. He sees the rise of a global capitalism characterized by an extreme neoliberal emphasis on the market and private property (as discussed in some length in the articles on the nation-state in the global economy), producing the opportunities for a new kind of labor movement. The social unionism he refers to requires a restructuring of the labor movement itself as well as a reevaluation of its goals. Trade unionism that seeks only to improve wages and working conditions for its members is increasingly irrelevant in an economy in which corporations can move production and other operations to find the cheapest possible source of labor. Unions must confront the issue of power and must do so on an international scale, and this will require greater attention to expanding democracy within unions.

Naomi Klein offers an analysis of the antisweatshop movement that emphasizes a particular weakness in the power of corporations. As corporate brands have become more central to our lives as consumers, there are more opportunities for activists to challenge the corporation for not living up to the image of its brand. If Nike asks us to "just do it," activists can ask the question whether the Indonesian women workers who assemble sneakers for a Nike contractor can "just do it" in the context of low wages and repressive labor practices. In this situation, the image of the corporation becomes an important resource that anticorporate activists can use to communicate their message to the public.

Despite the considerable power that social institutions have in shaping our lives, the sociological study of social movements provides evidence of the great potential for people to change these institutions. Each success, no matter how small, changes the field of struggle. This forces authorities to change their strategies for maintaining order, shifting the balance between consent and coercion depending on the situation. This, in turn, leads to the development of new strategies and tactics by existing social movements and the emergence of new movements. Even when social movement organizations do not succeed in achieving their stated goals, they leave cultural resources that can be used by others. Social movements must thus be seen, especially by the people who are active in them, as part of a broad historical process of change. They require simultaneously a utopian vision, by which we mean an ability to see beyond the boundaries defined for us by social institutions, and a systematic analysis of the opportunities for change present in existing institutions.

References

McAdam, Doug, and David A. Snow. 1997. *Social Movements: Readings on Their Emergence, Mobilization, and Dynamics.* Los Angeles: Roxbury Publishing Company.

Tarrow, Sidney. 1994. *Power in Movement: Social Movements, Collective Action, and Politics.* New York: Cambridge University Press.

THE STRUCTURING OF PROTEST

FRANCES FOX PIVEN AND RICHARD A. CLOWARD

Common sense and historical experience combine to suggest a simple but compelling view of the roots of power in any society. Crudely but clearly stated, those who control the means of physical coercion, and those who control the means of producing wealth, have power over those who do not. This much is true whether the means of coercion consists in the primitive force of a warrior caste or the technological force of a modern army. And it is true whether the control of production consists in control by priests of the mysteries of the calendar on which agriculture depends, or control by financiers of the large-scale capital on which industrial production depends. Since coercive force can be used to gain control of the means of producing wealth, and since control of wealth can be used to gain coercive force, these two sources of power tend over time to be drawn together within one ruling class.

Common sense and historical experience also combine to suggest that these sources of power are protected and enlarged by the use of that power not only to control the actions of men and women, but also to control their beliefs. What some call superstructure, and what others call culture, includes an elaborate system of beliefs and ritual behaviors which defines for people what is right and what is wrong and why; what is possible and what is impossible; and the behavioral imperatives that follow from these beliefs. Because this superstructure of beliefs and rituals is evolved in the context of unequal power, it is inevitable that beliefs and rituals reinforce inequality, by rendering the powerful divine and the challengers evil. Thus the class struggles that might otherwise be inevitable in sharply unequal societies ordinarily do not seem either possible or right from the perspective of those who live within the structure of belief and ritual fashioned by those societies. People whose only possible recourse in struggle is to defy the beliefs and rituals laid down by their rulers ordinarily do not.

The emergence of a protest movement entails a transformation both of consciousness and of behavior. The change in consciousness has at least three distinct aspects. First, "the system"—or those aspects of the system that people experience and perceive—loses legitimacy. Large numbers of men and women who ordinarily accept the authority of their rulers and legitimacy of institutional arrangements come to believe in some measure that these rulers and these arrangements are unjust and wrong. Second, people who are ordinarily fatalistic, who believe that existing arrangements are inevitable, begin to assert "rights" that imply demands for change. Third, there is a new sense of efficacy; people who ordinarily consider themselves helpless come to believe that they have some capacity to alter their lot.

The change in behavior is equally striking, and usually more easily recognized, at least when it takes the form of mass strikes or marches or riots. Such behavior seems to us to involve two distinguishing elements. First, masses of people become defiant; they violate the traditions and laws to which they ordinarily acquiesce, and they flaunt the authorities to whom they ordinarily defer. And second, their defiance is acted out collectively, as members of a group, and not as isolated individuals. Strikes and riots are clearly forms of collective action, but even some forms of defiance which appear to be individual acts, such as crime or school truancy or incendiarism, while more ambiguous, may have a collective dimension, for those who engage in these acts may consider themselves to be part of a larger movement. Such apparently atomized acts of defiance can be considered movement events when those involved perceive themselves to be acting as members of a group, and when they share a common set of protest beliefs.

■ ■ ■ ■

Institutional Limits on the Incidence of Mass Insurgency

Aristotle believed that the chief cause of internal warfare was inequality, that the lesser rebel in order to be equal. But human experience has proved him wrong, most of the time. Sharp inequality has been constant, but rebellion infrequent. Aristotle underestimated the controlling force of the social structure on political life. However hard their lot may be, people usually remain acquiescent, conforming to the accustomed patterns of daily life in their community, and believing those patterns to be both inevitable and just. Men and women till the fields each day, or stoke the furnaces, or tend the looms, obeying the rules and rhythms of earning a livelihood; they mate and bear children hopefully, and mutely watch them die; they abide by the laws of church and community and defer to their rulers, striving to earn a little grace and esteem. In other words most of the time people conform to the institutional arrangements which enmesh them, which regulate the rewards and penalties of daily life, and which appear to be the only possible reality.

Those for whom the rewards are most meager, who are the most oppressed by inequality, are also acquiescent. Sometimes they are the most acquiescent, for they have little defense against the penalties that can be imposed for defiance. Moreover, at most times and in most places, and especially in the United States, the poor are led to believe that their destitution is deserved, and that the riches and power that others command are also deserved. In more traditional societies sharp inequalities are thought to be divinely ordained, or to be a part of the natural order of things. In more modern societies, such as the United States, riches and power are ascribed to personal qualities of industry or talent; it follows that those who have little or nothing have only what they deserve. . . .

■ ■ ■ ■

Ordinarily, in short, the lower classes accept their lot, and that acceptance can be taken for granted; it need not be bargained for by their rulers. This capacity of the institutions of a society to enforce political docility is the most obvious way in which protest is socially structured, in the sense that it is structurally precluded most of the time.

Sometimes, however, the poor do become defiant. They challenge traditional authorities, and the rules laid down by those authorities. They demand redress for their grievances. American history is punctuated by such events, from the first uprisings by freeholders, tenants, and slaves in colonial America, to the postrevolutionary debtor rebellions, through the periodic eruptions of strikes and riots by industrial workers, to the ghetto riots of the twentieth century. In each instance, masses of the poor were somehow able, if only briefly, to overcome the shame bred by a culture which blames them for their plight; somehow they were able to break the bonds of conformity enforced by work, by family, by community, by every strand of institutional life; somehow they were able to overcome the fears induced by police, by militia, by company guards.

When protest does arise, when masses of those who are ordinarily docile become defiant, a major transformation has occurred. . . . [T]he emergence of popular uprisings reflects profound changes in the larger society. . . . [O]nly under exceptional conditions will the lower classes become defiant—and thus, in our terms, *only under exceptional conditions are the lower classes afforded the socially determined opportunity to press for their own interests.*

. . . This argues that it not only requires a major social dislocation before protest can emerge, but that a sequence or combination of dislocations probably must occur before the anger that underlies protest builds to a high pitch, and before that anger can find expression in collective defiance.

■ ■ ■ ■

And with that said, the implication for an understanding of the potential for political influence among the poor becomes virtually self-evident: *since periods of profound social dislocations are infrequent, so too are opportunities for protest among the lower classes.*

The Patterning of Insurgency

Just as quiescence is enforced by institutional life, and just as the eruption of discontent is determined by changes in institutional life, the forms of political protest are also determined by the institutional context in which people live and work. . . .

The Electoral System as a Structuring Institution

In the United States the principal structuring institution, at least in the early phases of protest, is the electoral-representative system. The significance of this assertion is not that the electoral system provides an avenue of influence under normal circumstances. To the contrary, . . . it is usually when unrest among the lower classes breaks out of the confines of electoral procedures that the poor may have some influence, for the instability and polarization they then threaten to create by their actions in the factories or in the streets may force some response from electoral leaders. But whether action emerges in the factories or the streets may depend on the course of the early phase of protest at the polls.

Ordinarily defiance is first expressed in the voting booth simply because, whether defiant or not, people have been socialized within a political culture that defines voting as the mechanism through which political change can and should properly occur. The vitality of this political culture, the controlling force of the norms that guide political discontent into electoral channels, is not understood merely by asserting the pervasiveness of liberal political ideology in the United States and the absence of competing ideologies, for that is precisely what has to be explained. Some illumination is provided by certain features of the electoral system itself, by its rituals and celebrations and rewards, for these practices help to ensure the persistence of confidence in electoral procedures. Thus it is significant that the franchise was extended to white working-class men at a very early period in the history of the United States, and that a vigorous system of local government developed. Through these mechanisms, large proportions of the population were embraced by the rituals of electoral campaigns, and shared in the symbolic rewards of the electoral system, while some also shared in the tangible rewards of a relatively freely dispensed government patronage. Beliefs thus nurtured do not erode readily.

Accordingly, one of the first signs of popular discontent in the contemporary United States is usually a sharp shift in traditional voting patterns. In a sense, the electoral system serves to measure and register the extent of the emerging disaffection. Thus, the urban working class reacted to economic catastrophe in the landslide election of 1932 by turning against the Republican Party to which it had given its allegiance more or less since 1896. Similarly, the political impact of the forces of modernization and migration was first evident in the crucial presidential elections of 1956 and 1960. Urban blacks, who had voted Democratic in successively larger proportions since the election of 1936, began to defect to Republican columns or to stay away from the polls.

These early signs of political instability ordinarily prompt efforts by contending political leaders to placate the defecting groups, usually at this stage with conciliatory pronouncements. The more serious the electoral defections, or the keener the competition among political elites, the more likely that such symbolic appeasements will be offered. But if the sources of disturbance and anger are severe—and only if they are severe and persistent—conciliations are likely merely to fuel mass arousal, for in effect they imply that some of the highest leaders of the land identify with the indignation of the lowly masses.

Moreover, just as political leaders play an influential role in stimulating mass arousal, so do they play an important role in shaping the demands of the aroused.[1] What are intended to serve as merely symbolic appeasements may instead provide a focus for the still inchoate anxieties and diffuse anger that drive the masses. Thus early rhetorical pronouncements by liberal political leaders, including presidents of the United States, about the "rights" of workers and the "rights" of blacks not only helped to fuel the discontents of workers and blacks, but helped to concentrate those discontents on demands articulated by leading officials of the nation.

But when people are thus encouraged in spirit without being appeased in fact, their defiance may escape the boundaries of electoral rituals, and escape the boundaries established by the political norms of the electoral-representative system in general. They may indeed become rebellious, but while their rebellion often appears chaotic from the perspective of conventional American politics, or from the perspective of some organizers, it is not chaotic at all; it is structured political behavior. When people riot in the streets, their behavior is socially patterned, and within those patterns, their actions are to some extent deliberate and purposeful.

Social Location and Forms of Defiance

■ ■ ■ ■

Just as electoral political institutions channel protest into voter activity in the United States, and may even confine it within these spheres if the disturbance is not severe and the electoral system appears responsive, so do other features of institutional life determine the forms that protest takes when it breaks out of the boundaries of electoral politics. Thus, it is no accident that some people strike, others riot, or loot the granaries, or burn the machines, for just as the patterns of daily life ordinarily assure mass quiescence, so do these same patterns influence the form defiance will take when it erupts.

First, people experience deprivation and oppression within a concrete setting, not as the end product of large and abstract processes, and it is the concrete experience that molds their discontent into specific grievances against specific targets. Workers experience the factory, the speeding rhythm of the assembly line, the foreman, the spies and the guards, the owner and the paycheck. They do not experience monopoly capitalism. People on relief experience the shabby waiting rooms, the overseer or the caseworker, and the dole. They do not experience American social welfare policy. Tenants experience the leaking ceilings and cold radiators, and they recognize the landlord. They do not recognize the banking, real estate, and construction systems. No small wonder, therefore, that when the poor rebel they so often rebel against the overseer of the poor, or the slumlord, or the middling merchant, and not against the banks or the governing elites to whom the overseer, the slumlord, and the merchant also defer. In other words, it is the daily experience of people that shapes their grievances, establishes the measure of their demands, and points out the targets of their anger.

Second, institutional patterns shape mass movements by shaping the collectivity out of which protest can arise. Institutional life aggregates people or disperses them, molds group identities, and draws people into the settings within which collective action can erupt. Thus factory work gathers men and women together, educates them in a common experience, and educates them to the possibilities of cooperation and collective action. Casual laborers or petty entrepreneurs, by contrast, are dispersed by their occupations, and are therefore less likely to perceive their commonalities of position, and less likely to join together in collective action.

Third, and most important, institutional roles determine the strategic opportunities for defiance, for it is typically by rebelling against the rules and authorities associated with their everyday activities that people protest. Thus workers protest by striking. They are able to do so because they are drawn together in the factory setting, and their protests consist mainly in defying the rules and authorities associated with the workplace. The unemployed do not and cannot strike, even when they perceive that those who own the factories and businesses are to blame for their troubles. Instead, they riot in the streets where they are forced to linger, or storm the relief centers, and it is difficult to imagine them doing otherwise.

That they should do otherwise, however, is constantly asserted, and it is in such statements that the influence (as well as the absurdity) of the pluralist view becomes so evident. By denying the constraints which are imposed by institutional location, protest is readily discredited, as when insurgents are denounced for having ignored the true centers of power by attacking the wrong target by the wrong means. Thus welfare administrators admonish recipients for disrupting relief offices and propose instead that they learn how to lobby in the state legislature or Congress. But welfare clients cannot easily go to the state or national capital, and when a few do, they are of course ignored. Sometimes, however, they can disrupt relief offices, and that is harder to ignore.

In the same vein, a favorite criticism of the student peace movement, often made by erstwhile sympathizers, was that it was foolish of the students to protest the Vietnam War by demonstrating at the universities and attacking blameless administrators and faculties. It was obviously not the universities that were waging the war, critics argued, but the military-industrial complex. The students were not so foolish, however. The exigencies of mass action are such that they were constrained to act out their defiance within the universities where they were physically located and could thus act collectively, and where they played a role on which an institution depended, so that their defiance mattered.

Since our examples might suggest otherwise, we should note at this juncture that the tendency to impute freedom of choice in the evolution of political strategies is not peculiar to those who have large stakes in the preservation of some institution, whether welfare administrators or university professors. Nor is the tendency peculiar to those of more conservative political persuasion. Radical organizers make precisely the same assumption when they call upon the working class to organize in one way or another and to pursue one political strategy or another, even in the face of overwhelming evidence that social conditions preclude the exercise of such options. Opportunities for defiance are not created by analyses of power structures. If there is a genius in organizing, it is the capacity to sense what it is possible for people to do under given conditions, and to then help them do it. In point of fact, however, most organizing ventures ask that people do what they cannot do, and the result is failure.

It is our second general point, then, that the opportunities for defiance are structured by features of institutional life.[2] *Simply put, people cannot defy institutions to which they have no access, and to which they make no contribution.*

The Limited Impact of Mass Defiance

If mass defiance is neither freely available nor the forms it takes freely determined, it must also be said that it is generally of limited political impact. Still, some forms of protest appear to have more impact than others, thus posing an analytical question of considerable importance.

It is our judgment that *the most useful way to think about the effectiveness of protest is to examine the disruptive effects on institutions of different forms of mass defiance, and then to examine the political reverberations of those disruptions.* The impact of mass defiance is, in other words, not so much directly as indirectly felt. Protest is more likely to have a seriously disruptive impact when the protestors play a central role in an institution, and it is more likely to evoke wider political reverberations when powerful groups have large stakes in the disrupted institution. . . .

The Limits of Institutional Disruption

To refer to an institutional disruption is simply to note the obvious fact that institutional life depends upon conformity with established roles and compliance with established rules. Defiance may thus obstruct the normal operations of institutions. Factories are shut down when workers walk out or sit down; welfare bureaucracies are thrown into chaos when crowds demand relief; landlords may be bankrupted when tenants refuse to pay rent. In each of these cases, *people cease to conform to accustomed institutional roles; they withhold their accustomed cooperation, and by doing so, cause institutional disruptions.*

By our definition, disruption is simply the application of a negative sanction, the withdrawal of a crucial contribution on which others depend, and it is therefore a natural resource for exerting power over others. This form of power is, in fact, regularly employed by individuals and groups linked together in many kinds of cooperative interaction, and particularly by producer groups. Farmers, for example, keep their products off the market in order to force up the price offered by buyers; doctors refuse to provide treatment unless their price is met; oil companies withhold supplies until price concessions are made.

But the amount of leverage that a group gains by applying such negative sanctions is widely variable. Influence depends, first of all, on whether or not the contribution withheld is crucial to others; second, on whether or not those who have been affected by the disruption have resources to be conceded; and third, on whether the obstructionist group can protect itself adequately from reprisals. Once these criteria are stated, it becomes evident that the poor are usually in the least strategic position to benefit from defiance.

Thus, in comparison with most producer groups, the lower classes are often in weak institutional locations to use disruption as a tactic for influence. Many among the lower class are in locations that make their cooperation less than crucial to the operation of major institutions. Those who work in economically marginal enterprises, or who perform marginally necessary functions in major enterprises, or those who are unemployed, do not perform roles on which major institutions depend. Indeed, some of the poor are sometimes so isolated from significant institutional participation that the only "contribution" they can withhold is that of quiescence in civil life: they can riot.

Moreover, those who manage the institutions in which many of the lower classes find themselves often have little to concede to disruptors. When lower-class groups do play an important role in an institution, as they do in sweatshops or in slum tenements, these institutions—operated as they often are by marginal entrepreneurs—may be incapable of yielding very much in response to disruptive pressure.

Finally, lower-class groups have little ability to protect themselves against reprisals that can be employed by institutional managers. The poor do not have to be historians of the occasions when protestors have been jailed or shot down to understand this point. The lesson of their vulnerability is engraved in everyday life; it is evident in every police beating, in every eviction, in every lost job, in every relief termination. The very labels used to describe defiance by the lower classes—the pejorative labels of illegality and violence—testify to this vulnerability and serve to justify severe reprisals when they are imposed. By taking such labels for granted, we fail to recognize what these events really represent: a structure of political coercion inherent in the everyday life of the lower classes.

We can now comment on the association of disruption with spontaneity, perhaps another relic of traditional ways of thinking about lower-class uprisings, although here the issue is a little more complicated. Disruption itself is not necessarily spontaneous, but lower-class disruptions often are, in the sense that they are not planned and executed by formal organizations. In part, this testifies to the paucity of stable organizational resources among the poor, as well as to the cautious and moderate character of such organizations as are able to survive. But even if formal organizations existed, and even if they were not committed by the exigencies of their own survival to more cautious tactics, the circumstance that lead to mass defiance by the lower class are extremely difficult to predict; and once defiance erupts, its direction is difficult for leaders to control. . . .

Still, if the lower classes do not ordinarily have great disruptive power, and if the use of even that kind of power is not planned, it is the only power they do have. Their use of that power, the weighing of gains and risks, is not calculated in board rooms; it wells up out of the terrible travails that people experience at times of rupture and stress. And at such times, disruptions by the poor may have reverberations that go beyond the institutions in which the disruption is acted out.

The Limits of Political Disruption

It is not the impact of disruptions on particular institutions that finally tests the power of the poor; it is the political impact of these disruptions. At this level, however, a new set of structuring mechanisms intervenes, for the political impact of institutional disruptions is mediated by the electoral-representative system.

Responses to disruption vary depending on electoral conditions. Ordinarily, during periods of stability, governmental leaders have three rather obvious options when an institutional disruption occurs. They may ignore it; they may employ punitive measures against the disruptors; or they may attempt to conciliate them. If the disruptive group has little political leverage in its own right, as is true of lower-class groups, it will either be ignored or repressed. It is more likely to be ignored when the disrupted institution is not central to the society as a whole, or to other more important groups. Thus if men and women run amok, disrupting the fabric of their own communities, as in the immigrant slums of the nineteenth century, the spectacle may be frightening, but it can be contained within the slums; it will not necessarily have much impact on the society as a whole, or on the well-being of other important groups. Similarly, when impoverished mobs demand relief, they may cause havoc in the relief offices, but chaotic relief offices are not a large problem for the society as a whole, or for important groups. Repression is more likely to be employed when central institutions are affected, as when railroad workers struck and rioted in the late nineteenth century, or when the police struck in Boston after the First World War. Either way, to be ignored or punished is what the poor ordinarily expect from government, because these are the responses they ordinarily evoke.

But protest movements do not arise during ordinary periods; they arise when large-scale changes undermine political stability. It is this context, as we said earlier, that gives the poor hope and makes insurgency possible in the first place. It is this context that also makes political leaders somewhat vulnerable to protests by the poor.

At times of rapid economic and social change, political leaders are far less free either to ignore disturbances or to employ punitive measures. At such times, the relationship of political leaders to their constituents is likely to become uncertain. This unsettled state of political affairs makes the regime far more sensitive to disturbances, for it is not only more likely that previously uninvolved groups will be activated—the scope of conflict will be widened—but that the scope of conflict will be widened at a time when political alignments have already become unpredictable.

When a political leadership becomes unsure of its support, even disturbances that are isolated within peripheral institutions cannot be so safely ignored, for the mere appearance of trouble and disorder is more threatening when political alignments are unstable. And when the disrupted institutions are central to economic production or to the stability of social life, it becomes imperative that normal operations be restored if the regime is to maintain support among its constituents. Thus when industrial workers joined in massive strikes during the 1930s, they threatened the entire economy of the nation and, given the electoral instability of the times, threatened the future of the nation's political leadership. Under these circumstances, government could hardly ignore the disturbances.

Yet neither could government run the risks entailed by using massive force to subdue the strikers in the 1930s. It could not, in other words, simply avail itself of the option of repression. For one thing the striking workers, like the civil rights demonstrators in the 1960s, had aroused strong sympathy among groups that were crucial supporters of the regime. For another, unless insurgent groups are virtually of outcast status, permitting leaders of the regime to mobilize popular hatred against them, politically unstable conditions make the use of force risky, since the reactions of other aroused groups cannot be safely predicted. When government is unable to ignore the insurgents, and is unwilling to risk the uncertain repercussions of the use of force, it will make efforts to conciliate and disarm the protestors.

These placating efforts will usually take several forms. First and most obviously, political leaders will offer concessions, or press elites in the private sector to offer concessions, to remedy some of the immediate grievances, both symbolic and tangible, of the disruptive group. Thus mobs of unemployed workers were granted relief in the 1930s; striking industrial workers won higher pay and shorter hours; and angry civil rights demonstrators were granted the right to desegregated public accommodations in the 1960s.

Whether one takes such measures as evidence of the capacity of American political institutions for reform, or brushes them aside as mere tokenism, such concessions were not offered readily by government leaders. In each case, and in some cases more than in others, reform required a break with an established pattern of government accommodation to private elites. Thus the New Deal's liberal relief policy was maintained despite widespread opposition from the business community. Striking workers in the mid-1930s succeeded in obtaining wage concessions from private industry only because state and national political leaders abandoned the age-old policy of using the coercive power of the state to curb strikes. The granting of desegregated public accommodations required that national Democratic leaders turn against their traditional allies among southern plantation elites. In such instances concessions were won by the protestors only when political leaders were finally forced, out of a concern for their own survival, to act in ways which aroused the fierce opposition of economic elites. In short, under conditions of severe electoral instability, the alliance of public and private power is sometimes weakened, if only briefly, and at these moments a defiant poor may make gains.

Second, political leaders, or elites allied with them, will try to quiet disturbances not only by dealing with immediate grievances, but by making efforts to channel the energies and angers of the protestors into more legitimate and less disruptive forms of political behavior, in part by offering incentives to movement leaders or, in other words, by coopting them. Thus relief demonstrators in both the 1930s and the 1960s were encouraged to learn to use administrative grievance procedures as an alternative to "merely" disrupting relief offices, while their leaders were offered positions as advisors to relief administrators. In the 1960s civil rights organizers left the streets to take jobs in the Great Society programs; and as rioting spread in the northern cities, street leaders in the ghettos were encouraged to join in "dialogues" with municipal officials, and some were offered positions in municipal agencies.

Third, the measures promulgated by government at times of disturbance may be designed not to conciliate the protestors, but to undermine whatever sympathy the protesting group has been able to command from a wider public. Usually this is achieved through new programs that appear to meet the moral demands of the movement, and thus rob it of support without actually yielding much by way of tangible gains. A striking example was the passage of the pension provisions of the Social Security Act. The organized aged in the Townsend Movement were demanding pensions of $200 a month, with no strings attached, and they had managed to induce some 25 million people to sign supporting petitions. As it turned out, the Social Security Act, while it provided a measure of security for many of the future aged, did nothing for the members of the Townsend Movement, none of whom would be covered by a work-related insurance scheme since they were no longer working, and most of whom would in any case be dead when the payments were to begin some seven years later. But the pension provisions of the Social Security Act answered the *moral* claims of the movement. In principle, government had acted to protect America's aged, thus severing any identification between those who would be old in the future and those who were already old. The Social Security Act effectively dampened public support for the Townsend Plan while yielding the old people nothing. Other examples of responses which undermine public support abound. The widely heralded federal programs for the ghettos in the 1960s were neither designed nor funded in a way that made it possible for them to have substantial impact on poverty or on the traumas of ghetto life. But the publicity attached to the programs—the din and blare about a "war on poverty" and the development of "model cities"—did much to appease the liberal sympathizers with urban blacks.

Finally, these apparently conciliatory measures make it possible for government to safely employ repressive measures as well. Typically, leaders and groups who are more disruptive, or who spurn the concessions offered, are singled out for arbitrary police action or for more formal legal harassment through congressional investigations or through the courts. In the context of much-publicized efforts by government to ease the grievances of disaffected groups, coercive measures of this kind are not likely to arouse indignation among sympathetic publics. Indeed, this dual strategy is useful in another way, for it serves to cast an aura of balance and judiciousness over government action.

The main point, however, is simply that *the political impact of institutional disruptions depends upon electoral conditions.* Even serious disruptions, such as industrial strikes, will force concessions only when the calculus of electoral instability favors the protestors. And even then, when the protestors succeed in forcing government to respond, they do not dictate the content of those responses. As to the variety of specific circumstances which determine how much the protestors will gain and how much they will lose, we still have a great deal to learn.

The Demise of Protest

It is not surprising that, taken together, these efforts to conciliate and disarm usually lead to the demise of the protest movement, partly by transforming the movement itself, and partly by transforming the political climate which nourishes protest. With these changes, the array of institutional controls which ordinarily restrain protest is restored, and political influence is once more denied to the lower class.

We said that one form of government response was to make concessions to the protestors, yielding them something of what they demanded, either symbolic or material. But the mere granting of such concessions is probably not very important in accounting for the demise of a movement. For one thing, whatever is yielded is usually modest if not meager; for another, even modest concessions demonstrate that protest "works," a circumstance that might as easily be expected to fuel a movement as to pacify it.

But concessions are rarely unencumbered. If they are given at all, they are usually part and parcel of measures to reintegrate the movement into normal political channels and to absorb its leaders into stable institutional roles. Thus the right of industrial workers to unionize, won in response to massive and disruptive strikes in the 1930s, meant that workers were encouraged to use newly established grievance procedures in place of the sit-down or the wildcat strike; and the new union leaders, now absorbed in relations with factory management and in the councils of the Democratic Party, become the ideological proponents and organizational leaders of this strategy of normalcy and moderation. Similarly, when blacks won the vote in the South and a share of patronage in the municipalities of the North in response to the disturbances of the 1960s, black leaders were absorbed into electoral and bureaucratic politics and became the ideological proponents of the shift "from protest to politics" (Rustin).

This feature of government action deserves some explanation because the main reintegrative measures—the right to organize, the right to vote, black representation in city government—were also responses to specific demands made by the protestors themselves. To all appearances, government simply acted to redress felt grievances. But the process was by no means as straightforward as that. As we suggested earlier, the movements had arisen through interaction with elites, and had been led to make the demands they made in response to early encouragement by political leaders. Nor was it fortuitous that political leaders came to proclaim as just such causes as the right to organize or the right to vote or the right to "citizen participation." In each case, elites responded to discontent by proposing reforms with which they had experience, and which consisted mainly of extending established procedures to new groups or to new institutional arenas. Collective bargaining was not invented in the 1930s, nor the franchise in the 1960s. Driven by turmoil, political leaders proposed reforms that were in a sense prefigured by institutional arrangements that already existed, that were drawn from a repertoire provided by existing traditions. And an aroused people responded by demanding simply what political leaders had said they should have. If through some accident of history they had done otherwise, if industrial workers had demanded public ownership of factories, they would probably have still gotten unionism, if they got anything at all; and if impoverished southern blacks had demanded land reform, they would probably have still gotten the vote.

At the same time that government makes efforts to reintegrate disaffected groups, and to guide them into less politically disturbing forms of behavior, it also moves to isolate them from potential supporters and, by doing so, diminishes the morale of the movement. Finally, while the movement is eroding under these influences, its leaders attracted by new opportunities, its followers conciliated, confused, or discouraged, the show of repressive force against recalcitrant elements demolishes the few who are left.

However, the more far-reaching changes do not occur within the movement, but in the political context which nourished the movement in the first place. The agitated and defiant people who compose the movement are but a small proportion of the discontented population on which it draws. Presumably if some leaders were coopted, new leaders would arise; if some participants were appeased or discouraged, others would take their place. But this does not happen, because government's responses not only destroy the movement, they also transform the political climate which makes protest possible. The concessions to the protestors, the efforts to "bring them into the system," and in particular the measures aimed at potential supporters, all work to create a powerful image of a benevolent and responsive government that answers grievances and solves problems. As a result, whatever support might have existed among the larger population dwindles. Moreover, the display of government benevolence stimulates antagonist groups, and triggers the antagonistic sentiments of more neutral sectors. The "tide of public opinion" begins to turn—against labor in the late 1930s, against blacks in the late 1960s. And as it does, the definitions put forward by political leaders also change, particularly when prodded by contenders for political office who sense the shift in popular mood, and the weaknesses it reveals in an incumbent's support. Thus in the late 1960s, Republican leaders took advantage of white resentment against blacks to attract Democratic voters, raising cries of "law and order" and "workfare not welfare"—the code words for racial antagonism. Such a change is ominous. Where once the powerful voices of the land enunciated a rhetoric that gave courage to the poor, now they enunciate a rhetoric that erases hope, and implants fear. The point should be evident that as these various circumstances combine defiance is no longer possible.

The Residue of Reform

When protest subsides, concessions may be withdrawn. Thus when the unemployed become docile, the relief rolls are cut even though many are still unemployed; when the ghetto becomes quiescent, evictions are resumed. The reason is simple enough. Since the poor no longer pose the threat of disruption, they no longer exert leverage on political leaders; there is no need for conciliation. This is particularly the case in a climate of growing political hostility, for the concessions granted are likely to become the focus of resentment by other groups.

But some concessions are not withdrawn. As the tide of turbulence recedes, major institutional changes sometimes remain. Thus the right of workers to join unions was not rescinded when turmoil subsided (although some of the rights ceded to unions were withdrawn). And it is not likely that the franchise granted to blacks in the South will be taken back (although just that happened in the post-Reconstruction period). Why, then, are some concessions withdrawn while others become permanent institutional reforms?

The answer, perhaps, is that while some of the reforms granted during periods of turmoil are costly or repugnant to various groups in the society, and are therefore suffered only under duress, other innovations turn out to be compatible (or at least not incompatible) with the interests of more powerful groups, most importantly with the interests of dominant economic groups. Such an assertion has the aura of a conspiracy theory, but in fact the process is not conspiratorial at all. Major industrialists had resisted unionization, but once forced to concede it as the price of industrial peace, they gradually discovered that labor unions constituted a useful mechanism to regulate the labor force. The problem of disciplining industrial labor had been developing over the course of a century. The depression produced the political turmoil through which a solution was forged. Nor was the solution simply snatched from the air. As noted earlier, collective bargaining was a tried and tested method of dealing with labor disturbances. The tumult of the 1930s made the use of this method imperative; once implemented, the reforms were institutionalized because they continued to prove useful.

Similarly, southern economic elites had no interest in ceding southern blacks the franchise. But their stakes in disfranchising blacks had diminished. The old plantation economy was losing ground to new industrial enterprises; plantation-based elites were losing ground to economic dominants based in industry. The feudal political arrangements on which a plantation economy had relied were no longer of central importance, and certainly they were not of central importance to the new economic elites. Black uprisings, by forcing the extension of the franchise and the modernization of southern politics, thus helped seal a fissure in the institutional fabric of American society, a fissure resulting from the growing inconsistency between the economic and political institutions of the South.

What these examples suggest is that *protesters win, if they win at all, what historical circumstances have already made ready to be conceded.* Still, as Alan Wolfe has said, governments do no change magically through some "historical radical transformation," but only through the actual struggles of the time (154). When people are finally roused to protest against great odds, they take the only options available to them within the limits imposed by their social circumstances. . . .

A Note on the Role of Protest Leadership

The main point of this chapter is that both the limitations and opportunities for mass protest are shaped by social conditions. The implications for the role of leadership in protest movements can be briefly summarized.

Protest wells up in response to momentous changes in the institutional order. It is not created by organizers and leaders.

Once protest erupts, the specific forms it takes are largely determined by features of social structure. Organizers and leaders who contrive strategies that ignore the social location of the people they seek to mobilize can only fail.

Elites respond to the institutional disruptions that protest causes, as well as to other powerful institutional imperatives. Elite responses are not significantly shaped by the demands of leaders and organizers. Nor are elite responses significantly shaped by formally structured organizations of the poor. Whatever influence lower-class groups occasionally exert in American politics does not result from organization, but from mass protest and the disruptive consequences of protest.

Finally, protest in the United States has been episodic and transient, for as it gains momentum, so too do various forms of institutional accommodation and coercion that have the effect of restoring quiescence. Organizers and leaders cannot prevent the ebbing of protest, nor the erosion of whatever influence protest yielded the lower class. They can only try to win whatever can be won while it can be won.

In these major ways protest movements are shaped by institutional conditions, and not by the purposive efforts of leaders and organizers. The limitations are large and unyielding. Yet within the boundaries created by these limitations, some latitude for purposive effort remains. Organizers and leaders choose to do one thing, or they choose to do another, and what they choose to do affects to some degree the course of the protest movement. If the area of latitude is less than leaders and organizers would prefer, it is also not enlarged when they proceed as if institutional limitations did not in fact exist by undertaking strategies which fly in the face of these constraints. The wiser course is to understand these limitations, and to exploit whatever latitude remains to enlarge the potential influence of the lower class. And if our conclusions are correct, what this means is that strategies must be pursued that escalate the momentum and impact of disruptive protest at each stage in its emergence and evolution.

Notes

1. Edelman ascribes the influence of public officials as "powerful shapers of perceptions" to their virtual monopoly on certain kinds of information, to the legitimacy of the regime with which they are identified, and to the intense identification of people with the state (101–102).
2. This is perhaps what C. L. R. James means when he writes: "Workers are at their very best in collective action in the circumstances of their daily activity or crises arising from it" (95). Richard Flacks has also made a related argument regarding the importance of what he calls "everyday life" in shaping popular movements.

References

Edelman, Murray. *Politics as Symbolic Action.* New Haven: Yale University Press, 1971.

Flacks, Richard. "Making History vs. Making Life: Dilemmas of an American Left." *Working Papers for a New Society* 2 (Summer 1974).

James, C. L. R.; Lee, Grace C.; and Chaulieu, Pierre. *Facing Reality.* Detroit: Bewick Editions, 1974.

Rustin, Bayard. "From Protest to Politics." *Commentary* 39 (February 1965).

Wolfe, Alan. "New Directions in the Marxist Theory of Politics." *Politics and Society* 4 (Winter 1974).

CAN FEMINIST ORGANIZATIONS BE EFFECTIVE?

SUZANNE STAGGENBORG

The literature on feminist organizations is replete with examples of organizations that are torn apart by internal conflict, of leaders who are "trashed," and of groups that dissolve before accomplishing their goals. Such difficulties are certainly not unique to feminist organizations; New Left organizations struggled with many of the same problems (see Breines 1989; Miller 1987). They are of particular concern, however, given the commonplace feminist goal of fostering democratic and caring kinds of organizations that empower participants. Indeed, feminist organizations have been the main carriers of the "participatory democratic" mode of social movement organization since the 1960s, and feminists have been influential in spreading this form of organization to other movements with similar concerns, such as the antinuclear power movement (see Epstein 1991). Tales of infighting, marathon meetings at which nothing is decided, and other organizational disasters raise the question of whether these groups can be effective.

To answer this question, I begin with the definitions of success that have been employed by social movement theorists and some of the problems involved in assessing movement outcomes. Next, I examine the characteristics of feminist organizations that are related to their effectiveness. I then focus on a particular type of feminist organization for which effectiveness has been especially problematic: the informal, "radical" feminist organization. I compare organizations that have had problems accomplishing their goals with others that have enjoyed more success. I conclude that feminist organizations can be considered effective if a broad definition of movement "success" is adopted. At the same time, I specify some of the obstacles to success confronted by different types of feminist organizations.

Definitions of Social Movement Success

Surprisingly little attention has been paid to the outcomes of collective action and to the question of what determines success in social movements, despite its obvious importance. Gamson's *The Strategy of Social Protest* (1990; first published in 1975) continues to stand as one of the few empirical and theoretical treatments of the problem. The criteria of movement success employed in his widely cited work are (1) *acceptance* of a challenging group as a legitimate representative of a constituency by the target of collective action, and (2) *new advantages* won by a challenger. One issue in an evaluation of the usefulness of these criteria is the extent to which they capture a broad range of outcomes that advance the cause of a movement.

It is perhaps easiest to think about acceptance and new advantages in narrow political terms, as some of Gamson's examples suggest. When representatives of a challenging group are routinely invited to testify at congressional hearings, this is a sign of acceptance (Gamson 1990, 32). When a new law is passed, a new advantage has been won. The model suggested is that of "outside" challenging groups trying to gain specific policy outcomes along with "membership" in the polity (Tilly 1978).

Burstein, Einwohner, and Hollander (1991) adopt such a focus on political movements and point out that Gamson's criteria of success need to be expanded to take into account other aspects of the political process. Drawing on the work of Schumaker (1975) and Kitschelt (1986), they argue that in addition to acceptance (or, in Schumaker's terms, "access responsiveness") and new advantages (or "policy responsiveness"), success involves getting movement demands on the political agenda, getting new policies implemented, actually having the intended impact on an aggrieved population, and transforming political structures. (One might argue that these can be subsumed under Gamson's categories, but I think it is useful to elaborate these political and policy outcomes.)

Beyond expanding the definition of how success is achieved through the political process, we can also look at movement success in broader cultural terms. Although his work lends itself to a narrow political interpretation, Gamson makes clear that a number of different types of outcomes are included in his definition of success. For example, the target of collective action may be public opinion, and "acceptance" may occur when the public changes its view of the challenging group promoting the change (Gamson 1990, 33). The "new advantage" won by a challenging group may be a change in public values or practices (Gamson 1990, 35). In comments written for the second edition of *The Strategy of Social Protest*, Gamson (1990, 149–50) emphasizes the importance of the mass media and suggests that influencing the framing of an issue by the media is a kind of success.

Others have explicitly advocated that a broad definition of social movement outcomes be adopted in assessing the influence of social movements. Gusfield (1981) advances a "fluid" concept of social movements, which leads to concern with a variety of consequences of social movements beyond the achievement of programmatic goals. One consequence is the activation of a pool of people who can be drawn into subsequent movements. Another is the broader change in public and private values and meanings created by movements as new vocabularies and new ideas are introduced and disseminated, often by the mass media. In Gusfield's (1981, 326) view, movements affect far more people than those who participate in collective action, and they have cultural consequences beyond the impact of their organized and public activities.

Mueller (1987) is similarly concerned with the broader cultural outcomes of social movements, which she links theoretically to the political and policy outcomes of movements. She points to the development of a "collective consciousness" as one type of movement "success," which can then affect future mobilization and the ability to bring about political and policy outcomes. Some movements, like the women's movement, need first to challenge existing ideas, cultural practices, and means of socialization before achieving more substantive goals, and these outcomes should be treated as successes (Mueller 1987, 93). In place of Gamson's distinction between "acceptance" and "new advantages," Mueller (1987, 104 n. 2) proposes that success be measured in terms of "substantive reforms" and "outcomes that create resources for future mobilization."

Based on these and other discussions of the problems involved in assessing the effectiveness, success, or consequences of a social movement, three main categories of movement outcomes can be identified: (1) political and policy outcomes; (2) mobilization outcomes; and (3) cultural outcomes. The first category, perhaps the most straightforward, includes various steps in the process of bringing about substantive changes through the political system. The category of mobilization outcomes focuses on organizational successes and the ability to carry out collective action. Cultural outcomes include changes in social norms, behaviors, and ways of thinking among a public that extends beyond movement constituents or beneficiaries, as well as the creation of a collective consciousness among groups such as women.

Consideration of these different types of outcomes encourages a long-range, processual view of social movements. Because movements are characterized by multiple rather than single outcomes, an interesting question is how different outcomes are linked to one another. One type of success may have a bearing on another type, and outcomes occurring at one point in time affect future outcomes (Snyder and Kelly 1979). Rupp and Taylor (1987), for instance, show that the ongoing mobilization of the National Women's Party in the period from 1945 to the 1960s was quite important to the subsequent resurgence of the women's movement; in particular, it bequeathed the struggle for the Equal Rights Amendment, which provided a unifying goal that mobilized many activists in the 1970s and early 1980s. Mueller's (1987) work is important in revealing something about the process whereby political outsiders become insiders. She shows how the creation of a collective consciousness among women legitimated their political ambitions and led in the 1970s to the first significant rise in the number of women elected to public office—a result with important implications for future outcomes of the women's movement. Feminist organizations did not become important in providing resources for women candidates until the late 1970s, after the first round of "self-starters" had already gotten themselves elected.

Movements, then, can be successful in introducing new ideas and creating new social norms, and these outcomes may produce subsequent achievements. Moreover, this sort of cultural "success" can typically be attributed not to the actions of any one social movement *organization* (SMO) but rather to a less clearly defined *movement*. In assessing movement successes and their determinants, we have to live with the fact that we cannot stay solely within the bounds of that convenient unit of analysis, the SMO. Not only are some outcomes the product of less organized aspects of a movement, but some movement organizations have less distinct boundaries than others. It is important to look at variations in the characteristics of organizations and to understand groups as *movement* entities rather than only as organizations.

Characteristics of Feminist Organizations

Feminist organizations vary in a number of ways that are important to their effectiveness. Martin (1990) argues persuasively that there are no essential characteristics of feminist organizations. Although some activists and scholars have viewed a collectivist or nonhierarchical organizational structure as the hallmark of a feminist organization, there are many organizations—such as the National Organization for Women—that do not have such structures but must surely be regarded as "feminist." Martin's proposal that a feminist organization be defined as one that meets any one of several criteria seems more useful.[1] In recognizing that there are different types of feminist organizations, we can look at which types are most effective in producing which kinds of outcomes.

Existing work suggests that there are two particularly important influences on the effectiveness of feminist organizations: (1) organizational structure and (2) ideology and related goals. As Martin (1990, 195) notes, the main distinction that has been made with regard to organizational structure is between organizations that are "collectivist" or "participatory" and those that are "bureaucratic" or "hierarchical." Feminist ideologies have been characterized in a variety of ways (see, e.g., Black 1989; Tong 1989), but one basic way in which feminist organizations vary is the extent to which they adopt "radical" ideologies and goals (see, Ferree and Hess 1985; Taylor 1989). Buechler (1990a, 108) defines a "radical" movement or SMO as "one whose ideology, goals and program pose a fundamental challenge to a particular system of power relations."

The problems of "collectivist" organizations, which tend to have radical ideologies, are well documented (see, e.g., Freeman 1972; Mansbridge 1973; Riger 1984; Baker 1986; Hansen 1986). Feminist organizations that stress collective decision-making and empowerment of individual members often focus on group process at the expense of other goals. The emotional intensity of interactions in such groups, and the level of commitment expected, lead to high levels of "burnout." The lack of an established division of labor makes it difficult to complete organizational tasks, and the refusal to recognize official leaders leads in many groups to unofficial domination by persons tied into friendship networks who lack accountability to the group. Because of these and other internal conflicts, collectivist organizations often do not survive for very long.

Bureaucratic or formalized organizations, which are often assumed to have less radical goals, tend to be more stable organizationally and better able to bring about specific policy outcomes. Gelb and Palley show how such organizations have been involved in bringing about change in several areas of public policy. They argue (1987, 22) that groups such as NOW, which have become increasingly hierarchical and professionalized, nevertheless "have not fallen prey to the perils of bureaucratization" predicted by Max Weber and Robert Michels but "have remained agents for change in the status of women in society even as they have worked to broaden understanding for the goals of the movement." Others have similarly shown how the women's lobby in Washington, made up of formalized movement organizations in alliance with established organizations, has become increasingly effective (Fraser 1983; Costain 1988). There are, however, limitations on the ability of these organizations to effect change, which can be attributed both to internal organizational features and to external political constraints.

The distinction between "bureaucratic" and "collectivist" feminist organizations has been useful in focusing attention on organizational as well as ideological differences in the women's movement. It is clearly inadequate, however, for the purpose of characterizing the range of structural dimensions of feminist organizations related to their effectiveness and elaborating the kinds of social changes that are achieved by different types of feminist organizations. Gamson's (1990) formulation is somewhat more helpful in identifying both centralization and bureaucratization as key characteristics related to success. In my own work (Staggenborg 1989) I have argued that an informal, decentralized structure makes organizational maintenance difficult but tends to encourage strategic and tactical innovation, whereas a formalized and centralized structure promotes maintenance while narrowing strategic choices. Other more specific features of feminist organizations, such as the way in which boards of directors are constructed and the nature of relations between staff and volunteers, can also be expected to influence various kinds of movement outcomes.

Among formalized organizations, groups that have grassroots components, such as NOW, need to be distinguished from others that are more strictly professional. NOW and other national women's movement organizations have succeeded and failed not only in achieving specific policy changes but with regard to all the kinds of political outcomes elaborated by Burstein, Einwohner, and Hollander (1991). Their achievements and inadequacies are related to their organizational structures as well as to external constraints, and some apparent "failures" are actually "successes" of a sort. For example, NOW has recently received a great deal of criticism, including some from other feminist organizations, for its proposal to create a third political party on the grounds that neither the Democratic nor the Republican Party adequately addresses the concerns of women and minorities. Although critics find the idea of a third party unrealistic, such a party might be successful in pressuring the major parties to address the issues it raises, if not in electing candidates (see Rothschild 1989). Whether or not such success is possible, the relationship between the strategic choice and NOW's organizational structure is of interest. For example, empirical research might show how grassroots activists influence NOW's strategies—and hence its successes and failures—and perhaps how the organization's structure discourages the kind of coalition work with other groups that might prevent such strategic choices.

Informal organizations, similarly, are not all "collectivist," and differences among such groups produce varying outcomes. Many are "radical" insofar as they seek fundamental changes in power relations, but they vary in both their ideologies and their structures. Looking at some differences among groups of this type helps to clarify the issues involved in assessing their impacts. Different types of informal and radical organizations do have difficulties associated with their organizational structures and ideologies, but they are also effective in ways that are generally not recognized.

Informal, Radical Feminist Organizations and Social Change

The organizations considered here are part of the "younger branch" of the women's movement (Freeman 1975), which some would argue no longer exists or has merged with the "older branch" of the movement (Carden 1977). This branch once included socialist feminist unions, most of which declined in the 1970s (see Hansen 1986), as well as radical feminist groups, a tendency within the women's movement that some claim has given way to "cultural feminism" (see Echols 1989). In a narrow sense, these groups can be considered complete failures because they had radical goals—such as changing the structure of capitalist and patriarchal society—but dissolved before achieving any of them. In a broader sense, however, they enjoyed a number of successes, albeit ones that are less easily measured than policy outcomes.

Take the case of the Chicago Women's Liberation Union (CWLU), a socialist feminist organization formed in 1969 and dissolved in 1977. Viewed as an *organization*, the CWLU enjoyed only limited success. It established an office and provided some coordination of various activities of the Chicago women's liberation movement, but it also had serious problems. It had trouble integrating into the Union new people who wanted to become active; it was always short of money; its resources were spread so thin that many projects never got off the ground; and it was devastated by internal conflict. In evaluating the achievements of the CWLU, however, it is more useful to view the group as part of a *social movement community* (Buechler 1990b) than as a task- and goal-oriented organization.

When the CWLU was founded in 1969, the antiwar movement was in disarray, but the younger branch of the women's movement that emerged from it was flourishing throughout the country. Growth of the CWLU came quickly, as there was already a constituency eager to work on the burning issues of the women's liberation movement. In other words, the CWLU was not an organization in the position of trying to create a movement; there was no need for issue "entrepreneurs" to create grievances (McCarthy and Zald 1973, 1977). The constituents and the issues—the movement—were *there*; networks of women were already mobilized, and phone calls from other interested women poured in. The CWLU had only to find ways to harness the existing energy and excitement.

As a kind of movement center (Morris 1984) around which the small groups revolved, the CWLU was successful for a time in attracting many energetic activists to its work groups (which were more numerous and active than its "chapters"). The Union's informal structure and orientation to the movement community was important in allowing the group to reach women who were not necessarily "members." For example, in 1972 its Liberation School enrolled over 220 women in twenty classes, and the Action Coalition for Decent Childcare organized a public hearing attended by some two hundred people (Rothstein and Weisstein 1972). The CWLU was not able to sustain such levels of mobilization after the early 1970s, however, in part because the cycle of protest that generated the larger movement had declined.

Beyond its temporary capacity to act as the center for a vibrant social movement community, the CWLU was also "successful" in that it contributed to later rounds of feminist collective action in several ways. First, the organization created alternative institutions that endured beyond its own demise, including two women's health centers and the Health Evaluation and Referral Service (HERS). Beyond whatever cultural impact these alternative institutions had, they later played a role in the local pro-choice movement by bringing together persons in the left-feminist community interested in fighting threats to abortion rights. Second, the Union helped to develop a pool of activists who went on to participate in other existing organizations, such as NOW, or to create new organizations such as the Chicago Women's Health Task Force, a group that also became involved in abortion rights work (see Staggenborg 1991).

Work groups of the Union also created models for collective action that could potentially influence other groups. An organizer of the Liberation School talked of the project as "a new, woman-controlled approach to women's studies which we hope will provide a model for other institutions" (Rothstein and Weisstein 1972, 6). Although it is difficult to know what, if any, impact the Liberation School and many other CWLU projects actually had, one work group, the Abortion Counseling Service—better known as "Jane"—has achieved almost mythic stature within the women's movement. As a collective of women who started out providing abortion referrals and ended up performing abortions themselves before legalization in 1973, Jane was and still is seen as a model of feminist service delivery (see Bart 1987; Addelson 1988). Not only did Jane influence other projects in Chicago, including HERS and the women's health clinics, but some have suggested that the model will be copied by many if abortion is again made illegal (e.g., Van Gelder 1991); in fact, former Jane members were asked to speak at the National Women's Studies Association conference in 1990 for just this reason (Blakely 1990).

Finally, the ideology developed by the CWLU and other socialist feminist groups across the country continued to motivate and attract adherents in later years. This can be seen in the concern of the women's health and reproductive rights movements with issues involving both class and gender, such as sterilization abuse and public funding of abortions. In Chicago, both former CWLU members and new activists were drawn into the abortion rights movement in 1977 in response to a threatened cutoff of state funding of abortions, and again in 1980 in response to the closing of the Cook County Hospital abortion clinic, which served poor women.

Thus, a feminist organization that exerted little direct influence on public policy and accomplished none of its radical goals can be seen as effective if we take into account its mobilization outcomes and broader cultural outcomes. The legacy of the CWLU also calls into question assertions that socialist feminism is no longer influential in activist circles. (B. Epstein 1991, 178–80; Buechler 1990b, 116–19). The CWLU is one socialist feminist organization that has influenced subsequent feminist concerns and produced alternative institutions and individual activists who carry on this tradition of feminism; it would be surprising if other socialist feminist groups did not have similar impacts.

The influences of such groups are no doubt neglected because of the many difficulties involved in tracing "fluid" kinds of outcomes of feminist organizations. It may not be possible to attribute some achievements to any particular movement organization, and it may be difficult to figure out what role, if any, movement activities played in producing a given outcome (a problem that also arises in assessing political and policy outcomes). The ideas of a movement, for instance, may spread, but how does this occur? Movement organizations may actively promote their positions through public education campaigns; actors outside of SMOs or movements may take up their ideologies; there may be larger social and political reasons why particular ideologies are accepted or rejected at different times.

In some cases, such as the reproductive rights movement that emerged in the late 1970s, it may be relatively easy to trace the roots of the movement to an earlier mobilization. In Chicago, women who had been members of the CWLU organized the Chicago Women's Health Task Force, and activists from that group formed Women Organized for Reproductive Choice (WORC). Some of the same individuals were involved in each succeeding organization, and there were clear ideological continuities. But even where there are direct links between organizations, it would be a mistake to think of the movement and its maintenance only in terms of its SMOs. Here, Buechler's (1990b) notion of a social movement community is useful in explaining the continuity in ideology and mobilization. It was the creation not only of a small organization called the Chicago Women's Health Task Force (consisting of fewer than twenty activists) that sustained socialist feminist activity in Chicago in the mid-1970s, but of a whole network of small women's health projects and alternative institutions such as HERS. Although many movement organizations were dissolving, there were events and networks that kept a social movement community alive.[2]

Thus, social movement communities operate to sustain movements and bring about social change in a number of ways. Even movements and movement organizations that seem to die out may be successful in influencing individuals or changing the collective consciousness of some group (McAdam 1988). For example, the reproductive rights movement of the late 1970s and early 1980s had a difficult time achieving its goals, and the Reproductive Rights National Network (known as R2N2), formed in 1978, dissolved in 1984 (see Staggenborg 1991 for details). Aspects of the movement, including its ideology, seem to have survived, however.

One of the new organizations that I discovered in researching the recent history of the prochoice movement is a student-based organization called Students Organizing Students (SOS). I obtained some literature from the organization and later interviewed one of its staff members. I was interested to see that SOS's literature presented a perspective strikingly similar to that of the Reproductive Rights National Network. Both talk about the importance of abortion rights in connection with other health and reproductive rights issues, including sterilization abuse. In addition, SOS calls for "free abortion on demand," the very slogan used by the CWLU and other women's liberation groups before the legalization of abortion. I asked the SOS staff member, a college student, whether she knew of the earlier reproductive rights movement, and she did not. Yet somehow the ideas of earlier movements and organizations were present in the literature of a student organization that was formed after the 1989 Supreme Court decision threatening abortion rights.

When this kind of outcome is taken into account, the hidden successes of feminist organizations become visible. On the other hand, informal organizations with radical goals do encounter real difficulties that should not be glossed over. Comparisons among feminist organizations are helpful in revealing the organizational characteristics that are responsible for both their successes and their failures. Here, I compare two reproductive rights organizations that are no longer in existence, the Reproductive Rights National Network and its Chicago affiliate, Women Organized for Reproductive Choice, with two other groups that have managed to survive, the National Women's Health Network and the National Women's Music Festival.

R2N2 was similar to the Chicago Women's Liberation Union in that it was able to grow quickly at a time when mobilization came easily. For the CWLU, the cycle of protest under way in the late 1960s generated activism; for R2N2, events in the abortion conflict in the late 1970s and early 1980s, including the cutoff of Medicaid funding of abortion and the election of Ronald Reagan, mobilized participants. Neither organization was able to endure for very long once these external impetuses disappeared. WORC did survive the demise of R2N2, remaining in existence until 1989, but for many of its years it was a very tiny organization held together in large part by one individual (see Staggenborg 1991). Although these organizations had some successes of the sort discussed above, they certainly did not accomplish their radical goals, and they had many organizational problems. What were the sources of these difficulties?

One obvious problem for groups with radical goals is that their aims are hard to achieve, and, in the absence of progress toward goal achievement, it is difficult to remain mobilized. Part of the dilemma associated with radical goals is tactical. The reproductive rights movement formed as a result of concern that the "pro-choice" movement had become completely reactive, responding in a narrow, single-issue manner to the New Right. Reproductive rights activists wanted to turn this situation around and, at least in the long run, advance a more comprehensive notion of reproductive "choice," one focused not only on abortion but on other issues—such as access to health care, employment, and day care—that are involved in making the decision to have a child a real choice for women. But reproductive rights groups had problems finding ways to advance this agenda and little or no success in achieving their goals in the late 1970s and early 1980s.

When asked about strategy, participants in such radical groups as the CWLU and R2N2 often talk of the consciousness-raising aspects of their activities. In explaining their early work on abortion rights, for example, a member of the CWLU commented: "[We] were doing political education about what people's rights in fact were. . . . We wanted a situation where abortion was not only available on demand, but ultimately where we had a health care system which did not allow profiteering on people's abortions, etc., etc., so it was couched in terms which would set up a debate which would allow all of these issues which we thought were consciousness-raising to be elaborated." One of the founders of the Reproductive Rights National Network explained in an interview that R2N2 intended to do "mass education" while groups like the National Abortion Rights Action League engaged in legislative lobbying and the like. R2N2 did hold some demonstrations and petition drives as a means of implementing this strategy, but it was difficult to keep them up indefinitely, and leaders became frustrated by tactical limitations. As my informant commented: "In general, R2N2 was not too innovative. The problem is that most of the fight is at the legislative level and we didn't want to get involved in that. So we concentrated on educational things . . . but it's really difficult to find an arena for R2N2's activity—so we ended up doing petitions, postcards as a means of educational outreach." Such activists may be successful insofar as they alter public opinion or create adherents for a particular feminist position, but it is extremely difficult to assess their impact. And without visible victories, it is difficult to keep supporters involved for long periods of time.

Feminist organizations with radical goals also try to achieve more concrete changes, but the political opposition they encounter creates tactical dilemmas. For example, Women Organized for Reproductive Choice continued in the 1980s to try to fight for poor women's access to abortions, particularly to reopen the Cook County Hospital abortion clinic, which had been closed in 1980. Because they could not alter the power structure in Chicago, they were unable to make any headway, and after a few years WORC simply ran out of tactics that could mobilize supporters in the absence of any progress toward victory.

Another difficulty for organizations like R2N2 and WORC is structural. Although R2N2's founders wanted to create a national organization that could coordinate local efforts and help build a larger movement, they were also wary of bureaucratic and centralized organizations. Consequently, they never tried to build a formalized organization with professional staff. Board members from local groups were supposed to provide leadership to the organization with assistance from one paid coordinator. The result was what a former board member called "the classic leadership problem" of feminist organizations. Because participants feared hierarchy, they failed to create an organization with a division of labor that would ensure that organizational tasks were completed and that persons with the appropriate skills were available.

The demise of R2N2 and other reproductive rights organizations cannot be attributed solely to their lack of formalized structures. Nevertheless, comparison with some other radical types of feminist organizations reveals that more formalized structures do promote longevity and do not necessarily preclude the empowerment of individual participants. The National Women's Health Network is an example of a national movement organization that has survived since its founding in 1975, despite ups and downs. Paid staff, first hired in the late 1970s, have been one important ingredient in the Network's survival. Staff members, together with national board members, have kept the organization visible and stable through the production of high-quality literature, through expert testimony to Congress, and through the generation of grant money. Direct-mail techniques, first used in the early 1980s, have generated members and additional funds. The NWHN has not had much success in activating a grassroots constituency, but it has remained alive by adopting a somewhat formalized structure (see Staggenborg 1991 for details.) At the same time, the Network has continued to take positions that are radical in the sense that they challenge existing power relations in the health care system.[3]

The National Women's Music Festival (NWMF) is another type of feminist organization that has successfully employed a formalized structure without sacrificing feminist principles (Eder, Staggenborg, and Sudderth 1995). The organization was originally a feminist collective that began in 1974 to produce a women's music festival on the campus of the University of Illinois in Champaign. The festival was held annually until 1981; there was none that year because of the group's large debts and the unwillingness of the university to permit the festival to be held on campus any longer. In 1982 a group formed to revive the festival at Indiana University in Bloomington, where it has taken place ever since. The group that revived the festival also tried to operate as a collective but after a few years was again in danger of extinction. At this point a festival producer took charge and made the NWMF into a formalized organization with an intricate division of labor and clear chain of command. Although there have always been some internal conflicts, the structural changes appear to be responsible for the organization's ability to survive and, in recent years, to attract large numbers of participants.

The festival producer responsible for this accomplishment commented on the difficulties of the earlier collective in a 1991 interview: "The problem with this group—and the problem with consensus decision-making—is that *everyone* has to be involved in *every* decision and has to agree on all of it, and no one wanted to give away any power. Everyone wanted input into *everything*. So, we would have huge meetings that would take *forever* and we'd get a couple of decisions made and, you know, we were getting further and further behind because we weren't getting things done. No one would allow someone to go off and take care of something." Although there was no bureaucracy in the collective organization, power was actually more centralized there than in the more formalized organization that followed. When a division of labor was created, different women became responsible for overseeing different areas of the festival production—workshops, services, music, and so forth—so that although there is hierarchy within the organization, responsibility and decision-making power are more dispersed than they were in the collective.

When asked if she considered the NWMF a feminist organization, the festival producer responsible for its structure replied:

> Yeah, definitely. Well, because we empower people. I think that by the time anybody's worked with us for a year or two, they're not

> afraid of figures, they're not afraid of budgets, they know how to read one, they know how to put things together. Basically, I think each of them learns how to be a producer in their own right. Actually, what they're doing, if they're doing spirituality, or if they're doing the health series, they are actually producing a health series. . . . I think that the empowering, and allowing everybody on every level—that as soon as you take on responsibility, you get the power in order to deal with that responsibility and then the accountability. The power and responsibility and accountability—having all those together, I think that that's very feminist oriented.

Conclusion

Feminist organizations can be effective at the same time that they self-destruct as organizations and fail to achieve changes in public policy. Groups that are unsuccessful in terms of organizational maintenance and policy outcomes may be effective as the centers of movement communities and as the originators of cultural changes. Although the successes of many feminist organizations tend to be hidden, they are likely to have an impact on subsequent rounds of collective action. The women's movement is perpetuated not only by its movement organizations but also by its cultural achievements. As I have argued, these achievements include the creation of alternative institutions that serve as movement community centers, pools of activists who remain involved in movement activities, models of collective action that are employed by subsequent activists, and ideologies that continue to attract adherents.

Informal, radical feminist organizations that are committed to participatory democracy and to the empowerment of participants as well as to the achievement of more instrumental goals are often used as the standard for what a feminist organization is. They are also the subject of much of the debate regarding the effectiveness of feminist organizations. I have argued that the cultural outcomes often produced by such groups in lieu of substantive reforms must be taken into account in judging their effectiveness. At the same time, I have identified some of the problems of such groups, which stem from both their ideologies and their structures. Because they have radical agendas, some feminist groups have a difficult time finding specific targets and tactics; consequently, they have trouble producing the victories needed to keep supporters mobilized. And because their ideologies are radical, such groups are likely to meet with powerful external opposition. Internally, informally organized groups lack the division of labor necessary for longtime organizational maintenance.

In focusing on informal, radical feminist organizations, I do not mean to imply that the operation of more formalized and less radical movement organizations is unproblematic. Detailed empirical research is needed to assess the strengths and weaknesses of all kinds of feminist organizations and to specify the important dimensions on which feminist organizations vary. Comparing organizations with different types of structures and ideologies is particularly useful in identifying the sources of their successes and failures.

My analysis in this paper provides some direction for future study of the outcomes of feminist organizations. It suggests that feminist organizations need to be considered in the context of a larger social movement community. Movements consist not only of political movement organizations, but of individuals, alternative institutions, and ideas, which are often perpetuated beyond the lives of the organizations. Feminist organizations can be effective in a variety of ways; studies are needed of the processes whereby they have the effects that I have identified. Key questions include how social movement communities extend beyond the bounds and lifetimes of movement organizations; how alternative institutions function; how individuals are kept within community networks; and how the ideas of movements get disseminated. Among the detailed investigations needed for an understanding of the outcomes of feminist organizations are studies that trace the movement careers of individual activists; examinations of how alternative institutions created by movements function and how they affect subsequent collective action; and reports on the role of women's studies courses and other likely avenues for spreading feminist ideas and assisting new mobilizations.

Notes

Acknowledgments: I thank Myra Marx Ferree and Verta Taylor for helpful comments on an earlier draft of this essay.

1. Martin (1990, 185) argues that "an organization is feminist if it meets any one of the following criteria: (a) has feminist ideology; (b) has feminist guiding values; (c) has feminist goals; (d) produced feminist outcomes; (e) was founded during the women's movement as part of the women's movement." I think these are useful criteria, although I would argue that feminist outcomes must be produced *intentionally*; one can well imagine an antifeminist organization that inadvertently produces feminist outcomes (e.g., by creating a feminist mobilization in response to its actions), but we would not want to call such an organization "feminist."

2. In 1975, for instance, a socialist feminist conference was held in Yellow Springs, Ohio, even as many socialist feminist organizations were dissolving. Although the conference was divisive, activists from Chicago whom I interviewed recalled that Helen Rodriguez-Trias spoke about sterilization abuse at the conference and that her speech was an important impetus for the growth of the Committee to End Sterilization Abuse (CESA). The issue became quite important to the women's health movement in the mid-1970s and was linked to the abortion issue, particularly through the founding of the Committee for Abortion Rights and against Sterilization Abuse (CARASA) in 1977.

3. The goals of the National Women's Health Network and those of the Reproductive Rights National Network seem equally radical. The NWHN focuses more narrowly on the health care system, however, and this may also be a key to its success in that it does not have the same tactical dilemmas as R2N2 and WORC. Similarly, the National Women's Music Festival has radical goals but focuses on the task of putting on a festival.

Bibliography

Addelson, Katherine Pyne. 1988. "Moral Revolution." *Radical America* 22 (5): 36–43.

Baker, Andrea J. 1986. "The Problem of Authority in Radical Movement Groups: A Case Study of Lesbian-Feminist Organization." In *Leaders and Followers: Challengers for the Future*, ed. L. A. Zurcher, 135–55. Greenwich, Conn.: JAI Press.

Bart, Pauline. 1987. "Seizing the Means of Reproduction: An Illegal Feminist Abortion Collective—How and Why it Worked." *Qualitative Sociology* 10(4): 339–57.

Black, Naomi. 1989. *Social Feminism.* Ithaca, N.Y.: Cornell University Press.

Blakely, Mary Kay. 1990. "Remembering Jane." *New York Times Magazine*, September 23.

Breines, Wini. 1989. *Community and Organization in the New Left: The Great Refusal.* Rev. ed. New Brunswick, N.J., Rutgers University Press.

Buechler, Steven M. 1990a. "Conceptualizing Radicalism and Transformation in Social Movements: The Case of the Woman Suffrage Movement." *Perspectives on Social Problems* 2: 105–18.

———. 1990b. *Women's Movements in the United States: Women's Suffrage, Equal Rights, and Beyond.* New Brunswick, N.J.: Rutgers University Press.

Burstein, Paul, Rachel Einwohner, and Jocelyn Hollander. 1991. "Political Movements and Their Consequences: Lessons from the U.S. Experience." Paper presented at the annual meetings of the American Sociological Association, Cincinnati, Ohio.

Carden, Maren Lockwood. 1977. *Feminism in the Mid-1970s: The Non-Establishment, the Establishment, and the Future.* Report to the Ford Foundation. New York: Ford Foundation.

Costain, Anne N. 1988. "Representing Women: The Transition from Social Movement to Interest Group" (revised). In *Women, Power, and Policy: Toward the Year 2000*, 2d ed., ed. Ellen Boneparth and Emily Stoper, 26–47. New York: Pergamon Press.

Echols, Alice. 1989. *Daring to Be Bad: Radical Feminism in America, 1967–1975.* Minneapolis: University of Minnesota Press.

Eder, Donna, Suzanne Staggenborg, and Lori Sudderth. 1995. "The National Women's Music Festival, Collective Identity and Diversity in a Lesbian-Feminist Community." *Journal of Contemporary Ethnography* 23 (January):485–515.

Epstein, Barbara. 1991. *Political Protest and Cultural Revolution: Nonviolent Direct Action in the 1970s and 1980s.* Berkeley: University of California Press.

Ferree, Myra Marx, and Beth B. Hess. 1985. *Controversy and Coalition: The New Feminist Movement.* Boston: Twayne.

Fraser, Arvonne S. 1983. "Insiders and Outsiders: Women in the Political Arena." In *Women in Washington: Advocates for Public Policy*, ed. Irene Tinker, 120–39. Beverly Hills, Calif.: Sage.

Freeman, Jo. 1972. "The Tyranny of Structurelessness." *The Second Wave* 2 (1): 20. Rpt. in *Berkeley Journal of Sociology* 17 (1972–73): 155–64; *Radical Feminism*, ed. Anne Koedt, Ellen Levine, and Anita Rapone (New York: Quadrangle Books, 1973), 285; *Women in Politics*, ed. Jane Jaquette (New York: Wiley, 1974), 202–14. Rev. in *Ms.*, July 1973, p. 76.

———. 1975. *The Politics of Women's Liberation: A Case Study of an Emerging Social Movement and Its Relation to the Policy Process.* New York: David McKay.

Gamson, William A. 1990. *The Strategy of Social Protest.* Homewood, Ill.: Dorsey Press, 1975; 2d ed., Belmont, Calif.: Wadsworth.

Gelb, Joyce, and Marion Lief Palley, eds. 1987. *Women and Public Policies.* Rev. ed. Princeton, N.J.: Princeton University Press.

Gusfield, Joseph R. 1981. "Social Movements and Social Change: Perspectives of Linearity and Fluidity." *Social Movements, Conflict, and Change* 4: 317–39.

Hansen, Karen V. 1986. "The Women's Unions and the Search for a Political Identity." *Socialist Review* 16 (2): 67–95.

Kitschelt, Herbert P. 1986. "Political Opportunity Structures and Political Protest: Anti Nuclear Movements in Four Democracies." *British Journal of Political Science* 16: 57–85.

McAdam, Doug. 1988. *Freedom Summer.* New York: Oxford University Press.

McCarthy, John D., and Mayer N. Zald. 1973. *The Trend of Social Movements in America: Professionalization and Resource Mobilization.* Morristown, N.J.: General Learning Press.

———. 1977. "Resource Mobilization and Social Movements: A Partial Theory." *American Journal of Sociology* 82 (6): 1212–41.

Mansbridge, Jane J. 1973. "Time, Emotion, and Inequality: Three Problems of Participatory Groups." *Journal of Applied Behavioral Science* 9: 351–68.

Martin, Patricia Yancey. 1990. "Rethinking Feminist Organizations." *Gender & Society* 4: 182–206.

Miller, James. 1987. *"Democracy Is in the Streets": From Port Huron to the Siege of Chicago.* New York: Simon & Schuster.

Morris, Aldon. 1984. *The Origins of the Civil Rights Movement: Black Communities Organizing for Change.* New York: Free Press.

Mueller, Carol McClurg. 1987. "Collective Consciousness, Identity Transformation, and the Rise of Women in Public Office in the United States." In *The Women's Movements in the United States and Western Europe: Consciousness, Political Opportunity, and Public Policy,* ed. Mary Fainsod Katzenstein and Carol McClurg Mueller, 89–108. Philadelphia: Temple University Press.

Riger, Stephanie. 1984. "Vehicles for Empowerment: The Case of Feminist Movement Organizations." In *Studies in Empowerment: Steps Toward Understanding and Action,* ed. J. Rappaport, C. Smith, and R. Hess, 99–117. New York: Haworth Press.

Rothschild, Mathew. 1989. "Third Party Time?" *The Progressive* 53 (10): 20–25.

Rothstein, Vivian, and Naomi Weisstein. 1972. "Chicago Women's Liberation Union." *Women: A Journal of Liberation* 2 (4): 2–9.

Rupp, Leila J., and Verta Taylor. 1987. *Survival in the Doldrums: The American Women's Rights Movement, 1945 to the 1960s.* New York: Oxford University Press.

Schumaker, Paul. 1975. "Policy Responsiveness to Protest Group Demands." *Journal of Politics* 37: 488–521.

Snyder, David, and William R. Kelly. 1979. "Strategies for Investigating Violence and Social Change." In *The Dynamics of Social Movements,* ed. Mayer N. Zald and John D. McCarthy, 212–37. Cambridge, Mass.: Winthrop.

Staggenborg, Suzanne. 1989. "Stability and Innovation in the Women's Movement: A Comparison of Two Movement Organizations." *Social Problems* 36 (1): 75–92.

———. 1991. *The Pro-Choice Movement: Organization and Activism in the Abortion Conflict.* New York: Oxford University Press.

Taylor, Verta. 1989. "The Future of Feminism: A Social Movement Analysis." In *Feminist Frontiers II,* ed. Laurel Richardson and Verta Taylor, 473–90. New York: Random House.

Tilly, Charles. 1978. *From Mobilization to Revolution.* Reading, Mass.: Addison-Wesley.

Tong, Rosemary. 1989. *Feminist Thought.* Boulder, Colo.: Westview Press.

Van Gelder, Lindsy. 1991. "The Jane Collective: Seizing Control." *Ms.*, September–October, pp. 83–85.

RIGHT-WING POPULISM IN AMERICA

CHIP BERLET AND MATTHEW N. LYONS

Right-wing politics in the United States has taken many forms since the end of the Cold War. The rise of the armed citizens militias accompanied electoral support for Patrick Buchanan's xenophobic economic nationalism. Christian evangelical groups at times dominated the Republican Party while the Promise Keepers filled stadiums with praying men. Major politicians denounced undocumented immigrants and poor single mothers while libertarian antigovernment attitudes flourished. On talk radio, discussions of black helicopters, secret teams, and sinister elites envisioned a massive global conspiracy. Some boldly asserted that President Clinton assisted drug smugglers, ran a hit squad that killed his political enemies, and covered up the assassination of his aide Vincent Foster. In 1995 a powerful homemade bomb—delivered in a rental truck driven by a fresh-faced American neonazi named Timothy McVeigh—destroyed the Murrah Federal Building in Oklahoma City. The blast killed 167 persons (including 19 children in an onsite day care center), and injured over 650 more. One rescue worker died. Violence from the Far Right continued, targeting abortion providers, people of color, gay men and lesbians, and Jews.

. . . [W]e show how all of these phenomena involve some form of right-wing populism—a concept we think is crucial to understanding not just the U.S. political Right, but also our history as a nation. Right-wing populist movements often defy conventional explanations of "extremism" because they combine attacks on socially oppressed groups with grassroots mass mobilization and distorted forms of antielitism based on scapegoating. . . .

One of the most visible right-wing populist movements from the mid-1990s to the present has been the armed citizens militias. As the militant cutting edge of a much larger "Patriot" movement, the militias collected weapons, conducted paramilitary training, advocated armed self-defense against what they saw as an increasingly repressive federal government, and warned of a vast elite conspiracy to subject the United States to a tyrannical "New World Order."[1]

Militias and Patriot groups were complicated—bringing together hardcore neonazis with a much wider array of right-wing antigovernment activists. The movement was pervaded by conspiracy theories historically rooted in antisemitism, and by arcane constitutional doctrines that implicitly rejected women's suffrage, citizenship rights for people of color, and the abolition of slavery. Yet many supporters seemed unaware of (or indifferent to) the history or politics of these oppressive ideas. Most of the militias disavowed ethnic bigotry, and some of them included a handful of Jews and people of color as members. Here was a movement that seemingly blurred the line between hate ideology and inclusiveness, and that mixed reactionary scapegoating with progressive-sounding attacks on economic injustice, political elitism, and government repression.

As is true for the militias, members of other recent right-wing populist movements have often spoken or acted in ways that challenged outsiders' expectations. Despite a history of close collaboration between law enforcement agencies and paramilitary rightists, sections of the neonazi–Klan movement undertook armed combat against the U.S. government beginning in the 1980s. Although the Right has regularly championed private enterprise and business interests, ultraconservative leader Patrick Buchanan denounced multinational corporations and "unfettered capitalism." Despite its traditional superpatriotism, large sections of the Right opposed the U.S.-led war on Iraq in 1990–1991, and the U.S.-led bombing of Yugoslavia in 1999. Although the Christian Right was virulently antifeminist and staunchly Eurocentric, major sections of that movement urged women to become politically active and to develop leadership skills, or made genuine efforts to build alliances with conservative Black, Latino, and Asian organizations.

This type of political complexity is not new. We . . . place the Christian Right, the Buchananites, and the militias in a long line of right-wing populist movements such as Father Coughlin's movement in the 1930s, the anti-Chinese crusade of the 1880s, and the Ku Klux Klan. Right-wing populist movements often borrow political slogans, tactics, and forms of organization from the Left, but harness them to rightist goals. They attract people who often have genuine grievances against elites, but channel such resentments in ways that reinforce social, cultural, political, or economic power and privilege.

Historically, right-wing populist movements have reflected the interests of two different kinds of social groups, often in combination:

1. Middle-level groups in the social hierarchy, notably middle- and working-class Whites, who have a stake in traditional social privilege but resent the power of upper-class elites over them, and,
2. "Outsider" factions of the elite itself, who sometimes use distorted forms of antielitism as part of their own bid for greater power.

The original Ku Klux Klan of the late 1860s, for example, represented an alliance between some lower- and middle-class southern Whites (outraged that Black emancipation and Reconstruction had eroded their social privilege), and southern planters (who sought to win back some of the power they had lost to northern capitalists in the Civil War). The Klan combined racist terrorism against Black people and their allies with demagogic antielite rhetoric about northern "military despotism."

While the original Klan is generally remembered today as an "extremist" movement, its politics reflected traditions considered mainstream. For example, Jacksonianism in the early nineteenth century (on which the modern-day Democratic Party is founded), is typically thought of as a progressive reform movement that championed "the common man" and helped to democratize the U.S. political system. Yet the Jacksonian political reforms, such as Pennsylvania's 1838 Constitution, disenfranchised Black men while giving the vote to poor White men. The Jacksonians spearheaded the murderous forced expulsion of American Indians, as in the 1838 Trail of Tears, when thousands of Cherokees died after being driven from their homes at gunpoint. And the Jacksonians denounced "the money power" of federal central banking as an evil conspiracy, yet upheld class inequality. Jacksonianism represented an alliance between lower-class Whites and certain factions of the elite. When the Klan emerged a few years later as the first truly right-wing populist movement, its constituency, doctrine, and rhetoric were largely Jacksonian.

Right-wing populist movements are subject to the same basic dynamics as other social movements, and their members are, for the most part, average people motivated by a combination of material and ideological grievances and aspirations. Despite widespread popular rhetoric, it is neither accurate nor useful to portray right-wing populists as a "lunatic fringe" of marginal "extremists." Right-wing populists are dangerous not because they are crazy irrational zealots—but because they are not. These people may be our neighbors, our coworkers, and our relatives.

■ ■ ■ ■

Populism

There is much confusion over the term *populism.* Margaret Canovan, in one of the few in-depth studies of the subject, mapped populism into two main branches—agrarian and political—with seven overlapping subcategories.[2] Although we do not use her typology, it shows how many different kinds of political movements and phenomena have been labeled as populist. Canovan's categories look like this:

Agrarian populism includes:

- Commodity farmer movements with radical economic agendas such as the U.S. People's Party of the late 1800s.
- Subsistence peasant movements such as eastern Europe's Green Rising movement after World War I.
- Intellectuals who wistfully romanticize hard-working farmers and peasants and build

radical agrarian movements like the late-nineteenth-century Russian narodniki or the U.S. back-to-the-land movement in the 1960s.

Political populism includes:

- Populist democracy, including calls for more political participation, such as the use of referenda; recent examples include the general perspective of columnists Jim Hightower and Molly Ivins.
- Politicians' populism marked by vague appeals for "the people" to build a unified coalition such as used by Ross Perot in his presidential campaigns in the 1990s.
- Reactionary populism such as the White backlash against civil rights that was harvested by George Wallace in the 1960s and 1970s and reseeded to some extent by Patrick Buchanan in the 1990s.
- Populist dictatorship such as that established by Juan Peron in Argentina in 1945–1955 or envisioned by some U.S. neonazi groups.

Across this wide range of categories there are only two universal elements, Canovan argues: all forms of populism "involve some kind of exaltation of and appeal to 'the people,' and all are in one sense or another antielitist."[3] We take these two elements—celebration of "the people" plus some form of antielitism—as a working definition of populism. A populist movement—as opposed, for example, to one-shot populist appeals in an election campaign—uses populist themes to mobilize a mass constituency as a sustained political or social force. Our discussion of populism will focus mainly on populist movements.

Michael Kazin calls populism a style of organizing.[4] Populist movements can be on the right, the left, or in the center. They can be egalitarian or authoritarian, and can rely on decentralized networks or a charismatic leader. They can advocate new social and political relations or romanticize the past. Especially important for our purposes, populist movements can promote forms of antielitism that target either genuine structures of oppression or scapegoats alleged to be part of a secret conspiracy. And they can define "the people" in ways that are inclusive and challenge traditional hierarchies, or in ways that silence or demonize oppressed groups.

Repressive Populism and Right-Wing Populism

We use the term *repressive populist movement* to describe a populist movement that combines antielite scapegoating . . . with efforts to maintain or intensify systems of social privilege and power. Repressive populist movements are fueled in large part by people's grievances against their own oppression but they deflect popular discontent away from positive social change by targeting only small sections of the elite or groups falsely identified with the elite, and especially by channeling most anger against oppressed or marginalized groups that offer more vulnerable targets.

Right-wing populist movements are a subset of repressive populist movements. A *right-wing populist movement*, as we use the term, is a repressive populist movement motivated or defined centrally by a backlash against liberation movements, social reform, or revolution. This does not mean that right-wing populism's goals are only defensive or reactive, but rather that its growth is fueled in a central way by fears of the Left and its political gains. The first U.S. populist movement we would unequivocally describe as right wing was the Reconstruction-era Ku Klux Klan, which was a counterrevolutionary backlash against the overthrow of slavery and Black people's mass mobilization and empowerment in the post-Civil War South. Earlier repressive populist movements paved the way for right-wing populism, but did not have this same backlash quality as a central feature.

The term "right wing" requires some attention. We do not accept the conventional definition of right wing as meaning "conservative or reactionary," because many of the movements we consider right-wing populist have advocated some form of social change, not simply preserving or restoring old institutions and relations. Conventional classifications of populist movements on a right–left spectrum are often misleading as well. . . .

Sociologist Sara Diamond has offered a simple but nuanced definition: "To be right-wing means to support the state in its capacity as *enforcer* of order and to oppose the state as *distributor* of wealth and power downward and more equitably in society."[5] This accurately describes many movements generally regarded as rightist, and has the advantage of cutting through claims that the Right consistently opposes "big government." But Diamond's definition does not cover all cases. Some rightist movements, such as Father Coughlin's Social Justice movement in the 1930s and George Wallace's American Independent Party in the 1960s, have advocated downward redistribution of wealth and power—not to everyone, but to certain groups below the elite. And some right-wing movements, such as the Ku Klux Klan of the late 1860s or various Patriot/militia groups in the 1990s, have rejected the state altogether and have sought to overthrow it, in the process rejecting and disrupting the state's order–enforcement role.

■ ■ ■ ■

Characteristics of Right-Wing Populism

Producerism

One of the staples of repressive and right-wing populist ideology has been *producerism*, a doctrine that champions the so-called producers in society against both "unproductive" elites and subordinate groups defined as lazy or immoral. The Jacksonians were the first major U.S. movement to rely on producerism. Their vision of the producing classes included White farmers, laborers, artisans, slave-owning planters, and "productive" entrepreneurs; it excluded bankers, speculators, monopolists—and people of color. In this way, producerism bolstered White supremacy, blurred actual class divisions, and embraced some elite groups while scapegoating others.

After the Jacksonian era, producerism was a central tenet of the anti-Chinese crusade in the late nineteenth century. Kazin points out that as it developed in the nineteenth century,

> the romance of producerism had a cultural blind spot; it left unchallenged strong prejudices toward not just African-Americans but also toward recent immigrants who had not learned or would not employ the language and rituals of this variant of the civic religion. . . . Even those native-born activists who reached out to immigrant laborers assumed that men of Anglo-American origins had invented political democracy, prideful work habits, and well-governed communities of the middling classes.[6]

In the 1920s industrial philosophy of Henry Ford, and Father Coughlin's fascist doctrine in the 1930s, producerism fused with antisemitic attacks against "parasitic" Jews. Producerism, with its baggage of prejudice, remains today the most common populist narrative on the right, and it facilitates the use of demonization and scapegoating as political tools.[7]

Demonization and Scapegoating

Gunning down children in a Jewish community center in Los Angeles makes sense if you think Jews run the world and are thus responsible for all that is wrong in the country as a whole and your life in particular. Shooting a postal worker who is a person of color makes sense if you think lazy people of color are conspiring with the Jewish-controlled Zionist Occupational Government to rob the hardworking taxpayer. The gunman accused of committing both these acts in California in 1999 is Buford O'Neal Furrow, Jr. He emerged from a neonazi milieu where Christian Identity is the dominant religious philosophy. Christian Identity argues that Jews are in league with Satan and that Blacks and other people of color are subhuman. The battle of Armageddon prophesied in the Bible is envisioned by Christian identity as a race war. This is an extreme example of demonization, but it is hardly new. An earlier example happened during the depression of 1837–1843 when there was a wave of attacks against Catholic immigrants to the United States. Catholics were demonized in popular culture as lazy and treacherous and the resulting scapegoating generated violence. Jean Hardisty argues that the contemporary Right has frequently relied on "mobilizing resentment" as an organizing process.[8]

Demonization of an enemy often begins with marginalization, the ideological process in which targeted individuals or groups are placed outside the circle of wholesome mainstream society through political propaganda and age-old prejudice. This creates an us–them or good–bad dynamic of dualism, which acknowledges no complexity or nuance and forecloses meaningful civil debate or practical political compromise.

The next step is objectification or dehumanization, the process of negatively labeling a person or group of people so they become perceived more as objects than as real people. Dehumanization often is associated with the belief that a particular group of people is inferior or threatening. The final step is demonization; the person or group is framed as totally malevolent, sinful, and evil. It is easier to rationalize stereotyping, prejudice, discrimination, scapegoating and even violence against those who are dehumanized or demonized.[9]

▪ ▪ ▪ ▪

We use the term *scapegoating* to describe the social process whereby the hostility and grievances of an angry, frustrated group are directed away from the real causes of a social problem onto a target group demonized as malevolent wrongdoers. The scapegoat bears the blame, while the scapegoaters feel a sense of righteousness and increased unity. The social problem may be real or imaginary, the grievances legitimate or illegitimate, and members of the targeted group may be wholly innocent or partly culpable. What matters is that the scapegoats are wrongfully stereotyped as all sharing the same negative trait, or are singled out for blame while other major culprits are let off the hook.[10]

Scapegoating often targets socially disempowered or marginalized groups. At the same time, the scapegoat is often portrayed as powerful or privileged. In this way, scapegoating feeds on people's anger about their own disempowerment, but diverts this anger away from the real systems of power and oppression. A certain level of scapegoating is endemic in most societies, but it more readily becomes an important political force in times of social competition or upheaval. At such times, especially, scapegoating can be an effective way to mobilize mass support and activism during a struggle for power.

Conspiracism

Conspiracism is a particular narrative form of scapegoating that frames the enemy as part of a vast insidious plot against the common good, while it valorizes the scapegoater as a hero for sounding the alarm. Like other forms of scapegoating, conspiracism often, though not always, targets oppressed or stigmatized groups. In many cases, conspiracism uses coded language to mask ethnic or racial bigotry, for example, attacking the Federal Reserve in ways that evoke common stereotypes about "Jewish bankers." Far-right groups have often used such conspiracy theories as an opening wedge for more explicit hate ideology.

▪ ▪ ▪ ▪

Mark Fenster describes how broader groups of people who are not necessarily caught up in far-right bigotry can still use conspiracism to construct a theory of power that fails to recognize how real power relations work in modern society. He argues that the phenomenon "should not be dismissed and analyzed simply as pathology," and suggests that "conspiracy theory and the contemporary practices of populist politics require a cultural analysis that can complement an ideological and empirical 'debunking.' "

According to Fenster,

> just because overarching conspiracy theories are wrong does not mean that they are not on to something. Specifically, they ideologically address real structural inequities, and constitute a response to a withering civil society and the concentration of the ownership of the means of production, which together leave the political subject without the ability to be recognized or to signify in the public realm.[11]

Certainly, real conspiracies exist: plotting in secret is one of the ways in which power is exercised (and resisted). The U.S. political scene has been littered with examples of illegal political, corporate, and government conspiracies such as Watergate, the FBI's Counterintelligence Program (COINTELPRO) of spying and dirty tricks against dissidents, the Iran–Contra scandal, and the systematic looting of the savings and loan industry. But as Bruce Cumings argues,

> if conspiracies exist, they rarely move history; they make a difference at the

> margins from time to time, but with the unforeseen consequences of a logic outside the control of their authors: and this is what is wrong with "conspiracy theory." History is moved by the broad forces and large structures of human collectivities.[12]

Conspiracism differs in several ways from legitimate efforts to expose secret plots. First, the conspiracist worldview assigns tiny cabals of evildoers a superhuman power to control events; it regards such plots as the major motor of history. Conspiracism blames individualized and subjective forces for political, economic, and social problems rather than analyzing conflict in terms of systems, institutions, and structures of power.

Second, conspiracism tends to frame social conflict in terms of a transcendant struggle between Good and Evil that reflects the influence of the apocalyptic paradigm.

Third, in its efforts to trace all wrongdoing to one vast plot, conspiracism plays fast and loose with the facts. While conspiracy theorists often start with a grain of truth and "document" their claims exhaustively, they make leaps of logic in analyzing evidence, such as seeing guilt by association or treating allegations as proven fact.[13]

Conspiracist attacks can be directed either "upward" or "downward." *Antielite conspiracism* (or *antielite scapegoating*) targets groups seen as sinister elites abusing their power from above. *Countersubversive scapegoating* targets groups portrayed as subversives trying to overturn the established order from below or from within.

Antielite conspiracism has deep roots in U.S. political culture. In some versions, antielite scapegoating attacks groups who do not really dominate society (such as Jews or Catholics); in other cases, it targets subgroups within the elite power structure (such as bankers, the Trilateral Commission, the Central Intelligence Agency, or the World Trade Organization). What these versions share, and what especially defines antielite conspiracism, is that the scapegoat is seen as a subjective, alien force that distorts the normal workings of society. Thus, despite its "radical" veneer, antielite conspiracism shares the mainstream assumptions that the United States is fundamentally democratic, and that any injustice results from selfish special interest groups, not from underlying systems of power and oppression.

U.S. elites, meanwhile, have long propagated fears of subversive conspiracies: bloodthirsty slaves plotting mass murder, disloyal immigrants undermining U.S. institutions, labor unionists spreading criminal anarchy, or godless Reds bent on global dictatorship. Whether cynical constructs or projections of the elite's own nightmares, such images have been used to demonize antioppression struggles by playing on people's fears of disorder, violence, invasion, and moral collapse.

As Frank J. Donner noted, propaganda based on a myth of the enemy "other" has helped to justify antidemocratic activities by state security forces and their allies, including spying, harassment, judicial persecution, forced removal, and physical violence. And, Donner argued, "In a period of social and economic change during which traditional institutions are under the greatest strain, the need for the myth is especially strong as a means of transferring blame, an outlet for the despair [people] face when normal channels of protest and change are closed."[14] In these ways, countersubversive scapegoating has played an important role in this country's system of social control, bolstering elite privilege and power.

Apocalyptic Narratives and Millennial Visions

The poisoned fruit of conspiracist scapegoating is baked into the American apple pie, and its ingredients include destructive versions of apocalyptic fears and millennialist expectations. This is true whether we are studying Christian-based right-wing movements consciously influenced by biblical prophecy, or more secularized right-wing movements for which Bible-based apocalypticism and millennialism have faded into unconscious—yet still influential—metaphors.[15]

Apocalypticism—the anticipation of a righteous struggle against evil conspiracies—has influenced social and political movements throughout U.S. history.[16] Early Christian settlers saw America as a battlefield for a prophetic struggle between good and evil. Starting in the 1620s, witch hunts swept New England for a century.[17] Many of the insurgent colonists who brought about the American Revolution invoked apocalyptic and millennial themes, as did the Antimasons and Jacksonians who denounced banks in the 1830s. Apocalypticism infused the evangelical Protestant revival that contributed to the Ku Klux Klan's rise in the 1920s and influenced both fascist and nonfascist rightists during the Great Depression of the 1930s. Today, apocalypticism remains a central narrative in our nation's religious, secular, political, and cultural discourse.[18] Numerous authors have noted that the contemporary Christian Right is significantly motivated and mobilized by apocalyptic and millennialist themes.[19] Yet as Richard Landes observes, apocalyptic activities rarely "receive more than a passing mention in 'mainstream' analyses."[20]

In its generic sense, the word apocalypse has come to mean the belief in an approaching confrontation, cataclysmic event, or transformation of epochal proportion, about which a select few have forewarning so they can make appropriate preparations. Those who believe in a coming apocalypse might be optimistic about the outcome of the apocalyptic moment, anticipating a chance for positive transformational change; or they might be pessimistic, anticipating a doomsday; or they might anticipate a period of violence or chaos with an uncertain outcome.[21] Christian apocalyptic fervor appears, often at seemingly random dates, throughout Western history.[22] A major U.S. episode of Christian millennialist fervor occurred among the Millerites in the 1840s, some of whom sold their worldly belongings and pilgrimaged to a mountaintop to experience the Rapture that they hoped in vain would sweep them up into God's protective embrace.[23] The apocalyptic tradition also exists in Judaism, Islam, and other religions.[24]

Apocalypticism is the principal source for what Richard Hofstadter called the "paranoid style" in American politics. According to Damian Thompson:

> Richard Hofstadter was right to emphasise the startling affinities between the paranoid style and apocalyptic belief—the demonisation of opponents, the sense of time running out, and so on. But he stopped short of making a more direct connection between the two. He did not consider the possibility that the paranoia he identified actually derived from apocalyptic belief.[25]

The process of demonization, a consistent factor in scapegoating, takes on special features during periods of apocalyptic fear or millennial expectation. Apocalyptic thinking meshes readily with producerism, since the good (and often Godly) people are counterposed against the traitorous elites and their lazy and sinful allies.

Millennialism is a specific form of apocalyptic expectation.[26] Most contemporary Christian fundamentalists believe that when Christ returns, he will reign for a period of 1,000 years—a millennium. Yet not all contemporary Christians promote apocalyptic demonization. Within Christianity, there are two competing views of how to interpret the apocalyptic and millennial themes in the Bible, especially the book of Revelation. One view identifies evil with specific persons and groups, seeking to identify those in league with the Devil. A more optimistic form of interpreting apocalyptic prophecy is promoted by those Christians who see evil in the will to dominate and oppress.[27] Apocalyptic thinking, in this case, seeks justice for the poor and weak. The two interpretations represent a deep division within Christianity. The dangerous form of millennialism comes not from Christianity per se, but from Christians who combine biblical literalism, apocalyptic timetables, demonization, and oppressive prejudices.

Christian apocalypticism and millennialism are based on many sources in the Bible, including the Old Testament books of Daniel and Ezekiel, and the New Testament Gospel of Matthew. The primary biblical source, however, is the book of Revelation, the last book of the Christian New Testament. Many Christians on the political Right who are looking for the "signs of the End Times" adopt a particular demonizing way of interpreting prophecy in the book of Revelation.

In this view, a powerful and charismatic agent of the Devil—the Antichrist—comes to earth along with his ally—the False Prophet. They appear disguised in the form of widely respected political and religious leaders. Promising peace and prosperity, these leaders launch a popular campaign to build a one-world government and a one-world religion. Many Christians are fooled, but a few recognize that these leaders are the prophesized Antichrist and the False Prophet, and thus actually Satanic traitors. Agents of the Antichrist try to force devout Christians to accept the Mark of the Beast (sometimes the number 666) which would mean they reject Christ. A wave of political and religious repression sweeps the world, with devout Christians rounded up and persecuted for their beliefs. Christians with this view read the book of Revelation as a warning about a government conspiracy and betrayal by trusted political and religious leaders in the End Times. A secular version of this narrative appears in conspiracy theories about liberal collectivists building a global new world order through the United Nations.

These apocalyptic themes buttress the producerist narrative in right-wing populist movements. This is the narrative of Pat Robertson's *700 Club* TV broadcasts, the newsletter of Beverly LaHaye's Concerned Women for America, and scores of other Christian Right media outlets. As the year 2000 approached a number of apocalyptic and millennial social movements surged in excitement and activism. Some were religious, such as the Promise Keepers, some were secular, such as the armed militias. These social movements sought to influence public policy, social conduct, and cultural attitudes, sometimes coming into conflict with the established order and state power.

Social Movements and Social Structures

While they may express apocalyptic fervor or millennialist expectation, mass political and social movements are composed of people motivated by a sense of grievance—legitimate or illegimate—who mobilize to seek redress of their grievances through a variety of methods often including, but seldom limited to, the electoral process.[28] These grievances flow from social, cultural, and economic tensions that combine and vary over time. Most participants in these groups and movements try to organize others using rational strategies and tactics—even if their claims seem bizarre or conspiracist and their goals are illegitimate and prejudiced—and in defense of disproportionate access to power, wealth, and privilege.[29]

Our view of social movements is hardly unique. As Christian Smith observes,

> The 1970s saw a major break in the social-movement literature with earlier theories—e.g., mass society, collective behavior, status discontent, and relative deprivation theories—that emphasized the irrational and emotional nature of social movements. . . . There was at the time a decisive pendulum-swing away from these "classical" theories toward the view of social movements as rational, strategically calculating, politically instrumental phenomena.[30]

While these newer and more complex social movement theories have shaped some popular discussions of liberal and radical social change movements, they have been less successful in changing the public discourse about right-wing movements.

We see two common pitfalls in contemporary discussions of right-wing populist movements. On one side, many liberals and moderate conservatives routinely portray such movements as paranoid fringe phenomena fundamentally at odds with the political mainstream. A standard premise is that the U.S. political system has an essence of democracy and freedom—a vital center of pragmatism, rationality, and tolerance—but that this essence is threatened by extremists from the left and right. This *centrist/extremist* model, as we call it, obscures the rational choices and partially legitimate grievances that help to fuel right-wing populist movements, and hides the fact that right-wing bigotry and scapegoating are firmly rooted in the mainstream social and political order. Centrist/extremist theory is the dominant model used by government agencies, mass media, and major human relations groups to portray right-wing movements. It is based to a large degree on the pessimistic studies of populism by Daniel Bell, Seymour Martin Lipset, Earl Raab, and others.

Centrist/extremist theory does not stand up to the field work done by social scientists who have studied members of right-wing (and left-wing) movements and groups and found them no more or less mentally unbalanced, politically dysfunctional, or "fringe" than their neighbors.[31] Nor does centrist/extremist theory allow us to recognize the frequent direct linkages—ideological, organizational, and economic—between right-wing and mainstream political forces.

Centrist/extremist theory fosters a dangerous complacency about mainstream politics and institutions. It has often been used to rally support for moderate versions of oppressive politics—for example, to attack Republicans and bolster the Democratic Party, even as Democratic leaders embrace traditionally right-wing positions. In addition, because it logically relies on government crackdowns to protect us from the "irrational zealots," centrist/extremist theory fuels the growth of state repression, and can serve as a rationale for aiding repressive government surveillance operations.[32]

On the other side of the coin, some left-leaning people have portrayed sections of the insurgent Right, especially the militias, as positive expressions of grassroots discontent, and as legitimate allies against the state and the elite.[33] In addition, some liberals and leftists have echoed right-wing conspiracy theories about the U.S. government and big business.[34] These positions romanticize populist activism and overlook the immediate and long-term dangers posed by right-wing movements. They also help blur the dividing line between an analysis of systemic and institutionalized oppression and conspiracist scapegoating, which is often rooted in and facilitates ethnic bigotry.

In contrast to both centrist/extremist doctrine and the left-romanticist view, we see right-wing populist movements as having a complex relationship with the established power structure: both rooted in it and distinct from it, opposing it in some ways yet bolstering it in others. Such movements often have close links with economic and political elites, yet they are not simply ruling-class puppets, but rather autonomous social forces with their own agendas and mass appeal. Right-wing populist movements often help to strengthen social oppression, yet they are themselves fueled by popular discontent at elite privilege and power.

The contradictions within right-wing populism point to tensions and complexities in the larger social order. We describe the U.S. political system as *pluralist*, meaning that a certain range of political debate and conflict between different political organizations, factions, and tendencies is accepted as legitimate, and civil liberties are protected to a degree. Yet we do not believe that this system has lived up to its image as a democracy, because most political and economic power is held by a tiny wealthy elite.[35] In our view, class hierarchy, racial and national oppression, male dominance, and other systems of social control have always been central to U.S. society.

At the same time, the social power structure is not divided neatly between oppressors and oppressed. Because there are many different intersecting lines of power, the majority of people occupy contradictory positions in society: they are oppressed in some ways but hold varying degrees of relative privilege in other ways. Such privilege brings social, political, or economic benefits that give many people a tangible stake in the very system that keeps them down. Even elite forces, while sharing basic interests, are internally divided. As business conflict theorists have argued, factional divisions within the elite play a major role in political life.[36] In some situations, both intraelite conflict and people's contradictory status can foster a kind of double-edged politics: a dissatisfaction with the people in charge, coupled with a desire to preserve or strengthen certain social inequalities. This double-edged politics often finds expression in repressive populist movements.

Mapping the Right

Since the 1970s, the political center of gravity in the United States has moved dramatically to the right. This shift is often identified with the Republican Party of Ronald Reagan and Newt Gingrich, but the Democratic Party, too, has largely embraced traditional right-wing positions regarding "welfare reform," "crime," "illegal aliens," and a host of other issues. The right turn has been driven by both elite policymakers and a range of mass-based political movements, from the electoral activism of the Christian Coalition to the insurrectionism of citizen militias.

We use various terms to describe specific gradations of right-wing politics, populist and otherwise. The *Reactionary Right* seeks to turn the clock back toward an idealized past. *Conservatism* emphasizes stability and order, and generally some combination of cultural traditionalism and "free-market" economics. *Ultraconservatism* goes beyond the conservative defense of the established order while stopping short of demands to fully eliminate pluralist institutions. The *Christian Right* is motivated by religious interpretations of cultural, social, and economic issues, and has branches that otherwise fall into all the other sectors of the Right, including the Hard Right and the Far Right.

The *Hard Right* takes an inflexible approach to politics and rejects pluralistic discourse in principle or in practice. Hard rightists may be either elitist or mass activist in their organizing, and may include both ultraconservatives and far rightists. The *Far Right* squarely rejects the existing political system, and pluralist institutions generally, in favor of some form of authoritarianism.

Fascism, in our usage, is the most virulent form of far-right populism. Fascism glorifies national, racial, or cultural unity and collective rebirth while seeking to purge imagined enemies, and attacks both revolutionary socialism and liberal pluralism in favor of militarized, totalitarian mass politics.[37] There are many definitions of fascism, and the term is often misused. Fascist movements are a product of the twentieth century, and first crystallized in Europe in response to the Bolshevik Revolution and the devastation of World War I. In the United States, fascist movements have blended European ideological imports with homegrown repressive populist traditions, and first became a significant political force during the Great Depression of the 1930s.

Today, in addition to the openly fascist organizations of the neonazi Right, fascist groupings (and more broadly, fascist tendencies) play a significant role in larger right-wing populist movements. Certain fascistic tendencies can be detected in the militias, the Buchananites, and in the most militant authoritarian sectors of the Christian Right.

Although the role of fascism in right-wing movements needs to be addressed, it is frequently overstated, and it would be a serious mistake to regard a "fascist takeover" as the main threat of right-wing populism. The danger associated with right-wing populism comes not only from its real or potential bids for power, or even from its day-to-day violence, bigotry, and scapegoating, but also from its interactions with other political forces and with the government.

The 1990s saw a dangerous interplay, for example, between right-wing paramilitarism and state repression. The government's response to the militias following the 1995 Oklahoma City bombing made it clear that anti-democratic initiatives do not only come from hard-right political movements. President Bill Clinton exploited fears of the Right to promote sweeping "counterterrorism" legislation that represented a serious attack on civil liberties. This in turn bolstered widespread fears of state repression, some of which militia groups were able to exploit. (The Terrorism Prevention and Effective Death Penalty Act, signed by Clinton in April 1996, was promoted based on claims that the militia movement bombed the Oklahoma City federal building, and claims that TWA Flight 800 bound for Paris was sent into the sea by a terrorist bomb. Both claims were false. All credible evidence suggests that Timothy McVeigh, convicted in the Oklahoma City bombing, was a neonazi trying to move the less militant and largely defensive militia movement into more aggressive insurrectionist action, and that Flight 800 was downed by a mechanical flaw.)

Here and in many other instances, we see a dynamic tension between right-wing populist movements, including the insurrectionist Far Right, and mainstream electoral politics. Such movements help pull the entire political spectrum to the right and make mainstream forms of brutality and injustice look more acceptable by comparison.

Notes

1. Neiwert, *In God's Country*; Dyer, *Harvest of Rage*; Stern, *Force Upon the Plain*; Burghart and Crawford, *Guns and Gavels.*

2. Canovan, *Populism,* pp. 13, 128–138.

3. Ibid., pp. 289, 293, 294. Canovan notes that there are "a great many interconnections" among her seven forms of populism, and that "many phenomena—perhaps most—belong in more than one category." She adds that "given the contradictions" between some of the categories, "none could ever satisfy all the conditions at once."

4. Kazin, *Populist Persuasion.* See also Harrison, *Of Passionate Interest.*

5. Diamond, *Roads to Dominion,* p. 9.

6. Kazin, *Populist Persuasion,* p. 35.

7. Our conception of producerism is derived from Alexander Saxton's discussion of the "Producer Ethic" as an ideology of the early White labor movement that "emphasized an egalitarianism reserved for whites" (Saxton, *Rise and Fall of the White Republic,* p. 313). See also p. 298; and *Indispensable Enemy,* pp. 21–22, 52, 265–269.

Our conception is also deeply influenced by Moishe Postone's discussion of how modern antisemitism draws a false dichotomy between "productive" industrial capital and "parasitic" finance capital. See Postone, "Anti-Semitism and National Socialism," especially pp. 106–113.

We use the term producerism in a different way than Catherine McNicol Stock does in her book *Rural Radicals.* Stock portrays producerism simply as a form of populist antielitism, separate from (though sometimes coinciding with) attacks on socially oppressed groups. In our view, producerism intrinsically involves a dual-edged combination of antielitism and oppression (in the U.S. setting, usually in the form of racism or antisemitism, but also sexism and homophobia) and it is precisely this combination that must be addressed.

8. Hardisty, *Mobilizing Resentment.*

9. Aho, *This Thing of Darkness,* pp. 107–121. See also Young-Bruehl, *Anatomy of Prejudices*; and Noël, *Intolerance, A General Survey.*

10. See Allport, *Nature of Prejudice,* pp. 243–260; Girard, *Scapegoat.*

11. Fenster, *Conspiracy Theories,* pp. 67, 74. For additional views of the cultural context of conspiracism, see Dean, *Aliens in America*; Schultz, ed., *Fear Itself*; and Marcus, ed., *Paranoia within Reason*; Melley, *Empire of Conspiracy.*

12. Cumings, *Origins of the Korean War: Vol. 2,* p. 767. See also Albert, "Conspiracy? . . . Not!"; "Conspiracy? . . . Not, Again."

13. Hofstadter, *Paranoid Style in American Politics,* pp. 37–38.

14. Donner, *Age of Surveillance,* p. 11.

15. This analysis of apocalyptic demonization and millennialism is drawn primarily from the following sources:

For apocalypticism: Boyer, *When Time Shall Be No More*; Strozier, *Apocalypse*; O'Leary, *Arguing the Apocalypse*; Fuller, *Naming the Antichrist*; Lamy, *Millennium Rage*; Thompson, *End of Time*; Fenn, *End of Time.*

For Christian critiques of conspiracist apocalyptics: Camp, *Selling Fear*; Abanes, *End-Time Visions*; and Sine, *Cease Fire.*

For a progressive challenge to apocalyptic thinking: Quinby, *Anti-Apocalypse.*

For apocalyptic demonization: Pagels, *Origins of Satan*, and Cohn, *Cosmos, Chaos and the World to Come*; Aho, *This Thing of Darkness.*

16. The word *apocalypse* comes from the Greek, "*apokalypsis*" which means unveiling hidden information or revealing secret knowledge concerning unfolding human events. The word "revelation" is another way to translate the idea of *apokalypsis.* Thus, the words "apocalypse," "revelation," and "prophecy" are closely related. Prophets, by definition, are apocalyptic. See LaHaye, *Revelation,* p. 9.

17. Devout Christians in Salem, Massachusetts, and other towns sought to expose witches and their allies as conspiring with the Devil (Fuller, *Naming the Antichrist,* pp. 56–61, 63.) Modern scholarship has shown that persons accused of being witches were disproportionately women who did not conform to societal expectations, and that there was frequently an economic dimension to the charge, such as a disputed inheritance. See Karlsen, *Devil in the Shape of a Woman,* pp. 46–116.

18. This can be found in a wide range of sources; see O'Sullivan, "Satanism Scare"; Victor, "Search for Scapegoat Deviants"; Zeskind, "Some Ideas on Conspiracy Theories"; Blee, "Engendering Conspiracy"; Harrington, "Conspiracy Theories and Paranoia"; Stern, "Militias and the Religious Right"; Price, "Antichrist Superstar"; and Stix, "Apocalypse Shmapocalypse"; Daniels, ed., *Doomsday Reader.*

19. See, for example, Boyer, *When Time Shall Be No More,* pp. 254–339; Strozier, *Apocalypse,* pp. 108–129; O'Leary, *Arguing the Apocalypse,* pp. 134–193; Fuller, *Naming the Antichrist,* pp. 165–190; Frances FitzGerald, "American Millennium"; Halsell, *Prophecy and Politics*; Harding, "Imagining the Last Days; Diamond, *Not by Politics Alone,* pp. 197–215; *Spiritual Warfare,* pp. 130–136; and "Political Millennialism"; Clarkson, *Eternal Hostility,* pp. 125–138; Kintz, *Between Jesus and the Market,* pp. 8–9. 134–139, 266–267; Herman, *Antigay Agenda,* pp. 19–24, 35–44, 125–128, 171–172.

20. Landes, "On Owls, Roosters, and Apocalyptic Time."

21. Bromley, "Constructing Apocalypticism"; and Wessinger, "Millennialism With and Without the Mayhem."

22. Cohn, *Pursuit of the Millennium.*

23. Boyer, *When Time Shall Be No More,* pp. 80–85.

24. See, generally, Cohn, *Cosmos, Chaos and the World to Come.*

25. Thompson, *End of Time,* p. 307.

26. The word millennium refers to a span of 1,000 years, but also has many deeper meanings. It has come to mean the point at which one period of a thousand years ends and the next begins, and for some this has important religious, social, or political significance. This was certainly the case as the year 2000 approached. All millennial movements are apocalyptic in some sense, even when positive and hopeful; but not all apocalyptic movements are millennial.

27. See, for example, Berrigan, *Ezekiel*; Gomes, *Good Book*; Camp, *Selling Fear.*

28. We reject narrow definitions of what constitutes a social movement applied by some academics. Challenges to centrist/extremist theory by social scientists who study the Right include Rogin, *Intellectuals and McCarthy,* pp. 261–282; Curry and Brown, eds., "Introduction," pp. xi–xii; Ribuffo, *Old Christian Right,* pp. 237–257; Canovan, *Populism,* pp. 46–51, 179–190; Himmelstein, *To the Right,* pp. 1–5, 72–76, 152–164; Diamond, *Roads to Dominion,* pp. 5–6, 40–41; Kazin, *Populist Persuasion,* pp. 190–193. Hixson, in *Search for the American Right Wing,* analyzes Rogin's criticisms.

29. For reviews of social movement theory in transition, see Buechler, *Social Movements in Advanced Capitalism,* pp. 3–57; and Garner and Tenuto, *Social Movement Theory and Research,* pp. 1–48.

30. Smith, "Correcting a Curious Neglect," p. 3.

31. Aho, *This Thing of Darkness.*

32. The Anti-Defamation League (ADL) is a prime example of centrist/extremist theory being used to help rationalize collaboration with state repression. On the ADL's spying against progressive organizations and collaboration with U.S., South African, and Israeli espionage agencies, see

Friedman, "Enemy Within"; Dennis King and Chip Berlet, "A.D.L. Under Fire"; "ADLgate"; Jane Hunter, "Who was the ADL spying for?"; Jabara, "Anti-Defamation League."

33. An example of leftist romanticization of the militia movement is Murray, "Chiapas & Montana." For a critique of this type of portrayal, see Biehl, "Militia Fever"; and Biehl and Staudenmaier, *Ecofascism.*

34. See Berlet, *Right Woos Left.*

35. Domhoff, *Powers That Be; Who Rules America?*; Mills, *Power Elite.*

36. For an overview of business conflict analysis in comparison with other theories of politics, see Gibbs, *Political Economy of Third World Intervention,* ch. 1. For other examples of business conflict analysis, see Ferguson and Rogers, *Right Turn;* Ferguson, *Golden Rule;* Cumings, *Origins of the Korean War: Vol. 2,* chs. 2 and 3; Davis, *Prisoners of the American Dream,* pp. 167–176; Ansell, "Business Mobilization and the New Right"; Bodenheimer and Gould, *Rollback!;* Cox, *Power and Profits;* Lyons, "Business Conflict and Right Wing Movements."

37. Lyons, "What is Fascism?"

The literature on fascism is vast. A few general discussions we have found particularly useful are Griffin, *Nature of Fascism;* Payne, *Fascism;* Eley, "What Produces Fascism," pp. 69–99; and Mayer, *Dynamics of Counterrevolution in Europe.*

Bibliography

Abanes, Richard. (1998). *End-Time Visions: The Road to Armageddon?* New York: Four Walls Eight Windows.

Aho, James A. (1994). *This Thing of Darkness: A Sociology of the Enemy.* Seattle: University of Washington Press.

Albert, Michael. (1992). "Conspiracy? . . . Not!" Venting Spleen column. *Z Magazine,* January, pp. 17–19.

Albert, Michael. (1992). "Conspiracy? . . . Not, Again." Venting Spleen column. *Z Magazine,* May, pp. 86–88.

Allport, Gordon W. (1954). *The Nature of Prejudice.* Cambridge, MA: Addison-Wesley.

Ansell, Amy Elizabeth. (1996). "Business Mobilization and the New Right: Currents in U.S. Foreign Policy." In Ronald W. Cox (Ed.), *Business and the State in International Relations.* Boulder, CO: Westview Press.

Berlet, Chip. (1994 [1990]). *Right Woos Left: Populist Party, LaRouchian, and Other Neo-fascist Overtures to Progressives and Why They Must Be Rejected.* Cambridge, MA: Political Research Associates.

Berrigan, Daniel. (1997). *Ezekiel: Vision in the Dust.* Maryknoll, New York: Orbis Books.

Biehl, Janet. (1996). "Militia Fever: The Fallacy of 'Neither Left nor Right,' " *Green Perspectives, A Social Ecology Publication,* no. 37, April. Online at http://www.nwcitizen.com/publicgood/reports/milfev2.html.

Biehl, Janet, and Peter Staudenmaier. (1995). *Ecofascism: Lessons from the German Experience.* San Francisco: AK Press.

Blee, Kathleen M. (1996). "Engendering Conspiracy: Women in Rightist Theories and Movements." In Eric Ward (Ed.), *Conspiracies: Real Grievances, Paranoia, and Mass Movements* (pp. 91–112). Seattle: Northwest Coalition Against Malicious Harassment, Peanut Butter Publishing.

Bodenheimer, Thomas, and Robert Gould. (1989). *Rollback! Right-wing Power in U.S. Foreign Policy.* Boston: South End Press.

Boyer, Paul. (1992). *When Time Shall Be No More: Prophecy Belief in Modern American Culture.* Cambridge, MA: Belknap/Harvard University Press.

Bromley, David G. (1997). "Constructing Apocalypticism." In Thomas Robbins and Susan J. Palmer (Eds.), *Millennium, Messiahs, and Mayhem: Contemporary Apocalyptic Movements* (pp. 31–45). New York: Routledge.

Buechler, Steven M. (2000). *Social Movements in Advanced Capitalism: The Political Economy and Cultural Construction of Social Activism.* New York: Oxford University Press.

Burghart, Devin, and Robert Crawford. (1996). *Guns & Gavels: Common Law Courts, Militias & White Supremacy.* Portland, OR: Coalition for Human Dignity.

Camp, Gregory S. (1997). *Selling Fear: Conspiracy Theories and End-Times Paranoia.* Grand Rapids, MI: Baker Books.

Canovan, Margaret. (1981). *Populism.* New York: Harcourt Brace Jovanovich.

Clarkson, Frederick. (1997). *Eternal Hostility: The Struggle Between Theocracy and Democracy.* Monroe, ME: Common Courage.

Cohn, Norman. (1970 [1957]). *The Pursuit of the Millennium.* New York: Oxford University Press.

Cohn, Norman. (1993). *Cosmos, Chaos and the World to Come: The Ancient Roots of Apocalyptic Faith.* New Haven: Yale University Press.

Cox, Ronald W. (1994). *Power and Profits: U.S. Policy In Central America.* Lexington: The University Press of Kentucky.

Cumings, Bruce. (1990). *The Origins of the Korean War: Vol. 2. The Roaring of the Cataract, 1947–1950.* Princeton, NJ: Princeton University Press.

Curry, Richard O., and Thomas M. Brown. (1972). "Introduction." In Richard O. Curry and Thomas M. Brown (Eds.), *Conspiracy: The Fear Of Subversion In American History* (pp. vii–xi) New York: Holt, Rinehart and Winston.

Daniels, Ted (Ed.). (1999). *A Doomsday Reader: Prophets, Predictors, and Hucksters of Salvation.* New York: New York University Press.

Davis, Mike. (1986). *Prisoners of the American Dream: Politics and Economy in the History of the US Working Class.* London: Verso.

Dean, Jodi. (1998). *Aliens in America: Conspiracy Cultures from Outerspace to Cyberspace.* Ithaca, NY: Cornell University Press.

Diamond, Sara. (1989). *Spiritual Warfare: The Politics of the Christian Right.* Boston: South End Press.

Diamond, Sara. (1995). *Roads to Dominion: Right-Wing Movements and Political Power in the United States.* New York: Guilford Press.

Diamond, Sara. (1997). "Political Millennialism within the Evangelical Subculture." In Charles B. Strozier and Michael Flynn (Eds.), *The Year 2000: Essays on the End* (pp. 206–216). New York: New York University Press.

Diamond, Sara. (1998). *Not by Politics Alone: The Enduring Influence of the Christian Right.* New York: Guilford Press.

Domhoff, G. William. (1979). *The Powers That Be: Processes of Ruling Class Domination in America.* New York: Vintage Books.

Domhoff, G. William. (1998). *Who Rules America? Power and Politics in the Year 2000.* Mountain View, CA: Mayfield Publishing.

Donner, Frank J. (1980). *The Age of Surveillance: The Aims and Methods of America's Political Intelligence System.* New York: Alfred A. Knopf.

Dyer, Joel. (1998). *Harvest of Rage: Why Oklahoma City is Only the Beginning.* Revised. Boulder, CO: Westview.

Eley, Geoff. (1989). "What Produces Fascism: Preindustrial Traditions or a Crisis of the Capitalist State?" In Michael N. Dobkowski and Isidor Walliman (Eds.), *Radical Perspectives on the Rise of Fascism in Germany, 1919–1945* (pp. 69–99). New York: Monthly Review Press.

Fenn, Richard K. (1997). *The End of Time: Religion, Ritual, and the Forging of the Soul.* Cleveland: Pilgrim Press.

Fenster, Mark. (1999). *Conspiracy Theories: Secrecy and Power in American Culture.* Minneapolis: University of Minnesota Press.

Ferguson, Thomas. (1995). *Golden Rule: The Investment Theory of Party Competition and the Logic of Money-Driven Political Systems.* Chicago: The University of Chicago Press.

Ferguson, Thomas, and Joel Rogers. (1986). *Right Turn: The Decline of the Democrats and the Future of American Politics.* New York: Hill and Wang.

FitzGerald, Frances. (1985). "The American Millennium." *The New Yorker,* November 11, pp. 105–196.

Friedman, Robert I. (1993). "The Enemy Within." *The Village Voice,* May 11, pp. 27–32.

Fuller, Robert C. (1995). *Naming the Antichrist: The History of an American Obsession.* New York: Oxford University Press.

Garner, Roberta, and John Tenuto. (1997). *Social Movement Theory and Research: An Annotated Guide.* Magill Bibliographies. Lanham, MD: Scarecrow Press, Pasadena, CA: Salem Press.

Gibbs, David N. (1991). *The Political Economy of Third World Intervention: Mines, Money, and U.S. Policy in the Congo Crisis.* Chicago: The University of Chicago Press.

Girard, René. (1986). *The Scapegoat.* Baltimore: John Hopkins University Press.

Gomes, Peter J. (1996). *The Good Book: Reading the Bible with Mind and Heart.* New York: William Morrow.

Griffin, Roger. (1991). *The Nature of Fascism.* New York: St. Martin's Press.

Halsell, Grace. (1986). *Prophecy and Politics: Militant Evangelists on the Road to Nuclear War.* Westport, CT: Lawrence Hill.

Harding, Susan. (1994). "Imagining the Last Days: The Politics of Apocalyptic Language." In Martin E. Marty and R. Scott Appleby (Eds.), *Accounting for Fundamentalisms: Vol. 4. The Fundamentalism Project* (pp. 57–78). Chicago: University of Chicago Press.

Hardisty, Jean V. (1999). *Mobilizing Resentment: Conservative Resurgence from the John Birch Society to the Promise Keepers.* Boston: Beacon.

Harrington, Evan. (1996). "Conspiracy Theories and Paranoia: Notes from a Mind-Control Conference." *Skeptical Inquirer,* September–October, pp. 35–52.

Harrison, Trevor. (1995). *Of Passionate Intensity: Right-wing Populism and the Reform Party of Canada.* Toronto: University of Toronto Press.

Herman, Didi. (1997). *The Antigay Agenda: Orthodox Vision and the Christian Right.* Chicago: University of Chicago Press.

Himmelstein, Jerome L. (1990). *To the Right: The Transformation of American Conservatism.* Berkeley: University of California Press.

Hixson, William B., Jr. (1992). *Search for the American Right Wing: An Analysis of the Social Science Record, 1955–1987.* Princeton, NJ: Princeton University Press.

Hofstadter, Richard. (1965). *The Paranoid Style in American Politics and Other Essays.* New York: Knopf.

Hunter, Jane. (1993). "Who was the ADL Spying For?" *Israeli Foreign Affairs,* vol. 9, no. 4, May 11, pp. 1–2, 5–8.

Jabara, Abdeen. (1993). "The Anti-Defamation League: Civil Rights and Wrongs," *CovertAction Quarterly,* no. 45, Summer, pp. 28–35.

Karlsen, Carol F. (1998). *The Devil in the Shape of a Woman: Witchcraft in Colonial New England.* New York: Norton.

Kazin, Michael. (1995). *The Populist Persuasion: An American History.* New York: Basic Books.

King, Dennis, and Chip Berlet. (1993). "ADLgate." *Tikkun* magazine, vol. 8, no. 4.

King, Dennis, and Chip Berlet. (1993). "The A.D.L. Under Fire." Op-ed. *The New York Times,* May 28.

Kintz, Linda. (1997). *Between Jesus and the Market: The Emotions that Matter in Right-Wing America.* Durham, NC: Duke University Press.

LaHaye, Tim. (1975). *Revelation: Illustrated and Made Plain.* Grand Rapids, MI: Zondervan.

Lamy, Philip. (1996). *Millennium Rage: Survivalists, White Supremacists, and the Doomsday Prophecy,* New York: Plenum.

Landes, Richard. (1996). "On Owls, Roosters, and Apocalyptic Time: A Historical Method for Reading a Refractory Documentation." *Union Seminary Quarterly Review*, vol. 49, nos. 1–2, pp. 165–185.

Lyons, Matthew N. (1995). "What is Fascism? Some General Ideological Features." In Chip Berlet (Ed.), *Eyes Right! Challenging the Right Wing Backlash* (pp. 244–245). Boston: South End Press.

Lyons, Matthew N. (1998). "Business Conflict and Right-Wing Movements." In Amy E. Ansell (Ed.), *Unraveling the Right: The New Conservatism in American Thought and Politics* (pp. 80–102). Boulder, CO: Westview.

Marcus, George E. (Ed.). (1999). *Paranoia Within Reason: A Casebook on Conspiracy Explanation*. Chicago: University of Chicago Press.

Mayer, Arno J. (1971). *Dynamics of Counterrevolution in Europe, 1870–1956: An Analytic Framework*. New York: Harper & Row, Publishers.

Melley, Timothy. (1999). *Empire of Conspiracy: The Culture of Paranoia in Postwar America*. Ithaca, NY: Cornell University Press.

Mills, C. Wright. (1956). *The Power Elite*. New York: Oxford University Press.

Murray, James. (1998). "Chiapas and Montana: Tierra Y Libertad." *Race Traitor*, no. 8, Winter, pp. 39–50.

Neiwert, David A. (1999). *In God's Country: The Patriot Movement and the Pacific Northwest*. Pullman: Washington State University Press.

Noël, Lise. (1994). *Intolerance: A General Survey*. Translated by Arnold Bennett. Montreal: McGill-Queen's University Press.

O'Leary, Stephen D. (1994). *Arguing the Apocalypse: A Theory of Millennial Rhetoric*. New York: Oxford University Press.

O'Sullivan, Gerry. (1991). "The Satanism Scare." *Postmodern Culture*, vol. 1, no. 2, January.

Pagels, Elaine. (1996). *The Origin of Satan*. New York: Vintage.

Payne, Stanley G. (1980). *Fascism: Comparison and Definition*. Madison, WI: The University of Wisconsin Press.

Postone, Moishe. (1980). "Anti-Semitism and National Socialism: Notes on the German Reaction to 'Holocaust.' " *new german critique*, no. 19, Winter, pp. 97–115.

Price, Robert M. (1997). "Antichrist Superstar and the Paperback Apocalypse: Rapturous Fiction and Fictitious Rapture." In special report, "On the Millennium." *Deolog* (online journal), January–February. Online at http://www.stealth.net/~deolog/Price297.html.

Quinby, Lee. (1994). *Anti-Apocalypse: Exercises in Genealogical Criticism*. Minneapolis: University of Minnesota Press.

Ribuffo, Leo P. (1983). *The Old Christian Right: The Protestant Far Right from the Great Depression to the Cold War*. Philadelphia: Temple University Press.

Rogin, Michael Paul. (1967). *The Intellectuals and McCarthy: The Radical Specter*. Cambridge, MA: MIT Press.

Saxton, Alexander. (1971). *The Indispensable Enemy: Labor and the Anti Chinese Movement in California*. Berkeley: University of California Press.

Saxton, Alexander. (1990). *The Rise and Fall of the White Republic: Class Politics and Mass Culture in Nineteenth-Century America*. New York: Verso.

Schultz, Nancy Lusignan. (1999). *Fear Itself: Enemies Real & Imagined in American Culture*. West Lafayette, IN: Purdue University Press.

Sine, Tom. (1995). *Cease Fire: Searching for Sanity in America's Culture Wars*. Grand Rapids, MI: William B. Eerdmans.

Smith, Christian. (1996). "Correcting a Curious Neglect, or Bringing Religion Back In." In Christian Smith (Ed.), *Disruptive Religion: The Force of Faith in Social-Movement Activism*. New York: Routledge.

Stern, Kenneth S. (1996). *A Force Upon the Plain: The American Militia Movement and the Politics of Hate*. New York: Simon and Schuster.

Stern, Kenneth S. (1996). "Militias and the Religious Right." *Freedom Writer*, Institute for First Amendment Studies, October.

Stix, Nicholas. (1997). "Apocalypse, Shmapocalypse: You Say You Want a Revolution." In special report, "On the Millennium." *Deolog* (online journal), January–February. Online at http://www.stealth.net/~deolog/297.html.

Stock, Catherine McNicol. (1996). *Rural Radicals: Righteous Rage in the American Grain*. Ithaca, NY: Cornell University Press.

Strozier, Charles B. (1994). *Apocalypse: On the Psychology of Fundamentalism in America*. Boston: Beacon Press.

Thompson, Damian. (1996). *The End of Time: Faith and Fear in the Shadow of the Millennium*. Great Britain: Sinclair Stevenson.

Victor, Jeffrey. (1992). "The Search for Scapegoat Deviants." *The Humanist*, September–October, pp. 10–13.

Wessinger, Catherine. (1997). "Millennialism With and Without the Mayhem." In Thomas Robbins and Susan J. Palmer (Eds.), *Millennium, Messiahs, and Mayhem: Contemporary Apocalyptic Movements* (pp. 47–59). New York: Routledge.

Young-Bruehl, Elisabeth. (1996). *The Anatomy of Prejudices*. Cambridge, MA: Harvard University Press.

Zeskind, Leonard. (1996). "Some Ideas on Conspiracy Theories for a New Historical Period." In Eric Ward (Ed.), *Conspiracies: Real Grievances, Paranoia, and Mass Movements* (pp. 11–33). Seattle: Northwest Coalition Against Malicious Harassment, Peanut Butter Publishing.

ENVIRONMENTALISM AND SOCIAL JUSTICE

ROBERT D. BULLARD

The environmental movement in the United States emerged with agendas that focused on such areas as wilderness and wildlife preservation, resource conservation, pollution abatement, and population control. It was supported primarily by middle- and upper-middle-class whites. Although concern about the environment cut across racial and class lines, environmental activism has been most pronounced among individuals who have above-average education, greater access to economic resources, and a greater sense of personal efficacy.[1]

Mainstream environmental organizations were late in broadening their base of support to include blacks and other minorities, the poor, and working-class persons. The "energy crisis" in the 1970s provided a major impetus for many environmentalists to embrace equity issues confronting the poor in this country and in the countries of the Third World.[2] Over the years, environmentalism has shifted from a "participatory" to a "power" strategy, where the "core of the active environmental movement is focused on litigation, political lobbying, and technical evaluation rather than on mass mobilization for protest marches."[3]

An abundance of documentation shows blacks, lower-income groups, and working-class persons are subjected to a disproportionately large amount of pollution and other environmental stressors in their neighborhoods as well as in their workplaces.[4] However, these groups have only been marginally involved in the nation's environmental movement. Problems facing the black community have been topics of much discussion in recent years. (Here, we use sociologist James Blackwell's definition of the black community, "a highly diversified set of interrelated structures and aggregates of people who are held together by forces of white oppression and racism."[5]) Race has not been eliminated as a factor in the allocation of community amenities.

Research on environmental quality in black communities has been minimal. Attention has been focused on such problems as crime, drugs, poverty, unemployment, and family crisis. Nevertheless, pollution is exacting a heavy toll (in health and environmental costs) on black communities across the nation. There are few studies that document, for example, the way blacks cope with environmental stressors such as municipal solid-waste facilities, hazardous-waste landfills, toxic-waste dumps, chemical emissions from industrial plants, and on-the-job hazards that pose extreme risks to their health. . . .

. . . This oversight is rooted in historical and ideological factors and in the composition of the core environmental movement and its largely white middle-class profile.

Many of the interactions that emerged among core environmentalists, the poor, and blacks can be traced to distributional equity questions. How are the benefits and burdens of environmental reform distributed? Who gets what, where, and why? Are environmental inequities a result of racism or class barriers or a combination of both? After more than two decades of modern environmentalism, the equity issues have not been resolved. There has been, however, some change in the way environmental problems are presented by mainstream environmental organizations. More important, environmental equity has now become a major item on the local (grassroots) as well as national civil rights agenda.[6]

Much of the leadership in the civil rights movement came from historically black colleges and universities (HBCUs). Black college students were on the "cutting edge" in leading sit-in demonstrations at lunch counters, libraries, parks, and public transit systems that operated under Jim Crow laws. In *The Origins of the Civil Rights Movement*, Aldon D. Morris wrote:

> The tradition of protest is transmitted across generations by older relatives, black institutions, churches, and protest organizations. Blacks interested in social change

> inevitably gravitate to this "protest community," where they hope to find solutions to a complex problem.
>
> The modern civil rights movement fits solidly into this rich tradition of protest. Like the slave revolts, the Garvey Movement, and the March on Washington, it was highly organized. Its significant use of the black religious community to accomplish political goals also linked the modern movement to the earlier mass movements which also relied heavily on the church.[7]

Social justice and the elimination of institutionalized discrimination were the major goals of the civil rights movement. Many of the HBCUs are located in some of the most environmentally polluted communities in the nation. These institutions and their students, thus, have a vested interest in seeing that improvements are made in local environmental quality. Unlike their move to challenge other forms of inequity, black student-activists have been conspicuously silent and relatively inactive on environmental problems. Moreover, the resources and talents of the faculties at these institutions have also been underutilized in assisting affected communities in their struggle against polluters, including government and private industries.

The problem of polluted black communities is not a new phenomenon. Historically, toxic dumping and the location of locally unwanted land uses (LULUs) have followed the "path of least resistance," meaning black and poor communities have been disproportionately burdened with these types of externalities. However, organized black resistance to toxic dumping, municipal waste facility siting, and discriminatory environmental and land-use decisions is a relatively recent phenomenon.[8] Black environmental concern has been present but too often has not been followed up with action.

Ecological concern has remained moderately high across nearly all segments of the population. Social equity and concern about distributive impacts, however, have not fared so well over the years. Low-income and minority communities have had few advocates and lobbyists at the national level and within the mainstream environmental movement. Things are changing as environmental problems become more "potent political issues [and] become increasingly viewed as threatening public health."[9]

The environmental movement of the 1960s and 1970s, dominated by the middle class, built an impressive political base for environmental reform and regulatory relief. Many environmental problems of the 1980s and 1990s, however, have social impacts that differ somewhat from earlier ones. Specifically, environmental problems have had serious regressive impacts. These impacts have been widely publicized in the media, as in the case of the hazardous-waste problems at Love Canal and Times Beach. The plight of polluted minority communities is not as well known as the New York and Missouri tragedies. Nevertheless, a disproportionate burden of pollution is carried by the urban poor and minorities.[10]

Few environmentalists realized the sociological implications of the not-in-my-backyard (NIMBY) phenomenon.[11] Given the political climate of the times, the hazardous wastes, garbage dumps, and polluting industries were likely to end up in somebody's backyard. But whose backyard? More often than not, these LULUs ended up in poor, powerless, black communities rather than in affluent suburbs. This pattern has proven to be the rule, even though the benefits derived from industrial waste production are directly related to affluence.[12] Public officials and private industry have in many cases responded to the NIMBY phenomenon using the place-in-blacks'-backyard (PIBBY) principle.[13]

Social activists have begun to move environmentalism to the left in an effort to address some of the distributional impact and equity issues.[14] Documentation of civil rights violations has strengthened the move to make environmental quality a basic right of all individuals. Rising energy costs and a continued erosion of the economy's ability to provide jobs (but not promises) are factors that favor blending the objectives of labor, minorities, and other "underdogs" with those of middle-class environmentalists.[15] Although ecological sustainability and socioeconomic equality have not been fully achieved, there is clear evidence that the 1980s ushered in a new era of cooperation between environmental and social justice groups. While there is by no means a consensus on complex environmental problems, the converging points of view represent the notion that "environmental problems and . . . material problems have common roots."[16]

When analyzing the convergence of these groups, it is important to note the relative emphasis that environmental and social justice organizations give to "instrumental" versus "expressive" activities.[17] Environmental organizations have relied heavily on environmentally oriented expressive activities (outdoor recreation, field trips, social functions, etc.), while the social justice movements have made greater use of goal-oriented instrumental activities (protest demonstrations, mass rallies, sit-ins, boycotts, etc.) in their effort to produce social change.[18]

The push for environmental equity in the black community has much in common with the development of the modern civil rights movement that began in the South. That is, protest against discrimination has evolved from "organizing efforts of activists functioning through a well-developed indigenous base."[19] Indigenous black institutions, organizations, leaders, and networks are coming together against polluting industries and discriminatory environmental policies. . . .

The Theoretical Basis of Environmental Conflict

Environmentalism in the United States grew out of the progressive conservation movement that began in the 1890s. The modern environmental movement, however, has its roots in the civil rights and antiwar movements of the late 1960s.[20] The more radical student activists splintered off from the civil rights and antiwar movements to form the core of the environmental movement in the early 1970s. The student environmental activists affected by the 1970 Earth Day enthusiasm in colleges and universities across the nation had hopes of bringing environmental reforms to the urban poor. They saw their role as environmental advocates for the poor since the poor had not taken action on their own.[21] They were, however, met with resistance and suspicion. Poor and minority residents saw environmentalism as a disguise for oppression and as another "elitist" movement.[22]

Environmental elitism has been grouped into three categories: (1) *compositional elitism* implies that environmentalists come from privileged class strata, (2) *ideological elitism* implies that environmental reforms are a subterfuge for distributing the benefits to environmentalists and costs to nonenvironmentalists, and (3) *impact elitism* implies that environmental reforms have regressive distributional impacts.[23]

Impact elitism has been the major sore point between environmentalists and advocates for social justice who see some reform proposals creating, exacerbating, and sustaining social inequities. Conflict centered largely on the "jobs versus environment" argument. Imbedded in this argument are three competing advocacy groups: (1) *environmentalists* are concerned about leisure and recreation, wildlife and wilderness preservation, resource conservation, pollution abatement, and industry regulation, (2) *social justice advocates'* major concerns include basic civil rights, social equity, expanded opportunity, economic mobility, and institutional discrimination, and (3) *economic boosters* have as their chief concerns maximizing profits, industrial expansion, economic stability, laissez-faire operation, and deregulation.

Economic boosters and pro-growth advocates convinced minority leaders that environmental regulations were bad for business, even when locational decisions had adverse impacts on the less advantaged. Pro-growth advocates used a number of strategies to advance their goals, including public relations campaigns, lobbying public officials, evoking police powers of government, paying off or co-opting dissidents, and granting small concessions when plans could be modified.[24] Environmental reform proposals were presented as prescriptions for plant closures, layoffs, and economic dislocation. Kazis and Grossman referred to this practice as "job blackmail." They insisted that by "threatening their employees with a 'choice' between their jobs and their health, employers seek to make the public believe there are no alternatives to 'business as usual.' "[25]

Pro-growth advocates have claimed the workplace is an arena in which unavoidable trade-offs must be made between jobs and hazards: If workers want to keep their jobs, they must work under conditions that may be hazardous to them, their families, and their community. Black workers are especially vulnerable to job blackmail because of the threat of unemployment and their concentration in certain types of occupations. The black workforce remains overrepresented in low-paying, low-skill, high-risk blue collar and service occupations where there is a more than adequate supply of replacement labor. Black workers are twice as likely to be unemployed as their white counterparts. Fear of unemployment acts as a potent incentive for many blacks to stay in and accept jobs they know are health threatening.

There is inherent conflict between the interest of capital and of labor. Employers have the power to move jobs (and sometimes hazards) as they wish. For example, firms may choose to move their operations from the Northeast and Midwest to the South and Sunbelt, or they may move the jobs to Third World countries where labor is cheaper and there are fewer health and environmental regulations. Moreover, labor unions may feel it necessary to scale down their demands for improved work safety conditions in a depressed economy for fear of layoffs, plant closings, or relocation of industries (e.g., moving to right-to-work states that proliferate in the South). The conflicts, fears, and anxieties manifested by workers are usually built on the false assumption that environmental regulations are automatically linked to job loss.

The offer of a job (any job) to an unemployed worker appears to have served a more immediate need than the promise of a clean environment. There is evidence that new jobs have been created as a direct result of environmental reforms.[26] Who got these new jobs? The newly created jobs are often taken by people who already have jobs or by migrants who possess skills greater than the indigenous workforce. More often than not, "newcomers intervene between the jobs and the local residents, especially the disadvantaged."[27]

Minority residents can point to a steady stream of industrial jobs leaving their communities. Moreover, social justice advocates take note of the miserable track record that environmentalists and preservationists have on improving environmental quality in the nation's racially segregated inner cities and hazardous industrial workplaces, and on providing housing for low-income groups. Decent and affordable housing, for example, is a top environmental problem for inner-city blacks. On the other hand, environmentalists' continued emphasis on wilderness and wildlife preservation appeal to a population that can afford leisure time and travel to these distant locations. This does not mean that poor people and people of color are not interested in leisure or outdoor activities. Many wilderness areas and national parks remain inaccessible to the typical inner-city resident because of inadequate transportation. Physical isolation, thus, serves as a major impediment to black activism in mainstream conservation and resource management activities.

Translating Concern into Action

A considerable body of literature shows that the socioeconomic makeup of environmental activists and the environmentally concerned are markedly different. Activists tend to be drawn disproportionately from the upper middle class, while environmentally concerned individuals tend to come from all socioeconomic strata.[28] Since our focus is on activism rather than concern, social participation models seem most appropriate in explaining the varying levels of environmental activity within the black community. Two of the most prevalent perspectives on social participation rates are expressed in the "social psychological" and "resource mobilization" models.

The basic assumption of the social psychological perspective is that personal characteristics, such as deprivation, status inconsistencies, grievances, and alienation, are useful in explaining motivation for social movement involvement.[29] The resource mobilization perspective, on the other hand, places greater confidence in structural conditions that make individual participation more accessible, including economic resources, organization affiliation, leaders, communication networks, and mastery skills gained through wearing "multiple hats."[30] Given the issues that have drawn minorities into the environmental movement (e.g., social justice and equity issues) and the indigenous black institutions that have initiated and sustained the movement, an integrated model is used to explain the emergence of environmentalism in black communities.[31] That is, both psychological factors (e.g., environmental quality rating, deprivation and sense of inequitable treatment, personal efficacy, and acceptance of trade-offs) as well as structural factors (e.g., social class and organization affiliation) are important predictors of environmental activism that is emerging in black communities.

There is no single agenda or integrated political philosophy in the hundreds of environmental organizations found in the nation. The type of issues that environmental organizations choose can greatly influence the type of constituents they attract.[32] The issues that are most likely to attract the interests of black community residents are those that have been couched in a civil rights or equity framework. They include those that (1) focus on inequality and distributional impacts, (2) endorse the "politics of equity" and direct action, (3) appeal to urban mobilized groups, (4) advocate safeguards against environmental blackmail with a strong pro-development stance, and (5) are ideologically aligned with policies that favor social and political "underdogs."

Mainstream environmental organizations, including the "classic" and "mature" groups, have had a great deal of influence in shaping the nation's environmental policy. Classic environmentalism continues to have a heavy emphasis on preservation and outdoor recreation, while mature environmentalism is busy in the area of "tightening regulations, seeking adequate funding for agencies, occasionally focusing on compliance with existing statutes through court action, and opposing corporate efforts to repeal environmental legislation or weaken standards."[33] These organizations, however, have not had a great deal of success in attracting working-class persons, the large black population in the nation's inner cities, and the rural poor. Many of these individuals do not see the mainstream environmental movement as a vehicle that is championing the causes of the "little man," the "underdog," or the "oppressed."[34]

Recently emerged grassroots environmental groups, some of which are affiliated with mainstream environmental organizations, have begun to bridge the class and ideological gap between core environmentalists (e.g., the Sierra Club) and grassroots organizations (e.g., local activist groups in southeast Louisiana). In some cases, these groups mirror their larger counterparts at the national level in terms of problems and issues selected, membership, ideological alignment, and tactics. Grassroots groups often are organized around area-specific and single-issue problems. They are, however, more inclusive than mainstream environmental organizations in that they focus primarily on local problems. Grassroots environmental organizations, however, may or may not choose to focus on equity, distributional impacts, and economic-environmental trade-off issues. These groups do appeal to some black community residents, especially those who have been active in other confrontational protest activities.

Environmental groups in the black community quite often emerge out of established social action organizations. For example, black leadership has deep roots in the black church and other voluntary associations. These black institutions usually have a track record built on opposition to social injustice and racial discrimination. Many black community residents are affiliated with civic clubs, neighborhood associations, community improvement groups, and an array of antipoverty and antidiscrimination organizations. The infrastructure, thus, is already in place for the emergence of a sustained environmental equity movement in the black community. Black sociologist Aldon Morris contends that the black community "possesses (1) certain basic resources, (2) social activists with strong ties to mass-based indigenous institutions, and (3) tactics and strategies that can be effectively employed against a system of domination."[35]

Social action groups that take on environmental issues as part of their agenda are often on the political Left. They broaden their base of support and sphere of influence by incorporating environmental equity issues as agenda items that favor the disenfranchised. The push for environmental equity is an extension of the civil rights movement, a movement in which direct confrontation and the politics of protest have been real weapons. In short, social action environmental organizations retain much of their civil rights flavor.

Other environmental groups that have appealed to black community residents grew out of coalitions between environmentalists (mainstream and grassroots), social action advocates, and organized labor.[36] These somewhat fragile coalitions operate from the position that social justice and environmental quality are compatible goals. Although these groups are beginning to formulate agendas for action, mistrust still persists as a limiting factor. These groups are often biracial with membership cutting across class and geographic boundaries. There is a down side to these types of coalition groups. For example, compositional factors may engender less group solidarity and sense of "control" among black members, compared to the indigenous social action or grassroots environmental groups where blacks are in the majority and make the decisions. The question of "who is calling the shots" is ever present.

Environmentalists, thus, have had a difficult task convincing blacks and the poor that they are on their side. Mistrust is engendered among economically and politically oppressed groups in this country when they see environmental reforms being used to direct social and economic resources away from problems of the poor toward priorities of the affluent. For example, tighter government regulations and public opposition to disposal facility siting have opened up the Third World as the new dumping ground for this nation's toxic wastes. Few of these poor countries have laws or the infrastructure to handle the wastes from the United States and other Western industrialized nations.[37] Blacks and other ethnic minorities in this country also see their communities being inundated with all types of toxics. This has been especially the case for the southern United States (one of the most underdeveloped regions of the nation) where more than one-half of all blacks live.

Environmentalism and Civil Rights

The civil rights movement has its roots in the southern United States. Southern racism deprived blacks of "political rights, economic opportunity, social justice, and human dignity."[38] The new environmental equity movement also is centered in the South, a region where marked ecological disparities exist between black and white communities.[39] The 1980s have seen the emergence of a small cadre of blacks who see environmental discrimination as a civil rights issue. A fragile alliance has been forged between organized labor, blacks, and environmental groups as exhibited by the 1983 Urban Environment Conference workshops held in New Orleans.[40] Environmental and civil rights issues were presented as compatible agenda items by the conference organizers. Environmental protection and social justice are not necessarily incompatible goals.[41]

The Commission for Racial Justice's 1987 study *Toxic Wastes and Race in the United States* is a clear indication that environmental concerns have reached the civil rights agenda. Reverend Ben Chavis, the commission's executive director, stated:

> Race is a major factor related to the presence of hazardous wastes in residential communities throughout the United States. As a national church-based civil rights agency, we believe that time has come for all church and civil rights organizations to take this issue seriously. We realize that involvement in this type of research is a departure from our traditional protest methodology. However, if we are to advance our struggle in the future, it will depend largely on the availability of timely and reliable information.[42]

A growing number of grassroots organizations and their leaders have begun to incorporate more problem-focused coping strategies (e.g., protests, neighborhood demonstrations, picketing, political pressure, litigation, etc.) to reduce and eliminate environmental stressors. The national black political leadership has demonstrated a willingness to take a strong pro-environmental stance. The League of Conservation Voters, for example, assigned the Congressional Black Caucus high marks for having one of the best pro-environment voting records.[43]

Many black communities, however, still do not have the organization, financial resources, or personnel to mount and sustain effective long-term challenges to such unpopular facilities as municipal and hazardous-waste landfills, toxic waste dumps, incinerators, and industrial plants that may pose a threat to their health and safety. Some battles are being waged on "shoestring" budgets. The problem is complicated by the fact that blacks in many cases must go outside their community to find experts on environmental issues. Lawyers, toxicologists, hydrologists, and environmental engineers in today's market are not cheap.

Institutional racism continues to affect policy decisions related to the enforcement of environmental regulations. Slowly, blacks, lower-income groups, and working-class persons are awakening to the dangers of living in a polluted environment. They are beginning to file and win lawsuits challenging governments and private industry that would turn their communities into dumping grounds for all type of unwanted substances and activities. Whether it is a matter of deciding where a municipal landfill or hazardous-waste facility will be located, or getting a local chemical plant to develop better emergency notification, or trying to secure federal assistance to clean up an area that has already been contaminated by health-threatening chemicals, it is apparent that blacks and other minority groups must become more involved in environmental issues if they want to live healthier lives.

Black communities, mostly in the South, are beginning to initiate action (protests, demonstrations, picketing, political pressure, litigation, and other forms of direct action) against industries and governmental agencies that have targeted their neighborhoods for nonresidential uses including municipal garbage, hazardous wastes, and polluting industries. The environmental "time bombs" that are ticking away in these communities are not high on the agendas of mainstream environmentalists nor have they received much attention from mainstream civil rights advocates. Moreover, polluted black communities have received little national media coverage or remedial action from governmental agencies charged with cleanup of health-threatening pollution problems. The time is long overdue for placing toxics and minority health concerns (including stress induced from living in contaminated communities) on the agenda of federal and state environmental protection and regulatory agencies. The Commission for Racial Justice's *Toxic Wastes and Race* has at least started government officials, academicians, and grassroots activists talking about environmental problems that disproportionately affect minority communities.

Nevertheless, "Black Love Canals" exist and many go unnoticed. A case in point is the contamination of Triana, a small, all-black town in northern Alabama. Barbara Reynolds in *National Wildlife* described Triana as the "unhealthiest town in America."[44] Residents of this rural town of about 1,000 people were tested by the Center for Disease Control and were found to be contaminated with the pesticide DDT and the highly toxic industrial chemical PCB (polychlorinated biphenyl). Some of the residents were contaminated with the highest levels of DDT ever recorded. The source of the PCBs was not determined. However, the DDT was produced at nearby Redstone Arsenal Army missile base from 1947 to 1971 by Olin Chemical Company. DDT was banned in the United States in 1971. The manufacturing plant was torn down and over 4,000 tons of DDT residue remained buried in the area and eventually worked its way into Indian Creek, a popular fishing place of the Triana residents. Indian Creek is a tributary of the Tennessee River and is under the jurisdiction of the Tennessee Valley Authority (TVA).

While the elevated level of contamination of these black residents was documented as early as 1978, actions on part of the U.S. Army or the federal government did not materialize. Clyde Foster, then mayor of Triana, spoke to this lack of concern and inaction on the part of government:

> I did not want a confrontation. I just wanted the scientific investigation to speak for itself. Why did the TVA suggest Triana be studied if DDT was not at all dangerous? How can it kill insects, fish, and birds and not be potentially harmful to people? I knew the stuff was real stable, that it stays in a body for years. Who knows what effects massive doses could have over a long period of time? The TVA has known about the presence of DDT in the fish of Indian Creek for years, and I found later that the Army checked in 1977 and found a fish with one hundred times the safe DDT level. We received the TVA analysis of the fish from our freezers. Our fish had even higher DDT levels than those they had first tested. . . . Many of us eat its [Indian Creek's] fish every day. Already there is a hardship among the very poor people who customarily derive sustenance from the river. Our whole community is upset. We needed some help.[45]

It was not until Mayor Foster filed a class-action lawsuit in 1980 against Olin Chemical Company that the problems of these citizens were taken seriously.[46] After many delays and attempts to co-opt the local citizens, the lawsuit was settled out of court in 1983 for $25 million.

The settlement agreement had three main points. Olin Chemical Company agreed to (1) clean up residue chemicals, (2) set aside $5 million to pay for long-term medical surveillance and health care of Triana residents, and (3) pay "cash-in-pocket" settlements to each resident. The legal claim against the federal government was withdrawn in order to make the settlement with Olin. The tragedy at Triana is not an isolated incident. There are numerous other cases of poor, black, and powerless communities that are victimized and ignored when it comes to enforcing environmental quality standards equitably. These disparities form the basis for . . . the environmental equity movement.

Notes

1. See Frederick R. Buttel and William L. Flinn, "Social Class and Mass Environmental Beliefs: A Reconsideration," *Environment and Behavior* 10 (September 1978): 433–450; Kenneth M. Bachrach and Alex J. Zautra, "Coping with Community Stress: The Threat of a Hazardous Waste Landfill," *Journal of Health and Social Behavior* 26 (June 1985): 127–141; Paul Mohai, "Public Concern and Elite Involvement in Environmental-Conservation Issues," *Social Science Quarterly* 66 (December 1985): 820–838.
2. Denton E. Morrison, "The Soft Cutting Edge of Environmentalism: Why and How the Appropriate Technology Notion Is Changing the Movement," *Natural Resources Journal* 20 (April 1980): 275–298.
3. Allan Schnaiberg, *The Environment: From Surplus to Scarcity* (New York: Oxford University Press, 1980): pp. 366–377.
4. See Morris E. Davis, "The Impact of Workplace Health and Safety on Black Workers: Assessment and Prognosis," *Labor Studies Journal* 4 (Spring 1981): 29–40; Richard Kazis and Richard Grossman, *Fear at Work: Job Blackmail, Labor, and the Environment* (New York: Pilgrim Press, 1983), Chapter 1; W. J. Kruvant, "People, Energy, and Pollution," in Dorothy K. Newman and Dawn Day, eds., *The American Energy Consumer* (Cambridge, Mass.: Ballinger, 1975), pp. 125–167; Robert D. Bullard, "Solid Waste Sites and the Black Houston Community," *Sociological Inquiry* 53 (Spring 1983): 273–288; Robert D. Bullard, "Endangered Environs: The Price of Unplanned Growth in Boomtown Houston," *California Sociologist* 7 (Summer 1984): 85–101; Robert D. Bullard and Beverly H. Wright, "Dumping Grounds in a Sunbelt City," *Urban Resources* 2 (Winter 1985): 37–39.
5. James E. Blackwell, *The Black Community: Diversity and Unity* (New York: Harper and Row, 1985), p. xiii.
6. Robert D. Bullard and Beverly H. Wright, "Environmentalism and the Politics of Equity: Emergent Trends in the Black Community," *Mid-American Review of Sociology* 12 (Winter 1987): 21–37.
7. Aldon D. Morris, *The Origins of the Civil Rights Movement: Black Communities Organizing for Change* (New York: Free Press, 1984), p. x.
8. See Robert D. Bullard and Beverly H. Wright, "Blacks and the Environment," *Humboldt Journal of Social Relations* 14 (Summer 1987): 165–184; Bullard, "Solid Waste Sites and the Black Houston Community," pp. 273–288; Bullard, "Endangered Environs," pp. 84–102.
9. Riley E. Dunlap, "Public Opinion on the Environment in the Reagan Era: Polls, Pollution, and Politics Revisited," *Environment* 29 (July/August 1987): 6–11, 32–37.
10. Brian J. L. Berry, ed., *The Social Burden of Environmental Pollution: A Comparative Metropolitan Data Source* (Cambridge, Mass.: Ballinger, 1977); Sam Love, "Ecology and Social Justice: Is There a Conflict," *Environmental Action* 4 (1972): 3–6; Julian McCaull, "Discriminatory Air Pollution: If the Poor Don't Breathe," *Environment* 19 (March 1976): 26–32; Vernon Jordon, "Sins of Omission," *Environmental Action* 11 (April 1980): 26–30.
11. Denton E. Morrison, "How and Why Environmental Consciousness Has Trickled Down," in Allan Schnaiberg, Nicholas Watts, and Klaus Zimmermann, eds., *Distributional Conflict in Environmental-Resource Policy* (New York: St. Martin's Press, 1986), pp. 187–220.
12. Robert D. Bullard and Beverly H. Wright, "The Politics of Pollution: Implications for the Black Community," *Phylon* 47 (March 1986): 71–78.
13. Bullard and Wright, "Environmentalism and the Politics of Equity," p. 28.
14. Richard P. Gale, "The Environmental Movement and the Left: Antagonists or Allies?" *Sociological Inquiry* 53 (Spring 1983): 179–199.
15. Craig R. Humphrey and Frederick R. Buttel, *Environment, Energy, and Society* (Belmont, Calif.: Wadsworth Publishing Co., 1982), p. 253.
16. Ibid.
17. Arthur P. Jacoby and Nicholas Babchuk, "Instrumental Versus Expressive Voluntary Associations," *Sociology and Social Research* 47 (1973): 461–471.
18. Gale, "The Environmental Movement and the Left," p. 191.
19. Morris, *The Origins of the Civil Rights Movement*, p. xii.
20. Humphrey and Buttel, *Environment, Energy, and Society*, pp. 11–136; Gale, "The Environmental Movement and the Left," pp. 179–199.
21. Samuel P. Hays, *Beauty, Health, and Permanence: Environmental Politics in the United States, 1955–1985* (Cambridge, Mass.: Cambridge University Press, 1987), p. 269.
22. David L. Sills, "The Environmental Movement and Its Critics," *Human Ecology* 13 (1975): 1–41; Morrison, "The Soft Cutting Edge of Environmentalism," pp. 275–298;

Allan Schnaiberg, "Redistributive Goals Versus Distributive Politics: Social Equity Limits in Environmentalism and Appropriate Technology Movements," *Sociological Inquiry* 53 (Spring 1983): 200–219.

23. Denton E. Morrison and Riley E. Dunlap, "Environmentalism and Elitism: A Conceptual and Empirical Analysis," *Environmental Management* 10 (1986): 581–589.

24. John R. Logan and Harvey L. Molotch, *Urban Fortunes: The Political Economy of Place* (Berkeley: University of California Press, 1987), pp. 50–98.

25. Kazis and Grossman, *Fear at Work*, p. 37.

26. Alan S. Miller, "Toward an Environment/Labor Coalition," *Environment* 22 (June 1980): 32–39.

27. See Barry Bluestone and Bennett Harrison, *The Deindustrialization of America* (New York: Basic Books, 1982), p. 90.

28. Buttel and Flinn, "Social Class and Mass Environmental Beliefs," pp. 433–450; Robert Cameron Mitchell, "Silent Spring/Solid Majorities," *Public Opinion* 2 (August/September 1979): 16–20; Robert Cameron Mitchell, "Public Opinion and Environmental Politics," in N. J. Vig and M. E. Kraft, eds., *Environmental Policy in the 1980's: Reagan's New Agenda* (Washington, D.C.: Congressional Quarterly Press, 1984), pp. 51–73; Mohai, "Public Concern and Elite Involvement," p. 821; Dorceta E. Taylor, "Blacks and the Environment: Toward an Explanation of the Concern and Action Gap Between Blacks and Whites," *Environment and Behavior* 21 (March 1989): 175–205.

29. See Ron E. Roberts and Robert Marsh Kloss, *Social Movements: Between the Balcony and the Barricade*, 2nd ed. (St. Louis: C. V. Mosby, 1979); James L. Wood and Maurice Jackson, eds., *Social Movements: Development, Participation and Dynamics* (Belmont, Calif.: Wadsworth, 1982).

30. For a detailed discussion of the resource mobilization model, see Anthony Oberschall, *Social Conflict and Social Movement* (Englewood Cliffs, N.J.: Prentice-Hall, 1973); John D. McCarthy and Mayer Zald, *The Trend of Social Movements in America: Professionalism and Resource Mobilization* (Morristown, N.J.: General Learning Press, 1979); William Gamson, *The Study of Social Protest* (Homewood, Ill.: Dorsey Press, 1975); Charles Tilly, *From Mobilization to Revolution* (Reading, Mass.: Addison-Wesley, 1978); Craig J. Jenkins, "Resource Mobilization Theory and the Study of Social Movements," *Annual Review of Sociology* 9 (1983): 27–53.

31. Edward J. Walsh and Rex Warland, "Social Movement Involvement in the Wake of a Nuclear Accident: Activists and Free-Riders in the TMI Area," *American Sociological Review* 48 (December 1983): 764–780; Mohai, "Public Concern and Elite Involvement," pp. 822–823.

32. The discussion of issues that are likely to attract blacks to the environmental movement was adapted from Gale, "The Environmental Movement and the Left," pp. 182–186.

33. Ibid., p. 184.

34. See Ronald A. Taylor, "Do Environmentalists Care About Poor People?" *U.S. News and World Report* 96 (April 2, 1982): 51–55; Bullard, "Endangered Environs," p. 98; Bullard and Wright, "The Politics of Pollution," pp. 71–78.

35. Morris, *The Origins of the Civil Rights Movement*, p. 282.

36. Miller, "Toward an Environment/Labor Coalition," pp. 32–39; Sue Pollack and JoAnn Grozuczak, *Reagan, Toxics and Minorities* (Washington, D.C.: Urban Environmental Conference, Inc., 1984), Chapter 1; Kazis and Grossman, *Fear at Work*, pp. 3–35.

37. Andrew Porterfield and David Weir, "The Export of Hazardous Waste," *Nation* 245 (October 3, 1987): 340–344; Jim Vallette, *The International Trade in Wastes: A Greenpeace Inventory* (Washington, D.C.: Greenpeace, 1989), pp. 7–16.

38. Jack Bloom, *Class, Race and the Civil Rights Movement* (Bloomington: Indiana University Press, 1987), p. 18.

39. Bullard and Wright, "Environmentalism and the Politics of Equity," p. 32.

40. Urban Environment Conference, Inc., *Taking Back Our Health: An Institute on Surviving the Toxic Threat to Minority Communities* (Washington, D.C.: Urban Environment Conference, Inc., 1985), p. 29.

41. Bullard and Wright, "Environmentalism and the Politics of Equity," pp. 32–33.

42. Commission for Racial Justice, *Toxic Wastes and Race: A National Report on the Racial and Socioeconomic Characteristics of Communities with Hazardous Waste Sites* (New York: United Church of Christ, 1987), p. x.

43. Taylor, "Do Environmentalists Care About Poor People?" pp. 51–52.

44. Barbara Reynolds, "Triana, Alabama: The Unhealthiest Town in America," *National Wildlife* 18 (August 1980): 33; Bullard and Wright, "The Politics of Pollution," p. 75.

45. Michael Haggerty, "Crisis at Indian Creek," *Atlanta Journal and Constitution Magazine* (January 20, 1980): 14–25.

46. Ibid.

TOWARD AN INTERNATIONAL SOCIAL-MOVEMENT UNIONISM

Kim Moody

By the late 1990s, the structure of world capitalism had become clear. Capitalism was now global, but the world economy it produced was fragmented and highly uneven. The old North–South divide had widened in terms of the incomes of the majority. The South was locked into the role of low-wage provider for corporations based in the North. Corporate-dominated systems of production crossed this North–South boundary, producing primarily for the markets of the North. The North itself was now divided into a Triad of major economic regions, which in turn crossed the North–South divide. Astride this divided world were the TNCs operating in each Triad region and beyond. The multilateral agreements and institutions that were said to regulate this process had been rigged to discipline governments and encourage centrifugal market forces. Together, these structures and forces sponsored a virtual race to the economic and social bottom for the workers of the world.

As the twenty-first century approached, however, a rebellion against capitalist globalization, its structures, and its effects had begun. The rebellion took shape on both sides of the North–South economic divide and, in varying degrees, within all three of the major Triad regions. It confronted the most basic effects of the process of globalization at the workplace level as conditions became intolerable. It confronted the conservative neoliberal agenda at the national level and, no matter how indirectly, the plans of capital's rickety multilateral regime at the international level. Its explosive force in some places surprised friends and foes alike. At the center of the rebellion were the working class and its most basic organization, the trade union.

This very class was in the midst of change: its composition was becoming more diverse in most places, as women and immigrants composed a larger proportion of the workforce, and its organizations were in flux—somewhere still declining, somewhere growing, everywhere changing. The rebellion was international in scope, but it was taking place mostly on national terrain. The need to create unity in action across racial, ethnic, and gender lines within the nation and across borders and seas was more apparent than ever. The difficulty of doing so was still daunting.

The rebellion had seemed unlikely because so many of its official leaders were reluctant warriors. The Brazilians, South Africans, Argentines, Venezuelans, Colombians, Ecuadoreans, and South Koreans might want to pick a fight with global capital or its local neoliberal representatives, but what about the "social partners" in Europe, the enterprise unionists in Japan, and the business unionists in North America? The change from paralysis to resistance could be explained by the specifics of each nation, but something lay beneath these specifics that drove labor in so many places toward confrontation.

The turn taken in so many countries in so short a period of time is all the harder to explain in the developed industrial nations because, with notable exceptions, many top trade union leaders had embraced a new "realism" that said competitive business considerations must be adhered to, cooperation with management was the means to that end, and partnership with national or regional capital was the road to employment stabilization. *Business Week* identified a new generation of European labor leaders willing to "deliver on needed cuts in pay and benefits." . . . What they had in common was a commitment to "flexibility" in the workplace and the labor market.[1] . . .

It is not so different in North America. The United Auto Workers' new president, Steve Yokich, could approve a dozen or so local strikes against GM, but still permit even more flexibility in the national contracts negotiated in 1996. The new president of the AFL–CIO could call for more militancy in organizing, but call on business leaders to engage in partnership. In Canada, reluctant leaders from the Canadian divisions of the American-dominated international unions resisted the Days of Action behind the scenes, but were forced to go along in the end. Even within some of the newer labor movements of the Third World, voices of moderation and "partnership" could be heard. Yet, the strikes continued.

The reason for this lay partly in the very nature of trade unions. They are ambiguous organizations. On the one hand, they are poised to fight capital in defense of labor. On the other hand, at the top level, they attempt to hold the lines of defense through long-term stable bargaining relations, a rudimentary type of social partnership. The step to a more ideological or even institutional "partnership" between the labor bureaucracy and capital's bureaucracy is not always a big one. But then the winds of economic change and competition come along and the house of cards collapses.

The lines of defense can no longer be held through the routine exercise of the bargaining relationship. A fight is called for and sometimes waged by these same leaders. Typically, it is waged in the name of the old stable relationship. For the top leaders there is no contradiction. There is, however, an underlying contradiction between the new demands of capital and the union's old line of defense. Stability is gone, but the paradise lost of stability and normal bargaining continues to inform the actions of the leaders even when they are confrontational. Their actions sometimes push forward even though their eyes are focused clearly on the past. That this contradiction is likely to limit the effectiveness of the unions is obvious, but it does not preclude such action.

This new generation of top labor leaders took office in a moment of transition across much of the developed industrial world. Most of them built their upward-bound careers during the long period of paralysis and restructuring of the 1980s. They tended to embrace the cooperation agenda of those years as something appropriate to the new global era. Expedience often took on a more ideological shape as the new leaders saw themselves as exponents of a "new realism" or "industrial democracy." They did so without strong opposition from a membership still in shock from the enormous changes. The activists in the workplace might be more suspicious of the new ambience of cooperation that inevitably pushed for more work and longer hours, on the one hand, and destroyed good jobs, on the other. But for most of this period they could not move their rank-and-file to action. The activists were themselves divided over what to do.

But the pressures of lean production, neoliberal austerity, and international competition bore down on more and more sectors of the working classes of more and more nations. The mass strikes of 1994–97 did not come out of nowhere. In most countries where these occurred there was already a pre-history of resistance in specific workplaces. Strikes in France's public-sector industries, such as Air France, France Télécom, the national railroad, and Paris transit began in 1992 or 1993. In fact, they began even earlier among rail workers and nurses in 1987, led by the rank-and-file "coordinations." Spain saw a long string of strikes in important industries as well as earlier mass strikes in 1993 and 1994. Italy had seen strikes called by unofficial "Cobas" among public-sector workers. In the US strikes returned in both the public and private sectors in the early 1990s.[2]

By the time the new leaders took office in the 1990s the mood of the ranks and of the activists was already beginning to change—or become more torn between fear and action. While fear of job loss remained a powerful force among the ranks and activists, it had become impossible to believe the promises of human resources management (HRM), team concept, total quality, or whatever name the new ways of working were known by. The new workplace, whether in the private or public sector, was worse, not better, in most cases. Job loss continued through downsizing and re-engineering. And national social safety nets were being cut back or even dismantled—threatening public employment, on the one hand, and the quality of life for more and more workers, on the other.

The return to action in the 1990s differed from the industrial upheaval of 1967–75 in a number of ways. While it was not on the scale of the 1960s, not yet an upheaval, it was more general—affecting not only more developed nations, but also many of the industrializing nations of the Third World. Like the processes that pushed more groups of workers into action, the rebellion itself was more truly global than any in the past. It pointed to one of the more suggestive strategic ideas of the period: the potential for joint action between the old unions in the North, which were beginning to change, and the new social movement unions in the most industrial nations of the South, which provided a model suited to the new era.

To a greater extent than the 1967–75 upheaval or that of the 1930s or 1940s, this was a rebellion led by public-sector workers.[3] While it was often the more "blue-collar" workers who initiated these events, this wave of mass strikes saw health-care workers, teachers, and others play an important role almost everywhere. Indeed, the more heavily female public-sector occupations swelled the ranks of these mass strikes from the beginning in many countries, reflecting the new role of women in both the workforce and the unions.

Looked at both nationally and internationally, the strikes and struggles that emerged in the mid-1990s reflected many of the changes in the workforce that were supposed to represent fragmentation. In the heat of mass action, however, international differences, ethnic and gender diversity, and old sectoral divisions, for example between public- and private-sector unions, appeared as strengths among both the strikers and the working-class public that expressed almost universal support for these movements. The 1996 strike by Oregon state workers might seem less spectacular than France's 1995 public-sector general strike, but it mobilized the same diversity of manual, service, and professional men and women workers of many races. Similarly, Ontario's one-day general strikes might appear almost tame compared with the struggles in South Korea or France, but this same mixture, in which women play a much larger role and racial and occupational diversity are taken as the norm, was apparent.

The new leaders who came to head many unions and federations in this changing context reflected the past in both ideology and, with some notable exceptions, ethnic or gender composition. Whether or not they were popular, they would certainly linger on for some time as the hesitant generals in a fight they never chose. While debate was growing and in some places oppositional movements forming, the ability of top leaders to hold on is one of the great problems of most trade-union structures. The lack of democracy and leadership accountability was a basic flaw and, under the new circumstances, a serious weakness for unions pushed into a fight. So, the fight for union democracy would have to become part of the agenda for change, if unions were to play an effective role.

Nowhere was the need for political change more apparent than in the area of internationalism. The top leaders who assumed office in the 1990s were certainly more aware of the international dimensions of collective bargaining than those they replaced. Indeed, global competitiveness routinely provided the argument for making concessions and taking retreats in stride. As globally minded as they might be in this sense, however, they still saw the unions and federations they governed in national and nationalist terms, as Dan Gallin pointed out.[4] Writing in *Labor Notes* after reading AFL–CIO president John Sweeney's book, *America Needs a Raise*, one German shop steward said, "I was shocked about the extreme nationalist viewpoint of Brother Sweeney."[5] But, in truth, much the same could be said of the leaders of most national labor federations in the industrial countries. Indeed, that is precisely what acceptance of the corporate competitiveness agenda means—a commitment to a specious "job security" at the national level by supporting the globally active employers of that country.

So, while the contours and vulnerabilities of international production chains may be well enough known in labor circles, very few unions actually acted on this basis. There were important exceptions, such as the UE's new plan to build cross-border networks on an industrial or corporate basis, FLOC's alliance with SNTOAC, Comisiones Obreras' attempts to build alliances with related unions in North Africa, or the CAW–Teamster–TGWU alliance at Air Canada, or the Canadian Auto Workers' work with unions in Mexico. Yet, while most union leaders across the industrial world were quick to send messages or even delegations of solidarity to South Korea or South Africa, or to attend the consensus or ceremonial meetings that pass for official labor internationalism, the more difficult work of building cross-border industrial alliances and networks remained a low priority. The International Trade Secretariats could have played a bigger role in this, but were limited by the nationalism of the affiliates that tend to dominate them.

The problem is not simply that today's leaders for the most part don't do enough on the international level. Most of the struggle against the structures and effects of globalization necessarily occurs on a national plane. That, after all, is where workers live, work, and fight. That also is the lesson of the first round of mass strikes and even the more localized struggles against the global regime of capital. The most basic feature of an effective internationalism for this period is the ability of the working class to mount opposition to the entire agenda of transnational capital and its politicians in their own "back yard." For this agenda, too, is ultimately carried out at the national level. It is the caution in the occasional battle and the open embrace of the enemy in the daily relationship of labor bureaucracy to corporate bureaucracy that is the fundamental problem. It is the ideology of partnership held by so many union leaders and institutionalized in the publications, educational programs, and official positions of the unions and federations that is a barrier to a clear course of action.

The often reluctant leadership is, nevertheless, engaging in battles with capital and the state at the national level. This new level of struggle, in turn, has a transformative power. It is in these kinds of struggle that people and their consciousness change. The inactive or fearful rank and file become the heroes of the street, whether it is in a mass demonstration or a more limited fight around workplace issues. Perceptions of what is possible change as new forces come into the struggle and the power of the class, long denied and hidden, becomes visible. Yesterday's competing ethnic or gender group is today's ally. The activists who have agitated for this fight now have a base; the conservatives in the union are, for the moment, isolated.

It is not possible to predict whether we are entering a period of intensified class struggle or whether the actions of recent years will fade as rapidly as they appeared. The political and economic pressures that produced these strikes and movements, however, will not go away. Neither lean production nor the rule of the market has alleviated the crisis of profitability. Indeed, the storms of international competition are, if anything, more destructive today. If history is any guide, the current period of renewed class conflict is likely to continue for at least a few years, perhaps a decade. These are the kinds of periods in which bigger changes in the organization of class become possible. This, in turn, alters what is possible in the realm of politics.

It is in such periods that the working class can glimpse the possibilities of social change or even revolution. It is in this kind of milieu of struggle and mass motion that answers to Margaret Thatcher's questions about free market capitalism, "What is the alternative?", become more apparent. It is also in such periods that certain demands and changes in working-class organization come to the fore: the demand for the eight-hour day in the 1880s; workplace organization and shop stewards in 1914–21; industrial unionism in the 1930s; the forty-hour work week in the 1930s. These ideas motivated millions across the world in earlier times and gave focus to the strike movements, political fights, and new organizations that arose in those times.

The vision appropriate to the era of globalization is social-movement unionism. It has already been born in South Africa, Brazil, South Korea, and elsewhere in the more industrialized parts of the Third World. Within the industrial North it is implied in many of the ideas put forth by oppositional groups within unions, national cross-union networks of union activists, international solidarity networks and committees, official and unofficial cross-border networks, and the only global grassroots industrially based network, TIE. These forces are small, even marginal in some cases, but they speak with a clear voice and offer ideas pertinent to the epoch of capitalist globalization.

Social-Movement Unionism and Union Democracy

Social-movement unionism isn't about jurisdiction or structure, as is craft or industrial unionism. . . .

■ ■ ■ ■

In social-movement unionism neither the unions nor their members are passive in any sense. Unions take an active lead in the streets, as well as in politics. They ally with other social movements, but provide a class vision and content that make for a stronger glue than that which usually holds electoral or temporary coalitions together. That content is not simply the demands of the movements, but the activation of the mass of union members as the leaders of the charge—those who in most cases have the greatest social and economic leverage in capitalist society. Social-movement unionism implies an active strategic orientation that uses the strongest of society's oppressed and exploited, generally organized workers, to mobilize those who are less able to sustain self-mobilization: the poor, the unemployed, the casualized workers, the neighborhood organizations.

The current debate in the US labor movement is often organized around the counterposition of the old business-union "service model" versus the newer "mobilizing" or "organizing" models. While the organizing or mobilizing concepts are obviously an improvement on the passive-service model, most versions of this counterposition narrow the debate in at least two ways. First, they leave the question of union hierarchy, the lack of membership control or leadership accountability, out of the debate. This is usually intentional, since much of this debate goes on among labor professionals and staff organizers who are employed by the hierarchy.[6]

As union organizer Michael Eisenscher argues, however, democracy is closely related to a union's ability effectively to mobilize and act. . . . [H]e writes:

> In confronting more powerful economic and social forces, democracy is an instrument for building solidarity, for establishing accountability, and for determining appropriate strategies—all of which are critical for sustaining and advancing worker and union interests. Union democracy is not synonymous with either union activism or militancy. Members can be mobilized for activities over which they have little or no control, for objectives determined for them rather than by them. Given that unions are institutions for the exercise of workers' power, their responsiveness to membership aspirations and needs is determined, in part, by the extent to which members can and do assert effective control over their political objectives, bargaining strategies, disposition of resources, accountability of staff and officers, and innumerable other aspects of organizational performance.[7]

Second, casting the debate as simply one between the "organizing" and "service" models also narrows the discussion by focusing exclusively on the union as an institution—its growth through organizing or its effectiveness in bargaining through occasional membership mobilization from above. But the idea of social-movement unionism is a labor movement "whose constituencies spread far beyond the factory gates and whose demands include broad social and economic change," as one study of the South African and Brazilian labor movements put it.[8] It is a movement in which unions provide much of the economic leverage and organizational resources, while social-movement organizations, like the popular urban movements in Latin America, provide greater numbers and a connection to the less well organized or positioned sections of the working class.

The activation of union members in order to reach and mobilize these broader constituencies is interwoven with the question of union democracy and leadership accountability. The members must have a hand in shaping the union's agenda at both the bargaining and the broad social level if they are going to invest the time and energy demanded by this kind of unionism. . . .

It is typical of social-movement unions like those in Brazil, South Africa, and Canada that open debates on tough issues take place regularly. To be sure, these unions, too, face a tendency toward bureaucratization. But the members have enough experience in union affairs to resist this trend. In America's bureaucratic business unions or Europe's top-down political unions, the opening of debate is something new and very incomplete. It often has to be forced by grassroots-based opposition movement from within.

Members' involvement in union affairs and power over their leaders are also key to new organizing and recruitment if unions are to become powerful once again. Experience shows that active union members are better recruiters than paid organizers. A recent study done in the United States showed that unions won 73% of representation elections when members did the organizing, compared with 27% when it was done by professional organizers.[9] A passive membership is not likely to devote the time it takes to organize other workers, and passivity is largely a product of bureaucracy.

The fight for union democracy does not come out of nowhere. It is usually a function of conflict within the unions—differences over direction. It is typically the "dissidents" fighting from the ranks or the activist layer for some sort of alternative program of action who demand greater democracy. This process is visible not only in the US, where challenges and "reform" movements have become widespread, but across many of the older unions in the developed industrial nations.

Harmonizing Collective Bargaining and Class Interests

The demands put forth by unions are another key to social-movement unionism. In many countries unions are seen as, or cast by the experts as, the organizations of a privileged minority, a sort of "labor aristocracy." Overcoming this is not simply a matter of the union raising some broad political demands. Most unions, even very conservative ones, do that already. It is, rather, a matter of shaping even the union's bargaining demands in a way that has a positive impact on other working-class people, harmonizing the demands of the union with the broader needs of the class.

■ ■ ■ ■

... [T]his harmonization of the interests of the workers covered in collective bargaining and the broader working-class public can begin to move unions toward a broader social agenda. Harmonization can touch on many of the issues of the crisis of working-class life. For example, when local unions win additional jobs, they also alleviate the health-and-safety or stress epidemic within the plants, taking some pressure off family life as well as improving workplace conditions. Contract demands for child care, pay equity (equal pay for comparable work), immigrant rights on the job, and affirmative action (positive discrimination in the UK) in hiring and promotions to reduce racial and gender inequalities at work can provide bridges across racial, national, and gender lines. White and/or male workers are much less likely to see such demands as threatening if the unions are fighting for and wining more jobs, relief from workplace stress, and growing incomes.

Most of the rebellion against capitalist globalization and its impact occurs on national terrain or even at the level of the workplace. Mass political strikes are, after all, directed at national or local states, which are still the mediators of the international regime. But even these strikes cannot be sustained or repeated regularly. Furthermore, the power and durability of the movement will depend on the strength of organization at the industry and workplace levels. Among other things this means there cannot be a trade-off between organizing and recruitment, on the one hand, and strong democratic workplace organization, on the other.

■ ■ ■ ■

Internationalizing Union Practice

To say that most struggle is ultimately national or even local is not to say that international links, coordination, organization, and action are not critical to the success of social-movement unionism in today's globalizing international economy. Internationalism must be part of the perspective and practice of union leaders, activists, and members if global capital is to be contained at all.

The analysis presented earlier points toward the centrality of international production chains in developing a multi-layered strategy for dealing with TNCs. While only a minority of workers are employed directly by TNCs, their potential impact at the heart of the world economy gives these workers a uniquely strategic position. Clearly, the TNCs dominate many nominally independent employers, set the world-wide trends in working conditions, and preserve the unequal wage levels that perpetuate competition among workers even in the same TNC. These giant corporations have deep pockets to resist strikes or other forms of action, but they are also vulnerable at many points of their cross-border production chains.

The strong tendency of cross-border production systems to be located within one or another of the Triad regions gives unions in that region the more manageable task of making the links, exchanging information on company tactics or conditions, and eventually coordinating actions with specific goals and demands on a regional basis. The similar tendency of many industries to be geographically concentrated within each nation also lessens some of the difficulties in organizing and coordinating actions that one would find in a truly global production system.

Mapping the course of production and ownership and its weak points is by now a fairly well known science.

Simply drawing up abstract plans for crippling internationalized production will be an exercise in futility, however, if the unions involved are too bureaucratic to mobilize their members for the fight and the leaders are committed to partnership and the nationalist thinking it implies. The International Trade Secretariats, which would be a logical forum for international coordination, tend to be dominated by partnership-minded union leaders from the US, Japan, Germany, and Britain. It should be obvious that the real difficulties and conflicts of interest between groups of workers in different countries are daunting enough. Union leaders who are ideologically and institutionally committed to the "competitiveness" of TNCs based in their own country through some kind of partnership program are unlikely to have the vision to overcome these very real stumbling blocks.

Much the same can be said of regionally based cross-border alliances. Simple alliances between leaders, like that between the leaders of the CWA, STRM, and CEP in the NAFTA region, will not be sufficient. At best, they will conduct worthwhile pressure campaigns such as the Sprint "Conexión Familiar" campaign. At worst, such an alliance will only reflect the existing caution of the union bureaucracy. This could be the fate of the cross-border contacts provided by the European Works Councils as well, if they are not based on workplace representation. Just as national leaders often need to be pushed into bolder actions from below, so cross-border alliances of these same leaders will need to be pressured from the ranks, and local unions to turn these top-down connections into action and grapple with the workplace crisis facing most workers.

The importance of official efforts like the UE–FAT alliance has been their willingness to involve workplace-level activists and leaders. The UE proposal to bring together local unions within the same company across borders will be one of the first official experiments in North America to attempt such grassroots linkages. So far, however, it is the exception.

The unofficial transnational worker networks, like those organized through TIE or the UAW Local 879-Ford Workers' Democratic Movement pact, have an important transformative role to play as more unions experiment with different types of cross-border activities. By themselves, they lack the power and resources of the unions, but they have roots in the workplaces of the industries where they exist. Their role in the overall process of union transformation, of creating an international social-movement unionism, is not primarily as a pressure group. Rather it is to set examples and to act as ginger groups that set people in motion. Right now it is difficult for them to do more than provide information and an overview, but in doing so they contribute to the growth of a current working to change their unions and to a deepening of the international outlook of workplace activists.

All this occurs in a context where enormous economic and social pressures are pushing workers and their unions to act, where action is transforming more and more people and widening their perspectives, and where the old unions have increasingly become the sites of internal challenges and debates over direction. In this situation, the transnational worker networks should serve not as internal opposition groups, but as daily educators on the importance of international work, and the cultural and political tools needed to carry it out. The conferences, meetings, and tours conducted by these networks have an important role in broadening the outlook of the activist layer in particular. Such actions as the networks can mount also play a worker-to-worker educational role, just as local and national actions do.

Local strikes in key locations can be part of this strategy where they can close down international production systems in whole or part. Thus, in situations where a workplace union is part of the transnational worker network, they can go beyond education and symbolic actions actually to influence management decisions, whether this is in defense of victimized workers at home or abroad, or in a fight for common demands in the interests of the workers in all the affected countries. Common cross-border actions by local unions in different countries can cripple even the largest TNCs in their major markets. As the perception of this possibility becomes more widely recognized, the rules of the game will change.

■ ■ ■ ■

Against Neoliberalism: A Labor Politics for the Moment

As "oppositions that never become governments," unions must fight from the outside. Indeed, in today's world, workers and their unions are more and more cast as outsiders when they refuse or resist the corporate competitiveness agenda and the race to the bottom it implies. The alternative on offer is the paralysis of partnership. Many union leaders hope to have it both ways, but capital's contemporary agenda and the very goals the unions are fighting for, when they fight, are too much at odds. In taking to the streets in opposition to government austerity plans and cut-backs, the unions have found different allies across the working class. Top leaders will continue to waver between these alternatives, at times undermining the struggle, but the direction of this struggle seems clear.

In the realm of politics, it is largely a defensive direction for the moment. The defense of welfare measures, pensions, health-care provision, unemployment benefits, and existing public services has been the motivation for most of the mass and general strikes of the past few years. It has also become necessary to defend social gains of specific groups, such as affirmative action or immigrant rights, where they exist. Occasionally, in the area of collective bargaining, unions make some advances, as with the French truckers or the fight for the shorter work week in Germany, but mostly it is inherent in the period that most struggles will be defensive until labor builds and expands its power nationally and internationally.

There is a tendency on the political left and among supporters of organized labor to see defensive struggles as somehow bad or inadequate. Yet, almost all labor upheavals and advances in history have originated in defensive struggles—when employers and/or governments attempt to take back something previously won or simply make matters worse. In this process, the defensive struggles provide the time and context in which labor recruits and builds or rebuilds its organizations. The siren voices of "partnership," however, advise that defensive struggles are: (a) hopeless in this global economy, or (b) conservative and backward-looking. They propose instead various forms of broader social partnership that are supposed to mend the economy, providing, of course, that unions abandon their hopeless fight for material improvements on the job, in incomes, or in broader social provisions. These various forms of social partnership or social contract are meant as alternatives to struggle—an easy road to renewed prosperity.

■■■■

These various stakeholder and stockholder proposals always rest on an analysis that dissolves real power relations. The capitalist corporation becomes just one more porous institution with neutral goals and various "stakeholders" whose interests can be harmonized with one another and with society as a whole. . . .

■■■■

The problems with all these alternatives to struggle is that today's corporations, led by the TNCs, are clearly predators waging class war to expand their world-wide empires and restore the legendary profit rates of decades ago. Governments are following their lead, coming more and more under the influence of "the commercial economy," not less. Under these circumstances something more than an amorphous "civil society" is needed as a counterweight, and that is the organized working class and its allies. Finally, of course, there is nothing in these proposals that guarantees real job creation, since the basic mechanisms of investment and internal profitability are left untouched.

The current emphasis on social safety-net issues and increased equality within the class, material issues from which working-class people can gain and strengthen their position, offers the best way to gather in broader forces and increase the power of the working class. All the various schemes for representation in the institutions of capital end up as versions of partnership in which unions or other members of "civil society" are dragged into the war that is real capitalist competition, which is more likely to destroy jobs than create them. Labor cannot advance through such competition. Its historic role is to limit and eventually suppress this destructive force. Social safety-net demands are one more way in which unions and their working-class allies can "take labor out of competition."

The fight for shorter work time, labor's major offensive issue, can and should also become a political fight as it did in the nineteenth century and the 1930s. The struggle to preserve publicly funded pensions, Social Security in the US, is a part of this fight to reduce total work time. But a national standard of thirty-five hours a week or less (with no pay reductions and no strings) implemented through legislation would contribute immediately to employment growth, strengthening the position of the working class. It is obvious that in most countries the old political parties of the left and the working class are unwilling, perhaps unable, to wage such a fight. It falls once again to the "oppositions that never become governments."

In the realm of international policy, renegotiating trade agreements would be part of a long-range program. But in terms of the politics of the moment, there is one goal that would do more to bring about "upward leveling" across the world than any other—cancellation of the Third World debt. . . .

The cancellation of this debt or even its progressive reduction would free billions of dollars in interest paid annually to banks or bond-holders in the North by governments of the South. Where unions and other organizations were able to fight for the proper distribution of the new resources this would free up, social programs that provide the necessary safety net for so many in the Third World could be restored or even expanded. The parameters of struggle would be altered across the Third World. Obviously, a constructive redistribution of this potential wealth would require strong labor movements in both North and South. But it is a common goal that could do much to bind the movements in these two parts of the world that capital has sought to play against one another.

Toward a World-Wide Social-Movement Union Current

The pressures of globalization and lean production, the transforming powers of renewed struggle, and the fresh forces that have come to the working class in recent decades are all pushing the working class and its organizations in a more aggressive and confrontational direction. Because so many top leaders still think and act in terms of the corporate competitiveness/partnership agenda, this process often begins with or includes internal union conflict. Debate and challenges are more common within unions and there are new social–movement unions in parts of the economic South to provide "role models" for activists in the North. Yet, there is nothing inevitable about the outcomes of these debates or challenges.

As noted earlier, the newest generation of top leaders in much of the North are the products of the 1980s, deeply committed to one or another form of partnership with capital. In fact, the end of the Cold War and the gathering in of more federations and unions in the ICFTU and the ITSs, on the one hand, and the rise in influence of the US, German, Japanese, and British leaders in these bodies, on the other, mean that the partnership advocates have a wider audience than in the past. They have behind them a seductive chorus of social-democratic politicians, and threats and promises from many of the TNCs themselves.

The context for a debate over the direction of world labor may be more favorable, but a fight is required. An international current is needed to promote the ideas and practices of social-movement unionism. The material for such a current is already at hand in unions such as those in South Korea, South Africa, Brazil, and other newer unions in Asia; in major tendencies within changing Latin American unions; in a few unions in the North, like the Canadian Auto Workers, the United Electrical Workers in the US, and SUD in France, among others; in oppositional or reform groups within unions; in the national networks of activists around publications such as *Labor Notes*; those in the international solidarity networks such as APWSL, CJM, US–GLEP, and the Maquiladora Workers' Support Committee; and the industrial networks of TIE.

Obviously, this is a diverse current and not an ideologically defined, left political tendency. It includes people from a variety of tendencies and even more of those with no left background. It contains organizations as different as unions and oppositional networks. It is world-wide, cutting across the North–South divide and spanning the three Triad regions.

What this current shares is not a single organization or a central leadership, but a view of what unionism can be in today's globalizing world. Central to this view of social-movement unionism are union democracy and leadership accountability, membership activation and involvement, a commitment to union growth and recruitment, a vision and practice that reach beyond even an expanding union membership to other sectors and organizations of the working class. This view sees unions as taking an active, leading role in the struggles against international and domestic capital and their neoliberal political allies.

Social-movement unionism is an orientation guided by these ideas and visions. It is not an attempt to reshape national labor-relations systems or make all unions have the same structure. While an industrial strategic approach is important, social-movement unionism can guide the actions of today's typical, merged general unions, as the case of the CAW indicates. It can be the practice and outlook of a single occupational union such as the California Nurses' Association, or of a government department or agency-based union such as SUD in France's telecom and postal systems. It can be a region of a national labor federation, such as the Catalan CCOO. What matters most is that its practice is a rank-and-file practice and not simply a matter of the progressive politics of a small group of leaders.

Above all, social-movement unionism is a perspective to be fought for on an international scale. The recognition of a common perspective by activists in different countries will both facilitate an internationalist practice and reinforce the struggle for this orientation at every level of existing working-class organization. It is a perspective that can maximize working-class power by drawing together the different sectors within the class around those organizations with the greatest existing and potential power at this juncture, the unions. It is a perspective that embraces the diversity of the working class in order to overcome its fragmentation. While it is not about "reforming" the old mass parties of the left, it is far more likely to move them off center than any amount of lobbying or conventional "boring within." It is, above all, a means, a rehearsal, for self-emancipation from below.

Notes

1. *Business Week*, December 16, 1996, pp. 61–65.
2. P. K. Edwards and Richard Hyman, "Strikes and Industrial Conflict: Peace in Europe?" in Richard Hyman and Anthony Ferner, eds. *New Frontiers in European Industrial Relations*, Oxford, Basil Blackwell Ltd., 1994, pp. 250–277; Daniel Bensaid, "Neo-Liberal Reform and Popular Rebellion." *New Left Review* 215, January/February 1996, pp. 109–116.
3. For a detailed view of the upheaval of 1967–75 in various US industries, see Glenn Perusek and Kent Worcester, *Trade Union Politics: American Unions and Economic Change 1960s–1990s*, Atlantic Highlands, NJ, Humanities Press, 1995.
4. Dan Gallin, "Inside the New World Order: Drawing the Battle Lines." *New Politics* 5(1), Summer 1994, pp. 127–128.
5. *Labor Notes:* Number 214, January 1997.
6. See, for example, Stephen Lerner, "Reviving Unions: A Call to Action," and responses in *Boston Review* 21(2). April/May 1996, 21(3/4) summer 1996, pp. 1–5.
7. Michael Eisenscher, "Critical Juncture: Unionism at the Crossroads," Center for Labor Research, University of Massachusetts-Boston, working paper, May 2, 1996. p. 3.
8. Gay W. Seidman, *Manufacturing Militance: Workers' Movements in Brazil and South Africa, 1970–1985.* Berkeley, University of California Press, 1984, p. 2.
9. *Business Week*, February 17, 1997, p. 57.

BAD MOOD RISING

The New Anticorporate Activism

NAOMI KLEIN

The Earth is not dying, it is being killed. And those that are killing it have names and addresses.

UTAH PHILLIPS

How do we tell Steve that his dad owns a sweatshop?!?

TORI SPELLING, AS THE CHARACTER DONNA ON *BEVERLY HILLS 90210*, AFTER DISCOVERING THAT HER OWN LINE OF DESIGNER CLOTHING WAS BEING MANUFACTURED BY IMMIGRANT WOMEN IN AN L.A. SWEATSHOP, OCTOBER 15,1997

While the latter half of the 1990s has seen enormous growth in the brands' ubiquity, a parallel phenomenon has emerged on the margins: a network of environmental, labor and human-rights activists determined to expose the damage being done behind the slick veneer. Dozens of new organizations and publications have been founded for the sole purpose of "outing" corporations that are benefiting from repressive government policies around the globe. Older groups, previously focused on monitoring governments, have reconfigured their mandates so that their primary role is tracking violations committed by multinational corporations. As John Vidal, environmental editor of *The Guardian*, puts it, "A lot of activists are attaching themselves leech-like onto the sides of the bodies corporate."

This leech-like attachment takes many forms, from the socially respectable to the near-terrorist. Since 1994, the Massachusetts-based Program on Corporations, Law & Democracy, for instance, has been developing policy alternatives designed to "contest the authority of corporations to govern." The Oxford-based Corporate Watch, meanwhile, focuses on researching—and helping others to research—corporate crime. (Not to be confused with the San Francisco-based Corporate Watch, which sprang up at about the same time with a nearly identical mission for the U.S.) JUSTICE. DO IT NIKE! is a group of scrappy Oregon activists devoted to haranguing Nike about its labor practices in its own backyard. The Yellow Pages, on the other hand, is an underground international cabal of hackers who have declared war on the computer networks of those corporations that have successfully lobbied to delink human rights from trade with China. "In effect, businessmen started dictating foreign policy," says Blondie Wong, director of Hong Kong Blondes, a group of Chinese pro-democracy hackers now living in exile. "By taking the side of profit over conscience, business has set our struggle back so far that they have become our oppressors too."[1]

Taking a distinctly lower-tech (some might say primitive) approach is Belgian Noel Godin and his global band of political pie slingers. Although politicians and movie stars have faced flying pies, the corporate sector has been the primary target: Microsoft CEO Bill Gates, Monsanto CEO Robert Shapiro, Chevron CEO Ken Derr, World Trade Organization director Renato Ruggiero have all been hit, as well as that architect of global free trade, Milton Friedman. "To their lies, we respond with pies," says Agent Blueberry, of the Biotic Baking Brigade.[2]

The fad got so out of hand that in May 1999, Tesco, one of the largest supermarket chains in England, conducted a series of tests on its pies to see which ones made for the best slinging. "We like to keep abreast of what the customers are doing, and that's why we have to do the testing," said company spokesperson Melodie Schuster. Her recommendation: "The custard tart gives total face coverage."[3] Oh, and rest assured that none of the Tesco tarts contain any ingredients that have been genetically modified. The chain banned those from its products a month earlier—a response to a groundswell of anticorporate sentiment directed at Monsanto and the other agribusiness giants.

. . . Tesco made its decision to disassociate itself from genetically modified foods after a series of protests against "Frankenfoods" were held on its doorstep—part of an increasingly popular strategy among activist groups. Political rallies, which once wound their predictable course in front of government buildings and consulates, are now just as likely to take place in front of the stores of the corporate giants: outside Nike Town. . . . Foot Locker, the Disney Store and Shell gas pumps; on the roof of the corporate headquarters of Monsanto or BP; through malls and around Gap outlets; and even at supermarkets.

In short, the triumph of economic globalization has inspired a wave of techno-savvy investigative activists who are as globally minded as the corporations they track. This powerful form of activism reaches well beyond traditional trade unions. Its members are young and old; they come from elementary schools and college campuses suffering from branding fatigue and from church groups with large investment portfolios worried that corporations are behaving "sinfully." They are parents worried about their children's slavish devotion to "logo tribes," and they are also the political intelligentsia and social marketers who are more concerned with the quality of community life than with increased sales. In fact, by October 1997 there were so many disparate anticorporate protests going on around the world—against Nike, Shell, Disney, McDonald's and Monsanto—that Earth First! printed up an impromptu calendar with all the key dates and declared it the first annual End Corporate Dominance Month. About a month later, *The Wall Street Journal* ran a story headlined "Hurry! There Are Only 27 More Protesting Days Until Christmas."

"The Year of the Sweatshop"

In North America, much of this activity can be traced back to 1995–96, the period that Andrew Ross, director of American Studies at New York University, has called "The Year of the Sweatshop." For a time that year, North Americans couldn't turn on their televisions without hearing shameful stories about the exploitative labor practices behind the most popular, mass-marketed labels on the brandscape. In August 1995, the Gap's freshly scrubbed façade was further exfoliated to reveal a lawless factory in El Salvador where the manager responded to a union drive by firing 150 people and vowing that "blood will flow" if organizing continued.[4] In May 1996, U.S. labor activists discovered that chat-show host Kathie Lee Gifford's eponymous line of sportswear (sold exclusively at Wal-Mart) was being stitched by a ghastly combination of child laborers in Honduras and illegal sweatshop workers in New York. At about the same time, Guess jeans, which had built its image with sultry black-and-white photographs of supermodel Claudia Schiffer, was in open warfare with the U.S. Department of Labor over a failure on the part of its California-based contractors to pay the minimum wage. Even Mickey Mouse was letting his sweatshops show after a Disney contractor in Haiti was caught making Pocahontas pajamas under such impoverished conditions that workers had to nourish their babies with sugar water.

More outrage flowed after NBC aired an investigation of Mattel and Disney just days before Christmas 1996. With the help of hidden cameras, the reporter showed that children in Indonesia and China were working in virtual slavery "so that children in America can put frilly dresses on America's favorite doll."[5] In June 1996, *Life* magazine created more waves with photographs of Pakistani kids—looking shockingly young and paid as little as six cents an hour—hunched over soccer balls that bore the unmistakable Nike swoosh. But it wasn't just Nike. Adidas, Reebok, Umbro, Mitre, and Brine were all manufacturing balls in Pakistan where an estimated 10,000 children worked in the industry, many of them sold as indentured slave laborers to their employers and branded like livestock.[6] The *Life* images were so chilling that they galvanized parents, students and educators alike, many of whom made the photographs into placards and held them up in protest outside sporting-goods stores across the United States and Canada.

Running alongside all this was the story of Nike's sneakers. The Nike saga started before the Year of the Sweatshop began and has only grown stronger as other corporate controversies have slipped in and out of the public eye. Scandal has dogged Nike, with new revelations about factory conditions trailing the company's own global flight patterns. First came the reports of union crackdowns in South Korea; when the contractors fled and set up shop in Indonesia, the watchdogs followed, filing stories on starvation wages and military intimidation of workers. In March 1996,

The New York Times reported that after a wildcat strike at one Javanese factory, twenty-two workers were fired and one man who had been singled out as an organizer was locked in a room inside the factory and interrogated by soldiers for seven days. When Nike began moving production to Vietnam, the accusations moved too, with videotaped testimony of wage cheating and workers being beaten over the head with shoe uppers. When production moved decisively to China, the controversies over wages and the factories' "boot camp" style of management were right behind.

It wasn't only the superbrands and their celebrity endorsers who felt the sting of the Year of the Sweatshop—clothing-store chains, big-box retailers and department stores also found themselves being held responsible for the conditions under which the toys and fashions on their racks were produced. The issue came home for America in August 1995, when an apartment complex in El Monte, California, was raided by the U.S. Department of Labor. Seventy-two Thai garment workers were being held in bonded slavery—some had been in the compound for as long as seven years. The factory owner was a minor player in the industry, but the clothes the women were sewing were sold by such retail giants as Target, Sears and Nordstrom.

It is Wal-Mart, however, that has taken it on the chin most frequently since sweatshops made their big nineties comeback. As the world's largest retailer Wal-Mart is the primary distributor of many of the branded goods attracting controversy: Kathie Lee Gifford's clothing line, Disney's Haitian-made pajamas, child-produced clothing from Bangladesh, sweatshop-produced toys and sports gear from Asia. Why, consumers demanded, if Wal-Mart had the power to lower prices, alter CD covers and influence magazine content, did it not also have the power to demand and enforce ethical labor standards from its suppliers?

Though the revelations came out in the press one at a time, the incidents coalesced to give us a rare look under the hood of branded America. Few liked what they saw. The unsettling combination of celebrated brand names and impoverished production conditions have turned Nike, Disney and Wal-Mart, among others, into powerful metaphors for a brutal new way of doing business. In a single image, the brand-name sweatshop tells the story of the obscene disparities of the global economy: corporate executives and celebrities raking in salaries so high they defy comprehension, billions of dollars spent on branding and advertising—all propped up by a system of shantytowns, squalid factories and the misery and trampled expectations of young women . . . struggling to survive.

The Year of the Brand Attack

Gradually, the Year of the Sweatshop turned into the Year of the Brand Attack. Having been introduced to the laborers behind their toys and clothing, shoppers met the people who grew their coffee at the local Starbucks; according to the U.S. Guatemalan Labor Education Project, some of the coffee frothed at the chain was cultivated with the use of child labor, unsafe pesticides and subsubsistence wages. But it was in a courtroom in London, England, that the branded world was most thoroughly turned inside out. The highly publicized McLibel Trial began with McDonald's 1990 attempt to suppress a leaflet that accused the company of a host of abuses—from busting unions to depleting rain forests and littering the city streets. McDonald's denied the allegations and sued two London-based environmental activists for libel. The activists defended themselves by subjecting McDonald's to the corporate equivalent of a colonoscopy: the case lasted for seven years, and no infraction committed by the company was considered too minor to bring up in court or to post on the Internet.

The McLibel defendants' allegations about food safety dovetailed with another anticorporate movement taking off across Europe at the same time: the campaign against Monsanto and its bioengineered agricultural crops. At the center of this dispute was Monsanto's refusal to inform consumers which of the foods they bought at the supermarket were the product of genetic engineering, setting off a wave of direct action that included the uprooting of Monsanto test crops.

As if that weren't enough, multinationals also found themselves under the microscope for their involvement with some of the world's most violent and repressive regimes: Burma, Indonesia, Colombia, Nigeria and Chinese-occupied Tibet. The issue was by no means new, but like the

McDonald's and Monsanto campaigns, it came to a new prominence in the mid- to late nineties, with much of the activity focusing on the host of familiar brand names operating in Burma (now officially known as Myanmar). The bloody coup that brought the current military regime to power in Burma took place in 1988, but international awareness about brutal conditions inside the Asian country skyrocketed in 1995 when opposition leader and Nobel laureate Aung San Suu Kyi was released from six years of house arrest. In a videotaped appeal smuggled out of the country, Suu Kyi condemned foreign investors for propping up the junta that had disregarded her party's overwhelming election victory in 1990. Companies operating in Burma, she stated, are directly or indirectly profiting from state-run slave-labor camps. "Foreign investors should realize there could be no economic growth and opportunities in Burma until there is agreement on the country's political future."[7]

The first response from human-rights activists was to lobby governments in North America, Europe and Scandinavia to impose trade sanctions on the Burmese government. When this failed to halt the flow of trade, they began targeting individual companies based in the activists' own home countries. In Denmark, the protests centered on the national brewer, Carlsberg, which had entered into a large contract to build a brewery in Burma. In Holland, the target was Heineken; in the U.S. and Canada, Liz Claiborne, Unocal, Disney, Pepsi and Ralph Lauren were in the crosshairs.

But the most significant landmark in the growth of anticorporate activism also came in 1995, when the world lost Ken Saro-Wiwa. The revered Nigerian writer and environmental leader was imprisoned by his country's oppressive regime for spearheading the Ogoni people's campaign against the devastating human and ecological effects of Royal Dutch/Shell's oil drilling in the Niger Delta. Human-rights groups rallied their governments to interfere, and some economic sanctions were imposed, but they had little effect. In November 1995, Saro-Wiwa and eight other Ogoni activists were executed by a military government who had enriched themselves with Shell's oil money and through their own people's repression.

The Year of the Brand Attack stretched into two years, then three and now shows no sign of receding. In February 1999, a new report revealed that workers sewing Disney clothes in several Chinese factories were earning as little as 13.5 cents an hour and were forced to put in hours of overtime.[8] In May 1999, ABC's *20/20* returned to the island of Saipan and brought back footage of young women locked inside sweatshop factories sewing for the Gap, Tommy Hilfiger and Polo Ralph Lauren. New revelations have also come out about violent clashes surrounding Chevron's drilling activities in the Niger Delta, and about Talisman Energy's plans to drill on contested territory in war-torn Sudan.

The volume and the tenacity of public outrage directed against them has blindsided the corporations, in large part because the activities for which they were being condemned were not particularly new. McDonald's has never been a friend of the working poor; oil companies have a long and uninterrupted history of collaborating with repressive governments to extract valuable resources with little concern for the people who live near them; Nike has produced its sneakers in Asian sweatshops since the early seventies, and many of the clothing chains have been doing so for even longer. As *The Wall Street Journal*'s Bob Ortega writes, labor unions had been collecting evidence of child laborers in Bangladesh making clothing sold at Wal-Mart since 1991, "But even though the unions had photos of children on the assembly lines . . . the accusations didn't get much play, in print or on television."[9]

Obviously much of the current focus on corporate abuses has to do with the tenacity of activists organizing around these issues. But since so many of the abuses being highlighted have been going on for decades, the current groundswell of resistance raises the question, Why now? Why did 1995–96 become the Year of the Sweatshop, turning quickly into the Years of the Brand Attack? Why not 1976, 1984, 1988, or, perhaps most relevant of all, why not 1993? It was in May of that year that the Kader toy factory in Bangkok burned to the ground. The building was a textbook firetrap, and when the piles of plush fabric ignited, the flames raced through the locked factory, killing 188 workers and injuring 469 more. Kader was the worst fire in industrial history, taking more lives than the Triangle Shirtwaist Company fire that killed 146 young workers in New York City in 1911. The parallels between Triangle and Kader—separated from each other by half a world, and eighty-two years of so-called development—are chilling: it was as if time hadn't moved forward, but had simply shifted locations.

■ ■ ■ ■

The Triangle Shirtwaist Company fire was the defining incident of the first anti-sweatshop movement in the United States. It catalyzed hundreds of thousands of workers into militancy and promoted a government response that eventually led to a fifty-four-hour weekly cap on overtime, no work past 9 p.m. and breakthroughs in health and fire regulations. Perhaps the most significant advance as a result of the fire was the introduction of what today would be called independent monitoring—the founding of the New York Factory Investigation Commission, which was authorized to stage surprise raids on suspected sweatshop operators.

So what did the 188 deaths in the Kader fire accomplish? Sadly, despite the fact that several international labor and development groups stepped in to denounce the unlawful factory operator, Kader didn't become a symbol of the desperate need for reform the way Triangle Shirtwaist had done. In *One World, Ready or Not*, William Greider describes visiting Thailand and meeting victims and activists who had been fighting hard for retribution. "Some of them were under the impression that a worldwide boycott of Kader products was underway, organized by conscience-stricken Americans and Europeans. I had to inform them that the civilized world had barely noticed their tragedy. . . . A fire in Bangkok was like a typhoon in Bangladesh, an earthquake in Turkey." Little wonder, then, that only six months after Kader, another devastating sweatshop fire—this one at the Zhili toy factory in Shenzhen, China—took the lives of another 87 young workers.

At the time, it didn't seem to register with the international community that the toys the Kader women had been sewing were destined for the joyful aisles of Toys 'R' Us, to be wrapped and placed under Christmas trees in Europe, the United States and Canada. Many news reports failed even to mention the names of the brands being stitched in the factory. As Greider writes, "The Kader fire might have been more meaningful for Americans if they could have seen the thousands of soot-stained dolls that spilled from the wreckage, macabre litter scattered among the dead. Bugs Bunny, Bart Simpson and the Muppets. Big Bird and other *Sesame Street* dolls. Playskool 'Water Pets.' "[10]

But in 1993 few people in the West—and certainly not in the Western media—were ready to make the connection between the burned-out building in Bangkok, buried on page six or ten of their newspapers, and the brand-name toys filling North American and European homes. That is no longer the case today. What happened in 1995 was kind of a collective "click" on the part of both the media and the public. The cumulative response to the horror stories of Chinese prison labor, the scenes of teenage girls being paid pennies in the Mexican maquiladoras, and burning in fires in Bangkok, has been a slow but noticeable shift in how people in the West see workers in the developing world. "They're getting our jobs" is giving way to a more humane reaction: "Our corporations are stealing their lives."

Much of this has to do with timing. Concerns expressed about child labor in India and Pakistan had remained at the level of a steady drone for more than a decade. But by 1995, the question of linking trade policies to human rights had been pushed so far off most governments' agendas that when thirteen-year-old Craig Kielburger deliberately disrupted Canadian prime minister Jean Chrétien's trade mission to India to talk about the children who were working there in bonded slavery, the issue seemed urgent and exotic. Moreover, in North America, the total usurpation of foreign policy by the free-trade agenda invited disruption—the world was ready to listen.

The same is true of corporate crime in general. It may be nothing new for consumer goods to be produced under oppressive conditions, but what clearly *is* new is the tremendously expanded role consumer-goods companies are playing in our culture. Anticorporate activism is on the rise because many of us feel the international brand-name connections that crisscross the globe more keenly than we ever have before—and we feel them precisely because we have never been as "branded" as we are today.

Branding . . . has taken a fairly straightforward relationship between buyer and seller and—through the quest to turn brands into media providers, arts producers, town squares and social philosophers—transformed it into something much more invasive and profound. For the past decade, multinationals like Nike, Microsoft and Starbucks have sought to become the chief communicators of all that is good and cherished in our culture: art, sports, community, connection, equality. But the more successful this project is, the more vulnerable these companies become: if brands are indeed intimately entangled with our culture and our identities, when they do wrong, their crimes are not dismissed as merely the misdemeanors of another corporation trying to make a buck. Instead, many of the people who inhabit their branded worlds feel complicit in their wrongs, both guilty and connected. But this connection is a volatile one: it is not the old-style loyalty between lifelong employee and corporate boss; rather, this is a connection more akin to the relationship of fan and celebrity: emotionally intense but shallow enough to turn on a dime.

This volatility is the unintended consequence of brand managers striving for unprecedented intimacy with the consumer while forging a more casual role with the workforce. In reaching brand-not-products nirvana, these companies have lost two things that may prove more precious in the long run: consumer detachment from their global activities and citizen investment in their economic success.

It has taken us a while, but if another Kader happened tomorrow, the first question journalists would ask would be, "What toys were being produced?" "Where were they being shipped?" and "Which companies hired the contractors?" Labor activists in Thailand would be in instant communication with solidarity groups in Hong Kong, Washington, Berlin, Amsterdam, Sydney, London and Toronto. E-mails would be fired off from Washington-based Campaign for Labor Rights, from the Clean Clothes Campaign out of Amsterdam, and forwarded through a network of Web sites, listserves and fax trees. The National Labor Committee, UNITE!, the Labour Behind the Label Coalition and the World Development Movement would be organizing protests outside Toys 'R' Us, shouting, "Our children don't need bloodstained toys!" University students would dress up as the cartoon characters of their childhood and hand out pamphlets comparing Bugs Bunny's payout for *Space Jam* to the cost of putting in a fire exit at Kader. Meetings would be scheduled with national associations of toy manufacturers; new and tougher codes of conduct would be highlighted for consideration. The public mind is not only able but eager to make the global connections that William Grieder searched for but did not find after the Kader fire.

Though anticorporate activism is seeing a renewal unparalleled since the thirties, there have, of course, been some significant anticorporate campaigns scattered between the thirties and their present-day revival. The granddaddy of modern brand-based actions is the boycott against Nestlé, which peaked in the late seventies. The campaign targeted the Swiss company for its aggressive marketing of costly baby formula as a "safer" alternative to breast-feeding in the developing world. The Nestlé case has a strong parallel with the McLibel Trial . . . largely because the issue didn't really capture the world's attention until the food company made the mistake of suing a Swiss activist group for libel in 1976.[11] As with McLibel, the ensuing court case put Nestlé under intense scrutiny and led to an international boycott campaign, launched in 1977.

The eighties saw the largest industrial accident in human history: a massive toxic leak in 1984 at a Union Carbide pesticide factory in Bhopal, India, killed two thousand people immediately and has taken five thousand more lives in the years since. Today, graffiti on the wall of the dilapidated and abandoned factory reads "Bhopal = Hiroshima.[12] Despite this tragedy, widely recognized to be the result of weak safety precautions including a switched-off alarm system, the eighties were a dry spell for most political movements that questioned the beneficial power of capital. Although there was a broad recognition during the Central American wars that U.S. multinationals were propping up various dictatorships, solidarity work in North America focused primarily on the actions of governments, as opposed to multinational corporations. As one report on the subject notes, "attacking [corporations] tended to be seen as a hangover from the 'silly seventies.' "[13]

There was, however, one major exception to this rule: the anti-apartheid movement. Frustrated by the international community's refusal to impose meaningful trade sanctions on South Africa, anti-apartheid activists developed a series of alternative roadblocks designed, if not to prevent multinationals from profiting from the racist regime, at least to inconvenience them if they persisted in doing so. Students and faculty members at several universities set up tent cities demanding that schools divest themselves of their endowments from any company doing business with the African nation. Church groups disrupted corporate shareholder meetings with demands for immediate withdrawal, while more moderate investors pushed corporate boards to adopt the Sullivan principles—a set of rules for companies in South Africa that purported to minimize their complicity with the apartheid regime. Meanwhile, trade unions pulled their pensions and bank accounts from institutions issuing loans to the South African government, and dozens of municipal governments passed selective purchasing agreements canceling large contracts with companies invested in South Africa. The most creative blockades were erected by the international trade-union movement. Several times a year, the unions would call a day of action, during which dock workers refused to unload cargo that had come from South Africa, and airline ticket agents refused to book flights to and from Johannesburg. In the words of campaign organizer Ken Luckhardt, workers become "activists at the point of production."[14]

Though there are definite similarities, there is one key difference between the apartheid actions and the kind of anticorporate campaigning gaining momentum today. The South Africa boycott was an antiracist campaign that happened to use trade (whether the importing of wine or the exporting of General Motors dollars) as a tool to bring down the South African political system. Many of the current anticorporate campaigns are also rooted in a political attack—but what they are attacking is as much a global economic system as a national political one. During the years of apartheid, companies such as the Royal Bank of Canada, Barclays Bank in England and General Motors were generally regarded as morally neutral forces that happened to be entangled with an aberrantly racist government. Today, more and more campaigners are treating multinationals, and the policies that give them free rein, as the root cause of political injustices around the globe. Sometimes the companies commit these violations in collusion with governments, sometimes they commit them despite a government's best efforts.

This systemic critique has been embraced, in recent years, by several established human-rights groups like Amnesty International, PEN and Human Rights Watch, as well as environmental rights organizations like the Sierra Club. For many of these organizations, this represents a significant shift in policy. Until the mid-eighties foreign corporate investment in the Third World was seen in the mainstream development community as a key to alleviating poverty and misery. By 1996, however, that concept was being openly questioned, and it was recognized that many governments in the developing world were protecting lucrative investments—mines, dams, oil fields, power plants and export processing zones—by deliberately turning a blind eye to egregious rights violations by foreign corporations against their people. And in the enthusiasm for increased trade, the Western nations where most of these offending corporations were based also chose to look the other way, unwilling to risk their own global competitiveness for some other country's problems. The bottom line was that in parts of Asia, Central and South America and Africa, the promise that investment would bring greater freedom and democracy was starting to look like a cruel hoax. And worse: in case after case, foreign corporations were found to be soliciting, even directly contracting, the local police and military to perform such unsavory tasks as evicting peasants and tribespeople from their land; cracking down on striking factory workers; and arresting and killing peaceful protestors—all in the name of safeguarding the smooth flow of trade. Corporations, in other words, were stunting human development, rather than contributing to it.

Arvind Ganesan, a researcher with Human Rights Watch, is blunt about what his organization refers to as "a shift in the terms of the debate over corporate responsibility for human rights."[15] Rather than improved human rights flowing from increased trade, "governments ignore human rights in favor of perceived trade advantages."[16] Ganesan points out that the severing of the connection between investment and human-rights improvements is today clearest in Nigeria, where the long-awaited transition to democracy has been coupled with a renewed wave of military brutality against Niger Delta communities protesting against the oil companies.

Amnesty International, in a departure from its focus on prisoners persecuted for either their religious or political beliefs, is also beginning to treat multinational corporations as major players in the denial of human rights worldwide. More and more, recent Amnesty reports have found that people such as the late Ken Saro-Wiwa have been persecuted for what a government sees as a destabilizing anticorporate stance. In a 1997 report, the group documents the fact that Indian villagers and tribal peoples were violently arrested, and some killed, for peacefully resisting the development of private power plants and luxury hotels on their lands. A democratic country, in other words, was becoming less democratic as a result of corporate intervention. "Development," Amnesty warned, is "being pursued at the expense of human rights. . . . "

> This pattern highlights the degree to which the central and state authorities in India are prepared to deploy state force and utilize provisions of the law in the interests of development projects, curtailing the right of freedom of association, expression and assembly. India's moves to liberalize its economy and develop new industries and infrastructure have in many areas marginalized and displaced communities and contributed to further violations of their human rights.[17]

India's situation, the report states, is not "the only or the worst" one, but is part of a trend toward the disregarding of human rights in favor of "development" in the global economy.

Where the Power Is

At the heart of this convergence of anticorporate activism and research is the recognition that corporations are much more than purveyors of the products we all want; they are also the most powerful political forces of our time. By now, we've all heard the statistics: how corporations like Shell and Wal-Mart bask in budgets bigger than the gross domestic product of most nations; how, of the top hundred economies, fifty-one are multinationals and only forty-nine are countries. We have read (or heard about) how a handful of powerful CEOs are writing the new rules for the global economy, engineering what Canadian writer John Ralston Saul has called "a *coup d'état* in slow motion." In his book about corporate power, *Silent Coup*, Tony Clarke takes this theory one step further when he argues that citizens must go after corporations not because we don't like their products, but because corporations have become the ruling political bodies of our era, setting the agenda of globalization. We must confront them, in other words, because that is where the power is.

So although the media often describe campaigns like the one against Nike as "consumer boycotts," that tells only part of the story. It is more accurate to describe them as political campaigns that use consumer goods as readily accessible targets, as public-relations levers and as popular-education tools. In contrast to the consumer boycotts of the seventies, there is a more diffuse relationship between lifestyle choices (what to eat, what to smoke, what to wear) and the larger questions of how the global corporation—its size, political clout and lack of transparency—is reorganizing the world economy. Behind the protests outside Nike Town, behind the pie in Bill Gates's face and the bottle shattering the McDonald's window in Prague, there is something too visceral for most conventional measures to track—a kind of bad mood rising. And the corporate hijacking of political power is as responsible for this mood as the brands' cultural looting of public and mental space. I also like to think it has to do with the arrogance of branding itself: the seeds of discontent are part of its very DNA.

■ ■ ■ ■

. . . The continuing attacks on brands like Nike, Shell and McDonald's not only reflect genuine indignation at sweatshops, oil spills and corporate censorship, they also reflect how large the antagonistic audience has become. The desire (and ability) to back up free-floating anticorporate malaise with legitimate facts, figures and real-life anecdotes is so widespread that it even transcends old rivalries within the social and ecological movements. The United Food and

Commercial Workers' union, which started targeting Wal-Mart because of its low wages and union-busting tactics, now collects and disseminates information on Wal-Mart stores being built on sacred Native burial grounds. Since when did a grocery-store workers' union weigh in on indigenous land claims? Since puncturing Wal-Mart became a cause in and of itself. Why did the London eco-anarchists behind the McLibel Trial—who don't believe in working for the Man in any form—take up the plight of teenage McDonald's workers? Because, for them, it's another angle from which to attack the golden beast.

The political backdrop to this phenomenon is well known. Many citizens' movements have tried to reverse conservative economic trends over the last decade by electing liberal, labor or democratic-socialist governments, only to find that economic policy remains unchanged or caters even more directly to the whims of global corporations. Centuries of democratic reforms that had won greater transparency in government suddenly appeared ineffective in the new climate of multinational power. What good was an open and accountable Parliament or Congress if opaque corporations were setting so much of the global political agenda in the back rooms?

Disillusionment with the political process has been even more pronounced on the international stage, where attempts to regulate multinationals through the United Nations and trade regulatory bodies have been blocked at every turn. A significant setback came in 1986 when the U.S. government effectively killed the little-known United Nations Commission on Transnational Corporations. Started in the mid-seventies, the commission set out to draft a universal code of conduct for multinational corporations. Its goals were preventing corporate abuses such as companies dumping, in the Third World, drugs that are illegal in the West; examining the environmental and labor impacts of export factories and resource extraction; and pushing the private sector toward greater transparency and accountability.

The merit of these goals seems self-evident today but the commission, in many ways, was a casualty of its time. American industry was opposed to its creation from the start and in the heat of Cold War mania managed to secure their government's withdrawal on the grounds that the commission was a Communist plot and that the Soviets were using it for espionage. Why, they demanded, were Soviet-bloc national enterprises not subject to the same probing as American companies? During this era, criticisms of the abuses of multinational corporations were so bound up in anti-Communist paranoia that when the Bhopal tragedy happened in 1984, the immediate response of a U.S. embassy official in New Delhi was not to express horror but to say, "This is a feast for the Communists. They'll go with it for weeks."[18]

More recently, attempts to force the World Trade Organization to include enforcement of basic labor laws as a condition of global trade have been dismissed by member nations who insist such enforcement is the job of the UN's International Labor Organization. The ILO "is the competent body to determine and deal with these standards, and we affirm our support for its work in promoting them," states the WTO's Singapore Ministerial Declaration of December 13, 1996. However, when the ILO embarked on an initiative to draft a meaningful corporate code of conduct, it too was blocked.

At first, these failures to regulate capital left many reform and opposition movements in a state of near-paralysis: citizens, it seemed, had lost their say. Slowly, however, a handful of non-governmental organizations and groups of progressive intellectuals have been developing a political strategy that recognizes that multinational brands, because of their high profile, can be far more galvanizing targets than the politicians whom they bankroll. And once the corporations are feeling the heat, they have learned, it becomes much easier to get the attention of elected politicians. In explaining why he has chosen to focus his activism on the Nike corporation, Washington-based labor activist Jeff Ballinger says bluntly, "Because we have more influence on a brand name than we do with our own governments."[19] Besides, adds John Vidal, "Activists always target the people who have the power . . . so if the power moves from government to industry to transnational corporations, so the swivel will move onto these people."[20]

Already, a common imperative is emerging from the disparate movements taking on multinational corporations: the people's right to know. If multinationals have become larger and more powerful than governments, the argument goes, then why shouldn't they be subject to the same accountability controls and transparency that we demand of our public institutions? So anti-sweatshop activists have been demanding that Wal-Mart hand over lists of all the factories around the world that supply the chain with finished products. University students . . . are demanding the same information about factories that produce clothing with their school insignia. Environmentalists, meanwhile, have used the courts to X-ray the inner working of McDonald's. And all over the world, consumers are demanding that companies like Monsanto provide clear labeling of genetically modified food and open their research to outside scrutiny.

Placing demands like these on private companies, whose only legal duty is to their shareholders, has generated a surprising number of successes. The reason is that many multinationals have a rather sizable weak spot. . . . [A]ctivists around the world are making liberal use of the very factor that has been the subject of this book so far: the brand. Brand image, the source of so much corporate wealth, is also, it turns out, the corporate Achilles' heel.

Notes

1. From an interview conducted by Oxblood Ruffin of the hacker group Cult of the Dead Cow. Authenticity of the interview confirmed with source.
2. "Derr Pied!" Biotic Baking Brigade press release, 10 March 1999.
3. "Entarteurs Take Note: Custard Wins Test of Best Pies for Throwing," *Wall Street Journal*, 26 May 1999.
4. Kitty Krupat, "From War Zone to Free Trade Zone," in *No Sweat*, 56.
5. "Toy Story," *Dateline*, NBC, 17 December 1996.
6. Sydney H. Schamberg, "Six Cents an Hour," *Life*, June 1996.
7. "Suu Kyi Calls for Halt to Investment in Burma," *Australian Herald*, 4 September 1995.
8. "Disney Labor Abuses in China," report produced by the Hong Kong Christian Industrial Committee.
9. Bob Ortega, *In Sam We Trust.* (New York: Times Books, 1998), 236.
10. William Greider, *One World, Ready or Not* (New York: Simon & Schuster, 1997), 338.
11. The libel suit was against "a Swiss group who translated War on Want's publication *The Baby Killer* . . . " Source: "Baby Milk: Destruction of a World Resource" (London: Catholic Institute for International Relations, 1993), 3.
12. Fred Pearce, "Legacy of a Nightmare," *Guardian*, 8 August 1998. These numbers represent conservative estimates. Satinath Sarangi, a researcher based in Bhopal, puts the death toll at 16,000.
13. Myriam Vander Stichele and Peter Pennartz, *Making It Our Business: European NGO Campaigns on Transnational Corporations* (London: Catholic Institute for International Relations, 1996).
14. Personal interview.
15. "Corporations and Human Rights," *Human Rights Watch 1997 World Report.*
16. Julie Light, "Repression, Inc.: The Assault on Human Rights," *Corporate Watch*, 4 February 1999.
17. "The 'Enron Project' in Maharashtra: Protests Suppressed in the Name of Development," Amnesty International, 17 July 1997, 2.
18. Pico Iyer, "India's Night of Death," *Time*, 17 December 1984.
19. Personal interview.
20. Personal interview.

CREDITS

Mimi Abramovitz, "A Feminist Theory of the State" from *Regulating the Lives of Women: Social Welfare Policy from Colonial Times to the Present.* 1996. Used by permission of South End Press.

Giovanni Arrighi, Terence K. Hopkins, and Immanuel Wallerstein, "The Liberation of Class Struggle?" from *Antisystemic Movements,* 1999. Reprinted with permission of Verso.

Chip Berlet and Matthew N. Lyons, "Right-Wing Populism in America" from *Right-Wing Populism in America,* New York: The Guilford Press, 2000, pp. 1–17. Reprinted with permission.

Fred Block, "Political Choice and the Multiple 'Logics' of Capital" from *Theory and Society* 15 (1986): 175–196. Used by permission of Kluwer Academic Publishers.

Robert D. Bullard, "Environmentalism and Social Justice" from *Dumping in Dixie, 2/e* by Robert Bullard. Copyright 1990 by Westview Press. Reprinted by permission of Westview Press, a member of Perseus Books. L.L.C.

Ward Churchill, "The United States and the Genocide Convention: A Half-Century of Obfuscation and Obstruction" from *A Little Matter of Genocide.* Copyright 1997 by Ward Churchill. Reprinted by permission of City Lights Books.

Dan Clawson, Alan Neustadtl, and Mark Weller, "Follow the Money" as it appears in *Dollars and Votes,* by Dan Clawson, Alan Neustadtl, and Mark Weller. Reprinted by permission of Temple University Press. Copyright 1998 by Temple University. All Rights Reserved.

Mike Davis, "Ecology of Fear" from "Beyond Blade Runner" from *Ecology of Fear* by Mike Davis. Copyright 1998 by Mike Davis. Reprinted by permission of Henry Holt and Company, LLC.

Bogdan Denitch, "Ethnic Nationalism as It Really Exists" from *Ethnic Nationalism: The Tragic Death of Yugoslavia,* Revised Edition. Copyright 1994, 1996 by the Regents of the University of Minnesota.

G. William Domhoff, "Defining the Class Dominance View" from *State Autonomy or Class Dominance?* Used by permission of Aldine de Gruyter, a division of Walter de Gruyter Inc.

G. William Domhoff, "How the Power Elite Dominate Government" from *Who Rules America? Power and Politics* by G. William Domhoff. Copyright 2001 by McGraw-Hill. Reproduced with permission of The McGraw-Hill Companies.

Hal Draper, "The State as Superstructure" from *Karl Marx's Theory of Revolution.* Reprinted with permission. New York: Monthly Review Press, 1977, pp. 250–252 portions and 253–262.

Gøsta Esping-Andersen, "The Three Worlds of Welfare Capitalism" from *The Three Worlds of Welfare Capitalism.* Copyright 1990 by Princeton University Press. Reprinted by permission of Princeton University Press.

John Foran, "Magical Realism: How Might the Revolutions of the Future Have Better End(ing)s?" from *The Future of Revolutions: Rethinking Radical Change in the Age of Globalization* (London: Zed Books, Ltd. 2003). Reprinted with permission.

Michel Foucault, "The Body of the Condemned" from *Discipline and Punish.* English translation copyright 1977 by Alan Sheridan (New York: Pantheon). Originally published in French as *Surveiller et Punir,* copyright 1975 by Editions Gallimard. Reprinted by permission of Georges Borchardt, Inc., for Editions Gallimard.

Linda Gordon, "Who Deserves Help? Who Must Provide?" from *Annals of The American Academy of Political & Social Science,* vol. 577, pp. 14, 15–18, 19, 20–25, copyright 2001 by Sage Publications. Reprinted by permission of Sage Publications, Inc.

Antonio Gramsci, "Hegemony" from *Selections from the Prison Notebooks.* Reprinted with permission from Antonio Gramsci, *Selections from the Prison Notebooks,* New York: International Publishers, 1971, pp. 12, 258–260 portions.

Lani Guinier, *The Tyranny of the Majority.* Reprinted with the permission of The Free Press, a Division of Simon & Schuster Adult

Publishing Group, from *The Tyranny of the Majority: Fundamental Fairness in Representative Democracy* by Lani Guinier. Copyright 1994 by Lani Guinier.

Edward S. Herman and Noam Chomsky, "Manufacturing Consent" from *Manufacturing Consent* by Edward S. Herman and Noam Chomsky, copyright 1988 by Edward S. Herman and Noam Chomsky. Used by permission of Pantheon Books, a division of Random House, Inc.

Naomi Klein, "Bad Mood Rising: The New Anticorporate Activism," Copyright 2000 by Naomi Klein. From*No Logo: Taking Aim at the Brand Bullies* by Naomi Klein. Reprinted by permission of Picador, an imprint of St. Martin's Press, LLC.

Gabriel Kolko, "The Making of American Foreign Policy: Successes and Failures" from *Another Century of War?* Copyright 2002 *Another Century of War?* by Gabriel Kolko. Reprinted by permission of The New Press. (800) 233–4830.

Jerry Lembcke, "Yellow Ribbons and Spat-Upon Veterans: Making Soldiers the Means and Ends of War" from *The Spitting Image.* Reprinted with permission. New York: New York University Press, 1998, pp. 11–26.

George Lipsitz, "The Possessive Investment in Whiteness" as it appears in *The Possessive Investment in Whiteness: How White People Profit from Identity Politics,* by George Lipsitz. Reprinted by permission of Temple University Press. Copyright 1998 by Temple University. All Rights Reserved.

Herbert Marcuse, "The New Forms of Control" from *One Dimensional Man* by Herbert Marcuse. Copyright 1964 by Herbert Marcuse. Reprinted by permission of Beacon Press, Boston.

Karl Marx, "The Fetishism of Commodities" from *Capital, Vol. 1,* 1974. Reprinted with permission from International Publishers, New York.

Kim Moody, "Toward an International Social-Movement Unionism" from *Workers in a Lean World,* 1997. Reprinted with permission of Verso.

Tom Nairn, "Demonising Nationality" from *Faces of Nationalism,* 1997. Reprinted with permission of Verso.

Mark Neocleous, "Fascism: Revolution Against the Revolution," in "Revolution Against the Revolution I: Capitalism, State Power, and the Conservative Revolution" from *Fascism* (University of Minnesota Press, 1997) pp. 38–58. Copyright 1997 by Mark Neocleous.

Kenneth J. Neubeck and Noel A. Cazenave, "Welfare Racism as Population Control." Copyright 2001 from *Welfare Racism: Playing the Race Card Against America's Poor* by Kenneth J. Neubeck and Noel Cazenave. Reproduced by permission of Routledge/Taylor & Francis Books, Inc.

Robert O'Brien, Anne Marie Goetz, Jan Aart Scholte, and Marc Williams, "The World Bank and Women's Movements" from *Contesting Global Governance: Multilateral Economic Institutions and Global Social Movements,* 2000. Reprinted with permission of Cambridge University Press.

Robert Perrucci and Early Wysong, "The Pacification of Everyday Life" as it appears in *The New Class Society* by Robert Perrucci and Earl Wysong, 2003, pp. 262–273. Published by Rowman & Littlefield Publishers, Inc. Used by permission.

James Petras and Henry Veltmeyer, "'Globalization' or 'Imperialism'?" from *Globalization Unmasked.* Reprinted with permission. London: Zed Books, 2001, chapter 1.

Anne Phillips, "Public Spaces, Private Lives" from *Engendering Democracy.* University Park, The Pennsylvania State University Press, 1991, pp. 92–97, 101–103, 106–107, 109–112, 119. Copyright 1991 by The Pennsylvania State University. Reproduced by permission from the publisher.

Frances Fox Piven and Richard A. Cloward, "Does Voting Matter?" from *Why Americans Still Don't Vote* by Frances Fox Piven and Richard A. Cloward. Copyright 2000 by Frances Fox Piven and Richard A. Cloward. Reprinted by permission of Beacon Press, Boston.

Frances Fox Piven and Richard A. Cloward, "Relief, Labor, and Civil Disorder: An Overview" from *Regulating the Poor* by Frances Fox Piven and Richard A. Cloward, copyright 1971 by Frances Fox Piven and Richard A.

Cloward. Used by permission of Pantheon Books, a division of Random House, Inc.

Frances Fox Piven and Richard A. Cloward, "The Structuring of Protest" from *Poor People's Movements: Why They Succeed, How They Fail* by Richard A. Cloward and Frances Fox Piven, copyright 1977 by Richard A. Cloward and Francis Fox Piven. Used by permission of Pantheon Books, a division of Random House, Inc.

Stephen A. Resnick and Richard D. Wolff, "Class Contradictions and the Collapse of the Soviet Union" from *Class Theory and History.* Copyright 2002 from *Class Theory and History* by Stephen Resnick and Richard Wolff. Reproduced by permission of Routledge/Taylor & Francis Books, Inc.

Suzanne Staggenborg, "Can Feminist Organizations Be Effective?" from "Can Feminist Organizations Be Effective?" by Suzanne Staggenborg as it appears in *Feminist Organizations: Harvest of the New Women's Movement,* by Myra Marx Ferree and Patricia Yancey Martin. Reprinted by permission of Temple University Press. Copyright 1995 by Temple University. All rights reserved.

Manfred Steger, "Five Central Claims of Globalism" from *Globalism: The New Market Ideology,* 2001. Used by permission of Rowman & Littlefield Publishers, Inc.

Charles Tilly, "War Making and State Making as Organized Crime" from *Bringing the State Back In* by Peter B. Evans, Dietrich Rueschmeyer, and Theda Skocpol (eds.), 1985. Reprinted with the permission of Cambridge University Press.